READINGS IN MORAL THEOLOGY NO. 3:
THE MAGISTERIUM AND MORALITY

READINGS IN MORAL THEOLOGY

No. 3:

The Magisterium and Morality

Edited by
Charles E. Curran
and
Richard A. McCormick, S.J.

PAULIST PRESS
New York/Ramsey

ACKNOWLEDGMENTS

The articles reprinted in *Readings in Moral Theology, No. 3: The Magisterium and Morality* first appeared in the following publications and are reprinted with permission: John C. Ford, S.J. and Gerald Kelly, S.J., "Doctrinal Value and Interpretation of Papal Teaching," from *Contemporary Moral Theology* I, 19–32, Newman Press, 1958; Bruno Schüller, S.J., "Some Remarks on the Authentic Teaching of the Church's Magisterium," from *Theologie und Philosophie* 42 (1967), 534–551; Daniel C. Maguire, "Morality and the Magisterium," from *Cross Currents* 18 (1968), 41–65; Joseph A. Komonchak, "Ordinary Papal Magisterium and Religious Assent," from *Contraception: Authority and Dissent*, ed. Charles Curran (New York: Herder and Herder, 1969, 101–126; Italian Moral Theologians, Italian Bishops, and Antonio de Marino, S.J., "Morality and the Magisterium at Padua" from *Rassenga di Teologia* 11 (1970) Supplemento, 73, 74 and 80–94; "The Dispute Concerning the Church's Teaching Office," from *Theological Investigations* XIV, edited by Karl Rahner. Copyright © Darton, Longman & Todd Ltd. 1976. Reprinted by permission of The Seabury Press, Inc.; Karl Rahner, "Open Questions in Dogma Considered by the Institutional Church as Definitively Answered," from *Journal of Ecumenical Studies* 15 (Spring 1978), 211–226; International Theological Commission, "Theses on the Relationship Between the Ecclesiastical Magisterium and Theology," with a commentary by Otto Semmelroth, S.J. and Karl Lehmann, Publication Office, USCC, 1977. (This publication in its entirety may be purchased from the Publications Office of the United States Catholic Conference, 1312 Massachusetts Ave., N.W., Washington, D.C. 20005.); Christopher Butler, O.S.B., "Authority and the Christian Conscience," from *American Benedictine Review* 25 (1974), 411–426; John Francis Whealon, "Magisterium," Reprinted with permission from: *Homiletic & Pastoral Review* 76 (July 1976), 10–19; Juan Arzube, "Criteria for Dissent in the Church." Taken from a talk given in San Diego, California, at the Catholic Press Association Convention Mass on April 26, 1978; Robert Coffy, "Magisterium and Theology," from Irish Theological Quarterly 43 (1976), 247–259; Giovanni B. Guzzetti, "The Magisterium of the Church in the Area of Morality," from *La Revista del Clero Italiano* 57 (1976), 834–847; "Doctrinal Authority for a Pilgrim Church" from *The Resilient Church* by Avery Dulles, S.J. Copyright © 1977 by Avery Dulles. Reprinted by permission of Doubleday & Company, Inc.; John R. Quinn, "Magisterium and the Field of Theology," from *Origins* 7 (1977), 341–343; Raymond E. Brown, S.S., "Bishops and Theologians: 'Dispute' Surrounded by Fiction," from *Origins* 7 (1978), 673–682; Yves M. Congar, O.P., "A Semantic History of the Term 'Magisterium'," from *Revue des sciences et theologiques* 60 (1976), 85–98; Yves Congar, O.P., "A Brief History of the Forms of the 'Magisterium' and Its Relations with Scholars," from *Revue des sciences philosophiques et theologiques* 60 (1976), 99–112; Thomas Dubay, S.M., "The State of Moral Theology: A Critical Appraisal." Reprinted, with permission, from *Theological Studies* 35 (1974) 482–506; Charles E. Curran, "Pluralism in Catholic Moral Theology," from *Ongoing Revision in Moral Theology* (Notre Dame: Fides, 1975); Charles E. Curran, "Academic Freedom: The Catholic University and Catholic Theology." Published by permission from *Academe: Bulletin of the AAUP*, April 1980; Philippe Delhaye, "The Collaboration of the Hierarchy and of All Christians in the Formulation of Moral Norms," from *L'Annee Canonique* 22 (1978), 44–60; John Boyle, "The Natural Law and the Magisterium," from *Proceedings of the Catholic Theological Society of America* 34 (1979), 189–210; Richard A. McCormick, S.J., "Thomas Dubay and the State of Moral Theology," from *Theological Studies* 36 (1975), 79–85; "Theologians and the Magisterium," *Theological Studies* 38 (1977), 84–100; "The Ordinary Magisterium in History," *Theological Studies* 40 (1979), 88–97; "Theologians and Academic Freedom," *Theological Studies* 41 (1980), 113–123.

Contents

Foreword

This volume of our series *Readings in Moral Theology* is concerned with the realtionship between the magisterium and morality. The very usage "*the* magisterium" has implications that are subject to discussion, as several essays make clear, especially those of Congar. Nevertheless, we have retained the usage in our title because it is a standard usage and because it states clearly the problem that the various readings address.

That problem is basically the relationship of theological inquiry to authoritative formulation of moral teaching. In her ordinary day-to-day teaching—what is known as the "ordinary magisterium" of Popes, the college of bishops, and the individual bishop in union with the Pope—the Church has taken authoritative stands on moral issues such as abortion, the means of birth control and sexual ethics more generally, religious liberty, war and peace, the right to private property, the duties of the state, etc.

As soon as the term "authoritative" is used, a whole host of questions arise. For instance, what is the meaning of "authoritative"? What is the proper Catholic response to such teachings? Is there a place for dissent vis-à-vis such teachings? What is the nature of the magisterial function of the Church? How should we conceive the contributions of scholars in this function? What part does reception of a teaching play in determining its overall significance? Are authoritative teachings independent of evidence and analysis for their validity? What is meant by the special assistance of the Holy Spirit granted to official teachers in the Church as they formulate Catholic doctrine? Is the teaching function of the Church similar in all eras and cultures?

Questions such as these are addressed in this volume. We believe that they are of great importance in themselves but they also have very profound pastoral implications. For instance, discussion of nearly every difficult and delicate moral problem of our time, the type of problem that touches people's lives, very often becomes a discussion of authority and ecclesiology. And it is no secret that as the model of the Church shifts from age to age, so does that of authority and its exercise in the Church. Thus we think it very important in the healing of a divided Church that the discussion of the magisterium occur at a high and well informed level.

We are also convinced that these readings can be of significant ecumenical value. The bilateral conversations between the Catholic Church and other Christian churches have produced significant results in some broad areas of doctrinal concern (e.g., the Petrine ministry, the sacraments). Yet no significant progress has been made in specific matters of morality, as "The Research Report on the Bilateral Consultations" (*Proceedings of the Thirty-fourth Annual Convention*, CTSA, 1979) makes clear. If fruitful discussion is to occur in the future on these matters, it must occur within a nuanced and historically well informed notion of the Church's magisterium in the area of morality.

Once again we have attempted to present several points of view in this volume, basically because several points of view exist in the Catholic Church on the magisterium and morality.

Charles E. Curran
Richard A. McCormick, S.J.

Doctrinal Value
and Interpretation
of Papal Teaching

John C. Ford, S.J. and Gerald Kelly, S.J.

At the annual meeting of the Catholic Theological Society of America in 1949, a paper read by Eugene M. Burke, C.S.P.,[1] devoted considerable space to the methods of teaching used by the magisterium, especially by the Roman Pontiff, and to the doctrinal value of these methods. At the meeting of the same society in 1951, the entire paper read by Edmond D. Benard concerned the doctrinal value of the ordinary teaching of the Holy Father.[2] The discussion evoked by both papers showed that the topics were of speculative interest and practical moment. This response was not surprising. Problems relative to the doctrinal value of ecclesiastical pronouncements have always been of special interest to theologians; and it is safe to say that this interest has never been more intense, nor of more immediate practicality, than during the reign of Pope Pius XII.

MORAL TEACHING OF PIUS XII

An earnest student of papal pronouncements, Vincent A. Yzermans, estimated that during the first fifteen years of his pontificate Pius XII gave almost one thousand public addresses and radio messages.[3] If we add to these the apostolic constitutions, the encyclicals, and so forth, during that same period of fifteen years, and add furthermore all the papal statements during the subsequent years, we have well over a thousand papal documents. It is true, of course, that many of these were not concerned with faith or morals; yet certainly a very large percentage, if not the vast majority, were concerned with either faith or morality. The moralist in particular has only to think of the stream of pronouncements on international peace, on labor relations, on family morality, on medicine and so forth, to realize that his own work is profoundly affected.

Merely from the point of view of volume, therefore, one can readily appreciate that it was not mere facetiousness that led a theologian to remark that, even if the Holy See were now to remain silent for ten years, the theologians would have plenty to do in classifying and evaluating the theological significance of Pius XII's public statements. And it may be added that the theologians' problem is created not merely by the number and variety of the papal statements, but also by the fact that many of them are in modern languages rather than in the traditional Latin, and that they were given in a more or less oratorical setting. We mention these as added problems because, whatever be the disadvantages of Latin, it has the theological advantage of an "established terminology"; and oratory, though perhaps more pleasing than the cut-and-dried theological statement, forces the theologian to dig for the theological core of a statement.

Among these numerous pronouncements of Pope Pius XII, one (*Munificentissimus Deus*[4]) is certainly an *ex cathedra* definition, and another (*Sacramentum Ordinis*[5]) seems to be such. Of these, only the second pertains to moral theology, and that more or less indirectly. In general, the teaching of the Holy Father on moral matters has been given in encyclicals, radio messages, and allocutions—which are normally the media of his authentic, but not infallible, teaching. This is not to say that such media could not contain *ex cathedra* pronouncements; but usually they do not, and there seems to be no reason for saying that during the reign of Pius XII these media have contained any infallible definitions concerning morality. By this we do not mean, however, that none of the moral teaching of Pius XII could be characterized as infallible. It is hardly conceivable that the papal teaching on such things as divorce, contraception, the direct killing of the innocent, and the possibility of observing continence with the grace of God is anything short of infallible. However, aside from such cases, we may safely assume that the moral teaching of Pius XII need not be characterized as infallible but rather belongs to the authentic, though not infallible, magisterium of the Church. Regarding this non-infallible teaching, questions of special interest concern (1) its doctrinal value, and (2) the function of theologians in their use of such teaching.

II

DOCTRINAL VALUE

Since the non-infallible moral teaching of Pius XII has been given through the medium of encyclicals, radio messages, and allocutions (as well as through papally approved decrees and instructions of the Roman congregations), something should be said here about the doctrinal value of these various media. Obviously, lest we turn this chapter into a book, we must be carefully selective in this matter. On the basis of such selectivity, the principal place must be given to the Pope's own statement in *Humani Generis*, which is concerned primarily, but not exclusively, with encyclicals. After criticizing the exponents of "the new theology" for their lack of appreciation of the ordinary magisterium (perhaps this expression is an understatement), the Pope adds the following now celebrated paragraph:

> Nor must it be thought that what is contained in encyclical letters does not of itself demand assent, on the pretext that the Popes do not exercise in them the supreme power of their teaching authority. Rather, such teachings belong to the ordinary magisterium, of which it is true to say: "He who heareth you, heareth me"; very often, too, what is expounded and inculcated in encyclical letters already appertains to Catholic doctrine for other reasons. But if the Supreme Pontiffs in their official documents purposely pass judgment on a matter debated until then, it is obvious to all that the matter, according to the mind and will of the same Pontiffs, cannot

be considered any longer a question open for discussion among theologians.[6]

There have been many excellent commentaries on the *Humani Generis* in general and on this paragraph in particular. Typical among these, and especially notable, we think, for its simplicity and clarity, is the explanation given by Father Cotter under the heading, "Authentic Teaching of the Magisterium." We quote this in full:

The Pope has no doubt that those Catholic theologians whom he has in mind throughout the encyclical are willing to abide by the definitive decisions of the magisterium, those handed down *solemni iudicio*. They are neither heretics nor schismatics. But he complains that they ignore papal pronouncements that come to them with less authority, such as encyclicals. If reputable theologians have disagreed in the past, they assume that nothing less than a solemn definition can settle the matter; and as long as none such is forthcoming, everyone is presumed free to construe papal documents according to his own interpretation of Tradition (27).

In reply, the Pope reminds them that encyclicals, besides often containing matters of dogma, may intend to settle points hitherto disputed, and that such decisions demand of themselves a positive assent on the part of the faithful, theologians included. In issuing them the Popes exercise what is technically known as the ordinary or authentic magisterium, of which it is true to say: "He who heareth you, heareth me." The reason for all this is that to the living magisterium alone has God entrusted the official interpretation of the deposit of faith (21, 23).

According to theologians, the doctrinal decrees of the Holy Office and responses of the Biblical Commission belong in the same category because of the close connection of these two Roman congregations with the Pope. Also their decisions demand per se the positive assent of the faithful (Denzinger 2113).

This is technically known as "religious assent." It is a true internal assent, not a mere *silentium obsequiosum* such as the Jansenists were willing to give the papal decrees issued against them. Yet it is not the assent of either divine or ecclesiastical faith; its motive is not the authority of God speaking nor the infallibility of the magisterium, but the official position of the living magisterium in the Church assigned to it by Christ.

Complaints have been raised against this doctrine as if it were putting shackles on the Catholic theologian (18). Yes and no. First of all, there are any number of problems in Catholic theology on which the magisterium has said nothing so far either definitely or authentically; witness the numerous probable theses or assertions in our manuals and the questions freely disputed in our reviews. Secondly, the authentic decisions of the magisterium, when examined closely, are generally seen to leave the door open for further study of the problem; witness especially the responses of the Biblical Commission. And if a reputable scholar should arrive at a different solution, theologians advise him to communicate his findings to the respective Roman congregation, but not to broadcast them, in defiance, as it were, of the magisterium. Thirdly, even when the decision is definitive, progress is still possible and desirable (21), and that means, partly at least, further research on the same matter by theologians.[7]

As Father Cotter notes, though the papal statement refers primarily to encyclicals, it is not restricted to these. Rather, it covers the whole range of what is called the "ordinary magisterium" of the Holy Father. Everything that has been said, therefore, could apply to the papal radio messages and allocutions; yet, since these have played such a prominent part in the moral teaching of Pope Pius XII, they merit some special attention.

On at least one occasion, the Pope himself made it strikingly clear that his discourses, even when given to small groups, can contain authoritative teaching for the whole Church. Thus, in his radio message on the education of the Christian conscience, he said:

Mindful, however, of the right and duty of the Apostolic See to intervene authoritatively, when need arises, in moral questions, in the address of 29th October last we set out to enlighten men's consciences on the problems of married life. With the self-same authority we declare today to educators and to young people also that the divine commandment of purity of soul and body still holds without any lesser obligation for the youth of today.[8]

At the conclusion of a commentary on this radio message and the subsequent allocution on the "new morality" (situation ethics),[9] F. X. Hürth, S.J., made a brief analysis of the doctrinal value of such pronouncements.[10] His conclusion was that, in general, they have about the same doctrinal value as encyclicals: they are an integral part of the ordinary teaching of the Pope; and, as such, though not infallible, they require both internal and external acceptance. An analysis of their content, said Father Hürth, shows that they consist largely of matters of faith or morals or of natural truths in their relation to faith and morals. The audience varies from the whole world (as in some of the radio messages) to a small professional group (as in an allocution to doctors); but even in the latter case the message assumes a universal character when, by command of the Supreme Pontiff, it is published in the *Acta apostolicae sedis.* As for the speaker, though the Pope may, if he wishes, speak as a private person, Father Hürth thinks it obvious that such is not his intention when he professedly speaks on matters pertaining to faith and morals in these various public messages.

Joseph Creusen, S.J., who, like Father Hürth, was a consultor of the Holy Office, offers the following observations to help determine when, and to what extent, papal discourses should be considered authoritative teaching:

What is important to us here is the character of the allocution: Has the Pope the intention of teaching, and in what measure does he invoke his authority? Apart from an express declaration, his intention can be manifested by the quality and number of the persons to whom he speaks, and by the subject-matter of the discourse.

If the Holy Father, in an audience granted to a sports association, praises the physical and moral effects of sports, everyone remains quite at liberty not to share this or that opinion of the Holy Father in the matter. His praise will often be the delicate expression of an invitation to seek in the use of sports, or of any other human activity, progress in moral values, in nobility of soul, in the duties of one's state well done. But the more the number of members of a congress increases, the greater the importance of their profession, of their responsibilities, and of their influence, the more we see the Holy Father select the subject-matter of his discourse and inculcate the duty of conforming oneself to his teaching and directives.[11]

Furthermore, Father Creusen tells us in another place, it would not make sense to restrict the obligation of assent and obedience merely to those who are present at the papal discourse:

In our case [the allocution on conjugal morality] there is no doubt that the obligation of internal submission cannot be restricted to those whom the Pope addressed. An obligation of this kind cannot be defined by the distance one happens to be from the Pope during his discourse. But perhaps someone will say: we are not obliged to read the allocutions of the Pope! Certainly, but we are all obliged to know our duties, especially those of our profession.

The "how" is not relevant, whether we come to know them by means of sermons, reading good books, lectures, or conversations with learned and reputable men.[12]

III
NORMS OF INTERPRETATION

The foregoing seems to be sufficient discussion of our first point: the doctrinal value of the various media of the ordinary teaching of the Holy Father. As for the second point — the function of theologians in their use of this teaching—we must first observe that the theologians have the same duty as the faithful in general to give the religious assent required by the papal teaching, as was stated by Pope Pius XII and explained by Father Cotter.

But the distinctive function of the theologian goes much beyond this acceptance of the papal teaching; as a theologian he must study the papal pronouncements and incorporate them into his teaching and his writing. One writer has deplored the tendency of theologians to "interpret" the papal statements; according to him the theologians' function is to explain the papal teaching, not to interpret it. In practice, this is a distinction without a difference. To fulfill his acknowledged duty of explaining the papal teaching, a theologian must in some measure interpret it; and all that can be reasonably demanded of him is that he follow sound theological norms of interpretation. Unfortunately, we do not have an official set of norms for interpreting pronouncements on the moral law such as we have, for example, regarding canon law; nevertheless, there seem to be at least three basic norms of interpretation that are in conformity with the mind and practice of the Holy See.

One such norm concerns the verbal formulas used in the moral pronouncements. These formulas are very important and should be carefully studied by theologians. Nevertheless, the words themselves are not the ultimate criterion of the true sense of the papal pronouncement; they can be obscure and admit of reformulation. This can be illustrated by the *acta* of both Pius XI and Pius XII relative to punitive sterilization, as well as by the tenor of canon law and by the reactions of eminent theologians to certain aspects of significant moral pronouncements.

In the originally published text of *Casti Connubii*, the words of Pius XI at least strongly implied that he was condemning punitive sterilization; but a *notandum* in the next fascicle of the *Acta apostolicae sedis* contained a rewording of the passage which showed that the Pope did not intend to commit himself on the controversy among theologians about the licitness of punitive sterilization.[13] Ten years later the Holy Office, with the approval of Pius XII, condemned direct sterilization, without qualification, as being contrary to the natural law.[14] That was in 1940. But in 1951, and again in 1953, Pope Pius XII, when referring to this condemnation, restricted it to the direct sterilization of the innocent.[15] In both these instances, the Popes apparently realized that, though perfectly apt for condemning the errors at which they were aimed, the formulas were broader than their own intention.

The very fact that Popes themselves have gone out of their way to clarify or restrict their moral pronouncements indicates that a theologian is not necessarily irreverent or disloyal in supposing that other such statements may need clarification or restriction or rephrasing. This is confirmed, it seems to us, by the rules for the interpretation of canon law, as well as by theologians' reactions to some recent and very important papal pronouncements on the social order. In canon law, the Church explicitly admits that the meaning of some laws may be dubious or obscure. The reason for this is surely not that the legislator wanted to be obscure but rather that he failed to make his own intention clear when framing the law. It is true, of course, that this concerns canon law, not pronouncements regarding moral law. But we do not think this affects the point we are stressing: namely, that the words themselves may fail to express the mind of the Holy See. That this has actually been the case concerning some important moral pronouncements seems evident from the controversies among eminent and unquestionably orthodox moralists regarding the meaning of social justice, the title to a family wage and so forth. In these cases, as in the framing of ecclesiastical laws, the Popes were certainly not intentionally obscure. They must have had something definite in mind, but this was not expressed with sufficient clarity — otherwise, how explain the controversies among learned commentators?

From the foregoing it follows that the words alone do not always give us the sense, the true meaning, of a papal pronouncement. To get to the true sense, the theologian must study not only the words, but their context and the papal intention in making the pronouncement. By the context we mean not so much the verbal context as the historical setting, because it is there particularly that we are apt to find the true meaning of the statement. For example, if the Pope is settling a controversy, his words should be taken in conjunction with the controversy; if he is condemning an error, the words should be interpreted with reference to the error and so forth.[16]

In *Humani Generis*, Pope Pius XII made it clear that even a non-infallible pronouncement can close a controversy among theologians. We feel sure, however, that the Pope himself would agree that this decisive character of the pronouncement must be evident. That is in accord with canon 1323, § 3, which states that nothing is to be understood as dogmatically declared or defined unless this is clearly manifested. The canon refers to infallible teachings; yet the same norm seems to apply with at least equal force to the binding character of non-infallible teaching, especially when there is question of pronouncements that would close a controversy.

To summarize briefly the main points of this section: A theologian must study and use and, to some extent, interpret papal pronouncements. In interpreting them, he should have regard not only for verbal formulas but also—and, it seems to us, especially—for the papal intention as manifested in the historical context of the pronouncement. When there is question of official teaching that would end legitimate controversy, this decisive character should be evident.

Notes

1. Cf. "The Scientific Teaching of Theology in the Seminary,"*Proceedings of the Fourth Annual Convention* of The Catholic Theological Society of America, pp. 129-73.

2. "The Doctrinal Value of the Ordinary Teaching of the Holy Father in View of *Humani Generis,*" *Proceedings of the Sixth Annual Convention*, CTSA, pp. 78-107. Father Benard (*ibid.*, pp. 84-85) gives the following explanation of the terms *ordinary* and *extraordinary magisterium*: "(1) *The Pope employs his Extraordinary Magisterium when he speaks* ex cathedra. *This Extraordinary Magisterium is* de se, *always, and necessarily infallible* . . . . (2) The Pope employs his Ordinary Magisterium when he speaks to the faithful, indeed as their supreme Pastor and Teacher, but in order to expound, explain, present Catholic teaching, or to admonish, persuade, enlighten, warn, and encourage the faithful, without calling upon the supreme exercise of his Apostolic Authority, and without, in the strict sense, defining a doctrine. *In this case he does not speak* ex cathedra *and the Ordinary Magisterium is hence not* de se *infallible.* (3) *However, the Pope may, if he chooses, employ a usual organ or*

vehicle of the Ordinary Magisterium as the medium of an ex cathedra *pronouncement.* In this case, an Encyclical Letter, for example — certainly a type of document usually associated with the Ordinary Magisterium — may be used as the vehicle of the Extraordinary Magisterium, and hence as the vehicle of an infallible pronouncement . . . ."

3. Cf. *The Catholic Mind*, 53 (1955), 252. Father Yzermans wrote originally in *Columbia,* for January 1955. The complete quotation given in *The Catholic Mind* is interesting: "Some five years ago I began to dream of an American work that would record all the addresses of His Holiness, Pope Pius XII. So I set to work in search of the sources. Little did I dream I would be so quickly disillusioned! To my utter dismay I discovered that our Holy Father has spoken so often that the mere recording of his words would be a super-human task. It would entail, first of all, the collection of all the addresses from an innumerable variety of sources. During the first fifteen years of his pontificate, from March 2, 1939 to March 2, 1954, the Supreme Pontiff delivered almost 1,000 public addresses, allocutions and radio messages. Over and above the mere recording of these addresses there would be the added task of translating them from the various languages in which they were delivered. Of the total number of addresses only a little more than a third have been translated into English."

A recent advertisement for *The Pope Speaks* carries this information: "In the course of a year, the Holy Father delivers 80 to 100 public messages — encyclicals, allocutions, radio messages, letters, addresses to audiences from all over the world." And the Autumn 1956 number of the same publication begins with the following paragraph:

"The Holy Father has temporarily overwhelmed our hopes of printing translations of all his important and interesting messages in a given quarter. In the second three months of this year (the period covered in this issue), Pope Pius XII addressed over *sixty* messages to various groups or to the world at large. And this includes only those which appeared in the *Acta* or *Osservatore Romano*. These messages range in length from the booklet-sized encyclical on devotion to the Sacred Heart . . . to several one-page letters . . . ."

4. Nov. 1, 1950; AAS, 42 (1950), 753-71.

5. Nov. 30, 1947; AAS, 40 (1948), 5-7.

6. AAS, 42 (1950), 568; for translation, cf. Cotter, *op. cit.*, pp. 21-23.

7. *Ibid.*, pp. 75-77. The numbers Father Cotter has in parentheses refer to the paragraph numbers of the encyclical as given in his book. The question of the "assensus religiosus" that must be given to non-infallible teaching is an intriguing one. Closely connected with this, of course, is the problem of divine assistance for the magisterium in this kind of teaching. Dogmatic theologians give different explanations. For more about this, see the paper by Father Benard (*supra*, note 2); also Charles Journet, *The Church of the Word Incarnate: I. The Apostolic Hierarchy* (New York:

Sheed and Ward, 1955), esp. pp. 351-53; and Wernz-Vidal, as cited *infra*, chapter 3, footnote 6. And for the replies of the Biblical Commission in particular, see the remarks of E. A., Sutcliffe, S.J., in *A Catholic Commentary on Holy Scripture* (New York: Thomas Nelson and Sons, 1953), pp. 67-68. Father Sutcliffe's explanation is very complete and it shows that in some questions the submission required of the Catholic exegete may consist only "in not opposing by word or writing the decisions of the Biblical Commission."

8. AAS, 44 (1952), 275; English translation based on *Catholic Documents*, 8 (July, 1952), 5. The address of October 29, 1951, to which the Pope refers in this quotation, was given to the Italian Society of Obstetrical Nurses, and it was certainly one of the most important moral pronouncements of his reign. Cf. AAS, 43 (1951), 835-54. It is often referred to as the allocution to the "midwives"; but it seems that the Italian is better translated by "obstetrical nurses," or perhaps "obstetrical social workers."

9. For a more detailed consideration of these papal statements, as well as the subsequent instruction of the Holy Office on situation ethics, cf. chapters 7 and 8.

10. Cf. *Periodica*, 41 (1952), 245-49. See also Father Hürth's brief remarks about the doctrinal value of decrees of the Holy Office, *ibid.*, 45 (1956), 141; cf. supra, note 7.

11. *Bulletin social des industriels*, 24 (1952), 153. P. DeLetter, S.J., summarizes the teaching of Father Creusen and Father Hürth, in *Clergy Monthly*, 17 (1953), 181-83.

12. Cf. *Problemi di vita conjugale* (Rome: S.A.L.E.S., 1955), p. 31. It should be noted that Father Creusen is referring to the duties discussed in the allocutions on conjugal morality. These duties are obviously of universal application. But in some cases the practical applications of papal directives are not universal. Thus, Father Creusen himself later notes that such applications "can be obligatory in one country and not in another, they are also subject to change in accordance with changing circumstances" (*ibid.*, p. 32).

13. Cf. AAS, 22 (1930), 565, 604.

14. *Ibid.*, 32 (1940), 73.

15. Cf. *Ibid.*, 43 (1951), 844; 45 (1953), 606.

16. What is said in this paragraph seems to be in keeping with the spirit of the Church as manifested in canon 18, which prescribes that words are to be taken according to their prior meaning as indicated by text and context, and that in case of doubt one should consider the purpose and circumstances of a law and the mind of the legislator. As for verbal formulas alone, one might note the following quotation from *Quamquam Pluries* of Leo XIII: "*Certe matris Dei tam in excelso dignitas est, ut nihil fieri maius queat. Sed tamen quia intercessit Josepho cum Virgine beatissima maritale vinculum, ad illam praestantissimam dignitatem, qua naturis creatis om-*

nibus longissime Deipara antecellit, non est dubium quin accesserit ipse, ut nemo magis." Cf. ASS, 22 (1889-90), 66. The Pope's meaning is obvious; yet a stickler for the primacy of verbal formulas would have no little difficulty with the expressions we have italicized.

Remarks on the Authentic Teaching of the Magisterium of the Church

Bruno Schuller, S.J.

By now the discussion in the Catholic Church about the moral evaluation of contraceptive means has been going on for quite a number of years. Yet the results of this discussion have hardly been satisfactory. How can that be explained? To be sure, we may not underestimate the difficulties which arise in judging artificial contraception by its inherent characteristics (*ex visceribus rei*). But sometimes one gets the impression that to many Catholics these difficulties would appear less serious if the Church's magisterium had not already taken an unequivocal stance, plainly denouncing the use of contraceptive means as morally wrong. It is true that in general one does not regard this judgment of the magisterium as infallible in the dogmatic sense of the word. But to many people the mere possibility that the magisterium could have erred in a matter of such importance is simply unimaginable. For decades, people have trusted firmly and unreservedly in its judgment and have formed their consciences accordingly. Couples have attempted, often with the greatest of internal conflict, to obey it in the intimacy of their marriage relationship. Meanwhile, confessors have shared this burden with married couples, usually without knowing how to help, for they did not feel authorized to tamper with what, relying on the magisterium, they regarded as an unmistakable divine command.

That the Church could be faced with the necessity of revising its current position on contraception is difficult for many to accept.

How could it be possible that all the agony and misery, all the sacrifice, was needless and in vain? How could God allow such a thing in his Church, which he has promised to guide with his Spirit? It would undeniably be a hard and bitter experience if the magisterium eventually revised its position on the use of contraceptive means.

But there is serious reason to question whether at any time or in any place God promised that those who trust in the magisterium to guide their moral lives would be spared such a bitter experience. In establishing the magisterium, Christ entrusted to it the task of proclaiming the Gospel and the law not only infallibly, but also just authentically (that is, non-infallibly). Is it therefore not legitimate to conclude that at least implicitly Christ gave us to understand that even those who listen to the magisterium cannot recognize the moral will of God in all things without error? The basis for this conclusion will be presented below. If the arguments are convincing, it would mean this: Catholics should not be surprised if now and then they fall into error because they have trusted in the magisterium for moral direction; whoever understands what kind of competence Christ intended for the authentic magisterium must be resigned to such occurrences.

I

AUTHENTIC MAGISTERIUM
AS FALLIBLE TEACHING AUTHORITY

In our brief remarks about the authentic teaching of the Church's magisterium, we shall presume the distinction of the two forms of magisterium as found in traditional theology: the infallible and the merely authentic.[1] We have nothing new to add to that. Besides, it has been treated by so many theologians that it would be superfluous to repeat it here. Rather, starting from what theology has to say about the authentic proclamation of the magisterium, we shall attempt to work out expressly what is implicit in it and to draw some consequences which, it seems, are usually not drawn clearly and resolutely enough.

Theology says that even in its (merely) authentic teaching, the magisterium speaks with genuine authority, even though it is not infallible. That the authentic magisterium speaks with genuine authority means that it speaks with the special assistance of the Holy Spirit which Christ has guaranteed, and consequently from a superior insight into Christ's Gospel and law, an insight which protects it in a special way from error. Thus it can vouch for the truth of what it teaches and proclaims, and it deserves to be trusted. One is allowed to believe its teaching and is even morally bound to do so, insofar as he who understands himself called upon to accept the truth of Christ's Gospel and law must also recognize himself bound to listen to an authority which he knows will transmit this truth in a dependable way.

Make no mistake: teaching authority consists primarily of superior insight.[2] Teaching is the transmission of truth and presupposes insight into the truth which is transmitted. But truth can no longer be transmitted through teaching to one who already knows it. Thus by definition a teacher is superior to the student in knowledge and insight. However, an unconditional obligation for the one who is inferior in knowledge—to let himself be taught by his superior—is given only when it has to do with something that is morally necessary for him. This applies especially to that in which the insight of the authentic magisterium of the Church is superior: the Gospel and law of Christ.[3] Accordingly, the authentic magisterium has binding authority for believers because through the assistance of the Holy Spirit it has superior insight into Christ's truth which is binding upon believers for their salvation.

Concretely, one is obligated to let himself be taught by authority only as often as he needs such instruction to find the truth. This is the case when a person through his own unaided insight either cannot find out a truth at all or at least cannot do so with sufficient certainty. In a sense, every authoritative transmission of the truth has a merely subsidiary character. It would be unnecessary if the individual alone were always in the position to recognize the truth through his own independent insight. One need not be taught what he already knows with certainty. Let us assume that someone through his own reasoning came to the insight that religious liberty is a fundamental human right. Later on, he learns that the Second

Vatican Council in virtue of its teaching authority has taken exactly the same stand on religious liberty. Would he then be obliged trustingly to let the Council teach him what he already knows? Not in the least. The magisterium ought to help the faithful to discover the truth. But it is impossible to help someone look for what he has already found. In short, because the magisterium is not an end in itself but rather a means to recognizing the truth, one is obligated to it only to the extent that one needs help in finding the truth. The believer's correct moral stance vis-à-vis the magisterium is not to expect everything from it, not merely to listen and to accept in trust without making an attempt through one's own individual insight to understand Christ's Gospel and law more correctly, fully, and deeply; rather, the proper recognition of the magisterium consists in one's readiness to trustfully allow himself to be taught as often as he needs it.

The magisterium in its merely authentic teaching is *not infallible.* In its authentic judgments and decisions, it can occasionally err. Then how can the faithful be obliged to trust the magisterium? They must always consider the possibility that they will be disappointed in their trust, that they will be led into error and not into the truth. And how can authority itself claim any trustworthiness when it knows from the very beginning that it is fallible and that it will at times unwillingly disappoint the trust that people put in it? The problem can be stated simply: Is fallible authority real authority? When the question is so put, then we may conclude: the authority that the magisterium exercises is formally like every other kind of authority that men exercise. Fallibility is an unavoidable human characteristic. Thus all authority, insofar as it is exercised by humans, is *eo ipso* fallible authority. Hence infallibility can hardly be constitutive for authority, or else there would be absolutely no human authority whatsoever.

Nevertheless there is still this problem: To what degree is "fallible authority" not a contradiction in terms? Every sick person who goes to a doctor and every youngster who willingly obeys his parents have already resolved the difficulty for their own life-situation. When a sick person entrusts himself to a doctor, he submits himself to his authority, that is, he shows himself willing to follow the doctor's directions, even though he is normally not in a position to determine from his own insight whether the doctor's directions in this particular case are correct. Likewise, when the doctor undertakes the treatment of the sick person, he ascribes to himself both authority and trustworthiness with regard to the patient. No doctor is able, of course, to assume that as a doctor he is infallible; he cannot vouch absolutely that he would never make a wrong diagnosis or prescribe the wrong treatment. No doctor, not even the most capable, would deny that he would ever err, even if he were most conscientious, nor that under certain conditions he might unwillingly make the patient's condition worse rather than better. How can a doctor claim authority and trustworthiness with regard to this patient in spite of this unavoidable possibility? He can do it to the extent that he can say that certainly there are "exceptional cases" when he might make a wrong diagnosis or prescribe the wrong treatment but that "as a rule" he does find the right answers and help his patients as far as they can be helped.

No one who exercises authority can claim more than that. No one need say more than that in order to show his authority and have it recognized. A teacher or superior who "as a rule" gives the correct instructions and only "in exceptional cases" acts incorrectly exercises authority in the only way humanly possible. In short, fallible authority proves to be authority by what it does "as a rule" (*per se*); it shows its fallibility by its failures "in exceptional cases" (*per accidens*). Clearly this formula leaves room for varying degrees of authority. Fallible authority is greater to the degree that its "exceptional cases" are less frequent; it is weaker to the degree that its failures are more frequent. It ceases altogether to be authority when its "exceptions" start to become "the rule" and thus are no longer exceptions.

No matter how seldom it fails, fallible authority is unavoidably somewhat unreliable. One cannot trust it without risking the possibility of being disappointed. Of course, no one reasonably accepts such a risk when it can be avoided without harm or disadvantage. Faced with a choice between fallible and infallible authority, no one would choose the former. But there is no infallible authority among men. Hence, when he sees that in this or that circumstance he needs authoritative direction, one has no other choice than to trust in a fallible authority. He unavoidably accepts the risk of being led into error to his own disadvantage. But since that authority is superior to him in insight, knowledge, and experience, he would without its authoritative direction be dependent upon lesser insight and experience and thus run a greater risk of falling into error. Thus one cannot totally avoid the risk of error; one can only be careful to prefer the lesser risk to the greater. And in general one does that naturally. No doubt parents do some harm to their children by mistakes in child-rearing. But no reasonable person would conclude that children should therefore be left to themselves. Doctors have harmed some patients' health or even life itself through medical errors, culpable or inculpable. But no matter how bad an individual case may be, on the whole it does not outweigh the good which doctors have done for their patients. In short, no one can exercise authority without running the risk of doing harm where he wants to help and ought to help; no one can submit himself to authority without running the risk of being misled instead of led. This risk can and must be faced. It is at the very least the lesser evil.

Granted, the authentic magisterium owes its authority to the founding intention of Christ, and this distinguishes it from other forms of authority which we encounter in human society; because of its basic fallibility, however, it can have no greater formal validity than any other fallible authority.[4] Based upon the guaranteed assistance of the Holy Spirit, the authentic magisterium can claim that its judgments and decisions in questions of faith and morals are "as a rule" correct and only "in exceptional cases" wrong. When it calls upon the faithful to trust in its leadership, even claiming that they are obliged to do so, it presupposes two things. First, although fallible, it is better protected against error than are the faithful, having in general superior insight into Christ's Gospel and law. Second, the magisterium itself, in those cases where it makes merely authentic decisions, is not certain in any absolute way that it is empowered to decide infallibly; it guarantees the faithful, in their search for truth, no absolutely dependable help, but in given circumstances offers the help that is generally the most dependable. Correspondingly, it offers the faithful this prospect: in the trust they give to it, they will "as a rule" find support and only "in exceptional cases" be disappointed.

From this, it follows for those who possess the authentic magisterium that they have to reckon with the possibility that they can err in their decisions and thus mislead the people subject to them. They must also be prepared to recall a previous decision as soon as it is recognized as erroneous. The kind of teaching authority which they have received from Christ cannot protect those who possess the authentic magisterium from the public confession, "*Erravimus*" (We have erred). From the fundamental fallibility of the authentic magisterium, it can happen that something which on account of the teaching of the authentic magisterium the faithful take to be wrong and rejectable may later be seen to be true and tenable — through the teaching of the same magisterium. Is that an overdemanding claim? It is bitter and hard, but it is not overdemanding. Because the faithful themselves are fallible, they simply cannot be spared the demand to correct themselves, rejecting as false and bad what they erroneously held to be true and good. They will not avoid this demand when they trust in the authentic magisterium but they will encounter it less often — only "in exceptional cases."

It is a position of the authentic magisterium on a question of moral law that has given rise to our present considerations. Therefore it may now be appropriate to focus our whole attention on the magisterium's competence of interpreting and proclaiming the *law* of Christ. In questions of the moral law, it is in no way the case that the faithful have access to the truth only through the mediation of the Church's magisterium. Whether one holds that the law of Christ contains concrete ethical demands that go beyond the natural moral law or whether one contests that assertion, there can never be the slightest doubt that each person possesses his own faculty of ethical judgment by means of which he is fundamentally capable of determining "what is the will of God, what is good, pleasing, and perfect" (Rom. 12:2). As often as the Church's magisterium authoritatively mediates knowledge of moral obligations, it fulfills a simply subsidiary responsibility.[5] Because it is basically fallible, the authentic magisterium can hold only a *relative* superiority to the faculty of ethical judgment which the individual believer possesses. It is only *better* protected from error than the individual believer; it has fundamentally more insight but it does not have the only insight into the will of God. Each believer possesses that.

Thus it follows that when in a question of the moral law, the judgment of the authentic magisterium and that of the individual believer are in conflict, one may not say simply that the magisterium is *always* right, and therefore is right also in this case. No, one may only say that in such a conflict of judgment, the authentic magisterium will be right "as a rule," but that "in exceptional cases" it may also happen that the believer and not the magisterium is right.

In a particular concrete case, how can we determine whether the rule holds (that the magisterium has judged correctly) or whether we have an exception to the rule—an error of the magisterium which the believer has recognized? Must both parties, magisterium and believer, present in like fashion the reasons for their decisions so that it can be determined which reasons are sound and who therefore is right? To demand this would imply that the authentic magisterium and the individual believer possess fundamentally the same faculty of ethical judgment, so that it would remain completely open which judgment in the end would prove true and correct. But this implication is false in general. The authentic magisterium is superior in moral insight. Therefore it has to be regarded as *likely* that its teaching will prove correct. Similarly the eventuality that prior insight rather than the magisterium has found the truth is rather unlikely, though in principle it is possible. In theological and canonical language, the assumption of what is likely to be true or correct is called *praesumptio veritatis.* Thus one may say that there is the general presumption that the judgments of the authentic magisterium are correct.[6] Error is not fundamentally excluded by such a presumption; but since it is unlikely, it must be proven in each individual case. Thus when a believer contends that in a question of the moral law he must judge differently from the authentic magisterium, he bears the burden of proof: he must prove that the unlikely case has arisen—a deviation from the rule, an error by the authentic magisterium.[7]

The following is self-evident: as soon as one comes to the conclusion that the decision of the authentic magisterium misses the truth, he may no longer assent to that decision. He is obliged to withdraw his previous approval. It is primarily the truth to which we are obligated; only insofar as the authentic magisterium mediates the truth are we obliged to listen to it. Obedience to the authentic magisterium as a fallible authority is governed by the same ethical rules as obedience to any other fallible authority. If someone obeys an authority although he knows that its rules violate the moral law, he sins against God. To approve in questions of faith and morals what one recognizes as error is to violate the will of God. Thus we read in Wernz-Vidal[8] that the interior approval of the faithful to an authentic teaching "has something of the provisional to it and is founded on the presumption that the authentic teacher of doctrine does not err unless there is a strong suspicion to the contrary. Therefore we owe obedience of the intellect to the teacher much as we owe obedience of the will to a superior issuing a legitimate command—unless there is a strong suspicion that he is commanding something morally wrong."

II
Signs of Unjustified Partiality
to the Authentic Magisterium

What we have said thus far about the authentic magisterium is the traditional and dominant teaching of Catholic theology. It can be found in the appropriate manuals of fundamental theology. But one will find little there about the risk one runs in trusting the authentic magisterium, and nothing at all about possible obligation on the part of those who exercise the magisterium to admit that an authentic decision is wrong. This appears to us to be significant. One gets the impression that when theologians write about the authentic magisterium, they see a need to fight in the interest of authority against an open or latent tendency among the faithful toward insubordination. They explain in great detail what is apt to set the authority of the authentic magisterium in its proper perspective. They cannot do enough to show why the faithful are strictly obliged to put their faith also in the merely authentic magisterium. That the faithful run the risk of being misled now and then and that they might even have to disobey the leadership of the authentic magisterium for the sake of Christ's truth—theologians speak of that (if at all) in a few sentences, as though it had hardly any practical application. This recalls the way that some theologians of a few decades ago treated *epikeia* in the manuals. They could not be completely silent about it. But they put very little trust in the sense of responsibility of most people. They entertained rather the suspicion that more often than not *epikeia* is used as a mere disguise for disobedience—reason enough to mention it only as briefly as possible. No doubt, it is important to specify without any omission the appropriate preference of every authority to those who are subject to it. But is it not just as important to point out the limits of any humanly exercised authority—even the limits of ecclesiastical authority, whenever there are limits? And in point of fact Christ did establish limits for the authentic magisterium.

It is worth the effort to point out some signs of unjustified partiality to the authentic magisterium on the part of theologians. F. Gallati has written a worthwhile monograph on the authentic magisterium entitled "When the Popes Speak."[9] Out of two hundred and one pages of text, a total of five pages is devoted to the question of how a Catholic should act when he determines that an authentic decision of the magisterium is erroneous.[10] Of significance is a tendency which, with variations, appears several times. "If the error [by the authentic magisterium] is certain, the obligation of acceptance ceases" (p. 172). The title of the chapter where this statement is found reads, "Permitted [!] Withdrawal of Internal Assent" (p. 171). Gallati finally states the basic principle: "When the grounds" which speak against the teaching "are clear and cogent, above all, when they are shared by a number of serious and loyal theologians, then it is permitted [!] to differ from the decree or at least to withdraw one's agreement for the present time" (p. 175). One might suppose that what one is merely "permitted" to do, one may also neglect to do. If the agreement to a judgment máy be withdrawn (only) by permission, then it may also remain by permission. Does Gallati mean to say that whoever recognizes a decision of the authentic magisterium as erroneous may choose whether or not he wants to agree to it? That would be absurd. When one has discovered an error on "clear and cogent" grounds, he is not only allowed, he is *strictly obliged* to reject the error, regardless of who is teaching it. If one says that it is "permitted" to withdraw one's agreement from the magisterium when it is shown to be in error, that sounds like a mere concession to the faithful, the recognition of a ground which excuses them from obedience. In reality it has to mean that one has to obey the truth more than any fallible teaching authority.[11]

After Gallati states that it is permissible to withdraw one's internal agreement to the authentic magisterium if it is shown to be in error, he immediately adds: "But it is not permissible, out of respect for the holy power of the Apostolic See, to take a public position against it [i.e., against the erroneous decision]; rather, one should undertake a respectful silence, or the difficulty may be presented to the Apostolic See" (p. 175). Gallati apparently considers this position so obvious that he sees no need to justify it. But is it really so obvious? Definitely not. How could it be a lack of respect and honor to point out to someone in error, even if it is the Church's magisterium, that he is in error?'

Is it not even an obligation to explain the error to the one who makes it, insofar as that is possible? Of course—*Unusquisque sit memor condicionis suae!* (Let everyone be mindful of his own condition.) It is not proper for anyone to assume a donnish attitude toward the magisterium. But if only due respect is maintained in form and appearance, why should the obligation to reveal an error cease when the one in error is an authority figure? There could be certain circumstances which oblige one to leave the erring person in his error—for example, when one could disclose the error only by causing an evil to be judged greater than the error left unexposed. This was probably the earlier attitude: when someone "publicly" contended that the Apostolic See had made an erroneous decision, he brought the prestige and trustworthiness of the authentic magisterium into question in the eyes of the faithful. This would be a greater evil than allowing the error to go unnoticed. But suppose this erroneous decision of the authentic magisterium brings the faithful into a most serious conflict of conscience by imposing upon them a burden which is beyond their strength? Would the magisterium's possible loss of trustworthiness be a greater evil than an unacknowledged error? In this case, doesn't one have to say rather that the error must be admitted as quickly as possible, both for the sake of the conscience of the faithful and for the sake of the trustworthiness of the magisterium? The temptation to the faithful to withdraw their trust from the magisterium will increase the longer and the more they have to suffer from this error of the magisterium. The authentic magisterium is not a private person. When it makes an erroneous decision, the evil affects the whole Church. Thus it is all the more urgent to assist in removing a possible error by the authentic magisterium than by a private person.

Finally, it is not apparent why the authentic magisterium, if it were informed on "telling" grounds of an erroneous decision, would lose trustworthiness in the eyes of the faithful if only they were taught with appropriate clarity that there is in the Church not only the infallible magisterium but also a merely authentic one and that it is appropriate to trust the latter only with reservation. To the extent that the faithful were really conscious of this, it would not then be a cause for amazement if now and then the authentic magisterium found it necessary to admit to an erroneous decision. Indeed, anyone who has discussed the authority of the Church's magisterium at meetings and conferences has discovered how little the faithful are aware that there is such a thing as a merely authentic magisterium and what its particular characteristics are.

We can grant that to "publicly" criticize a recognized erroneous decision of the authentic magisterium would in general be morally inadmissible if it were sufficient for the removal of the error to immediately present to those who exercise the magisterium what the grounds of the error are. Gallati probably presumes that this procedure would be sufficient in every case and thus be the only allowable one. This assumption, however, is not valid universally but only most probable, as the history of the authentic magisterium would show. Such a history, unfortunately, has not yet been written. This lack in the common teaching about the authentic magisterium can for the most part be explained as follows. One begins a priori to explain by analysis of terms, as we have done, what kind of obligations the judgments and decisions of a fallible authority impose. This procedure is undoubtedly suitable to the issue and remains fundamental. But it has to be supplemented by evaluating the experiences of the Church with the authentic magisterium throughout its history. A pure analysis of terms shows that the magisterium errs in its authentic decisions only in exceptional cases. The exceptional case is by definition a rare event in comparison to the normal case. But such a rarity can be greater or lesser; an exception to the rule can occur more often or less. In light of this, what is to be said in this respect about erroneous decisions of the authentic magisterium ? Are they exceptions which occur only once or twice in a century, or much more often? This question cannot be answered a priori, but only a posteriori from the history of the authentic magisterium.

One gets the impression that theologians in general simply presume that erroneous decisions of the authentic magisterium, because they are exceptions, have been extremely rare occurrences in the past and that this will most likely continue to be so in the future. They presume this without offering any proof from the history of the authentic magisterium. But what if history were to show that exceptions to the rule in the magisterium occurred much more often? Wouldn't that have practical consequences both for those who exercise the magisterium and for the faithful who are subject to it? It would be just as important to know how erroneous decisions of the magisterium in the past were recognized and revised, what role the magisterium played and what role theologians or the faithful themselves played, which factor brought about the recognition of the error and which hindered it.

As we have said, there is not enough historical research to give sufficient information on these points. But when, in dealing with the systematic treatment of ethical questions, one follows the history of a problem, one immediately encounters facts which lead to the cautious assumption that erroneous decisions of the authentic magisterium were not all that rare in the past and that a more critical attitude toward the Apostolic See by theologians would sometimes have been helpful in the search for ethical truths.

Let us briefly consider an example of how moral theologians let themselves be misled and put off in resolving an ethical question by putting too much trust in Church authority, although it is certain that in this case Popes and bishops did not reach an authentic decision at all. From the seventeenth to the nineteenth century, an impressive number of Catholic moral theologians taught that the castration of boys for the purpose of achieving and preserving high-pitched voices for religious and secular choirs was morally licit, at least, *probabiliter*. They presented objective arguments. But one might feel, as Peter Browe has written,[12] that it was not because of the objective grounds that moral theologians held castration to be permissible; rather, these grounds "were thought up in order to justify the existing custom and thus to protect and defend the Church from the accusation that it allowed and made use of an abominable practice." For three hundred years, *castrati* sang in the Sistine Chapel. This period spanned the reign of thirty-two Popes. Not one of them spoke against it. Leo XIII was the first to direct that no new *castrati* be accepted into the Sistine Choir. Certainly the silence of all these Popes to this practice is not a formal judgment of the authentic magisterium. But, as moral theologians of the time argued, would the Popes allow *castrati* to sing regularly in the Sistine Chapel if castration for the sake of preserving high-pitched voices were considered immoral? Thus they concluded, as Bartholomeus Mastrius de Meldula (d. 1673), did: "Daily practice, especially that of the Roman curia where such eunuchs were permitted for the service of sacred music and the churches, renders more probable" the permissibility of castration.[13] At the same time, there were moral theologians who held on objective grounds that castration was not permissible. But "because the Pope and many bishops allowed or approved it, many doubted the conclusiveness of their evidence and credited the other position with at least the right to exist and with a certain probability."[14]

This example is also instructive in showing how overdone apologetic zeal can lead to justifying a dubious practice or teaching of the Church's authority by every available means—even means which are not easily reconcilable with intellectual honesty. The current discussion about the moral evaluation of contraception has already led one or another theologian to resort to rather questionable means in order to spare the authentic magisterium the eventuality of admitting that it has erred and must correct itself. In analyzing again and again those passages from *Casti Connubii* which ever since its publication have been understood by everyone as an unequivocal condemnation of the use of contraceptive means, one wonders whether these passages allow perhaps a different interpretation. Have they not invariably been misunderstood? It would be a relief for the authentic magisterium to be able to answer "yes" They would thus remain free from having erred. But wouldn't the authentic magisterium then be subject to a most terrible accusation? No doubt Pius XI knew exactly how the relevant passages of *Casti Connubii* had been received by the whole Church—namely, as a categorical condemnation of the use of contraceptive means. But had the Pope not meant to make such a condemnation, would he not have been obliged to remove the misunderstanding immediately and completely? One cannot reasonably make any kind of reproach against the authentic magisterium, fallible as it is, that it makes a mistake. *But a Pope who knows that in an important matter he has been misunderstood by the whole Church and does nothing to resolve the misunderstanding is liable to a most frightful reproach.*

Today, with so much being thought and even more being said about the historical dimension of man, overdone apologetic zeal has found a new way of sparing the authentic magisterium from having erred. Teachings which today are seen to be wrong need only be interpreted in light of their historical situation to be seen as actually true and correct. Certainly it is a commonplace of hermeneutics that a statement finds its meaning only when it is read in its historical setting. But this does not mean that once it is understood how a statement was originally intended in its historical context, it is true of necessity. If that were so, historical relativism would be valid. What is the nature of the reluctance of some Catholics to admit that the authentic magisterium may possibly have erred, when it induces them to choose ways out which lead to things much worse than an error of the magisterium would be?[15]

A not always satisfactory chapter in the history of Christian moral theology is sexual ethics. That cannot be doubted. The historical studies to date are more than sufficient to demonstrate that. Now, matters would have gone very oddly in the Church if throughout the centuries, a certain kind of sexual ethics could have prevailed without being approved or promoted by the authentic magisterium in some form or another. The position would therefore be extremely unlikely that, in taking a stand on sexual ethics, the authentic magisterium had never supported a false development, not in fifteen hundred years. One need not go back that many years to test whether this position is tenable. It would be enough to compare the teaching on marriage of the encyclical *Casti Connubii* with the corresponding chapters of the *Pastoral Constitution on the Church in the Modern World* of the Second Vatican Council. Is there really a direct, unbroken line of development from the one to the other? Could the magisterium speak about marriage as it does in that pastoral constitution without distancing itself from earlier teachings and thus silently admitting that it had earlier misrepresented the truth in part? How much has the magisterium learned to better understand marriage from theologians whom it censured twenty or thirty years ago?[16]

It would take more than one article to arrive at a halfway satisfactory answer to these questions. Simpler are those which pertain to another problem that likewise triggered a lively debate in the Catholic Church in the last few decades: Is there a general right to religious liberty? In the *Declaration on Religious Liberty,* the Second Vatican Council put an end to the discussion by unmistakably recognizing religious liberty as a general right. Not a few of the Council Fathers were convinced only after a long debate that such a right really exists. This fact alone lets us presume that the Council in its decree did not merely repeat or broaden what the Church's magisterium had taught always and everywhere. And actually the cardinals and bishops who first could not conceive of recognizing a general right to religious liberty appealed to Pius XII. In his 1953 allocution *Ci riesce* he taught otherwise—namely, that a general freedom of religion could exist only as a requirement of toleration. In doing so (as those bishops pointed out), Piux XII and his teaching on toleration stood within a long ecclesiastical tradition, one which Leo XIII in particular had repeated before him. In comparing this allocution of Pius XII with the teaching of the Council on religious liberty, one cannot avoid the following: the Council does not teach the same thing which Pius XII taught; the Council has corrected Pius XII and the long tradition from which he spoke. We have developed this matter elsewhere at greater length.[17] The Council has admitted in silence that in the question of religious liberty, the authentic magisterium has for a long time partially misrepresented the truth—or, to say it more clearly, it has erred. As we said, the Council makes this admission *in silence* by teaching something different from what Pius XII taught. It does not specifically say at any time that it must now distance itself from a traditional authentic teaching because of a better insight into the matter. Why not? Is it because such a free admission does not belong to the style of the Church's teaching authority? Or did the Council want to avoid a loss of respect for the authentic magisterium in the eyes of the Catholic people? Now, even if one would have liked a more open style of speaking, the Council still had to be at liberty to present the correction of the traditional teaching in silence. But a few conciliar statements give the unpleasant impression that they wanted rather to cover up this correction; they speak suggestively of a continuity between the new teaching and the previous one. Thus in its introduction the Declaration asserts: "This Vatican Synod takes careful note of these desires in the minds of men. It proposes to declare them to be greatly in accord with truth and justice. To this end, it searches into the sacred tradition and doctrine of the Church—the treasury out of which the Church continually brings forth new things that are in harmony with the things that are old (*nova semper cum veteribus congruentia profert*)." The introduction closes with this statement: "In taking up the matter of religious freedom this Sacred Synod intends to develop (*evolvere intendit*) the doctrine of recent Popes on the inviolable rights of the human person and on the constitutional order of society." Now, no matter how these statements were intended, it was certainly difficult for a large number of the Council Fathers to come to the conclusion that in the question of religious liberty, the Church's magisterium had for a long time partially misrepresented the truth. This error affected first of all not Catholics themselves, but rather those of other beliefs who lived in predominately Catholic countries. But in no way does that make the error less bitter and hard.

The small amount of historical material which has been presented here allows the cautious assumption that the erroneous decisions of the authentic magisterium were not as infrequent as one might have presumed. One may conclude that Christ never guaranteed to protect his Church from serious errors in all practical problems of life.[18] Let us mention only one consequence to be derived from that.[19] When one learns from experience that he is not protected from error to the extent that he thought he was, he then has to be prepared to re-examine all his previous judgments—not so that he will be right in the end, but rather so that the truth may be recognized. In particular, one cannot deduce a priori in detail from divine revelation just which errors Christ promised to guard his Church against; one has to examine the Church's history, free from all prejudice. If now and then the authentic magisterium misunderstands the moral will of God and thus unwittingly misleads the faithful, that will generally lead to bitter consequences. But a conscience correctly informed in all matters is obviously an illusion, not a real possibility for any person, even a Christian. Soberly acknowledged, this fact *can* be a temptation to resignation or skepticism. But it *ought* to be taken as a challenge to seek more seriously, more energetically, and more thoroughly what was earlier perhaps too quickly and too certainly thought to have been found: the will of God.

Notes

1. On the authentic teaching of the magisterium and its relationship to infallible teaching, see above all the excellent work of J. Beumer, "Das authentische Lehramt der Kirche," in *Theologie und Glaube* 38 (1948), pp. 273-289. "Authentic teaching" is the same as "non-infallible teaching." This designation is not yet standard, but many theologians do use it.
2. This is true of all authority. See B. Schüller, *Gesetz und Freiheit* (Düsseldorf, 1966), pp. 31-41. H. G. Gadamer, *Wahrheit und Methode* (Tübingen, 2nd ed. 1965), pp. 263f., speaks in a similar vein: "Personal authority has its ultimate foundation not in an act of submission and abdication of reason, but rather in an act of acknowledgment and recognition—namely, recognition that the judgment of another takes preference over one's judgment."
3. Because it is founded upon the special assistance of the Holy Spirit, the superior insight of the Church's magisterium has a charismatic character; it is, if you will, charismatic insight—but nevertheless real insight and understanding. Those who exercise the magisterium know and understand what they teach and proclaim; they act as persons in the fullest sense of this word.
4. Some theologians may find this statement rather strange. They are accustomed to looking at the Church's teaching authority as something ful-

ly unique and incomparable. Now, the Church's teaching authority is unique insofar as it is charismatically grounded through the assistance of the Holy Spirit and has Christ's Gospel and law for its theme. But what applies to fallible authority as such must also apply to the authentic magisteɪium if authority and fallibility have any meaning at all in speaking of the authentic magisterium. Further, one repeatedly discovers at meetings that non-theologians see their expected trust in the authentic proclamation of the magisterium as an *obsequium rationale* only when it is clear to them that a person in his actual human condition is dependent upon the trust he puts in the leadership of fallible authority in all possible dimensions of his life.

5. If the law of Christ did possess concrete ethical demands that go beyond the natural moral law, the Church's magisterium would have a responsibility in relationship to this that would not be subsidiary only. See B. Schüller, "Zur theologischen Diskussion über die lex naturalis," in *Theologie und Philosophie* 41 (1966), pp. 481-503.

6. M. Scheeben, *Kath. Dogmatik I* (Ges. Schriften, III [Freiburg i. Br., 1948]), p. 265: "Except with the *approbatio solemnis* of the Holy See, the doctrinal decrees of the particular councils are not infallible. Therefore [!] they possess only a greater or lesser presumption of truth." According to Scheeben, authoritative but non-infallible decisions are identified in that their truth can be "presumed." The term *praesumtio veritatis* seems to some theologians to be extremely juridical since they find it so often in canon law. Actually canon law has adopted a rule from the general process for the establishment of truth, which a person cannot renounce as the "ultimate reason" and necessary essence of authoritative leadership. H. G. Gadamer (pp. 250-268) calls the convictions and values taken over from fallible authority "pre-judgments" (*praejudicia*) and demonstrates their legitimacy and indispensability. K. Rahner ("Thoughts on the Possibility of Belief Today" in *Theological Investigations V* [Baltimore, 1966], p. 4) applies the same rule: "If a man does not want to abandon his very self, then he must basically regard what is already there as something to be taken over and to be preserved until he has proof of the contrary."

7. Genuine human tradition also possesses the character of fallible authority; thus the rules presented here apply to it as well. In this sense, T. E. Jessop writes in *The Christian Morality* (London, 1960), p. 12, about who bears the burden of proof—the one who asserts the validity of morality or the one who denies it: "Given, however, the age-long tradition of morality, it may fairly be contended that the onus of proof lies rather on those who would reject the moral attitude than on those who accept it. As a rule, it is the rebel who has to prove his case, for the accepted position usually has behind it a large volume of social experience."

8. Ius Canonicum IV/2 (Romae, 1835), n. 617.

9. "Wenn die Päpste sprechen," published in Vienna in 1960.

10. J. Ford and G. Kelly, *Contemporary Moral Theology*, Vol. I

(Westminster, Maryland, 1958), pp. 3-41, treat the authority of the Church's magisterium rather more one-sidedly.

11. The *clausula Petri* (Acts 5:29) presents an ethical principle which is valid for a person's relationship to fallible authority. Normally one obeys God by obeying God-given authority. But when one recognizes in an exceptional case that such an authority misses the moral good or the truth in its directives, there is a conflict between divine authority and human authority. One must then obey God (the truth) more than men.

12. Peter Browe, *Zur Geschichte der Entmannung* (Breslau, 1936), p. 112. The evidence for the following information can be found here.

13. Cited in Browe, p. 112, n. 100.

14. *Ibid.,* p. 113.

15. J. Beumer *(loc. cit.)* correctly states: "Because the possibility of an error [by the authentic magisterium] cannot be doubted, we may not hold back from establishing its actual existence . . . . Many things which were said against papal infallibility at the time of the Vatican Council actually belong here. If the points which were then attacked were definitely not *ex cathedra* decisions, then there can hardly be any doubt that here and there a more or less authentic proclamation was involved. A clear example is the case of Galileo. More recently, we could cite the declaration of the Holy Office on the *comma Joanneum* and its subsequent 'interpretation,' which was practically a withdrawal, and the various positions on the question of evolution and on exegetical problems in the Old Testament."

16. Valuable material can be found in John T. Noonan, *Contraception. A History of Its Treatment by the Catholic Theologians and Canonists* (Cambridge, Massachusetts, 1965).

17. B. Schüller, "Die Religionsfreiheit nach dem 2. Vatikanum," in *Kirche in Not,* Band XIV (Königstein, 1967), pp. 13-29. See also *Herder Korrespondenz* (Freiburg/Br., 1966), p. 272, where it says that the Council's *Declaration on Religious Liberty* "demonstrates an essential step forward in ecclesiastical thinking, whose continuity with the teaching of the last few Popes is difficult to prove. One must (or may) speak here rather of a *caesura* in the utterances of the Church's magisterium." See further G. de Broglie, *Problèmes chrétiens sur la liberté religieuse* (Paris, 1965), p. 8, where it says that in the question of religious liberty, the tradition has given "une réponse opposée [!] à celle à laquelle le Concile va se rallier."

18. Such errors produce in the faithful an erroneous conscience. If it is inculpable, it is not an immediate threat to the salvation of the individual. Therefore one may say with certainty that the Church's magisterium, if it errs in the merely authentic proclamation of the moral will of God, does not endanger the salvation of those who entrust themselves to it. See B. Schüller, "Das irrige Gewissen," in *Theologische Akademie* 2 (Frankfurt a. M., 1965), pp. 7-28.

19. See B. Schüller, "Die Autorität der Kirche und die Gewissensfreiheit der Gläubigen," in *Der Männerseelsorger* (September/October, 1966), pp. 130-143.

Morality and Magisterium

Daniel C. Maguire

History does not commend a simple view of the magisterium of the Church, which may be described as its active competence to teach and bear witness to the nature and consequences of God's revelation in Christ. Although this competence has been in the Church from the beginning, its object, as well as its subject and manner of realization, shows the creative and passive-reactive shifts and changes that mark the history of man. Indeed, one may say that the way in which the magisterium appears in history depends on the prevailing ecclesiology, the status of communications, and the cultural views of authority and truth.

"Teaching" is not a univocal term. History presents a variety of teaching forms, and a teacher can be anything from an authority figure who imposes information on his subjects to a prodding stimulator of thought. It must be remembered, too, that the Church acting is also the Church teaching. In the beginning, liturgy was a primary means of teaching the good news. Important sections of the inspired Scriptures are actually liturgical documents. The teaching office in the early Church was not relegated to a "department"; the community itself was magisterial. The community, seen as a concrete and living norm of Christian existence, came to be called "the Way" (Acts 9:2; 19:9; 22:4). Councils and synods became a favored technique for tapping ecclesial wisdom and for revealing the Church's prevalent state of doctrinal consciousness. Particular weight was also attached to the traditions of the communities in the great cities which had been the starting points of Christianization. At times, the most important magisterium figures on the scene were individual bishops who through their eloquence and extraordinary abilities obtained a voice and influence not suggested by their sees. In the period from the sixth to the eleventh centuries, the monasteries attained magisterial prominence through the penitential books. Centralization became a notable phenomenon in the modern Church with teaching and administrative burdens shifting more to the Roman See—a situation now being altered by an application of the principles of collegiality and subsidiarity—but no study of the magisterium can ignore the variety of forms that has characterized it in history. It is not enough to look to conciliar or Roman decrees to know what the Church has taught.

Our specific concern here is with the Church teaching morality. This is not to say that the moral and dogmatic magisterium do not face many common problems. Both are affected by the fallibility of language, the nature of judgment and propositional formulations of truth, and recent refinements in the area of biblical exegesis. Advances in the understanding of both the content and mode of revelation require a "demythologizing" of formal magisterial pronouncements of the past on questions such as original sin, the preternatural gifts, the knowledge of Christ, the eternity of hell, the virgin birth and other Marian dogmas. We must also examine the myths that gird our understanding of the Church itself. The nature of morality, however, is such as to present special problems and to justify a distinct consideration of the Church's authentic teaching competence in this area.[1]

I

THE THEOLOGY OF THE MAGISTERIUM

The theology of the magisterium has been until recently a neglected subject. Customarily, the magisterium is spoken of as either *ordinary* or *extraordinary*. The extraordinary magisterium comprises the *ex cathedra* statements of the Pope and the solemn statements of bishops convoked in council in union with the Pope to define the faith. The ordinary magisterium refers to the normal daily teaching of the bishops throughout the world.

As regards infallibility, the ordinary magisterium is considered infallible when there is "unanimity of the episcopal magisterium."[2]

The concept of an infallible ordinary magisterium presents some special problems. First of all, the determination of what constitutes unanimity is not always an obvious matter, especially in specific questions of morality. Secondly, unanimity or consensus can be of various kinds. There can be reflective or non-reflective consensus. Unanimity on some moral matters might represent only a legacy received uncritically from another age, a non-reflective consensus, which has serious limitations.

The discussion of infallibility has come to center more on the extraordinary magisterium, with the *Pastor Aeternus* of Vatican I offering the most solemn expression of the consciousness of the Church concerning its magisterial role. This constitution centered, with unfortunate exclusiveness, on the infallibility of the Pope. Since, however, it emphasized that the Pope had the same infallibility that Christ willed his Church to have, its statement provides much insight into the understanding of infallibility in general that existed in the Church of Vatican I.

The Council declared it a divinely revealed dogma that the Roman Pontiff, when he speaks ex cathedra, that is, when in discharge of the office of pastor and doctor of all Christians, by virtue of his supreme apostolic authority, he defines a doctrine regarding faith or morals to be held by the universal Church, by the divine assistance promised to him in blessed Peter, is possessed of that infallibility with which the divine Redeemer willed that his Church should be endowed for defining doctrine regarding faith or morals, and that therefore such definitions of the Roman Pontiff are irreformable of themselves, and not from the consent of the Church.

This definition was the result of prolonged and intense conciliar discussion and debate. Its meaning is precise and finely nuanced, but a study of the text alone would not reveal that. The context must be carefully considered if we are to capture the meaning of this important definition. This is needed all the more today inasmuch as the *Constitution on the Church* of Vatican II repeats the words of Vatican I, without, of course, assuming the theologian's task of analyzing their original import (chapter 3).

Competent theological inquiry has never neglected the task of research into the *acta* of Church councils in order to discover the true significance of conciliar texts. Thanks to new understanding of the evolution of doctrine and of the historical and cultural conditioning of human thought and language, modern theologians are becoming more aware of the need for contextual analysis of past magisterial pronouncements. Recent advances in the interpretation of Scripture have also been instructive in this regard. Vatican II gives this advice to the biblical exegete:

> The interpreter must investigate what meaning the sacred writer intended to express and actually expressed in particular circumstances as he used contemporary literary forms in accordance with the situation of his own time and culture. For the correct understanding of what the sacred author wanted to assert, due attention must be paid to the customary and characteristic styles of perceiving, speaking, and narrating which prevailed at the time of the sacred writer. . . . [3]

Since magisterial Church pronouncements can hardly be more immune to the influence of context and culture than Scripture, the task of the theologian is obvious. He must face the problems of language, the influence of epistemological and theological presuppositions, the presence of limiting polemical perspectives, and the reality of dogmatic development. And when past magisterial pronouncements on morality are involved, the theologian must consider the statements in the light of the development of moral insight and the circumstances and conditions that affected the statements. To do anything less is to strip the original statement of its reality.

Vatican I had originally proposed to develop a vast schema on the Church of Christ. Chapters one to ten would treat of the Church in general; eleven and twelve would treat of the primacy of the Pope. Through internal and external pressures, the decision was made to drop all the chapters except those on the Pope, but many bishops felt that a separate discussion of the infallibility of the Pope without treatment of the role of the bishops was ill-considered.[4] Bishop Moriarity of Kerry, for example, testified that in the Irish Church neither the ordinary preaching nor the catechisms stressed the infallibility of the Pope, but that the subject of infallibility was always said to be the Church. In practice this meant the bishops in agreement with the Pope.[5] The proposed definition seemed to be giving a power to the Pope which was too "personal, separate, and absolute." These words were spoken in concern by so many that Bishop d'Avanzo remarked that the council could become known in history as "the council of three words."[6] To quell these anxieties, the Deputation of the Faith, the committee which had drafted the document, gave close attention to the clarification of these terms as well as to the notion and object of infallibility in the Church.

Speaking for the Deputation, d'Avanzo stressed that the anti-Gallican expression of the definition *ex sese non autem ex consensu ecclesiae* did not purport to separate the Pope from the Church. He pointed out, first, that it was the same Holy Spirit who was operative in Pope, bishops, and faithful. Second, the Pope teaching infallibly did not do so in virtue of a new revelation but, rather, with the help of the Holy Spirit; his role was to discover the truth already contained in the fonts of revelation. Third, it was obvious that the Pope did not work privately with the Holy Spirit, but rather that he must seek out the truth in the living witness of the Church.[7]

A more complete elucidation is found in the monumental speech of Bishop Gasser, the outstanding theologian and spokesman of the Deputation. He centered his discourse on the "three words." The infallibility of the Pope was "personal" only in the sense that the Pope was a public person and head of the Church.[8] This is better explained when he discusses the second word, "separate." He begins by saying that the word "distinct" would be more precise. The Pope is part of the Church, and indeed when he speaks infallibly he speaks as one who represents the universal Church. The essential concurrence and cooperation of the Church is not excluded by the definition.[9] Since the Pope has no new revelation on which to base his statement, he is bound to seek out the truth in the Church by various means. This is an obvious duty which binds him in conscience.[10]

Is the definition, then, really maintaining a union between the Pope and the consenting Church? Yes. Anything other than such a union is unthinkable.[11] What kind of consent does the definition exclude? It excludes consent of the Gallican style (cf. Denz. 1322-1326). To make consent a *de iure conditio* would create insoluble problems, such as determining how many bishops had to be consulted, and so forth.[12] When the truth is obvious it would be foolish to bind the Pope to an extensive investigation. It is in this limited sense that the consent of the Church is not required.[13]

Concerning the question of infallibility, Gasser said: (1) Absolute infallibility is ascribed only to God. The infallibility of the Church is limited. (2) The limited infallibility of the Church, whether exercised by the Pope or in some other fashion, extends to the same ambit of truths. (3) It certainly extends to the revealed truths contained in the deposit of faith. (4) The infallibility extends to those truths which, though not revealed, are necessary for the defense and explanation of the deposit. Whether the infallibility extended to these matters in such a way as to constitute them dogmatic truths (the denial of which would be heresy) was an unsolved theological question and the Deputation decided unanimously to leave the question open.[14] Doctrines noted as theologically certain (or with lesser notes) are not within the range of *de fide* infallible statements.[15]

More space than is available here would be required to discuss the total context of Vatican I and the deficiencies under which the Council labored. In any event, the Church's present understanding of the doctrines discussed at Vatican I has grown and widened. As Vatican II says, "There is a growth in the understanding of the realities and the words which have been handed down."[16] Important areas touched by Vatican I have known vast development: the interpretation of Scripture, the relationship of Scripture and tradition, the concept of "Church," including the acknowledgment of genuine ecclesial reality in the Protestant Churches, the increased respect for the *sensus fidelium* and the magisterial role of the laity.[17] We cannot concede the genuine ecclesiality of the Protestant Christian Churches and then deny them magisterial significance. The doctrinal positions of all Christian bodies must now be viewed with a new seriousness. This appreciation does not simplify the theology of the magisterium, but it is a reality from which we may not flee.

Let us now focus on certain elements of the teaching of Vatican I that are vital to our understanding of the moral magisterium. It is an important fact that Vatican I did not give special attention to the distinct problems involved in teaching morality. This is not surprising, since the nineteenth century may represent the nadir of Catholic moral theology. Repetitious manuals that taught morality like a code had trained the Council bishops and theologians. The in-depth expositions of Aquinas were not seminary fare; indeed, until *Aeterni Patris* of Leo XIII in 1879, a heavily Cartesian spirit per-vaded Catholic thought.[18] The Cartesian stress on clarity as the mark of truth did not dispose its students to grasp the ambiguities and complexities that are met in applying moral principles to the in-finitely diverse circumstances of life.[19]

Vatican I said that "infallibility" extended at least to the truths contained in the "deposit of faith." It should be clear, however, that we no longer look to the "deposit of faith" for specific answers to modern ethical questions. For example, no longer does anyone look in Scripture for explicit answers to questions of interest-taking. Also, however much the ingredients of peace were in the doctrine of Jesus, he never took a position on the question of war. As Rudolf Schnackenburg observes: "Jesus no more intended to change the social system than he did the political order. He never assumed a definite attitude on economic and social problems."[20] Revelation did not answer the multiple questions of sexual ethics, the moral right to silence, religious liberty, business ethics and international law. Even when Jesus was apparently quite specific on the divorce issue, he did not close the case. Father Schillebeeckx writes:

> It is important to bear in mind that, although Christ declared that marriage was indissoluble, he did not tell us where the ele-ment that constituted marriage was situated—what in fact made a marriage a marriage, what made it the reality which he called absolutely indissoluble. This is a problem of anthropology. . . . [21]

The so-called "Pauline Privilege" (canons 1120-1124, 1126) which permits a person to contract a second valid marriage for reasons of faith while the first partner still lives is not found in St. Paul. Schnackenburg points out that the permission is based on 1 Corinthians 7:15ff.; he makes clear that "Paul is dealing with the question whether separation is permissible in such a case; he does not speak of remarriage."[22] In other words, the Church went beyond Scripture here and decided that the ideal of indissolubility did not apply in this case. In this instance divorce and remarriage were seen as a value even though without scriptural warranty.

Clearly then, the "deposit of faith," whatever riches it contains for morality, does not do the moralist's work. Although Vatican I defined that infallibility in faith and morals extends to guarding and exposing the deposit of faith (Denz. 1836), it obviously does not extend to answers that are not there. Gasser, however, explained that it extends in some theologically undetermined fashion to those matters that, though not revealed, are necessary to guard, explain, and define the deposit of faith (Mansi 52:1226).

It would be no simple matter to show that the various moral questions we have mentioned above are necessary for guarding, explaining, and defining the deposit of faith. Indeed Cardinal Berardi, immediately after the distribution of the final schema for the infallibility definition, pointed out the vagueness of the definition with regard to practical moral matters. He said that the wording even implied that the infallibility did not extend to decisions about the morality of actions *in concreto spectatae*.[23] His difficulty was not relieved the next day by the final exposition of Gasser.

Whatever problems the definition presents in this regard, the Council intended to say that in some way the teaching authority of the Church does extend to the area of morals. The practice of the hierarchical magisterium at the time and the general tone of the Council leave no doubt of it. What the Council did not do was explain how this teaching competence is best realized and explained.

Traditionally the Church has claimed authority to teach "faith and morals." What is meant by "morals" in this expression is not clear, but the dominant opinion of late has been that it refers to the general and specific questions of natural moral law. Pius XII asserted this unambiguously:

> The power of the Church is not bound by the limits of "matters strictly religious," as they say, but the whole matter of the natural law, its foundation, its interpretation, and its application, so far as their moral aspect extends, are within the Church's power.[24]

Pope John XXIII, speaking of the moral principles of the social order, said:

> For it must not be forgotten that the Church has the right and the duty to intervene authoritatively with its children in the

temporal sphere when there is a question of judging the application of those principles to concrete cases.[25]

Recent discussion, however, comes to center more and more upon whether to term this competency "infallible." Gregory Baum writes: "The Church speaks with great authority in the area of human values but when it is not dealing with the ethics revealed in the Gospel, it is not exercising an infallible teaching office."[26] However, since the Church is entrusted with the whole of revelation, it seems obvious to John J. Reed, S.J., that it may teach the natural law infallibly. In some way the natural law is contained in revelation. Since this allegation is bristling with difficulties, Father Reed explains: "Evidently, as with matters of dogmatic truth, a particular demand of natural law may be contained only obscurely, implicitly, or virtually in the deposit of revelation."[27] Richard A. McCormick, S.J. applauds this position, but notes that the disagreement between Baum and Reed "is representative of a growing body of opinion on both sides of the question."[28] I think that the term "infallible" does not in fact aptly describe the nature or function of the moral magisterium, and that we should discontinue using that term in describing the moral magisterium. My reasons are the following:

1. It is commonplace in discussions of infallibly defined doctrine to refer to the norm of canon 1323, #3, which says that nothing is to be taken as a definition unless it is seen to be such beyond all reasonable doubt: *nisi id manifeste constiterit.* Certainly since Vatican I, and even before that Council, it is difficult to find an example of a pronouncement in the area of natural moral law that meets this requirement. The lack of examples in the writings of the defenders of the infallible moral magisterium is thus not surprising.[29]

The Church's non-use of the prerogative of infallibility is theologically instructive. It seems to mean that in practice, despite its firm grasp of the moral vision of the Gospel, the Church seems to realize (though the theologians have been slow to acknowledge it) that it does not enjoy an infallibly guaranteed competence to apply the moral vision of the Gospel to complex natural law questions such as are presented by medical ethics, genetics, business ethics, international law, social reconstruction, and war and peace. To allege that the Church can teach the natural law infallibly suggests the weird spectacle of a Church that has the power to settle these questions in a definitive fashion and does not do so. It is also a position that must suffer considerable embarrassment from the data of history.

The infallibilist position also claims that the natural law is contained implicitly or virtually in the deposit of revelation. This is not a little baffling, since all ethical theory grants that concrete and changing circumstances enter essentially into the constitution of the "moral object." Hence there is an essential presentiality (*parcas*) in the natural law which precludes its being pre-given even in an implicit and virtual way, in any "deposit."[30] Knowledge of the empirical data is essential to moral judgment; no moral judgment may be made without such knowledge.

Moral principles and examples may be pre-given; they may have been acquired from past experience or revelation. They enter into moral judgment but they are not the only requisite for moral science, which is not simply a deductive science. For particular demands of the natural law to be contained in revelation it would be necessary to say that a foreknowledge of the ethical implications of the particularities and circumstances of subsequent centuries is somehow contained in that revelation. Such a contention is certainly not supported by an uncritical repetition of past magisterial formulations or by the Church's abstinence in the use of this infallibility.

2. In Thomistic ethics, moral principles are, by reason of the ethical implications of circumstances, not universally applicable. The completely general principles such as "Do good and avoid evil" can be called absolute and universal precisely because of their lack of circumstantial content. When, however, you begin to apply specific principles to particular contexts, they admit of exceptions.

This does not mean that there are no stable values in the moral realm; for example, the sacredness of human life must always be respected. However, in certain cases a man may kill; the ethical task is to determine what instances of killing are, because of special circumstances, compatible with a respect for life. To say in advance that no circumstance whatever could ever justify a particular action implies a foreknowledge of the ethical import of all possible circumstances. The epistemological problem here should be obvious. In actions involving other human beings history should have taught us that the unpredictables and imponderables should not be adjudicated in advance.

Indeed, it can be stated that as the complexity of life increases, "exceptional" cases become more frequent. As Karl Rahner says: "What used to be an extreme borderline case in a moral situation which hardly ever occurred has now become almost the 'normal' case."[31] Compare the ethical problems of a general store in the country a century ago with the ethical problems of a corporation like General Motors today to see what complexification does to ethics. Infallible guidance is not anticipated in such a situation; what is needed is a meaningful and effective dialogue of experts in particular fields with moralists and other representatives of the moral magisterium of the Church.

3. The very nature of truth should make us cautious in speaking of infallibility. Reality always exceeds our conceptualizations and knowledge of it. As Piet Fransen writes, the magisterial ministry "is a diaconia of the Holy Spirit and also of divine truth. This truth possesses the Church but we do not possess it."[32] Morality involves the mysterious truth of personal contact and relationship of God and man. No matter how wise we become in explaining this mystery, we remain unprofitable servants and we still know only "in part." "The truth lives in us as something open, a disposition for more truth, for correction and completion."[33] In a sense, human knowledge is never free of error inasmuch as it is never complete. This is not to say that it is invalid; it embodies the real, but for *homo viator* it is never complete or entirely error-free.

This notion was quite alien to the men of Vatican I, who sought to grasp truth *nullo admixto errore* (Denz. 1786). The term "infallibility" seems to imply a completion that our groping knowledge of reality does not allow. It conforms better to Cartesian assumptions than to modern views of truth.

4. There is a conflict in the concept of an infallible statement made through the medium of fallible language. A form of words can symbolize "an indefinite number of diverse propositions."[34] Communication, which is the goal of language, can be blocked by

"a lack of shared presuppositions or shared universe of discourse."[35] Meaning has a tendency to slip out from under verbal formulae; through usage, new meanings succeed in attaching themselves to old expressions. It can happen that a verbal change is essential to recapture and conserve the original meaning. This appreciation of the character of language is not entirely new. St. Thomas, for example, taught that the act of the believer did not terminate at the proposition but at the reality (IIa, IIae, q.1, a. 2, ad 2). But it is modern linguistic analysis that has presented this insight with force.

5. Even this brief look at the history of our moral teaching should prompt us to describe our teaching competence in more modest terms. Either we must admit a drastic relativism which would allege that all of that teaching was right in its day or we must admit the presence of error in the history of the pilgrim Church. To stress this point: The decree of Gratian which taught that it was "meritorious" to kill the infidel, the teaching of Gregory XVI and Pius IX that it was "madness" to allege religious freedom as a right of man and a necessity in society, and the proclamation of Vatican II that such freedom is a right and necessity in society—such teachings are not consistent or mutually reconcilable. Even full recognition of the historical context that spawned these statements does not establish doctrinal continuity. The change on interest-taking cannot honestly be explained by alleging simply that the nature of money has changed. Interest-taking could have served some economic purposes in the fifteenth century at the height of the Church's condemnation. Certainly the nature of sexuality has not changed so much as to permit our justification of the opinions once taught by the universal ordinary magisterium. Similarly for the right to silence, and the others.

This, of course, is not to deny that notable good often resulted from positions taken. So, for example, the ravages of a usurious economy that have wracked other civilizations were largely averted. The attitude toward contraception did much to underline the sacredness of life and the life-giving processes. Analysis of the historical context often makes it quite understandable why a particular position was taken. These traditions, however much awry they may have been in their conceptualizations and conclusions, usually embodied basic and enduring value judgments about the dignity of man and the urgency of love.

Still, to assert that in all of this there is not change but simply development is to play semantic games. Some react to the discovery of past error by insisting that the doctrine in question was not infallibly taught. When the doctrine has come to be seen as largely wrong, its non-infallibility is hardly debatable. Behind this protest, however, there seems to be a docetist tendency to deny the incarnationalism of the Christian experience and the essential characteristics of human thought and language. Implicit in it is the failure to accept the fact that we are a pilgrim people who move slowly and not always directly toward the beckoning God of truth.

6. The *acta* of Vatican I show that some of the bishops were not at all happy with the word "infallible."[36] Furthermore, the use of the word in conciliar discussion shows marked ambiguity. Gasser explained that infallibility—which had become by this point synonymous with the teaching authority of the Church—extended also, in some way, to positions noted as rash, scandalous, or dangerous.[37] Clearly Gasser intended to assert teaching competence concerning matters related to the data of revelation. Describing this as yet theologically unrefined competence as "infallibility" was not felicitous. We are not, of course, bound to this expression.

7. We have already noted some of the difficulties encountered by the defenders of the infallible moral magisterium. We touched upon the position of Father Reed, who maintains that the natural law is contained implicitly and obscurely in the "deposit." Of interest here are the remarks of Richard A. McCormick as he comments with regrettable brevity on the position of Father Baum: "The Church's prerogative to propose infallibly the Gospel morality would be no more than nugatory without the power to teach the natural law infallibly."[38] He argues from the ambiguous position that the natural law is integral to the Gospel; hence the Church can teach it infallibly.

Saying that the natural law is integral to the Gospel could mean that principles concerning human dignity, the sacredness of life, the idea of morality as an operation of love, and the like, are integral to both natural law and the Gospel. From this, however, it does not at all follow that the Church has the power to proceed infallibly through the multiple judgments and informational processes required to apply these natural and Gospel values to special natural law problems. The Christian experience is certainly an enrichment of the natural law. The magisterium, if it is faithful to this experience, has much to offer those who struggle for the realization of human values, but this contribution need not be considered infallible.

McCormick elaborates his argument by saying that natural law is essential to the protection and proposal of Christian morality. He concludes again that particular demands of the natural law are capable of definition. Given the many meaningful and important ways that the Church can treat natural law questions, and given the way that it does in fact treat them, this seems to be a case of *qui nimis probat nihil probat.*

McCormick's concluding statement is more helpful:

> Would not, therefore, the ability to teach infallibly the dignity of man (certainly a revealed truth) without being able to exclude infallibly forms of conduct incompatible with this dignity be the ability infallibly to propose a cliché?[39]

There seems to be a legitimate concern here to avoid an irrelevant proclamation of the Gospel ethos without applying it to modern life. One can readily agree that the Church must enter into the specific questions of the day in a quite specific fashion. The Church must recognize in so doing, however, that the position it in good faith assumes may, as has happened often in the past, later have to be changed because of subsequent data and insights. Infallibility is not the only escape from platitudinous clichés.

A final word on McCormick's statement about excluding forms of conduct that are incompatible with a proposed ideal: the claim that this can be done is more modest and nuanced than "teaching the natural law infallibly." The essential problem, however, remains. The Church might declare with much certitude (infallibly, if you will) that murder (unjust killing) is incompatible with human dignity. This statement is self-evident if not tautological. It is a general statement which allows for certitude precisely because of the lack of circumstantial content. To be certain about this does not mean that you can be equally certain (or at all certain) that a particular instance of killing is murder. The certitude of the general principle does not pass over into the discussion of cases such as the liceity of certain abortions or pills that prevent implantation. Here moral intuition, empirical data, philosophical probings, and various forms of expertise are relevant, and the certainty of unapplied principle does not obtain.

Baum's view of the magisterium has the merit of an historical consciousness:

> We must face the fact that the development in the understanding and presentation of the Gospel has not always been positive in the Church and may not always be positive. It would not be difficult to establish the fact that certain themes of divine revelation have not always been announced and taught by the ecclesiastical magisterium with the same clarity.[40]

He still feels bound to assert some area of infallibility, however, and he formulates the idea that the Church is infallible only in regard to the ethics revealed in the Gospel. But as McCormick observed, such an infallible power would be nugatory, since most of the current ethical questions are not answered in the Gospel. Much of the ethics of the Gospel is applied to the situation existing at that time and must be reapplied today to be of value. If Baum meant to say that the Church can be expected to have a basic sureness about the Gospel's moral ideals he might well have stated it without resorting to infallibility, and balanced it off with his realisitic perception of how the sinful Church can at times obscure the Gospel light.

8. In the polemics of the past century the word "infallible" has acquired connotations that are offensive and confusing to many. "The manner and order in which Catholic belief is expressed should in no way become an obstacle to dialogue with our brethren"; Catholic doctrine should be presented "in ways and in terminology which our separated brethren too can really understand."[41] Words, like persons, have a history and a set of relationships from which one may not prescind. There is probably no word which more readily suggests to non-Catholic Christians the objectionable aspects of the Catholic pre-conciliar mind-set than this word "infallible."

II
THE AUTHENTIC, NON-INFALLIBLE MAGISTERIUM

Since the question of infallibility has tended to loom over Catholic moral theology casting an inhibiting shadow, it was necessary to deal with it at some length. Of more practical importance, however, is the authentic and admittedly fallible magisterium. In the *Constitution on the Church*, Vatican II speaks of this magisterium and the response due it:

> In matters of faith and morals, the bishops speak in the name of Christ and the faithful are to accept their teaching and adhere to it with a religious assent [*obsequio*] of soul. This religious submission [*obsequium*] of will and mind must be shown in a special way to the authentic teaching authority of the Roman Pontiff, even when he is not speaking *ex cathedra*.[42]

Pope John XXIII wrote:

> It is clear, however, that when the hierarchy has issued a precept or decision on a point at issue, Catholics are bound to obey their directives. The reason is that the Church has the right and obligation, not merely to guard the purity of ethical and religious principles, but also to intervene authoritatively when there is question of judging the application of these principles to concrete cases.[43]

We will impose upon John Reed again for an example of the way in which many theologians explained the effect of the authentic, non-infallible magisterium. From such teaching, he says, "two consequences follow, one external and absolute, the other internal and conditional. In the external order there results the obligation not to contradict the doctrine in public speech or writing." Theologians may enter into a "speculative discussion" of the doctrine taught, "supposing a discreet selection of audience and method of discourse." Still, even in such discreet discussions the

matter in question "is not to be approached as something on which either side is of equal standing or could be equally followed."
So much for the external order.

> In the internal order there results per se the obligation of intellectual assent to and acceptance of the teaching. But since, in the supposition, the teaching is not infallible and there remains the possibility of the opposite, there must remain also the absolute possibility that someone, exceptionally qualified in some aspect of the question upon which the conclusion depends, may have grave reason to think that the proposition is not certainly true. In this event the individual, while bound by the teaching in the external order, would not be obliged to yield internal assent.[44]

Before commenting on this particular approach to the papal and episcopal magisterium it seems necessary to introduce more recent philosophical and theological perspectives without which the discussion is doomed to become a narrow exercise in legalistic quibbling.

Catholics have always believed in ecclesiastical offices, and linked these offices to a teaching role. It is partially in terms of teaching that theology explains the nature of the offices of deacon, priest, bishop, and Pope. Catholic theology has emphasized those scriptural texts that promised the grace and blessings of God upon the preaching and teaching offices of the Church (Mt. 16:18; 28:19; Jn. 21:15ff; 1 Tim. 4:14; 5:22; 2 Tim. 1:6; 2 Pet. *passim*).

As often happens in any science, certain aspects of a truth might be overly stressed due to cultural and polemical factors, with the result that other elements are neglected and an imbalance ensues. Regarding the ecclesiastical office, theological science should be especially wary. There is a deep-rooted tendency observable in man's religious history to magnify the role of religious authority figures and to view their teachings as oracular.[45]

To preserve us from a false estimation of the authority of the teaching office in the Church the office must be seen not only in terms of a *gift* of the Spirit but also in terms of a *task* imposed by the Spirit. We must continue to stress the supportive presence of

God in the teaching Church, but we must acknowledge that the divine assistance is not foisted upon us without our cooperation and a disposition of openness on our part. Neither history nor theology will permit us to say that constant fidelity to the Spirit is guaranteed by the promise of the ultimate victory of Christ. We must never forget that the Church which is holy by the presence of God's Spirit is sinful by the presence of man: "The Church is a sinful Church: that is a truth of faith, not just a fact of its primitive experience. And it is a shattering truth."[46] If we forget this truth of faith in our discussion of the magisterium, as though the magisterium were removed from the possibility of sin, we imply that God's help is given without human cooperation. To remove the spots and smooth the wrinkles that we find in ourselves, in the Church, or in magisterial pronouncements is a service to the Lord who works with us.

Discussions of the Church teaching tend to ignore how equivocal, mutable, and culturally conditioned the notion of teacher is. Recognizing with the recent Council that "the human race has passed from a rather static concept of reality to a more dynamic, evolutionary one,"[47] we should also view the teaching offices of the Church in an evolutionary perspective. "The living conditions of modern man have been so profoundly changed in their social and cultural dimensions that we can speak of a new age in human history." Thus Vatican II.[48] A new mode of teaching in this new age should be expected. It might differ from past forms as profoundly as a forty-year-old man differs from the infant he once was *without loss of identity*.

In a paternalistic culture where there was general illiteracy, little insight into God's presence in non-Catholic and non-Christian experiences, and a view of truth as something static and given, paternalistic magisterial figures were understandable. They could take over the task of reflection, formulation, and preservation of the faith; their teaching was truly analogous to the work of a shepherd feeding his sheep.

The laity today are not aptly compared to sheep, and the Church in dialogue does not present itself in the guise of the all-knowing schoolmaster teaching by rote. In moral matters in the past, Church leaders could be expected to act like a parent dealing with immature children who need extensive help in making particular decisions. Today, however, Vatican II emphasizes that even children have a "sacred right" to weigh moral values with an upright conscience and to embrace them by personal choice.[49]

What the Council says of children is obviously more true of adults. We can expect the maturing hierarchical Church to give fewer detailed rules of conduct to the maturing laity and to teach rather by giving broad outlines. Vatican II's reminder is a good one here: "Let the layman not imagine that his pastors are always such experts that to every problem which arises, however complicated, they can readily give him a concrete solution, or even that such is their mission."[50] Moreover, what their pastors on the scene cannot do should not be expected from the bishop or the Pope. The nature of ethics in a world of mounting complexification makes this quite impossible.

It seems today that the notion of teacher does not imply the imposition of information and decisions on largely passive recipients. Rather, the effective teacher in this age should be a stimulator of thought. He should seek to dissipate the immature desire for unreal certitudes. He should seek always to enlarge a debate and not to close it.

Let it not be thought that we are suggesting here that the hierarchical magisterium make an instant conversion to a kind of nondirective counseling technique. Whatever the ideal and whatever the progress thus far, many people will continue to function at an immature level and will continue to need very specific directions. But as we attend to these needs which our pastoral practice has helped to create, let us see the situation for what it is.

Regarding the various sciences, there is an expansion not only of data and expertise but also of our appreciation of the ethical significance of the sciences. Acknowledgment of this is frequent in the documents of Vatican II. We are directed to the many new and active *ancillae* of theology: psychology, sociology, the social sciences, the science of communications, and biology.[51] Small wonder that the Council said that the sciences have so expanded "that the ideal of 'the universal man' is disappearing more and more."[52]

So too is the ideal of "the universal magisterium" disappearing. Magisterial pronouncements will perhaps have an even greater value in such an age as man's social consciousness grows and his need to tap communal wisdom is more felt. The magisterium must try to provide this wisdom by being as sensitive as possible to the movements of the ubiquitous Spirit. Still, both moralist and moral magisterium will have a very new look.

In a simpler age the moralist could attempt to acquire enough technical expertise to make judgments about the moral problems of the scientist. Technological growth and "the information explosion" make this impossible. In facing the moral questions posed, for example, by the science of genetics, two possibilities are conceivable: the moralist must become a geneticist or the geneticist must be made morally alert by a continuing dialogue with the ethical experts. The second is obviously preferable. The geneticist must not prescind from the moral dimensions of his science (and indeed he does not even if he pretends to). The moral questions cannot be answered by him alone, but they cannot be answered without him.

This point about ecumenism can be made briefly. The Church has entered into dialogue with other Christians, with non-Christians, and with non-believers. This means that we have something to learn from them. None of the faithful, lay or clergy, can ignore the witness of these people in the pursuit of moral truth—although emotionally, it would seem, we are more ready to say this than to do it. The hierarchy may not merely proclaim their teaching prerogatives if they are not engaged in *real* dialogue with the laity, theologians, and all others who are also anointed with the spirit of truth and prophecy.

With these considerations in mind it is hoped that we will attain to some useful refinements by turning to the statements of Reed and McCormick concerning the authentic magisterium. John Reed asserts that, given a pronouncement of the authentic magisterium, there is an "obligation not to contradict the doctrine in public speech and writing."[53] This statement, for some years, was a truism among Catholic moralists and canonists. It is hardly defensible today. Reed, we saw, says that theologians may enter into speculative discussion about magisterial statements "supposing a discreet selection of audience." Presumably, if discussion is called for, theologians around the world can hardly communicate by word of mouth. They must write, and by now it would be obvious that there is no written word on theological subjects that might not be proclaimed from the housetops. Vital theological discussions can no longer be kept "under wraps." Pastoral difficulties result from this and must be met, but this new fact of life must be accepted.

More important is the internal intellectual assent which Reed states is *per se* due magisterial statements (p. 59). Enlarging on this Reed says that "it will not easily or commonly happen that the ordinary faithful, the ordinary priest, or even the ordinary theologian will be in a position to depart from the sort of authentic teaching at issue here" (p. 60). Anyone going against a particular moral teaching would appear to be imprudently exposing himself "to the danger of violating the moral law" (p. 57). The reason: "For the assistance of the Holy Spirit is always present to the vicar of Christ and the other bishops, and in their purposeful pronouncements they will have used more than ordinary human means as well" (p. 57). (Since the Holy Spirit is also present to the laity and theologians and non-Catholics, this reason is limp. It also ignores the times when hierarchical teachings were amended at the initiative of the faithful.)

Reed does, however, make an important admission. There is an "absolute possibility" that someone "exceptionally qualified" could disagree with the teaching in question and even act according to his own opinion as long as he does not shake "the external order" (p. 59). This, of course, is "a rather extraordinary thing" (p. 60).

This admission, I repeat, is important. It is, I think, quite gratuitous to assert that it is "a rather extraordinary thing" to find persons sufficiently qualified to dissent with a particular teaching. In the present question of contraception, for example, given the wide publicity afforded important studies on the subject and the deep convictions of the persons and groups with whom we are in dialogue, it seems to me that the number of those "exceptionally qualified" to dissent could be quite large. Clearly it is a matter of judgment. Reed mentions the possibility that the Church could in a particular case wish to impose a norm of conduct by using its "jurisdictional authority." If we apply this possibility to the contraception question, then the debate is no longer about natural law but is a case of positive law; positive law, of course, is open to the soothing influence of *epikeia*.

Several points made by Richard McCormick deserve attention. He writes: "Certain truths about man's nature penetrate his consciousness gradually by historical processes and for the same reason are maintained only with difficulty."[54] He points out that it is not always easy to demonstrate the reasonableness of certain moral evaluations. Because of this, an authoritative magisterium makes sense.

It is certainly true that it is not always easy to give a fully satisfactory explanation of certain moral convictions which emerge gradually in human consciousness. The magisterium can exercise an important preservative influence here. It can preserve these nascent appreciations from an iconoclastic rationalism. We would only add to this that the developing understanding in history of a truth can also be arrested at a particular point by an inflexible magisterium. which is not open to the implications of an expanding historical consciousness. The magisterium can easily fall prey to a bad spirit of conservatism. This too should be admitted and guarded against.

McCormick continues:

> Is it not, up to a point, precisely because arguments are not clear, or at least not universally persuasive, that a magisterium makes sense in this area? At what point does our healthy impatience to understand muffle the voice most likely to speed the process? (p. 613)

Three comments suggest themselves here. First, precisely because the arguments are not clear it makes sense for the magisterium to be flexible and open to the possibility that when the arguments are clarified another position may be indicated.

Second, precisely because the arguments are not clear, the magisterium, however forcefully it presses its position, may not impose a certain obligation that only clarity makes possible. *In dubiis libertas* contains an insight that may not be invalidated by any juridical power.

Finally, one should view history closely before saying that the magisterium is "the voice most likely to speed the process." At times, it has been such a voice, but at other times it has failed.

To conclude this section on the authentic, non-infallible magisterium: How should we react to this kind of papal and episcopal teaching? Pius XII in *Humani Generis* said that "if the Supreme Pontiffs in their official documents purposely pass judgment on a matter debated until then, it is obvious to all that the matter, according to the mind and will of the same Pontiffs, cannot be considered any longer a question open for discussion among theologians" (*quaestionem liberae inter theologos disceptationis iam haberi non posse*).[55] Vatican II, as we have seen, said that the ordinary magisterium of Popes and bishops should be met with a *religiosum obsequium* (in *Documents of Vatican II, "obsequium"* is translated "assent" and "submission," perhaps not too felicitously). To determine the authority of papal statements which are not *ex cathedra* the Council offers some criteria: they are to be adhered to in accordance with the "manifest mind and will" of the Pope (same paragraph). "His mind and will in the matter may be known chiefly either from the character of the documents, from his frequent repetition of the same doctrine, or from his manner of speaking" ("The Church," n. 25, p. 48).

Concerning the celebrated statement of Pius XII in *Humani Generis*, Ford and Kelly are ready to concede that "even a non-infallible pronouncement can close a controversy among theologians." They add something of a reservation:

> We feel sure, however, that the Pope himself would agree that this decisive character of the pronouncement must be evident. That is in accord with canon 1323, #3, which states that nothing is to be understood as dogmatically declared or defined unless this is clearly manifested. The canon refers to infallible teachings; yet the same norm seems to apply with at least equal force to the binding character of non-infallible teaching, especially when there is question of pronouncements that would close a controversy.[56]

We need not belabor the problems of such a position. *An admittedly fallible statement could close off discussion of the question among theologians with the possibility of error thus going un-checked.* The reservation expressed by Ford and Kelly indicates that they were not unaware of this difficulty. They do not, however, exclude the possibility of closing a controversy with fallible teaching.

John Reed prefers to translate the final words of the statement from *Humani Generis* in this way: " . . . cannot be any longer considered a matter of open debate."[57] He feels that Pius XII meant that the debate could go on but that both sides of the question cannot "be held and followed with equal freedom."[58] The precise cause of this limitation of freedom is not made manifest. It seems to me that whatever the presumptive value of a particular fallible papal teaching and however respectfully one receives it and studies it, it is difficult to see why the discussion should thereby have been rendered less free. At any rate, I do not think that many theologians would deny that the theology of the magisterium has advanced considerably since *Humani Generis*, and that the magisteriological controversy was obviously not closed by that encyclical.

The statement of Vatican II concerning the criteria for judging the binding power of the authentic papal magisterium is not satisfying. It seems to say that the teaching is as binding as the Pope wills it to be. This would be voluntarism. It also would lead theologians into fantastic probes to discover the mind and intent of the Pontiff on certain questions. Some theologians, for example, trying to discover the mind of Pius XII on psychiatry after he had warned against certain attitudes and techniques, felt the need to do more than analyze his text. They also sought out "a subsequent 'inspired' comment in the pages of *Osservatore Romano* [which] made it very clear that he had not intended to condemn psychiatry in general or psychoanalysis in particular."[59] They also thought it relevant to report that "his *cordial* reception of the psychiatrists and psychoanalysists and the friendly words with which he closed his address showed a spirit far removed from hostility to this modern branch of science."[60]

Let us think of the statements of Pius IX on religious freedom. His manner of speaking, his frequent repetitions, and the solemn character of the language he used indicated the utmost seriousness of intention. I would not be inclined to say that those who respectfully disagreed with Pius' stand, preferring something more akin to the subsequent teachings of Vatican II on religious liberty, would have deserved any reproach.

The language of the code of canon law on the related question of the episcopal magisterium seems better: "While the bishops, whether teaching individually or gathered in particular Councils, are not endowed with infallibility, yet with regard to the faithful entrusted to their care they are truly teachers and masters (*veri doctores seu magistri*)" (can. 1326). The Pope and the bishops are truly teachers. Their teachings should receive deep respect. Their statements represent serious interventions by officers of the Church. Hopefully, these teachings are representative of ecclesial wisdom and thus merit religious reverence, but it is religious also to recognize that they are not infallible; they might at times come from a period when vitally relevant data, since come to light, were lacking. These teachings, after all — and we must say this to avoid a kind of magisteriolatry — are not the word of God. Indeed they must stand under the judgment of the word of God. It is not an act of disloyalty but rather a duty of the theologian to test these statements to see if they can withstand the cutting power of the two-edged sword.

To develop a new kind of magisterial approach to a new kind of world is a massive task. A thousand questions beginning with "how" await research and reply. Here I presume only to present certain terms which might more accurately describe the essential characteristics of the Church's moral magisterium. Two terms seem particularly apt: prophetic (closely allied to creative) and dialogical.

1. *Prophetic:* The magisterium is called to prophecy. The prophet is distinguished not so much for his insight into the future as for his insight into the present. His call is to pierce the blinding clouds which inevitably envelop human consciousness. Inherent in our history is a tendency to develop a myopic and insensitive code morality which evades the agonies of the moral call to authentic personhood. This insensitive ethos tends to grip society and defy penetration. The prophet must see and penetrate.

The Church in history has had great moments of powerful prophecy. In the early centuries it became a powerful social force, championing the dignity of persons, the rights of conscience, and the power of unselfish love. It was its religious and moral intensity that made it so important on the imperial scene that Decius himself had to admit that he was more concerned over the election of a bishop in Rome than over the revolt of a political rival.[61] It was not Constantine who gave the Church status. Historians tell us: "Sooner or later some emperor after Constantine would have had to seek an understanding with the victorious Church."[62] The Church's work in education and the care of the sick and the poor gave many effective, prophetic lessons in compassion and love of truth to the medieval world. The social encyclicals in modern times that braved charges of left-wing radicalism to call for social reconstruction were genuinely prophetic. Recent papal calls for peace merit the same encomium.

On the other hand, prophecy melted in the warmth of Constantinian favor. In the medieval age of violence the Church imbibed the barbarian spirit of violence. It did not pierce the enveloping cloud. Christian consciousness was seduced by the rigors of Roman law and Stoicism for centuries. It followed when it should have led. The treatment of "heretics" and unbelievers was harsh and often ruthless. The use of torture and the ordeal provide us no happy memories. The lessons taught by these practices were not prophetic or Christian. The evils of anti-Semitism, colonialization, slavery, right-wing totalitarianism, and racism were not met with distinguished prophecy.

The bane of prophecy, often enough, is a stifling traditionalism which confuses tenure with authenticity, forgetting that error too can become traditional. Traditions must be respected; they must also be critically examined to see if they enshrine insensitivity and blindness.

Creativity breaks through the status quo. An institution which has allowed itself to center on survival will thus be tempted to crush the creative spirit. The long list of creative theologians who have been condemned shows that this danger is not illusory in the Church. The harassment of theologians whose work was later to find conciliar blessing in Vatican II gives a poignant lesson in this regard.[63]

2. *Dialogical:* Truth is not reached in solitude but in the processes of communitarian existence. If the Church would bear witness on the human scene, it must recognize itself as a participant in these processes. It must not enter conversation trying to say the last word; rather it must say meaningful words drawn from its vast memory and rich Christian experience. The magisterium must be honest and not pretend to data it does not have. Obviously the moral magisterium must not feel bound, by a kind of institutional pride, to past magisterial documents that through lack of insight and information taught something that can now be seen as inaccurate and unacceptable. Respect for the wisdom of the past does not impose the perpetuation of past deficiencies.

An example of a dialogical magisterium can be found in the statement on the Vietnamese war issued by the American bishops in November 1966. Indeed, it could serve as a paradigm for the Church teaching on many moral questions:

> We realize that citizens of all faiths and of differing political loyalties differ among themselves over the moral issues involved in this tragic conflict. While we do not claim to be able to resolve these issues authoritatively, in the light of the facts as they are known to us, it is reasonable to argue. . . .

The bishops then went on to acknowledge that Catholics were free to be conscientious objectors to the position that their bishops had presented. The bishops did not content themselves with reiterating the Gospel message of love and peace. They made an effort to see how this applied to the present war situation. But they allowed that Catholics with other viewpoints and insights could responsibly reach another opinion.

There is no reason why this approach could not be taken in other areas. The doctrine of conscientious objection involves a respect for the individual conscience and for the complexity of ethical decision-making. These factors obtain in questions other than war. Persons of all faiths and differing loyalties differ among themselves and with us on issues such as contraception, abortion, divorce, civil disobedience, political philosophy, business ethics, etc. With the same honesty that our bishops showed in this instance, all spokesmen for the teaching Church should admit that we do not have a comprehensive knowledge of all the factors needed for a solution to these questions.

Any other practice pretends to an omniscience regarding all relevant essential circumstances and places an obstacle before the guidance of the Spirit whose grace is the new law. We are not suggesting that the Church succumb to the weakness of consensus politics and become an insipid and bland voice. Dialogue cannot always be reserved or agreeable; neither can it be reduced to a gentle, inoffensive bleating geared to the creation of a false unanimity and fellowship. Its prophetic character would thereby be lost. However, it must acknowledge a *de facto* pluralism in many moral matters, especially those which have been profoundly affected by changing conditions and new knowledge. It is naive and self-deceiving to seek one "official" Catholic position on all questions. (It would, for example, be naive and self-deceiving to allege that Catholics are one in theory and practice on the question of contraception.) However, in such less ambiguous questions as racial integration, and even in ambiguous questions, churchmen should speak out with sufficient force and specificity to be influential in national and international discussions.

Agencies should be erected also to make it possible for strong minority opinions in the Church to enter the public forum effectively as "Catholic."

A dialogical magisterium does not forget the integral magisterial role of the laity. The laity, Pius XII said, "are the Church" (AAS 38:141). Vatican II taught: "The body of the faithful as a whole, anointed as they are by the Holy One, cannot err in matters of belief."[64] Neither the magisterium nor the Church is simply hierarchical. In fact, since there are and should be various agencies of witness and influence in the Church, it would be better to speak of the *magisteria* of the Church. We would then consider not just the papal and episcopal magisteria but the equally authentic magisterium of the laity and the magisterium of the theologians. Each of these has a role of creative service to the truth; none can be considered as having a juridical power to stifle or invalidate the other. Rather, each magisterium must be seen as open to the corrective influence of the other magisteria.

Mutual respect for the distinct but complementary magisteria of Pope, bishop, theologian, and layman must be the goal. The theologian must respect the bishops' concern for the integrity of the kerygma; bishops should presume a similar concern on the part of theologians. Episcopal consecration does not convey theological expertise.

Theologians whose teachings or prudence are questioned should have the advantage of judgment by their peers. Those not active in the theological community might easily miss the implications of current debate and judge a man unjustly. Error is inevitable in the development of any science. The only way to stop it is to stop all thought.

Will a moral magisterium that does not call itself infallible command respect? Yes. Will an authentic magisterium that is conscious of its limitations as well as of its strength be able to exert a positive influence? Yes. In the first place, it will spare many Catholics the anguish of unexpected change that wracks so many of our people today. Unaware that the Church can in many ways change and has changed often in the past, many Catholics today are shaken in their faith. Future Catholics, schooled in the reality of being a pilgrim people, will greet progress with joy and not with panic. Formal magisterial pronouncements which give faithful voice to Christian consciousness will be received with respect. In matters moral, such pronouncements will be seen as an invaluable aid but not as a substitute for conscience, since no agency can substitute for the unique role of conscience.

Secondly, non-Catholics will react to our honesty as they did to the honesty of Vatican II. No man of good will will think less of us if he hears in our voices the echo of him who was meek and humble of heart. A Church that is distinguished by a fervent religious life and an unmistakable concern for the good of mankind will be a powerful force for good. Its involvement, its love, and its absence of pretense will give it superb credentials in the modern world.

Catholic moral teaching will be more realistic and pertinent. The collegial character of the magisterium will free it from the impossibilities attached to overcentralization and the attempt to impose moral absolutes universally and transculturally without sufficient regard to varying contexts. The magisterium will not be thought of as merely papal or merely episcopal. Rather the service of the hierarchy will be to vitalize and encourage the witness of the entire Church. This is the magisterial Church that will give to the world the word that is life.

Notes

1. Space permitting, it would obviate detached and rationalistic theorizing about the nature of the teaching Church if we could survey the success and failures of the moral magisterium in the course of history. Recent studies make such a survey possible. Cf. my essay "Modern War and Christian Conscience," *On the Other Side* (Englewood Cliffs, N.J., 1968); Roland H. Bainton, *Christian Attitudes Toward War and Peace* (Nashville, 1960); Stanley Windass, *Christianity Versus Violence* (London, 1964); E. Schillebeeckx, O.P., *Marriage, Human Reality and Saving Mystery* (New York, 1965); John T. Noonan, Jr., *Contraception* (Cambridge, Mass., 1965), *The Scholastic Analysis of Usury* (Cambridge, Mass., 1957), and "Authority, Usury and Contraception," *Cross Currents*, 16 (1966), pp. 55-79; Patrick Granfield, O.S.B., "The Right to Silence," *Theological Studies*, 26 (1965), pp. 280-298; Edward H. Flannery, *The Anguish of the Jews* (New York, 1965); George H. Tavard, *Two Centuries of Ecumenism* (New York, 1962); John Courtney Murray, S.J., "The Problem of Religious Freedom," *Woodstock Papers*, No. 7 (1965); and Pius Augustin, O.S.B., *Religious Freedom in Church and State* (Baltimore, 1966).

2. Louis Bouyer, *Dictionary of Theology* (New York, 1965), p. 237.

3. *Constitution on Divine Revelation*, n. 12, *The Documents of Vatican II*, p. 120.

4. Cf. Butler, *op. cit.*, vol. II, chap. XIX; cf. also Hans Küng, *The Council, Reform and Reunion* (New York, 1962), p. 161.

5. Manṣi 51:1026B.

6. Mansi 52:761.

7. Mansi 52:764.

8. Mansi 52:1212.

9. Mansi 52:1213.

10. Mansi 52:1214.

11. *Ibid.*

12. Mansi 52:1217.

13. Cf., Mansi 52:1216-1217.

14. Mansi 52:1226.

15. Mansi 52:1227.

16. *Constitution on Divine Revelation,* n. 8, *The Documents of Vatican II,* p. 116.

17. *Constitution on the Church*, n. 12 and n. 15, *The Documents of Vatican II*, p. 29 and pp. 33-34.

18. Edgar Hocedez, *Histoire de la Théologie au XIXe siècle*, Vol. I, (Brussels, 1947-1952), pp. 67-69; 132.

19. Given the inevitable dependence of a Council on the philosophical tools available to it, it is perhaps not useless to speculate on how a strong Thomistic revival before Vatican I would have influenced the outcome of that Council. The Council Fathers would have been well served by St. Thomas' reminder of the *quasi infinitae diversitates* that characterize the material of ethics (*S. Th.*, IIa, IIae, q. 29, a. 3). Thomas also realistically appreciated the essential plasticity of moral principles which are applicable most of the time (*in pluribus*) although they may not be applicable in every case (Ia, IIae, q. 94, a. 4, a. 5). Thomas was not at all inclined to do ethics by the use of principles conceived as static derivatives of an immutable nature. "The nature of man," he taught, "is mutable" (IIa, IIae, q. 57, a. 2, ad 1; cf. Supp. 41, 1, ad 3, 65, 2 ad 1; *De Malo*, 2, 4, ad 13). Almost anticipating the modern realization of the difficulty of teaching morality transculturally, Thomas wrote that law is not everywhere the same "because of the mutability of the nature of man and the diverse conditions of men and of things, according to the diversity of places and of times" (*De Malo*, 2, 4, ad 13).

20. Rudolf Schnackenburg, *The Moral Teaching of the New Testament* (New York, 1965), p. 122.

21. Schillebeeckx, *op. cit.*, p. 389.

22. Schnackenburg, *op. cit.*, p. 249.

23. Mansi 52:1235.

24. Pius XII, "Allocution Magnificate Dominum," Nov. 2, 1954; *AAS*, 46 (1950), p. 561.

25. John XXIII, Encyclical *Pacem in terris*, Apr. 11, 1963; AAS, 55 (1963), p. 301.

26. Gregory Baum, O.S.A., "The Christian Adventure—Risk and Renewal," *Critic*, 23 (1965), 44.

27. John J. Reed, S.J., "Natural Law, Theology, and the Church," *Theological Studies*, 26 (1965), 55.

28. Richard A. McCormick, S.J. "Notes on Moral Theology," *Theological Studies*, 26 (1965), 614.

29. Even the strong stand of Trent on marriage and divorce is not seen today as prohibiting the growing debate concerning those matters.

30. For St. Thomas' appreciation of the essential role of circumstances, cf. Ia, IIae, q. 18, a. 10; *ibid.*, q. 73, a. 7; *Sent.*, 4 d. 16, q. 3, a. 2; *De Malo*, q. 2, a. 6, 7.

31. Karl Rahner, S.J., *Nature and Grace* (New York, 1964), p. 41.

32. Fransen, *art. cit.*, p. 366.

33. Jan. H. Walgrave, O.P., "Is Morality Static or Dynamic?" *Concilium*, V (London, 1965), p. 20.

34. Alfred North Whitehead, *Process and Reality* (New York, 1960), p. 297.

35. John Macquarrie, *God-Talk: An Examination of the Language and Logic of Theology* (London, 1967), p. 127.

36. Butler, *op. cit.*, I, 101; II, 215-216; Rondet, *op. cit.*, p. 126.

37. Mansi 52:1133-1134; 1226-1228.

38. Richard A. McCormick, S.J., *art. cit.*, 615.

39. *Ibid.*, 615.

40. Gregory Baum, O.S.A., *art. cit.*, 52.

41. *Decree on Ecumenism*, 11, *The Documents of Vatican II*, p. 354.

42. *Constitution on the Church*, 25, *The Documents of Vatican II*, p. 48.

43. Encyclical *Mater et Magistra*, n. 239; AAS, 53 (1961), p. 457.

44. Reed, *art. cit.*, 59. For a similar interpretation and citations from other authors, cf. Ford and Kelly, *Contemporary Moral Theology*, Vol. I (Westminster, Md., 1963), pp. 19-41.

45. A rather clear example of this is found in the history of the Church. The proclamations of Councils in the early Church came to be viewed as inspired by the Holy Spirit. It became a widely held view that the first four Councils were inspired and on a par with the four Gospels. This tradition continued through the Middle Ages and was carried on by various Synods and Popes as well as by canonists and theologians. Only after Trent did all traces of the tradition die out in Catholic theology.

46. Karl Rahner, S.J., "The Church of Sinners," *Cross Currents*, I (1951), 68.

47. *The Church in the Modern World*, 5, *Documents of Vatican II*, p. 204. My frequent use of the documents of Vatican II in this development is not without recognition that this Council, perhaps more than most others, contains the fruit of many theologies and does not represent a synthesis of these theologies. I think it important, however, that philosophical and theological theories which support my analysis did find a place in the Council.

48. *Ibid.*, n. 54, p. 260.

49. *Declaration on Christian Education*, 1, *The Documents of Vatican II*, p. 640.

50. *The Church in the Modern World*, 43, *The Documents of Vatican II*, p. 244.

51. *Ibid.*, n. 5, pp. 203-204.

52. *Ibid.*, n. 61, p. 267.

53. Reed, *art. cit.*, 59. From here on, reference to this article will be given in the text.

54. McCormick, *art. cit.*, 613. Hereafter reference to this article will be made in the text.

55. AAS, 42 (1950), 568.

56. Ford and Kelly, *op. cit.*, p. 32.

66 / *Daniel C. Maguire*

57. Reed, *art. cit.*, 57.
58. *Ibid.*, note 30.
59. Ford and Kelly, *op. cit.*, vol. I, p. 314.
60. *Ibid.*, p. 315.
61. Cyprian, Ep. 55, 9; cf. *Handbook of Church History*, p. 380.
62. *Handbook of Church History*, p. 427.
63. Cf. Y. Congar, *Chrétiens en Dialogue* (Paris, 1964).
64. *Constitution on the Church*, 12, *The Documents of Vatican II*, p. 29.

Ordinary Papal Magisterium and Religious Assent

Joseph A. Komonchak

Humanae Vitae is a document about marriage, love, and procreation, but the controversy that has followed its publication has not centered around those matters, but around authority in the Church and, specifically, around the authority to teach. The questions now under discussion are not new, but the encyclical has forced them to be asked with a concern and an urgency that have been lacking in the recent past. This article speaks of some of those problems.

I
LUMEN GENTIUM

In paragraph 28 of *Humanae Vitae,* Pope Paul VI urges priests to "loyal internal and external obedience to the teaching authority of the Church." "That obedience, as you well know," the Pope continues, "obliges not only because of the reasons adduced, but rather because of the light of the Holy Spirit, which is given in a particular way to the pastors of the Church in order that they may illustrate the truth." A footnote at this point refers to paragraph 25 of *Lumen Gentium,* where the Second Vatican Council teaches:

> Religious allegiance of the will and intellect should be given in an entirely special way to the authentic teaching authority of the Roman Pontiff, even when he is not speaking *ex cathedra;* this should be done in such a way that his supreme teaching

68 / *Joseph A. Komonchak*

authority is respectfully acknowledged, while the judgments given by him are sincerely adhered to according to his manifest intention and desire, as this is made known by the nature of his documents, or by his frequent repetition of the same judgment, or by his way of speaking.

That it is to this statement about *religiosum voluntatis et intellectus obsequium* that the Pope is referring, and not to other statements in paragraph 25, is clear from the Pope's own manner of speaking in the encyclical and from the remarks of Monsignor Lambruschini in presenting the encyclical to the press. In order to understand what response the Pope himself is seeking, then, it will be of aid to examine the background and import of paragraph 25.

A section dealing with the ordinary teaching authority of the Pope was included in the original *schema, De Ecclesia et de B. Maria Virgine,* presented to the Council at the first session in 1962:

To the authentic teaching authority of the Roman Pontiff, even when he is not speaking *ex cathedra,* religious allegiance of will and intellect should be given; this should be done in such a way that his supreme teaching authority is respectfully acknowledged, while the judgment given by him is sincerely adhered to according to his manifest intention and desire, as that is made known by the nature of the documents, by his frequent repetition of the same judgment, or by his way of speaking. The intention and desire of the Roman Pontiffs is made manifest especially through those doctrinal acts that concern the whole Church, such as certain apostolic constitutions or encyclical letters or their more solemn addresses; for these are the principal documents of the ordinary teaching authority of the Church, they are the principal ways in which it is declared and formed, and what is taught and inculcated in them often already belongs, for other reasons, to Catholic doctrine. And when the Roman Pontiffs go out of their way to pronounce on some subject which has hitherto been controverted, it must be clear to everyone that, in the mind and intention of those Pontiffs, this subject can no longer be regarded as a matter for free debate among theologians.[1]

In support of the general obligation of assent, the text refers to the First Vatican Council, the Code of Canon Law, Leo XIII's *Sapientiae Christianae,* and Pius XI's *Casti Connubii.*[2] A second footnote identifies the last lines of the passage as a direct citation from Pius XII's *Humani Generis.*[3]

The first *schema* on the Church was rejected by the Council at the first session. Between the first and second sessions a new *schema* was elaborated, which was presented to the second session and accepted as a basis for discussion. In the new *schema,* the paragraph on the teaching office of the Church (n. 19) was entitled, *"De Episcoporum munere docendi,"* and formed part of the new Chapter III, *"De Constitutione Hierarchica Ecclesiae et in specie de Episcopatu."* The section on the ordinary magisterium of the Pope is the last part of paragraph 19 and is, except for very minor differences, the same text cited above from *Lumen Gentium.*[4] But it should be noted that in the new *schema* the explanation of the concrete mode of exercise of the magisterium and the warning against continued public theological discussion are both omitted. Apparently the warning was not dropped without opposition, for among the suggested *emendationes* distributed along with the second schema was that of five bishops who asked that the statement from *Humani Generis* be replaced in the text.[5] This suggestion was not accepted, nor was that of Bishop Cleary who proposed that the text include a statement about freedom of investigation.[6] No explanation for either refusal is given.

The last stage in the history of *Lumen Gentium* was the presentation and acceptance of the revised second *schema* at the third session. Very slight changes were made in the text of the section on the ordinary magisterium of the Pope (now n. 25); but its position in the paragraph was changed, so that, as it was explained, "it might be clearer that the discussion of the teaching office of the Roman Pontiff was being carried on *in the context of the teaching office of the entire college of bishops,* which is the subject of this paragraph."[7]

Three *modi* were presented to the doctrinal commission for paragraph 25. The *modi* and the answers they received are important for our purpose:

Modus 159 is the suggestion of three bishops who "invoke the particular case, at least theoretically possible, in which an educated person [*eruditus quidam*], confronted with a teaching proposed non-infallibly, cannot, for solid reasons, give his *internal* assent." The response of the commission is, "For this case approved theological explanations should be consulted."[8]

Modus 160 is the proposal of three bishops that the text read: "... and that the judgments given by him are sincerely adhered to, *although not with an absolute and irreformable* assent." The reason for the addition is to make clear the distinction between the response owed to the infallible magisterium and that owed to the authoritative but non-infallible magisterium.[9] The reply is, "The ordinary teaching office often proposes doctrines which already belong to the Catholic faith itself, so that the proposed addition would itself have to be completed. Therefore, it is better to refer to the approved authors."[10]

Finally, *modus* 161 is the proposal of one bishop that an addition be made indicating the freedom to be permitted for further investigation and for doctrinal progress. The reply is, "The observation is true, but does not need to be brought in at this point."[11]

This review of the *modi* and the replies they received indicates that paragraph 25 of *Lumen Gentium* is to be read in the light of the presentation of the ordinary magisterium given by the *auctores probati.* The problems that arise when an educated person cannot assent to a non-infallible declaration and the differences between the various kinds of responses expected from a Catholic to the magisterium are all to be studied from the manuals. It is not, then, an idle exercise in historical theology to examine the manuals' presentation, but a work that is necessary in order correctly to understand the teaching of Vatican II on the subject.

II
THE "AUCTORES PROBATI"

For the sake of clarity, "manuals" here will be understood as textbook presentations of theology, usually intended for use in seminary theology courses. They are a distinct *genus litterarium,* whose historical origin, methodological presuppositions, and theological *Denkformen* deserve study.[12] The manuals used for the following study date from 1891 to 1963 and do not represent any particular "tendency," whether theological or regional. [13]

In the first place, the manuals describe the "ordinary" teaching office of the Church as the day-to-day proposal of the faith that the Pope carries out in his sermons, addresses, and encyclicals, "that exercise of his teaching office by which the Pope intends to teach, but does not make clear his intention of imposing his judgment as absolutely definitive and irreformable." [14]

The ordinary teaching office of the Pope is commonly regarded by theologians as being non-infallible. [15] But, the manualists say, even when it is non-infallible, the Pope's ordinary teaching office is "authoritative"; that is, unlike the teacher whose teaching stands or falls by the merit and strength of the arguments he presents, the Pope has been given an authority to teach which can require assent even when his reasons are not in themselves convincing. [16] His is a *magisterium authenticum,* where *authenticum* means not "authentic," but "authoritative" or "official." [17]

To every authority there corresponds an obligation on the part of its subjects. In the case of the ordinary magisterium, the obligation is to "internal, religious assent." Assent is required, that is, an act "by which what is contained in the decree is affirmed to be true." [18] The assent must be internal and sincere; external conformity or respectful silence is not sufficient. [19] Finally, the assent is termed "religious," because its motive lies in the fact that the Pope has been given authority to teach by Christ. [20]

But this "internal religious assent" must be distinguished from the assent of divine faith. [21] The motive for an act of divine faith is the unfailing authority of God; the motive for "internal religious assent" is the authority of the teaching office in question. [22] Divine faith is absolutely certain and *super omnia firma*; internal religious assent is not absolutely or metaphysically certain. [23] Most of the authors speak of it as "morally certain," [24] that is, not excluding the possibility of error but only its present likelihood. Finally, divine faith is given without qualification or condition, but this is not true of internal religious assent. Most of the authors say explicitly that it is conditional; [25] Palmieri and Pesch do not use that word but imply it by the mere fact that they acknowledge the possibility of dissent. [26]

While the manualists agree that internal religious assent has its conditions, they are rather general in describing them. Salaverri expresses the condition as "unless by an equal or superior authority the Church should decree otherwise."[27] For Sullivan, it is "unless the Church should at some time decide otherwise or unless the contrary should become evident."[28] For Lercher, it is "unless a grave suspicion should arise that the presumption is not verified."[29] Pesch speaks of the binding force of pronouncements "so long as it does not become positively clear that they are wrong," and adds that "assent is prudently suspended when there first appear sufficient motives for doubting."[30] Straub is quoted by Salaverri as holding that it is licit to dissent, to doubt, or to continue to regard the opposite opinion as probable, "if the decree should appear to someone to be certainly false or to be opposed to so solid a reason that the force of this reason cannot be shattered even by the weight of the sacred authority."[31] And Palmieri says that "religious assent is owed when there is nothing which could prudently persuade one to suspend his assent. . . . The assent is morally certain; therefore, should motives appear, whether they be true or false (but from inculpable error), motives which persuade one to a different view, then in those circumstances the will would not act imprudently in suspending assent."[32]

Apart from Salaverri, then, the manualists admit the possibility of a Catholic's having reasons which could justify his withholding his assent to a teaching of the ordinary magisterium of the Pope. Dieckmann and Salaverri suggest that only a theologian could find himself in such a position;[33] the others are quite general in their statements. Nor do these authors suggest that the reasons for dissent must be new ones, not previously considered by the magisterium.[34]

On the other hand, the authors insist that the presumption in the beginning is always with the teaching of the ordinary magisterium, and that assent may not be suspended rashly, casually, out of pride, "excessive love of one's own opinions," or "overconfidence in one's own genius."[35] Generally, they think it extremely unlikely that error would ever be taught officially by the ordinary magisterium.[36] Palmieri, however, at least suggests that certain historical cases, such as Celestine III's permission of divorce and remarriage in the case of the heresy of a spouse, or the Galileo case, may prove "both the exception that we have allowed for and that metaphysically certain assent is not required."[37] And Sullivan implies error in the ordinary magisterium on the part of Liberius, Vigilius, and Honorius.[38]

The manuals are generally rather negative on the possibility of public dissent or disagreement. The only one that can be regarded as leaving any door open for public dissent is Hervé, who speaks of "external reverence"[39] where the others require "*obsequium silentii*"; but his mention of the possibility of one's presenting one's reasons to the proper authorities leaves reason to doubt that he is any more liberal on the point than the others. Palmieri would permit public discussion if the Pope should allow it, and he suggests two reasons among others why the Pope might allow it: "either so that the truth might shine out more clearly or in order to complete the stage of investigation before a solemn definition."[40]

Three of the manuals explore more fully than the others the possibility of error and of its correction. Sullivan admits the possibility of a Pope's making a mistake on one or another occasion, but not that it would ever become the "constant and traditional teaching of the Holy See."[41] Against the claim of infallibility for the ordinary magisterium of the Pope, he argues:

> It seems to be possible that a Pope, teaching *modo ordinario*, might propose a judgment that would have to be corrected afterward, without the whole Church being drawn into error thereby. In such a case, the divine assistance would be enough to assure that the error would be corrected before it was generally accepted by the Church and to prevent the erroneous teaching from becoming the traditional teaching of the Holy See.[42]

On the following page, he acknowledges again that "an error in the ordinary magisterium could be corrected before the whole Church was led into error."[43] But at no point does he indicate how that might be accomplished in fact.

Dieckmann makes a rather important statement in a discussion of the assistance of the Holy Spirit that accompanies the daily exercise of the ordinary magisterium:

It must be conceded that the influence of this assistance cannot be determined accurately, so that each doctrinal act could be said to have been made under this special assistance which preserves one from error. If that were true, all the acts would be infallible. The assertion is rather a universal one: generally the Holy Spirit will preserve the organs of the authoritative magisterium from the error, especially in those decisions which are prepared and issued with the necessary diligence, caution and scholarship.[44]

The remark is chiefly of value against the assumption that to acknowledge the possibility or fact of error is to deny the assistance of the Holy Spirit.

In Pesch the problem is also approached obliquely, in a discussion of inquiry into the reasons for a pronouncement:

Since the Pope's congregations[45] do not *per se* supply an absolutely certain argument for their teaching, one can and, it may be, one must inquire into the reasons for the teaching. In this way it may come about either that the teaching in question will slowly be received by the whole Church and thus be raised to the level of infallibility, or that the error will be detected.[46]

When error is present, it can be detected by inquiry into the reasons for some pronouncement.

What the other three authors are perhaps only hinting at is stated more explicitly by Lercher:

If the Supreme Pontiff, exercising his authority, but not at its highest level, obliges all to assent to a thing as true (because revealed or coherent with revelation), he does not seem to be infallible *de jure*; nor is it necessary to say that the Holy Spirit would never permit such a decree to be issued, if it should be erroneous.

It is true that the Holy Spirit will never allow the Church to be led into error by such a decree. The way in which error would be excluded would more probably consist in the assistance of the Holy Spirit given to the head of the Church, by which such an erroneous decree would be prevented. But it is not entirely out of the question that the error might be excluded by the Holy Spirit in this way, namely, by the subjects of the decree detecting its error and ceasing to give it their internal assent.[47]

A few lines earlier, Lercher had make a similar comment about the decrees of the papal congregations made *in forma communi*: "If by such a decree the affirmation of the truth of some matter should be prescribed for the whole Church and the thing should be objectively false, the Holy Spirit would not permit error; probably by his assistance he would not move the bishops and faithful to give a firm internal assent."[48] A few pages later he repeats the notion: "It is not out of the question that the Holy Spirit might assist individual bishops or even individual members of the faithful, so that they would not err, when the magisterium teaches authoritatively but not infallibly."[49]

The cogency of these statements is not affected by the fact that Lercher is extremely skeptical that such a situation will ever arise. He is the only manualist who explicitates how concretely the Church might correct an error taught by the ordinary magisterium. That correction would be the work of the Holy Spirit and it would take the concrete form of refraining from internal dissent. It should also be noted that Lercher does not exclude the faithful from the possibility of such dissent for the sake of preserving the Church from error.

Lercher's position, acknowledging at least the possibility of the Church's correcting the Pope, fits in well with such views as Newman's "on consulting the faithful in matters of doctrine," or even with the insistence of Bishop Gasser, the official *relator* at Vatican I, that the Pope has a moral obligation to consult the Church before approaching an infallible declaration.[50] But it calls to mind even more a set of traditional discussions which recent scholarship has recalled to our attention. I am referring to the discussions, which can be fully documented from the eleventh century on, of the possibility of a Pope becoming a heretic or a schismatic.[51] Popes, canonists, and theologians can be cited who acknowledged the possibility of heresy or schismatic action in a Pope, and some nine centuries of theological and canonical discussion have included consideration of what the Church at large could do in such a case.[52] The whole discussion demonstrates at least this much: that there do remain within the Church at large norms of doctrine and practice which are not dependent on the Pope, that there are circumstances (however unlikely one may judge them to be) in which it could be necessary for the Church to judge and correct the Pope,[53] and that the Church is not unreservedly committed into the hands of any Pope.[54] By no means is this digression meant to suggest that the present circumstances constitute a case of heresy or schism; it is merely intended to recall that quite traditional positions in canon law and in theology acknowledge that there could be circumstances in which the Spirit might not be speaking or acting through the Pope but through the bishops and/or faithful in opposition to the Pope.

So far as I know, the history of the theology of the teaching office in the Church still remains to be written. The manuals offer no help in tracing the tradition they endorse back beyond 1863, and the single encyclopedia article I have discovered to treat the matter at all is too sketchy to be of much use.[55] Congar observes that the explicit distinction between an "extraordinary" and an "ordinary" papal magisterium dates only from the mid-nineteenth century.[56] If that is so, it is understandable that there is so little evidence for our subject in such post-Tridentine writers as Bellarmine, Duval, Billuart, and Ballerini. These authors normally distinguish only between the Pope as a *doctor privatus*, capable of error, and the Pope as *caput Ecclesiae*, acting and speaking infallibly.[57] The center of controversy for these men was the *locus* within the Church of a *judex controversiarum infallibilis*, and this context did not suggest such distinctions as we make today.

Whatever the earlier history may reveal, it was not until the middle of the nineteenth century that the duty of internal religious assent to non-infallible teaching is stated explicitly in Church documents. The earliest references anyone gives are to Pius IX's "Munich Brief" and its restatement in the Syllabus of Errors.[58] After those references, the manuals also refer to a *monitum* at

Vatican I,[59] and to documents of Leo XIII, Pius X, Pius XI, and Pius XII.[60] To these can now be added the *Constitution on the Church*, paragraph 25, the doctrinal statement of the Synod of Bishops,[61] and *Humanae Vitae*. The theological note attached to their thesis by the manuals varies from Lercher's *doctrina communis et satis c̈erta* to Sullivan's and Salaverri's *doctrina catholica*.[62] It might then be remarked that the obligation of "internal religious assent" to the ordinary magisterium has never been taught by the extraordinary magisterium (with the consequence that internal, religious assent and not divine faith is due to the proposition that "internal religious assent" is due to the ordinary magisterium).

The tradition reflected by the manuals, then, teaches at once the duty of internal religious assent to ordinary teaching and the possible legitimacy of dissent. Any author who discussed the authority of such teaching also considered (at least *in abstracto*) the circumstances under which it would no longer require assent.[63] It was to this tradition that the six hundred and fifty theologians who have signed the American theologians' statement were appealing when they said, "It is common teaching in the Church that Catholics may dissent from authoritative, noninfallible teachings of the magisterium when sufficient reasons for so doing exist." The same tradition underlies the 1967 statement of the German bishops[64] and the statement of the Belgian hierarchy on *Humanae Vitae*.[65] This tradition did not find its way into the 1967 pastoral of the American bishops.[66]

After this review of the manuals, something should be said of the perspective in which they discuss the matter. That perspective suffers from some serious philosophical and theological limitations. For one thing, the manuals' analysis of the nature of assent is quite inadequate and quite unaware of the kind of questions raised by Newman in *A Grammar of Assent*.[67] They tend to pass rather quickly over the problems created by using such words as "authority" and "obedience" when speaking of "teaching."[68] Not much effort is expended in distinguishing the part of the mind and the part of the will in assent, with the result that the movement from "assent" to "obedience" and vice versa is often made too easily. Perhaps these difficulties derive from a too close association (not to say identification) of the magisterial and juridical functions of authority.[69] Such an association would cause misgivings even if the notion of law involved were properly intellectualist, but when it is voluntaristic itself the danger is greatly increased of a voluntaristic notion of truth as whatever authority happens to be teaching.[70] All these questions are much too large for extensive discussion here. For our purposes, it is enough to have shown that even within the perspective of the manuals, dissent from authoritative teaching is not regarded as entirely out of the question.

III

SOME PERSPECTIVES FROM VATICAN II

The possibility of dissent is, if anything, strengthened by more recent theological developments in ecclesiology and especially by several positions adopted by the Second Vatican Council. The following paragraphs briefly indicate a few of those positions.

There is, first of all, the very experience of the Council. The conciliar documents did not descend full-grown from above, but were arrived at only after long and sometimes bitter debate. If we believe the Spirit to have presided over Vatican II, it remains true that the Spirit guided its course precisely through the human dialectic of disagreement, discussion, and compromise. Nor was this dialectic a closed debate among members of "the teaching Church"; it involved consultation with theologians, with the non-Catholic observers present, and even, through the press, with the non-Christian world. Whatever progress was made at the Council was in varying measures due to all these factors, and it would be difficult to restrict the working of the Spirit to any single one of them.

Secondly, there is the perspective in which Vatican II discussed the infallibility of the Church. *Lumen Gentium* deliberately refrained from speaking of the infallibility of the Church *in credendo* as a "passive" thing, deriving from the "active" infallibility of the magisterium as an effect from a cause.[71] The Council Fathers do indeed speak of the Church's "faithful obedience" to "the guidance of the sacred teaching authority" (*Lumen Gentium* 12), but they do so in a context in which it has also been explained to them that respected post-Tridentine theologians saw no danger to the hierarchy in arguing "from the faithful to the hierarchy" or from infallibility *in credendo* to infallibility *in docendo.*[72]

Along the same lines is the Council's insistence on the freedom and responsibility of the laity to make known to Church authorities their needs, desires and opinions (*L.G.* 37). In *Gaudium et Spes* (62), the Council refers to that paragraph in *Lumen Gentium* to indicate that "all the faithful, clerical and lay, possess a lawful freedom of inquiry and of thought, and the freedom to express their minds humbly and courageously about those matters in which they enjoy competence."[73] Such comments are, perhaps, not without connection with conciliar statements on charisms in the Church (*L.G.* 12).

In such statements the Council may be considered to be thematizing its own experience. Another indication of the same thing can be found in the Council's acknowledgment that it is not only from within the Roman Catholic Church that proceed the forces leading toward the growth of the Church's understanding of itself and of its mission and message. God's grace and truth also exist outside the Roman Catholic community: in non-Catholic Christians and their communities (*Unitatis Redintegratio* 3, 20, 21; *L.G.* 8, 15-16; *G.S.* 40), in non-Christian religions (*Nostra Aetate* 1-2), and in the world (*G.S.* 22, 26, 34, 36, 38). From dialogue with non-Catholics, the Church grows in its self-knowledge and self-criticism (*U.R.* 4, 9). With the world and aided by it, the Church, which does not have solutions to all men's problems, commits itself to search for them (*G.S.* 10, 11, 33). From the world which it helps, the Church has, in its turn, derived abundant and various helps in preparing the way for the Gospel (*G.S.* 40, 44, 57) and even in its presentation of the knowledge of God (*G.S.* 62).

The chief point of this brief summary is to recall that the Second Vatican Council, while restating the place and role of the teaching office in the Church, at the same time recognizes and emphasizes, as the manuals did not, the activity of the Spirit in many and differing ways in the Church and in the world. It is from all these workings of the Spirit that the Church grows in its understanding and accomplishment of its mission, and it may be suggested that by all these workings the Spirit may operate for the correction of mistaken teachings.

IV
SOME OBJECTIONS

Arguments can be brought against the position maintained in the previous pages, and in considering them, it might be well to make the discussion concrete by particular reference to *Humanae Vitae.*

An important objection asks: If *Humanae Vitae* does not require assent, is there any teaching of the ordinary magisterium of the Pope which must be considered to require assent? It can be replied that *Humanae Vitae* does require assent, in the sense outlined above; that is, the fact that the encyclical comes from the supreme teacher in the Church, whose office was instituted by Christ and is guided by the Holy Spirit, establishes a presumption in favor of its truth. Therefore, assent to it can be suspended only because serious, personally convincing arguments lead a person to believe that the general presumption is not verified in this instance. Further, depending on the weight of the authority in question in each case, any other authoritative teaching also requires assent and can be dissented from only for reasons that are similarly sound and convincing. Nor does this reply say anything that is not already implied in the recognition that such teaching is not infallible. If it is fallible, it may be mistaken. If it may be mistaken, no unqualified assent may be given to it. If it is mistaken, it has no claim on assent.[74] If a person is convinced that it is mistaken, then he may, indeed he must, suspend assent to it. This is the teaching of the manuals, the teaching presupposed by *Lumen Gentium* 25, and it is hard to see how *Humanae Vitae* can be exempted from it. It does not undermine papal teaching authority to maintain that in one or another, even in a very serious case, it has been wrong. The authors of the manuals could consider the possibility without suspecting that they were thereby undermining the papal teaching office.

Secondly, it may be objected that if the papal position on artificial birth control is wrong, we are faced with an extremely serious doctrinal error. For many centuries the Church would have been giving incorrect moral guidance, and there are theologians who believe it impossible for the Spirit ever to permit the Church to fall that seriously into error. In reply, it can be pointed out that it is a very risky business to try to predict how much of evil (whether the evil of sin or the evil of error) God might permit to creep into the Church.[75] There are enough cases in which the Church has been wrong in the past, and there are no *a priori* grounds on which it can be demonstrated that it could not be wrong again.

Others object, however, that even if the teaching of *Humanae Vitae* is reformable, even if objectively it is wrong, still this encyclical represents what the Spirit, speaking through the Pope, wants us, historically conditioned creatures that we are, to do here and now. We must live by our present lights, and this is all the light the Spirit is now giving. In reply, it can be noted that, first of all, the teaching of *Humanae Vitae*, as any other teaching, requires assent only to the extent that it is objectively true; that, while one may be required to obey a *law* that one may believe to be incorrect, no one can be required to assent to a *teaching* he believes to be incorrect. Secondly, it cannot be excluded *a priori* that the Spirit may make his will known independently of the Pope; it cannot be demonstrated *a priori* that it is not the Spirit who is leading individuals to dissent in this case; and therefore it cannot be excluded *a priori* that the Spirit may be using such dissent to correct more quickly than would otherwise be possible a teaching that is, as all agree, at least reformable and possibly incorrect.

V
THE QUESTION OF PUBLIC DISSENT

We have already seen that the authors of the manuals generally do not allow public disagreement to authoritative teaching. With regard to the manuals, however, it should be recalled that Palmieri had offered two reasons why the Pope might feel it helpful to permit public discussion—to confirm the truth of the teaching or to prepare the way for an infallible statement.[76] Pesch, similarly, saw as one of the possible results of inquiry into the reasons for a teaching its acceptance by the whole Church, but saw another one in the possible detection of its error.[77] Further discussion and inquiry, then, could either confirm the truth or discover a mistake, but in either case the Church would only be served. Both possibilities ought to be kept in mind in the debate about the legitimacy of making the inquiry and discussion public.

To advance a first, less important argument in support of public dissent, the fact that the discussion of *Humanae Vitae* concerns a matter that is not speculative and practically indifferent (such as, for example, subsistent relations in the Trinity, or the quality of Adam's original justice), but rather a matter of immediate and urgent practical consequence for millions of persons, both Catholic and not, has already moved the matter from the remote and private rooms of the theologians out into the forum of public concern.

Secondly, for what it is worth, it should be recalled that a prohibition of further public discussion after a papal pronouncement, included in the first draft of the Constitution *De Ecclesia* at Vatican II, was dropped in the second *schema*.

More importantly, arguments in favor of public discussion and dissent can be drawn from points already touched upon: the necessity of dialogue between the teaching and believing Church and the possibility, acknowledged by all,[78] that the teaching of *Humanae Vitae* may be incorrect. Dialogue has always played a major role in the development of Church teaching in the past, as the most casual reading of the history of the Councils makes abundantly clear. Defined Catholic teaching generally represents a consensus arrived at by an all too human dialectic of disagreement and debate, of compromise and conciliation, of honesty and humility. An end to such a process was considered to have come only with a definitive pronouncement of Pope and/or Council. There is no reason why such a dialogue should be stopped before such a pronouncement in the present case.

Now it must be granted that such a dialogue could continue without having to be public and that the dialogue would eventually make the truth or error of the teaching clear. But it may be suggested that if the dialogue is conducted in private, the process of confirmation or of correction would take a much longer time.

While the Church might not suffer if the process of confirmation were to be prolonged, it would be hard to establish that whatever value there may be in private discussion outweighs the harm that could be done to the Church if the process of correction were prolonged. The general good of the Church can be invoked on both sides.

Again, given the real possibility of error, is there not a responsibility imposed upon each qualified member of the Church, who believes he has detected an error, to seek to correct it? Does he not have this responsibility to truth itself? *Magis amica veritas.* By the same token, does he not have a responsibility to the Church, "light of the world," "pillar and ground of truth"? Does not the qualified person who believes dissent to be necessary have a responsibility toward the members of the Church who regard a particular teaching as unacceptable and, because of it, are tempted to leave the Church? Finally, does not the more qualified person have the obligation to speak publicly to avoid misunderstandings and over-simplifications which can so readily occur in the mass media? In the light of an affirmative answer to these questions, what I have called the possibility of public dissent can well be described as the right, or indeed the obligation, to dissent publicly.

Further, if there is a real possibility of error, may it not be argued that the Church has nothing to fear from public discussion? If the teaching is correct, the Spirit will show (as has not yet been shown) why it is correct. If the teaching is incorrect, it can only be corrected if there is given to bishop and to theologian the freedom to explore the matter. Since collaboration is a necessary part of the theological endeavor, it is difficult to see how such exploration can remain private. No theological journal is so abstruse and no language so arcane that its publication cannot overnight become known to the world. It is not certain that one can even speak of private discussion or dissent any longer.

Finally, much of the fear expressed about the laity's losing respect for the teaching authority of the Church when debate is public arises at least in part from the fact that the faithful have not generally been taught what are the respective and mutual roles of teacher and believer in the Church. Commonly they are unaware that all pronouncements on religious matters are not of equal authoritative weight and that the response they owe differs accordingly. If they were to possess a more adequate notion of the teaching office, then perhaps the danger of scandal and disrespect might be considerably less than many feel it to be today. It was also the strong recommendation of the Synod of Bishops in 1967 that "clearly and in ways adapted to the contemporary mentality" the faithful be taught their responsibilities before the magisterium.[79] Even if, therefore, someone may still be convinced that public dissent in the Church may do more harm than good, only good can come from a clear and intelligent explanation of the various responses a Catholic owes to the various exercises of the Church's teaching office, an explanation that would have to include as well a discussion of the circumstances under which it is quite legitimate and even necessary for a Catholic to suspend his assent.

Notes

1. *Schemata Constitutionum et Decretorum de quibus disceptabitur in Concilii sessionibus: Series Secunda, De Ecclesia et de B. Maria Virgine* (Vatican Press, 1962), pp. 48-49.

2. *Ibid.*, p. 57.

3. *Ibid.*

4. *Schema Constitutionis Dogmaticae De Ecclesia*, Pars I (Vatican Press, 1963), p. 30.

5. *Emendationes a Concilii Patribus scripto exhibitae super schema Constitutionis Dogmaticae De Ecclesia,* Pars I (Vatican Press, 1963), pp. 43-44.

6. *Ibid.*, p. 43. Bishop Cleary's proposed text reads: "Romani Pontificis authentico magisterio, etiam cum non ex cathedra loquitur, religiosum obsequium iuxta regulas prudentiae praestandum est; sed nihil impedit quominus periti omni qua par est moderatione et temperentia, argumentis hinc inde accurate perpensis, rem plenius investigent, dummodo profiteantur se paratos esse stare iudicio Ecclesiae."

7. *Schema Constitutionis De Ecclesia* (Vatican Press, 1964), p. 96; italics in the original text here and elsewhere unless otherwise indicated.

8. *Schema Constitutionis Dogmaticae De Ecclesia: Modi a Patribus conciliaribus propositi a commissione doctrinali examinati, III: Caput III: De constitutione hierarchica Ecclesiae et in specie de Episcopatu* (Vatican Press, 1964), p. 42.

9. *Ibid.*

10. *Ibid.*

11. *Ibid.*

12. See Y. Congar, "Théologie," in *Dictionnaire de Théologie Catholique*, XV, cols. 431-444 (ET: *A History of Theology* [New York, 1968], pp. 177-95). Karl Rahner's strictures against *Schultheologie* are well known.

13. D. Palmieri, *De Romano Pontifice cum prolegomeno De Ecclesia* (2nd ed.; Prato, 1891); C. Pesch, *Praelectiones Dogmaticae*, I: *Institutiones Propaedeuticae ad Sacram Theologiam* (Freiburg, 1915); H. Dieckmann, *De Ecclesia*, II (Freiburg, 1925); J. M. Hervé. *Manuale Theologiae Dogmaticae*, I (Paris, 1934); L. Lercher, *Institutiones Theologiae Dogmaticae* (5th ed. by F. Schlagenhaufen), I (Barcelona, 1951); J. Salaverri, "De Ecclesia Christi," in *Sacrae Theologiae Summa*, I (Madrid, 1955); F. A. Sullivan, *De Ecclesia*, I: *Quaestiones Theologiae Fundamentalis* (Rome, 1963).

14. Sullivan, p. 349; see Lercher, p. 296, and Dieckmann, p. 91. Congar remarks that the distinction between ordinary and extraordinary magisterium, always implicit *via facti*, was not made in those explicit terms until Pius IX's *Tuas libenter* in 1863. See *La Foi et la Théologie* (Tournai, 1962), p. 158.

15. For the discussion, see Sullivan, pp. 348-352; Salaverri, pp. 709-710; J. Hamer, *The Church Is a Communion* (New York, 1962), pp. 29-34.

16. Palmieri, p. 719; Pesch, p. 370; Dieckmann, p. 116; Lercher, pp. 297-298; Salaverri, pp. 716, 718; Sullivan, pp. 345, 348.

17. The manuals distinguish between a *magisterium mere docens seu scientificum*, to which assent is given because of the reasons the teacher offers, and a *magisterium auctoritativum*, to which assent is given because of the authority of the teacher. See Sullivan, pp. 258-259; Salaverri, pp. 662-663; Lercher, pp. 158, 275; Palmieri, p. 167.

18. Lercher, p. 297; see Dieckmann, p. 116; Salaverri, p. 716; Sullivan, p. 347.

19. Palmieri, p. 719; Pesch, p. 370; Dieckmann, p. 116; Lercher, p. 297; Salaverri, p. 716; Sullivan, p. 347.

20. Pesch, p. 370; Dieckmann, p. 116; Lercher, p. 297; Salaverri, p. 716; Sullivan, p. 347, and see 345, 259. Palmieri (p. 719) calls the assent "religious" both because of its object and because of its motive, Christ's establishing of teachers in the Church and God's special providence over them.

21. There has long been a dispute whether between divine faith and "religious assent" there is not a third category of assent, called "ecclesiastical faith," which regards those infallible statements of the Church that do not concern matters formally revealed. See Congar, "Faits dogmatiques et 'foi ecclésiastique'," in *Catholicisme*, IV, cols. 1059-1067, reprinted in *Sainte Eglise* (Paris, 1963), pp. 357-373. This discussion is not of importance for this study.

22. Palmieri, p. 719; Pesch, p. 393.

23. Palmieri, p. 719; Pesch, p. 370; Dieckmann, p. 116; Salaverri, p. 716.

24. Palmieri, pp. 719, 720: "maxime probabile causas erroris deesse"; Pesch, p. 370: "certitudine morali quadam latiore"; Dieckmann, p. 116; Sullivan, p. 348; Salaverri's "certitudo relativa" is identical with what the others mean by "certitudo moralis." Lercher speaks of religious assent as "non objective certus" because resting "upon a motive that does not exclude the possibility of error and is known to be such." The presumption, however, is that in any concrete case the magisterium is not in error (p. 297; see p. 275).

25. Dieckmann (quoting Maroto), p. 116; Lercher, p. 297; Sullivan, pp. 348, 354; Salaverri, pp. 716, 719, where he cites other authors.

26. Palmieri, p. 719; Pesch, p. 370.

27. Salaverri, pp. 716, 720.

28. Sullivan, pp. 348, 354.

29. Lercher, p. 297.

30. Pesch, p. 370.

31. See Salaverri, p. 719; Straub's manual, De Ecclesia Christi, published in 1912, was not available for my use.

32. Palmieri, p. 719.

33. Dieckmann (again quoting Maroto), p. 116; Salaverri, p. 720; see Hervé, p. 523.

34. Diekamp, who can be cited in favor of restricting the possibility of dissent to the scholar, does not require new reasons to justify such dissent but only "a new, scrupulous examination of all the elements." See F. Diekamp, Katholische Dogmatik, I (11th ed.; Münster, 1949), p. 64.

35. Lercher, pp. 298, 307; Salaverri, p. 720.

36. See Lercher: "periculum erroris fere nullum," p. 298.

37. Palmieri, p. 72; see pp. 731-737.

38. Sullivan, pp. 349-350; see. pp. 331-340.

39. Hervé, p. 523.

40. Palmieri, p. 719.

41. Sullivan, p. 345.

42. Ibid., p. 350.

43. Ibid., p. 351.

44. Dieckmann, pp. 117-118.

45. Pesch's exposition of "internal religious assent" is made in terms of the respect due to the papal doctrinal congregations, but he adds that his remarks "nullo negotio applicantur ad decreta summi pontificis, quae non pro suprema sua auctoritate emittit" (p. 370).

46. Pesch, p. 370.

47. Lercher, p. 297.

48. Ibid.

49. Ibid., p. 307.

50. See *Collectio Lacensis*, vol. VII (Freiburg, 1892), p. 401.
51. See B. Tierney, *Foundations of the Conciliar Theory* (Cambridge, 1955); H. Küng, *Structures of the Church* (New York, 1964), pp. 249-319. See also the controversy about the force and significance of the *"Sacrosancta"* decree of the Council of Constance, for example in P. de Vooght, *Les pouvoirs du Concile et l'autorité du Pape au Concile de Constance* (Paris, 1965), or the reviews of this book in *The Downside Review* 84 (1966), pp. 432-435, and in the *Revue des Sciences Religieuses* 40 (1966), pp. 195-196. Nor was this discussion only within the context of conciliarism; see the references to Adrian II, Gratian, and Innocent III below.
52. The problem did not concern the Pope only as *persona privata*; see A. Duval, *De Suprema R. Pontificis in Ecclesiam Potestate* (1614), 19th ed. (Paris, 1877), pp. 255-257. And the remarks of Adrian II about Honorius cannot be restricted to his "private" opinions: "Siquidem Romanorum Pontificum de omnium Ecclesiarum praesulibus judicasse legimus, de eo vero quemquam judicasse non legimus. Licet enim Honorio ab Oriental*bus post mortem anathema sit dictum, sciendum tamen est quia fuerat super haeresi accusatus, propter quam solam licitum est minoribus majorum suorum motibus resistendi vel pravos sensus libere respuendi," *PL* 129, 110.
53. See Gratian, "Cunctos ipse Papa judicaturus a nemine est judicandus, nisi deprehendatur a fide devius." *Decretum,* dist. 40, c. 6; or Innocent III, "In tantum fides mihi necessaria est, ut cum de ceteris peccatis solum Deum iudicem habeam, propter solum peccatum quod in fide committerem, possum ab Ecclesia iudicari." *PL* 217, 656.
54. See the interesting reply of the doctrinal commission at Vatican II to Pope Paul VI's suggested formula on the Pope: "ipse uno Domino devinctus." After observing that the intention of the proposed formula, namely, to exclude any higher human authority, is sufficiently expressed in earlier statements, the commission replies: "Formula est *nimis simplificata*: Romanus Pontifex enim etiam observare tenetur ipsam Revelationem, structuram fundamentalem Ecclesiae, sacramenta, definitiones priorum Conciliorum, etc. Quae omnia enumerari nequeunt." *Schema Constitutionis De Ecclesia* (Vatican Press, 1964), p. 93. See also Karl Rahner's comment on the relationship between the Pope and the college of bishops: "There are no juridical norms for the behavior of the Pope with regard to the college of bishops whose breach could invalidate his actual decision about the amount of cooperation allowed them. There is no process of law through which the Pope in such a case could be made answerable to an earthly authority distinct from himself. But the Pope is obviously bound by the ethical norms of the Gospel, justice, fairness and the objective relationships which result from the fact that an entity founded by Christ with a constitution . . . may not be condemned to atrophy by being disregarded and left out of account, or allowed to exist only in name. . . . And though there is no legal authority to see that these ethical norms are observed, and to question the validity of the Pope's decision if they are not, the

charismatic and prophetic quality of the Church still makes 'open opposition' (Gal. 2:11) possible": *Commentary on the Documents of Vatican II*, ed. H. Vorgrimler, Vol. I (New York, 1967), p. 202.

55. See E. Dublanchy in *Dictionnaire de Théologie Catholique*, VII, cols. 1710-1711.

56. See above, note 14. It is surely not accidental that the distinction was explicitated at the same time that the most frequently used means of ordinary teaching by the Popes, encyclical letters, was coming into its own under Gregory XVI and Pius IX. See Congar, *La Foi et la Théologie*, p. 159.

57. For example, Billuart, *Cursus Theologiae iuxta mentem Divi Thomae*, vol. V (Paris, 1839), p. 174; P. Ballerini, *De vi ac ratione Primatus Romanorum Pontificum* (1766), in Migne, *Theologiae Cursus Completus*, III (Paris, 1842), cols. 1217-1218. A study of the ecclesiology of this period is much needed, for it is the immediate background of the nineteenth century and of Vatican I.

58. DS 2879-2880, 2895, 2922. A study of the reaction to the "Munich Brief" and to the *Syllabus of Errors* provides an excellent background for the contemporary discussion. For the reaction in England, see J. Altholz, *The Liberal Catholic Movement in England* (London, 1962); H. A. MacDougall, *The Acton-Newman Relations* (New York, 1962); D. McElrath, *The Syllabus of Pius IX: Some Reactions in England* (Louvain, 1964).

59. DS 3045; see *Collectio Lacensis*, vol. VII, pp. 83-84, 209-212.

60. Leo XIII, *Immortale Dei*, DB 1880; *Sapientiae Christianae, ASS* 22 (1889-1890), p. 395; Pius X, *Lamentabili*, DS 3409-3410; *Praestantia Scripturae*, DS 3505; Pius XI, *Casti Connubii, AAS* 22 (1930), p. 580; Pius XII, *Humani Generis*, DS 3885.

61. "Omnes autem christifideles clare edocendi sunt, modis mentalitati hodiernae adaptatis, de filiali obedientia et sincera adhaesione quae declarationibus magisterii Ecclesiae praestanda est, ratione utique diversa pro diversis earum indole." II, 2.

62. Lercher, p. 298; Sullivan, p. 354; Salaverri, p. 717.

63. See also the following encyclopedia articles: O. Karrer, "Papst," in H. Fries (ed.), *Handbuch Theologischer Grundbegriffe*, vol. II (Munich, 1963), p. 274; J. R. Lerch, "Teaching Authority of the Church," in *New Catholic Encyclopedia*, vol. XIII (New York, 1967), pp. 364-365; S. E. Donlon, "Freedom of Speech," in *ibid.*, vol. VI, pp. 122-123.

64. See *Documentation Catholique* 65 (1968), pp. 321-324.

65. "If we do not find ourselves considering a statement which is infallible and therefore unchangeable . . . we are not bound to an unconditional and absolute adherence such as is demanded for a dogmatic definition. Even in the case, however, where the Pope . . . does not use the fullness of his teaching power, the doctrines which he teaches, in virtue of the power entrusted to him, demand in principle on the part of the faithful, strengthened by a spirit of faith, a religious submission of will and mind. . . . This adherence does not depend so much on the arguments proposed

in the statement as on the religious motivation to which the teaching authority, sacramentally instituted in the Church, appeals. Someone, however, who is competent in the matter under consideration and capable of forming a personal and well-founded judgment—which necessarily presupposes sufficient information—may, after a serious examination before God, come to other conclusions on certain points. In such a case he has the right to follow his conviction, provided that he remains sincerely disposed to continue his inquiry. Even in this case, he must maintain sincerely his adherence to Christ and to his Church and respectfully acknowledge the importance of the supreme teaching authority of the Church. . . . He must also beware of compromising the common good and the salvation of his brothers by creating an unhealthy unrest or, *a fortiori*, by questioning the very principle of authority" (as quoted in the *National Catholic Reporter*, September 11, 1968, p. 7).

66. *The Church in Our Day* breaks with the usual theological vocabulary to speak of "religious assent" as a generic term including at once the faith that responds to an infallible dogmatic definition (such as the real presence), the response due to the ordinary magisterium, and obedience to disciplinary decisions (such as clerical celibacy). This new use could easily confuse what must be kept distinct. Despite a long treatment of conscience, supposedly under the guidance of Newman, the document does not mention the possibility of dissent.

67. What, for example, would the manualists have made of Newman's view that assent is by nature unconditional? "No one can hold conditionally what by the same act he holds to be true": *A Grammar of Assent* (London, Longmans, Green & Co., 1906), p. 172. The discussion of what Newman terms "opinion" is also of interest to the discussion of "assent" that is the "presumption" of truth (*ibid.*, pp. 58-60).

68. The association of the words "teaching" and "authority" is not without its ambiguity. Surely the use of the word "authority" with regard to teaching is at best analogous to its use with regard to law. Does "authority" to teach derive from another source than from the possession of truth? The manuals seem to think so; Palmieri (pp. 240-241) and Pesch (pp. 193-194) add to the obligation to assent to a word from God that derives from natural law (not to mention common sense) another obligation that derives from the "authority" of the Church. The manuals can argue from the fact that the magisterium possess a *vis coactiva* to its infallibility, for otherwise, the whole Church would be required to assent to error. Is not the sole ground on which a person (whether God, the Pope, or a private individual) can claim assent his assurance of possessing the truth?

69. For the discussion of the relationship between these two functions, see Salaverri, pp. 964-987 and Hamer, pp. 118-124. Hamer's discussion of the Thomist virtue of *"docilitas"* (pp. 25-26) is illuminating.

70. On the dangers of "juridicism" in the interpretation of Church documents, see Congar, *The Meaning of Tradition* (New York, 1964), pp. 120-124; W. Kasper, *Dogme et évangile* (Tournai, 1967); and the remark of

a prominent contemporary theologian, "Rome seems to regard truth as a law to be imposed." The shift in theological ideal from the medieval quest for understanding to the post-Tridentine passion for certainty is also not without its importance for the development of the kind of perspective present in the manuals.

71. See *Schema Constitutionis De Ecclesia* (Vatican Press, 1964), p. 46.

72. *Ibid.*, p. 46.

73. See the use of this text in the first draft of the doctrinal report of the Synod of Bishops: "As far as doctrine is concerned, we must distinguish between truths infallibly defined by the magisterium of the Church and those which are authentically proposed but without the intention of defining. While preserving that (*sic*) obedience to the magisterium, 'the just freedom of research is recognized for faithful and clerics, as also freedom of thought and of expressing their opinion with courage and humility in those matters in which they are competent.' " See P. Hebblethwaite, *Inside the Synod: Rome, 1967* (New York, 1968), pp. 132-133.

74. See St. Thomas: "Notandum autem quod cum multi scriberent de catholica veritate, haec est differentia, quia illi qui scripserunt canonicam Scripturam, sicut Evangelistae et Apostoli, et alii hujusmodi, ita constanter eam asserunt quod nihil dubitandum relinquunt. Et ideo dicit, 'Et scimus quia verum est testimonium ejus' (Gal. 1:9). 'Si quis vobis evangelizaverit praeter id quod accepistis, anathema sit.' Cujus ratio est quia sola canonica scriptura est regula fidei. Alii autem sic edisserunt de veritate, quod *nolunt sibi credi nisi in his quae vera dicunt.*" *Super Ioannem XXI,* lectio VI, 2; no. 2656 in the Marietti edition; my emphasis.

75. Compare J. M. Cameron's criticism of Charles Davis for failing to place ecclesiastical failure and sin against the larger background of the enormous evils that exist in the world but do not shake our belief in God's existence or providence: *New Blackfriars* 49 (1968), p. 333.

76. Palmieri, p. 719.

77. Pesch, p. 370.

78. There is the possibility that some would maintain that the practical conclusions of *Humanae Vitae* are infallible not because of the encyclical but because of a constant tradition in the Church. Obviously, I have assumed throughout that the practical conclusions are not infallible. In 1964 Pope Paul VI, by speaking of a possible duty to reform the tradition, implied that the tradition to that point was not irreformable. Nothing in the subsequent discussion can be said to have strengthened the force of the tradition. And in *Humanae Vitae* itself, Paul's quest for assent is built not upon the infallibility of the tradition or of his restatement of it, but upon the authority of the ordinary magisterium. This is also the assumption of the great majority of those bishops who have commented on the encyclical and its authoritative force.

79. See Hebblethwaite, p. 155.

Morality and the Magisterium

Congress of Italian Moral Theologians
The Italian Episcopal Conference

Antonio di Marino, S.J.

The Congress of Italian Moral Theologians met at Padua from March 31 to April 3, 1970 to discuss the topic of "Morality and the Magisterium." The papers delivered at this meeting have been published by Edizioni Dehoniane under the title "Magistero e Morale." A concluding note at the end of this volume indicates that ecclesiastical authority forbade the publication in this volume of the final document representing the conclusions of the meeting. Subsequently, these conclusions were published. Our present selection includes three parts: the final document and conclusions of the Congress of Italian Moral Theologians, a "Note" from the Italian Bishops' Conference on this final document, and an article disagreeing with the final document written by moral theologian Antonio di Marino, S.J., who was a participant at the Congress. This whole discussion took place in the aftermath of the promulgation of the encyclical "Humanae Vitae.'

1
Final Document of the
Congress of Italian
Moral Theologians

I

The Function of the Magisterium
in the Realm of Morality

1. Vatican II highlighted the reality of the Church as the people of God: the responsibility of carrying forward through time the message of salvation, which is Christ himself, is one incumbent on the people of God as a whole.

2. Within the context of this overall responsibility, the magisterium has its own specific function of listening and dialoguing, entailing discernment (confirmation and guarantee) and prophecy.

3. Given the incarnational character of the Christian message on the one hand and the overall responsibility of the people of God on the other hand, today the Christian message cannot find satisfactory expression except through pluralistic and dialogic articulations under the guidance of the Spirit.

4. The moral life — i.e., the response of concrete, individual human beings to their divine vocation — is always tied up with the understanding that human beings have of themselves both as individuals and members of a group. To be faithful to its task, then, moral reflection is to a large extent conditioned culturally and historically; hence it must take cognizance of these inevitable limits.

5. The moral reflection of the Church does not escape this law but it remains ever tied to a constant datum, Christ, the total call of God and the one and only perfect human response to God. Christ is present to the Church both in the written word and as a happening in the faith-experience. Thus the method for exercising this sort of reflection will be dialogue between the many and varied experiences of fidelity to the unique Word, in the unique Spirit.

6. The moral magisterium will be exercised, first of all, in the context of differing cultural and historical conditions, and hence as the witness of the local church. On the worldwide level the magisterium will ordinarily be the meeting ground between the reciprocal proposals arising amid the people of God and, in the event, the place where an effort is made to bring unity into the manifold experiences in the light of the unique Word.

7. The establishing of norms having juridical force is not the characteristic function of the magisterium in the area of morality; that particular task is per se inherent in the function of governing, though it could entail a choice of a magisterial character.

8. Today the ordinary function of the magisterium in the moral realm is predominantly one of maintaining the thrust toward authentically evangelical values, and of encouraging their historical concretization in the conscientious choices of individuals and groups.

9. Particularly in the social realm the magisterium, in exercising its function, will maintain the eschatological tension of the Church's pilgrimage through time. In that pilgrimage the Church is to remain open to present opportunities and to the full realization of Christ's mystery: i.e., the total salvation of the human being. Hence the magisterium must increasingly assume its prophetic function in the encounters of the whole human family. That is to say, it must bear witness and testimony, on both the local and worldwide levels, to the inadequacy of all the structures which inevitably condition human existence and concrete experience.

II

The Function of Moral Theology
as a Servant of the Magisterium and the People of God
in Interpreting the Signs of the Times
(Mediation from the Bottom Up)

Vatican II encourages us to pay heed to the signs of the times, as we try to perceive the presence of Christ in and through the growth of humanity as persons and as community.

1. Moral theologians have their own proper competence within the ambiguity of reality. The task of the moral theologian is to help people to grasp the operation of the salvific happening and the import of the Christian vocation, which is to bear the fruits of charity for the life of the world. Hence the moral theologian has an obligation to pinpoint the process of humanization in the signs of the times, to note the relationship between ethical action and the

constantly changing historical situation, and to point out these matters to the magisterium so that it may guide the people of God.

2. This demands that moral theologians:

(a) have real contact with the human sciences;

(b) have experiential knowledge of the needs of the day and point them out;

(c) have an innate feel for what the Spirit is suggesting to the churches;

(d) compare the fonts of the Christian life with present-day historical realities in a scholarly, scientific way.

3. Hence we would like to see the following:

(a) more dynamic presentation of moral theology, one that would be more rigorously scientific and also more attentive to the signs of the times;

(b) joint reflection by Italian moral theologians on some of the major signs in our community that deserve a prompt and specific response;

(c) more serious consideration by the magisterium, on both the local and universal level, of the contribution that moral theologians can make to reading and interpreting the signs of the times.

III

MORAL THEOLOGY AS A SERVANT OF THE PEOPLE OF GOD
IN MEDIATIONS COMING DOWN FROM THE MAGISTERIUM

The Christian conscience derives the moral norm from the word of God and from the human situation viewed in the light of Christ (*kairos*). The magisterium represents an authoritative help in this effort. We must affirm the complementarity existing between the value of conscience and the function of the magisterium. For an adequate formation of conscience various factors must come together: e.g., the word of God, the grace of the Spirit, personal experience, critical reflection, community encounter, and the authentic teaching of the magisterium.

The task of moral theologians is:

1. to present the magisterium in the framework of the whole of revelation and Christian life;

2. to encourage and help the faithful to integrate the teaching of the magisterium with the fruits of their personal experience and that of the whole people of God;

3. to stimulate an adult, responsible discernment vis-à-vis the magisterium. Such discernment would include docility and charitable respect toward authority as well as a sense of co-responsibility shared with the Church and the world. Today a particular concern would be to form people in the Gospel spirit of nonviolence;

4. to make the faithful aware that in a conflict-ridden situation respect for the magisterium itself forbids us to have recourse to one single principle alone. Such respect obliges us to integrate a full and complete view of the scale of values with the compelling urgency of particular values, in line with the law of growth that properly belongs to the wayfaring Church. Hence moral theologians will help believing Christians to serenely follow their own sincere conscience even though in a given situation it cannot be clearly seen how their complete choice is to be reconciled with a particular goal that has been authoritatively proposed by the magisterium—provided that they seem to be on the road toward the ideal envisioned by the total teaching.

Theologians fully realize that their work of interpretation and research on the signs of the times may well scandalize members of the faithful who are less prepared. Hence they should make every effort to express their working hypotheses in a way that will not call into question respect for the doctrine and discipline of the Church that is now in force. But the faithful must also be taught not to place such hypotheses on the same level as the authoritative pronouncements of the magisterium. New theories and research-findings often call for patient discussion and further qualification before they can prove their pastoral fruitfulness and their fidelity to the Christian message.

IV
MORAL THEOLOGIANS AND PAST DOCUMENTS OF THE MAGISTERIUM

1. Hermeneutic work on the documents of the magisterium should aim not only for historical and semantic-philological inter-

pretation but also, and even mainly, for a theological interpretation.
2. In a theological interpretation the theologian seeks to grasp the underlying, and as such ever valid, import of the Church's overall teaching. Thus the theologian is concerned with receptiveness to the mystery of Christ as it is lived by the Church in a specific moral area.
3. Theologians note a certain amount of difficulty with respect to past documents of the magisterium. This difficulty often stems from the fact that such documents seem to attribute excessive importance to conceptual formulations which are held to be definitive but which do not always express the life of the ecclesial community.

2
Note of the
Italian Episcopal Conference
on the Conclusions of the
Italian Moral Theologians

I

First of all we feel that we should express our thanks to the moral theologians for devoting themselves to the task of confronting real, central problems. Efforts to examine and reflect upon such problems are a real service to the Church.

Nor is it really surprising that in their initial stage of study and exploration they might succumb to a certain degree of one-sidedness and even ambiguity. Good intentions and deeper, well-guided reflection can correct both matters.

To achieve this result, it seems necessary to underline two conditions that must be verified:

1. Discretion is needed at the time of research, particularly in moral matters, to avoid the danger of distorted presentations of their labors by organs of the press and public opinion — whether such distortions be committed in good faith or something less than

good faith. If there is to be calm, serious research in the service of the Church, then it seems that efforts must be made to avoid premature publication of conclusions that may confuse people.

2. One must point out the differing competence of the magisterium and of moral theologians as guides for the people of God in everything having to do with the path to salvation. In the supernatural order the primary guarantee of truth derives from the gifts of the Holy Spirit. If moral theology is to avoid the danger of harmful deviations in that order, then it must be animated by a lively sense of spiritual and intellectual communion with the magisterium. Or, to use the words of *Lumen Gentium*, it must proffer "religious assent of intellect and will" (n. 25) to those who have received "not only the office of sanctifying but also the offices of teaching and ruling" (n. 21). This attitude does not rule out proper freedom for scholarly research, and hence an evaluation of the teachings of the magisterium in terms of sound theological methodology. But it remains the necessary presupposition for any fruitful *science of moral theology*. It is the basis of the "connatural judgment" which is the chief factor for progress in the moral field, as the moral theologians at Padua themselves pointed out in one of their texts. In a treatment of "the magisterium and moral theology," it would have been gratifying to see a suitable amount of reflection on this condition governing the science of moral theology. Indeed this was officially suggested in Cardinal Garrone's letter to the participants of the Congress when he called attention to the import of the Church's spiritual and doctrinal *tradition*.

II

Insofar as the Conclusions of the Congress are concerned, several observations seem necessary. The following ones seem to be particularly imporant.

1. *A Basic Defect*

We accept as true and sincere the statement contained in the "Report of the Padua Congress (March 31 to April 3)," which mentions the unreserved acceptance by all the participants of Vatican II's teaching on the magisterium (*Lumen Gentium*, n. 25). Hence we find a basic defect in the drafting of the "Conclusions" insofar as no reference is made to the *binding* aspect of teachings from the authentic magisterium. Reference is made solely to the dialoguing aspect. This defect is all the more serious insofar as some of the conclusions seem to directly contradict this aspect of the authentic magisterium (especially III/4), and also insofar as such a one-sided presentation of only one aspect of the relationship between theology and the magisterium may lead less well-prepared readers to conclude that the Conclusions present an exact and adequate view of the whole relationship. Indeed some comments in the press would seem to suggest such a conclusion (see *Il Regno*, n. 9, 1 May 1970).

It is necessary, therefore, to complete and spell out the Conclusions more precisely and to frame them in a context which describes the relationsip between theology and the magisterium in more adequate and correct terms. As they now stand, they could not be offered as guidelines for what moral theology has to say about this subject.

Now we would like to offer some observations on various points contained in the text of the Conclusions as we have it. Additional observations arose from the Commission's careful study of the text, but here we will restrict ourselves to those observations which seem to be most pertinent and important.

2. The Function of the Magisterium in the Realm of Morality
Section I of Conclusions

Regarding Conclusion 2: Our basic observation is contained in the point made just above. Due to the aforementioned onesidedness, no mention is made of the fact that the *primary and proper* task of the magisterium is the *authentic proclamation* of the Christian message. And it is by adhering to this authentic proclamation (see *Lumen Gentium*, n. 12) that the Christian people and moral theologians develop the *sensus fidei* which enables them to work out *in Christian terms* the solution to problems of concrete life and history, perhaps even anticipating future solutions of the magisterium itself. In other words, the "experience of faith" cannot be genuine if it is not illuminated by the word of God authentically interpreted by the magisterium (see *Gaudium et Spes*, n. 50).

Regarding Conclusion 5: "Christ is present to the Church both in the written word and as a happening in the faith-experience." There is no reference whatsoever to the doctrinal and spiritual *tradition* of the Church. This tradition, with the positive assistance of the Holy Spirit, has interpreted both written and unwritten revelation, thus constituting the unbroken basis of the Church's fidelity to the Lord's teaching through the course of history.

This may well be the most important point raised in the letter issued by Cardinal Garrone.

Regarding Conclusion 6: The suggested approach for the formation of the universal magisterium's teaching is incorrect and one-sided. The elaboration of an authentic teaching may have a local origin or an immediately universal one, depending on the problems and the needs at issue. For the task of the personal, universal magisterium of the Supreme Pontiff is not just to be the *expression* of a teaching that already exists in the local churches. It can *also* be, *if necessary*, the anticipatory forerunner and guide for the individual teachers in the local churches. If individual members of the faithful, theologians, and bishops can propose new solutions for new problems by virtue of their charisms, then certainly the Vicar of Christ can do this with even more justification by virtue of his singular charism, for Christ's flock, the people of God, has been entrusted to him primarily and in a wholly singular way.

Regarding Conclusion 7: The formulation of this section is not readily comprehensible to the average reader. Because of its ambiguity, it readily lends itself to unacceptable interpretations. In reality it must be said that the moral magisterium is *per se doctrinal, with morally binding efficacy* for the formation of conscience and the conduct of life, but it can have different characteristics and functions. It can be definitively doctrinal, prudentially doctrinal, and so forth. In short, it can teach some norm, which interprets the Gospel law or natural law, as an absolute norm for all times and places, or it can present some norm as the *historical application* of an indeterminate and dynamic Gospel law.

The historicity *of the origin and formulation* of many of the magisterium's moral norms should not lead people to the conclusion that *all of them are always* historically conditioned insofar as their value is concerned, and hence changeable as cultures change.

It is precisely that task of moral theology to bring out the distinction between what is absolute and what is relative (or historical) in the formulations of the magisterium. It must distinguish the varying degrees of depth and seriousness in the norms and the varying degrees of obligatory commitment which the conscience of the faithful must give to the teaching of the magisterium. In the texts under consideration, however, no adequate distinction is made between various fields of application and various forms of exercising the magisterium. That leads to undue and improper generalizations.

Regarding Conclusion 8: The statement is incomplete. The magisterium cannot maintain "the thrust toward authentically evangelical values," except by teaching and imposing as well the *moral obligations* included in the will of God, whether that will be divinely revealed or made manifest in natural law (see Mt. 7:21). This conclusion, then, needs to be completed and clarified.

3. *Moral Theology in the Service
of the People of God
(Section III of the Conclusions)*

The initial paragraph offers an inadequate illustration of the formation of conscience, and it tends toward an incorrect view, for it enumerates the various factors without pointing up their reciprocal relations, thus giving the false impression that they are equal in value and binding force.

Regarding Conclusion 2: The task here assigned to moral theologians is proper and fitting, provided that in each and every case one clearly specifies the relationship between the magisterium, personal experience, and the experience of the whole people of God.

Regarding Conclusion 3: The text talks about "adult, responsible *discernment* vis-à-vis the magisterium," which would include "docility and charitable respect toward authority as well as a sense of co-responsibility shared with the Church and the world." This does not correctly express all that the teaching of the Church demands with respect to "religious assent of intellect and will" (*Lumen Gentium*, n. 25).

Regarding Conclusion 4: The preceding ambiguities and inadequacies explain this section. Its formulation readily inclines people to the error that in particular individual cases something is licit in conscience which may even have been declared illicit in absolute terms by the authentic magisterium.

As it is formulated, this section cannot be accepted as a correct statement of a *moral-theology teaching that is faithful* to the magisterium of the Church. Hence it cannot be proposed in teaching moral theology without failing in the duty that theologians have to the magisterium, which entrusts them with the task of teaching.

N.B. Nothing essential has been detected in Section II of the Conclusions.

III

We would like to close by thanking the Padua Congress for its efforts at serious reflection. However, we feel it necessary to urge the executive board of the Association to rethink the "Conclusions." They should be formulated in a more complete and, in some cases, more accurate way. Then the new emphases, which are properly brought out, will clearly not contradict, or seem to contradict, the spiritual and doctrinal tradition of the Church. Instead of seeming to break with that tradition, they will clearly be in continuity with it. And that tradition has undoubtedly been assisted by the Holy Spirit in past centuries as well.

To give a more accurate picture of the Congress and episcopal involvement at it, you should also be sure to publish the introductory discourse of Bishop Bortignon and the concluding discourse of Bishop Luciani, which laid stress on the points that were passed over in silence in the Conclusions.

3
The Church's Magisterium
in the Field of Morality

Antonio Di Marino, S.J.

The Significance of the Church's Magisterium
in the Field of Morality

There is no more practical problem than the one of determining how we are to form the moral convictions that guide the choices and behavior patterns of daily life.

In solving this problem, are we to trust to the judgment and conscience of the individual? But can the latter do without external teachers here, any more than we can do without them in other areas of knowledge? Are we to be governed in this area by the prevailing opinion of a given time and place? And how are we to detect the emergence of a shared or common moral conviction? Can we say, perhaps, that in the Church it is the magisterium, the ordinary magisterium at least, which is the organ to detect such emerging convictions amid the pluralism of differing opinions? But how are we to distinguish the wheat from the chaff, even in God's field?

The solving of these questions by the Church is a matter of concern for all humanity, since the Church is a standard raised aloft amid the nations: therefore I think we would do well to take a brief look at the task and essential function of the Church in order to sketch the outlines of an answer to these questions.

The Church is the assembly of those who visibly heed the summons to salvation which God addresses to humanity through Christ, his incarnate Word. God constitutes them as an elect people in which his glory dwells as in a temple and he offers them his friendship and divine life in a covenant agreement. In the Church, Christ is the head who gives life to his members through his Spirit. The Spirit in turn is two things at once. He is the principle of unity who unites the members with each other and with their head. He is also the teacher of truth; throughout the centuries he enables the members to see and understand what Christ revealed. Thus in the Church unity and truth are mutually related and affect one another. The Church's saving truth makes headway insofar as its members are united, and unity can be sustained only on the basis of the truth. Charity grows out of faith, and faith flowers in charity.

The Church has probably exercised its magisterium more massively in the realm of dogmatic truths relating to the faith than in the realm of moral truths relating to the practice of charity. For the shining glory of charity, like the leaves of trees, spontaneously produces its fruit when the roots and trunk of faith are sound and secure. When people of faith believe in God's revealed message, which tells them that he loves us, then it becomes easy to love him in return and do his will, for we then know that he wills what is good for all human beings.

In other words, the Spirit of Christ enkindles friendship and charity toward God the Father in the Church. The Spirit renews the paschal mystery in the Church, arousing in the faithful the sentiments of Christ himself, who adhered to God's will even though it meant the sacrifice of his own life. The Spirit infuses his own charity into the faithful, bringing them together visibly or sacramentally in eucharistic communion. This union is prolonged in the liturgy of Christian living, which is made up of mutual service (*diakonia*) and mutual, fraternal love (*agape*).

Charity Is Union,
the Source of Knowing Moral Truths

As indicated above, then, the Holy Spirit pours out love for God and human beings. However, the Holy Spirit also reveals the ways to attain this union.

Charity, or love, is the union which the Spirit effects between human beings themselves and between human beings and God. It effects a greater likeness and harmony between the parties involved. As the old expression put it: *Simile simili gaudet; amicitia aequales invenit aut facit.* To be authentic and solid, accord between human beings must take place on a level that is both deeply personal and universally shared. It must take place on the level that makes them truly human, which is to say, on the level of uprightness and moral goodness. Accord with God, too, demands that human beings respect their dignity as such. In fact it was the human being without sin who realized for all human beings the mystery of communion with the life and friendship of God. Love for God, who cannot be seen, takes on shape and substance in love for one's fellow human being who can be seen. And since human beings have been created in the image and likeness of God, we can understand why Christ taught that things done for the lowliest human being would be regarded as favors done to himself.

Thus the will of God is carried out by obeying that of human beings, and his love is shown in service to one's fellow human beings.

In other words, divine charity cannot co-exist with sin, which also represents a failure to live up to one's human dignity. For the love of God demands love for human beings. It requires the other human or moral virtues, just as light presupposes the design of flowers for us to delight in the sight of them.

Now the Church is the locale and instrument of the loving encounter of human beings with each other and with God. As such, it must have a specific role to play in the realm of the moral life and hence its magisterium is also competent in this realm.

The Moral Magisterium of the Church in the Evolving Course of Time

It is easy enough to accept the fact that the magisterium of the Church should be involved with moral problems. The acceptance of this magisterium might also be easy to accept, at least mentally, if its teachings concerned a stable, unchanging human situation. But human circumstances are mutable and changing, like everything that takes place in time. Here again, then, we face the problem of reconciling the eternal with the temporal, the salvation achieved once and for all by Christ in the Church with the history of human beings who are traveling through this vale of tears.

The history of salvation is a living thing, even as the Church itself is a body, the mystical body of Christ. Life grows and nourishes itself by taking in food. Only part of the latter is assimilated, and even that part is eliminated once its quota of energy is consumed. So even what was once useful, needed food and sustenance becomes noxious material to be expelled.

The same applies to the Church and salvation history. Its vital principle must know enough to expel what has become decadent, even as it must expel poisons and harmful nutriments.

It was in this light that the Fathers of the Church interpreted the action of the Church promoted by the apostle Paul with regard to Old Testament prescriptions. It is a vital action, though die-hard conservatives may feel cut to the quick. It is also a living, evolving process that may escape the superficial observer or seem like immobilism to those who impatiently demand reform at any price.

There was a time, not so long ago and not completely over yet, when Sacred Scripture, the privileged organ of divine revelation, was supposed to be read and interpreted in such a naive, traditionalist way that insurmountable difficulties were created. The case of Galileo is a famous example. When a more scholarly and mature exegesis was developed, a sound distinction was made between culture and scientific notions of hagiography on the one hand and the teaching connected with God's saving plan and revelation on the other.

Now can this hermeneutic criterion, which has rendered such good service in the reading and interpretation of Sacred Scripture, be extended to the interpretation of the ecclesiastical magisterium as well? The analogy is not without problems since the magisterium generally uses an idiom that is more precise and spare than the literary idiom of hagiography, and its didactic intent is more explicit. But since God's original revelation has managed to reach us despite the cultural factors conditioning its first witnesses, one may legitimately assume that its preservation and explanation by the Church's hierarchical magisterium would be guaranteed despite the inevitable cultural and philosophical conditioning factors employed by the drafters of the magisterium's documents. It is conceivable that deeper theological investigations would not only bring out the true import of earlier documents from the magisterium but also distinguish the salvific relevance of that teaching for our day from doctrinal content suited to past situations; it could also separate the teaching intended by the magisterium from opinions that were naturally limited by the culture of another day.

In short, it is the salvific intent, not the scientific or cultural one, which the Spirit guarantees in Scripture, tradition, and both the ordinary and extraordinary magisterium of the Church. From this standpoint we can deduce that a pronouncement by the magisterium is not supposed to be read or interpreted in anachronistic terms. Even though some statement by the magisterium may seem dated and outmoded, not only in terms of present-day reality but also in terms of later interventions by the magisterium, a closer examination of it may reveal that in its own day it was highly effective in enabling people to hear the voice of the Spirit.

Moreover, if knowledge of the truth of salvation were bound up with the letter of Sacred Scripture and that of magisterial documents, then it seems inexplicable that Christ did not write any books, and that he devoted his time instead to the training of living witnesses.

Christ's Witnesses

If it is not the letter of Scripture or of the magisterium that guarantees us an understanding of the truth about salvation, neither is it solely the exegesis or hermeneutics of that letter which ensures us what we need to know to be saved in our day.

Just as the Father's logos became tangible in Christ, so Christ's presence and voice is perceived through those he sent out with the words: "He who hears you hears me" (Lk. 10:16).

The living witness of the apostles continues, thanks to an uninterrupted tradition, in the Pope and the bishops united with him. The Spirit, who guided the nascent Church through the apostles, has never ceased to assist the Church through the Pope and the bishops united with him during the course of centuries and changing human circumstances.

At this point we might raise another question. As we noted earlier, morality has to do with salvation and hence falls under the competence of the magisterium. But since it is undoubtedly a cultural datum, is it not also entrusted to the competence of human beings and their conscience? Indeed another question arises here relating specifically to the salvific aspect of morality. Since Vatican II stressed the importance of the whole people of God, wouldn't the individual faithful be capable of comprehending what the Spirit says to the churches, even in the moral realm as it relates to salvation? Hence, in the last analysis, wouldn't the conscience of each upright human being, and that of the faithful moved by the Spirit in particular, be sovereign in making decisions in the moral realm?

Morality certainly is an affair for the conscience of each human being, since all of us have been given intelligence, self-awareness, and knowledge of what belongs to us. Conscience, indeed, is awareness of self as a personal totality that reflects God as his image and attributes to him all that rightfully should be so attributed.

But who can deny that human beings, even the best intentioned ones, are subject to many errors and uncertainties, even in the area of moral norms and the discernment of moral good and evil? As Scripture put it: "For the reasoning of mortals is worthless, and our designs are likely to fail" (Wis. 9:14). Incarnate Wisdom, living in the Church, teaches human beings to recognize the paths of righteousness promptly and thus paves the way for them to reach salvation. As completely self-taught people, we do not make a great deal of progress in learning sciences or technical skills, even though these areas of culture are within the capability of human beings. The help of a teacher is not an obstacle to the intelligence of the pupil, even in the case of highly gifted people.

In like manner the ecclesiastical magisterium is not opposed to the moral conscience of human beings. It encourages that conscience, smoothing the way to salvation for it. Moreover, the journey to salvation requires moral virtue, as I noted earlier.

This is all the more true in the bosom of the Church, the sacrament of Christ and his salvation. The requirements of salvation call for the intervention of the magisterium, which is assisted by the Spirit of Wisdom, in order to prepare the way of the Lord with moral teaching.

Now and then one gets the impression that people would like to apply to the internal life of the Church everything that has happened historically in the government of civil society. In the latter area we have moved from royal absolutism, which saw monarchs directly invested by God, to a democratic view that theoretically attributes to all citizens the authority which in fact is exercised by a group of people who are more or less capable and lucky in politics.

I am not suggesting that people would go so far as to apply to the Church, the people of God, some sort of pan-pneumatism or populist pantheism that would equate God and the people. But even excessive stress on an analogy between democracy and the highly distinctive structures of the Church can lead us far from the truth. Some, it seems, would prefer to think that each member possesses the Spirit to such a degree that each is prophetically authorized to proclaim what the Spirit has to say to the churches. According to this view, the institutional magisterium should limit itself to promoting encounters between pluralistic views and opinions. Its only contribution would be to point out which way the majority is leaning. Its only weight would reside in the reasons it manages to marshal in support of its own positions. This view, however, is in danger of fostering the confusion that once appeared in the church of Corinth, and it would not be able to rely on the authority of the apostle Paul to put things in order and effect agreement. Yet such agreement is essential to the Christian life, as Paul himself tells the Corinthians: "Agree with one another, live in peace, and the God of love and peace will be with you" (2 Cor. 13:11).

If the democratic outlook of the present day is not to regard the hierarchical magisterium of the Catholic Church as a stumbling block, then it must resort to the fundamental principle that salvation is a grace, a gratuitous gift, from God. That gratuitousness is expressed visibly—or, as people prefer to say today, sacramentally—in God's salvific deeds: i.e., the incarnation of the Word and the mission of his Spirit in the apostolic, hierarchical Church.

The fact is that Christ, even as a human being, was given as a gift to humanity. He was not a product of humanity resulting from natural generation. He is the son of the Virgin who conceived by the Holy Spirit. In like manner Christ's prophetic presence in the Church, or the ecclesiastical magisterium, does not emerge from the human will of the faithful, as in a parliamentary democracy. It is given and made incarnate, as it were, in a visible charism, through apostolic succession and tradition. As the Father visibly sent the Incarnate Word, so Jesus visibly sent his apostles and their successors until the end of time. In this way Jesus has remained ever present in his Church, just as he promised.

Without this visible apostolic tradition and without this quasi-sacramental sign of the hierarchical magisterium, no member of the Church, however much united with the Spirit, could enjoy the guarantee of the Church, the pillar of truth, in distinguishing the voice of Christ's Spirit from that of the spirit of evil. The latter spirit is still alive and operative, seeking people to devour (1 Pet. 5:8). But when the members of the Church more docile to the Holy Spirit enjoy the backing and assured support of the hierarchical magisterium, then they certainly can enrich the Christian community. This is what happened in past centuries. They can even provide charisms and illuminations more copiously than those enjoyed by the trustees of the magisterium itself. The Fathers and Doctors of the Church operated usefully in that vein. Even moralists and the ordinary faithful of today can contribute much in the same vein.

From the help provided by well-prepared members of the Church and by theologians who sensitively grasp the meaning of history and the values being discovered and experienced by humanity as a whole in the evolving course of history under the guidance of divine providence, the magisterium is indirectly prompted to encourage and undertake interventions suited to the new situations facing humanity.

The fact is that the exercise of the magisterium is a human one. Exegetes tell us that the activity of those who wrote the inspired books of the Bible was conditioned by the culture of their time. If this is true, then how much more is it true that the training and study of those who enjoy the charism of the ecclesiastical magisterium will condition the efficacy and utility of their interventions.

Fallible and Infallible Interventions
of the Magisterium

As we know, not all the interventions of the magisterium are solemn and infallible. Some are fallible interventions, and they are the most frequent ones in the realm of morals. That does not mean that fallible interventions are in fact erroneous. It simply means that there is no absolute guarantee that they are not erroneous. One might be tempted to ask, therefore, what purpose is served by that kind of magisterium. The purpose served is the very same purpose sought by practical or moral truth. The aim is to serve charity and promote agreement between minds in the Church, the body of Christ. When some truth comes more clearly to the fore, perhaps even through the understanding of ordinary members of the Church who see things more correctly than their pastor does, it is not meant to be a wedge driven between the community and the pastoral authorities. Instead it is to be presented as a gift that will unite the community even more closely in its search for what is good. The Church and its pastors may seem to deserve reproach for having made a mistake. Nevertheless they "cannot do anything against the truth, but only for the truth" (see 2 Cor. 13:7ff.). Only by "speaking the truth in love" (Eph. 4:15) does the body of Christ grow through the activity of each of its members. It is a body which grows and develops in the warmth of charity.

Moreover, to win acceptance of a truth, there is no argument better than kindness and an understanding of the other person's reasons. Now, the authenticity and the guarantee behind the hierarchical magisterium derive from the assistance of the Spirit. It is that very Spirit who is the force of supernatural love knitting the Church into visible oneness around Christ, now invisible, and Christ's visible Vicar. There is a difference between the private individual in the Church and the Church's hierarchical teachers. There is no denying that the private individual might know the truth better than the hierarchical teachers. But the real difference between them lies in the fact that private individuals do not have the authority or power to demand that others give internal assent to their affirmations. Thus if we wish to enjoy union and avoid damaging charity, we must agree with that authority which, by very definition, unifies the ecclesiastical community.

Truth and unity go together of necessity. A dawning truth spontaneously unites minds. And the union of intentions in reciprocal love enables people to grasp the practical truths needed to choose prudently between the possible choices provided by a contingent reality. Prudence and the Christian conscience might be described as the sense of love which knows how to discern what unites human beings and fortifies their union on the road to salvation.

The great dogma, revealed by God and taught infallibly, which lies at the basis of all Christian morality is that God loves human beings and wills for them to dwell in their liberty in order to love him with heartfelt sincerity and human works. The other practical truths of morality are more or less like kindling wood meant to stoke this fire of God's Spirit. Not all the wood turns into flame, but a residue of ashes does not prevent charity from blazing out in the Church. Yet it would be good if the heap of ashes did not grow too big. It is fitting, therefore, that the moral magisterium of the Church be kept zealously immune from potential errors even though such errors are not at all impossible for anyone or anything that remains human, even if it is the case of a magisterium aided by the Spirit of Truth. It is not just the fallible magisterium that is exposed to error. So is the infallible magisterium, when it is misunderstood or expanded.

Insofar as the hermeneutic problem is concerned, it seems obvious enough that if we examine the formulas of the magisterium from a bygone day in a careful, scholarly fashion, and then compare them intelligently with present-day situations, we should be able to shed new light on the rich patrimony of the Gospel message, which takes in *nova et vetera*.

On the other hand I cannot see what useful results are to be achieved by another hermeneutic approach. This particular approach would see the *kenosis* of the salvation mystery embodied in even erroneous formulas of the magisterium, and then seek a *glorification* of this mystery through a sacramental interpretation of those formulas.

And what are we to say about the relationship between conscience and the magisterium? Certainly one is correct in maintaining that the relationship between the two is the relationship existing between the understanding of the pupil and the teaching of the teacher. One is in the service of the other. And it is also true that moral goodness is achieved in the liberty which accepts the judgment of conscience. But are we talking about good conscience when we are talking about a conscience which, while acknowledging the ideal goodness of some teaching by the magisterium, calmly sets it aside in its concrete choices? An affirmative answer hardly seems tenable. We are dealing with a very different case, of course, when we are talking about someone who in good faith, but out of *invincible* ignorance as the manuals put it, chooses to act in disagreement with the teaching of the magisterium or even in the case of those who, with definite and certain competence, decide that it would be a mistake to apply the teaching of the magisterium to their case.

The Dispute Concerning the Teaching Office of the Church

Karl Rahner, S.J.

In 1967, in the course of what may be accounted an initial period following upon the Second Vatican Council, the German bishops undertook to produce a document in which they attempted to apply the claims of the Council to the special circumstances of the German Church. It is not our intention here to examine this document in its entirety. We shall confine ourselves rather to a few observations on a single brief passage in the document, and, moreover, from the standpoint of a particular episode of which we shall shortly have to speak in more detail.

I
THE DOCUMENT OF THE GERMAN BISHOPS

In order to avoid imposing upon the reader the wearisome task of having to search out the text referred to for himself,[1] let us repeat the relevant section of the document here:

17. At this point a difficult problem arises, calling for realistic discussion. It is one which today more than formerly threatens either the faith of many Catholics or their attitude of free and unreserved trust toward the teaching authorities of the Church. We refer to the fact that in the exercise of its official function this teaching authority of the Church can, and on occasion actually does, fall into errors. The fact that such a thing is possible is something of which the Church has always been aware and which it has actually expressed in its theology. Moreover it has evolved rules of conduct to cater

for the kind of situations which arise from this. This possibility of error refers not to those statements of doctrine which are proclaimed as propositions to be embraced with the absolute assent of faith, whether by a solemn definition on the part of the Pope, a general council, or by the exercise of the ordinary *magisterium*. Historically speaking it is also incorrect to maintain that any error has subsequently arisen in such dogmas as proclaimed by the Church. This is of course not to dispute the fact that even in the case of such a dogma, while we must uphold its original meaning, it is always possible and always necessary for a development in our understanding of it to take place, involving a progressive elimination of any misinterpretations which may perhaps have been attached to it hitherto. Nor should we confuse the question which we have raised here with the manifest fact that side by side with the immutable divine law there is also a human law in the Church which is subject to change. Changes in this latter have from the outset nothing to do with error. At most they raise the question of how far some juridical decision in the remote or recent past was opportune.

18. Now let us consider the possibility or the fact of error in non-defined statements of doctrine on the part of the Church, recognizing that these themselves in turn may differ very widely among themselves in their degree of binding force. The first point to be recognized resolutely and realistically is that human life, even at a wholly general level, must always be lived "by doing one's best according to one's lights" and by recognized principles which, while at the theoretical level they cannot be recognized as absolutely certain, nevertheless command our respect in the "here and now" as valid norms of thinking and acting because in the existing circumstances they are the best that can be found. This is something that everyone recognizes from the concrete experience of his own life. Every doctor in his diagnoses, every statesman in the political judgments he arrives at on particular situations and the decisions he bases on these, is aware of this fact. The Church too in its doctrine and practice cannot always and in every case allow itself to be caught in the

dilemma of either arriving at a doctrinal decision which is ultimately binding or simply being silent and leaving everything to the free opinion of the individual. In order to maintain the true and ultimate substance of faith it must, even at the risk of error in points of detail, give expression to doctrinal directives which have a certain degree of binding force and yet, since they are not *de fide* definitions, involve a certain element of the provisional even to the point of being capable of including error. Otherwise it would be quite impossible for the Church to preach cr interpret its faith as a decisive force in real life or to apply it to each new situation in human life as it arises. In such a case the position of the individual Christian in regard to the Church is analogous to that of a man who knows that he is bound to accept the decision of a specialist even while recognizing that it is not infallible.

19. At any rate any opinion which runs contrary to a current statement of doctrine on the part of the Church has no place in preaching or catechesis, even though the faithful may, under certain circumstances, have to be instructed as to the nature of, and the limited weight to be attached to, a current doctrinal decision of this kind. This is a point which has already been discussed. Anyone who believes that he is justified in holding, as a matter of his own private opinion, that he has already even now arrived at some better insight which the Church will come to in the future must ask himself in all sober self-criticism before God and his conscience whether he has the necessary breadth and depth of specialized theological knowledge to permit himself in his private theory and practice to depart from the current teaching of the official Church. Such a case is conceivable in principle, but subjective presumptuousness and an unwarranted attitude of knowing better will be called to account before the judgment-seat of God.

20. It belongs intrinsically to the right attitude of faith of any Catholic seriously to strive to attach a positive value to even a provisional statement of doctrine on the part of the Church, and to make it his own. In secular life too far-

reaching decisions have to be taken on the basis of fallible findings on the part of others, which have been arrived at according to their best lights. And it is no less true in Church matters that the individual need not feel any shame or diminishment of his own personality if in his findings he relies upon the Church's teaching even in cases in which it cannot be accounted as definitive from the outset. It is possible that in specific cases the development of the Church's doctrine proceeds too slowly. But even in arriving at a judgment of this kind we must be prudent and humble. For in any such development of doctrine within a Church made up of men subject to historical conditions time is needed. For it cannot proceed any faster than the task permits of preserving the substance of the faith without loss.

21. We do not need to fear that in adopting the positions of the Church in the manner described we are failing to respond to the claims of our own age. Often enough the serious questions raised for us by our own age, and which we are called upon to answer on the basis of our faith, make it necessary for us to think out the truths of our faith afresh. It is perfectly possible that in this process fresh points will come to be emphasized. But this is not to call the faith itself in question. Rather it contributes to a deeper grasp of the truths of divine revelation and of the Church's teaching. For we are firmly convinced, and we see that experience confirms us in this, that we need neither deny any truth for the Catholic faith, nor deny the Catholic faith for the sake of any truth, provided only that we understand this faith in the spirit of the Church and seek always to achieve a deeper grasp of it.[2]

At a later stage we shall have a few brief remarks to make on the theological importance of this document in general and of the passage quoted in particular. The only observation to be made at this point is that an Italian version of the document appeared in *Osservatore Romano* of 15 December 1967 (in a translation commissioned, so it is reported, by the Secretariat of State). Incidentally I know that the document was read in the refectory in the presence of the learned professors of the Gregorianum and was received most favorably there. (It can hardly be as bad, therefore, as it is judged to be in the text which we are about to quote.) This text is particularly remarkable to the extent that so far as I know this is the first occasion on which this problem has been explicitly tackled at all in a (relatively) official document. Previously it had been left solely to the theologians to discuss.

II
CRITIQUE OF THE DOCUMENT

At the current time (and probably for some time previously) a mimeographed paper has been circulating among higher ecclesiastical circles which amounts to a critique of this document. The passage in this text which is of special interest to us here is that which is concerned with the passage in the document of the German bishops cited above. On this it has the following to say:

The "Document of the German Bishops Addressed to All Members of the Church who are Commissioned to Preach the Faith" of the 22nd September 1967 has made a very favorable impression here. Nevertheless the document is in error in the distinction it draws between the concept of a "provisional" statement of doctrine and an infallible doctrinal decision and when it says on this: "In such a case the position of the individual Christian in regard to the Church is first and foremost analogous to that of a man who knows that he is bound to accept the decision of a specialist even while recognizing that it is not infallible" (p. 13).[3] A statement of doctrine on the part of the Church which does not claim to be infallible can *per accidens* prove erroneous, but this does not mean that it can be characterized as provisional. Whoever speaks in the name of the Church's teaching authority can speak and should speak only if he is convinced of the fact that the doctrine to be put forward is *true*. This means that he never meets the individual Christian in the role of a specialist, either "first and foremost" or at all. A specialist is subject to the basic principle: "*Tantum valet quantum probat.*" In any statement of doctrine on the part of the Church the arguments adduced in support of it have in all cases merely the character of aids to the free and voluntary acceptance of the decision concerned, and it is in this again that the radical difference is to be found between the Church's teaching authority and theological science. The wrong estimation of the force of a non-infallible decision of doctrine has led, not least in the question of the acceptance of *Humanae Vitae*, to the following journalistic formula appearing even in the Church's own press: "No infallible decision — conscience decides." This represents a complete distortion of the real function of conscience. A point that is overlooked is that in *any and every* human act the conscience is called upon to play its part, even in the case of accepting an infallible decision of doctrine. And a further point no longer recognized here is that the conscience of the Christian needs to be guided and directed by Christ, and so by her whom the Lord has entrusted with his mission.

What is to be said of this paper? In a single word I maintain that this critique of the bishops' document is theologically and practically speaking radically mistaken.

III

INTERIOR CONTRADICTIONS WITHIN THE CRITIQUE

First and primarily: the reader of this critique may ask himself with some amazement how in all logic the writer manages to make the accusation that the document concerned undervalues that very teaching office of the Church which derives exactly and precisely from the bishops and their teaching. After all we cannot, as a matter of sound logic, uphold an authority for the bishops which they themselves authoritatively reject. Of course it is possible to say that an episcopal document is not necessarily either infallible or correct in all its points, and so that one is justified in disagreeing with a document of this kind or with individual points in it provided that one has good reasons for doing so and has given full and mature consideration to it. That is perfectly correct. But the critic quoted above is in fact disputing the very conditions which make it possible for a critique to exist, and prescribes a more or less unconditional obedience to such doctrinal declarations even though they themselves make no explicit claim to be infallible, and even though *in this particular case* the author of the critique we have quoted is in fact contradicting his own general principle in regarding doctrinal pronouncements of this kind as not being beyond dispute. The real situation, however, is in fact this: our present-day Catholic authoritarians are only too ready to uphold Pope and bishop so long as they teach what they themselves regard as right. Otherwise they dispense themselves from that very attitude of unconditional obedience to doctrine which they defend indiscriminately against the "modernists" of today as a sacred principle. One of the points which, so the critique asserts, has been overlooked in the bishops' document is that the doctrinal authority of the bishops and the Pope (even in cases in which no definitions are arrived at) is a distinct entity in its own right such that on the one hand we are obliged to assent to it and on the other it has to be distinguished from the material arguments adduced in support of the official doctrinal declaration and has a value of its own independent of these. Now in the authoritative doctrinal statement of the bishops there is no attempt whatever to identify in any sense these two factors: the material theological arguments and the teaching authority of the Church. The *comparison* which has led the critic to this totally false imputation is precisely one which, in common with all comparisons, has to be taken with a grain of salt. It is actually a sound and intelligible comparison. For when someone finds himself in certain circumstances obliged to submit himself to the (non-infallible) diagnosis of a doctor, then in this situation too he is acting not on the basis of the arguments put to him by the doctor, and which he is quite incapable of understanding, but on the basis of the doctor's authority, albeit this is, ultimately speaking, different in kind from the teaching authority of the Church. Are we unable to understand a comparison of this kind? After all the true *tertium comparationis* consists simply in the fact that one individual is presenting another with a decision which is clearly recognized by both parties to be non-infallible and capable of error. Hence while there are indeed solid grounds to support the decision (including, among other factors, that of "authority" of the most varied kinds), still, since it is not infallible, the party addressed retains the right, under certain circumstances (notice we say "circumstances," not mere capriciousness), to reject the proposal that he shall come to this decision (in doctrinal matters, etc.) so long as he believes that his reasons for doing so are good or better than those of the person proposing the decision to him.

Now it might be said that while it is true that formally speaking all this is quite correct it is not applicable to our present case because an individual Catholic theologian, or even a layman, is never in a position here and now (unless the decision concerned is revised by the teaching authorities themselves) to be *capable* of having good or better reasons to depart from the decision of the teaching authorities even though in principle it is conceded by both sides that this official doctrinal decision on the part of the Church is in itself and at basis capable of being revised. In such cases the position may be compared to that of a stone-breaker who declares that he regards the most recent theory of Professor XY on plasma physics as erroneous, for this professor does in fact admit that his theory is not absolutely certain. It is not for one moment to be denied that there can be, and often are, *cases of this kind* of dissent from the noninfallible doctrinal decisions of the Church, a dissent which is theoretically false and morally unjustified. Those who wish can confidently and reasonably go beyond this in maintaining that in cases of such dissent it is to be presumed that they are of this kind (whereas the opposite presumption is invalid). The bishops' doctrinal document too leaves no room for doubt that there are such cases and that any Christian who presumptuously or without grave reasons departs from the Church's teaching even when it does not contain any definition will have to answer for it before God.

But the alternative case is precisely possible too, and this is a point which is boldly and honestly expressed in the bishops' document. Cases may perfectly well arise in which a Catholic Christian has a right and, under certain circumstances, a moral duty to depart from some official doctrine of the Church of this kind. This is something which the critic refuses to recognize yet which is true. This is not the place to give a more detailed exposition of the question of whether a distinction is to be drawn in this principle between the rights and duties of specialist theologians on the one hand and laymen on the other (any such distinction would be strongly dependent upon the nature of the individual case). Nor do we intend here to adopt a casuistic approach in enlarging upon the question of *what precise form* the attitude of the dissenter should take in such cases according to the traditional principles of fundamental theology and morals. Nor shall we attempt to establish, on the grounds of wholly traditional theology, the point that the principle expressed in the bishops' document is itself traditional. All this would take us too far afield.

IV
EXAMPLES OF ERRONEOUS DECISIONS

I will adopt another approach by putting a simple question, arising from the practice of theologians, to the critic and giving some explanation of this. A brief but true anecdote may serve by way of introduction. During the modernist period the great Dominican exegete Lagrange had to listen to the following reproach from a friend in the course of a private conversation: "In fact on this point (an anti-modernist declaration on the part of the doctrinal authorities of the Church of that time on a question of exegesis) the only response you can manage is a *'silentium obsequiosum'* (meaning that while you do indeed hold your tongue, you in fact interiorly reject this declaration)." To this Lagrange replied: "That is true. But I would actually be committing a mortal sin (against my own conscience with regard to truth) if I were to act in any other way."

Now let us consider the question itself in fuller detail. I have no time to search through Denzinger for official doctrinal decisions belonging to the last few decades which have proved false, and which virtually no Catholic theologian any longer accepts nowadays. Accordingly I will merely rummage a little through my own memory. For my purpose the fact that my examples are primarily of an exegetical kind makes no very great difference. Not all of them are of this kind however. For it has been explicitly stated at an

earlier stage that the same weight is to be attached to such exegetical decisions as to the doctrinal decisions of other Roman
authorities. Again we must ask to be excused if our approach is
very unsystematic, and I shall not extend my researches further
back than our own century. If these doctrinal decisions were all
true or still valid for me today (they are never officially taken back
with the same degree of explicitness and weight with which they
were promulgated) then I would still today have to give my assent
to propositions such as the following: Most of the psalms are by
David himself; there are no post-exilic psalms; there are no
Deutero-Pauline epistles; the discourses of Jesus in John are not
theological compositions; the Gospels were written in the same se-
quence in which we enumerate them today; there is no "Q" Source;
there is no Deutero-Isaiah; the Epistle to the Hebrews was written
by Paul; the Pentateuch is "a Mosaic text" (written virtually in its
entirety by Moses himself), and not (as a French exegete once
maliciously put it) "une mosaïque de textes." I must maintain it as
certain that the baptismal formula in Matthew 28 was laid down by
Jesus himself. I must be convinced that the Lucan Gospel was written prior to the destruction of Jerusalem; I should be convinced
that it is *ipso facto* modernism for me to call for any alteration to
the Holy Office or to support the abolition of the Index; I would
not be allowed to give even a modest support to the idea that so-
called polygenism is reconcilable with a right interpretation of the
doctrine of original sin; I should regard any participation of clergy
and laity in the government of the Church, whatever form it took,
as *ipso facto* modernist. As I have said, I am quoting from
memory. But the reader too, even without having to look up any of
the numbers in Denzinger, can rely on the fact that these points are
valid. Every specialist theologian is aware of them. And over and
above these and similar examples we might quote many other propositions in which the condemnation of one implies, in practice, the
acceptance of its alternative even though this is far from being
much of an improvement upon the condemned proposition, and
even though under certain circumstances condemnation may have
been just.

In referring to these propositions I have no intention of writing
a *chronique scandaleuse* of the life of the Church during the first

half of the twentieth century. Anyone who takes the references I have given in this sense is being foolish, knows nothing of the burden of history upon the Church, is failing to take due cognizance of the context in which such erroneous decisions were taken, a context which also exists even though it cannot be included in our presentation here, and is failing to understand how inevitable it is that even in the Church the developing awareness of faith and doctrine must proceed slowly (even though I hold the opinion that sometimes it has proceeded more slowly than was necessary).

V

PROVISIONAL DECISIONS AND THE ADVANCE OF DOCTRINE

My intention in this section is to put the following question to the critic of the bishops' document: What is my lord the critic's view, working from *his own* principles, of the advance which the Church has made in overcoming these erroneous decisions, the advance which has been achieved, at least tacitly on many points, since the decisions were initially promulgated? In terms of his principles I cannot find any place for it at all within my purview. But I certainly can find one according to the principles underlying the bishops' document. For whence can we achieve the insight we need into the erroneousness of such wrong decisions if, at least in practice (if not in theory as well), theologians and layfolk have nothing else to do than to regard these wrong official decisions in matters of doctrine as *absolutely* binding norms in virtue of the authority of the Church's official teachers as the critic recommends? Anyone at all — and this includes any member of the Catholic Church itself — must, after all, take the initiative in saying that this or that point is simply not true and showing the reasons why. He must take this initiative even though according to Denzinger 2007 an "interior assent" (*assensus internus*) is required of him, and Denzinger 2113 threatens that the exegete incurs "grave guilt" (*culpa gravis*) if he does not submit to the decisions of the Biblical Commission. And all this even though no trouble is taken to draw even a few of the necessary distinctions, and even though it would have been possible even at that time to find from "approved authors" that on this point those very distinctions have to be drawn which the German bishops have drawn in our own times.

Formerly anyone entertaining such doubts on a doctrinal decision of this kind was advised to keep silent about them even though they were, in the nature of the case, authorized. He was advised simply to be patient, and in the meantime to observe a *silentium obsequiosum*. One point to be made about this is that in contemporary society the constantly increasing communication of everyone with everyone else, reaching down into the most private spheres of human life, makes any such *silentium obsequiosum* quite impossible to maintain any longer. But quite apart from this the situation today is such that time is running out too quickly for us to be able to wait patiently in every case until the mental attitude of the official teachers who set the standards has changed spontaneously and without conscious thought in such a way that they themselves, without noticing it, have, of their own volition, undertaken to bring about this change of views or feel that such a change as put forward by others no longer in any sense constitutes a deviation from earlier doctrines. (I recall an episode from the period of the Council in which a Roman cardinal assured me in all seriousness that in Rome there had *never* been any objection to the theory that on his physical side man is descended from animals.) Such cases of a gradual and unconscious change in theological views within the Church may still be going on even today. (One such instance can be found in the attitude of optimism of the Second Vatican Council with regard to the possibility of salvation for all men.)

But in general it is no longer possible to proceed by these methods alone. We have become too consciously aware of the factors involved and time is running out too quickly for this. Hence the question to the critic: How in your view is such a change to take place in the Church's awareness (not in the true and ultimate substance of its faith but in opinions which are put forward as matters of official doctrine yet are nevertheless erroneous) if there is never any case in which a Christian has the right to disagree with a doctrine of the Church on well-considered grounds and, moreover, not merely some decades after this doctrine has been promulgated? The fact that the principle relevant to this question and expressed in the bishops' document can be misused does not make any difference to its correctness. Any example of such misuse in relation to such a principle has just as little to do with the question of its truth as if I (with perfect justice and adducing historical proofs which are ready to hand) were to say that the principle of the critic leads to heresy hunting, stagnation in Catholic theology, and the falling away of many from the faith.

Nor is it any argument against this to say that the principle expressed in the bishops' document is not in fact the sole principle, so that the application of it to a particular concrete case leads to delicate situations of conscience for the individual in which each one remains fairly isolated in his relationship with God and with his own conscience. The same might also be said of innumerable other cases in Christian life. For instance my eternal salvation may perhaps to a large extent depend on my choosing the right vocation. Here too I find myself thrown on my own resources by the official Church (apart from very general principles in matters the details of which involve life-and-death decisions) and rightly so. For this is how God has willed it to be. Now according to Catholic doctrine there is in fact no authority in this world constituting an absolute norm for the individual without the personal decision of his own conscience. The existence and justification of the Church's teaching office is something which each individual must in fact recognize and accept as such *without* being able to base himself on the authority of this teaching office. In other words he must act solely "at his own risk." And if this is the case, then why should it be so particularly surprising to concede that even *after* acknowledging the validity of this teaching office in principle, situations of personal risk of this kind still continue constantly to be present, *analogous* to those which existed and still exist prior to the individual accepting the validity of the teaching office (for this acceptance in fact constitutes a decision requiring constantly to be renewed)?

Obviously we should not overlook the point that "the conscience of the Christian needs to be guided by Christ and so by that which the Lord has entrusted with his mission." But is not this point constantly being reiterated throughout the whole of the bishops' document itself? And is this statement of the necessity of this guidance gainsaid when the document draws the distinction it does, and points out that in particular cases this guidance is, after all, precisely a provisional one and *therefore* gives the one so guided, under certain circumstances a right and a duty, as a matter of concrete practice and not merely of abstract theory, to take such guidance for what it is and for what it is intended to be and nothing more, namely as provisional? And if the critic maintains that we should not describe a declaration of this kind of the teaching office as provisional on the grounds that in such a doctrine those entrusted with the teaching office are convinced that this doctrine is true, then his position becomes totally incomprehensible to me. Obviously the only doctrines they can teach are those which they are convinced are correct. But can they not be convinced in this way and yet, even in being so, be aware that they are *capable* of error? Or are they in that case no longer to teach at all? Yet even this course would in fact in its turn fail to measure up to the critic's statement that such a doctrine can be erroneous *per accidens*. After all a doctor may be convinced that his diagnosis is correct yet at the same time be aware that in this he can be mistaken. And he then has the right to express this diagnosis of his as correct and as something to be followed.

When, therefore, the critic quite explicitly condemns the term "provisional" as used in the document and as applied to non-infallible doctrines of the Church's teaching office of this kind, then I must once more raise the question: How then are we ever to be in a position to reject doctrines of this kind seeing that they are never at any stage claimed to be irreformable, and have often in the past been shown to be erroneous? Supposing I had been alive when Leo X declared, against Luther, that the practice of burning heretics is fully in accordance with the will of the Holy Spirit, could I not even then have been in a position to think to myself: "Thank God, this is only a provisional doctrine"?

By way of conclusion I may be permitted one more earnest observation, even though to many it may sound somewhat pathetic. A few days ago I received the copy of a letter (I accept its genuineness because I myself have often heard similar things from behind the Iron Curtain). The writer declares that he has spent twelve years in prison and suffered terrible things for his Catholic faith and his loyalty to the Pope. He then came to the West only to receive the impression that in the Church here everything which he had suffered for was being squandered in unbelief. He would rather return once more to live in such a prison, for he was happier in it. I can understand this, for I myself have friends of the same kind in the East. It may be that many of the factors included in this condemnation of the West are to be explained on historical and sociological grounds, and that his condemnation of them does not *merely* reflect the mentality of the saint. It may be true that a Christian of the West views this martyr for Christianity with a holy envy. But if anyone supposes that the problems of the Church of the West are to be solved by an attitude of stubborn conservatism and that the Church is thereby to be confirmed in its faith and unity he is deceiving himself.

Under God's disposing power history has presented us with these present-day problems, and only courage, truthfulness, resolution in the faith *and at the same time* in positive thinking, can solve them by God's grace. Remembering the theology of the cross, our attitude to martyrs can be very favorable, whereas our attitude to mere reactionaries who are just as well off as the rest of us prosperous citizens is less so. But if we intend to fulfill the tasks of the future for the Church of the West, then there are elements from the Church's past which must be overcome, and among the methods for overcoming them is to be numbered that principle which the German bishops have expressed in the document we have been discussing. It is to be hoped that they will not let themselves be held back from recognizing it and acting upon it as well. It may be said that the unity of the faith (which does not mean union with the opinion of Mr. XY), acknowledgement of Jesus Christ as our Lord and Savior, loyalty to the Church, and much else besides are factors which are *still more* important than the principle we are defending here. But this is something that we neo-modernists (the name which our opponents like to reproach us with) are aware of too. We would be happy not to be put in the position nowadays of having to conduct a special defense of this principle which the German bishops have taught us.

Notes

1. The text was published by the Secretariat of the Conference of German Bishops in the autumn of 1967 as a semi-private document and disseminated at diocesan level. Hence it is relatively difficult to achieve access to it. Cf. Herder-Korrespondenz 21 (1967), col. 549.

2. Cf. pp. 12-14 of the official text.

3. We should notice the word "analogous," which the critic reads as though it were equivalent to "absolutely the same."

Open Questions in Dogma Considered by the Institutional Church as Definitively Answered

Karl Rahner, S.J.

In using the term "institutional Church" here, we do so in a way that is somewhat vague. We are speaking of the institutional Church as it acts both in the everyday exercise of its public policies connected with teaching (the appointment of professors, the censorship of books—at least up to quite recent times—and the like) and the institutional Church as it acts in doctrinal statements that are "authentic" but not strict definitions. We are not referring, therefore, to strict definitions by the supreme teaching office, papal *ex cathedra* (infallible) definitions or conciliar definitions. Such definitions about dogmatic questions are treated here only insofar as these decisions can, without losing their absolutely binding character, still leave certain questions open—questions that have not been answered by such definitions either because a particular question was not envisioned at all, or because, even though it was thought that a question had already been answered, by closer examination of the appropriate definition it can be established that in fact the question had not been answered. In this sense, then, one can discover open questions even in connection with final definitions. These are questions that were only apparently answered by a definition. But when we speak of open questions which are considered by the institutional Church as already answered, we have in mind especially those "authentic" statements of the Church's magisterium, statements that are differentiated from those that "define" dogma. We may be referring also to those kinds of doctrines that in the traditional Scholastic theology, at least up to Vatican II, were qualified as *theologice certa* (theologically certain) on the basis of common agreement among theologians — teachings, therefore, that in practice were no longer considered as open questions. Such teachings can be included here, since even the Roman magisterium, when it sees itself obliged to publish a declaration on something or other, commonly makes use of such traditional teachings of theologians.

When we speak here of questions that the magisterium has only seemingly settled, questions that are really dogmatic but still open, we intend to discuss here only dogmatic questions and not questions connected with canon law or pastoral theology. For example, dogmatically it may be a completely open question whether the *materia* used in the Eucharist can be only bread made from wheat. Holding that this dogmatic question is open need not require the Church to change anything in its concrete practice. Just because the questions are dogmatically open does not necessarily mean that they will create a problem for the Church's practical course of action.

We are, of course, approaching our topic from an ecumenical viewpoint. Our wish is to reflect on those questions that have particular importance for ecumenical dialogue among the traditional Christian Churches. In our discussions, we deliberately leave aside all those questions nowadays much discussed about moral theology and which the Church's magisterium in our day touches upon in authentic statements. These statements of the magisterium, although they can make no claim to be definitive, are nonetheless presented in such a way as though in fact they are definitive. We will not treat here such problems of moral theology, although it cannot be denied that such statements from Roman congregations make ecumenical dialogue more difficult. We will also not treat here all those Roman decisions concerning exegesis and biblical theology dating back to the time of Pope Piux X. In these decisions, the magisterium of the Catholic Church overreacted to modernism and set down norms for Catholic exegetes that brought them into conflict with Protestant exegesis, thereby making ecumenical dialogue more difficult. Such questions can be omitted here since these anti-modernist expressions of the Church's teaching have by and large become obsolete and have been tacitly laid to rest by the Roman magisterium.

But even if we restrict ourselves to dogmatic questions in the strictest sense of the word, we need to clarify our theme still further. Per se, it would be meaningful and useful to set forth general, fundamental considerations about a theological theory of knowledge, and to do so in a general and fundamental way so as to explain why it is and how it happens that frequently an opinion can be formed within the Church's faith-consciousness (although not in a manner that engages its absolute act of faith) that a specific teaching is seen as the clear and definitive answer to a specific question, when in fact such is not the case at all. In such fundamental and general considerations about a theological theory of knowledge, one could try to show what are the cultural, historical and political reasons that led to the sudden discovery that traditional teachings do not at all answer those questions which we are asking today, although we used to think that they did. Since the amount of space available to us is quite limited and since the overall problem is quite complicated, it is impossible to study this question in any detailed way. Instead, we intend to restrict ourselves to some brief remarks about several specific dogmatic questions about which the magisterium and traditional "school theology" conclude too quickly and too confidently that they have an answer.

When we treat such questions, we can, I believe, leave aside, although it may sound rather strange, questions related to those three major clusters of questions that have been the subject of tension between Catholics and Protestants, questions that are summarized in the three slogans: *sola fide, sola Scriptura* and *sola gratia* (faith alone, Scripture alone, grace alone). With regard to the doctrine of justification, today it is no longer possible to maintain that it is certain that the doctrines of the *Confessio Augustana* (the Augsburg Confession of 1530, the basic statement of the faith of Lutheran churches) and the Council of Trent are clearly contradictory. The same may be said about justification by faith alone in the sense that Lutheran theology has insisted upon it. With regard to the principle of *sola Scriptura,* one would only have to point to the lively discussions that took place at Vatican II, which intentionally left open the question about the exact relationship between Scripture and tradition. In doing this, the Council made what since Trent had been a traditional teaching now an open question. I would argue, then, that we may for the time being leave aside those basic, traditionally controversial questions within the Western churches. Of course, it is another question altogether to ask how all the official churches in the exercise of their offices should handle the question about the proper course of action for their churches when there occurs a sudden realization that the disagreement that was once the only reason for lack of unity between these churches no longer exists. Rather we are only discussing several relatively secondary questions that, contrary to traditional teaching, we regard as open. We cannot here place much emphasis on a systematic presentation of these questions. In treating these very limited questions, we cannot attempt to offer a detailed comparison between Protestant convictions and positions which are absolutely binding for Catholics. We have to limit ourselves to simply noting open questions or possible different interpretations of traditional Catholic positions. In so doing, we hope to show that it is in no way clear and obvious, as it might seem, to speak of an absolute contradiction between a Protestant and a Catholic position on these matters.

I

The Sacraments

We would like to begin with several remarks about the doctrine of the sacraments in general (*de sacramentis in genere*). The Council of Trent teaches that there are seven sacraments instituted by Christ. Yet today, if we Catholics engage in honest historical research about the history of the sacraments, we will have to admit that the sacraments, as presently realized fundamental actions of the Church's nature, originate with the historical Jesus to the extent that the Church itself, "founded" by Jesus, originates with him. We need not necessarily try to locate or postulate express words of institution spoken by the historical Jesus, even if in the case of the

Eucharist such an expressly stated institutional word cannot be disputed.

Such an understanding of the sacraments in general here mere-ly briefly indicated — an understanding that regards the sacraments as the Church's actualization in word of itself as the fundamental sacrament or as the presence of God's invincible salvific activity in Jesus Christ — should be acceptable also to Protestants, since according to this presentation the proper meaning of the *opus operatum* (i.e., the efficaciousnes of the sacrament) can be made in-telligible and the sacraments can be understood as the most intense expression of the Gospel's exhibitive word. This is true even in Catholic perspective, since thereby present-day Protestant theology could be brought to appreciate (in accord with its own present-day biblical exegesis) that the origin of baptism with Jesus himself, recognized by the Reformation theologians as a sacrament, cannot be more clearly and assuredly demonstrated than can the other sacraments. Catholics also can recognize today that the concept of *jus divinum* (divine right) as applied to the sacraments can and must now be understood as a legitimate and irreversible foundational decision of the apostolic Church. There thus exists a possibility of an explanation of the Tridentine doctrine on the sacraments that could be acceptable to contemporary Protestant teaching about the sacraments. Of course, on the other hand, this way of explaining the Tridentine doctrine would open up for Catholics new questions, but at the same time it would offer more new possibilities for the Church's pastoral practice than previously thought of. From the point of view of a modern Catholic sacramental theology which is sensitive to the historical data, and on the basis of a theology that shows a long overdue but gradually developing Catholic theology of the word, it is no longer possible or even necessary to characterize the Catholic Church as the Church of the sacraments and the Prot-estant Churches as churches of the word. In this connection, one might note that there are many more open questions in the doctrine about the sacramental character of several particular sacraments than are clearly stated in our Scholastic theology. To the extent that the Church may wish to confer an irreversible ecclesial status through specific sacraments, a status it simply will not revoke and which it confers as irrevocable, then this in itself is what one would have to understand as the binding nature of a sacramental character; further deeply speculative considerations are out of place.

II
THE OFFICE OF MINISTRY

We now come to examine the Catholic Church's understanding of the office of ministry. Here, too, there are many more open questions connected with our understanding of the office of ministry than we normally suppose. According to a Catholic understanding of pastoral ministry in the Church, it is obvious that there must exist a ministry of leadership in the Church as an historical and social reality. The characteristics, tasks and powers of this ministry have to be understood and explained on the basis of the Church's nature. (For the time being, let us leave out of our consideration the papacy and its roles. We will have more to say on this subject later on.) Apart from this, what we have said about the ministry of leadership in the Church and its connection with the nature of the Church is all that can and must be said about the office of Church ministry with absolute dogmatic binding force. What we have said applies, of course, in the fullest sense to those who are traditionally called "bishops," those who exercise such pastoral ministry, who are responsible for the direction of a larger church, a church that may be called autonomous, apart from its necessary relationship to the worldwide Church. In point of fact, this one ministry, insofar as it is now sacramentally conferred in the Roman Catholic Church, has a threefold division: the episcopate, the presbyterate and the diaconate.

It does not seem to me as certain that this threefold division of pastoral office is strictly speaking *juris divini.* This threefold division of pastoral office certainly does not go back to an express word of institution by the historical Jesus. It seems to me to be a possibility, but not absolutely certain, that this threefold division developed in the primitive Church of apostolic times so irreversibly that in this way it is *juris divini* and unchangeable. The Church could still, even if one wants to recognize the threefold division as *juris divini,* further divide this one pastoral office and confer it according to different degrees. In practice, the Church already does this. There is no reason to conclude that the Church could not confer sacramentally other kinds or levels of participation in the one pastoral ministry of the Church. In light of the teaching during the Middle Ages about the sacramentality of minor orders, a negative opinion is not even probable. From all this, it follows that it is not a priori certain that Protestant Churches wishing to be united with Rome would have to adopt that division of pastoral ministry which now exists in the Roman Church.

From a purely dogmatic point of view, I would argue that it is not absolutely certain that the *potestas episcopalis* (the bishop's power) as described from Trent up to Vatican II, and which will always be valid, must necessarily be exercised by an individual person acting as a "monarchical" bishop. Practically and concretely, there is nothing to be said against the monarchical episcopacy. When the essence of the *potestas episcopalis,* the power of leadership of a large church, is described in Church teaching, this power, which is valid and will remain, is automatically described as held by a single individual, because in practice it is exercised universally in this way. It does not seem to me, however, that it is thereby dogmatically excluded that the one and whole episcopal power could also be exercised by a small collective body. The Catholic doctrine about the universal episcopacy as being the supreme leadership body within the Church proves that collegial constitutional structures cannot a priori be considered as foreign to the nature of the Catholic Church. At any rate, we should better distinguish two questions: (a) the question of the nature of ecclesial pastoral ministry, and (b) the question about the exercise of this office by an individual person or a collective body. The nature of pastoral ministry must be understood from the Church's nature. Clearly, the nature of leadership in the Church is different from that found in a secular society. Wherever these considerations in fact are now or eventually would be recognized by all sides in ecumenical dialogue, then very many other elements of the concrete structuring of pastoral ministry and in appointing pastoral ministers could be agreed upon freely within the one Church, which will be formed out of the many local churches each with its own historical traditions.

Pastoral ministry in the Church takes its origin from the theological nature of the Church and thus ultimately from Christ.

In this sense, pastoral ministry comes "from above" and not "from below" by means of a free decision by the basis of the Church. Still, how those who exercise such a pastoral ministry can and should be chosen and appointed is quite a different question and one that is still open. It is not, properly speaking, a dogmatic question. At most, it becomes a dogmatic question inasmuch as new bishops, to assume legitimately the episcopal function, need to be approved by the Pope and the universal episcopacy. This does not mean, however, that the choice and appointment of a bishop must reside *jure divino* only with the Pope. This can be a meaningful and useful arrangement established by positive canon law, but it is not something that pertains to the Pope *jure divino.* The long history of the episcopal office proves that. That one could arrive at the choice of a bishop through an election "from below," namely, through an historically conditioned elective body, is not contrary to the Church's nature. This is already clear from the simple fact that appointment to the supreme office (the papacy) nowadays takes place by means of a choice "from below," through the college of cardinals, an institution that has been markedly conditioned by history. It is true, of course, that one so chosen to be a bishop in any conceivable way "from below" only then possesses his total *potestas episcopalis,* when he not only is accepted into the unity and communion of the universal episcopacy, but also is sacramentally ordained by other bishops, thereby sharing in this respect also in apostolic succession. On the other hand, it does not follow that a choice "from below" is impossible and would contradict the nature of the Church. Unity and communion with the Apostolic See in Rome are fundamentally indispensable. But that does not mean that the conferral of this unity and communion must necessarily, from a dogmatic point of view, be the central and specific procedure for selecting one particular bearer of the episcopal office. The Pope would not be renouncing dogmatically indispensable prerogatives, but simply historically conditioned prerogatives, were he to renounce at the time of union with separated churches the practice of naming bishops according to the form presently required in the code of canon law for the Church of the Latin rite.

In connection with our theme, I wish to add some remarks about the complex question concerning the recognition of ministries in the Reformation churches. I have already expressed my views on this topic in my book, *Vorfragen zu einem ökumenischen Amtsverständnis* (Preliminary Questions Toward an Ecumenical Understanding of Office in the Church, Freiburg, 1974). The views I expressed there, to the extent that I can measure, have not received wide support and, furthermore, are regularly passed over in silence in official Church statements emanating from Rome or from Germany. Since these kinds of official statements certainly cannot claim to be irreformable, I still maintain that the views I outlined cautiously in my book are worthy of discussion. Since Vatican II, it cannot be questioned that these pastoral ministries as exercised in the separated Churches can have a positive salvific significance. But I would also further maintain that these ministries are legitimate and at least in many cases (that, of course, must be distinguished from other cases which are not legitimate) that they are sacramental both in their conferral (ordination) and in exercise of these ministries (the celebration of the Eucharist). This holds true not merely for the Churches of the East separated from Rome, but also for the Reformation Churches.

To make such a view intelligible, I would recommend that one reflect first of all on the fact that Catholics can no longer judge Reformation Churches as they did at the time of the Reformation (in principle correctly for the times) when the situation was one of becoming separated (*Trennung*) as distinct from the ongoing state of being separated (*Getrennstein*). We must further take into consideration that fundamentally there is such a thing as an "essential law" that precedes every piece of legislation, a law that follows simply from the nature of a particular person or society. Such a distinction between a law of fundamental nature and a right according to a piece of legislation is in principle conceivable even in the Church, since the Church has a nature that precedes its legislation and that stems from the final and irreversible salvific event of Jesus Christ and from faith in Christ, which necessarily follows from its definitive nature. From such an ultimate nature of the Church could also flow—at least in principle this is conceivable—certain sacramental realities, even when they cannot be realized through normal canonical procedures, when a procedure, for unavoidable reasons, cannot be followed.

Unless one accepts such a possibility, there is no possible way to make sense out of numerous events that have happened in the history of the Church. Would a priest or a bishop who possessed unchallenged ecclesiastical powers no longer be in possession of these powers if one were to assume that at some particular point in time their connection with apostolic succession had been broken according to normal canonical norms governing the sacraments? Was Martin V, who was recognized as Pope by the entire Church, a legitimate Pope only if it is certain that his predecessors either had been invalidly elected or had voluntarily abdicated? If a Catholic priest were to use rice bread in celebrating the Eucharist, because here and now in the foreseeable future no wheat bread would be available, would such a celebration really not be sacramental? How was it that theologians in the Middle Ages could consider confession of sins to a lay person in case of emergency as a real sacramental act?

If non-Catholic Christians marry and thereby celebrate a sacrament, a sacrament based on the fundamental sacramental nature of the Church, then their marriage is sacramental *not* because the Pope has decreed by a positive canonical act that for such Christians, although they do not use the Tridentine form, the form that they follow for the celebration of their marriage is the sacramental sign. Otherwise, one would have to draw the absurd conclusion that the Pope could prevent sacramental marriages for non-Catholics by demanding the application of the Tridentine form even for them. The sacramentality of these marriages derives immediately from the Church's fundamental sacramental nature, since baptized Christians possess a right to this sacrament and the sacrament for them because they are in good faith cannot be conferred through the normal sacramental sign.

It should also be taken into consideration that the rite of ordination in the Church is subject to the Church's own discretionary act and need not necessarily consist in the imposition of hands. On the basis of such considerations, which would of course need fuller and more precise development, it seems to be quite possible to recognize in the Reformation churches the sacramental character of both ordination and the exercise of ministerial acts to a much greater extent. As noted, I refer my readers to the short book I mentioned where they will get a fuller treatment of these questions that have important ramifications for possible Church unification. As Catholic theologians, we have a serious obligation to investigate carefully every conceivable means of serving the goal of Church unity. Therefore, we should avoid being satisfied with the traditional but cheap answer to questions about the recognition of ministries in the Reformation Churches.

III
THE PAPACY

We now come to the major obstacle to Church unification — the question of the papacy and the primacy of Rome. Pope Paul VI himself recognized that the papacy is today the principal obstacle to church unity. There are in this matter also many more open questions than are usually supposed. Theologians and Popes today should give special attention to clarifying what in the doctrine and practice of the primacy of Rome really does or does not pertain to the truly indispensable content of faith. Catholic theologians, and especially Popes, should clarify much more lucidly what the elements are that do not belong to that content, although these elements are retained in practice. Such clarifications are all the more important since one can observe among Protestants a clear, growing inclination to recognize that a Petrine office in the Church is necessary for, or at least not in conflict with, the Church's nature. And yet, in Rome we can hardly see any indications that would lead us to expect from Rome, in a way dogmatically possible and desirable for the needs of today, a clear self-limitation of the Roman primacy. We do not see signs coming from Rome indicating that they wish to take the first step toward unity in this matter. There can be no doubt whatsoever that much of what is claimed by the Roman See as historically acquired powers and rights of the Roman See does not in fact pertain dogmatically to the inalienable essence of the primacy. Of course, even in Rome there is no doubt about this. But Rome should state clearly what does not pertain to the essence of the primacy and what it is prepared to renounce in dealing with Churches that seek unity with Rome.

It is still another question that we do not wish to go into now whether such renunciations should be offered only toward those Churches prepared to enter union with Rome, or whether they should not also be extended to the Latin Church of the West. The fundamental question should probably be addressed not by listing those elements Rome could in principle renounce, but by giving a description of those elements that Rome, because of its own dogmatic principles, could not renounce. In so doing, a more exact answer would have to be given to the question of what it means (and does not mean) to say that the Pope enjoys universal primacy of jurisdiction over all Churches as *potestas ordinaria* (the authority pertaining to the papal office as such). We need not offer specific proof for the fact that in this there are still very many open questions and that from the perspective of dogmatic theology many things are not foregone conclusions that, in fact, Rome in exercising its primacy of jurisdiction continues to regard as foregone conclusions. (We have already mentioned various possible ways whereby Rome could open up the way to ratifying the appointment of bishops. We have also underlined the considerable presbyterial, collective, constitutional elements within the Catholic Church or in its particular churches that are not dogmatically excluded.)

We need to explore and state more clearly when we speak of the canonically unlimited rights of the Roman primacy such considerations as the following. In this canonically unlimited *potestas*, the Pope is not only subject to limits in that he may not alter what is *jure divino* the nature of the Church—for example, he may not abolish the episcopacy as articulated in Vatican II—but neither may he even in practice diminish the episcopate's proper characteristics to such an extent that bishops would become, for all intents and purposes, only regional representatives of the Pope. This danger has not yet been eliminated even today. Furthermore, what is a canonically unlimited primacy is limited by another consideration which should be much more clearly stated than actually happens in practice. We mean by this the following: The exercise of the full primacy of jurisdiction is bound to Christian moral norms, including some that are not always the same materially, but vary according to the historical situation. People act in the Church as if this were self-evident and as if no one could doubt that a Pope would always observe these moral limitations of his power. That this is generally so will not be disputed. But that it is always the case can be doubted. It is quite conceivable that certain moral limitations which derive necessarily from a modern social and cultural situation are objectively present but not recognized and therefore not respected. For example, it is in principle quite conceivable that Pope Paul VI, by the publication of the encyclical *Humanae Vitae* (1968), though in good faith, still offended in practice norms governing the Pope's reaching a judgment.

It is also quite conceivable that members of the Roman curia interfere in the private affairs of local churches so as to offend objectively the principle of subsidiarity in the Church. For me it is not self-evident and obvious that the regulation about sacerdotal celibacy should be unilaterally determined for the Church by Rome. It is not clear that every papal claim to exercise universal primacy is in fact always and in every case morally justified. (If, for example, a general ecclesiastical regulation in the matter of celibacy by Rome alone is morally justified, then the Pope would in principle also have the right to make regulations vis-à-vis the Churches of the East. But can one seriously argue that the Pope has the moral right to forbid priests even in all the Uniate Churches of the East from marrying?) One could, of course, debate the details about what precisely are the limits of the Pope's universal power of jurisdiction as set forth in moral principles, including some which are time-conditioned and ever-changing. But there should be open and straightforward dialogue in the Church about this, even though our presumption is that the Pope is acting correctly in cases of doubt and that he is not commanding anything that is clearly immoral. For ecumenical progress it would be highly desirable if Rome were itself concretely, clearly and in detail to list those exercises of jurisdiction which it can forego consistently with its own self-understanding.

Ecumenically, the most difficult question within the whole congeries of questions connected with the papacy is doubtlessly the definition of the Pope's infallible primacy of teaching. We cannot eliminate this difficulty once and for all, as Küng does, simply by denying the Pope's infallibility in *ex cathedra* definitions. But we could make much clearer the meaning of this Catholic dogma, as well as what it does not mean. In the past, only one major difficulty has arisen in fact concerning the exercise of this infallible teaching of the Pope: the definition of the two Marian dogmas by Pius IX and Pius XII. These difficulties can be cleared up satisfactorily, as we will later attempt to do. The special difficulty for Protestant Christians is the possibility that in the future the Pope could conceivably promulgate further *ex cathedra* definitions. Protestant Christians who in principle would be prepared to recognize a Petrine office do not feel justified in handing over to the Pope for the future a blank check, as it were. It does not appear clear and obvious to a Protestant believer that the same divine providence that maintains the Church in the truth of Christ must necessarily and ineluctably be operative when the Pope defines something, rather than in another place and in another way.

Protestant Christians find the Catholic concentration of the sure charism of truth bestowed upon the Church, precisely in a specific and juridically determinable papal act, as one example of the human temptation to objectivize and juridicize the charism of truth. Furthermore, Protestants find this emphasis unworthy of belief for two reasons: (a) on the one hand, the ordinary teaching office of the Pope, at least in its authentic doctrinal decisions, often contains errors, even up to our own day; (b) secondly, Rome normally presents and pushes doctrinal decisions that are per se reformable as though there were no doubt whatsoever about their definitive correctness and as though any further discussion about the matter by Catholic theologians would be inappropriate. These are the sorts of hesitations that Protestants experience. Purely theological arguments on our part will have very little prospect of offsetting such hesitations. What we could do is try to show better than we have done before that those concrete procedures that are used before formulating and in the course of formulating a papal *ex cathedra* definition will now and in the future be so carefully followed that practically and concretely Protestant Christians would not have to fear that their blank check would be made out to include a papal teaching which would contradict their own credal conscience. In this regard, two further considerations might be useful.

First of all, it is clear conciliar doctrine that a Pope who in promulgating *ex cathedra* definitions is not introducing new revelation must make use of every human means available to him in the given situation in preparing *ex cathedra* definitions. What moral norms are implicitly connected with such a procedure can today be much more clearly articulated and codified, even though in a concrete case the following of these norms would not be subject to legal examination by a court of appeal higher than the Pope. Such procedural norms need to be drawn up and followed in papal definitions. (By and large, even in the past, we can assume that proper norms were observed, but nowadays and in the future they can and must be much more explicit.) These norms need to be explicitly formulated and codified; then Protestant Christians would in large measure feel that their fears about a future papal *ex cathedra* definition in conflict with their own credal conviction would be minimized. At Vatican I and II, it was stated that the Pope, or, more accurately, the Pope's definitions, are infallible *ex sese, non autem ex consensu Ecclesiae* (by themselves, rather than by consent of the Church). This only means that *ex cathedra* definitions gain their definitive weight not through a subsequent legal examination of their correctness by a higher court of appeal in the Church other than the Pope. This "ex sese" of the Vatican Councils does not mean that the Pope enjoys an infallibility independently from God's irreversibly successful promise made to the Church universal. In reaching *ex cathedra* definitions, the Pope acts as head of the Catholic Church and of the worldwide episcopate, as *an* instance that is conditioned by the Church universal and its infallible faith.

In preparing *ex cathedra* definitions, the Pope must of necessity have recourse to the *sensus fidei* of the universal Church. If this were not the case and were unnecessary, then a papal *ex cathedra* definition would be a promulgation of a new revelation. But a Pope does not have or receive such a revelation. He is the authoritative spokesperson who brings to verbal expression the Church's *sensus fidei*. The assistance of the Holy Spirit that the Pope possesses for this purpose need be thought of not as a psychological inspiration but rather as the ability, ultimately rooted in God, to be able to reach back successfully into the infallible faith-consciousness of the Church universal. This connection with the consciousness of faith (*sensus fidei*) in the Church universal has, of course, in various historical phases of the Church shown itself in different ways, according to the possibilities that were available. For such an exercise of office today, there is a moral obligation, absolutely necessary objectively, to conduct some sort of inquiry among the worldwide episcopate.

This inquiry may once again be thought of in a variety of ways. But today such a practice is an absolute requirement, not simply a praiseworthy practice that both Pius IX and Pius XII followed (even though perhaps the modes they employed were not completely felicitous). In our modern world, the technical means for administering such an inquiry are readily available. Therefore this practice is a moral obligation. How else nowadays could a Pope honestly be able to say that he has done everything that was morally possible within human means to reach human certitude about the definitive presence of his teaching within the faith-consciousness of the Church universal if he were to refuse to conduct such an inquiry among the worldwide episcopacy? It is completely obvious, then, that such an inquiry today has to take place according to the specific ways available to us, in an atmosphere that permits dialogue, consultation of theologians and research into the faithful's *sensus fidei*. Such a procedure has to be clear to the public. All of this is obvious even though apparently in Rome these conclusions are not yet sufficiently reflected upon or put into practice, as shown even in very recent times by the actual methods used to gather information for publishing doctrinal statements intended not as strict definitions but as "authentic" doctrine. If such procedures are clearly articulated, expressly stated as being in force and then followed in practice, Protestant Christians would be freed in large measure from the fear of an arbitrary exercise of papal authority which is seen as contradicting the true spirit of Jesus and of the Church.

In addition to this first consideration, there is a second consideration. Catholic faith in the existence of a papal teaching authority that pertains to the continuous nature of the Church does not imply that the actual exercise of this papal authority is the same at all times (which would not be true of the past). It does not imply, either, that this authority is free from all historical or changing pre-conditioning factors. We have become accustomed by the history of dogma during the Church's first two millennia to consider this history of dogma as a continuing, ever-developing process of explication and articulation of the faith's final substance through an increasing number of new explications, and to conceive of the Pope's teaching power as active in producing new and differentiated statements of this sort. We think of the exercise of the Pope's teaching primacy when speaking *ex cathedra* as the declaration of statements that are *materialiter* new, not previously explicitly seen (even though, in the last analysis, they would be seen as implicitly present in the tradition of the faith). Examples would be the dogma of the immaculate conception, the assumption of Mary into heaven or the teaching, proposed up to twenty years ago as ready to be raised to the level of dogma, about Mary as the mediatrix of grace.

But it is quite unproved that in the future the exercise of the Pope's teaching authority will occur in this way; further, it seems thoroughly improbable that it will. What the history of doctrine in Christianity and in the Church will see in the future, it seems to me, will be not further material differentiation of the substance of Christian belief, but rather new expressions of the ultimate fundamental substance of Christianity required and made possible by new cultural and socio-political situations. One should think correspondingly about the exercise of the Pope's teaching authority as it will be practiced in the future. Unfortunately, we cannot offer here a more detailed justification for my prognosis about the future course of developments in the history of dogma and the concrete way that the Pope's teaching authority will be exercised. Otherwise, we would have to provide, for example, a more detailed analysis of the cultural situation in the world and its civilization, an analysis of the present irreversible pluralism in a world that still remains one, and an analysis of the presuppositions in the secular world that affect the faith-life of our modern contemporary worldwide Church. Such analyses are not possible here, but I am convinced that on this basis such a prognosis for future exercise of papal teaching authority would be possible.

Such a prognosis would make it clear to Protestant Christians that in the future the papal magisterium would unavoidably and willingly concentrate on the defense and the contemporary expression of the fundamental substance of Christianity, a substance that is just as precious and certain to these Christians as it is to Catholics. To summarize this point, I might say: If the future agenda and tendency of papal teaching authority were to be made clear and were to be expressed by Rome itself in an open manner, and if, at the same time, the methods that are possible and necessary for us in the exploration of truth and of decision making are made more clear by Rome and are observed more carefully, then the Vatican doctrine about papal teaching primacy would no longer remain, as it has in the past, that scary specter that is so unsettling to the faith convictions of Protestant Christians. It is another question altogether whether in the foreseeable future we are to expect papal *ex cathedra* definitions at all or whether for a variety of reasons these are improbable.

Finally, we need to make some comments about those open questions connected with the two Marian dogmas of Pius IX and Pius XII. Of themselves and as the only concrete examples of *ex cathedra* papal definitions, they are among the major stumbling blocks for Protestant and Orthodox Christians in their attitude toward the Roman Church since Trent. As for the first Marian dogma, I would dare to suggest that one can indicate much more easily the connection of this with revelation as such, by further possible orthodox developments of the dogma concerning original sin in general. This would have the effect of eliminating for Protestant Christians those obstacles that are found to be inconsistent with their own faith. If we seek today to clarify the dogma of original sin with reference to all persons, and at the same time to state just as clearly and unequivocally our faith that all human beings since Adam, even after the fall, find themselves from the very outset always under the supernatural sanctifying salvific will of God — under a salvific will which implies not only a design on God's part but also a supernatural existential connected with God's continually and universally offered gift of supernatural grace — then this means that the fact of original sin implies not simply a condition that temporally precedes the offer of grace to human freedom, but rather implies a condition which co-exists dialectically with the offer to human beings of salvation and grace. Humans remain, therefore, in a condition of freedom, simultaneously always and everywhere persons who originate in Adam and in Christ and who have to ratify freely either one or the other situation of their freedom.

If one considers that even Mary is redeemed by Christ, and hence is in need of redemption, and that this fact belongs to the ongoing existential factors of her life, then the difference between ordinary infralapsarian man or woman and Mary does not consist in the difference of the temporal period dating from the beginning of her existence, but rather in the fact that Mary receives the offer of grace extended to her freedom on the basis of her predestination to be the mother of Jesus; consequently, this offer of grace is victorious and recognizable as such in salvation history. This difference should not be an obstacle for a Protestant theology which emphasizes the efficacy of pure grace by itself. There is no necessary implication in the dogma of the immaculate conception that Mary's beginning at a point in time is different from our own, since it is not just at the moment of baptism that we ourselves receive grace as the permanent existential of our freedom drawing us to salvation.

With regard to the second Marian dogma, we could reach an easier consensus with Protestant theology. Its content does not imply that the "bodily" assumption of Mary into heaven is a privilege granted, apart from Jesus, only to her. The Church Fathers, for example, felt it was obvious that the souls in limbo entered heaven with their bodies at the resurrection of Jesus. If today we use a way of thinking that differs from a platonizing interpretation of the "separation of body and soul" at the time of death and hold that all of us at death take on our resurrection body already "even at that very moment" (to the extent that the use of such a temporal concept is legitimate), which view is frequently proposed even in Protestant theology, and which, with some appropriate demythologizing, can be quite legitimate, then what is stated in the dogma of Mary's assumption is not an exclusive occurrence since, as a matter of fact, it happens to all the saints. What is claimed is that what happens to Mary belongs to her in a special way because of her role in salvation history and therefore is more readily perceived by the Church's faith-consciousness than in the case of other human beings.

Thus we can say that in regard to both Marian dogmas there need be no insurmountable points of controversy if we are willing to admit those open questions which, without doubt, are present in these dogmas.

All things considered, a Catholic theologian may maintain that today there are no theological opinions that with certainty can be pointed to as absolutely binding on Catholics or Protestants of such a nature as to require or to legitimate the separation of Churches. Note that we say "today." One could, of course, object that if today there are no differences of opinion that legitimate a separation of Churches, they could not have existed in the past either, which is quite improbable. Against this objection one can argue that an always possible fundamental unity in credal affirmations still requires conscious recognition and that, for this, time and history are necessary, the exact length of which cannot be determined or measured in advance. Furthermore, we need to remember that the separation of the Churches in the sixteenth century not only meant that the time had not yet come for conscious awareness of agreement, but was also an illegitimate form of dissent from official regulation of terminology by the Catholic Church, for which both sides were to blame. Perhaps this refusal to reach a common terminology did not necessarily imply the presence of heresy, but it did certainly imply a schismatic situation, even if this is perhaps not everywhere present today.

If we maintain that contemporary theology no longer knows any insuperable dogmatic controversial points, or no opposing points in which the doctrines of the existing Churches clearly take contradictory views, if we maintain that in ecumenical questions the major responsibility lies no longer strictly speaking with theologians but with Church officials who today in their exercise of their ecumenical responsibilities can no longer simply shrug their shoulders with regret about the dissent among theologians, then we do not mean to imply that theologians have no further ecumenical tasks. The consensus that is possible and that already exists and continues to be strengthened between the doctrines of the separated Churches still needs to be further clarified and to be worked out in greater detail. Catholic theologians have the responsibility to make it clear to the ecclesiastical magisterium in Rome (which is far from

having appropriated modern, thoroughly orthodox theology sufficiently) that today there already exists a theological consensus or at
least that one is possible without further ado. These Catholic
theologians must try to bring Rome to appreciate other theological
languages that the separated Churches legitimately wish to bring
with them into the unity of the Church. They must try to bring
Rome to appreciate that there can be a legitimate pluralism in the
theologies of the one Church confessing the one faith, a pluralism
that can have an effect on the understanding of the faith and the
practical life of the local churches.

Even if one believes in the possibility today of dogmatic unity
among the separated Churches, there still remains the question of
who on the Protestant side can be the authorized partner for determining with binding force the presence of a consensus in faith. It is
obvious that within the Protestant Churches there are groups and
theologies with which such a consensus cannot be established, since
these groups and theologies clearly contradict the fundamental
substance of the Christian faith. They therefore cannot be positively included in this consensus. This opens up new questions which
we cannot go into now.

The traditional neo-Scholastic theology out of which all of us
have come and which in Rome, despite Vatican II, still enjoys more
or less unquestioned hegemony, a theology that is used quite
unabashedly even in recent Roman declarations, has failed to see
that many questions are still open questions—left open by the
Church's dogma that requires our assent. The failure to recognize
these open questions leads all too easily to a narrow interpretation
of these dogmas that do require assent, an interpretation that
discourages further discussion. Open questions and dogma are
mixed together, as though this interpretation of dogmas were an interior moment of the dogmas themselves. Thus, misunderstandings
arise about real dogmas, which make it difficult or impossible for
Protestant Christians to see their own Christian faith reflected in
Catholic doctrine. Here lies an important task for contemporary
Catholic theology in its ecumenical dimension. It is not only a question of misunderstandings arising for Protestant Christians in
regard to Catholic dogmas, but a question of misunderstandings
that we ourselves as Catholic Christians and theologians still possess

and which we incorrectly identify with Catholic dogma. Our work consists, then, not only in enlightening non-Catholic Christians and theologians, but first of all in enlightening ourselves and in purifying our own faith from misunderstandings that we ourselves continue to convey out of inertia or out of an exaggerated confidence in our own convictions.

The Ecclesiastical Magisterium and Theology

International Theological Commission
Otto Semmelroth, S.J. and Karl Lehmann

These theses on the relationship between the ecclesiastical magisterium and theology summarize the conclusions of a plenary session of the International Theological Commission held from September 25 to October 1, 1975. They were drawn up by Otto Semmelroth, S.J. and Karl Lehmann and were approved by the great majority of the Commission. Following the theses is a commentary by Semmelroth and Lehmann.

1
Theses on the Relationship Between the Ecclesiastical Magisterium and Theology

International Theological Commission

INTRODUCTION

"The relations between the magisterium and theology not only . . . are of the greatest importance but must also be considered to be of very great contemporary interest today."[1] The following pages are an attempt to clarify the relationship between "the mandate given to the ecclesiastical magisterium to protect divine revelation and the task given to theologians to investigate and explain the doctrine of the faith."[2]

Thesis 1

By "ecclesiastical magisterium" is meant the task of teaching which by Christ's institution is proper to the college of bishops or to individual bishops linked in hierarchical communion with the Supreme Pontiff. By "theologians" are meant those members of the Church who by their studies and life in the community of the Church's faith are qualified to pursue, in the scientific manner proper to theology, a deeper understanding of the word of God and also to teach that word by virtue of a canonical mission. When the New Testament and the subsequent tradition discussed the magisterium of pastors, theologians or teachers, and the relationship between them, they spoke analogously, in terms both of similarity and dissimilarity; along with continuity, there are rather profound modifications. The concrete forms in which they have been related to one another and coordinated have been rather varied in the course of time.

I
Elements Common to the Magisterium
and to Theologians in the Exercise of Their Tasks

Thesis 2

The element common to the tasks of both the magisterium and theologians, though it is realized in analogous and distinct fashions, is "to preserve the sacred deposit of revelation, to examine it more deeply, to explain, teach and defend it,"[3] for the service of the people of God and for the whole world's salvation.

Above all, this service must defend the certainty of faith; this is a work done differently by the magisterium and by the ministry of theologians, but it is neither necessary nor possible to establish a hard and fast separation between them.

Thesis 3

In this common service of the truth, the magisterium and theologians are both bound by certain obligations:

1. They are bound by the word of God. For "the magisterium is not above the word of God, but serves it, teaching only what has been handed down, as . . . it listens to this, guards it scrupulously, and expounds it faithfully; and it draws from this one deposit of faith all that it proposes as being divinely revealed."[4] For its part, "sacred theology relies on the written word of God along with sacred tradition as on a permanent foundation, and by this word it is most firmly strengthened and constantly rejuvenated as it searches out, under the light of faith, all the truth stored up in the mystery of Christ."[5]

2. They are both bound by the "sensus fidei" (supernatural appreciation of the faith) of the Church of this and previous times. For the word of God pervades all time in a living manner through the supernatural appreciation of the faith (*communi sensu fidei*) of the whole people of God, in which "the whole body of the faithful, anointed by the Holy One, cannot err in believing,"[6] if "in maintaining, practicing and confessing the faith that has been handed down, there is a harmony between the bishops and the faithful."[7]

3. Both are bound by the documents of the tradition in which the common faith of the people of God has been set forth. Although the magisterium and the theologians have different tasks with regard to these documents, neither of them can neglect these traces of the faith left in the history of salvation of God's people.

4. In exercising their tasks, both are bound by pastoral and missionary concern for the world. Although the magisterium of the Supreme Pontiff and of the bishops is specifically called "pastoral," the scientific character of their work does not free theologians from

pastoral and missionary responsibility, especially given the publicity which modern communications media so quickly give to even scientific matters. Besides, theology, as a vital function in and for the people of God, must have a pastoral and missionary intent and effect.

Thesis 4

Common to both, although also different in each, is the manner, at once collegial and personal, in which the task of both the magisterium and the theologians is carried out. If the charism of infallibility is promised to "the whole body of the faithful,"[8] to the college of bishops in communion with the successor of Peter, and the Supreme Pontiff himself, the head of that college,[9] then it should be put into practice in a co-responsible, cooperative, and collegial association of the members of the magisterium and of individual theologians. And this joint effort should also be realized as much among the members of the magisterium as among the members of the theological enterprise, and also between the magisterium on the one hand and the theologians on the other. It should also preserve the personal and indispensable responsibility of individual theologians, without which the science of faith would make no progress.

II
DIFFERENCES BETWEEN THE MAGISTERIUM AND THEOLOGIANS

Thesis 5

Something must first be said about the difference in the functions proper to the magisterium and to theologians.

1. It is the magisterium's task authoritatively to defend the catholic integrity and unity of faith and morals. From this follow specific functions; and, although at first glance they seem particularly to be of a rather negative character, they are, rather, a positive ministry for the life of the Church. These are: "the task of

authoritatively interpreting the word of God, written and handed down,"[10] the censuring of opinions which endanger the faith and morals proper to the Church, and the proposing of truths which are of particular contemporary relevance. Although it is not the work of the magisterium to propose theological syntheses, still, because of its concern for unity, it must consider individual truths in the light of the whole, since integrating a particular truth into the whole belongs to the very nature of truth.

2. The theologians' function in some way mediates between the magisterium and the people of God. For "theology has a two-fold relation with the magisterium of the Church and with the universal community of Christians. In the first place, it occupies a sort of midway position between the faith of the Church and its magisterium."[11] On the one hand, "in each of the great socio-cultural regions . . . theological reflection must submit to a new examination, guided by the tradition of the universal Church, the facts and words revealed by God, contained in the Scriptures, and explained by the Fathers of the Church and by the magisterium."[12] For "recent research and discoveries in the sciences, in history and philosophy, bring up new questions which . . . require new investigations by theologians."[13] In this way, theology "is to lend its aid to make the magisterium in its turn the enduring light and norm of the Church."[14]

On the other hand, by their work of interpretation, teaching and translation into contemporary modes of thought, theologians insert the teaching and warnings of the magisterium into a wider, synthetic context and thus contribute to a better knowledge on the part of the people of God. In this way, "they lend their aid to the task of spreading, clarifying, confirming and defending the truth which the magisterium authoritatively propounds."[15]

Thesis 6

The magisterium and the theologians also differ in the quality of the authority with which they carry out their tasks.

1. The magisterium derives its authority from sacramental ordination which "along with the task of sanctifying confers also

the tasks of teaching and ruling."[16] This "formal authority," as it is called, is at once charismatic and juridical, and it founds the right and the duty of the magisterium insofar as it is a share in the authority of Christ. Care should be taken that personal authority and the authority that derives from the very matter being proposed also be brought to bear when this ministerial authority is being put into effect.

2. Theologians derive their specifically theological authority from their scientific qualifications, but these cannot be separated from the proper character of this discipline as the science of faith which cannot be carried through without a living experience and practice of the faith. For this reason, the authority that belongs to theology in the Church is not merely profane and scientific, but is a genuinely ecclesial authority, inserted into the order of authorities that derive from the word of God and are confirmed by canonical mission.

Thesis 7

There is also a certain difference in the way in which the magisterium and the theologians are connected with the Church. It is obvious that both the magisterium and the theologians work in and for the Church, but still there is a difference in this ecclesial reference.

1. The magisterium is an official ecclesial task conferred by the sacrament of orders. Therefore, as an institutional element of the Church, it can only exist in the Church, so that the individual members of the magisterium use their authority and sacred power to build up their flocks in truth and holiness.[17] This responsibility applies not only to the particular churches under their charge, but, "as members of the episcopal college . . . each of them must by Christ's institution and command show a care for the universal Church which . . . would be a great benefit for the universal Church."[18]

2. Even when it is not exercised in virtue of an explicit "canonical mission," theology can only be done in a living communion with the faith of the Church. For this reason, all the bap-

tized, insofar as they both really live the life of the Church and enjoy scientific competence, can carry out the task of the theologian, a task which derives its own force from the life of the Holy Spirit in the Church which is communicated by the sacraments, the preaching of the word of God, and the communion of love.

Thesis 8

The difference between the magisterium and the theologians takes on a special character when one considers the freedom proper to them and the critical function that follows from it with regard to the faithful, to the world, and even to one another.

1. By its nature and institution, the magisterium is clearly free in carrying out its task. This freedom carries with it a great responsibility. For that reason, it is often difficult, although necessary, to use it in such a way that it not appear to theologians and to others of the faithful to be arbitrary or excessive. There are some theologians who prize scientific theology too highly, not taking enough account of the fact that respect for the magisterium is one of the specific elements of the science of theology. Besides, contemporary democratic sentiments often give rise to a movement of solidarity against what the magisterium does in carrying out its task of protecting the teaching of faith and morals from any harm. Still, it is necessary, though not easy, to find always a mode of procedure which is both free and forceful, yet not arbitrary or destructive of communion in the Church.

2. To the freedom of the magisterium there corresponds in its own way the freedom that derives from the true scientific responsibility of theologians. It is not an unlimited freedom, for, besides being bound to the truth, it is also true of theology that "in the use of any freedom, the moral principle of personal and social responsibility must be observed."[19] But the theologians' task of interpreting the documents of the past and present magisterium, of putting them in the context of the whole of revealed truth, and of finding a better understanding of them by the use of hermeneutics brings with it a somewhat critical function which obviously should be exercised positively rather than destructively.

Thesis 9

The exercise of their tasks by the magisterium and theologians often gives rise to a certain tension. But this is not surprising, nor should one expect that such tension will ever be fully resolved here on earth. On the contrary, wherever there is genuine life, tension also exists. Such tension need not be interpreted as hostility or real opposition, but can be seen as a vital force and an incentive to a common carrying out of the respective tasks by way of dialogue.

III
A METHOD FOR PROMOTING TODAY THE RELATIONSHIP
BETWEEN THEOLOGIANS AND THE MAGISTERIUM

Thesis 10

The basis and condition for the possibility of this dialogue between theologians and the magisterium are community in the faith of the Church and service in building up the Church. They embrace the diverse functions of the magisterium and theologians. On the one hand, this unity in the communication and participation in the truth is a habitual association which is antecedent to every concrete dialogue; on the other, it is itself strengthened and enlivened by the various relations that dialogue entails. Thus dialogue provides excellent reciprocal assistance: the magisterium can gain a greater understanding as it defends and preaches the truth of faith and morals, and the theological understanding of faith and morals gains in certainty from corroboration by the magisterium.

Thesis 11

The dialogue between the magisterium and theologians is limited only by the truth of faith which must be served and explained. For this reason, the whole vast field of truth lies open to such dialogue. But this truth is not something uncertain and utterly unknown, always having to be sought; it has been revealed and handed on to the Church to be faithfully kept. Therefore, the dialogue reaches its limits when the limits of the faith are reached. This goal of the dialogue, the service of the truth, is often endangered. The following types of behavior especially limit the possibility of dialogue: wherever the dialogue becomes an "instrument" for gaining some end "politically," that is, by applying pressure and ultimately abstracting from the question of truth, the effort is bound to fail; if a person "unilaterally" claims the whole field of the dialogue, he violates the rules of discussion; the dialogue between the magisterium and theologians is especially violated if the level of argument and discussion is prematurely abandoned and means of coercion, threat, and sanction are immediately brought to bear; the same thing holds when the discussion between theologians and the magisterium is carried out by means of publicity, whether within or outside the Church, which is not sufficiently expert in the matter, and thus "pressures" from without have a great deal of influence, e.g. the mass media.

Thesis 12

Before opening an official examination of a theologian's writings, the competent authority should exhaust all the ordinary possibilities of reaching agreement through dialogue on a doubtful opinion (e.g., personal conversation, or inquiries and replies in correspondence). If by these forms of dialogue no real consensus can be reached, the magisterium should employ a full and flexible stock of responses, beginning with various forms of warning, "verbal sanctions," etc. In a very serious case, the magisterium — after consulting theologians of various schools and having exhausted the means of dialogue — for its part must necessarily clarify the compromised truth and safeguard the faith of the believers.

According to the classical rules, the fact of one's professing "heresy" can only be definitely established if the accused theologian has demonstrated "obstinacy," that is, if he closes himself off from all discussion meant to clarify an opinion contrary to the faith and, in effect, refuses the dialogue. The fact of heresy can be established only after all the rules of the hermeneutics of dogmas and all the theological qualifications have been applied. In this way, even in decisions which cannot be avoided, the true "ethos" of the dialogue-procedure can be preserved.

Notes

1. Pope Paul VI, "Address to the International Congress on the Theology of Vatican II," October 1, 1966, *Acta Apostolicae Sedis,* 58 (1966), 890.

2. *Ibid.*

3. *Ibid.,* p. 891.

4. Vatican II, *Dei Verbum,* no. 10.

5. *Ibid.,* no. 24.

6. Vatican II, *Lumen Gentium,* no. 12.

7. Vatican II, *Dei Verbum,* no. 10.

8. Vatican II, *Lumen Gentium,* no. 12.

9. *Ibid.,* no. 25.

10. Vatican II, *Dei Verbum,* no. 10.

11. Pope Paul VI, *loc. cit.,* p. 892.

12. Vatican II, *Ad Gentes,* no. 22.

13. Vatican II, *Gaudium et Spes,* no. 62.

14. Pope Paul VI, *loc. cit.,* p. 892.

15. *Ibid.,* p. 891.

16. Vatican II, *Lumen Gentium,* no. 12.

17. *Ibid.,* no. 27.

18. *Ibid.,* no. 23.

19. Vatican II, *Dignitatis Humanae,* no. 7.

2
Commentary on the Theses

Otto Semmelroth, S.J., and Karl Lehmann

INTRODUCTION

The theme which the International Theological Commission discussed in its October 1975 meeting is the same topic which Pope

Paul VI spoke about in his address to the International Congress on the Theology of the Second Vatican Council, October 1, 1966. It seems only fitting, then, to refer to some of the views he expressed then.

In particular, it should be noted that the relationship between the ecclesiastical magisterium and theology is a close one. By way of introduction, this relationship might perhaps be explained as follows: it is the task of the whole Church, and therefore of those organs especially delegated for it, to proclaim to men the word which it has heard. Two tasks, then, have to be carried out simultaneously: hearing the word of God and proclaiming it by a witness of both word and life. This latter must be undertaken by the common witness of all the faithful, but in a special way by the witness of those equipped for this either by official ministry or by scientific qualifications, This indivisible unity of hearing and teaching has a different nuance in the two different ways in which the task of teaching is carried out, ministerially or scientifically. One could perhaps say that the theologians' primary task is the hearing of the word of God—in a qualified, scientific way, of course—while the task of the ecclesiastical magisterium is more that of proclaiming the word of God it has heard, but with the help of theological experts.

Thesis 1

Two questions are considered in this thesis. First it is necessary to discuss what is meant by the terms "ecclesiastical magisterium" and "theologians." Both of them in fact can be understood to have a teaching office, for the task of teaching belongs both to bishops and to theologians, although in different ways. At the same time, it should be noted that discussion of the ecclesiastical magisterium and of teachers has not been carried on in univocal terms in every age of the Church. Analogy applies here, both with regard to the understanding of the two realities and with regard to the concrete way in which they are exercised. For example, in some earlier times more than in later ones, the office of bishop and the exercise of theology were undertaken by the same person. Later, the ecclesiastical magisterium and scientific theology were linked rather by way of cooperation.

I

Part I considers elements which are common to the ecclesiastical magisterium and to theologians as they carry out their tasks. For it is very important, while noting the diversity of the two tasks, not to forget that they must cooperate with one another as they fulfill their ecclesiastical functions.

Thesis 2

In fact, true theology, understood in the Catholic sense, is no less a task to be undertaken within the Church than is the ecclesiastical magisterium. Each task must safeguard the certainty of faith, whether by a deeper understanding and scientific defense of the faith, or by authoritatively proclaiming it and defending it against adversaries.

Thesis 3

Certain common obligations bind both the magisterium and the theologians. It is true that the authority which each enjoys differs from that of the other, but in both the magisterium and the theologians' task there is a genuine authority. For this reason, each must be aware that this authority is not absolute, but has to be exercised in the form of service, the service of the word of God. This hearing or "obedience of faith" (Rom. 1:5; 16:26) accomplished by theologians by means of their scientific investigations serves that better hearing which theologians offer to bishops, and this cooperation with them serves the proclamation of the word of God which bishops undertake.

In carrying out this common task, both theologians and the magisterium draw what the word of God has communicated to the Church from the common faith (*e communi sensu fidelium*) of the community in the past and in the present. For what belongs to the common patrimony of the Church's faith becomes manifest in the faith of the universal Church in its varied dimensions, the whole Church of today and the whole Church of past ages.

In the course of time, the Church has left records by which the faith by which the Church lived in past ages may be discerned. The investigations of theologians and the witness of the ecclesiastical magisterium are both bound to these, i.e., documents of various kinds which have come down to us, for they are the documents of the believing Church itself in its passage through history.

Theological investigations and the exercise of the magisterium's task are not undertaken purely for academic reasons or simply for the sake of polemical controversy. The reason why the truth of faith is investigated, why it is kept intact, why it is proclaimed as the Gospel, is pastoral and missionary. Men must be brought to live by faith. The pastoral character of the ecclesiastical magisterium is more apparent than that of the theologians. But the theologians themselves cannot undertake their task without some pastoral reference, and the care of souls is even an internal element of the theological enterprise itself. This pastoral character affects theology both negatively and positively. Negatively, it means that the theological effort must be careful that the faith of believers not suffer harm because difficult explanations and disputed questions reported in the public communications media are heard and seen by people who are unduly disturbed by such publications. Positively, it means that the theological effort is used in proclamation and preaching and in religious education. The theological effort, scientific as it is, not only cannot be kept behind closed doors; by its very purpose as a ministry in the service of the preaching of the word of God, it affects the life of the ecclesiastical and human community.

Thesis 4

This thesis draws attention to the collegial or communitarian nature of both the magisterium's task and the theologians' enterprise. Although each of them can and must be carried out through the personal work of an individual bishop or theologian, still the pertinent charism given to each member of the magisterial and theological communities is given because of their link with the college or the ecclesiastical community. This communion and collegiality must be respected in the carrying out of the office or of the scientific work. Special care should be taken for fostering community between the magisterial college and the community of those who devote themselves to the theological enterprise.

The Second Vatican Council made a special point of recalling the collegiality of the episcopal college, so that individual bishops neither should nor can perform their tasks without reference to the college. On the other hand, neither can theologians perform their work if they do not pay attention to the work and opinions of their colleagues, and this not merely because of the demands of scientific method, but also because of the needs of a living community which is both intellectual and charismatic.

II

The common elements which link the task of the ecclesiastical magisterium and the ministry of theologians do not eliminate the difference between them. They differ especially on four points: the function proper to each, the quality of authority proper to each, the different way in which each is linked with the Church, and the proper and specific freedom each enjoys.

Thesis 5

The magisterium exercises the role of defending the integrity and unity of faith and morals. This cannot be done merely by decree, but only according to the measure of the truth proposed in the exercise of the role. For this reason, it needs the help and cooperation of the science of the theologians who in fact attempt scientifically to uncover the truth of God's word hidden in the words of men. The task of defending the integrity and unity of the faith at first glance appears rather negative or restrictive. In fact, however, it is carried out in a positive way for the life of the Church, i.e., by the authoritative interpretation of the word of God, which includes at once the exclusion of opinions contrary to faith and, much more, an introduction into a deeper understanding of the faith.

The remarks in Thesis 5:2 about the somewhat mediatorial function of theologians between the magisterium and the people of God must not be understood exclusively. Still, it is a matter of great importance. For the things which the ecclesiastical magisterium proclaims as matters of faith or as ecclesiastical doctrines must be communicated with the help of theological interpretation and explanation to the people of God living here and now, who do not always correctly understand what the magisterium has taught in the past or is teaching now. On the other hand, the magisterium itself needs the cooperation of the theologians in order to discern what is true and what is erroneous in the faith of the Christian people, for the faith of the community of the people of God is also a norm for what the magisterium can proclaim and require all to accept. Since scientific means must be employed in carrying out this task, the ecclesiastical magisterium needs the serious cooperation of the theologians. And theologians themselves must, therefore, be aware of this ministry.

Thesis 6

While the sources of the authority with which the ecclesiastical magisterium and the theologians fulfill their roles are distinct, the valid distinction should not lead to a false opposition.

On the one hand, the specific authority of the ecclesiastical magisterium derives from the sacramental ordination by which its members are brought into the college of bishops to which as such belongs the highest pastoral authority in the Church. But it should be noted that this "formal authority" should coincide with a certain personal authority, deriving either from the person's own behavior or from the scientific authority which a theologian acquires for himself by his study and research. These need not be mutually exclusive, as is clear in the case of a man consecrated a bishop and pastor in the Church who has also acquired the other authority for himself in theological study, or of a man consecrated a bishop and teacher who makes use of the help and cooperation of an expert theologian as he carries out his task.

As for the authority of a theologian, it should be noted that this is not only an intellectual authority, but also derives from his share in the life of the Church whose living faith is investigated and explained by the theological enterprise.

Thesis 7

There is no doubt that, in exercising their tasks, both the ecclesiastical magisterium and theologians are bound to the Church, but the manner in which each is linked to the Church differs.

With regard to the ecclesiastical magisterium, the link with the Church derives from the fact that it is an office and ministry in and for the Church, which has no meaning outside the Church. And this is particularly true with regard to the office of teaching—magisterium—and all the more because this magisterium must be exercised in the manner of a judge who discerns the truth or falsehood of proposed opinions.

Similar comments hold also for theologians, when and to the degree that they carry out their task not only as researchers but also as teachers and do this by canonical mission. But even when the science of theology is pursued, not as an official exercise, but as personal research, it remains linked with the Church, for theology, as the science of faith, can only be carried out truly in the living context of the Church's faith. For the objective faith (*fides quae*) can only be investigated by those who live in the Church with a living subjective faith (*fides qua*).

Thesis 8

There is a great deal of talk today about the freedom of the science of theology, and this scientific freedom is often presented as incompatible with the restrictions which authority brings to bear.

As a result, it is often overlooked that genuine freedom belongs to both the ecclesiastical magisterium and theological science, and that the freedom proper to the one must be respected by the other. In discussing freedom, whether in the ecclesiastical magisterium or in scientific theology, it must not be forgotten that freedom is not license, but is linked with a great responsibility which necessarily puts restrictions on it. This remark must not destroy the scientific freedom of theologians, which itself, however, is not unlimited but is bound by the truth that has been proclaimed by the word of God and guarded by the magisterium. No doubt it is very difficult to preserve the freedom of both magisterium and theologians. It is a constant struggle to exercise this freedom without violating its necessary restrictions and to observe and guard the restrictions without destroying the freedom proper to the ministry of the truth.

Thesis 9

This thesis provides the transition to the third part which discusses a properly understood dialogue between the magisterium and theology. For from what has been said, it can hardly be doubted that tension will arise. Constant effort is required in order to keep in harmony the common and different elements. But such tension is always experienced whenever there are diverse elements which must co-exist but which are not easily synthesized. Dialogue is a means, if not simply for removing this tension, at least for making it fruitful.

III

Part III of the theses offers a contribution to prevent the tension between magisterium and theologians described in Thesis 9 from harming the common good of the Church. There are many means and instruments available to prevent this, among which dialogue stands out as the chief way and a valid method for setting up a fruitful relationship between theologians and magisterium.

The notion of dialogue must be properly understood. It is not a vague conversation, indefinite and interminable. Dialogue serves the search for truth. If dialogue even at the highest level serves the true freedom and "initiative" of all participants, it does not take the place of the role of the judges of the faith, and it must not impede decisions from the magisterium which are needed to defend the faith of the Church. Hence, "dialogue" must not be understood in a superficial and popular sense; it must be purified of these implications and be in accord with the Christian faith.

Thesis 10

Dialogue has certain presuppositions, without which it would not reach the truth. Every dialogue between the magisterium and theologians presupposes a basic "solidarity" which consists in the common faith of the Church. This unity respects and retains the diverse functions of the magisterium and of theology. True dialogue lives in and arises out of this common basis, and it would lack any sense if this profound community in the faith were absent or were simulated. For this reason, for a dialogue to lead to the truth, it must not be directed only by expertise, but above all by sincerity, by courage in stating the truth, and by eagerness to hear the truth. Since this community is often neglected or doubted today, it is necessary to emphasize this "basis," for all dialogue between magisterium and theologians must be stressed.

The thesis has another 'point: the proper functions of the magisterium and of theology must not be confused. If they keep to their own responsibilities, as these are set out at the end of the thesis, they will be an excellent help to one another. This thesis rejects the attempts of those who would more or less like to do away with the task of the magisterium and assign exclusive competency in matters of faith and morals to scientific theology and so to theologians.

Thesis 11

Consequently, the question arises of the limits of the dialogue between magisterium and theologians. Two points are of major importance: (1) If community in the faith is preserved, there is no intrinsic limit to the dialogue, although this does not mean an indefinite process in the search for truth. (2) The dialogue method reaches its limits where the truth of faith is harmed.

But there are dangers intrinsic to dialogue which can destroy conversation. The dialogue can easily be damaged, for example, if means of external coercion are employed. While today this is not a grave danger, there is a new situation in the relation between magisterium and theologians which has not existed in this form until now. At one time the dialogue between magisterium and theologians on doubtful matters was conducted *directly*, between the competent authority and the individual theologian. Today, in cases of conflict, "publicity" often intervenes between magisterium and theologians. Thus pressure is applied, tactical moves are considered, etc., in all of which the "atmosphere" of dialogue is lost. The authenticity of the dialogue is thus reduced. Facts of this sort constitute a new situation that certainly deserves further consideration.

Thesis 12

The theses do not intend to discuss specific questions and especially not juridical questions about the external structure of the dialogue, particularly in cases of conflict. But the thesis does intend to indicate the significance and the "locus" of the dialogue method before a formal doctrinal investigation is undertaken and, insofar as this is possible, even during the "Ratio Agendi" (title of a document of the Sacred Congregation for the Doctrine of the Faith outlining the steps of a doctrinal investigation, January 15, 1974; *AAS* 63 [1974], pp. 234-36). The doctrinal procedure represents the last and decisive step, when all the other forms (see the text) have become vain and useless. The thesis recommends the use of the dialogue method even to the magisterium in the sense that it make use of a "graduated store" of reactions to doubtful opinions (see the ones proposed in the text). The classical rules of the hermeneutics of dogmas provide good and clear help. But the thesis also clearly recognizes that dialogue comes to an end when the theologian definitely contradicts the truth of faith. In this case, it is the theologian himself who in the last analysis has refused the dialogue.

Authority and the Christian Conscience

Christopher Butler, O.S.B.

The interests of clarity require that I should say a few words about the use I intend to make of the three terms: authority, constraint and the Christian conscience.

I distinguish authority from constraint. Constraint, as I understand it, is an external limitation imposed upon the freedom of behavior of those upon whom constraint is exercised. Constraint, according to one theory, by impeding the passage of Greek merchant vessels through the Dardanelles and only allowing them to proceed on payment of customs charges to the Trojans, provoked the siege of Troy. Trojan constraint had limited the freedom of movement of the Greek sailors, and Greek constraint eventually destroyed the power of Troy and placed the constraint of death upon its king. Constraint, then, operates by limiting human freedom. This it can do not only by the actual exercise of force but by the threat of force—sanctions as we call them today. An unscrupulous citizen might be deterred from falsifying his tax returns only by the fear of civil punishment. In short, we may say that as constraint increases in range and effectiveness, so freedom is diminished.

Authority is often combined with constraint, and it is often held that authority and freedom are related in the same way as constraint and freedom, so that when authority increases in effectiveness and range, freedom is correspondingly diminished. I do not so understand authority.

True authority makes no attempt to diminish human freedom. On the contrary, it presupposes that freedom and, in principle, desires to see it functioning untrammeled. For authority does not dictate with the threat of sanctions; it appeals to freedom and invites freedom to come into the act. But the freedom it appeals to is responsible freedom. The characteristic language of authority is not the language of necessity ("you *must* do so or so — or else") but the language of duty: "You ought to behave in the way I propose, and in so behaving you will expand the area of your true freedom."

For freedom is not something that exists by and in itself. It is directed to a goal in which it will find its own full self-expression. It has an intention inscribed within it, and this intention summons it to become not mere freedom to do anything you like, but responsible freedom: a freedom that adjusts itself and its subject to the reality beyond itself, apart from which there can be no subject and no freedom.

Responsible freedom looks beyond itself to a norm of action that is conformed to reality. And it is to responsible freedom that authority addresses itself, not to constrain or to command but to illuminate and enable. At the moment when authority takes on the aspect of command and menace, it allows itself to be corrupted by constraint.

Authority is not absent from the world of science and intellectual growth. The world of science is maintained in actual existence by the collaboration of many scientists, and this collaboration depends on mutual confidence between scientists. If every scientist had to make for himself the discoveries, and give birth within himself, unaided and undirected, to the intuitions of an Einstein, there would be little progress in science. Very many scientists take their Einstein on trust because they have recognized his authority. Even those who prefer to rethink Einstein for themselves choose to do so because they recognize the authority of their predecessor, directing them to this set of questions and answers rather than to a myriad of alternatives that lack similar authority.

Note, however, that the authority of the great scientists is not something that imposes itself against the will of those on whom it is exercised. On the contrary, they welcome it and it is only as so welcomed and voluntarily accepted that it enlarges, instead of constraining, their thought.

Freedom, exercised with responsibility, is what I propose to call conscience, though I am aware that a respectable linguistic tradition prefers to use the word "conscience" always of an act of judgment and not of a habit of responsibility. The conscientious man, for me, is the same as the man of good will to whom the Second Vatican Council addressed its message in the *Constitution on the Church in the Modern World*. He is not necessarily a Christian believer, though he may be such.

The Christian conscience is the conscience of a man who has accepted as true, and wishes to follow as a guide for behavior, the self-disclosure of God in and as Christ. I hasten to add that, in my view, this acceptance and the resultant resolution for behavior are themselves, in one aspect, the fruit of responsible freedom. A Christian who has not yet reached years, as we used to say, of discretion, one who is not yet able to exercise responsible freedom because of his immaturity, is not capable of Christian responsibility in the full sense; he has no developed Christian conscience. A full Christian is one who has discovered that he will be what he has made himself, and that he has freedom and therefore an obligation to make himself such as he ought to be.

Christian faith, accepted by the believer in particular acts and then by a habit of responsible freedom, relates a man directly to God—directly, but mediately, and the mediator is Jesus Christ. Thus directed, the believer attains a certain knowledge of God. God is in himself the Absolute Mystery, the unattainable horizon and infinite support, of all created existence. And yet man has an unquenchable, if often hardly conscious, aspiration to penetrate that Mystery and to know the unknowable. And the Christian believes that "he that hath seen" Jesus of Nazareth "has seen the Father." We cannot know God by our own efforts, but God has spoken a word in our human language, a Word made flesh for our salvation—and not least for our intellectual salvation.

I
JESUS REVEALS GOD

Because God is unattainable by our own efforts, the word of God comes to us from beyond the horizon of our experience. But because we have a latent aspiration toward God, he comes to us as the reality for which we were made, and in whom we find our own full expansion and self-realization. Moreover, this latent aspiration of our being is fundamental to our existence. It slumbers in the very heart or apex of our being, and it is when the word of God is spoken within us that we begin really to live and not merely to exist. Only a personal word of a personal God could thus meet and supply the latent possibilities of our personhood. No general or abstract law, law of the material universe or law of natural morality, not even such a law revealed by God, could thus touch us and lift us at once beyond ourselves and into our full selfhood.

The word of God made flesh is thus not just our lawgiver. He is above all the one who speaks God to us, and who does so both by what he says and by what he is and does and suffers. He is, in the plenitude of his historical existence, not only the mediator but the fullness of divine self-disclosure and of divine self-giving.

What does he tell us of God by his words? He tells us that God is supremely and, it would seem, unconditionally generous. "He mades his sun rise on the evil and on the good, and sends his rain on the just and on the unjust." He is the shepherd who leaves the ninety and nine sheep on the mountainside while he goes in search of the one sheep that has strayed. He is the woman who, instead of rejoicing over the nine drachmas that she has not lost, searches high and low for the one lost coin, and when she has found it calls her friends together to rejoice with her. He is the father who does not wait for the prodigal's confession but runs to cast his arms about him and kiss him. He is even the owner of the vineyard who chooses, out of sheer and — to human eyes — even inequitable generosity to pay the eleventh-hour workers as much as those who have borne the labor and heat of the whole day. And he is the one who sent Jesus to summon "not the righteous but sinners to repentance."

Since Jesus Christ is not only the mediator of the message but himself the message, we can learn of God not only from his words but from his deeds. It is therefore not for nothing that we see Jesus healing the sick, giving sight to the blind and hearing to the deaf, casting out devils — and breaking through the conventions of Palestinian Judaism by consorting with publicans and sinners. And it is a revelation of God when we see Jesus suffering, crying out in agony on the cross the psalmist's words: "My God, my God, why hast thou forsaken me?" and dying in a final gesture of appeal to a world that had rejected him.

Jesus speaks God to us not only by his words about God, his deeds and his sufferings, but by what he was. What he was is only partiallv disclosed to us in his words. But he does speak of himself as "meek and humble of heart," as the teacher whose yoke is easy and his burden light — surely offering our philosophy unexpected insights on the God whom he reveals. And above all, Jesus is the one who addressed his prayers to his "heavenly Father," and who expressed the uniqueness of his relationship with him as a relationship of sonship. If the supreme revelation of God is one who prayed as a son to his Father, then this tells us something about God himself, who henceforth for Christain believers will be not supremely the Creator, the Lord of history, the Lord of hosts, the Almighty One (though he is all these things), but "the God and Father of our Lord Jesus Christ."

What seems to follow from such reflections is that, for the Christian conscience, the archetypal authority is the authority of a God who is totally generous and absolutely forgiving love, and that this authority, at its supreme moment of self-actualization, is an authority that not only appeals rather than commands, but appeals with the fullness of love. All authority, after all, is the self-presentation not of mere fact but of value to the subject addressed. The authority of truth, for instance, is anything but the brute constraint of fact. Science has no authority over us except in its quality of truth or attempted truth, and the authority of scientists is also an authority of personal and intellectual value. Love, for the Christian, is the supreme value. God is supreme love, and the authority of God is therefore something that comes to us with an appeal analogous to that of love as we know it in its best expressions in our human relations.

No one can constrain another to love him, and any so-called love that was caused by contraint would be less than satisfactory not only to the lover but to the beloved. Love only operates perfectly in perfect freedom. Love is tender and kind and respectful, exigent indeed but with an exigency that is identical with its patience and its respect for the person wooed. God has never made anyone

love him without the free consent, involving for adult human beings the possibility of withholding consent, to the offer of God's
self-giving that we call grace.

If such is authority in its supreme embodiment and self-disclosure, the very authority of God, it would seem that we have certain lessons to learn about authority in God's Church, the body of
Christ who is God self-revealed, self-offered and (if man does not
withhold his consent) self-given. We should suppose that authority
in the Church is most true to itself when those who wield it speak
not in terms of dictation and constraint, but in terms of loving appeal. Constraint limits freedom, and appeal enlarges it. And Christ
came that we might have life, and have it more abundantly. We
should perhaps be a little suspicious of the kind of father-confessor
who generally exacts "blind obedience" from his penitents and
those who come to him for spiritual direction. We should be happier with the director who spoke in such terms as were used by that
lay spiritual director, Baron Friedrich von Hügel:

> Religion is indeed authoritative, since only if felt and ac-
> cepted as not of our making but of God's giving is it religion
> at all. . . . Yes . . . authority is exercised and experienced in
> and through our human religious sense and conscience. . . .
> Hence . . . you will not for one moment strain or torture
> yourself, to think or do any of the things here proposed to
> you. Only in the degree and manner in which, after thinking
> them well over, in a prayerful and open disposition, they real-
> ly come home to your mind and really appeal to your own
> heart and conscience will you quietly accept them and try and
> work them into your life.[1]

A remarkable modern lay thinker writes of authority in what
he calls "a religion of appeal." He who wields authority in such a
religion should not see himself as

> a cog in a system of government but rather as one who helps
> each of his inferiors in their quest of what is spiritual. He
> knows that he cannot dictate this quest, nor even teach in a
> precise way how it should be conducted. So he exerts his

authority with modesty. . . . He will be slow to claim that what he prescribes is the will of God. . . . He claims no (personal) infallibility, but only a relative competence due to the specially favorable situation in which his office has put him. . . . At the final limit, authority would fain be silence and presence; at this term of perfection (never actually attained) authority would act upon man like the living memory of Jesus in the heart of his disciple. . . .The wielder of such authority has faith in men, and so he helps his subordinates, by his mode of behavior among them, to have faith in themselves and in God.[2]

For a modern example of authority exercised in this way, one could mention the present Pope's recent Exhortation on Devotion to Our Lady.

II
HUMAN ASPECTS

How comfortable it would be if we could end our discussion of authority and the Christian conscience at this point. But we have been discussing authority in its pure form and in its supreme exercise by God, and suggesting this as a model for the exercise of authority in the Church. The divine word, however, was vouchsafed to human recipients, and "whatever is received is received according to the modality of the recipient." We have, then, to consider authority not only in itself but as addressing itself to us human beings and to the human groupings in which we find ourselves.

There are two aspects of humanity that seem relevant here. The first is that man is not a static entity but a creature in progress, a growing creature. The child may indeed be the father of the man, but he does not start as an adult man. The Greek definition of man as a rational animal may be not too misleading when applied to adults, but animality seems to express itself outwardly more clearly than rationality in the very young. Bernard Lonergan has put the point well: we have to acknowledge "the priority of living to learning how to live, to acquiring the willingness to live rightly, to developing the adaptation that makes right living habitual."[3] Thus, the immature human is living in a situation that constantly demands more from him than he is capable of supplying, demands an effective reasonableness and rationality that is not yet his. This is particularly important in a consideration of authority, since pure authority is the self-presentation of some value, be it truth or justice or love or beauty, and until one is adultly rational and reasonable the appeal of value cannot be apprehended in its native essence. It is necessary, to quote the same author, that "the empirically, intelligently, rationally conscious subject of self-affirmation become a morally self-conscious subject,"[4] and until that occurs he can hear with his ears the voice, and catch the tones, of authority but he cannot adequately apprehend it in its true nature of appeal. In such circumstances, authority may have to go into alliance with constraint, consenting to a temporary limitation imposed upon the subordinate in order that he may reach the fullness of responsible freedom with a greater range of effective freedom at some later date or in some "absolute future."

The other relevant aspect of humanity is that, in fact, man is free, even when adult, not to respond to the appeal to authority, and that when he exercises his freedom in such refusal there results what in theology is called sin. Sin is not just a private affair between man and God; it usually has social repercussions, and the cumulative effect of sin is to build up a total human situation in which the innocent divagations of immaturity are reinforced in their effects by a positive distortion. In such a situation, and with his reasonableness already weakened by his own sins and the resultant habits, a man is more prone to further sin and less willing to hear the voice of authority.

Indeed, and even before the teachings of revealed religion are brought into the discussion, it seems possible to discern in man a corruption, a tendency to evil, that not only infects the human environment in which we all operate but that will take advantage of that environment to advance further on the downward slope of delinquency.

What, humanly speaking, prevents a total relapse into moral

anarchy is what I propose to call social structure. Social structure is the framework for shared living and mutual help, laboriously and always most imperfectly erected by the labors of individuals and groups who are not prepared to sink into worse than barbarism without a struggle.

The late Professor Sir Herbert Butterfield, in his book *Christianity and History,* wrote:

> The plain truth is that if you were to remove certain subtle safeguards in society many men who had been respectable all their lives would be transformed . . . weak men would apparently take to crime who had been kept on the rails by a certain balance in existing society. . . . We do not . . . reflect how precarious our civilized systems will always be, if, almost in absence of mind, we allow certain safeguards to be taken off. The virtues of Western society in modern times were in reality the product of much education, tradition and discipline; they needed centuries of patient cultivation. Even without great criminality in anybody—merely by forgetting certain safeguards—we could lose the tolerance and urbanities, the respect for human life and human personality, which are in reality the late blossoms of a highly developed civilization.[5]

It is in respect of human beings thus subject to the law of development and thus corrupted, in themselves and in their society and culture, by sin that ecclesiastical authority has to be exercised. Without drawing on the resources of constraint it cannot fulfill its task.

The baptized infant is introduced into the life of the Church in the Christian family governed by his Christian parents. The family is, as Vatican II teaches, "a sort of domestic Church" (*Lumen Gentium,* n. 11), and the child's parents are his first evangelists. There can be no doubt at all that the controlling spirit of the family should be Christian love, or that an atmosphere of stable and trustworthy love is among the child's primary needs. There can also be no doubt that the child will not be well brought up unless this caring and forgiving love is allied with constraint. Before the child can learn for himself and decide for himself not to play with fire, the parents must prevent him from doing so and, if disobedience is threatened, fortify their authority with prohibition and, if need be, sanction. Great harm has been done by a theory of the upbringing of children that has deprecated proper family discipline. And the indispensable need for such discipline is in no way diminished by our recognition of the fact that, as the children grow older, the element of constraint has to give way more and more to an attitude of trust; dictation in the end has to yield to persuasion and to appeal, and this in order that the children may become truly adult. It has been well said that if young people are prevented by constraint from doing what is wrong, they will never learn to do what is right by an act of self-determination. Nevertheless, while autonomy is the ideal to aim at, heteronomy has its place in the developmental process.

In Christ, God is our Father, and the Church, as tradition has long proclaimed, is our mother. The Church, from another point of view, is the family of God, and within that family there are many who are not yet fully adult in the moral sense, few who are completely adult. There are also many who, though "grown up" in the eyes of the world, are retarded by sin and in need of more help than pure authority can give them. Thus, as in the Christian family, an epitome of the Church, so also in the Church itself we shall expect and shall find an alliance of authority and constraint. The Church will not always speak only in tones of appeal; it will sometimes use the accents of command, indeed of dictation. Obedience thus becomes a Christian virtue.

I should be the last to deny that the element of constraint in the Church has at times been emphasized beyond measure, or that this has had a stunting effect upon the genuine development of Catholics. Constraint has its own dynamism, and although its lawful purposes are to reinforce authority, it can fascinate and corrupt those who wield authority and thus find themselves in possession of the power to constrain. From the era of Constantine onward the Church has been a powerful structure, sometimes in alliance with the state, and sometimes in confrontation with it. Both confrontation and collaboration have tended to strengthen the element of constraint in the Church. And, because the Church is habitually concerned with its own survival and influence in society, there has been a tendency for the Church's authority and power to constrain to take their stand in support of the political and social status quo against movements for reform and even revolution in which the real seeds of a happier future for mankind may have lain concealed. No such historical facts, however, suffice to make the alliance of authority and constraint in itself illegitimate. The recent ecumenical Council has emphasized the genuine Christian character of authority and was relatively silent about the legitimacy of constraint. In consequence, there have developed anarchical elements within the Church, and these, if they increase, could be dangerous.

Authority in the Church is further suffering from the difficulty experienced by those who wield it in adjusting their activities and their administration to the spirit of the Council. The habits engendered by long centuries of what today we should call authoritarianism are not easily discarded. Yet the documents of Vatican II are open to inspection by any interested Christian, and any discrepancy between the performance of officials and the spirit of these documents inevitably produces what today is recognized as a crisis of authority. It is far too simple to explain this crisis as due to a culpable diminution of respect for legitimate authority. The fact is that when authority speaks with one voice in the Council and with another voice in its day-to-day performances after the Council, the faithful find it difficult to determine where their duty of obedience lies. In the result, the Church finds itself passing through a dangerous and unhappy stage of its existence. Authority is of its essence, and constraint is a necessary ally of authority in this fallen and developing world. But authority, deriving its status from God, yet depends for its efficacy on a measure of consent from the faithful. Precisely that measure of consent is diminished by our present difficulties.

III
RESOURCES OF RESPONSIBLE FREEDOM

Perhaps, then, the time has come for us to turn our attention once again from authority to its correlative—responsible freedom. What resources does responsible freedom find within itself to render aid to the Church during such an abnormal period as that through which we are now passing?

First of all, the mature Christian must remind himself that authority in the Church is a derivation from the divine authority incarnate in Jesus Christ; and in its own nature it follows that ecclesiastical authority expects the sort of response that Christ himself called for, and not a different kind of response such as we might associate with a human monarch or legislative assembly.

Secondly, it must be borne in mind that authority is not located exclusively in the Pope and the bishops and in those who have received delegation from them. The authority of Christ in the Church is as extensive and as multifarious as the life of Christ in his mystical body. Thus there is a kind of authority appertaining to theology and sound scholarship, despite the fact that theologians do not constitute an ordained ministry in the Church. There is, as we have seen, a real authority of parents in respect of their young children, an authority that is, in the case of Christian parents, more than the natural authority of parents, since in a Christian home the parents represent the authority of the Church itself. There is also the undoubted authority of the Christian teacher in a Christian school, and, in general, the authority of elders in respect of their juniors.

It should be noted that the diffused and "unofficial" authority of which we are here speaking is not confined to matters of practical discipline, but extends to the sphere of Christian doctrinal and theological teaching. Despite a modern unfortunate use of the word *magisterium* to designate the bishops, the college of bishops, and the Pope, magisterial authority is not confined in the Church to official magisterial authority. It cannot reasonably be maintained, in the face of Vatican II, that the Church is divided into an *ecclesia docens* consisting of the Pope and the bishops and an *ecclesia discens* embracing all other baptized persons. On the contrary, everyone in the Church, from the Pope downward, belongs to the "learning Church" and has to receive information from his fellow believers, and everyone in the Church who has reached maturity has, at some time or another, to play the role of the teacher, the *magister,* the *ecclesia docens.*

What, then, is the special function of official authority in the Church?

The Church can usefully be seen as a "communion" or fellowship of believers. The notion of communion, in its full sense, includes that of a system of interpersonal relationships. This system, in Christianity, is built upon the sacraments and above all on the Eucharist. It is in common eucharistic worship that the relationship between Christian believers reaches its high point and finds its focus. Already in the epistles of Ignatius of Antioch the bishop is seen as at once the minister of the Eucharist and the personal focus of the local church as a communion.

Local unity, however, vital as it is, does not exhaust the idea of unity, and therefore of fellowship or communion, in the Church. While from one point of view the Church only becomes fully and existentially actual in the (necessarily local) eucharistic celebration, from another point of view the local church has validity only as a local expression of the universal Church, the one catholic, covenantal people of God. Hence, the role of the local bishop for his own local church has to be taken in conjunction with his role as a personal link between his own local church and the universal communion. And already very clearly in St. Cyprian of Carthage's writings we see the notion of the worldwide "college" of bishops not only adumbrated but given great prominence and an essential role. Subsequent development of theology answered the question how the college of bishops can be more than a mere "number" of individual bishops by combining the notion of an episcopal college with that of the primacy of the see of Rome as the focus of the college.

Can we not therefore say that a special function of official authority in the Church, that authority that belongs inherently to the Pope and college of bishops and derivatively to those to whom the Pope or bishops delegate authority, is to preserve and promote the local and universal unity or communion of the people of God? This unity is not a mere sociological value but belongs to the heart of our religion, since the Church which is the body of Christ is part of the one mystery of salvation.

The preservation and promotion of unity are the grounds of the disciplinary authority of bishops and Pope. A community is only really such if it has a measure of organization, and the disciplinary acts of official authority are (in their proper use) designed to sustain this organization. The Christian conscience will in principle acknowledge this authority and will direct the individual's behavior to conformity with it. Here, however, it is important to realize that this disciplinary authority is truest to its own ideal when it can and does use the accents not of command but of appeal and exhortation. But because the people of God is made up of individuals who are in various stages of development toward maturity, official Church authority can rightly ally itself with constraint, denying—for example—the full rights of communion to those who pertinaciously behave in ways contrary to the values of communion.

Official Church authority has also a doctrinal role. For the people of God is built both on faith, in its primordial sense of openness and surrender to the basic invitation of God self-revealed, and on those beliefs in which the content of faith, or its revealed "object," is articulated. These beliefs, as they are in their subjective aspect, are at the same time doctrines in the objective order, and it needs no long argument to show that heterodoxy is fatal to communion. Thus, the unitive role of Church authority has a doctrinal component and expresses itself and its function in what modern theology calls dogma.

Dogma, therefore, has authority over the Christian conscience. And if it be asked how I can be bound to believe doctrines or dogmas which do not commend themselves to me by their intrinsic force but only by their official character, it must be replied that without such doctrine the Church as a communion of believers could not survive, and that therefore the authority of dogma is derivatively the authority of God self-revealed in the Christian mystery.

Only when the position I have just outlined has been accepted can we profitably turn our attention to certain qualifications that have been brought into prominence in very recent discussions of authority and undoubtedly require consideration.

IV
CERTAIN QUALIFICATIONS

In the first place, then, the divine guarantee of doctrine appertains, in its fullest sense, only to those doctrines and dogmas to which the Church has fully committed itself, whether by the common consent of its believers (the *sensus fidelium*) or by the decisions of official authority. The claim of these doctrines on the adhesion of the believer is identical with the claim of the divine revelation itself. To require the same adhesion for doctrines that are indeed taught by officials with authority but to which the Church has not irrevocably committed itself is to abuse authority, and if this requirement is accompanied by threatened sanctions it is also to abuse the power of constraint. It would seem that, in order to preserve clearly the distinction between irrevocable and provisional doctrinal decisions, the word "assent" should be confined to the type of adhesion properly required for irrevocable doctrinal decisions.

Secondly, theology cannot fail to take account of the contingent character of all linguistic expression. There is no such thing as "timeless English"—or, for that matter, "timeless Latin." Except in mathematics and in the sciences so far as they express themselves in mathematical language, it is hardly too much to say that language is continually modified in the very process of its use. In particular, the Church's dogmas have often been expressed in language that reflected certain limited fields of theological or juridical interest or that was tributary to a philosophy that cannot claim to be part of the revealed deposit of Christian truth. In principle, then, it is always possible to distinguish between the intended meaning of a doctrinal formula and the contingent elements in its linguistic expression. Strictly speaking, the official teaching office of the Church does not define a formula; it defines a truth with the help of a formula. The truth is irreformable; the formula may be such as, in a different stage of linguistic development, to be positively misleading. It has long been admitted that the understanding of the biblical documents demands both exegesis and hermeneutics. The same admission needs to be made about the doctrinal formulas of the Church.

These qualifications with respect to the teachings of ecclesiastical authority have their importance for the Christian conscience. The object of Christian faith is God, divine truth, self-disclosed in the Christian mystery, which is at one and the same time the mystery of Christ Jesus and the mystery of the Church, his body. The divine revelation is the content of the faith of the Church as a communion or community and, in consequence, of the faith of the individual believer. This revelation has the supreme authority of God, for it is the revelaton *of* God in Christ. The Christian is thus led by his conscience to assent to this revelation both in its global wholeness and in those articulations of it that have in their support the *sensus fidei* or the irrevocable self-commitment of the Church through the solemn definitions of the official teaching authority within it. Such assent is to be seen not as a constraint upon the freedom of thought of the believer but as an expression of his responsible freedom and as his mode of access to the enriching values of revealed truth.

We have already agreed that official teaching is not confined to these solemn and irrevocable definitions. There is what is known today as the "ordinary magisterium"—of which the non-definitive teaching of ecumenical councils may be taken as an illustration. The two Vatican Councils themselves have, in this non-definitive way, taught that some doctrines of the ordinary magisterium can call for the assent of faith, but this is an area in which we lack the guidance of good theology today. Other non-definitive but official teaching cannot properly claim the assent of faith, but will be received by the Christian conscience with that respect that is due to the considered actions and utterances of those in positions of legitimate and official authority. In all cases, the mood of the devout believer will be not resentment at what appears to be a constraint upon his thinking, but a welcoming gratitude that goes along with the keen alertness of a critical mind and of a good will concerned to play its part both in the purification and the development of the Church's understanding of its inheritance.

While, however, a balanced view compels us to draw attention to the response of respect and consent that authority, even when allied with the power of constraint, calls for from the Christian conscience, it may well be that the more immediate need in the Church today is to remind those who exercise official authority in it that both the limits and the style of their authority are derived from the authority of God himself, the Father of our Lord Jesus Christ, who has disclosed himself to us in the Gospel as pure, all-generous, all-forgiving love, a love that cannot rest content with enforced obedience because, as St. Thérèse of Lisieux said (quoting St. John of the Cross), "love is only repaid by love." The divine love that is the very heart of reality is a love that, in its own pure self-expression, "throws away the rod" of constraint and entreats where it might command. And because it thus renounces constraint and trusts to its own appeal and attractiveness, it exercises over the Christian conscience a power that, by a shift of meaning of the word, the New Testament even calls constraint: "For the love of Christ constrains us, because we are convinced that one has died for all; therefore all have died. And he died for all, that those who live might live no longer for themselves but for him who for their sake died and was raised" (2 Cor. 5:14f.). If such is the authority of God in Christ, those who have a pastoral authority in the Church must always be ill at ease when the mode and style of their own exercise of authority does not immediately suggest to their subordinates and to onlookers the humble appeal of him whose yoke is easy and his burden light.

Notes

1. Letter to a young girl, March 11, 1918, quoted in Joseph P. Whelan, *The Spirituality of Friedrich von Hügel* (London, 1971), pp. 226f.
2. Marcel Légaut, *Introduction à l'intelligence du passé et de l'avenir du christianisme* (Paris, 1970), pp. 253-255.
3. Bernard Lonergan, *Insight* (New York, 1957), p. 693.
4. *Ibid.,* p. 599.

The Magisterium

John Francis Whealon

On January 16, 1976, the Sacred Congregation for the Doctrine of Faith released a significant document — *Declaration on Certain Questions Concerning Sexual Ethics*. Published with the specific approval of Pope Paul VI, this document is indisputably authoritative Catholic teaching.

Concerning premarital sex, living together without a marriage ceremony, homosexual relationships, masturbation, mortal sin and the ideal of chastity, this document presented no new teaching. The document in fact stated that it was emphasizing the constant Catholic doctrine so as to clarify doubts and confusion as to what the Church teaches.

What followed the release of this document? The secular and Catholic press gave it generous coverage. Simultaneously considerable coverage was given to public criticisms of the document by a few Catholic theologians. Little coverage was given to the many statements by bishops, bishops' conferences and theologians in praise of this document. The general impression, again, was left that the Church is divided on these teachings.

The problem here is not just the man-bites-dog approach of the press. A more serious problem is the lack of awareness by many Catholics of the teaching authority in the Lord's Catholic Church. They do not understand the magisterium and its benefits for their own faith.

This article speaks of the magisterium: not the rarely invoked, infallible extraordinary magisterium, but rather the ordinary magisterium — the day-to-day, year-to-year reformable teaching of the Bishop of Rome, the universal episcopate or the local diocesan bishop in union with the Pope (Denz. 3061, *Constitution on the Church,* n. 25). This ordinary magisterium does not operate in an ivory tower, and it presumes an interrelationship, a continuing symbiotic dialogue with all voices in the Church and especially with theologians.

For any priest or alert layman there is hardly any Catholic topic more alive, timely and helpful. Yet, considering the importance of the magisterium for Catholic faith and unity, surprisingly little has been written or spoken recently about it. The Consultation between Bishops and Theologians, held at the North American College of Rome in September 1974, had as a major theme the teaching authority of Pope and bishops, the relationship of the magisterium to theologians, and the effects of this on priests and laity.

I
TEACHING ON THE MAGISTERIUM

The magisterial aspect of the Catholic Church is indeed its least attractive feature. In Vatican II's masterwork, the Constitution on the Church, Chapter Two describes the Church as the people of God. This chapter is a fresh, attractive, biblically based presentation of the Church. It is a pleasure to read and to present to others through instruction and homily. But the next chapter of that same document is dramatically different in spirit. Chapter Three, treating the hierarchy and the magisterium of the Church, is theological, canonical, formal. This chapter is hardly attractive for teaching or preaching.

That Chapter Three is something like the skeleton of the mystical body. No beauty is there, especially when isolated or dissected. Yet like a skeleton it performs an essential function in the Church. So this unappealing concept of the operative ordinary magisterium is, intellectually speaking, a critical question in today's Church for the priest and for many laity.

The question is whether there exists in the Catholic Church an authority that ultimately persuades a Catholic to accept a teaching which that Catholic is not logically or psychologically disposed to accept. One recent example is the Constitution of Pope Gregory XVI in 1838, repeating papal teaching that slavery is immoral and that blacks are equal to others in human dignity and rights (Denz. 2745-46). This magisterial teaching, now universally accepted, was rejected by those who incredibly held that the negro had no soul and could be subjected to slavery. A second example is the magisterial teaching of Pius XI in *Casti Connubii* (1929), teaching that contraception is immoral. This teaching, essentially restated by the Second Vatican Council (1965) and by Paul VI in *Humanae Vitae* (1968), was rejected rather in its restatement by those Catholics who held that contraception is not intrinsically evil. Another current illustration is the teaching of the Second Vatican Council, restating Church doctrine that abortion is an unspeakable evil. Even this magisterial doctrine, frequently reasserted, is not accepted by some Catholics. A December 27, 1975, article in *America* expressed the impatience of the contributing author "with Catholic officialdom" and dissent from the unqualified magisterial teaching against abortion. The most recent example is the *Declaration on Certain Questions Concerning Sexual Ethics*.

There are different ways to approach the complex concept of magisterium. From the New Testament comes a conviction that the ultimate authority and the one authoritative teacher is Jesus, our Master. Also from the New Testament comes our belief that the Master gave teaching authority to Peter and the other apostles. The word authority holds the root *augere*: it is solely (as Robert Grosseteste said) to increase or build up the Church. The exercise of this authority is a service, in Christ and for the body of Christ. Also from the New Testament comes the lesson that Peter had a dominant authority in teaching. Mark's Gospel, as Peter's *didache*, was the foundation of the other Gospels. Cephas (Peter) influenced Paul also, stood first on the list of the apostles, and had the normative teaching. From Paul we get the picture that is essentially the concept of magisterium: there were false apostles and false teachers, but agreement with Cephas was the norm of Christian orthodoxy (cf. *Peter in the New Testament*, Paulist Press).

Theologically, the doctrine on the ordinary magisterium is presented in Chapter Three of the *Constitution on the Church*. This chapter begins with the teaching that the successor of Peter and the successors of the apostles—the Pope and the bishops—have inherited the responsibility and service in the Church that is magisterium.

The key text for understanding the ordinary magisterium is n. 25 of the *Constitution on the Church*.

Bishops, teaching in communion with the Roman Pontiff, are to be respected by all as witnesses to divine and Catholic truth. In matters of faith and morals, the bishops speak in the name of Christ and the faithful are to accept their teaching and adhere to it with a religious assent of soul. This religious submission of will and of mind must be shown in a special way to the authentic teaching authority of the Roman Pontiff, even when he is not speaking *ex cathedra*. That is, it must be shown in such a way that his supreme magisterium is acknowledged with reverence and the judgments made by him are sincerely adhered to, according to his manifest mind and will. His mind and will in the matter may be known chiefly either from the character of the documents, from his frequent repetition of the same doctrine, or from his manner of speaking.

Organizationally the Church's teaching authority is an immeasurable service to the entire Church. A Catholic can know what the Church teaches. Even when the question is a particularly controverted one, the Catholic need have no doubt concerning Catholic doctrine. In a real sense the magisterium is an identifying mark of the Catholic Church. Different Christian communities can be understood as to where they place ultimate ecclesial authority under Christ. For the Episcopalians it was the *episcopoi*; for the Presbyterians it was the presbytery; for the Congregationalists it was the individual congregation; for the Baptists, it was the individual follower of Christ who held authority. But for Catholics, as n. 25 of the *Constitution on the Church* teaches, final authority under Christ is found in the Pope and bishops, just as in the New Testament it reposed in Peter and the other apostles.

Psychologically, the very idea of magisterium is not well received in an age when all authority is challenged. The word magisterium comes from *magister* or "master." For us in the United States the master is one who dominates. We have lost the meaning, still found in England, of the master as the teacher. There is a certain tension in this, because this is teaching given with the authority of a teacher. The authority in the magisterium comes not from the person but rather from the doctrine. It must be teaching given in the name of Christ, in the Spirit of Truth. And the correlative to *magister* is *minister*. The spokesmen of this teaching of Christ are themselves subservient to it.

In this modern age there is a resistance to the inescapable intellectual humility, docility, and openness to acceptance that the magisterium demands. As teachers today testify, too few seem willing to learn. But a teacher makes no sense, functionally and philosophically, unless there are learners. There can be no *docentes* without *discentes*. Conceit and presumption cause special problems here, as the German bishops have noted. So psychologically the magisterium does not now receive an open reception, a fair hearing.

II
THEOLOGIANS AND THE MAGISTERIUM

An area of special importance is the relationship between Catholic theologians and the magisterium. (It is as difficult to define who a theologian is as it is easy to use this term in a univocal sense. I have a theology degree, teach theology and esteem highly my colleagues in Christ who do the same without having been ordained priests or bishops.)

It is important not to strain or worsen relationships between bishops and theologians. The trust that developed at the Second Vatican Council led to great progress in the Church. And both theologians and bishops must take care not to let that trust be eroded. Bishops must understand that theologians should be able to probe sensitive areas of doctrine while remaining loyal to the Church. And theologians, while making their theological probes, must understand that the magisterium carries ultimate responsibility for defining and specifying the content of Catholic doctrine. One of the more helpful statements on the difference between

magisterial teaching, freedom and theological speculation is found in the *Pastoral Instruction on the Means of Social Communication*:

117. There is an enormous area where members of the Church can express their views on domestic issues. It must be taken that the truths of the faith express the essence of the Church and therefore do not leave room for arbitrary interpretations. Nonetheless, the Church moves with the movement of man. It therefore has to adapt itself to the special circumstances that arise out of time and place. It has to consider how the truths of the faith may be explained in different times and cultures. It has to reach a multitude of decisions while adjusting its actions to the changes around it. While the individual Catholic follows the magisterium, he can and should engage in free research so that he may better understand revealed truths or explain them to a society subject to incessant change. . .

118. For this reason, a distinction must be borne in mind between, on the one hand, the area that is devoted to scientific investigation and, on the other, the area that concerns the teaching of the faithful. In the first, experts enjoy the freedom required by their work and are free to communicate to others, in books and commentaries, the fruits of their research. In the second, only those doctrines may be attributed to the Church which are declared to be such by its authentic magisterium. These last, obviously, can be aired in public without fear of giving scandal.

It sometimes happens, however, because of the very nature of social communication, that new opinions circulating among theologians, at times, circulate too soon and in the wrong places. Such opinions, which must not be confused with the authentic doctrine of the Church, should be examined critically. It must also be remembered that the real significance of such theories is often badly distorted by popularization and by the style of presentation used in the media.

III
Attitude of Bishops, Priests and Deacons Toward the Magisterium

What stance should any priest, deacon or bishop adopt in regard to magisterial teaching? How should anyone in holy orders think and speak when faced with a magisterial teaching which he does not understand or does not like or does not accept?

Certainly every priest, deacon and bishop must look upon himself as a *man of the Church*. We are, indeed, men of Christ. Every Christian, however, is to be another Christ. That which sets us apart from the others is our sacrament of orders. We are then placed in special relationship to Christ, and in particular relationship to the Church. We become ministers *of the Church* to the rest of God's people. We are not of our own. We are men of the Church.

Recently there has been considerable obscuring of the understanding by priests of themselves as churchmen. During the past ten years bishops have been made to feel occasionally almost isolated from priests and priest groups—as if somehow an adversary relationship exists between bishops and priests, so that a bishop must defend before priests the teachings of the Church. The unity of the presbyterium is important. And that unity will be stronger when bishops and priests sense themselves as united in holy orders and priestly ministry, together men of the Church. Certainly the relationship is never to be one of management vs. labor, with a senate of priests acting as an adversary labor union.

Considering oneself a man of the Church means considering oneself a man of Chapter Three of the *Constitution on the Church* —as a part of the hierarchy—as well as of Chapter Two. As that Chapter Three states: "Priests, prudent cooperators with the episcopal order as well as its aids and instruments, are called to serve the people of God. They constitute one priesthood with their bishop.. . . Associated with their bishop in a spirit of trust and generosity, priests make him present in a certain sense in the individual local congregation of the faithful . . . " (n. 28)

A second expectation is that the priest—as well as the bishop and deacon—will teach and preach as the Church's doctrine only that which the magisterium has presented as the Church's doctrine.

As men and ministers of the Church we are fully expected to present the Church's teachings — and not our own ideas or speculations, or the ideas and speculations of theologians *qua* theologians. This point — which is the expectation of the official and the general Church — is of paramount importance. The neglect of this principle has led to enormous confusion in the minds of the laity and some priests.

The entire concept of faculties to preach and teach illustrates how the spokesman for the Church must present the Church's doctrine. The bishop cannot give faculties to one who does not preach or teach the Church's doctrine.

How do we know what is the official teaching of the Church on a question of faith or morals? That doctrine is easily learned, especially in this age of rapid communications. A rule of thumb for the Catholic laity is to accept the teaching of a deacon or priest if he is in agreement with the local bishop, and to accept the teaching of the local bishop if he is in agreement with the Pope. And for a priest the rule of thumb is even more simple. The priest (or deacon) follows the teaching of his bishop if that worthy is in concert with the Pope, and in every final instance he follows the Pope. It is now as it was in New Testament times: Cephas is the norm for our doctrine; unity with Peter's successor is essential. The Petrine office is our guarantee of unity of faith and doctrine. And with modern communications so effective, no deacon or priest, no bishop or lay person, need long doubt as to what is Catholic teaching.

The magisterium, an enormous gift to the Church, is there to give guidance and bring peace of mind. We need the magisterium even more in this questioning, challenging, changing modern society.

What of the priest who does not reflect or express the official Church teaching in his public or private utterances? Here precisely is the cause of confusion. The simple Catholic trusts the priest and rightly expects that a priest would not teach a doctrine at variance with that of the local bishop or the Pope. Yet Frank Sheed, that doughty theologian and student of the Catholic scene, writes: "There is hardly a doctrine or practice of the Church I have not heard attacked by a priest" (*Is It the Same Church?*, p. xiv). Small wonder that there has been widespread confusion in the minds of

Catholic faithful. The duty of us ministers of the Church, particularly ordained ones, is to present publicly the Church's teaching, the whole Church's teaching, and (as formal doctrine) nothing but the Church's teaching, so help us God.

A scholion should be added concerning the statements of national hierarchies. What is the authority for a U.S. Catholic of a statement issued by the National Conference of Catholic Bishops here in the United States, or of a statement issued by the bishops of another episcopal conference—say the Canadian bishops, Mexican bishops, Dutch bishops or Indonesian bishops? This is an interesting question, little studied. In the Catholic Church, however, there exist only the various local dioceses or churches, united to Peter's See to make the one universal Catholic Church. Therefore there is no national Church, no U.S. Catholic Church. What then is the authority of the bishops' conference or of a statement adopted by the majority of bishops of a nation? Vatican II's *Decree on the Pastoral Office of Bishops* (n. 38) makes it clear that the juridical force of acts of a national episcopal conference comes not from the conference itself, but from the Holy See and only in certain specified areas. A statement from the NCCB, then, is as I understand it basically for the collegial guidance of the bishop of each local diocese. It has magisterial import only if accepted by the local bishop and taught by him to the local church. A statement from another episcopal conference has no direct relevance for bishops, priests and laity of another nation—and in every instance enjoys validity only if it is in harmony with Peter. This is helpful so that a Catholic does not get "hung up" as to what an NCCB statement said, by how many votes it was accepted, why negative votes were cast—or as to what this or that episcopal conference said, or was said to have said. Your only authentic teachers are your own bishop and the Pope.

Another scholion concerns the importance of what Catholics have traditionally referred to as the *imprimatur*. The magisterium carries a special responsibility to guarantee that Catholic doctrine not be falsely represented. The purity of faith must be safeguarded, and the mechanism for this guarantee is the *imprimatur*—a review of the manuscript by a *censor deputatus* who notifies the bishop that this manuscript holds nothing contrary to Catholic teaching, and the subsequent authorization from the bishop to print the manuscript as an expression of Catholic truth. Like the stamp of the Pure Food and Drug Commission, the *imprimatur* is a guarantee of the doctrinal purity or orthodoxy of the document. The obligation to follow the *imprimatur* procedure is specified in canon law, is incumbent on every Catholic, and in March 1975 was simplified, clarified and re-emphasized.

The *imprimatur* machinery is an expression of the Church's responsibility for sound doctrine. This is not and should never be an optional matter; a Church which does not safeguard what is presented as Catholic doctrine is inviting doctrinal chaos. The revised legislation protects the reasonable expectations of the ordinary Catholic while respecting the legitimate freedom of competent writers. Often in fact the mechanism of the *imprimatur* sets up a dialogue which leads to an improved text.

Any Catholic who does not obtain the *imprimatur* for a book on faith or morals, and any Catholic — especially a priest — who does not personally insist on an *imprimatur* for such texts is on dangerous grounds. Yet amid the confusion of the past several years there has been a neglect of the *imprimatur*, even in some texts which purport to teach the Catholic religion.

It is first for this reason that I find serious fault with a recently published book, *An American Catholic Catechism.* Described as "A Book of Faith for Every Catholic," it has no *imprimatur.* The total book, written by eighteen separate theologians, is most uneven. Some chapters are excellent. Other chapters, especially some on moral theology, are unfortunate. The entire work shows the lack of internal discipline through collaborative criticism and editing. It demonstrates sadly the lack of external discipline through an *imprimatur* granted after needed revisions were made. A chain is as weak as its weakest link. As a presentation of Catholic faith this book has several weak links: its teaching concerning ordination, the indissolubility of marriage, and intrinsic morality; its cavalier attitude toward the magisterium; its presentation on abortion, divorce and remarriage, and contraception; and (at a lower level of importance) its limited views on first confession and First Communion.

The special problem in this book is its occasional attempt to set up "reputable theologians" as a second teaching authority in the Church and its occasional presentation of the hierarchical magisterium as that which a Catholic should in conscience be schooled not to obey rather than to obey (cf. pp. 181-187).

This book illustrates well many of the current problematics in theology today. At the 1974 Theology Consultation in Rome, some of the major moral theologians explained to the bishops that at the present time moral theologians do not agree even with one another in regard to primary principles, so that the bishops have to judge as to what is right and prudent. In view of this current disarray in moral theology, it is incumbent on every priest to be prudent, to follow the magisterium, and to expect that every development in moral theology (as well as in dogmatic theology) be an organic development in keeping with Catholic tradition. To throw a flag down on the field over this book is regrettable. Theologians are at the service of the magisterium — and we are all together in serving Christ's truth and the entire Church. This book penalizes us all.

In his recent Apostolic Exhortation on Reconciliation, Pope Paul expressed clearly the unhealthy results of public dissent from the magisterium by Catholic theologians:

The process that we have described takes the form of doctrinal dissension, which claims the patronage of theological pluralism and is not infrequently taken to the point of dogmatic relativism which in various ways breaks up the integrity of faith. And even when it is not taken as far as dogmatic relativism, this pluralism is at times regarded as a legitimate theological stand that permits the taking up of positions contrary to the authentic magisterium of the Roman Pontiff himself and of the hierarchy of bishops, who are the sole authoritative interpreters of divine revelation contained in sacred tradition and Sacred Scripture.

We recognize that pluralism of research and thought which in various ways investigates and expounds dogma, but without disintegrating its identical objective meaning, has a legitimate right of citizenship in the Church, as a natural component part of its catholicity, and as a sign of the cultural richness and personal commitment of all who belong to it. We recognize also the inestimable values contributed by pluralism to the sphere of Christian spirituality, to ecclesial and religious institutions and to the spheres of liturgical expression and disciplinary norms. These are values which blend together into that "one common aspiration" that "is particularly splendid evidence of the catholicity of the undivided Church."

But what is to be said of that pluralism that considers the faith and its expression not as a common and therefore ecclesial heritage but as an individual discovery made by the free criticism and free examination of the word of God? In fact, without the mediation of the Church's magisterium, to which the apostles entrusted their own magisterium and which therefore teaches "only what has been handed on," the sure union with Christ through the apostles, who are the ones who hand on "what they themselves had received," is compromised. And once perseverance in the doctrine transmitted by the apostles is compromised, what happens is that, perhaps in a desire to avoid the difficulties of mystery, there is a quest for formulas deceptively easy to understand but which dissolve the real content of mystery. Thus there are built up teachings that do not hold fast to the objectivity of the faith or are plainly contrary to it and, what is more, become crystallized side-by-side with concepts that are even mutually contradictory. Furthermore, we must not shut our eyes to the fact that every concession in the matter of identity of faith also involves a lessening of mutual love.

We try hard to understand the root of this situation, and we compare it to the analogous situation in which contemporary civil society is living, a society which is divided by the splintering up into groups opposed one to another. Unfortunately, the Church too seems to be in some degree experiencing the repercussions of this condition. However it should not assimilate what is rather a pathological state. The Church must preserve its original character as a family unified in the diversity of its members. Indeed, it must be the leaven that will help society to react, as was said of the first Christians: "See how much they love one another." It is with this picture of the first community before our eyes—a picture that is certainly not

idyllic, but one that was matured through trials and suffering
— that we call upon all to overcome the illicit and dangerous
differences and to recognize one another as brethren united by
the love of Christ.

It is significant to note how the theologian John Henry
Newman regarded the magisterium. A Catholic parent asked
Newman if her son might enroll at Oxford University, even though
a rescript from the Holy See had cautioned Catholics against
attending Oxford or Cambridge. Newman replied: "Whether the
Pope be infallible or not (Newman's words were written before the
definition of papal infallibility), in any pronouncement he is to be
obeyed. . . . His facts and his warning may all be wrong. His
deliberations may have been biased. He may have been misled. Im-
periousness and craft, tyranny and cruelty may be patent in the conduct of his advisers and instruments. But when he speaks formally
and authoritatively, he speaks as our Lord would have him speak,
and all these imperfections are overruled for the result which our
Lord intends."

Our intellectual attitude toward the ordinary magisterium is indicated in the analogy given us by Christ himself. That analogy is
presented in the final chapter of the Fourth Gospel — undoubtedly
the last Gospel material to be written down. In that Gospel tradition
the apostle Peter, appointed shepherd of the Lord's flock, was told
to care for the old and young, the large and small members of the
flock. The magisterium is the way in which the shepherds of the
Lord's flock give theological care to the Church. The member of the
Lord's flock should, in adult and responsible fashion, be most
grateful for this pastoral guidance — grateful to Christ, whose flock
we are. The first task of the Church and particularly the
magisterium is to serve the man of today, to save man from the
disease of his increasingly secular intelligence.

The *Encyclopedia of Theology* (Seabury, 1975) expresses well
the need for a modern understanding of the magisterium: "In spite
of the individualism of later days, which is still very much the
prevailing temper of the West, a new understanding for the
magisterium of the Church must surely now be possible, in view of
our knowledge of the man of today and tomorrow. Man cannot

possess his truth as an isolated individual, since he is no such thing. . . . But in a post-individualistic epoch new possibilities of understanding may be opened up, even for the understanding of the magisterium of the Church." A better understanding of the Church's magisterium is indeed imperative for many contemporary Catholics. Until that better understanding is reached, confusion will continue.

Criteria for Dissent
in the Church

Juan Arzube

The basic message of Luke 12:15-31 is twofold: (l) we are passing through this life, so we must not cling to material goods as
though they were our lasting possessions; (2) we should have absolute confidence in the God who clothes even the grass in the fields.

Once we realize this, we should not then be merely concerned
about ethereal matters or the salvation of souls, but rather be involved in the liberation of the entire human being: body and soul.

In fact, I believe God wants us to consider life as a challenge, a
challenge to use in a positive and creative way our God-given
talents. If we are to be effective in our roles, I believe we need to
use our talents in a prophetic and positive manner.

A characteristic of a prophet is to point out something
beforehand, that is, before everyone else already accepts it or
believes it, because we are convinced, as a result of prayerful
meditation, of its validity and truth. I would say that we, Catholic
editors and bishops, are usually afraid of being prophetic and
prefer to wait until an issue is perfectly "safe" so that we can then
give it approval and publicity.

As prophets we must be guided by the two factors stressed in
today's Gospel: our responsibility to render an account on the day
of judgment of what we say and do, and a confidence in God's loving concern for us.

We should continuously look at or study moral and
theological concepts, liturgical practices, traditional points of view,

papal encyclicals, and bishops' pastoral letters from different points of view in order to grasp the truth more faithfully in accordance with contemporary knowledge. By studying contradictory opinions we are ultimately going to arrive at a greater conviction that one or the other is the truth, because I am convinced that the truth always wins out in the end and then we can pursue it and teach it with greater conviction.

A couple of years ago I took theology courses in Rome with other bishops from the United States, and as a result of them I became more aware, for instance, of the different way in which we are to accept infallible and non-infallible teachings in the Church.

An infallible definition represents a point of arrival in the development of doctrine, whereas ordinary, non-infallible teaching represents a stage along the way. An infallible definition is a point of no return. On the other hand, history shows us that in the process of the development of doctrine, ordinary teaching has sometimes had to undergo correction and change.

The Second Vatican Council itself shows us some examples of this. Consider, for instance, the difference between Vatican II's *Declaration on Religious Freedom* and the well-known teaching of previous Popes on the obligation of civil authorities in so-called Catholic states to suppress the teaching of so-called "heresy." Consider again the difference between Vatican II's *Decree on Ecumenism* and previous papal encyclicals such as *Mortalium Animos* of Pope Pius XI or even *Mystici Corporis* of Pius XII.

The question naturally arises: How could such development have taken place at Vatican II unless theologians and bishops had been free to be critical of papal teaching, to express views at variance with it, and thus to prepare the ground for the acceptance of their views at the Council? How can one reconcile such necessary freedom to dissent from papal teaching with the obligation to give interior assent to such teaching? It seems impossible to believe that such development of doctrine as has actually taken place through criticisms of papal teaching has taken place only through a "sinful" failure of some theologians to give the required assent to the papal teaching.

There must, then, be room for legitimate criticism of and dissent from the ordinary teaching of the Church, given the very real possibility of the development of the doctrine by way of correction and change of such teaching. To think otherwise is to sink our heads in the sand and hinder the work of the Spirit.

The basic fact involved here is that our faculty of judgment can give internal assent only to what presents itself to our minds as true. The judgment is not a free faculty, as the will is. The will can freely choose to obey even a command that is manifestly absurd, but our judgment is not free to assent to a proposition that the mind judges to be untrue.

Authoritative teaching carries with it a presumption of its truth, but such a presumption no longer has weight in the face of grave reasons to doubt the truth of a proposition. When we are dealing with infallible teaching, our faith in the divine assistance that guarantees the truth of infallible definition should be enough to resolve any doubts that might arise as to the truth of the defined dogma. But in the case of ordinary magisterium we have no such guarantee to help us resolve grave doubts that might arise. One simply cannot give sincere internal assent to a proposition in the face of enduring grave doubts as to its truth.

Under what conditions, then, is dissent from ordinary Church teaching legitimate? I submit, under the following conditions:

1. that those who dissent are competent to have an informed opinion in the matter;

2. that they have made a sincere and sustained prayerful effort to assent to the teaching;

3. that, despite such a sincere and sustained effort, the reasons for a contrary opinion remain so convincing as to make it truly impossible to assent.

This attitude is not something radical and new but in fact is sustained by and goes back to the time when St. Paul opposed St. Peter, as is told us in Paul's Letter to the Galatians 2:11-21, which reads in part, "But when Cephas came to Antioch I opposed him to his face . . . and with him the rest of the Jews acted insincerely, so even Barnabas was carried away by their insincerity. So when I saw that they were not straightforward about the truth of the Gospel, I said to Cephas before them all: 'If you, though a Jew, live like a Gentile and not like a Jew, how can you compel the Gentiles to live like Jews?' "

I am sure that even though Paul opposed Peter in this one instance he would not advocate dissent as a matter of practice. I, likewise, am not trying to promote dissent, but rather to give a perspective to its reality in the Church and our responsibility to consider it as something positive and constructive when it comes from a serious and competent source.

Time does not permit me to go on, but this should suffice to make us realize what a challenge it is to live in the twentieth century. Let us accept this challenge in which God invites us to use our talents in a prophetic and positive manner, and thus bring his message of faith, hope and love to all peoples.

The Magisterium and Theology

Robert Coffy

Before embarking on this specific topic of the relationship between bishops and theologians, I would like to make two preliminary remarks.

1. I will be very brief on the theological foundations of the magisterium, because I introduce my theme in the frame of the wider one of bishops as servants of the faith and would like to avoid repetition.

2. In this delicate question, I will try to place myself on the theologians' side. I know that these do not need a bishop to take up their defense and they are quite capable of defending themselves. But, as a bishop addressing bishops, I thought it useful to adopt this stance. Since it is a matter of picking up again the dialogue between bishops and theologians, it seems right that I examine our patterns of action and the context in which we are called to act.

I therefore merely offer food for thought to help us arrive at the right analysis.

I

An Overview of the Current Situation

During these last years, collaboration between bishops and theologians has encountered considerable difficulties. These are not peculiar to any single country but seem to belong to the whole Church. We here face a phenomenon which is independent of the situation of particular states and of individual personalities. It is so widely spread as to warrant the conclusion that, at this moment of history, it emerges as a basic problem of the relationship between the magisterium and theology. And it is quite possible that the magisterium may be called to exercise its ministry in a relatively novel manner.

Manifestations of This "Conflict"

We shall first examine a few examples of these difficulties and consider four manifestations of the "conflict" between those responsible for the magisterium and theologians. There are others, no doubt, but I will focus on those which, to one with a French cultural background like mine, seem to be the most characteristic. I will list them briefly.

1. *Theologians vindicate a certain amount of freedom vis-à-vis the magisterium.* In 1968, four theologians sent to the Cardinal Secretary of State a letter, later signed by over a thousand theologians from fifty-three different countries, in which they asked for the creation of the international commission of theologians envisaged by the 1967 Synod. They also expressed the desire for more freedom in theological research. The fact must not be given undue weight. One must admit, however, that it exposed latent feelings and that it stepped up the movement to request wider freedom for those engaged in theological studies.

2. *A difficulty in the discussion: the different theologies.* Theology is no longer marked by the unity it displayed in the past but now expresses many diverse points of view. The consequent diversity has important implications for the degree of collaboration existing between bishops and theologians on the local level. When, for example, bishops in plenary session undertake a basic study, they call for the help of theologians who seem to them best equipped to deal with the subject in question. But in their choice a few read an unexpressed intention to select those theologians who somehow would support the bishops in their particular theological views. One could make the same remark concerning other episcopal conferences who normally work with their theologians. And hence

there emerges the possible accusation, which certainly does not help their relationship: bishops select experts in the light of their particular theological options when they should be willing to be criticized and contradicted on them.

3. *A parallel magisterium.* It is clear that an article in a review or in the wider press, signed by a theologian or by a religious journalist, often receives a better hearing than a pastoral letter or a pontifical document. The language used and the problem posed are often more in line with the real concerns of the people than the style and wording of episcopal or pontifical documents. In the situation, many Christians accept the contents of these articles as proposals of faith for today when, in reality, they are only valid as working hypotheses. There is thus a teaching of the faith, presented in modern language, which escapes the magisterium of the Church. As regards such teaching bishops usually do not intervene but when they do they usually express reservations or warnings. This has the effect of identifying the magisterium as a repressive organism. This image of the magisterium does not improve the state of the relationship between bishops and theologians. On the other hand there develops a situation which does not make the mission of bishops, or their relationship with theologians, any easier: the magisterium no longer enjoys the monopoly of the teaching of the faith.

4. *The normative force of practice.* We live in an age of surveys and statistics. These are spread by the mass media and become carriers of new life styles. The action patterns of a large number of persons, as presented by the press, often become norms of behavior. This makes the intervention of bishops difficult and distorts their relationship with theologians once each party does not see the new fact from the same angle. This presents us with the problem of the *consensus fidelium.*

The Causes of the "Conflict"

One can, no doubt, point to other expressions of the differences between bishops and theologians. We will not delay over these, preferring to delve into the causes which explain the conflict situation, in order to outline some form of remedy or to come to a better understanding and be better able to grasp the real reasons which render collaboration between bishops and theologians more difficult now than it has ever been.

It seems to me that we are here facing two complexes of causes, one connected with the situation of theology, the other with that of the magisterium. The first complex of causes is a new status for theology, in response to the acculturation of the faith.

1. *The difficulties of theology today.* Today theologians face a difficult task. Humanity is currently experiencing a major cultural change, whose various elements would take too long to list. For believers, this means a certain degree of disorientation and a demand for a new language to express the faith. Christians want to confess, live and proclaim their faith in the emerging culture which constantly challenges them. And so they turn to their theologians and to their pastors, obliging them to respond to their needs. To meet this current demand, these must move forward from the mere repetition of formulas and from their personal comments on these, to search for fresh formulations. In other words, theology moves *from the state of a discipline* which is taught through the repetition and the perfection of formulas inherited from the past *to a stance of research* and of relative innovation.

Theology, in fact, is "the faith understanding itself, the rule for adequately expressing the revealed message" to contemporary men who live in specific cultural contexts. Now these men no longer live in the cultural worlds which witnessed the development of the existing propositions of faith and of the major theological systems. And it is quite normal that exploration becomes the characteristic stance of theology today. Still, the development of a new faith language is a delicate operation. It should cause no surprise that theologians do not hit the right formulas at once. Theologians would like that, in this difficult task, no one accuse them of ill will. They require a certain amount of freedom.

And they become the more sensitive to this freedom, the less they work at their desks as they struggle more with the concrete situations of dialogue with pastors, Christians, non-believers and experts of the various disciplines. For example, they help pastors reflect on the doctrinal implications of their pastoral practice and on their specific commitments. They are aware that they have to be very careful with a theology which justifies pastoral decisions, because pastoral work is only a *locus theologicus* to the extent that it reflects the discernment of spirits in the light of the Gospel. They are also not always responsible for the use that certain Christians in search of novelty make of their doctrinal insights, often turning working hypotheses into dogmas of faith. On the other hand, theologians like to move with pastors and committed Christians so that they themselves discover what, in their activity, is really at stake. They like to have the right to come, vis-à-vis pastors and Christians, to an understanding of their situations and of their problems. Such *moving together* and such *understanding* do not necessarily imply *approval*. They claim the freedom to face the new problems as these emerge and to formulate fresh working hypotheses. And here a conflict with the magisterium often develops as Christians who live in other situations do not face the same problems and reject the working hypotheses. It then happens that they ask bishops to make pronouncements on things they consider heretical but which, in fact, are only attempts at new expressions of the faith. If the bishops intervene, they are seen as total strangers to the problems. And this often happens because of their way of intervening. Hence emerges a serious source of conflict between bishops, theologians and pastors.

2. *The theological process*: There was a time when theology was the queen of the sciences. That was a time when humanity enjoyed a religious culture. Today the status of theology as a science is contested not only by unbelievers but also by some Christians who do not consider the development of rigorous reasoning about God as feasible for modern man and who thus proclaim the end of all theologies.

Faced with these situations, theologians strive to justify the possibility of theological investigation. But they are aware that their reasoning will be credible only to the extent that they submit it to rigorous and methodical verification.

3. *Theological pluralism*: Finally, one must add that the strains on the relationship between bishops and theologians also derive from the so-called *theological pluralism*. Different schools of theology existed in former times. The various and often famous

disputes which they engaged in are well known. But in this plurality of schools Karl Rahner says: "One was convinced of one's knowledge of the thought of one's opponents, of their terminology, of their premises, of the tone of the language used and this immediate, spontaneous, mutual understanding, from one side as well as from the other. The differences, if any, did not involve reflection." One can add that differences were regulated by the dictum *in necessariis unitas, in dubiis libertas, in omnibus charitas.* In other words, the plurality of theological schools was set against a background *of one common culture.*

The contemporary scene is so different that one can speak of a qualitative change. The term "theological pluralism" has come to define the present situation. One is aware that, during the last Synod, the Pope showed reservations in this respect. He considered it dangerous to speak of "theologies diversified according to continent and culture." Notwithstanding this, he proposed that this problem, with others, find "better definition, further study, completion and deepening"; without pronouncing ourselves on the question, we realize that, in fact, theology no longer appeals to one philosophy but to various philosophies. On the other hand it is obliged to take note of what the human sciences have to say of man. But what do these say? The answer is not univocal. There is an explosion of languages which speak of man. Theology is no longer a system which develops in its own orbit. It pays attention to what men experience, to their commitments (especially political commitments). What men are living through has many facets. How, then, can one theology respond to so many different situations? It is clear that we have moved quite far from the time when theologians understood one another as they debated the *quaestiones disputatae.* Do they understand one another today? In such a situation, how can the magisterium intervene? By selecting a theology to the detriment or condemnation of another? How can it judge without studying, in dialogue, the problem formulations of each theology? These are hot issues. Can they receive a clear answer today?

The second complex of causes is the situation of the magisterium. I have examined the causes of current difficulties existing between representatives of the magisterium and theologians by focusing on the present state of theology. The situation becomes worse when one embarks on an analysis of the context in which the magisterium is exercised. Indeed, this very exercise is often contested, and on several grounds. Of these, I will highlight four major ones.

1. In the Church, the magisterium is an authority—and we know how sharply criticized today is the way in which authority is exercised. We here face a particular aspect of a general phenomenon. Theologians do not deny the existence of a magisterium in the Church and they do not challenge its authority. What they claim is that this ecclesial ministry be exercised in new ways. Specifically they refuse to accept that there be condemnations without previous dialogue. Briefly, I would say that the difficulties encountered by the magisterium in carrying out its mission are the same as those experienced by people in the ministry of authority. They are, perhaps, more formidable. One of the reasons for this can be found in the nature of the interventions of the last century and of those of the beginning of this one. It is enough to recall the "syllabus" and the various pronouncements of the magisterium on the question of modernism. These interventions were clumsy and excessive. With more understanding and discussion, certain dramatic situations could have been avoided. It is certain that in this crisis the magisterium damaged its credibility. The trust people had in it suffered.

2. The situation gains in complexity as one accepts theological pluralism—and how can one do otherwise when faced by facts? To accept pluralism is to accept that the faith can legitimately express itself in different theologies. As one becomes aware that the faith never exists in a pure state, one recognizes that every profession of faith necessarily implies a theology. There can be no clear borderline between the faith and the theological intelligence of the faith. This explains the reaction of theologians when faced with certain interventions of the magisterium. They have the impression that the magisterium imposes on them its particular theology. What they ask is that it make explicit its theological options and abstain from presenting them as the only possible way of expressing the faith.

3. A third source of difficulties encountered by the

magisterium in the exercise of its ministry is more basic. Its correct presentation would require long explanations. I here limit myself to recalling it. It is a question of the relation between revelation and the magisterium which, of course, is commissioned to guarantee the authenticity of its transmission. This original thrust of the relationship has somehow changed and we must be aware of the fact.

Since the eighteenth century, in fact, apologetics developed in such a way as to focus on the defense of the specificity of the Christian religion vis-à-vis the theism which was rejecting positive revelation in order to come to some form of natural religion. It thus became a question of establishing the historical fact of the revelation, a fact rejected by the other side. To prove the historicity of revelation, apologetics resorted to external motives like miracles and the verification of prophecy. The act of faith in revelation is reasonable because the fact of revelation can be demonstrated "scientifically." And so apologetics created a kind of separation between the very fact of revelation and its meaning. The truth of revelation was not justified on its own merits but through something different from it — that is, the arguments which establish that it did happen. As a normal and — we can really say it — necessary consequence of this manner of demonstrating the credibility of the faith, people began to focus on demonstrating the need of the divine magisterium of the Catholic Church. It was from this magisterium that the credibility of the teaching of the Church was seen to derive directly. And so one arrived at a progressive consolidation of the magisterium of the Church, at times presented as the only basis for the credibility of the faith. One even forgot to recall that it was God's truth that was the final motive of faith.

To the extent that the magisterium was presented as the only basis of the credibility of the act of faith, it was normal for theology to develop from the premises of the more recent definitions or propositions of the magisterium and to go on to demonstrate their validity from Scripture and tradition. One recognizes here the model of the manuals of theology used in our major seminaries.

It seems that we can find, in this brief sketch, one of the reasons which explain both the place now occupied by the magisterium and the limitations imposed on its relevance. We also find here one of the reasons why the interventions of the magisterium have been so numerous and frequent. Today, however, the context is quite different and the magisterium-revelation relationship is being interpreted in a new manner. We live in an atheistic context which demands a clarification of the meaning of revelation. As a test of this change, we desire to move from apologetics to fundamental theology. This passage shows that one no longer appeals to external proofs to establish the truth of Christianity but, without ignoring those, one strives to demonstrate that revealed truth is the truth about man. The truth of revelation has no other justification but its very content. Revelation touches on the most basic aspirations of man and provides human existence, history, the universe, with ultimate and mysterious meaning. It makes man true. Henceforth, the effort required consists not just in guaranteeing the fact of revelation but in bringing to light the wealth of meaning contained in revelation for man.

The magisterium, consequently, responds by decentralizing and by focusing on the word of God, whose servant it now wants to be. And it does it in a somewhat novel way. For it must henceforth justify the quality of the motives it offers by starting from their very relevance. It must justify its interventions by stating its reasons for doing it, rather than by appealing to the formal right of intervention (which, of course, is not excluded).

4. A fourth source of difficulties encountered by the magisterium is still more basic than the preceding one. It is a matter of a deep change in the way of our approach to revealed truth and in our way of teaching it. Such a topic does not readily lend itself to a summary presentation. Indeed, this could appear more of a caricature. I therefore apologize for my formulation of the matter.

During the last century, no doubt under the influence of Platonism, revelation was conceived as the discovery of eternal truths which existed in their own right. These truths were considered as so many objective realities which, it was thought, could be translated into formulas, more or less effectively, even though this was never said in so many words. There existed propositions of the truth which were thought to be immutable. The role of the magisterium was identified as that of guaranteeing the correspondence of the formulas and the eternal truths. To put it sharply, truths were conceived as coming from above and as lending themselves to definitive translations into formulas quite capable of expressing them perfectly. In this question, the magisterium could draw the line between what was truth and what was error.

The question now appears in another light. With the Council behind us, it seems that the historical dimensions of revealed truth are now better recognized. Truth is discovered in history—and it happens gradually, bit by bit. Revelation is not the transmission of immutable formulas, or statements. It is a mystery: the mystery of God. That is also the mystery of man, already totally communicated in Christ but which can never be stated perfectly. It belongs to each generation, by bowing to the Scriptures understood and lived in the living tradition of the Church, to delve into this mystery of Christ as God and Man to show its inexhaustible depth.

All has been revealed in Christ, and revelation has been closed with the conclusion of the apostolic age. But revelation will never cease to bring out its wealth in this very becoming of history.

It emerges, from all this, that the ministry of the magisterium does not lend itself to an easy activation. Its interventions cannot pretend to be as clear-cut as they sometimes attempted to be. The magisterium cannot limit itself to the repetition of formulas inherited from the past. It must admit, when faced by the problem of its relationship to the Absolute of the mystery of Christ, the relativity of every formulation. Perhaps it could usefully foresee new styles of intervention.

And here my frame of reference begins to fail. I stressed the difficulties and the problems and I did it on purpose—to stimulate reflection. By now it should be crystal clear that, were there no difficulties, we would not be able to discuss them.

II

THE FUNCTION OF THE MAGISTERIUM
AND THE FUNCTION OF THEOLOGY

It is easier to point to the defects of the functioning of a social organism and to discover their causes than to state how it could be made to function smoothly. Consequently, this second section of my article will be briefer than the first. In effect we are here trying to seek together how to establish better guidelines for improving the state of collaboration between bishops and theologians. I can only show some ways our quest could take—and I will do so by recalling a few concepts of general application. I do not have to say, of course, that any criticism of the proposals offered is warmly welcome. I further state that these proposals take note of the situation just described. I will not pause to reaffirm recognized principles but will simply seek to show in which context they can be applied.

1. *The functions of the magisterium and of theology as quite distinct but also complementary*: The statement of this principle offers no difficulties and should find no objections. It remains to be seen, however, how far the effective performance of these two distinct functions, once we move into it, makes the establishment of the right frontier any easier. In point of fact, these have never been clearly traced. It would take too long to go into the history of the relationship between the magisterium and theology. We simply take note that historically many models have emerged, each with its particular advantages and disadvantages. Quite frequently , in practice, the relationship will escalate into conflict. Just to give some examples, we can remember that, during the first centuries, the majority of the Fathers and Doctors were also bishops and thus simultaneously guardians of the apostolic tradition, preachers and theologians. The convergence of these different roles in the same persons provided them with that authority which one continues to invoke even today. During the Middle Ages, when theology adopted the systematic model, the distinction became more frequent. The universities, however, often continued to perform the magisterial function. Closer to us, with, for example, Pius XII, we do not clearly see where the frontier between theologians and the representatives of the magisterium lies. These are only a few cases from a very complex story.

Even if difficult to define, the frontier between the magisterium and theology does exist, and, at least theoretically, we can take note of the distinction between the two functions.

The purpose of theology is to develop reasoning on the faith, reasoning of the scientific type. This last quality does not coincide with experimental or deductive activity but refers us to conscience reflecting on the intellectual steps, accessible to theologians and often taken by them as they seek to clarify the positive side of the faith in a given culture. Theology is not a science in the strict sense of the term. But its inner functioning belongs to the scientific category. Its reasoning is not cut off from time. It bears on contemporary man. And so theology today is the privileged ground for dialogue between the Church which professes faith in the Lord Jesus Christ and the world to which the same Church must proclaim this faith. To say that theology develops a faith discourse for modern man is equivalent to highlighting the specific character of its current effort. Is not this an activity which somehow is also pastoral? If theology remains scientific research, it can no longer be an activity of people tied to their desks.

The function of the magisterium is to ensure that the testimony given by the contemporary Church to Jesus Christ is the testimony of the apostles. It can only perform this function if it appeals to theology. In fact, there is no statement of the faith which is not also an understanding of this same faith in a given culture. If the frontier is difficult to fix, then it becomes vital to promote effective and habitual collaboration between the magisterium and theology.

Let us not confuse frontiers. Let us not confuse literary genera. A product of the magisterium does not belong to the same literary type adopted by the current theological effort. But the two functions remain complementary and the two products relate and refer to one another.

2. *The specific roles of the magisterium and of theology*: It could be necessary to commission a study of the term magisterium. Up to Pius IX it seems that the word meant authority in general. During the nineteenth century it acquired the specific meaning of doctrinal authority, and this happened in a given historical context in which faith was seen as, above all, intellectual acquiescence to a body of truths. And thus emerged a limitation of the meaning of the concept of magisterium. This now had the function of watching over the rectitude of the formulations of the faith. In a form closer to the truth, the faith is today presented as an assent of the whole being to the mystery of salvation. It is an assent to an act of God in our world, an action which simultaneously manifests and makes

present and establishes a new reality of a divine origin. This means that the truths of faith are no longer considered as mere conceptual constructs. They must tie up with the experiences and with the deeper aspirations of men.

By placing the magisterium in this frame of understanding the faith, we offer it a function which spans and embraces deeper and wider realities. The ministry of the magisterium, then, does not only seek the right expression of the faith but also the right way of praying, of behaving, of living the faith. The role of bishops can then be defined as that of "the heralds of the word of God," that is, that of watching (*episcopos*) that this word be proclaimed, and proclaimed in full fidelity to the Scriptures, that it be understood by contemporary men, that it be professed by Christians, that it be prayed and lived. In this way the ministry of the magisterium is not reduced to safeguarding doctrinal rectitude (orthodoxy) but extended to guarding over practical righteousness (orthopraxis), as in the celebration of the faith (liturgy).

The role of the magisterium can be summed up in the three words of *Christus Dominus*: moderator, promoter, guardian.

Moderator: the term is all-embracing. It means that the Pope and the bishops bear special responsibilities in the ecclesial mission of handing on the faith. These are made specific by the other terms, promoter and guardian.

Promoter: the magisterium enacts a positive role. It must act in such a way that the faith is taught and transmitted to men of all cultures. "Bishops must propose Christian doctrine in ways adapted to the needs of the moment, responding to the difficulties and to the problems which rend men's hearts" (*Christus Dominus*).

Guardian: the same quotation continues: "They must watch over this doctrine, teaching the very faithful to defend and spread it."

The magisterium is charged with watching so that the faith taught is that which comes to us from the apostles, through the long series of witnesses which constitutes the living tradition of the Church.

In the current situation, it seems to me indispensable that the mission of the magisterium be described by the two words "promoter" and "guardian."

The best way to guard is to promote, because fidelity to the testimony of the apostles doubtlessly today consists in finding new formulations of the faith, as well as in finding new ways of living and celebrating it.

The role of theologians is different. The specificity of theology seems to me to be well pinned down by the phrase "reasoning of a scientific kind," with all that this entails: knowledge of the word of God, of tradition, of the cultural contexts, of methodology. It rests, besides, with theologians to question the praxis and the commitments of Christians and to do it day in, day out, especially now. The different theologies, whether they deal with politics, revolution or development, demonstrate this point. In the process, theologians, on different levels, with different methods, and in different languages (their technical jargon), are obliged to become themselves also promoters and guardians — that is, to search how to proclaim, pray and live the faith today and to do it in full fidelity to the apostolic testimony.

To pin down the specificity of these two functions implies, simultaneously, the affirmation of their complementarity. The magisterium without theology runs the risk of repeating to modern man meaningless formulas. We also know the role played by theology, historically, in developing dogmatic formulas. On the other hand, theologians who today are obliged to specialize run the risk of ignoring the incidence of their working hypotheses and even of sowing confusion in the faith of Christians (when they propose formulations which these cannot appreciate with the required competence), should they lose contact with the magisterium. They also risk telling meaningless things when they focus on the too specific. They finally risk heresy, should the magisterium not be there to remind them of ecclesial communion and to draw their attention to the demands of helping Christian people live and profess their faith.

3. *Magisterium and theology at the service of the word of God for the service of the people of God:* To foster a spirit of collaboration between bishops and theologians, one must avoid repeating that theology is at the service of the magisterium. It is much better to state that the magisterium and theology are both at the service of the word of God, which must be announced for the service of the people of God, which must, in its turn, profess, celebrate, pray and

proclaim this same word. This does not mean putting the magisterium and theology on the same level or eliminating the specificity of each. It only means stressing their complementarity and the need for permanent collaboration. It means a refusal to put the magisterium and theology in the situation of a power struggle or of confrontation. It means one way of refusing to turn theology into an accelerator and the magisterium into a brake. As I have already stated, the magisterium, with its responsibilities of promoting and guarding the faith, must move in such a way that this task is assumed by the whole Christian people and, in the first place, by theologians. To recognize the function of an ecclesial institution does not mean that it is the only one that must perform it. It means that it must act in such a way that it be taken care of by the Christian people.

Magisterium and theology serve the word; both are called to adopt an attitude of welcome to this word, of obedience to it. They serve the people of God and are thus placed within this people. The ministry entrusted to the magisterium is general and all-embracing. It is oriented toward the whole process of the proposition of the faith. The service entrusted to theology follows a diversified course. Without the magisterium theology could be shattered and confined to limited and juxtaposed affirmations. Faith is found only in the global faith of the Church. It falls on the magisterium, therefore, to keep theology to its place and help it enact its specific role. I can only take one case, and just as an example: that of the quest for a new language of faith, a point which concerns us all. If theology has to play a primary role in this field, it is not going to be the sole actor. The quest has spiritual and intellectual dimensions. The language of faith, to be found in fidelity to Jesus Christ, cannot but be the result of a spiritual experience of living ecclesial communities incarnated in the very heart of modern culture—but of a spiritual experience that reflects on its own self. Such an effort implies "praying well" the faith, "acting well" on the faith, "stating well" the faith. The role of the magisterium (promoter and guardian) embraces all the spiritual and apostolic experiences of communities now "happening" in the Church. It means helping them check with one another. In this "confrontation," theologians play a very important role—but they are not the only counterparts of the magisterium.

The "spirituals" also have their place as do the committed Christians at work in building up a better world.

The outcome of all this is that the last word has to belong to the magisterium. Its institution by Christ is the unifying factor of it all. It is through it that every act of faith becomes an ecclesial act of faith. On this point we again find the hierarchy as the guarantee of the apostolic faith and of ecclesial community.

Magisterium and theology serve the people of God not in a passive sense—or, at least, they must cease to do it this way. This implies "dialogue between the magisterium-theology and the Christian People." It is here that we can place the "sensus fidelium," taking note, in the process, that even this concept today takes on a new meaning. There is a "sensus fidelium" because the Holy Spirit, who remains the interior Master, is at work in all Christians to lead them to the whole truth and to preserve them in their fidelity to Jesus Christ. Many insights and developments of the mystery of faith find their origins in the Christian people. The devotion to the Virgin, the current teaching on matrimony and the role of the laity are all good examples of this. One must, however, be aware that the faithful are becoming less of a mass of people who preserve, by repeating them, formulas inherited from the past. Christians are provoked by unbelief and by atheism. They are asking questions, and they like to know how to account for their faith. They want to know—and today they can—why the mass media spread expressions of faith and reflections on the Christian mysteries. The "sensus fidelium" has often been seen in the context of a time when the faithful people did not have other teachings on the faith besides that of the ordinary magisterium of bishops. Today journalists write of matters of faith and are read. There also exist various movements which promote reflection in the faith on their action and their commitments—and not always in line with the magisterium. The "sensus fidelium" becomes active. And there emerges a new demand on the ministry of the magisterium: to ensure its mission, it must, as far as possible, be present wherever research is in progress, first to listen, then to discern—and for this discernment it needs the light of theology.

III
CONCLUSION

To conclude, I would like to submit practical proposals. The volume of documents produced by the magisterium is considerable. It originates from various sources: the Holy See, plenary assemblies, bishops' conferences and individual bishops. Before this mass of documents, a question emerges: Does not the sheer volume of documents produced by the magisterium harm the credibility of its interventions?

In an age marked by research, as ours is, we must certainly intervene, and, at times, quite forcefully. But we must do it to recall basic certitudes. Should not allowance be made, in many cases, for that slow process which is indispensable for ideas to come to maturity? As regards the direct relationship with theologians, I would make the following points:

1. The magisterium must promote theological effort which today appears as a primary need. And so we must invest in the formation of theologians. We must also think of the formation of lay theologians.

2. It is important to encourage meetings between bishops and theologians. Once these acquire the habit of working together, their relationships and their work will meet with less problems, especially when the hot issues oblige them to collaborate closely. Here the bishops' secretariats could play an important role by promoting such meetings.

3. Finally, even if bishops lack the time to become specialists, should not some of them affirm, without any complexes, their theological options?

The Church's Magisterium in the Field of Morality

Giovanni B. Guzzetti

GENERAL CONSIDERATIONS

When we look at the teaching of the Church in the area of morality, we can readily see that its tasks in this area come down to four: faithful custody of divine teaching, suitable exposition, authentic interpretation, and timely application. All of this is carried out with special assistance from the Holy Spirit. That assistance can go so far as to guarantee the infallibility of the Church's teaching and hence oblige the faithful to loyal adherence.

Faithful Custody

Even the moral doctrine proposed by the Church is not generally something the Church has discovered or happened upon. It is a divine gift rather than the fruit of the Church's understanding, diligence, or hard work. The Church has the duty of faithfully guarding this doctrine.

Let me mention only St. Paul here, who followed Jesus, and his repeated insistence that he was only preaching what he had heard from the Father. St. Paul repeatedly points out that he is transmitting only what he himself has received. To the Corinthians he writes: "I received from the Lord what I also delivered to you"

(1 Cor. 11:23). To Timothy he writes: "I charge you to keep the commandment unstained and free from reproach until the appearance of our Lord Jesus Christ. . . . O Timothy, guard what has been entrusted to you. Avoid the godless chatter and contradictions of what is falsely called knowledge, for by professing it some have missed the mark as regards the faith" (1 Tim. 6:14-20). And we find the same sentiment reiterated by Pius XII: "The Church has received the deposit of eternal truth from God."[1]

For that reason the moral teaching of the Church today is what it was yesterday, and tomorrow it will be what it is today. In every age the Church simply offers to its age the immutable divine teaching, thus obeying Christ's command: "Go therefore and make disciples of all nations . . . teaching them to observe all that I have commanded you . . . " (Mt. 28:19-20).

Suitable Exposition

Recall the way Christ exposed his messiahship. He worked miracles and told people not to talk about them. He wrung a confession from Peter, then "strictly charged the disciples to tell no one that he was the Christ" (Mt. 16:20).

Recall the practice of the early Church from the third to the fifth centuries, which has come to be known as the *disciplina arcani* since the eighteenth century. It involved being very tight-lipped, or even completely silent, about the sacred rites and dogmas of the new religion when talking to outsiders.

Coming closer to Church practice in recent times, we recall the differing ways in which Leo XIII on the one hand and both Pius XI and Pius XII on the other hand dealt with the issue of government intervention in the economy. In *Rerum Novarum* Leo XIII urged government intervention: "Governments . . . should first of all abet national prosperity generally through the whole complex of political laws and institutions, regulating and administering the state in such a way that public and private prosperity is the natural result. This, in fact, is the service of civil prudence and the duty of rulers."[2]

By contrast, Pius XI and Pius XII warned against excessive government intervention. Said Pius XI: "It is clear and demonstrably true from history that, due to changes in circumstances, many things once demanded of small associations can now be carried out only by large associations. Nevertheless that very important principle of social philosophy still stands: just as it is illicit to take away from individuals and entrust to the community what individuals can do with their own resources and efforts, so it is not right to entrust to the larger and higher society what smaller and lower communities can do. . . . Such a course does grave damage, and it overturns proper societal order. . . . "[3] And so, in talking about the corporative setup of fascism, the Pope went on to express his fear of excessive government intervention: "With good reason some fear that the state is substituting itself for freely undertaken activity instead of limiting itself to adequate assistance and help when needed."[4]

One could put it this way. In proposing the unique and immutable Christian message, the Church acts like an intermediary between an optimist and a pessimist, each of whom has covered half of a journey and still has half to go. It reminds the optimist that half of the journey still lies ahead, while telling the pessimist that half of the journey is already over.

Authentic Interpretation

With regard to the Eucharist, we might recall interpretation of the Johannine passage: "Unless you *eat the flesh* of the Son of man and *drink his blood* . . . " (Jn. 6:53). What do the words mean? What was Christ's thinking exactly? When it comes to the Eucharist specifically, must one receive Communion under both species in order to be faithful to Christ's words? Or did his words simply mean that one must partake of the Eucharist, no determination being made as to whether it should be done under both species or one, and which one in the latter case?

We know that Christendom long remained divided over the correct answer to those questions and over its evaluation of the Western Church's practice of giving Communion under the species of bread alone. We also know that Trent stepped in to play a definitive role here. In the first and second canons of its twenty-first session it established that neither for lay people nor the clergy did there exist a divine precept or an obligation binding for salvation to receive Communion under both species and it asserted that the Latin Church's practice of giving Communion under the species of bread alone was grounded on correct and reasonable motives.[5]

Coming much closer to today, we need only recall the two well-known sections of the encyclical *Humanae Vitae*. Section 11 says: "Recalling human beings to the observance of the norms of natural law as interpreted by its constant doctrine, the Church teaches that every matrimonial act must remain open to the transmission of life." Section 14 says: "In conformity with these basic principles of the human and Christian vision of matrimony, we must once again declare that absolutely to be ruled out as a licit way of regulating births is the direct interruption of the generative process already initiated, and especially directly willed and procured abortion, even for therapeutic reasons. Equally ruled out, as the Church's magisterium has stated more than once, is direct sterilization of either the man or the woman, be it temporary or permanent. Also ruled out is any action which, in anticipation of the conjugal act, in its carrying out, or in the unfolding of its natural consequences, proposes as means or end to render procreation impossible."

Thus the Church has exercised the function of acting as the authentic interpreter of divine law. As a matter of fact, it has expressly defended that function. Talking about Sacred Scripture in *Humani Generis* (August 12, 1950), Pius XII reminded people that "together with these sacred fonts [God] has also given his Church the living magisterium to elucidate and develop those truths that are contained only obscurely and implicitly in the deposit of faith."[6] In *Humanae Vitae* Paul VI had this to say in talking about natural law: "None of the faithful would wish to deny that the Church's magisterium has the competence to interpret the natural moral law as well. It is simply incontestable, as our predecessors have repeatedly pointed out, that Jesus Christ, in communicating his authority to Peter and the apostles and sending them out to teach his commandments to all nations, constituted them authentic guardians and interpreters of the whole moral law: i.e., not only of the Gospel law but also of the natural law. The latter, too, is an expression of God's will. Faithful execution of it is equally necessary for salvation" (n. 4).

Timely Application

Let us go back to the example of the Eucharist. Christ talks about the necessity of eating his flesh and drinking his blood, but he does not say how often it is to be done. Should it be done once in a lifetime, as we do in the case of those festive meals which accompany and characterize fundamental decisions in life—e.g., marriage and priestly ordination—or should it be done every day, just as we eat and drink every day to sustain our lives? And how many times each day, if that is true: once, twice, three times, five times?

Here again the Church has intervened. It has established that Communion must be received no less than once a year, unless special circumstances exist. It has established that Communion is not to be received more than once a day, unless special conditions exist. And it has delicately prodded people toward more frequent Communion, indeed toward daily reception.

Another example, in the social sphere this time, might be noted here. Remember how Leo XIII forbade Catholic workers to get involved with socialists in the formation and activity of labor unions: "Clearly a wide variety of associations, particularly of workers, are on the increase today more than ever before. This is not the place to consider the origin, scope, and operation of many of the latter associations. But there is widespread opinion, confirmed by many indicators, that most of the time they are directed by hidden leaders and organized in a way that runs counter to the Christian spirit and the public welfare. Exercising monopoly power over industries, these leaders force those who refuse to go along with them to pay a heavy price. In such a situation, Christian workers have only two alternatives. Either they must join associations that jeopardize their religion, or else they must form their own associations and thus join forces to escape such unjust and intolerable oppression. If they do not wish to jeopardize the supreme good for human beings, how can they help but choose the second alternative?"[7]

In the socio-political sphere we cannot help but recall the prohibition against collaborating with communism. This prohibition was solemnly sanctioned in the encyclical *Divini Redemptoris* (March 19, 1937) and forcefully reiterated by the decree of the Holy Office on July 1, 1949. In the encyclical Pius XI told bishops: "See to it, venerable brothers, that the faithful do not let themselves be deceived. Communism is intrinsically perverse. In no area would there be room for collaboration between it and those who wish to save Christian civilization."[8] The Holy Office declared that it was illicit "to enroll in communist parties, support them, publish or spread or read their books, periodicals, and papers, or collaborate with them by contributing writings."[9]

Thus the Church has stepped in to apply principles to various situations and impose an obligation of compliance on the faithful. Indeed the Church has expressly defended that practice, upholding its right to intervene in the area of application as well. On this matter it will be helpful to recall a noteworthy section of John XXIII's encyclical *Pacem in Terris* where he commented on the relationship between false philosophical teachings about human nature and life and historical movements deriving from them:

False philosophical teachings regarding the nature, origin, and destiny of the universe and humanity cannot be equated with historical movements having economic, social, cultural, or political aims, not even when the movements originated from the philosophical teachings and still draw inspiration from the latter. This is so because the teachings always remain the same once they have been elaborated and defined. By contrast, the movements, operating in constantly evolving historical situations, cannot help but be subject to changes, and even profound changes. Moreover, who can deny the fact that in these movements, insofar as they conform to the dictates of right reason and interpret the legitimate aspirations of the human person, we find positive elements that are worthy of approval? (n. 159).[10]

Then John XXIII went on to draw his conclusion and application:

> It can happen, then, that meetings for the achievement of
> some practical end, which formerly were judged inopportune
> or pointless, might not be so judged today or tomorrow. Now
> deciding whether or not this moment has arrived, and also
> determining the ways and degrees of possible joint efforts to
> achieve sound and socially useful goals of an economic,
> political, cultural, or social nature—these are problems which
> can be solved only by using the virtue of prudence, the
> guiding virtue when it comes to the moral life of the in-
> dividual and society. As far as Catholics are concerned, such
> decisions rest first and foremost with those who live and work
> in the specific societal areas where the problems arise. They
> must, however, act in accordance with natural law, the social
> teaching of the Church, and ecclesiastical authority. None
> can forget the fact that the Church has the right and the duty
> to intervene authoritatively, not only to safeguard ethical and
> religious principles, but also to intervene authoritatively
> among its children in the temporal order when it comes to
> applying those principles to concrete cases (n. 160).[11]

Insofar as the duty of the faithful to respect such interventions
is concerned, we are immediately reminded of Pius XII's remarks
to Charles Flory on July 14, 1945. Flory had taken over the
presidency of the French *Semaines Sociales* from Eugène Duthoit.
Pius XII reminded Flory that there was an obligation to act in
accordance with "the imprescriptible teachings of the Gospel and
the salutary applications of those teachings which the papal
magisterium, by divine vocation, never ceases to make to different
temporal and geographical situations."[12]

Three years later, in his Christmas radio message on December 24,
1948, the same Pope acknowledged how serious was his burden of
having to "confirm the brethren" in the faith. He felt it ever more
deeply and keenly in exercising his apostolic ministry. As the Pope
put it, he had to "communicate to the episcopate and the faithful
around the world the teachings, norms, and exhortations which full
execution of the Church's saving mission required." Though the

substantive immutability of those teachings had to be preserved, they also had to be suitably adapted to "the ever changing circumstances of time and place." [13]

Clearly, then, the Church has not only exercised the power of stepping in to apply Christian moral principles to reality but has also upheld its right to do so.

The reason for these interventions is the necessity of helping the faithful to find concretely the right road to follow in order to be faithful to God's will. There may be religious immaturity, particular problems of spiritual upset, conflicting interests, or highly complicated situations. Therefore it may not be easy for the faithful to pinpoint the concrete way to implement principles, and so they may be in danger of going to extremes. To take the reception of Communion as an example, some people might feel that going to Communion once every three years is too much, while others might assume that going to Communion twice a day is not enough. Outside help is needed. Doesn't the same hold true in more commonplace matters? A person might not know exactly what food or drink to take. A doctor might be needed to prescribe or even dictate some dietary regimen. Even some sort of surgical intervention might be required. And who can offer better help in the area we are discussing than the hierarchy, which enjoys a special charism, a special sort of divine assistance, *for this*?

This means, first of all, that such an application stemming from outside intervention cannot be the norm, but only the exception. The *normal* subject in applying principles to concrete cases and situations is the party involved. The intervention of another is always an exception. Pope John XXIII made this point expressly in n. 160 of *Pacem in Terris* which I cited above. In writing about possible collaboration with movements deriving from false or anti-Christian teachings, he said: "As far as Catholics are concerned, such decisions rest *first and foremost* with those who live and work in the specific societal areas where the problems arise" (my italics). Therefore we cannot accept the position of those who maintain that the task of making correct applications of moral principles to concrete situations belongs *solely*, or even *primarily*, to the hierarchy.

The danger of such a position is that one may never find applications *cut to the measure of concrete reality*. Even worse is the danger of maintaining the faithful in a state of real infantilism. Do we not see a proof of this in the abandonment of *epikeia* in practice, insofar as Church laws are concerned? Who among the faithful are capable of having sound recourse to *epikeia*, of avoiding the two extremes of total non-use and capricious use? Take priests, for example. Consider all the priests who have every reason and justification for considering themselves excused from the recitation of the Divine Office on a certain day. The state of their health or sudden, unforeseen obligations clearly excuse them. But instead of having recourse to *epikeia*, instead of substituting some other feasible pious practice perhaps, they prefer to get through the Divine Office somehow, fighting off sleep at the end of the day or squeezing it into a few spare moments here and there.

The preference given to the hierarchy is not due primarily or mainly to any greater or better human preparation they enjoy. It is not due to their greater intelligence, diligence, experience, reflection, or whatever. It is due to the assistance of the Holy Spirit which has been granted to them specifically insofar as they are "pastors" of souls. Of course it would be fine if greater human preparation were to be found in them, and often this is the case. But that is not the real reason for the preference I have underlined above. We must be mindful of the problems connected with this sort of ultrahistorical reference. We must be mindful of the dangers it may entail—i.e., supernaturalism or a magical view of the hierarchical office. But such dangers are supposed to keep us on the alert so that we do not fall prey to them. They cannot and should not prevent us from recalling that the fundamental reason for the privileged position of the hierarchy is of a supernatural order. Such a reason, of course, cannot easily be perceived or appreciated by people who neither know nor are trying to live Christianity, and it should always be kept in mind by the members of the hierarchy themselves. They should constantly make an effort to open themselves up to the guidance of the Holy Spirit by living lives of prayer and union with God.

Moreover, both the hierarchy and the faithful should be constantly attentive to the underlying principle involved. They should remember that the intervention of the Church is merely an application of the principle, and that the observance of the application is to serve fuller implementation of the principle.

Take the case of abstinence from meat on fast days, as used to be the rule. Focusing solely on the application rather than on the underlying principle, one could readily delude oneself about having fulfilled the obligation when one had not. One might eat a sumptuous meatless meal and look down upon some poor person who had nothing to eat but a slice of bread and a chunk of sausage. But the application is a means to observe the principle, not an elegant way to evade the latter. Who can deny that it has often been used for such evasion, and may still be used that way? How often the harsh accusations of Jesus against the Pharisees might well be directed against Christians: "Woe to you, blind guides, who say, 'If anyone swears by the temple, it is nothing; but if anyone swears by the gold of the temple, he is bound by his oath. . . . If anyone swears by the altar, it is nothing; but if anyone swears by the gift on the altar, he is bound by his oath.' . . . Woe to you, scribes and Pharisees, hypocrites! for you tithe mint and dill and cummin, and have neglected the weightier matters of the law, justice and mercy and faith; these you ought to have done, without neglecting the others" (Mt. 23:16-23).

All that has been said above also means that the interventions of the hierarchy in the area of applications can and should change when there are changes in the circumstances of individuals, time, and place. It would be unacceptable for a doctor to impose a certain diet for every moment in the life of a person. It would be equally unacceptable if certain Church applications, introduced when a people were still little children in human or religious terms, were to be maintained when they had become adult in those terms. It is not that it was not a good thing to introduce the applications in the first instance. But since the people involved are no longer children, it is not good to keep treating them as if they were.

The same goes for changes in time and space. A law on the eucharistic fast calling for a total fast from midnight on clearly did not create much difficulty before electric lights came into being. Then people basically went to bed near sunset, and they gave no thought to receiving Communion shortly after midnight. They also worked in and around their homes. The situation changed greatly with the coming of electric lights and altered work conditions. People now went to bed later, even staying up beyond midnight. They might well think about receiving Communion shortly after midnight. Moreover, factory workers and others might not be able to get to Church before starting their working day. Thus the law now created serious difficulties. It was now possible for people to come to Communion with a full stomach, or to be deprived of it completely if they had to fast from midnight on.

These brief observations show us that there are two rather different kinds of moral norms. One type is made up of immutable, eternal principles, of prescriptions that are valid always and everywhere for every situation of life. The other type has to do with applications that can and should change. The two types must be clearly and accurately distinguished. Otherwise there is a danger that mere applications, which should vary in time and space, will be defended as immutable, eternal norms. Or, on the other side of the coin, there is a danger that true and strict principles, which are universally and eternally valid, will be considered as bound to certain limits of time and space.

Herein lies the root of certain errors and conflicts. Some people cannot look beyond their own little territory and their own time. They cling ferociously to norms which are mere applications and subject to the laws of time, and hence they are scandalized when the Church accepts or even promotes certain changes! Other people are uncritically, perhaps even neurotically, taken by the profound changes going on in our day and their dizzying pace. They would like to see revision and change even in eternal principles, in the norms that God has laid down for *all* humanity!

These observations also apply to space. They have to be kept in mind in the drafting of the new code of canon law. Otherwise there is a danger that too many norms of an applicatory type will be made binding on all Christendom. If we want norms that are truly adapted to all Christendom, then they must be very few and very general. For if the norms were to be truly adapted to all peoples, then we would practically have to have different norms from one people to the next.

I should also say something about the *obligation which arises for the faithful to adhere to the norms laid down*. Clearly the interventions of the Church, be they interpretations or applications, are not without impact on the conscience of the Christian. Since this is the intervention of one who has been sent by Christ to tend his faithful, it cannot be disregarded by them, whereas the opinion of theologians can be disregarded. Here an analogy might help. Consider a criminal and his relationship with an expert on penal law on the one hand and a sentencing court on the other. The criminal could well reject the expert's view as to how many years of jail he has merited by his act, but he cannot reject the sentence that the court imposes on him. In like manner the faithful can reject the opinion of some theologian, but they cannot do the same with the decision of the Church.

The obligation to adhere to such interventions, however, can vary in accordance with the type of Church intervention involved. The Church can intervene in an authentic and infallible way, or it can intervene in a way that is authentic only. The first form of intervention is definitive and irreformable; the second form could be reformable or revisable. I say "could be reformable" because merely authentic interventions may sometimes propose things that are irreformable insofar as they have already been the object of an infallible intervention, or of an intervention of the ordinary magisterium which proposes something in a definitive way. Do we not have an outstanding example of this in Vatican II as a whole? For its explicit declarations do not contain any infallible definitions, but they do contain many irreformable propositions.

And there is still more. The Church can intervene in a binding way or in a merely indicative and exhortative way. It can lay down an obligation, but it can also restrict itself to offering indications and exhortations. The intervention of the Church with regard to the frequency of confession and Communion is clearly of the second type.

These points should be clear from the study of theology, but I shall come back to them to some extent later on.

II
APPLICATIONS TO NATURAL LAW

The above considerations have to do with the whole field of moral law: i.e., both with the area of law derived from consideration of the nature of things, humanity, and God, and with the area of norms communicated expressly by God through the prophets and, ultimately, Christ.

Now we must examine more closely the role of the Church with regard to the first area of law just noted. For in recent times, especially with regard to the publication of the encyclical *Humanae Vitae*, much doubt, disagreement, and controversy has arisen over this matter.

Opponents of Magisterial Intervention

First of all, one group of theologians denies that natural law should be regarded as moral law. Hence these theologians deny that the Church has any right to touch upon this area in order to guide human consciences.

By way of example, let me mention the Jesuit R. Troisfontaines who is a professor on the faculty of Namur and at Louvain University. In an article on artificial insemination published in the *Nouvelle revue théologique* in 1973,[14] Troisfontaines maintained that "nature is something given prior to the intervention of liberty." [15] In other words, nature is the fruit of the spontaneous action and interaction of forces which precede the free intervention of the human being. By that very fact nature cannot be the norm of conduct. The latter consists of "interpersonal communion in freedom and love." [16] Logically, then, the author rejects the Church's teaching on artificial insemination.[17]

A second group of theologians, a rather sizable group, puts the main stress on the incompetence of the Church as such to intervene in the area of natural law. Let us consider a few examples.

To start with, there is the Jesuit Jakob David and what he has to say in his work on new aspects of the Church's teaching on marriage:[18]

The authority of the Church's magisterium has to do directly with the diffusion, explanation, conservation, delimitation, and defense of divine revelation. Hence it undoubtedly has the task and the right to reject explanations of natural law that contradict revelation. What is more, it can declare positively whether other doctrines are reconcilable with revealed truth. It can also draw conclusions from revealed doctrine, or clarify premises without which revealed truth cannot be considered, although in this case there can also be errors of interpretation. Nevertheless, all that is not enough to arrive at *doctrinal declarations that are fully binding in problems of merely natural law.*[19]

Although the author admits that ecclesiastical authority is said to have the right to intervene with competent declarations on problems of natural law and morality that are binding on the faithful, he notes that "the reasons give rise to difficulties and do not satisfy all."[20]

In the area of natural law the Church has a supplementary role to play. This role is valid so long as peoples and individuals are not in a position to serve as their own guides, but it cannot lay claim to infallibility. David calls it a "pastoral" function:

The Church has the duty to rule and guide the faithful in their moral conduct *so long as they have need of this guidance.* Clearly at times, and among people who are still backward, a more robust guide is necessary. But this should slacken gradually as their Christianity grows more mature and capable of passing judgment. Pastoral action must dovetail with the level of growth and development, the state of awareness and knowledge, the capacity for judgment, and the needs of the persons who are to be guided. Thus a particular people, or social class, or cultural level must be given the answers that peoples and social classes on a higher cultural level can find out for themselves. Parents, too, must give guidance to their children. But when the latter have grown up, they no longer have need of such guidance. They cannot look to such guidance, *much less accept it.*[21]

Here is another example, from the writings of the Redemptorist Bernard Haering: "From a careful study of the documents of Vatican I and Vatican II it seems possible to maintain the theological opinion that the Pope is not infallible in questions pertaining merely to natural law when, in pronouncing on them, he does not also and chiefly propose a truth of supernatural revelation." [22]

Enrico Chiavacci has this to say:

It is certain that the *sacra potestas* of the Church has the task of expressing itself on this matter also (i.e., on natural law), which is part of its teaching on morals. But it is equally certain that natural law has human reason itself for at least its instrument of discovery. Except in the light of the most general principles, and when it is communicated in revelation, every pronouncement attributed to it is always *fallible and correctible of its nature*. Every appeal to natural law is as valid as the reasoning that justifies it. [23]

More radical, it seems to me, is the final document of the Congress of Italian Moral Theologians held in Padua from March 31 to April 3, 1970. [24] Among other things, it states in Section I:

The moral magisterium will be exercised, first of all, in the context of differing cultural and historical conditions, and hence as the witness of the local Church. On the worldwide level the magisterium will ordinarily be the meeting ground between the reciprocal proposals arising amid the people of God and, in the event, the place where an effort is made to bring unity into the manifold experiences in the light of the unique word (n. 6).

Today the ordinary function of the magisterium in the moral realm is predominantly one of maintaining the thrust towards authentically evangelical values, and of encouraging their historical concretization in the conscientious choices of individuals and groups (n. 8).

Particularly in the social realm the magisterium, in exercising its function, will maintain the eschatological tension of the Church's pilgrimage through time. In that pilgrimage the Church is to remain open to present opportunities and to the full realization of Christ's mystery: i.e., the total salvation of the human being. Hence the magisterium must increasingly assume its prophetic function in the encounters of the whole human family. That is to say, it must bear witness and testimony, on both the local and worldwide levels, to the inadequacy of all the structures which inevitably condition human existence and concrete experience (n. 9).[25]

Supporters of Magisterial Intervention

On the other side we have moral theologians who uphold the right of the Church to intervene authoritatively in the area of natural law as well. They say that the Church can offer suitable exposition, authentic interpretation, and timely application of natural law, *even to the point of infallibility*, and a corresponding obligation on the part of the faithful, including theologians, to respond with a degree of adherence proportionate to the intervention itself.

Here again I will restrict myself to the mention of a few names. First, there is the Jesuit Marcellino Zalba, a professor at the Gregorian University, who wrote two long articles for *Doctor communis*.[26] One of the reasons Zalba offers in defense of his position is that the power of the Church extends "not only to the deposit of revelation in itself, but also to those things necessary for its effective custody and exposition."[27]

For the Jesuit Alberto di Giovanni, another reason is the fact that natural law, too, represents the will of God.[28] In an article deliberately confined to the philosophical aspect, he goes so far as to write the following:

The being of things does not just "document" their being "from God." It also documents what he wants with regard to them. . . . The being which all things have, insofar as they have received it from God, is *having* being from Another. Besides indicating that they are beings-from-God, this also reveals God's will for them. Thus the human creature, privileged to be a conscious and free subject, can not only see himself as a gift of and from God but also grasp God's will for himself. Knowing what-it-is (i.e., its own essence or way of participating in being), the human being can recognize and acknowledge what God wants it to be. It is, because God wills that it be. And it is "what" God wills and "how" he wills it to be: not a mineral or a plant but a human being, a being that has to exist in a human way.[29]

What are we to say, then? Let us begin by recalling a few notions associated with the magisterium; i.e., authentic, infallible, fallible, reformable, irreformable, extraordinary, ordinary.

Now, reading the first group of authors mentioned in the immediately preceding section, one gets the impression—to say the very least—that there is an opposition between the authentic magisterium and infallible magisterium, that the authentic magisterium is always fallible and hence reformable, that the non-infallible magisterium counts for nothing and almost habitually teaches error, and, finally, that infallibility belongs only to the extraordinary magisterium.

All that is not completely correct. First of all, it is not correct to set the infallible magisterium over against the authentic magisterium, claiming that the former is irreformable and the latter reformable. As Giulio Oggioni remarks:

All this . . . focuses on the difference in the effects of the various magisteriums, not on their specific, inner difference. The magisterium of the Church is called authentic or authoritative for the value it has, not by virtue of the force of the arguments it uses in proposing a doctrine, but by virtue of the charism which sustains it and the authority invested in those who do the proposing. This authority derives . . . from the gift of the Holy Spirit, which elevates the recipients to the dignity of teachers and guides in transmitting the deposit of faith. Thus the magisterium of the Church, when it is truly such, is always authentic, always authoritative, because it is always guaranteed by that charism of the Holy Spirit. At times this guarantee is such that the affirmation or exposition is preserved immune from error in a sure and certain way.[30]

At times, of course, it is not proposed in those terms. Thus we have two cases here. In the first case, described by Oggioni in the last sentence of the above citation, we are talking about a magisterium that is both authentic *and* infallible. In the other case, we are talking about a magisterium that is authentic but not infallible.

Furthermore, it is not correct to equate the authentic, non-infallible magisterium — or, simply, the authentic magisterium — with the reformable magisterium. The authentic but non-infallible magisterium is not irreformable *by virtue of the exposition which the Church makes*, but it could be by virtue of the nature of the things in question or by virtue of the presence of divine revelation. In other words, when we confront an infallible proposition, we know it is true and hence irreformable by virtue of the Church's exposition or proposal itself and by virtue of the way in which the Church proposes it, quite apart from our scientific consideration of the matter itself or of the content of revelation. A merely authentic presentation *does not afford the same guarantee in and of itself*. To decide upon the truth or falsity of the proposition, and hence its reformability or non-reformability, we must move on to an analysis of the reality in question or of the content of revelation. Therefore an infallible proposition is certainly irreformable, but an authentic, non-infallible proposition may be either reformable or not.

This explains how in the development of dogma the Church can move on from a non-infallible proposal to an infallible one. In other words, it explains how the Church can propose something which is true and hence irreformable, but without guaranteeing irreformability by its very proposal, and then, later, guarantee this irreformability by making an infallible exposition of it. Otherwise such a transition would imply a contradiction. Why? Because first the Church would be saying that a certain thing could be true or false, and that its own exposition could be revised or not revised, and then it would move on to say that the matter itself is true and hence its own exposition is irreformable.

Still less is it permissible to maintain that a proposition is reformable by the mere fact that the document in which it is contained is declared to be a non-definitive document. Even a document of that sort may contain irreformable declarations, either because they are already contained in an earlier definitory document or because they have been subjects considered by the *definitive* ordinary magisterium.[31]

Furthermore, it is not correct to equate the infallible magisterium with the extraordinary magisterium or the ordinary magisterium with the non-infallible magisterium. Even the ordinary magisterium can be infallible. This possibility is taught explicitly by Vatican II, which reiterates the traditional doctrine in this area as in so many others. Carlo Colombo has pointed out the fact and the pertinent reference.[32] Here is what *Lumen Gentium* has to say:

> Individual bishops do not enjoy the prerogative of infallibility. However, when the bishops, although dispersed throughout the world, but preserving their bond of communion with one another and with the successor of Peter, in their authentic teaching on matters of faith and morals come together in teaching a doctrine *as definitive*, they infallibly announce the doctrine of Christ (n. 25).

Neither is it correct to picture the non-infallible magisterium as an insignificant magisterium devoid of importance for Church members and theologians. As Carlo Colombo has pointed out, a non-infallible proposition does not rule out the possibility of error, the Johannine comma being a classic example where the magisterium made a mistaken declaration in the past (see Denz. 3681f.).[33] But as Colombo goes on to point out, it is mistaken to think or assert that the non-infallible magisterium

> *frequently* or *habitually* teaches error under the name and authority of Jesus Christ the teacher, whom it is commissioned to represent. . . . Through the bishops, and primarily through the Vicar of Christ, Jesus himself is mysteriously present and at work in his Church. As *Lumen Gentium* (n. 21) puts it: "Through the bishops . . . our Lord Jesus Christ, the high priest, is present in the midst of those who believe. Though he is seated at the right hand of God the Father, he is not absent from the assembly of his high priests. On the contrary, through their outstanding service above all, he preaches

the word of God to all nations and unceasingly administers
the sacraments of faith to believers; by their paternal office he
incorporates new members into his body through a supernatural rebirth; and, finally, by their wisdom and prudence he
guides and directs the people of the new covenant in their
pilgrimage toward eternal happiness.[34]

Now let us get back to the specific problem of the Church's
competence in the area of natural law. Here I shall limit myself to
two basic observations.

First of all, accepted teaching tells us that the competence of
the Church is not restricted to truths formally contained in divine
revelation. It also extends to those non-revealed doctrines and facts
which are necessarily bound up with revealed truths, with those
doctrines and facts which are necessary if the Church is to provide
faithful custody, suitable exposition, authentic interpretation, and
timely application of things formally revealed.

Now natural law is certainly bound up with the four functions
just mentioned. How are we to accept, and win acceptance for, the
obligations presented to us by God in divine revelation if we do not
first demonstrate the obligation to obey God on the basis of
reason? If we start from the premise that the "matter" of the sacrament of marriage is the "contract," then how can we know the
precise content of this sacrament if we do not first know the content of this term "contract"? How can we *effectively* guide people
to carry out the divine command to rule over all created things and
to transform them into the service of all human beings and every
human being if we do not also consider the problem of what incen-
tives are to be offered to fallen humanity, the kind of work
humanity is supposed to carry out, and the way goods are to be
distributed in the private and collective spheres?

Hence we must say that the competence of the Church also extends to natural law by the very fact that natural law is necessarily
bound up with the exposition and defense of revelation.[35] I
might also add here that in giving us the Our Father Christ exhorted
us to ask the Father that his will be done "on earth as it is in
heaven." Now doesn't God's will also show up in and through
creation, through the nature of things, through the natural law as
the Church understands it?

The second observation derives from the fact that the Church has constantly preached, interpreted, and applied the natural law as well. The Church has also defended this *modus operandi* against hostile attacks.

This practice has already been documented to some extent in the preceding pages of this article. I would just add here the statement of Pius XII in his address to cardinals and bishops who had gathered in Rome for the proclamation of the Queenship of Mary:

> It must be firmly and openly maintained that the power of the Church is in no way limited to what people call "strictly religious matters." The whole matter of natural law, its exposition, interpretation, and application, insofar as it is considered in its moral aspect, is within the competence of the Church. In fact, by divine disposition the observance of the natural law has to do with the way human beings are to move toward their supernatural end. Now on this road, insofar as it has a supernatural end, it is the Church that is the guide and guardian of human beings. From the time of the apostles and the earliest centuries of its history, the Church has consistently followed this norm, even as it does today. And it has not acted as a private guide and counselor, but by the will and mandate of the Lord. So when we are dealing with prescriptions and decisions issued on matters of natural law by the legitimate pastors—i.e., the Supreme Pontiff for the universal Church, and the bishops for the faithful entrusted to their care—the faithful should not have recourse to the dictum that is usually applied to private opinions: "The authority is as good as the arguments used." Hence the obligation to obey perdures, even though someone feels that some ecclesiastical prescription is not proved by the arguments offered.[36]

I might also add here another point with regard to *Humanae Vitae* specifically. In that document the teaching about the illicitness of contraceptives is presented as a traditional teaching (see sections 6, 10-12, and 14), and it is presented once again even in the face of serious objections and contrary arguments.

Now how could one think that a teaching and practice *of this nature*, so constant and broad, and presented once again in the face of objections and opposing arguments, could be in error? Wouldn't that compromise the very function of the hierarchy? Wouldn't it compromise its function as a guide? Wouldn't we have to say that the hierarchy has led us to error and perdition instead of leading us to the green pastures that nourish us for eternal life? If this hierarchy has for so long continued obstinately in a position that is erroneous and extremely dangerous socially, indeed downright corruptive, and if it has done so in circumstances that should have forced it to recant its mistakes, how could one continue to believe in it as a hierarchy?

These are questions for which satisfactory answers must be found by those who deny the right of the Church to intervene, even to the extent of infallibility, in the area of natural law. It certainly will not do to say that we are dealing here with a mere episode that does not invalidate the hierarchy's function as guide. For this is certainly not a mere episode; still less is it a fact that does no harm to the hierarchy's function as a spiritual guide.

It seems to me that a Church which allegedly does not even know its own powers and violates them so impudently could no longer be accepted as "Mother and Teacher."

A few final remarks remain to be said to the first group of theologians noted in the previous section of this article: i.e., those who say that the incompetence of the Church in this area derives from the fact that natural law is not a norm of conduct because it is simply the norm of reality before human beings intervene.

As I have already briefly noted, they must be reminded that the Church and the theologians they call "traditional" have never understood natural law in that sense. It is indeed surprising that authors of such prestige have fallen into such a gross error. The Church and "traditional" theologians have always understood natural law to be the end of the human being, its perfection and fulfillment. In that sense it refers to the happiness of human beings, to perfected human beings, to the human being we are called upon to fashion laboriously through our free choices, often fighting against the disordered inclinations that derive from the original fault. Putting it another way, we could say that the natural law proposed by the Church is the complete, harmonious development of the whole being of every human. It covers the whole gamut from their higher faculties down. It has to do with their complete dominion over things, full respect for the equal dignity of other human beings from the fertilized ovum to the moment of death, and loving concern for their welfare in complete subordination to God. The natural law is not the course of things before human beings intervene with their free decision, nor is it merely "interpersonal communion in liberty and love."

It may seem odd, but it bears repeating once again even after so many centuries: the Church mainly needs to be known, even by its most prestigious theologians.

Notes

1. See *Discorsi e radiomessaggi di Sua Santità Pio XII*, 10 (1948-1949), p. 192.
2. Italian text in Igino Giordani (ed.), *Le encicliche sociale* (Rome, 1956), p. 192.
3. *Ibid.*, p. 462.
4. *Ibid.*, p. 467.
5. Denz. 1731f.
6. Italian text in *La Civiltà cattolica*, III (1950), p. 464.
7. Italian text in I. Giordani, *Le encicliche sociale*, p. 204.
8. *Ibid.*, p. 627.
9. *AAS* 41 (1949), p. 334.
10. Italian text in *La Civiltà cattolica*, II (1963), p. 160.
11. *Ibid.*, p. 161.
12. *AAS* 37 (1945), p. 210.
13. *AAS* 41 (1949), p. 5.
14. R. Troisfontaines, "L'insémination artificielle: Problèmes éthiques," *Nouvelle revue théologique*, 1973, pp. 764-778.
15. *Ibid.*, p. 771.
16. *Ibid.*, p. 765.
17. *Ibid.*, p. 778: "If morality takes as its criterion conformity to nature, then artificial insemination is unacceptable. If morality refers to the communion of persons, then only artificial insemination of the wife by her husband seems to be legitimate."
18. Jakob David, *Nuovi aspetti della dottrina ecclesiastica sul matrimonio* (Rome, 1968), p. 190. See also *Il diritto naturale, problemi e chiarimenti: Un nuovo ripensamento critico* (Rome, 1968), p. 123.
19. J. David, *Nuovi aspetti*, p. 102. All italics are mine.
20. *Ibid.*, p. 101.

21. *Ibid.*, p. 119.

22. Bernard Haering, *La morale del discorso della montagna* (Alba, 1967), pp. 148f. See also *La morale è per la persona* (Alba, 1972), pp. 283f.; Eng. tr., *Morality Is For Persons* (New York, 1970).

23. In Enrico Chiavacci, Tullo Goffi, and Dalmazio Mongillo (eds.), *Humanae vitae: Note teologico-pastorali* (Brescia, 1968), pp. 68f. See also *La legge naturale ieri e oggi* (Brescia, 1969), pp. 84-87.

24. The Proceedings can be found in *Magistero e morale: Studi e ricerche* (Bologna, 1970). On page 390 in that volume the editors specifically mention that the absence of the final document from the published Proceedings was due to "a prohibition by higher ecclesiastical authorities."

25. See the final document and conclusions detailed earlier in this volume.

26. Marcellino Zalba, "Num magisterio ecclesiae commissa fuerit propositio et interpretatio declarativo-comprehensiva authentica iuris naturalis," *Doctor communis*, 22 (1969), pp. 109-144. *Idem*, "Magisterium infallibile in Conciliis vaticanis I et II," *Doctor communis*, 26 (1973), pp. 281-315.

27. Zalba, "Magisterium infallibile . . . " p. 314.

28. Alberto di Giovanni, "La natura come rivelazione del volere di Dio al cuore dell'uomo," *Rassegna di teologia*, 10 (1969), pp. 1-21.

29. *Ibid.*, pp. 2-4.

30. Giulio Oggioni, "Valore dell'Humanae vitae: autorità e ossequio religioso," *La scuola cattolica*, 97 (1969), p. 265. Justo Collantes asserts: "Some authors make a distinction between infallible magisterium and authentic magisterium, restricting the latter term to the non-infallible magisterium. This use of terminology strikes me as most unfortunate and confusing, since the infallible magisterium is just as authentic as the non-infallible magisterium": "Magisterio de la Iglesia y ley natural," *Estudios eclesiasticos*, 44 (1969), p. 66, n. 75.

31. Let us suppose, by way of example, that in a *non-infallible* document the Church recalled the fact that Mary was conceived without the stain of original sin. In such a case the affirmation would not be reformable, not because of the nature of the document that contains it but because of the nature of the thing contained in the document.

32. Carlo Colombo, "Obbedienza al magistero ordinario," *La rivista del clero italiano*, 49 (1968), p. 258.

33. *Ibid.*, p. 253.

34. *Ibid.*, pp. 255f.

35. It is worth repeating that natural law comes to be known by reason, not by revelation. The problem is not whether natural law is known by reason, but whether it is so bound up with the function of the hierarchy that the Church would not be able to fulfill its function effectively without the possibility of infallible interventions.

36. Italian text in *La Civiltá cattolica*, IV (1954), pp. 472f.

Doctrinal Authority
for a Pilgrim Church

Avery Dulles, S.J.

Enlightenment, according to Immanuel Kant, is the over-coming of self-caused immaturity. "Immaturity is the incapacity to use one's own intelligence without the guidance of another. The motto of the Enlightenment is 'sapere aude!' — have the courage to use your own intelligence."[1] Through laziness or cowardice, Kant goes on to say, a large portion of humankind gladly remains immature. It is more comfortable to be a minor, under the guardianship of others.

Kant recognized that in certain official functions one may take on an obligation to refrain from speaking according to one's own convictions and to abide by the teaching of an institution. For example, he notes, a pastor is obliged to teach his congregation according to the doctrine of the Church he serves. He has to state faithfully what the Church teaches, regardless of his own personal views. If he felt that the teaching of the Church were seriously wrong, he would no doubt have to resign his post. But as long as he is a priest he remains unfree, for he is executing the mandate of others.

Quite different, according to Kant, is the position of the scholar. He writes for the general public and in that capacity he is entitled, even obliged, to employ his own reason and to speak with complete candor.

Kant is typical of rationalism insofar as he presumes that reason is the best tool we have for getting at the truth, and that reason operates more effectively when unchecked by authority. Authority, he holds, is for the sake of the immature. It is only provisional. Tiue personal conviction depends not upon authority but upon rational insight.

The rebellion against authority at the time of the Enlightenment was a time-conditioned reaction against the excesses of ecclesiastical authoritarianism, which was carried to unprecedented lengths in early modern times. When authority becomes oppressive and violates the integrity of honest inquiry and conscientious decision, it generates the kind of negative image reflected in the writers of the Englightenment. The rejection of authority, however, is scarcely a sign of adulthood. Rather, it is a mark of adolescence. In practically all the affairs of daily living, mature persons rely upon authority in the sense that they depend on the advice of experienced and knowledgeable persons—those whom they have reason to regard as experts in the particular field. If we do this in law, in medicine, in history, and art criticism, why not in religion? In the case of a religion which, like Christianity, claims to rest on a definite revelation given in the past, belief is essentially linked with the acceptance of the testimony of those who, allegedly, were the prime recipients of the revelation. There is no way in which reason can prove by universally cogent arguments the truth of the interpretation that the New Testament and the creeds give to the figure of Jesus. If we antecedently refuse to take anything on authority, we cut ourselves off from the benefits of historical revelation. Christianity ceases to have any value except as a set of symbols for interpreting our own experience.

The acceptance of authority, as I understand it, does not mean the abandonment of reason. As I have explained more fully elsewhere, reason and authority are dialectically intertwined throughout the process of religious inquiry and the life of faith.[2] Reason is a necessary instrument for assessing the rival claims of various claimants to authority. Reason is also necessary to interpret authoritative statements, to judge whether the authority is speaking within its competence, and to reinterpret past statements to grasp their significance for new situations. Reason may at times detect false emphases or errors into which the authorities may have fallen. The critical thinking developed by Kant and the great philosophers of the Enlightenment can thus be helpful in guarding against the absolutization of authority. Contemporary Christians are indebted to the Enlightenment for having developed defenses against an unhealthy authoritarianism.

While acknowledging the importance of relativizing authority, I would contend, against certain liberal theologians, that authority has a central place in the Christian religion. For the vitality of the faith it is essential that the authorities function properly. If the authorities fail to speak with truth and power, the whole community of faith is in danger of disintegrating. The right question for Christians is not whether to accept authority but rather how to identify and relate to the authorities. Many Christians make the mistake of overlooking some authorities and of absolutizing others.

The standard loci of authority in the Christian system are well known: the Bible, the pastoral office, the sense of the faithful, the judgment of theologians, and the testimony of prophetically gifted individuals. Certain groups of Christians have traditionally accented some of the instances as against others.

Classical Protestantism at one time coined the slogan, "The Bible alone."[3] The position was a protest against the teachings that had been cumulatively built up by the Scholastic theologians and the Popes in the Middle Ages. The Reformation was, under one aspect, a radical call for simplification—for a return to primitive purity. The word "alone" in the formula has to be taken with a grain of salt, for no Protestants really ignored tradition. Luther and Calvin were scarcely less eager than the Roman Catholics to square their doctrine with the early ecumenical Councils. In their controversies they drew heavily on the Church Fathers and even, at times, on the medieval Doctors. But they insisted that any Christian teaching—including that of Councils and Church Fathers—had to be aligned with Scripture. If anything could not be shown to agree with Scripture, it had for them no authority. Very many contemporary Protestants hold approximately this position.

From a Catholic point of view we may agree that the Bible, taken as a whole, is the word of God. It is the fundamental document of Israelite and Christian revelation. The Bible, we believe, is the fundamental touchstone of our faith. No teaching that contradicts the Bible, taken as whole, could be true.

On the other hand, the Catholic will have many difficulties against the catchword "Scripture alone." Let me put some of the familiar difficulties under three headings:

1. The Bible did not collect itself. It is a selection of Jewish and early Christian writings made in the early centuries by the Church—and more specifically by the leaders of the local and regional churches, and ultimately by Councils. To put one's trust in the Bible, therefore, inevitably implies a certain trust in the Church that gathered up these writings and declared them to be authoritative for Christians. One cannot drive a wedge between the authority of the Church which canonized the Scriptures and that of the Scriptures which it canonized. To say "Bible alone" with the negative implication "not Church" is therefore unacceptable.

2. The Bible is not self-interpreting. It is a very complex collection of writings from different ages and situations. One can pick out sentences here and there that seem to teach error—things we know to be false from science, from history, or from faith. To gather up the meaning of the Scripture as a whole is an act of creative interpretation, in which all sorts of skills and funds of information are brought to bear. If the Bible is to speak to us today, its meaning must be mediated to us through other authorities—the exegete, the pastor, the believing community, or whatever. If the individual reader were handed a Bible outside of any ecclesial context, he would probably find it uninteresting, unintelligible, or seriously misleading.

3. According to the New Testament, Jesus has promised to remain forever present with his Church. The Holy Spirit, who previously "spoke by the prophets," remains at work in the Christian community to the end of time. Thus it may be presumed that Christians since biblical times have spoken with the special assistance of the Spirit. We should therefore make an effort to identify the occasions on which God may be judged to be speaking through persons who have lived since Christ and the apostles. To accept no authority but the Bible would be to reject, in part, the teaching of the Bible, which refers us to Christians who speak by the Spirit.

Among Catholics it is undisputed that the Holy Spirit who inspired the Scriptures is also at work in the Church, and therefore that there is living authority in the Church. But there are differences of opinion regarding the loci in which the presence of the Spirit is to be found: pastoral office, people of God, or a variety of charismatic leaders.

Since the Reformation, and especially since the eighteenth century, the Catholic emphasis has been upon the pastoral office and, more specifically, upon the papal and episcopal offices. In the Roman textbooks out of which most of the present clergy were taught in their seminary days, practically no other form of authority than that of the office-holder was acknowledged. The term "magisterium" came to be used to designate the teaching authority of Popes and bishops—and the tendency was to reduce every other kind of theological authority to this one font.

According to the theory of apostolicity then prevalent—and still prevalent in some circles—the bishops and they alone were successors of the apostles. Apostolic succession was conceived as giving the bishops a special "charism of truth" proper to themselves. The Pope, as head of the whole Church, was thought to have in himself as much authority as the entire body of bishops. Thus he was the supreme and universal teacher of all Christians, equipped with that infallibility with which Christ had endowed his Church.

This theory of authority, which may be called institutional or hierocratic, has real assets that should not be overlooked. For one thing it helps to safeguard the unity of the Church and its doctrinal continuity with the Church of apostolic times. If the Church is to cohere as a society, it must have ways of assembling a body of clearly identifiable, self-consistent, and certified teachings—qualities that are clearly fostered by the hierocratic model.

On the other hand, this model, taken in isolation, has certain liabilities.[4] By insisting as it does upon the formal and juridical aspects of authority, it encourages a kind of doctrinal extrinsicism, sometimes referred to as the "blank check" theory of assent. Furthermore, it does not sufficiently attend to the fact that the official teaching would not have power or credibility except that it emanates from a community of faith and is, so to speak, inscribed within this community. Official teaching has no force unless it somehow expresses the faith of the believing Church, and unless the teachers are bound by conviction to the community of believers. The doctrine of infallibility, in particular, becomes incredible if set forth in an automatic or mechanistic way, without taking account of the human and Christian character of the process by which faith is gathered up and distilled into doctrine.

Some modern ecclesiologists, seeking the limitations of the hierocratic model, have attempted to substitute what may be called a democratic view of authority.[5] Without saying explicitly that the Church is a democracy, they lean in that direction. They speak of the common priesthood of all the faithful and are uncomfortable with the idea that the priesthood, or authority, of the ordained would be essentially different from this. They would see the official teachers simply as those who publicly announce what is already the conviction of the faithful, or at least of a large majority of them. These democratic ecclesiologists strongly emphasize the "sense of the faithful" (*sensus fidelium*), which, according to Vatican II, is so assisted by the Holy Spirit that the people of God as a whole is infallible in its unanimous understanding of what constitutes a matter of faith.[6]

I am not sure whether any Catholic ecclesiologists go so far as to say that the Pope can be bound by a majority vote of the bishops or that the bishops can be bound by a majority vote of the priests and faithful of their diocese. Such a view would be difficult to reconcile with Vatican I and with the whole tenor of the Catholic tradition. But because of the doctrine that the Holy Spirit is present in the whole Church as well as the rulers, majorities do have to be taken seriously. In actual practice, Popes and bishops very rarely if ever seek to impose doctrines unless they believe that those doctrines are already accepted by a large majority.

The attention given in modern theology to the active role of the faithful is in many ways a welcome development. It corrects certain exaggerations to which the hierocratic model is prone—especially the unhealthy concentration of all active power in the hands of a small ruling class, with the corresponding reduction of the lower classes in the Church to a state of passivity scarcely consonant with lively Christian commitment.

The main weakness of the democratic theory is that, like the hierocratic, it labors under a certain juridicism. Concerned with the formal aspects of authority, it overlooks the authority of the Gospel or the content of revelation, which could conceivably be opposed to the drift of public opinion in the Church. Preoccupied with juridical structures, this theory leaves insufficient room for the inspirations and special graces bestowed by the Holy Spirit, who can raise up powerful voices of prophetic protest.

In contrast to some contemporary theologians of the Western world, I tend to be distrustful of majorities. I am fond of Kierkegaard's aphorism "The majority is always wrong." The *sensus fidelium*, as a theological font, should never be confused with the public-opinion poll. Not all in the Church are equally close to Christ and to the Holy Spirit. Many members of the Church are as much influenced by the mass media and the secular fashions of the day as they are by the Gospel and Christian tradition. This does not mean, of course, that by taking power from the people and transferring it to a power elite one gets closer to the truth. The officials can easily make decisions in the light of their class interests and professional biases rather than the Gospel itself. Where the teaching of the magisterium fails to resonate with the consciousness of the faithful at large, one has reason to suspect that the power of office has been incorrectly used.

In contradistinction to the hierocratic and democratic theories in their crude form, I should like to propose, as theologically more acceptable, a pluralistic theory of authority in the Church. The Church, I would maintain, depends for its health and vigor upon the co-existence of several distinct organs of authority, and hence on multiple groups of believers.[7] These authorities serve as mutual checks and balances. They exist in a state of natural tension and dialogue, and only when they spontaneously converge can authority make itself fully felt. The great French ecclesiologist Yves Congar has put the matter well:

If the question is to be considered theologically, it is impossible to restrict oneself to *a single* criterion, or to ancient texts without the "living magisterium," or to the living magisterium without the ancient texts, or to authority without the community, or to the latter without the former, or to the apostolicity of the ministry without the apostolicity of doctrine, or vice versa, or to the Roman Church separated from catholicity, or to the latter detached from the former. . . . All these criteria together should ensure a living faithfulness and identity in the full historicity of our lives and our knowledge. The fullness of the truth is associated with that of the means that God has given us to enable us to live by it, and with the totality of Christian existence.[8]

Among the authorities in the Church one must unquestionably include the documents which it recognizes as constitutive of its own beliefs. The canonical Scriptures, as we have said, serve as the basis and reference point of all Christian teaching. Anyone who seeks to impose beliefs and norms of conduct that evidently contravene the Scriptures will meet with deserved resistance. Even the magisterium of the Church, according to Vatican II, is not above the word of God, but serves it.[9] A sound historico-critical approach, as cultivated by the community of biblical scholars, can prevent the Bible from being misused to support whatever anyone wants to maintain on non-biblical grounds.

A second constitutive norm, which Catholics place on a par with the Bible, is sacred tradition. Tradition is known through various sedimentations, technically called the "monuments of tradition." They would include, most importantly, the solemn decisions of ecumenical councils. Unlike the Scriptures, these expressions of tradition, in Catholic theology, are not normally called the "word of God," but they bear witness to the word of God, and as such are authoritative.

Among the living voices that have authority in the Church I would mention, in the first place, the general sense of the faithful. This is to be obtained not simply by counting noses but by weighing opinions. The views of alert and committed Christians should be given more weight than those of indifferent or marginal Christians, but even the doubts of marginal persons should be attentively considered to see if they do not contain some prophetic message for the Church. The sense of the faithful should be seen not simply as a static index but as a process. If it becomes clear that large numbers of generous, intelligent, prayerful, and committed Christians who seriously study a given problem change their views in a certain direction, this may be evidence that the Holy Spirit is so inclining them.

But there is need for caution and discernment to avoid mistaking the influences of secular fashion for the inspirations of divine grace.

In addition to the general community of the faithful, there are persons who by reason of their particular gifts or positions in the Church have special qualifications to speak with authority. Here I think one must consider three sets of factors: first, learning and other natural personal endowments, such as prudence and common sense; second, spiritual gifts such as faith and prophetic insight, attributable to prayerful intimacy with God; third, regular appointment to an office in the Church with the graces, concerns, and experiences that go with the office in question.

These three sets of qualifications can be brought into some kind of loose correspondence with three types of ministry that have been recognized in the Church since biblical times: the doctoral, the prophetic, and the pastoral. For the first, the human gifts of intelligence and learning are of chief importance; for the second, docility to the Holy Spirit; for the third, regular appointment to office. It would be a mistake to overlook the special authority of each of these three types of witness.

The three classifications of ministry are not, of course, mutually exclusive. A qualified teacher in the Church must be something more than an intelligent and learned person; he must be open to the movements of the Spirit and sensitive to pastoral concerns. So, likewise, the prophet may stand to gain if he is theologically educated and pastorally responsive. The pastor, finally, should be sensitive to the demands of sound doctrine and to the promptings of the Holy Spirit. It is possible for teachers and prophets, as well as pastors, to have a recognized office in the Church, as they would seem to have had in New Testament times, at least at Antioch. It would be a mistake, therefore, to identify the official Church exclusively with pastoral administration or to look upon prophecy and teaching as merely private charisms. The three types of ministry, while remaining distinct, should somewhat overlap and interpenetrate.

Is there a hierarchy of dignity among teachers, prophets, and pastors? To judge from the listings of charisms in the New Testament (1 Cor. 12:27-31; Eph. 4:11), one would conclude that the highest of the three in dignity are the prophets, who rank immediately after the apostles in both listings.[10] The administrators (*kybernēseis*) in 1 Corinthians rank not only after prophets and teachers, but after wonder-workers and healers. In Ephesians, however, the pastors (*poimenes*) rank after prophets and before teachers, or perhaps, according to another interpretation, the pastors in this text are the same persons as the teachers. The presbyters (*presbyteroi*) and bishops (*episkopoi*) do not appear in either list, but they are perhaps to be equated with the administrators and/or pastors. The New Testament *episkopoi* are the ancestors of the modern bishops, but are not identical.[11] They seem to have been something like an executive board of the presbyters and to have combined in their persons some administrative and pastoral roles together with certain functions of proclaiming, teaching, and supervising doctrine. Like all the other officers, the *episkopoi* were subordinate to the apostles, so long as the apostles were still alive. Their authority, moreover, appears to have extended only to the local church.

Since biblical times the *episkopoi* have risen in status so as to occupy the highest rank in the ecclesiastical hierarchy. The term "successors of the apostles" is sometimes applied to the bishops and the bishops alone. This title could be misleading for three reasons. First, the apostles were founders of the Church, and as such they have no successors. Second, the apostles, as wandering missionaries, did not have regular administrative responsibility for any particular local church. Third, we have no clear biblical or historical evidence that the apostles designated any particular class of persons in the Church to take over their transmissible functions. Still, the expression "successors of the apostles" can, if necessary, be defended.[12] For the bishops, in modern ecclesiastical polity, have a kind of general supervision, on the highest level, of all the functions of the Church, and in this way they resemble the New Testament *apostoloi*, at least as portrayed in the early chapters of Acts.

The precise reasons for the emergence of the *episkopoi* as a kind of ruling class in the Church need not concern us here. Presumably the power shift had something to do with the necessity of strong organizational structures to ward off heresies such as Gnosticism, Marcionism, and Montanism and to equip the Church to stand up under the pressures of persecution. It seems likely, too, that religious leaders imitated, consciously or unconsciously, the civil structure of government in the Roman Empire.

In the post-Tridentine Church, and in the neo-Scholastic theology of the nineteenth and twentieth centuries, the dialectical tension between the charisms in the Church is virtually eliminated. All authentic teaching power is simply transferred to the episcopal order. The main disadvantage in this system is that the bishop is given an almost unbearable load of responsibility. He becomes in his diocese—at least theoretically—not only the highest administrator but also the chief priest and the supreme teacher. In this last capacity he is supposed to be in a position to settle intellectually all disputed doctrinal questions. To illustrate this awesome doctrinal responsibility, one may refer, for example, to the Ethical and Religious Directives for Catholic Health Facilities issued by the United States bishops in 1971, which state:

> The moral evaluation of new scientific developments and legitimately debated questions must be finally submitted to the teaching authority of the Church in the person of the local bishop, who has the ultimate responsibility for teaching Catholic doctrine.[13]

In order to encourage the vigorous exercise of this responsibility, and to facilitate compliance with the bishop's doctrinal decisions, the authors strongly emphasize the grace of the episcopal office. They frequently quote St. Irenaeus to the effect that the bishops have the "sure charism of truth" (*charisma veritatis certum*).[14] But they neglect to mention that Irenaeus in this passage acknowledges that presbyters as well as bishops have this "charisma." Furthermore, according to many commentators, *charisma veritatis* in this passage signifies not a subjective grace for discerning the truth but the objective deposit of faith, "the precious and spiritual gift entrusted to the Church."[15] Irenaeus, speaking to the situation of his own time, was presumably referring to the fact that the apostles had thoroughly instructed the persons to whom they turned over the leadership of the apostolic churches.

The neo-Scholastic theory, in my opinion, is very unconvincing. It fails to give a rationale for the kind of collaboration between bishops and theologians that has normally existed in the Church. There are ample resources for a better theory both in the New Testament and in the earlier theological tradition.

From Acts and the Pauline letters, one has the impression that there was a special class of individuals in the early Church recognized as having received from the Holy Spirit the gift of teaching Christian doctrine.[16] The *didaskaloi* could teach in their own right and were not viewed as mere representatives of *episkopoi* or *presbyteroi*. The *episkopos* was primarily an administrator or, perhaps better, a pastor—a true shepherd of the flock. The presbyter-bishop was expected, among other things, to be "an apt teacher" (1 Tim. 3:2; cf. Tit. 1:9), but he was not expected to be a paragon of learning or to appropriate all doctrinal functions to himself. In many passages the *didaskaloi* are seen as a distinct class. According to Paul's ecclesiastical polity, as set forth in 1 Corinthians, the various ministries in the Church are bound together by mutual interdependence, as are the organs in a living body. Just as the eye and the ear cannot say to each other, "I have no need of you," so the teacher, the prophet, and the administrator must recognize their dependence upon one another for the sake of better service to the entire Christian community.

If this is true, it would seem to follow that those who have the specialization of teaching in the Church should have a voice in doctrinal decisions. In the words of a contemporary New Testament scholar:

If there is any group in the Church which has the right to be heard when the Church makes decisions it is that composed of those to whom the charism of teaching has been given, the *didaskaloi*, who, in the list of 1 Cor. 12:28 rank third after the apostles and prophets. If this charism now exists in the Church apart from the hierarchy—and to deny that it does is utterly arbitrary—it is surely possessed by the theologians. If the "whole Church" is to have a part in the making of decisions, particularly in the making of decisions which bear upon the content of faith, the proper authority of the theologians must be given much more weight than is often the case in the present functioning of the Church.[17]

In the early centuries the concentration of authority in the episcopal office did no great harm because the bishops of those times were less heavily burdened with administrative responsibilities than are their modern successors. Many of them were charismatic leaders and theologians. Irenaeus and Cyprian, Augustine and Leo, Athanasius and Chrysostom, Cyril of Jerusalem and Cyril of Alexandria, Gregory of Nyssa and Gregory of Nazianzus—these and many other great patristic theologians were also bishops.

In the Middle Ages, the doctoral function once again had a certain autonomy. As the cathedral schools outgrew the personal control of the bishops and evolved into universities with theological faculties, the *magistri* and *doctores* were seen as the primary teachers. Thomas Aquinas, for instance, makes a sharp distinction between the *officium praelationis* (prelacy), possessed by the bishop, and the *officium magisterii* (magisterium), which belongs to the professional theologian.[18] In one text he does speak of a magisterium of bishops, but only in a qualified sense; for he draws a distinction between the *magisterium cathedrae pastoralis* (pastoral magisterium), which belongs to the bishop, and the *magisterium cathedrae magistralis* (magisterial magisterium), which pertains to the theologian.[19] The former, he holds, is concerned with the regulation of preaching and public order in the Church rather than with the intricacies of speculation.[20] The *magistri*, according to St. Thomas, teach by learning and argument rather than by appeal to their official status. The conclusions are no more valid than the evidence they are able to adduce. In this sense, therefore, the magisterium of the theologians is unauthoritative.[21]

In the course of the thirteenth century we see the beginnings of what Yves Congar calls a "magisterium of doctors" in the Church.[22] Over and above the task of scientific teaching, doctors and university faculties begin to acquire a certain decisive role, especially in judging cases of alleged heresy. The *studium* thus gradually takes its place as a third force in Christendom, alongside the *sacerdotium* and the *regnum*. By order of Pope Clement V, the decrees of the Council of Vienne (1311-12) were not made official until they had been submitted to the universities for approval. At a number of Councils in the later Middle Ages, including Constance and Basel, the theologians were given a deliberative vote even though they were not bishops.[23] Facts such as these call into question the correctness of the statement, so often made in the past century, that theologians do not belong to the magisterium.

I recognize, of course, that theologians, whose energies are so often taken up with subtle speculative questions, are not always well suited to make decisions of a practical nature concerning the government and public preaching of the Church. It is necessary that there be pastoral authorities whose main concern is to supervise the mission and good order of the Church as a community of faith and witness. On the other hand, it is important that questions touching on the order of revelation and theology should not be settled without regard for the demands of truth and scholarship. In questions of a mixed nature, involving both pastoral and academic considerations, there is need for close collaboration between bishops, as holders of the chief pastoral power, and theologians.[24]

In making this recommendation I feel that I am merely articulating what is in practice developing. At Vatican II the theologians had considerable visibility, and in some cases it was well known that they were the real authors of certain speeches given by bishops and of certain sections of conciliar documents. Since the Council Pope Paul VI has set up an International Theological Commission that, even with limited autonomy, speaks in its own name. In the United States, as elsewhere, efforts are being made to establish regular working relationships between the bishops and learned societies such as the Catholic Theological Society of America, the Canon Law Society of America, and others. Groups of theologians collaborate closely with the National Conference of Catholic Bishops, especially through its Commission for Ecumenical and Interreligious Affairs. Both in the United States and abroad, it is common for consensus statements emanating from ecumenical dialogues to be signed by bishops and by theologians as co-authors. This practice might in the course of time be extended to other statements, more properly magisterial in character.

The tendencies represented by these new initiatives are in my opinion signs of closer collaboration, without confusion, between the scholarly and the pastoral functions in the Church. As this process continues, it may become possible for scholars to have a greater initiative in selecting their colleagues who are to be in contact with the Pope and the bishops, lest those who do collaborate come to be labeled "court theologians." I would hope also that there could be regular consultations in which theologians would have an appropriate input into the agenda.

The proper balance of authority demands that theologians should not be merely apologists for what the pastoral leaders decide, nor mere consultors to the pastors (though they may well be this *also*), but that they have a recognized voice in the Church, with a certain relative autonomy to develop their own positions by their own methodology and to seek to gain acceptance for these positions by the pastoral magisterium.

In speaking of the scholar's independence I am by no means returning to the position of Kant, rejected at the beginning of this chapter, but I am, I would hope, recognizing what is sound in the Kantian thesis. With Kant I would hold that it is possible and necessary to assess authoritative pronouncements in the light of rational criteria, but against him I am maintaining that theology is as much concerned with truth as are philosophy and the natural sciences. The theologian can be a true scholar — one who asks the hard questions and honestly expresses his real convictions — without on that account being less bound to the community of faith or less respectful toward the authorities recognized in the Church. In fact the Catholic Christian, reflecting on the faith, will find positive aids to truth in all the types of authority discussed in the preceding pages — the Bible, the "sense of the faithful," and the decisions reached in previous ages through interaction among pastors, prophets, and theologians. None of these instances, in my opinion, is a peremptory authority in isolation from the others, but in combination they afford the guidance needed for the sustenance of Christian faith and the progress of theology. Christian theology, as I understand the term, presupposes a commitment to the saving truth disclosed in the Christian sources.[25]

To give a somewhat practical turn to what I have been saying about teaching authority, I should like to conclude with some observations on dissent. This problem is, I suspect, one that will never cease to recur both in civil society and in the Church. There will always be painful conflicts between some who are sincerely convinced that certain ideas are intolerable within the community of faith and others who believe these same ideas are true or at least compatible with Christian commitment. I cannot propose a full solution, but pastors and theologians can, I think, fruitfully ponder together the sources of the difficulty and the best ways of treating conflicts so that they do not become destructive.

Dissent, in the sense in which we are using the term, is a matter internal to the society in which the opposite position is normative. Dissent in the Church means that a member of the Church takes exception to the position that has become official. Dissent therefore cannot be absolute. It occurs within the context of a larger agreement — namely, the acceptance of Christ as the supreme revelation of God and of the Church as the place where Christ is made specially present and accessible.

Generally speaking, dissent pertains not to fundamental articles of faith, which are regarded as constitutive of membership, but to relatively secondary teachings. Dissent can exist within the Church because it is not usual, nor would it be proper, to impose the supreme penalty of excommunication for views not infallibly proclaimed as pertaining to the very substance of the faith. Thus it is possible to be a Christian and a member of the Church even when one disagrees with certain official teachings.

The problem of dissent has always existed in the Church, but has not always been equally acute. In the "fortress Church" of the past several centuries, dissent was kept to a minimum. Catholics felt a strong obligation to stick together for the sake of survival, and were therefore willing to subject their personal judgment to that of the ruling authorities. The ecclesiology of nineteenth-century neo-Scholasticism, with its heavy stress on "official charisms," tended to reinforce the authority structures. Dissent was handled by essentially the same moral principles as were applied to the case of an erroneous conscience, and thus insufficient consideration was given to the possibility that dissent might be a corrective force in the Church.[26]

The phenomenon of dissent has been intensified in recent years by all the factors that have tended to weaken the "hierocratic" view of authority and to substitute the kind of pluralistic or dialogic view I have attempted to sketch. Three aspects of the general climate of ideas may be singled out for special mention.

1. Under the influence of psychological and philosophical currents, our age has become particularly sensitive to the values of freedom and authenticity, and to the dignity of conscience as the ultimate norm for moral choice. Typical of our times is an abhorrence of laws and institutions that inhibit personal freedom, and a deep conviction that true religion should help its adherents to become mature, responsible persons. As previously explained, this does not mean a rejection of authority but it does involve a certain relativizing of authority.

2. Thanks to modern means of travel and communications, the believer almost inevitably lives in a pluralistic situation, at the intersection of many different cultures and traditions. This pluralism was sanctioned by Vatican II, which invited the Church to seek out new forms of solidarity with the various cultures of humankind. There are increasingly few protected havens in which the mind of the faithful is predominantly formed by official Catholic teaching.

3. The Freudian and Marxist critiques of ideology, combined with evident abuses of power on the part of leaders in the political and economic world, have made us acutely aware that officeholders are under a constant temptation to employ their power to bolster up their position. When Popes and bishops insist very heavily on apostolic succession, divine right, and the special graces attached to their office, they leave themselves open to the suspicion that ideology is at work.

Vatican II, in its formal discussion of the teaching authority of Popes and bishops, did not directly challenge the reigning neo-Scholastic theory. Article 25 of the *Constitution on the Church* may be interpreted as supporting the standard position of the day. It affirms the obligation to assent to the ordinary non-infallible teaching of the Roman Pontiff without any explicit mention of the right to dissent. Several bishops at the Council submitted a proposal that allowance should be made for the case of an educated person who for solid reasons finds himself unable to assent internally to such teaching. To this the Doctrinal Commission replied that "approved theological explanations should be consulted."[27] Thus the Council in its formal teaching did not advance the discussion of dissent beyond where it had been in the previous generation.

Indirectly, however, the Council worked powerfully to undermine the authoritarian theory and to legitimate dissent in the Church. This it did in part by insisting on the necessary freedom of the act of faith and by attributing a primary role to personal conscience in the moral life. By contrast, the neo-Scholastic doctrine of the magisterium, with its heavy accentuation of "blind obedience," minimizes the value of understanding and maturity in the life of faith.

Most importantly for our purposes, Vatican II quietly reversed the earlier positions of the Roman magisterium on a number of important issues. The obvious examples are well known. In biblical studies, for instance, the *Constitution on Divine Revelation* accepted a critical approach to the Bible, thus supporting the previous initiatives of Pius XII and delivering the Church once and for all from the incubus of the earlier decrees of the Biblical Commission. In the *Decree on Ecumenism*, the Council cordially greeted the ecumenical movement and involved the Catholic Church in the larger quest for Christian unity, thus putting an end to the hostility enshrined in Pius XII's *Mortalium animos*. In Church-state relations, the *Declaration on Religious Freedom* accepted the religiously neutral state, thus reversing the previously approved view that the state should formally profess the truth of Catholicism. In the theology of secular realities, the *Pastoral Constitution on the Church in the Modern World* adopted an evolutionary view of history and a modified optimism regarding secular systems of thought, thus terminating more than a century of vehement denunciations of modern civilization.[28]

As a result of these and other revisions, the Council rehabilitated many theologians who had suffered under severe restrictions with regard to their ability to teach and publish. The names of John Courtney Murray, Pierre Teilhard de Chardin, Henri de Lubac, and Yves Congar, all under a cloud of suspicion in the 1950's, suddenly became surrounded with a bright halo of enthusiasm.

By its actual practice of revision, the Council implicitly taught the legitimacy and even the value of dissent. In effect the Council said that the ordinary magisterium of the Roman Pontiff had fallen into error and had unjustly harmed the careers of loyal and able scholars. Some of the thinkers who had resisted official teaching in the pre-conciliar period were among the principal precursors and architects of Vatican II.

As a result of the conciliar experience, together with the general climate of ideas previously alluded to, dissent is today perceived by many sophisticated Catholics as an inevitable and potentially beneficial phenomenon. Many would not wish to have a situation, even if it were possible, in which every Catholic agreed with every stated position of the hierarchy. On the other hand, dissent can be a source of confusion and discord; it is not something to be desired for its own sake. To alleviate the harmful effects of dissent, I would submit the following recommendations:

1. The pastoral magisterium should keep in close touch with the theologians and other intellectuals in the Church. Popes and bishops would do well not to act without benefit of the best available scholarship, as happened, to the detriment of the Church, when the Biblical Commission issued some of its less enlightened decrees. Conversely, scholars in the Church should try to cultivate greater sensitivity to pastoral considerations.

2. Generally speaking, the pastoral leaders should not speak in a binding way unless a relatively wide consensus has first been achieved. For authentic consensus to develop, there is need of free discussion. Only when it becomes clear through such discussion that the weight of responsible opinion decisively favors one side over the other can true consensus arise.

3. Where no such consensus exists, it is well to acknowledge publicly that good Christians do in fact disagree. Such disagreement will hardly be scandalous in our times, when open clashes of opinion are common in the scientific and political worlds. It would, however, be scandalous for the holders of pastoral power to suppress freedom of expression and debate on issues where there is as yet no agreed solution.

4. Even where there is no consensus, Popes, bishops, and others in authority may clearly and candidly state their convictions on matters of pastoral importance and seek to win assent for their

own positions by giving testimony and adducing arguments. If they do this without trying to impose their views by juridical pressures, they will generally meet with a favorable response on the part of the faithful who are hungry for pastoral leadership.

5. When members of the Church find themselves sincerely unable to give assent to a given teaching of the pastoral authorities, they should not feel that they are on that account disloyal or unfaithful. Non-infallible teaching, as Richard A. McCormick has pointed out, does not bring with it an immediate obligation to assent. Rather, it calls for "religious docility and deference—always on the assumption, of course, that authority has proceeded properly."[29] In view of such deference, the dissenter will be reluctant to conclude that the official teaching is clearly erroneous; he will carefully reassess his own position in the light of that teaching, and he will behave in a manner that fosters respect and support for the pastoral magisterium, even though he continues to strive for a revision of the current official teaching.

6. Provided that they speak with evident loyalty and respect for authority, dissenters should not be silenced. As already noted, experience has shown that in many cases those who dissent from Church teaching in one generation are preparing the official positions of the Church in the future. Vatican II owes many of its successes to the very theologians who were under a cloud in the pontificate of Pius XII. The Church, like civil society, should cherish its "loyal opposition" as a precious asset.

These principles, although they seem quite evident in the light of the general ecclesiology governing this study, will be contested by some. There are still those who look upon the Church as an institution that must give oracular responses to all really important questions, and who consequently regard dissent as tantamount to disloyalty. My own point of view is governed by the vision of the Church as a pilgrim community renewing itself by creative interaction with its changing environment. The Church, "like a pilgrim in a foreign land," receives from the risen Lord not a clear vision of ultimate truth but the power "to show forth in the world the mystery of the Lord in a faithful though shadowed way, until at last it will be revealed in total splendor."[30] Thus the Church may in some sense be called a "Society of Explorers"—to borrow a term from Michael

Polanyi's prescription for the scientific community.[31] The Church, like any other society, needs outside criticism, and depends on all the help that its thoughtful members can provide in the task of discerning the real meaning of the Gospel for our time. Faith, then, is not simply a matter of accepting a fixed body of doctrine. More fundamentally, it is a committed and trustful participation in an ongoing process. In the course of responsible discussion, certain previously accepted doctrines will be modified. For progress to be achieved, there must be discussion, and for there to be discussion, all must be assured of their "lawful freedom of inquiry and of thought, and of the freedom to express their minds humbly and courageously about those matters in which they enjoy competence."[32] Without such freedom, and thus without the possibility of dissent, the Church would be deprived of that creative interaction which, as we have seen, is the key to authentic renewal.

Notes

1. Kant, "What Is Enlightenment?" in C. J. Friedrich, ed., *Kant's Moral and Political Writings* (New York: Modern Library, 1949), pp. 132-39.

2. See A. Dulles, *The Survival of Dogma* (Garden City: Doubleday, 971; Image Books, 1973), esp. chaps. 2 and 3.

3. William Chillingworth gave this principle its sharpest formulation: "The BIBLE, I say, the BIBLE only, is the Religion of Protestants" (*The Religion of Protestants, A Safe Way to Salvation*, published 1638). The so-called "material principle" of the Reformation, "Scripture alone," is ably criticized by Wolfhart Pannenberg in his essay "The Crisis of the Scripture Principle," *Basic Questions in Theology,* 1 (Philadelphia: Fortress, 1970), pp. 1-14. But Pannenberg, here and elsewhere, tends to exalt the role of reason to the detriment of authority. His positions are best understood as a reaction against the excesses of the "theology of the word" in some sections of contemporary European Protestantism.

4. For a critique, see K. Rahner, "The Teaching Office of the Church in the Present-Day Crisis of Authority," *Theological Investigations,* 12 (New York: Seabury, 1974), pp. 3-30.

5. See Alois Müller, ed., *Democratization of the Church,* Concilium Vol. 63 (New York: Herder and Herder, 1971). A nuanced presentation of the problem is given by Patrick Granfield in his *Ecclesial*

Cybernetics: A Study of Democracy in the Church (New York: Macmillan, 1973). While holding that the Catholic Church neither is nor should be a democracy (p. 186), Granfield contends that it is in need of "cybernetic reform through democratization" (p. 211). As a correction to the hierocratic model, this cybernetic model makes an important contribution.

6. *Lumen Gentium,* n. 12, in W. M. Abbott, ed., *The Documents of Vatican II* (New York: America Press, 1966), p. 29.

7. For a fuller statement of my position on this point see Dulles, *The Survival of Dogma,* chap. 5.

8. Y. Congar, "Norms of Christian Allegiance and Identity in the History of the Church," in E. Schillebeeckx, ed., *Truth and Certainty,* Concilium Vol. 83 (New York: Herder and Herder, 1973), pp. 24-25.

9. *Dei Verbum,* n. 10, in Abbott, p. 118.

10. See J. L. McKenzie, *Authority in the Church* (New York: Sheed and Ward, 1966), chap. 5.

11. A brief but very helpful study of the New Testament *episkopoi* may be found in R. E. Brown, *Priest and Bishop: Biblical Reflections* (New York: Paulist Press, 1970), esp, pp. 34-40.

12. See the paper drawn up by the International Theological Commission, "Apostolic Succession: A Clarification," *Origins,* 4, No. 13 (Sept. 19, 1974), pp. 193-200.

13. Text in John Dedek, *Contemporary Medical Ethics* (New York: Sheed and Ward, 1975), p. 208.

14. Irenaeus, *Adversus haereses* 4.26.2, in *Patrologia Graeca* 7:1053; Eng. trans. in *The Ante-Nicene Fathers* (New York: Scribner's 1899), Vol. 1, p. 497.

15. Y. Congar, *Tradition and Traditions:* (New York: Macmillan, 1967), p. 177. Congar is here following the view of K. Müller and D. van den Eynde. For an alternative interpretation see Louis Ligier, "Le *Charisma veritatis certum* des évêques," in *L'Homme devant Dieu: Mélanges offerts au Père Henri de Lubac* (Paris: Aubier, 1963), Vol. 1, pp. 247-68; also Norbert Brox, "Charisma vertatis certum," *Zeitschrift für Kirchengeschichte,* 75 (1964), pp. 327-31.

16. On teaching authority in the Church of the apostolic age, see McKenzie, *Authority in the Church,* chaps. 5 and 6.

17. Myles M. Bourke, "Collegial Decision-Making in the New Testament," in J. A. Coriden, ed., *Who Decides for the Church?* (Hartford: Canon Law Society of America, 1971), p. 13.

18. Thomas Aquinas, *In 4 Sent.,* Dist. 19, q. 2, a. 2, qua. 2, ad 4 (Parma ed., vol. 7, p. 852).

19. Thomas Aquinas, *Quodlibet* 3, qu. 4, art. 1 (Parma ed., vol. 9, p. 490).

20. See also Thomas Aquinas, *Contra Impugnantes Dei cultum et religionem,* chap. 2 (Parma ed., vol. 15, p. 7).

21. M. D. Chenu, " 'Authentica' et 'magistralia.' Deux lieux théologiques aux XII-XIII siècles," *Divus Thomas* (Piacenza), 28 (1925),

pp. 257-85. Cf. Chenu, *La théologie au douzième siècle,* 2nd ed. (Paris: Vrin, 1966), pp. 351-65.

22. Y. Congar, "Brève Histoire des Formes du 'Magistère' et ses relations avec les docteurs," *Rev. des sciences phil. et theol.,* 60 (1976), p. 104.

23. For some brief historical indications with further references see Dulles, *The Survival of Dogma,* chap. 6.

24. Collegial association of the members of the hierarchical magisterium and individual theologians is called for by the International Theological Commission in the fourth of its *Theses on the Relationship Between the Ecclesiastical Magisterium and Theology* (Washington, D.C.: USCC, 1977) p. 3. An excellent discussion of current relationships may be found in A. L. Descamps, "Théologie et magistère," *Ephemerides theologicae lovanienses,* 52, no. 1 (June 1976), pp. 82-133. In discussing the relations between bishops and theologians, one should not lose sight of what has been said earlier in this chapter about the authority of the whole body of the faithful. It goes without saying that both pastors and theologians should seek to maintain close contact with the laity, upon whom rests the chief burden of living out the faith in the circumstances of today's world.

25. I thus differ from those who hold that the Christian theologian need not write from the perspective of Christian belief and that the Christian texts should not function as norms for theology. David Tracy, in his *Blessed Rage for Order* (New York: Seabury Press, 1975), argues that the theologian's commitment should be to the "faith of secularity" which is shared in common by the secularist and the modern Christian (p. 8), and that the fundamental loyalty of the theologian should be to "that morality of scientific knowledge which he shares with his colleagues, the philosophers, historians, and social scientists" (p. 7). Tracy accordingly contends that the traditional Christian beliefs may not serve as warrants for theological arguments (*ibid.*). Richard P. McBrien, in his review, rightly points out that Tracy's position apparently rests on a positivistic conception of "the Christian fact" and that it "seems to erase the difference between theology and philosophy" (*Commonweal,* 103, No. 25 [Dec. 3, 1976], pp. 797-98). For a discussion of possible differences between Tracy and myself I refer again to my review article, "Method in Fundamental Theology," *Theological Studies,* 37 (1976), pp. 304-16.

26. A brief catena of quotations from typical manualists and other "approved authors" of the period between the two Vatican Councils may be found in H. J. McSorley, "Some Ecclesiological Reflections on *Humanae Vitae,*" *Bijdragen,* 30 (1969), pp. 3-8. For a fuller discussion of the same theme see J. A. Komonchak, "Ordinary Papal Magisterium and Religious Assent," in C. E. Curran, ed., *Contraception: Authority and Dissent* (New York: Herder and Herder, 1969), pp. 101-26.

27. See "Some Ecclesiological Reflections on *Humanae Vitae,*" McSorley, p. 3; Komonchak, "Ordinary Papal Magisterium and Religious Assent," pp. 104-05.

28. For some prudent reservations with regard to this last assertion, see L. J. O'Donovan, "Was Vatican II Evolutionary?" *Theological Studies*, 36 (1975), pp. 493-502.

29. R. A. McCormick, "The Magisterium: A New Model," *America*, 122, No. 25 (June 27, 1970), p. 675. See also McCormick's fuller discussions of the magisterium and dissent in *Theological Studies*, 29 (1968), pp. 714-18; 30 (1969), pp. 644-68; and 38 (1977), 84-100; and in *Proceedings of the Catholic Theological Society of America*, 24 (1969), pp. 239-54.

30. *Lumen Gentium*, n. 8, in Abbott, p. 24.

31. M. Polanyi, *The Tacit Dimension* (Garden City: Doubleday Anchor Books, 1967), pp. 53-92.

32. *Gaudium et Spes*, n. 62, in Abbott, p. 270.

The Magisterium and the Field of Theology

John R. Quinn

Contemporary problems touching the magisterium appear to be reducible to two main questions: 1. Which members of the Church hold the magisterial office? What are the conditions and limits of dissent from the papal-episcopal magisterium?

Historically I believe that the first question has risen out of the second, since it is the actual dissent of some theologians in recent years which has led to the more basic discussion of who holds the magisterial office. But there is a wider cultural and ideological background to the present discussion.

First is the dominance of the scientific method. The scientific method has gradually gained hegemony as the only acceptable way of knowing reality. What cannot be verified through the application of the scientific method is rather commonly thought to be unworthy of anything more than private opinion and speculation. This frame of mind, of course, excludes most forms of philosophical knowledge, and more so it excludes divine revelation and theology as valid avenues of true knowledge. This in turn has led to the present dichotomy between orthodoxy and orthopraxis which regards questions of truth as inconsequential and is exclusively concerned with practicalities.

The second factor making up the wider background of the problem is the cultural phenomenon of the new emphasis on human dignity, freedom and rights, the new personalism which so cherishes self-determination and self-fulfillment and tends to reject what would influence thought or opinion from outside or above.

I mention these factors not to reject them outright since it is obvious that there is a place for the scientific method as well as for a wholesome personalism. Yet these two factors carried beyond their proper sphere do have destructive and reprehensible features and both have some bearing on the present problem.

To return, then to the first question: the holders of the magisterial office in the Church. It is essential to the very being of the Church that it preserve and hand on to every age the apostolic heritage of the faith. It is therefore of paramount importance that the Church have some clear understanding as to whose primary responsibility that task is.

Not surprisingly, then, the Second Vatican Council dealt with that question. Of the sixteen major documents of the Council only four were called constitutions, and of these four only two were called "dogmatic" constitutions: the *Dogmatic Constitution on the Church* and the *Dogmatic Constitution on Divine Revelation*. They were so titled in order to indicate the mind of the Council that it intended to speak of principles and truths of the faith and the common belief of the Church.

In the *Dogmatic Constitution on the Church* the Second Vatican Council unfolds its teaching on the magisterium. It bases itself on Sacred Scripture, the Councils of Florence, Trent and the First Vatican Council as well as on Clement of R;me, Ignatius of Antioch, Tertullian and Irenaeus among others. I mention this simply because some have given the impression that the Second Vatican Council's position was only founded in the First Vatican Council or only rooted in Irenaeus.

The salient points of the teaching of the Second Vatican Council, then, may be summarized as follows:

1. The bishops together with the Pope are the successors of the college of the apostles.

2. As St. Peter held a primacy among the apostles, the Pope is the successor of St. Peter and head of the college of bishops.

3. The magisterium or teaching office belongs to the Pope in a special manner as the successor of St. Peter and to the bishops in communion with him as successors of the college of the apostles.

The Council then deals with various points concerning the obligation of the faithful to accept the teaching of the magisterium both when it is given *ex cathedra* and when it functions as the ordinary magisterium.

In the mind of the Council the Church does not now nor has it in the past understood anyone other than bishops and the Pope as comprising the magisterium. A new approach, however, has been presented recently by Fr. Avery Dulles. I admire and applaud his effort to try to probe this complex matter of the relationship of theologians to the magisterium, although I cannot agree in all respects with his conclusions.

After stating "I should like to propose, as theologically more acceptable, a pluralistic theory of authority in the Church," he goes on to say, "The Church, I would maintain, depends for its health and vigor upon the co-existence of several distinct organs of authority, and hence on multiple groups of believers. These authorities serve as mutual checks and balances. They exist in a state of natural tension and dialogue, and only when they converge can authority make itself fully felt" (Avery Dulles, S.J., *The Resilient Church*, Doubleday and Co., 1977, p. 99).

If I have understood him correctly, Fr. Dulles prefers the term authority to magisterium in enunciating his theory. As authorities he lists six things: Sacred Scripture, sacred tradition, the *sensus fidelium*, the pastoral office, theologians, and persons of great holiness.

The first two are considered constitutive of the Church and normative. But the major weakness of the theory is that it in effect proposes an undifferentiated or oligarchical magisterium of bishops, theologians and saints. In this case I do not see how there could be any point of real certitude for the faithful if the magisterium is conceived as a fugue of frequently dissonant voices forming a choir with no director.

The second weakness in Fr. Dulles' theory is his too limited understanding of the pastoral office. Thus he states, "From the Acts and the Pauline letters, one has the impression that there was a special class of individuals in the early Church recognized as having received from the Holy Spirit the gift of teaching Christian doctrine. The *didaskaloi* could teach in their own right, and were not viewed as mere representatives of *episcopoi* or *presbyteroi*. The *episcopos* was primarily an administrator or, perhaps better, a pastor — a true shepherd of the flock" (*ibid.*, p. 103).

This conception of the pastoral office of the bishop as primarily administrative or primarily concerned with people's everyday problems and needs at the practical level seems to me to do too little justice to the biblical concept of pastor as one who feeds the flock and to the biblical and patristic notion of "feeding" as including the teaching of the faith and sound doctrine. It also seems to me to do too little justice to the wealth of patristic teaching on the office of bishop as preacher and teacher of the flock and as the center and bond of communion for his church. This communion has never been understood as a mere social reality but above all as a unity of faith. To be the bond of the unity of faith necessarily makes the pastor a teacher and judge of the faith.

To take up the second question, the conditions and limits of dissent, I would begin by pointing out the dangers of two extremes. The first extreme is embodied in the affirmation that we are obligated to accept only what is defined and that everything else is an open question. The second extreme is to raise every pronouncement of the magisterium to the level of a definition.

The problem with the first extreme is that it paves the way for the rejection of defined teaching, since often what is defined was previously taught by the ordinary magisterium for some time. To make a sudden change from rejection of a doctrine to complete acceptance is to say the least psychologically very difficult and frequently impossible.

The problem with the second extreme is the failure to make appropriate differentiation between what is taught with a measure of tentativeness and what is taught with the full and complete support of the magisterium. When what is taught as somewhat tentative is later changed, as does happen, then there is the same tendency to reject what is defined as also being tentative.

In this connection I would agree with Fr. Dulles that the correct attitude would be characterized by religious docility and deference, by reluctance to conclude that the official teaching is clearly erroneous, and that it is always necessary to behave and speak in a manner which fosters respect and support for the magisterium (*ibid.*, p. 111).

On June 6, 1976, the International Theological Commission published *Twelve Theses on the Relationship Between the Ecclesiastical Magisterium and Theology* (English edition, USCC Publications Office, 1977). The twelve theses were agreed on by the great majority of the commission. These twelve theses offer sound guidelines for both the theory and practice of the relationship and I think may be summarized in this way:

1. The magisterium and theology have distinct roles in the Church and function with different methodologies but they are interdependent also.

2. Both share a common task though in analogous fashion. The common task is "'preserve the sacred deposit of revelation, to examine it more deeply, to explain, teach and defend it' for the service of the people of God and for the whole world's salvation."

3. "The magisterium and the theologians differ in the quality of the authority with which they carry out their tasks."

A. The authority of the magisterium derives from sacramental ordination.

B. Theologians derive their specifically theological authority from their scientific qualifications.

4. The difference between the magisterium and theology also calls for special consideration of the freedom proper to each:

A. "By its nature and institution, the magisterium is clearly free in carrying out its task. And while it is often difficult, it is nonetheless necessary that the magisterium use its proper freedom in such a way that it not appear to theologians or to the faithful at large to be arbitrary or excessive."

B. "To the freedom of the magisterium there corresponds in its own way the freedom that derives from the true scientific responsibility of theologians. It is not an unlimited freedom, for besides being bound to the truth, it is also true of theology that 'in the use of any freedom, the moral principle of personal and social responsibility must be observed.'"

Thesis Nine enunciates a truth which it will be the greater part of wisdom to remember: "The exercise of their tasks by the magisterium and theologians often gives rise to a certain tension. But this is not surprising, nor should one expect that such tension will ever be fully resolved here on earth. On the contrary, wherever there is genuine life, tension also exists. Such tension need not be interpreted as hostility or real opposition, but can be seen as a vital force and an incentive to a common carrying out of the respective tasks by way of dialogue."

The magisterium needs theologians not only to fulfill its task prudently but also to fulfill its task in a way that does justice to its sacred mission. Theologians also need the magisterium and need to be guided by the authoritative teaching of the magisterium.

Above the tangled casuistry of "Who is greatest in the kingdom?" rises the grand vision of the symphony of truth. As the crowd arrives the musicians are tuning their instruments in a rain of discordant scales and arpeggios. But there comes the moment when the piano sounds its A-major and all the many instruments form a single harmony of one note. As the symphony begins, each distinctive instrument plays its own assigned melody fashioned by the composer for the nature of that instrument, yet all together conspire to develop in concord and beauty the unifying theme of his genius.

In the plan of God, the Church is not only a body, it is also a symphony of truth and beauty and in that symphony all the instruments must play their part in the harmony of love and charity.

The Magisterium
vs. the Theologians:
Debunking Some Fictions

Raymond E. Brown, S.S.

I last spoke to the National Catholic Educational Association convention in New Orleans on the subject "Teaching Religion in a Time of Theological Change."[1] That topic was requested because of difficulties then being faced in designing guidelines and a directory for religious education. In overreaction to the challenge of Vatican II, some forms of religious education had concentrated on personal formation at the cost of content, and the bishops were wisely concerned. However, in the search to reinsert content there was a danger that voices of the extreme right, more vocal than their numbers would warrant, might have undue influence in shaping guidelines. My talk, insisting on content but a content that would not simply repeat past formulas with the naive assumption that they meet the problems of all times, was not likely to be appreciated by purists on either side of the dispute. All these memories flashed before me when the NCEA requested me to speak at this seventy-fifth anniversary convention on another "hot potato": How teachers might cope with disputes between the magisterium and theologians. Inevitably I repeated the old maxim: "With friends like these inviting me, I shall not want for enemies."

The fact that I accepted the invitation does not mean that I have superior wisdom on an already much discussed topic. If I understand correctly, the final form of the National Catechetical Directory has been submitted to Rome for approval, and it will contain some practical directions for teachers of religion in relation to this question. In earlier forms, the Directory showed balance in respecting necessary pluralism in theology and the rights of investigation; and so as regards principles, the Directory will probably be adequate and certainly needs no supplementation from me.

Nor am I interested in entering the debate about the term "magisterium." We all know that careful historical studies have shown that the equation of magisterium with the Pope and the bishops (in council or out) is relatively recent and does not do justice to the previously more active role of the *magister theologiae* (the medieval teacher of theology).

Be that as it may, I tend to be pragmatic about terminology. Many of my biblical confreres use the term "myth" in relation to the New Testament, arguing eloquently and correctly that it need not connote falsehood. But since it has a connotation of falsehood for most people, I avoid the term in my study of the New Testament simply because I think it raises more difficulty than it is worth, and that a circumlocution that does not cause resentment serves more effectively to communicate the nuance I desire.

Similarly magisterium is a fighting word; I think the attempt to reclaim it for theologians will not succeed; and I personally do not think the battle worth fighting so long as, under any other name, the legitimate role of theologians in shaping the teaching of the Church is respected.

In estimating that role I recognize that I may be more modest than some of my Catholic theologian friends. All that I want is that scholarly evidence be taken into account in the formulation or reformulation of Catholic doctrine and that theologians be sincerely treated as dialogue partners to be listened to (not obeyed). If I may be permitted to quote myself to show that I have remained very consistent on this point, in dealing with the sensitive topics of the virginal conception and bodily resurrection I stated:

A responsible answer to these questions must take into account the evidence as scholars view it today. Notice that what I ask is that the answer *take into account* the scholarly evidence. It would be sheer nonsense for me to pretend that scholars can give the Catholic answer to these questions.

When it is a question of doctrinal teaching, it is the Church through its various organs of teaching and belief that gives the answer. Thus I offer here no ammunition for the charge that theological scholars are usurping the rights of the magisterium of the Church by their investigations of past doctrines with an eye to possible modification. For the most part theologians are quite aware that the evidence they offer must be assessed within the wider context of the Church's life guided by the Spirit and are only too happy to put their evidence at the service of the magisterium.[2]

If that past statement of mine may seem to some theologians not to do justice to their understanding of the role they should have, I am sure that to some on the other side it will seem too slighting of their understanding of the magisterium. After all, I said that *the Church* gives the answer "through its various organs of teaching and belief"; I did not say that the magisterium alone gives the answers (and by "magisterium" consistently in the rest of this paper I mean the Pope and the bishops).

Perhaps both the magisterium and theologians need to be more sensitive in making claims to authority, lest we give the Church and the world the impression that we have confused the priorities of our Master. He criticized the heathen rulers for exercising authority over people and ordered: "It shall not be so among you" (Mk. 10:42-43). His statement does not negate the need for authority, but it warns us against making the struggle for authority a priority.

In discussing the question of teaching authority, there are two abuses to which we should be alert. The first is too simple an assignment of responsibilities; the second is too simple an understanding of the way in which one exercises the responsibility one has. A good example of a simplistic assignment of responsibilities is the unqualified equation of the Pope and bishops with the *Ecclesia docens* ("teaching Church") and theologians and everyone else with the *Ecclesia discens* ("learning Church"). At one time or another and in some way, everyone in the Church is part of the *Ecclesia docens* — and, indeed, very visibly, you women and men (the order of the sexes is deliberate) to whom parishes and schools have entrusted the formal religious education of the next generation. And, at one time or another and in some way, everyone in the Church is also part of the *Ecclesia discens*, including Pope and bishops. Again the words of our Master are almost a reproach: "You have only one Teacher — all the rest of you are brothers and sisters" (Mt. 23:8).

Once we have recognized that the responsibilities of teaching and learning are assigned in different ways to all, we must not exercise those responsibilities in independence of each other but by cooperation. I have said above that theologians must put their evidence at the service of the magisterium and not pretend to give *the* Catholic answer to disputed points. Similarly the magisterium must draw upon theologians in making its contribution to the Church's answer.

In one of my books I told a story that has been cited again and again in the ultraconservative press as an example of arrogance whereas I think it is a basic lesson about what should be in the Church. I mentioned that a bishop, now deceased, was welcoming several Scripture scholars into his diocese, and that he remarked that his own Scripture course in the seminary had been hopeless and consequently he never felt confident about even the exegesis of Scripture needed for preaching. Yet at the same time he cautioned the scholars that only the bishops could speak authoritatively about Scripture! And I remarked: "Here was a man innocently claiming that he could speak authoritatively about a subject in which, as he had just admitted, he had not even elementary competence."[3]

I would still make that remark: I do not think that the members of the magisterium can speak authoritatively about matters of theology or Scripture unless they have elementary competence in the field, either by their own learning or by consultation. I recognize fully that the office of Pope and bishop is a charism that involves divine help; but, as far as I know, in good Catholic theology grace is thought to cooperate with nature. To use properly the teaching role that is theirs by the charism of their office bishops must take the step of learning about what they are teaching — that is not only common sense; it is the age-old understanding of the Church. Ah, the charge will come back, you are saying that bishops must listen to the theologians and thus become their mouthpieces. No, I am saying that bishops must listen to theologians and acquire information, and pray over it, and think over it, and then teach pastorally what they judge the Church must hear. But, as part of the *Ecclesia discens* and *docens*, the first step of any Catholic is to listen and to learn.

I have made these general remarks about the magisterium and theologians and how I understand their roles simply that my own position may be clear. I have not the slightest intention of lecturing members of the hierarchy or my fellow theologians on their responsibilities. As will become clear, I think they both know their responsibilities and are exercising them well. My fear is that third parties do not always understand well the roles of bishops and of theologians and that some will use my talk on the subject to increase division rather than to increase cooperation, which is my goal. But before I turn to the heart of my talk, which is directed toward lessening the scope of division, let me make one more general observation to place this paper in focus.

I am speaking on this subject because I was asked to, and the request from the NCEA indicates that it is an important issue in the minds of many people—certainly some educators, presumably some bishops and some theologians. Important it may be; but I agree with Andrew Greeley that a division between the magisterium and theologians is not the number one problem or even the number two problem that faces the Church in the world or in the United States. One might give higher rank to the problem if it were phrased more broadly: "How does the Church teach with authority in these times?" But that would mean a recognition that there are more alternatives in the answer than "Listen to the magisterium" or "Listen to the theologians."

In New Testament times the man who wanted to know "What must I do to inherit eternal life?" did not go to the priests and the scribes (the Jewish equivalent of magisterium plus theologians); he went to the "Good Teacher" whose own life gave visible indication that he knew something about eternal life (Mk. 10:17). Today Mother Teresa of Calcutta can command a larger audience than either bishop or theologian when she talks about what it means to be a Christian. Saints teach authoritatively, and with a different kind of authority than either the magisterium or theologians. But even then we have not exhausted the alternatives, and the question of who teaches our Catholic people with authority is not always solved so positively. In fact, Catholics give tremendous authority to what they hear about religion on the media and to what other people are doing in matters of morals and religious observance.

The real significance of the question whether to listen to the magisterium or to the theologians may lie in the somewhat desperate hope that in making decisions Catholics get some "input" of substance whether by way of tradition or by way of responsible modern theology, and do not settle for gleanings from "pop" presentations. Neither papal encyclical, nor bishop's pastoral, nor theological tractate has the direct religious impact on many American Catholics of an article in the religion section of *Time* and *Newsweek* or of a half-hour prime-time treatment on national television. That realization not only relativizes the importance of the dispute between the magisterium and theologians; it makes such a dispute more tragic.

Yet I wish to give a hopeful note to most of this paper, for I think the dispute between theologians and the magisterium has been greatly exaggerated. This dispute is surrounded with fiction; and true to my vocation as a biblical scholar I would like to "demythologize" some of the fiction, if just this once I may cede to the frequent misuse of the term "demythologize."[4] Teachers will be asked to follow the guidance of the National Catechetical Directory in instances when the magisterium and theologians disagree, but that means that teachers must learn to diagnose correctly such disagreement. I wish to point out four fictions involved in the popular American Catholic presentation of the disagreement. If teachers succeed in debunking these fictions, they may be able to deal intelligently with the relatively few instances where there is real disagreement.

First fiction: In matters of Catholic doctrine the main opponents are the magisterium (Pope and bishops) and theologians.

In fact, third parties are much more frequently in public disagreement with both the magisterium and the main body of

Catholic theologians over doctrine than those two groups are in disagreement with each other. By "third parties" I think particularly of how the communications media have been employed by groups who stand at opposite ends of the religious spectrum. On the other hand there is a religious view that finds vocalization in the national television and the great secular newspapers which is quite critical of the Roman Catholic position on matters of morals and religious education. On the other hand, the ultraconservative bloc of Catholic newspapers and magazines is quite critical of what they regard as the dissolution of traditional Catholicism.

I think that both these critiques are much more acerbic than the critique of bishops by the theologians or vice versa. It is rare that you find a major theologian whose disagreement with the magisterium is not respectful; and it is increasingly rare for an American bishop to indulge in the "so-called theologians" calumny when he is disagreeing with theologians of note. I find that third parties are much less careful when they go after either theologians or bishops. Let me give some examples.

The liberal elements in the secular media do not indulge in invective (as sometimes do the liberal elements in the Catholic media). But when the Pope or bishops issue any statement contrary to the "with-it" trends of our times, especially in questions of sexual morals, there is thinly veiled contempt in the reporting. One way or another the audience is reminded that those who composed the statement are older celibates, religious leaders who do not have their feet on the ground and who are hewing to the party line.

To show that these leaders are out of touch with the Catholic laity, there is usually brought forward to comment on the statement a representative of a more contemporary Catholicism (a nun, a priest, or a lay person) who inevitably begins: "While I respect the position in the statement, I do not believe that this is where most Catholics are." What else can the audience conclude but that those who composed the Church statement are "out of it."

The liberal third party rarely extends the attack to modern Catholic theologians because of a belief (or a wish to create the illusion) that most Catholic theologians reject the Church statements as well. In fact, liberals are often genuinely nonplussed when they consult a Catholic theologian of note on such a matter and do not get a liberal answer. You can almost hear the silent surprise: "You are supposed to be on our side."

On the other side, the ultraconservative Catholic press is much less subtle in its assaults on both magisterium and theologians. The savage invective heaped upon Catholic theologians and biblical scholars in this press is well known: "so-called priests, Modernists, crypto-Protestants, Judases, latter-day Herods, subverters of the faith." More startling is the extension of this invective to the bishops. "Bishops in the dark" screams a headline on an article which charges that bishops are now the enthusiastic backers of the great rebellion against Catholic belief. High members of the Church are said to be in active collaboration with the Communists; a cardinal is villified as perhaps the greatest heretic the American Catholic Church has ever known; highly respected archbishops and bishops are denounced as undermining the faith of their people when they extend sponsorship to scholars disapproved of by the right; the Roman Pontifical Biblical Commission is described as having been taken over by Modernists; and American dioceses are charged with being in schism from Rome over the first confession-First Communion issue.

With increasing frequency the patronage of St. Thomas More is invoked: the gallant layman who stayed on the side of the Pope when almost all the bishops of England betrayed the faith; and, of course, the ultraconservatives think they are doing just that in face of the betrayal of the faith by the bishops of our time. (Alas St. Thomas, most subtle author of *Utopia*, to have survived the barbarism of an arrogant king only to be lionized by the unnuanced of a later age—the latter fate may be worse than the first.) If this ultraconservative press does not go all the way (as did Archbishop Lefebvre) and attack the Pope when they disagree with him, it is because they can present him as an old man, deceived by his liberal advisors, who does not know the iniquities of the American situation where the Church is increasingly passing into the hands of a Modernist hierarchy.

Of the two attacks on the magisterium and on theologians, challenging what they teach, the attack from the right may be noisier, but it speaks only to those already convinced and has no major effect on the thinking of American Catholics, especially now

that death and age are removing from the scene the very few sup-
porters that ultraconservatives have had in the hierarchy. The
liberal contempt for Church positions, particularly moral positions, is now far more serious, and, I think, does more to undermine the authority of the magisterium than does disagreement with
theologians. (Some may object that the theologians are on the side
of the secular liberals on moral matters; but that is calumny—the
position of responsible Catholic moral theologians, even when they
disagree with the bishops, is far more nuanced than the permissiveness encouraged in secular liberalism.)

It is not my intent in this paper to discuss how both the
magisterium and theologians should deal with attacks from the
right and the left. I simply wish to emphasize that the claim that
Catholic doctrine is imperiled because of quarrels between the
bishops and theologians is too simple. There is the massive presence
of those who would constitute a "third magisterium" and would vie
for authority in teaching with both bishops and theologians.

Leaving aside now third parties, let me explore some of the fiction about the extent of disagreement between the two recognized
parties.

*Second fiction: The prevailing relationship between the magis-
terium and Catholic theologians is one of disagreement.*

At times a significant group of noted Catholic theologians has
expressed dissent from official statements of the Pope or of the
bishops, especially in matters of sexual morals. But the amount and
frequency of this disagreement are seriously exaggerated in the
mind of many Catholics, and I see at least two obvious reasons for
this.

The first is the general negative thrust of "news." The air flight
that crashes makes the headlines; the thousand flights that arrive
safely are never mentioned. The general agreement of scholars with
the positions of their Church, inherent in the very fact that they are
practicing Roman Catholics, is not news; the occasional dissent is.
A theologian or biblical scholar can give conferences in dioceses all
over the country and be enthusiastically thanked by the respective
bishops for contributing to the welfare of the Church; his lectures

will be mentioned only in the local diocesan newspaper as part of the promotion. But let one bishop attack that scholar, and the item is on the NC News Service for distribution to every Catholic newspaper in the country. A book by a Catholic theologian on a sensitive subject may be distributed by thirty cardinals and bishops to every priest in their dioceses with the encouragement to read it; that is not a news item. The newspapers report only when a member of the hierarchy condemns a book.

The second factor that leads to an overstatement of disagreement is less inevitable and less innocent. Precisely because there are third parties who find the bishops too conservative or both the bishops and theologians too liberal, these third parties will tend to underline any sign of disagreement between bishops and theologians and exploit that disagreement to accomplish their own goal.

Let me concentrate for a moment on a spate of recent actions that does just this. In the last two years ultraconservative groups are making a big splash about founding *orthodox* Catholic colleges and *orthodox* catechetical institutes. The right to educate is not the issue of concern here; but their action is deliberately phrased so as to cast doubt on the orthodoxy of recognized theologians teaching at the main Catholic centers of learning. The stress that the new college or institute is orthodox is a broad hint that all others are not. Ultraconservatives plead for the restoration of the Index of Forbidden Books and do not hesitate to reprimand bishops for giving *imprimaturs* to books which in their judgment belong on the Index. Such pleas and charges are meant to make Catholics think that some very dangerous theologians are at work undermining the faith, when, in fact, those who are doing the protesting are often an alienated pressure group, so little open to change that their own orthodoxy may be questionable.

The same process is at work on the liberal side when the bishops are mocked as being clearly out of step with *modern* Catholic thought. Half the time when I read what newspapers characterize as "modern Catholic thought," my first reaction is, "Deliver us from evil." It is often a mélange of superficial nonsense to which no serious theologian in my ken would lend support. And again such nonsense is being manipulated to portray a disagreement between the magisterium and theologians.

There is one example that I want to concentrate on and expose as a deliberate attempt to inflate the disagreement between the magisterium and theologians. We have been treated lately to a flurry of writing on the theme that the bishops are too soft on theologians, that they are not acting with sufficient decisiveness to wipe out dissent on matters of doctrine, that they should crack down since a large percentage of Catholic theologians are in open rebellion against the magisterium. In a way these complaints are an eloquent proof that the bishops do *not* see disagreement with theologians to be such a great problem—certainly not as great as militant vigilantes would make it.

But as I look at such articles and note the names of the American theological scholars that the authors want condemned, the situation becomes even more paradoxical—many on the list are openly appreciated by the magisterium both here and abroad. In other words, the article entitled "Why Don't the Bishops Get Tough with the Theologians?" should really be titled "Why Are the American Bishops Listening to the Theologians Whom My Group Wants to Condemn?"

But do not take my word for this; rather join me in a little, informal poll that I have been conducting on the side and test my results. Ask knowledgeable people (bishops, religious educators, editors of diocesan newspapers, teachers of theology) this question: "Who are the ten most prominent Catholic theologians, moralists, and biblical scholars in the United States?"—not whether you like them or disagree with them—just the ten most prominent American Catholic scholars in these fields. Making allowances for different choices, I have come up with about fifteen names that appear on most lists. And I judge that seventy-five percent of the fifteen named are very acceptable to the American bishops, as judged by their meeting at least several of the following criteria: their books are recommended by bishops to the priests or people; they are frequently invited to dioceses under the auspices of bishops; they are appointed to commissions set up under episcopal supervision; their books regularly appear with Church approval. And I think this percentage is rather representative of the real relations between the magisterium and theologians in this country—seventy-five percent or higher agreement. And so I contend that agreement and cooperation in the task of Catholic teaching is the prevailing picture between bishops and theologians, not disagreement.

Third fiction: Theologians and the magisterium can be spoken of as if they were monolithic groups, all of whom see doctrinal issues the same way.

It is not an infrequent occurrence to see headlines like these: "Theologians deny papal infallibility"; "Biblical scholars deny the bodily resurrection"; "Catholic moralists disagree with Rome on homosexuality"; "Canonists say divorce is O.K." The first reaction to those headlines should be to ask: "Which Catholic theologians? Which Catholic scholars?" Theologians and biblical scholars and canonists are not a monolithic group. I do not mean to emphasize the obvious: that there are extremely liberal and extremely conservative theologians who disagree with the larger number of centrist theologians; I mean that even the centrists and moderate progressives are not a bloc.

I can think of a European Catholic theologian who denies infallibility; I can think of an American Catholic biblical scholar who denies the bodily resurrection of Jesus and another biblical scholar who denies the virginal conception; I can think of an American Catholic moralist who thinks that homosexuality can be an acceptable and moral lifestyle. But I can think of many reputable and famous centrist Catholic theologians and biblical scholars who disagree firmly with such positions and have written against them.

I take for granted that the chief task of theologians and biblical scholars is to use the tools of their trade to seek meaning and truth. As Roman Catholics, they conduct their search for truth within the general framework of the traditional teachings of the Church and with loyalty to that tradition. But they are not primarily defenders of past positions. And so I am not surprised that in the course of seeking truth, they have to ask new questions, and to wonder whether old questions were properly heard when they were asked, and whether past responses really meet the nuances of modern problems.

In asking such questions, one or the other theologian and biblical scholar may well emerge with a view startlingly different from the one that has been traditional in Catholicism. I am not surprised that those who have the primary pastoral responsibility for the faithful, the Pope and bishops, may not wish that such a startlingly different view be disseminated from the pulpit or on the more elementary levels of religious training. But that is not necessarily a dispute between the magisterium and theologians. A more sensitive scholar will *not* wish his views to be disseminated on such a popular level until they have been discussed and honed by critique. And inevitably there will be other theologians of equal competence and adventurousness who will be harsher than the bishops in their critique of the startlingly different view, not on the grounds that the view is dangerous, but because they judge it implausible by the rules of theological and biblical methodology.

If the centrist bloc of theologians is far from univocal, neither is the magisterium, although differences in the confraternity of the Pope and the bishops are expressed much more discreetly than differences among theologians. To the perceptive, it is clear that the majority of American bishops are not in complete agreement with certain Roman pastoral stances on the sacraments. Those who have sat in on the national meetings of the American bishops are impressed by the sharp differences of views expressed within that hierarchy. And when there have been votes on highly publicized issues, like Communion-in-the-hand, it becomes clear that one bishop may regard an action as healthy for the Church, while another may regard it as a diabolical innovation.

This should be remembered when a single bishop speaks out against theologians. It is perfectly possible, for instance, to have an ultraconservative member of the hierarchy align himself with right-wing forces and become their spokesman, condemning virtually every theologian in sight. This is not the magisterium vs. theologians; it is an extremist archbishop or bishop against theologians. It may be a mark both of sanity and of complete loyalty to present trends in the Church to have the disapproval of such a figure. His fellow bishops may judge his position as hopelessly exaggerated, even if they do not express their feelings as publicly as do theologians about an exaggerated member of their guild. Among themselves bishops are properly wary of the maverick hierarch who is being lionized either by conservatives or by liberals as the ideal spokesman of the hierarchy—that designation usually means a spokesman for what a particular group of Catholics would like to have all bishops say.

Perhaps it would be in order to make a passing remark about the bishop who wishes to write and speak as a theologian in his own right—a theologian left, right, or center—rather than as a member of the hierarchy speaking for the Church. That must be made very clear, for the tendency otherwise will be to give the bishop's remarks more value than they have in themselves because of his position.

If one wishes for the role of a theologian, one must meet the same standards as other theologians. The standard questions must be asked about the bishop-theologian: Was he ever trained beyond the seminary level in theology or biblical studies? Does he know the scientific literature? Does he control the languages? Above all, is he willing to submit an article, for example, to a magazine that has an editorial board which tests quality, like the *Catholic Biblical Quarterly* or *Theological Studies*?. One becomes immediately suspicious when a bishop's articles consistently appear in a journal or newspaper that is an organ of propaganda for the extreme right and that is obviously delighted to use his name to support an already established conservative position. Finally, the bishop-theologian must be willing to have his views handled as roughly by theologians as they would handle those of a non-bishop.

Returning to the main issue, I would judge that a real controversy exists between the magisterium and theologians only when the Pope or a whole group of bishops takes a stand opposed by a good number of theologians. The struggle between the majority on one side and the odd man out on the other is more a problem of eccentricity than of theology. But, since eccentricity can be exploited in these times by those who want to inflate the issue of disagreement, perhaps both theologians and bishops need more firmly to dissociate themselves from their respective eccentrics.

It may be objected that my comparison of diversity within the guild of theologians and diversity within the confraternity of bishops was not exact. I mentioned that theologians disagree with each other over things like the bodily resurrection, the virginal conception, the morality of homosexual behavior—in short, matters of faith and morals. Do bishops, representing the magisterium, disagree with each other on matters of Church doctrine? To some extent the answer to that question depends on what one considers Church doctrine, and this leads to a fourth fiction.

Fourth fiction: Theologians and the magisterium are in conflict because even centrist Catholic theologians deny many matters of Church doctrine.

Catholics are in a strange state of schizophrenia about Church pronouncements. Those who inhabit the extreme right of the Catholic spectrum are eager to burn at the stake any theologian who disagrees with Church pronouncements on sexual morality; but the necessity of accepting Church positions becomes very vague if the bishops suggest returning the Canal to Panama or come out in support of the farmworkers, or if Rome comes to an agreement with an Iron Curtain country. For this group, obedience is required in matters of faith and morals—and "morals" means sexual morals—but not in matters of social and political justice. On the other side of the spectrum, Catholic liberals taunt conservatives with non-observance of the social encyclicals, but preserve a glacial silence when the Pope or the bishops speak about sexual morality. For them, bishops should be listened to if they say something progressive, but when they repeat tradition, that is just the party line. A reference to infallibility in faith and morals is looked on as archaic.

Thus selectivity toward Church pronouncements has become a high art on all sides, and that should be kept in mind when theologians are said to disobey Church teachings. But I do not wish to excuse the disobedience of theologians on the grounds that "everyone is doing it." I wish rather to examine to what extent major theologians really do contradict Catholic doctrine. This can be answered only if one comes to grips, first, with inflated ideas about what constitutes Catholic doctrine, and, second, with the realization that doctrines change.

First, an inflated and inexact idea about what constitutes Catholic doctrine. We have not erased from the general Catholic psyche the view that everything people were taught in catechism was Catholic doctrine. Half the bitter struggle over Communion-in-the-hand and Communion-under-two-species reflects the fact that people were taught that only the consecrated fingers of the priest should touch the sacred species or the chalice. Those who got a more refined education learned to distinguish such a pious custom (of dubious theological basis) from doctrine, but most people did not. Naturally, then, if theologians challenge such pious customs, they are thought to be opposing Catholic doctrine.

Since the time I agreed to give this talk, I have noticed over and over again in the Catholic press instances where the reader would think that theologians were undermining Catholic doctrine but which did not involve matters of doctrine at all. For instance, a conservative group demands that a European theologian be censured for suggesting that the Pope have a limited term of office and that his election be conducted by a more representative group than the College of Cardinals. The demand for censuring surely implies a grave deviation, does it not? Yet a Catholic is perfectly free to hold any view he or she wants about papal terms and elections, and I know that one of the most distinguished cardinals of the Church shares on this point the views of the theologian in question.

Another example: a liberal reporter notes that this year, when the Epiphany was no longer a holy day of obligation in Italy, the Pope made a strong statement on the historicity of the Epiphany. (I doubt if any theologian would question that, since epiphany means the manifestation of the Son of God in human form, which is certainly the most basic historical claim of Christianity.) Yet the reporter went on to speculate that the Pope was implicitly criticizing biblical scholars who denied the historicity of the magi. Such gratuitous speculation creates theological confusion on many scores. The Pope never mentioned the historicity of the magi. I know of no great number of Catholic biblical scholars who are denying the historicity of the magi. Of course, I do know that most Catholic scholars recognize that Matthew 2:1-12 is not an historical narrative in the way that the accounts of Jesus' ministry are historical; but it would go beyond the limitations of biblical method and beyond proof to say: "There were no magi." And, finally, I have too much respect for the Pope to think that he would so stretch the credibility of his office as to state solemnly that there were magi. The last several Popes have been very discreet in not overcommitting themselves beyond questions of faith and morals, and most certainly the existence of the magi is not a matter of doctrine.

Still one more example of inflation going back to the conservative side: an editorial laments the evil fruit of recent biblical scholarship which has turned Catholics away from accepting the Scriptures and the Gospel as factual history. Certainly this is a sign of rebellion, is it not? Just the contrary — it is a sign of obedience, for the official teaching of the Catholic Church requires Catholics to hold that the Gospels are *not* literal accounts of the ministry of Jesus.[5] It is the editorial writer who is out of step with the Church's teaching.

I could go on and on, for the inflation of Catholic doctrine is often tendentious and deliberate on the part of those who wish to discredit centrist theologians. Statements of the Biblical Commission and of the Holy Office of the 1905-1920 anti-Modernist period are repeated over and over again as if they were Catholic doctrine, even though Church authorities have explicitly granted freedom with regard to many of these[6] and others have demonstrably passed into desuetude.[7] The statements in the *Syllabus* of Pius IX are quoted as if they all had the same value as binding Catholic teaching, even though the most authoritative collection of Church documents warns specifically against doing that.[8] Such crass misuse of doctrine fed to ordinary Catholics will inevitably confuse them about the loyalty of responsible theologians who seek to work within the freedom that the Church gives them.

Second, what constitutes Catholic doctrine is obscured if one does not recognize change in doctrine. There are explicit statements of the Doctrinal Congregation (Holy Office) in *Mysterium Ecclesiae* (1973)[9] about the historical conditioning of past Church pronouncements. This is the Church itself coming to grips with what centrist theologians have been insisting on for years: All Church dogma and doctrine have been phrased by human beings (with divine guidance, to be sure), and thus doctrine is conditioned by the limitations of those who did the phrasing.

The Holy Office declaration lists a series of limitations flowing from the expressive power of the language in use at a given time, from the fact that certain truths are expressed only partially, and that dogmas were meant to solve only certain questions, and were expressed in the changeable conceptions of a given epoch. Yes, it is the Doctrinal Congregation, not some wild-eyed theologian, that has taught solemnly and bindingly that the formulas of the past will not always be suitable for communicating the truth involved in them and that, with Church approval, they may need to give way to new formulations.

When it is claimed that some theologian is denying a past doctrine of the magisterium, one must remember this principle of the conditioned value of past formulas, and ask whether the theologian is really denying the truth affirmed in that formula (which would bring him into real conflict with the magisterium) or whether he is simply seeking a new formulation to meet a new problem not settled in the past (which is an investigation quite tolerable within the bonds of loyalty to the magisterium).

In summary, an intelligent understanding of the limits of Catholic doctrine within guidelines given by the magisterium itself means that very few modern theological investigations can be said to deny Catholic doctrine. In the fields of Christology and ecclesiology Rome has expressed its public concern about only a few named European theologians and, in fact, has never officially labeled any one of them as guilty of heresy. In this country the disputes between the body of bishops and any large number of theologians have been in the field of ethics. If the bishops have handled these disputes gingerly,[10] it is not because they are weak or indecisive, but rather because, like many of us, they are beginning to appreciate more fully the complexities of truth and the way in which it is revealed, preserved and discovered—an appreciation singularly lacking in some who despise the bishops for not crushing the theologians, presumably on the principle that the first and greatest of all the commandments is: "Hate one another for the love of God."

I have now finished my four fictions and hope that I have reduced to a more manageable size the relatively few times in which there is a direct conflict between the magisterium (Pope and bishops) and a large number of representative Catholic theologians on matters of Catholic doctrine. If one can get rid of all the inflation, misunderstood or deliberate, we are not in such bad shape theologically. There are pains, but I suspect they are growing pains, not the pains of the expiring.

Nevertheless, I have sympathy for those who are upset that even on a few issues there could be serious disagreement between the magisterium and theologians. I wish I could share with them a knowledge of Church history so that they could realize that moments of disagreement within the Church are far from infrequent, and we are not the first generation of Catholics to face this dilemma. Indeed, I would judge that the New Testament Church had far more factions within it than has Catholicism today.

And for those today who think that surely the end must be at hand because there are divisions, know that there was a New Testament author who thought the same (1 Jn. 2:18). Frustrated by the presence of teachers whom he thought were wrong but who would not listen to him, he tried to give a principle of guidance to people who were confused by hearing such different teachings from the author and from his opponents. The principle he gave is *not* adequate to solve all Church teaching problems for a long period of time, but it remains of help to those who think it a desperate problem that there are different teachers in the Church. The author of 1 John 2:27 wrote these words to those whom he called "little children":

> As for you, the anointing received from Christ abides in your hearts; and so you have no need for anyone to teach you. Rather, inasmuch as his anointing teaches you about all things, it is true and free from any lie. And just as it taught you, so must you abide in him.

In moments of confusion because of different teachers it is consoling to know that the Paraclete is given to everyone who loves Jesus and keeps his commandments (Jn. 14:15-16) and that this Spirit of truth does not leave us without guidance along the way of all truth (Jn. 16:13).

Notes

1. Reprinted in my *Biblical Reflections on Crises Facing the Church* (New York: Paulist, 1975), pp. 3-19.

2. R. E. Brown, *The Virginal Conception and Bodily Resurrection of Jesus* (New York: Paulist, 1973), p. 12.

3. R. E. Brown, *Priest and Bishop: Biblical Reflections* (New York: Paulist, 1970), pp. 76-77.

4. It is often used, as I misuse it here, to describe the removal of mythology from a narrative in order to reach historical fact. It really means to reinterpret the ancient mythological expressions into modern terms so that the point of the narrative may be more easily grasped.

5. "The truth of the story is not at all affected by the fact that the evangelists relate the words and deeds of the Lord in a different order, and express his sayings not literally but differently": *Instruction of the Pontifical Biblical Commission on the Historical Truth of the Gospels* (1964), Section IX. See my *Biblical Reflections* (note 1 above), pp. 111-115.

6. For the freedom granted by the secretary of the Pontifical Biblical Commission regarding decrees issued earlier in the century, see the 1955 statement quoted by Brown, *Biblical Reflections*, pp. 110-111.

7. For the basis of modifying the 1918 Holy Office statement on the human knowledge of Jesus by means of the responses to the Holy Office questionnaire of 1966, see R. E. Brown, *Jesus God and Man* (New York: Macmillan, 1967), p. 41, n. 6.

8. H. Denzinger and A. Schonmetzer, *Enchiridion Symbolorum* (22nd ed; Freiburg: Herder, 1963), p. 576.

9. Text given in Brown, *Biblical Reflections,* pp. 116-18.

10. The bishops have expressed clear disapproval of the *Human Sexuality* study, but they have not been nearly severe enough to satisfy those who want the book condemned and its authors dismissed from teaching.

A Semantic History
of the Term "Magisterium"

Yves Congar, O.P.

It is a question only of the *word*. In the Church there has always been a teaching ministry, connected either with charismata or an authority endowed with charisma. Here we can only draw attention, by way of example rather than as a catalogue, to a few of the terms which have expressed these realities: *didaskalos, didaskalia,* and the large number of words which, since the New Testament, have described preachers, teachers, those who bear the *parathèkà,* the mission of preaching (Clement of Rome, Cor. 42, 1-2), "Praedicatio Ecclesiae" (Irenaeus, A. H. III, 24, 1: PG 7, 966), "eos qui ab apostolis instituti sunt episcopi et successores eorum usque ad nos, qui nihil tale docuerunt . . . " (III, 3, 1: col. 848) and the famous "charisma veritatis certum" (IV, 26, 2: col. 1053) of which the meaning is still a matter of debate: an objective gift of the truth or functional charisma? It would be necessary to discuss what is involved in the words *cathedra*, "mater et magistra" applied to the Roman Church, *potestas, auctoritas.* St. Leo speaks of "docendi et praedicandi ius," "gradum praedicatoris assumere" (letter of June 11, 453: PL 54, 1045-46). In almost all periods people have spoken of "officium docendi." These are just a few examples to illustrate a preliminary remark: the word *magisterium,* which is the subject of our investigation, has not been, indeed has fallen far short of being, the only expression of the reality which we now describe in that term.

In French its use is comparatively recent: Robert's dictionary lists it but Littré's does not. What has been its use in Latin?

The word is rare in classical Latin: the article of Forcellini (*Totius Latinitatis Lexikon,* Vol. IV, Prato, 1668, p. 17) is very short: it defines our term as "magistri dignitas seu officium." *Magister* comes from *magis* (*major*), as *minister,* which is often coupled with it, comes from *minor.*[1] Antiquity and the Middle Ages knew innumerable applications of the title *magister,* which described the principal or leader in all sorts of activities and areas.[2] For example, there were *magister equitum, magister militum* (from which comes in Justinian's Code 2. 12. 25: law of 392, "magisterium militare"), *magister convivii, magister gladiatorum,* and so forth. *Magisterium,* the dignity or office of a *magister,* served to describe, first, all leadership positions: "munus, officium praefecti, rectoris, moderatoris."[3] Eustatius, in about 440, translates the *hegemonia* of St. Basil's *Hexameron* (PL 53, 911 D, "militum magisteria"). But the expression was very quickly applied more specifically to the function and activity of preceptor, professor, doctor, counselor, exemplar.[4] We shall find the same logical succession of meanings in Christian use of the term: a general sense of a position of authority, with special reference to teaching, until, from the official and even hierarchical function of teaching, the word comes to define the body of priests with authority to exercise this function: *the* magisterium. But this meaning, now current, seems not to have appeared before the nineteenth century.

Given the importance of St. Augustine in the literary history of Latin Christianity and the influence he has exercised in the West, we devote a first paragraph to the bishop of Hippo.

In St. Augustine *magisterium*'s first meaning refers to teaching; its second is most often reserved to God (to Christ), while men of the Church have only a *ministerium.*

The text of Matthew 23:10 ("Magister vester unus est Christus") had often been invoked: Ignatius of Antioch, *Eph.* 15, 1; *Martyrium Polycarpi,* 17, 3. In Augustine there is a profound conviction: "Magisterium in coelis habemus" (Sermo 298, 5: PL 38, 1367).[5]

"Sonus verborum nostrorum percutit, magister intus est. . . . Magisteria [teaching activities] forinsecus, adiutoria quaedam sunt et admonitiones. Cathedram in coelo habet qui corda docet" (*In Epist. Ioan.* tr. III, 13 [35, 2004]). "[In Christo] eo tempore quod oportunissimum ipse noverat, et ante saecula disposuerat, venit hominibus magisterium et adiutorium, ad lapescendam sempiternam salutem. Magisterium quidem ut ea quae hic ante dicta sunt utiliter vera, non solum a prophetis sanctis, qui omnia vera dixerunt, verum etiam a philosophis atque ipsis poetis . . . illius etiam in carne praesentata confirmaret auctoritas" (*Epist.* 137, 12: 33, 521). ". . . praeter cuius magisterium nemo discit" (*De pecc. meritis* I, 28, 55: 44, 141). "Sed ne ipso studio cognitionis, propter humanae mentis infirmitatem in pestem alicuius erroris incurrat, opus habet magisterio divino, cui certus obtemperet" (*De civ. Dei* XIX, 14; 41, 642). This divine teaching sometimes takes on the objective sense of "lesson": "si non tentaretur [Christus] tibi tentando vicendi magisterium non praeberet" (*En. in Ps.* 60, 2: 36, 724). Yet one finds "magisterii illius sarcinam deponere," leading Augustine to give up his teaching duties (*Confess.* IX, 2, 4; 32, 764).

Men have only one service, one *ministry:* "Animo tenentes nostrae officium servitutis, ut loquamur non tanquam magistri, sed tanquam ministri. . . . Magister autem unus est nobis, cuius schola in terra est, et cathedra in coelo" (*Sermo* 292, 1: 38, 1319ff.).[6] This coupling of *magister* and *minister* is classical.[7] We find it in Tertullian, in the *Cod. Theod.* 16, 5, 5, in Thomas Aquinas ("homo autem dicitur indulgentia pater, et magister ministerio": *Contra impugn.,* c. 2; *In Matt.,* c. 23; etc), in St. Bonaventure, for whom Christ is "principalis magister" (*Sermo* IV n. 20), and men only "ministeriales doctores" (*ibid.,* n. 24).

Magisterium means first of all the position and authority of the man in charge, *magister.* It kept this sense a long while. Applied to Christ or to priests of the Church, *magisterium* means the "power" conferred on them so that they may be ministers of salvation. At the beginning of the fourth century, Lactantius wrote that Christ came "ut . . . hominem ad Deum magisterio suo superata morte perduceret" (*Epitome* 39 [44]: Brandt 716, 13). Commenting on the gesture by which Jesus had the didrachma paid for himself, for Peter, and, in them, for all the apostles, Ambrosiaster, around 380, gives this explanation: "quia sicut in Salvatore erant omnes causa magisterii," because he was their leader, "ita et post Salvatorem in Petro omnes continentur" (*Quaest. Vet. et Nov.*

Test., LXXV: inter Opera Augustini, PL 35, 2270). In Eustatius, around 440, we find the old meaning when he writes: "Adde divitiis civilem quoque potentiam . . . militum magisteria" (Hexam. lib. V c. 2: PL 53, 911 D). In St. Leo (died 461) *magisterium* sometimes means authority, the quality of master and, for example, for the Roman Church, mistress (cf. *Sermo* 3, 3: PL 54, 146 C). In the Sacramentary attributed to St. Leo the presence of the apostles Peter and Paul in the Church is sought in these terms: "Da ecclesiae tuae toto terrarum orbe diffusae eorum semper moderamine gubernari per quos sumpsit religionis exordium,"[8] but the same prayer replaces "moderamine gubernari" by "magisterio gubernari."[9] According to St. Avitus (died around 525) the fact that the bishop is the *magister* of the faithful means that he governs them with *pietas* and firmness at the same time.[10] In the famous *Regula pastoralis* composed in 591, St. Gregory intends by *magisterium* the position and function of a leader, of *regimen* (I, proem.: PL 77, 13; I c. 1, col. 14 A: Ab imperitis ergo pastorale magisterium qua temeritate suscipitur, quanto ars artium regimen animarum").

For John XIX, in 1024, *magisterium Patri* means the authority of Peter, his power of binding and loosing.[11] For Alexander II, in 1063, *magisterium* means the competence of his legate Peter Damien, his authority to judge and decide.[12] For Alexander, *magisterium* means the authority which decides, even in the juridical point of view.[13] Under the name of the extraordinary "Norman anonymous," around 1100, *magisterium* means a position of authority and even superiority: no Church possesses it over another Church.[14]

"Master" in the Middle Ages was the title of the head of a corporation, *magisterium*, the dignity and responsibility of the master: it occurs thus in the bull *Benedictus Deus* by which, in 1175, Alexander III institutes a Master of the Knights of St. James (PL 200, 1025 D). Before that, in a speech in November 1159 about Frederick Barbarossa (cf. Bosan, *Vita Alexandrini III,* cited by L. Duchesne, *Liber Pontificalis,* II, p. 401), it was a question of the apostle Peter as "magister ac fundator" of the Roman Church. Urban III, approving in 1186 the statutes of a community of regular canons founded by the man who was to succeed him under the name Gregory VIII, wrote "si que vero ecclesie magsterio uestro se

decreuerint committendas,"[15] where *magisterium* means government, authority, direction. The term is found frequently in
Celestine III (1191-1198) to express the authority of the Roman
Church, "mater et magistra," to which belongs the plenitude of
power of binding and loosing.[16] His formula "magisterium et prin-
cipatus" becomes, with his successor Innocent III, "apostolicum
principi Petro magisterium contulit et primatum."[17] Innocent III
uses *magisterium* to express direction, government, the head's
authority.[18] When the word corresponds to the classical phrase
"mater et *magistra*," *magisterium* suggests the molding of disciples
by a master.[19] The same is true of Innocent's contemporary, the
Calabrian abbot Joachim of Flore.[20] Pope Clement IV (1265-1268)
or his chancellery begins a series of letters accrediting a legate to re-
establish understanding between the queen and bishops of Den-
mark with the words "Summi Regis magisterio."[21] Thomas Aquinas
who — as we shall see — clearly knows the special association with
instruction also uses the expression in its original meaning, that of a
leader's position (IIa-IIaa q. 185 a. 8: the bishop has "quoddam
perfectionis magisterium"), an authority which decides and judges
(Christ: IIIa q. 81 a. 2).

* * *

In classical Latin, the equivalent institution had received the
name *magistratus*.[22] Leo XIII, who was an excellent Latin scholar,
did not forget it and uses the term with this sense (enc. *Satia
cognitum,1896: D 1961; DSch 3309): "bini magistratus"* = the two
sovereign authorities.

It was natural that, having first described a position of
authority or command, *magisterium* should have been applied to a
teacher's role. Texts with this meaning abound. We have found
some in St. Augustine. His contemporary, Pope Celestine I, writing
after the Council of Ephesus to the clergy and people of Constantinople, says that the action of St. Cyril toward Nestorius: "Nisus
est labentem revocare collegam, porrexit dexteram magisterii
sui . . . " (PL 50, 552 A; Schwartz, A.C.O., / pp. 93-94). How can
this be translated? "He stretched out his hand to him as bishop and
doctor." Such, we believe, is the sense. "Magisterium" would not be

wrong, but would certainly be too precise, because, as we shall see, the word has taken on a more definite meaning. This is how St. Maximus of Turin (died 465) defines the role and respective merits of Peter and Paul: "Et licet in Petro fides emineat, in Paulo doctrina praecellet, et magisterium tamen Pauli fidei plenitudo est, et credulitas Petri doctrinae est fundamentum," in which *doctrina* means "teaching" in the active sense.[23] Maximus claims for Paul the "clavis scientiae" (for Peter the "clavis potentiae"), an expression that some have, since then, applied to the infallible magisterium. St. Peter Chrysologus says, still speaking of Paul, to describe his teaching both as content and activity, with regard to the abrogation of the law and with regard to grace: "Postquam Davidicam citharam . . . ad Apostolicum magisterium mox credidimus esse remeandum. . . .Videtis, fratres, beati Apostoli magnum coelestis magisterii documentum" (PL 52, 515 B and C).

St. Gregory, in whose writing we have already met the expression *"magisterium pastorale"* (= the pastorate),[24] says: "Quid vero per cathedram, nisi magisterii auctoritas designatur?" (*Mor. in Iob* XIX, 16 25: PL 76, 113 C), which defines pastoral authority as teaching authority. And here is how the *Missala Gothicum,* in seventh-century Gaul, introduced the Pater: "Divino magisterio edocti et divina institutione formati . . . " (ed. H. M. Bannister, p. 155 and 517). Fulbert of Chartres (died 1029) also said: "Patrum magisterio edocemur" (Tract.: PL 141, 277), and the Norman anonymous (around 1100) warned the man who did not want to "recedere a vestigiis Petri et apostolorum magisterio" (J 29: ed. Pellens p. 227). Peter Damien (died 1072) denied reason a "ius magisterii" in the interpretation of the Scriptures.[25] To accede "ad magisterium divinae lectionis" was to accede to worthiness to comment on the Scriptures. Abelard was accused of having done this "sine magistro" (*Hist. calamit.*, c. 8: PL 178, 140 A). Abelard often uses *magisterium* to signify the function and right to teach.[26] This was current at this time when the title *magister* was held for life by a man who had lectured in public.[27] In a sermon at Oxford on November 11, 1229, the blessed Jordan of Saxony warns those "qui docendi habent officium" against the temptation of desiring to raise themselves, as if to a dignity, "ad statum magisterii," to the pinnacle of the temple (ed. A.G. Little and D. Douie, in *The*

English Hist. Rev. 54 [1939] 12). People were always aware of the fact that God (the Holy Ghost) is the supreme master and possesses absolute teaching authority,[28] but they did not hesitate, despite St. Augustine, to attribute to men a *magisterium* which is plainly ministerial.[29] We have previously cited texts of St. Thomas; we could cite ones by St. Bonaventure.[30]

The medieval text in which the word *magisterium* comes closest to its current usage is unquestionably that of Bernard of Fontcaude criticizing shortly after 1185 the position of the disciples of Valdo who read the Scriptures and preached without submission to the authorities of the Church. After referring to the way in which Paul had been sent to Ananias (Acts 9:6) and Cornelius to Peter (Acts 10:5), he writes: "Ex quibus aperte datur intelligi, quod nullus praesumere debet docere aliquam viam perfectionis, nisi sit in civitate, id est in sancta Ecclesia, et Christi sit discipulus: cum Christus vel eius angelus Saulum vel centurionem docere noluerint, ut magisterium Ecclesiae inviolabiliter custodiendum esse ostenderent; et a nullis omnino attendandum, nisi ab his qui in loco discipulorum successerunt, id est ab episcopis et viris ecclesiasticis, quibus id officii Dominus delegavit, sicut scriptum est Malachia attestante *Labia sacerdotis custodient scientiam et legem requirent ex ora eius quia angelus domini exercituum est . . . (Liber contra Waldenses,* c. 2, 4: PL 204, 799).

From St. Thomas let us note here, without pretending that he is the only witness, the distinction clearly made between the pastoral "teaching office," that of a "prelate" having jurisdiction, and the "teaching office" of a doctor, expert in theology, in which one sees that the word did not have its modern sense (magisterium).

"Docere sacram Scripturam contingit dupliciter. Uno modo ex officio praelationis, sicut qui praedicat, docet. Non enim licet alicui praedicare nisi officium praelationis habeat, vel ex auctoritate alicuius praelationem habentis: Rom. 10:15, *Quomodo praedicabunt nisi mittantur*? Alio modo ex officio magisterii, sicut magistri theologiae docent" (In IV Sent. d. 19 q. 2 a. 2 qª 2 ad 4).

"Imminent pericula spiritualia his qui habent magisterii locum. Sed pericula magisterii cathedrae pastoralis devitat scientia cum claritate . . . pericula autem magisterii cathedrae magistralis vitat homo per scientiam" (Quodl. III, 9 ad 3).

If *magisterium* came to be applied particularly to teaching, it was natural for the word to be construed objectively and come to mean the content of teaching, a doctrine. Use of the word in this sense is very common in St. Cyprian.[31] We find the same usage by Innocent I in January 417 (*Inter Augustini Epp.* 182, 4: PL 33, 785), and by St. Leo, with a connotation of active teaching,[32] which occurs also in the Roman Council of March 27, 680 condemning monothelitism (D 288; DSch 548 end) and in the Second Nicean Council on the cult of images: D 302, DSch 600.[33] Rupert of Deutz wants the faithful to be "tanquam filii in domo patris sub fidei magisterio morumque disciplina eruditi" (*In Genas.* lib. I c. 25: PL 147, 549 D). The *Exordium Magnum* of Citeaux calls on monks to follow the teaching of salvation or the example (the *magisterium*) of the monastic founders and abbots. Let us mention finally the title of the great *Summary of Theology* composed by William of Auvergne between 1231 and 1235, the *magisterium divinala*.[34]

If *magisterium* expresses a position of authority and if the term very early became applied particularly to the order of doctrine, it is natural to find texts in which the modern usage of the term seems intended. There are cases among our earlier citations, but here are others probably of more significance.

The text of Alexander III that we have quoted (*Epist.* 1447 *bis*) speaks of the *magisterium* of the Roman Church (of Peter) and requires reference to it if a question arises. We can trace back to Alexander III a new development of awareness of the Pope's doctrinal authority.[35] Celestine III on February 20, 1196, wishing to advance the return of Cyprus to the unity of the Roman Church, wrote: "Fundavit Deus in unitate fidei supra petram ecclesia firmamentum, cuius a sui nascentis exordio, collata beato Petro eiusque vicariis potestate, Romane sedi primatiam contulit, et indulsit tocius magisterii principatum." The word might have only the primary sense of superiority, but it is a question of the unity of the faith, and the text goes on: "ex qua si quidem per partes orbis plurime et diverse in unius doctrine spiritu ecclesie, velut a matre filiae procreate, ab eiusdem uberibus in edificationem fidelium lacte nutriantur, necessaria suggerere documenta, et inde omnes suscipiant regulas magisterii ubi tocius ecclesie Christus posuit principatum, ut que uniuscuiusque sacerdota; os dignitatis mater esse dignoscitur, sit etiam allactandis filiis magistra ecclesiastice rationis."[36]

Without the word *magisterium*, what we understand by it became more precise in the theology of the great scholastics.[37] Brian Tierney has traced back to Jean-Pierre Olieu (Olivi) the assertion of the Pope's infallibility when he decides a point of faith.[38] Whatever the significance of this point in the history of doctrines, Olivi does not give the *words* "magisterium, magistralis" a sense beyond that we have already met, that of an authority to decide: he says "Romana Ecclesia, sui datum est universale magisterium."[39] Guy Terreni, who, before 1328, uses the word *infallibilis* (which Olivi does not), uses *magisterium* only in the familiar sense of teaching.[40] With traditional words one is nevertheless approaching the modern usage. Here, for example, is what Claude Lejay wrote in his memoir on apostolic traditions which he published in 1546 for the Council of Trent: "Viro catholico dubium non est, quin ecclesia eiusdem Spiritus sancti magisterio regatur, cuius instinctu Scripturae sacrae scriptae sunt, atque ita non sibi adversantur Scriptura sane intellecta et ecclesia" (*Conc. Trid.,* ed. Goerresgesellschaft, Vol. XII, *Tractatus,* pp. 522, 12-16).

If the Church is ruled by the *magisterium* of the Holy Ghost, it enjoys the Spirit's *instinctus*. The problem is to know who is the person, who is the subject of this charisma? Tradition was very definite: it is the *Ecclesia* itself. But from remote antiquity, *Ecclesia Romana*, "mater et magistra," has been declared and considered as verifying this charisma in a special way. Over the centuries it has been recognized that the churchly charisma is personified by pastors who, as ministers, *exercise* on the level of the historical life of the Church the doctrinal authority of Christ and of his Holy Ghost. This perception of things was clarified in the ecclesiology of the Counter-Reformation, then in the debates with the Jansenists, the Protestants and the critics of the time of the Enlightenment. Melchior Cano wrote in 1561: "Ecclesia in credendo errare non potest: non solum Ecclesia universalis, id est collectio fidelium hunc veritatis spiritum semper habet, sed eumdem habent etiam Ecclesiae principes et pastores" (*De locis theol.* lib. IV c. 4). Twenty years afterward, Bellarmine argued: "If the entire episcopate were mistaken, the entire Church would be mistaken also, since Christians are obliged to follow their pastors" (*Controv.* 4, lib. III c. 14). At the beginning and toward the middle of the eighteenth century a distinction was made between the instructing Church and the instructed Church, and the first was said to possess active infallibility and the second passive infallibility.[41] These categories became widespread in the catechisms of the early nineteenth century. Even a theologian of the Eucharist and member of the episcopal college like Martin Gerbert, abbot of Saint-Blaise (died 1793), speaks, for the faithful, of "passive communion" and concerns himself mainly with the "summi principes" (the bishops). He writes: "Tale ergo est ecclesiae magisterium, quod omni hominum statui graduique officia praescribat, idque summa auctorite, nimirum vicaria ipsius Dei, cui haud impune quis resistat" (*De legitima ecclesiastica potestate circa sacra et profana*, St. Blasien, 1761, p. 14).

This is still not exactly what we now call "*the* magisterium," that is, a definite hierarchical body; it is a question of the function of teaching of "the Church" (for human beings!), exercised with an authority which represents that of God before men, but we are very close to that meaning.

The expression "the magisterium" in its current usage was introduced by eighteenth-century theology but especially by German canonists at the beginning of the nineteenth century.[42] S. Brendel, who still belonged to the ethos of the Enlightenment, wrote: "Catholic doctrine understands as Church not the whole body of clergy members and laity together, but the teaching office, the teaching Church."[43] Mohler criticized this in his review in the *Theologische Quartalschrift* 6 (1824), pp. 84-113. But the innovation which concerns our theme most was the introduction by F. Walter, in the second edition of his *Lehrbuch des Kirchenrechts*, Bonn, 1823, of the tripartite distinction of the "powers" in the Church into a "potestas magisterii" beside a "potestas ministerii sive ordinis" and a "potestas iurisdictionis sive ecclesiastica in specie" (Pottmeyer 146). This distinction was taken up by G. Phillips (*Kirchenrecht*, 7 volumes, Regensburg, 1845ff.; Pottmeyer, pp. 154ff.), by J. B. Schwatz (*Theologia fundamentalis seu generalis*, Vienna, 1850; 4th ed. p. 392; Pottmeyer, p. 191), and so forth. From that time the term entered the ecclesiastical vocabulary.

We find it in Gregory XVI as early as 1835, in an encyclical addressed to the Swiss clergy on the arrangements of the Congress of Baden: "Habet Ecclesia ipsa, ex divina institutione potestatem, non Magisterii solum, ut res fidei et morum doceat ac definiat sacrasque litteras absque ullo erroris periculo interpretetur, verum etiam Regiminis . . . " (quoted in the schema *Supremi Pastoris* of January 21, 1870: Mansi 51, 583 note 18). Again in the short *Dum acerbissimas* against Hermes, September 26, 1835: Hermes has said absurd things, foreign to Catholic doctrine "in particular concerning the nature of faith, the rule of things to believe, tradition, revelation and *Ecclesiae magisterium*" (D 1620; DSch 2739). Pius IX, in the encyclical *Nostris et nobiscum* of December 8, 1849, after his return to Rome, after having strongly reaffirmed the privileges and authority of the "Petri cathedra," added: "One cannot rebel against the Catholic faith without at the same time rejecting the authority of the Roman Church, in which dwells *fidei irreformabile magisterium* a divino Redemptore fundatum et in quo propterea semper conservata fuit ea quae est ab Apostolis traditio." Pius IX takes up the expression again in the letter *Tuas libenter* to the archbishop of Munich criticizing the theological congress presided over by Döllinger, of December 21, 1863. They had failed in "oboedientia debita erga magisterium Ecclesiae . . . " (D 1679; DSch 2875). And this obedience is not called for solely by the express definitions of ecumenical Councils or Roman Pontiffs, but by what is given as revealed "ordinario totius Ecclesiae per orbem dispersae magisterio" (1683; 2879).

The Deputation of the theologico-dogmatic Commission ordered to prepare the Vatican Council of 1869 had defined, on April 20, 1868, the *subject* of infallibility in these terms: "Infallibilitas autem haec cuius finis est fidelium societatis in fide et moribus intemerata veritas, magisterio inest quod Christus, etc." (Mansi 49, 634 B).[44] Let us pass over an ecclesiology which did not sufficiently place "the *magisterium*" *within* the "fidelium societas" which God maintains in the truth. It is the usage of the word which interests us. The schema *Summi Pastoris* distributed to the Fathers on January 21, 1870, written mainly by Schrader, openly adopted the tripartite distribution of powers (c. 4: Mansi 51, 540 D), with that of a "visibile magisterium" coming first. On this occasion the word meant directly a function rather than a defined body, but this sense of the body of pastors is met with frequently in speakers at the Council and, mixed with the sense of office, in the second schema, *Tametsi Deus*, prepared by Kleutgen, chapter VII, *De ecclesiastico Magisterio* (Mansi 312, D-313 B).[45] In *Pastor aeternus*, discussed and ratified (as was not the case with *Tametsi*), Chapter IV is devoted to the infallible magisterium of the Roman Pontiff (D 1832ff.; DSch 3065ff.). Our term appears there twice, with the sense of office and of the activity of teaching. For Leo XIII on the contrary, the word refers to the body of pastors to whom "data divinitus facultas est perficiendi atque administrandi divina mysteria" (enc. *Satis cognitum*, June 29, 1896: ASS 28 [1896] 723; D 1957 [DSch 3305] and 1958 [omitted in DSch]). In St. Pius X's encyclical *Singulari quaedam*, September 24, 1912 (AAS 4 [1912] 658): "Ecclesie catholicae magisterio tradita" means both the function and those who exercise it.

Recent Popes, Pius XII and Paul VI, have used the word *magisterium* frequently. Without trying to make a complete list, here are a few examples.

Pius XII, in his encyclical *Mystici corporis*, June 29, 1943: AAS 35 (1943) 209, states the three functions, but without the word *magisterium*; on page 228 this word is applied *to Christ*.

In the encyclical *Humani generis*, August 12, 1950, the word defines *the* magisterium, that is to say, at once the function or the hierarchical activity of teaching and the body of pastors who are responsible for it: AAS 42 (1950) 567 to 569; DSch 3884 to 3886; it speaks of "magisterium vivum," an expression repeated by the Dogmatic Constitution of Vatican II, *Dei verbum*, n. 10, with reference to the encyclical. *Magisterium Ecclesiae* reappears often in the remainder of this text with the sense of "*the* magisterium": pp. 571, 575, 576; DSch 3892, 3896, 3897.

The Constitution *Munificentissimus* of November 1, 1950, establishing as a dogma the bodily assumption of the Virgin Mary, asserts: " . . . ordinarii Ecclesiae magisterii doctrinam concordemque christiani populi fidem, quam idem magisterium sustinet ac dirigit" (AAS 42 [1950] 756). It is *the* magisterium.

The speech *Si diligis*, May 31, 1954, for the canonization of Pius X, proclaims that after the apostles their legitimate successors, the bishops, are "veri doctores seu magistri," the Pope "supremus in Ecclesia magister," the theologians whom they would classify in the "magistri munere," summoned to teach "vi missionis quam a legitimo magisterio receperunt" (AAS 46 [1954] 314 and 315). It is *the* magisterium, the hierarchical body of doctors.[46]

The radio broadcast *Inter complures* of October 24, 1954 (p. 678) states: "Quod quidem depositum authentice illustrandum atque interpretandum Divinus Redemptor uni concredidit magisterio Ecclesiae" (same meaning).

In the Constitution *Sedes Sapientiae* of May 31, 1956, it is stated analogously and with the same meaning.

Thus for Pius XII our word often means *the* magisterium. It is clearer still in the speech "Di gran cuore" of September 14, 1956, warning theologians that they are not masters of the magisterium, "magistri magisterii" (AAS 48 [1956] 709) and in "Oculis Nostris" of January 14, 1958, speaking of the "institutionibus et decretis sacri magisterii" (AAS 50 [1958] 151). It was extremely well defined in the Pope's thinking. He spoke of "nostra sancta Mater Ecclesia hierarchica" (speech *Quamvis inquieti*, September 7, 1946: AAS 38 [1946] 384).

Paul VI has the same concepts and the same vocabulary as Pius XII in his writings. In his opening speech at the second period of Vatican Council II, *Salvate fratres*, he said: "Cum igitur magisterii ecclesiastici munus" (AAS 55 [1963] 845), where it is a question of the function, but in his speech of March 12, 1964, *Incensissimo desiderio*, the word means *the* magisterium: "Ecclesiae magisterio . . . cui profecto a divina institutione munus concreditum est fidei depositum fideliter custodire et infallibiliter declarare" (AAS 56 [1964] 365). Elsewhere the word means both the function ("potestate magisterii": speech *Singulari cum* of November 20, 1965: AAS 57 [1965] 986), the teaching and the hierarchical body of those who exercise it: speech *Libentissimo sane* of October 1, 1966 (AAS 58 [1966] 891). Addressing the bishops of the first Synod, Paul VI said: "vos partes agitis universi catholicae Ecclesiae corporis hierarchici" (speech *Deo Patri omnipotenti* of September 30, 1967: AAS 59 [1967] 971).

In the sense of "body of pastors" exercising authoritatively the function of teaching, *magisterium*, "*the* magisterium," seems to us to be of recent usage. It appears first with Gregory XVI and Pius IX, and it is contemporary with the series of encyclicals generally considered to begin with *Mirari vos* (August 15, 1832). It has become common under Pius XII and, although with less constancy, with Paul VI.

Notes

1. Ernout and Meillet: *Dictionnaire étymologique de la langue latine*, p. 674 for *magister*, 740 for minister.

2. Du Cange fills several pages with it. Forcellini, *op. cit.*, pp. 15-17, gives some sixty usages and defines it as "qui in aliqua societate vel in aliquo officio prae ceteris auctoritate pollet." Pauly-Wissowa-Kroll refers us to various articles. The *Thesaurus Linguae Latinae*, Vol. VIII (Leipzig, 1936-46) gives a multitude of texts and references, col. 76-88.

3. *Thesaurus Linguae Latinae* VIII, col. 88ff.

4. Cf. Forcellini; *Thes. Linguae Lat.*; Blaise-Chirat. Alvaro d'Ors cited *infra*.

5. The frequent theme of the internal master connects with this: *De magistro* 14, 58 (32, 1216); *In Ioann.* Ev. tr. XCVI, 4 (35, 1876); *De civ. Dei* XV, 6 (41, 442); *Confess.* IX, 9 (32, 773); *In Epist. Ioann.* III, 13 to IV, 1 (35, 2004-5); cf. J. Rimaud, "Le Maître intérieur," in *Saint Augustin* (*Cahiers de la Nouvelle Journée* 17) 1930, pp. 53-69. This is a frequent theme of the Fathers and the Middle Ages (references in Alfaro, *Gregorianum* 44 [1963] 779-780, n. 357 and Congar, *La Foi et la Théologie* [Paris, 1962], p. 17, n. l). St. Leo speaks of "Paracleti magisterio" (*Sermo* 78: PL 54, 416), St. Bernard "sub magisterio Spiritus Sancti" (*Epist.* 320, 2: PL 182, 525).

6. Cf. *Sermo* 316, 1 (38, 1431); 339, 3 (38, 1481); *Epist.* 188, 1 (33, 849); *In Ioan.* Ev. tr. LXXX, 2 (35, 1839); D. Zähringer, *Das kirchliche Priestertum nach dem hl. Augustinus* (Paderborn, 1931), pp. 144ff.

7. Cf. Alvaro d'Ors, "Ministerium," in *Teologia del Sacerdocio*, 4: *Teologia del Sacerdocio en los primeros siglos* (Burgos, 1972), pp. 315-328.

8. *In natale apostolorum Petri et Pauli*. or. VIII: L. C. Mohlberg, *Sacramentarium Veronense* (Rome, 1956), n. 303, p. 41.

9. Or. 1, n. 280, p. 37.

10. *Sermo in ordinatione episcopi: Oeuvres de S. Avit*, ed. U. Chevalier (Lyon, 1890), p. 318.

11. Cf. Hugues de Flavigny, *Chron.*: MGH.SS.VIII, 392.

12. Before Alexander sent Peter Damien, and when he did not know if he would be able to send him, he delegated Girelmus. But now Peter Damien is a legate, and the Pope writes: "Volumus ut si quid apud vos Girelmus coepit, ad Domini Petri magisterium veniat . . . " (PL 146, 1296 AB).

A Semantic History of the Term "Magisterium" / 311

13. Alexander II, *Epist*. XV, in 1063: PL 146, 1296 AB.
14. Treatises J 2 and J 23: *Die Texte des Normannischen Anonymus*, publ. by K. Pellens (Wiesbaden, 1966), pp. 17 and 125: "Divina institutione nullus inter apostolos maior fuit, nullus magisterium vel principatum in alios habuit."
15, Cf. P. Kehr, "Gregor VIII. als Ordensgründer," in *Miscellanea Fr. Ehrle*. *Scritti di Storia e Paleografia*, Vol. II (*Studi e Testi* 38) (Vatican, 1924), pp. 248-275 (n. 15 of the text, p. 270).
16. Thus *Epist*. 235 of December 23, 1195: "Cum sacrosancta Romana ecclesia . . . per beati Petri merita ecclesiarum omnium magisterium cepit et principatum" (PL 206, 1127 C).
17. Thus *Reg*. II, 218; II, 220; VII, 1; VII, 9 (PL 214, 777 A, 779 C; 215, 278 and 294).
18. Thus *Reg*. I, 354 to the patriarch of Constantinople, 1198 (PL 214, 328); II, 209, to the same, November 24, 1199 (762 C); II, 218, to Gregory, catholicos of the Armenians (776 D, 777 A and B); II, 220 to the king of the Armenians (779 C); VII, 1 to King Colojan of the Bulgars (215, 278 and 279 B); VII, 9 (294); *Sermo de tempore* XVIII (217, 395).
19. Thus *Reg*. II, 57 to Richard, king of England, April 28, 1199 (PL 214, 595).
20. "Romana Ecclesia, cui datum est universale magisterium et cuius mandato et licentia scripsi haec": end of the commentary on revelation, ed (Venice, 1527), fol. 224 (quoted by H. de Lubac, Exégèse médiévale, vol. II/1 [Paris, 1961], p. 475).
21. Letters of June 8, 1265, to the legate Guy; of June 12, 1265, to Waldemar, king of Sweden and to the prelates of Sweden: Potthast, nn. 19182, 19191 and 19192.
22. Pauly-Wissowa-Kroll, which is an "encyclopedia in itself," has a long article "Magistratus," by Kühlen.
23. *Homil*. 70 (PL 57, 398ff.); comp. Hom. 72 (57, 403ff.): "Paulo, tanquam idoneo doctori magisterium ecclesiasticae institutionis iniunxit. . . . "
24. *Supra*, p. 4; *Reg. Past*. I. c. 11: "Ad pastorale magisterium dignus qualiter veniat . . . " (PL 77, 26 C). The Council of Paris of 829 (I c. 12: MGH. Legum sectio III. Concil. II/2, p. 618) was to say that bishops have a "magisterium pastorale."
25. "Quae tamen artis humanae peritia si quando tractandis sacris eloquiis adhibetur, non debet ius magisterii sibimet arroganter arripere, sed velut ancilla . . . " (*De divina omnipotentia* [Opusc. 36] c. 5: PL 145, 603.)
26. G. Paré, A. Brunet, P. Tremblay, *La Renaissance du XIIe siècle. Les écoles et l'enseignement* (Paris-Ottawa, 1933), p. 59, n. 2, cite five passages. Let us add this strange testimony about the end of the Middle Ages: Pierre d'Ailly, Tract. II adv. Cancellarium Parisiensem: *An liceat pecuniam dare vel exigere pro docendi licentia?* "Magisterium . . . non est ultra licentiam . . . aliqua authoritas spiritualis. . . . Unde magisterium huiusmodi se habet ad licentiam sicut nuptiae ad sacramentum matrimonii" (inter *Opera Gersoni*, ed. Dupin, 1, 769 P).

27. In addition to *op. cit.* in note 26, cf. E. Lesne, *Histoire de la propriété ecclésiastique en France*, V: *Les écoles* (Lille, 1940), pp. 461-463; our article on "Maître Rufin et son *De bono pacis*," in *Rev. Sc. ph. th.* 41 (1957), 428-444; P. de Léo, "*Ricerche sul Liber ad Gebehardum di Manegoldo di Lautenbach*," in *Riv. di Storia e Letteratura religiosa* 10 (1974), pp. 112ff.

28. Richard of Saint-Victor, *De erudit. hom. int.* lib. II c. 6: "Absque dubio numquam proprie Scripturarum interpretatio fit sine eius magisterio qui eas inspiravit" (PL 196, 1305 AB).

29. St. Bernard, *In Cant.* sermo 27, 7, "sanctus ille Emmanuel servis intulit magisterium disciplinae coelestis" (PL 183, 216 C); Alexander III, after referring to the foundation of the authority of the Roman Church, continues: "ut quicumque de ovili Christi sunt Petri magisterio et doctrinae subiaceant . . . " (*Epist.* 1447 *bis*, in 1171: PL 200, 1259).

30. *Christus unus omnium magister*, n. 24: "Omnis doctrina ministerialis doctoris ad haec tria debet ordinari, ut sub illo magistro summo officium magisterii digne possit executioni mandare. . . . "

31. D. van den Eynde gives 18 references for this: *Les Normes de l'Enseignement chrétien dans la littérature patristique des trois premiers siècles* (Gembloux-Paris, 1933), p. 129 n. 5.

32. "In universa Ecclesia *Tu es Christus Filius Dei vivi* quotidie Petrus dicit et omnis lingua quae confitetur Dominum magisterio huius vocis imbuitur": *Sermo* 3, 3 (PL 54, 146 C).

33. *Conciliorum Oecumenicorum Decreta*, cur. J. Alberigo, 3rd ed. (Bologna, 1973), p. 135.

34. Cf. J. Kremp, "Des Wilhelm von Auvergne 'Magisterium divinale,'" in *Gregorianum* 1 (1920), pp. 538-584; 2 (1921) pp. 42-78, 174-187.

35. Cf. our *L'Eglise de S. Augustin à l'époque moderne* (Paris, 1970), p. 191.

36. L. de Mas Latrie, *Histoire de l'île de Chypre sous le règne des princes de la maison de Lusignan*, III (Paris, 1855), pp. 599-600.

37. Cf. Y. Congar, *op. cit.* (n. 14), pp. 244-248; "St. Thomas Aquinas and the Infallibility of the Papal Magisterium," in *The Thomist* 38 (1974), pp. 81-105.

38. Brian Tierney, *Origins of Papal Infallibility 1150-1350. A Study on the Concepts of Infallibility, Sovereignty and Tradition in the Middle Ages* (Leiden, 1972).

39. In R. Manselli, *La "Lectura super Apocalipsim" di Pietro di Giovanni Olivi* (Rome, 1955), p. 220, n. 2 (Tierney, p. 112, n. 1).

40. Contrary to the Joachimite idea of an era of the Holy Ghost, he says that the Son and the Holy Ghost have "una natura, una doctrina, unum magisterium" (*Concordia* in Jn 16:14: cited by Tierney p. 252, n. l, who translates "one teaching"). Cf. Guido Terreni, *Quaestio de magisterio infallibili Romani Pontificis*, ed. B.-M. Xiberta (Münster, 1926). The word *magisterium* is the editor's.

41. Cf. Congar, *op. cit.* (n. 14), p. 389.

42. This history is retraced by J. Fuchs, *Magisterium, Ministerium, Regime Vom Ursprung einer ekklesiologischen Trilogie* (Bonn, 1941)

(translated in *Rev. Sc. ph. th.* 53 [1969], pp. 185-211); J. Pottmeyer, *Unfehlbarkeit im System der ultramontanen Ekklesiologie des 19. Jahrhunderts* (Mainz, 1974) (reviewed in *Rev. Sc. ph. th.*, 59 [1975], pp. 489-493).

43. *Handbuch des katholischen und protestantischen Kirchenrechts* (Bamberg, 1823), p. 110 (Pottmeyer, p. 137).

44. The Deputation of the Faith summed up the intention of its text thus: "Declaretur Ecclesiam societatem esse conspicuam et visibilem per vincula, quibus continetur, externa, scilicet per visibile suum magisterium, ministerium et regimen" (Mansi 49, 744 D).

45. Cf. our work cited *supra* (n. 14), p. 447 n. 15 (references); J. Salaverri, *La triple potestad de la Iglesia* (Comillas, 1951); J.-P. Torrell, *La Théologie de l'épiscopat au premier concile du Vatican* (*Unam Sanctam* 37) (Paris, 1961).

46. The reader is referred to M. Seckler, "Die Theologie als kirchliche Wissenschaft nach Pius XII and Paulus VI," in *Theol. Quartalschr.* 149 (1969), pp. 209-234 (to whom we owe most of our references).

A Brief History of the Forms of the Magisterium and Its Relations with Scholars

Yves Congar, O.P.

This story has never been told in its entirety. There are many monographs on particular segments, and sometimes we find people taking care either to illustrate the orthodoxy of the writers and their submissiveness to instituted authority or to reduce the significance of the latter. Confessional predispositions have often had an impact even on the conclusions of excellent research. This study, prepared originally for the International Commission of Theologians, seeks only to clarify the main lines of a rich and complicated history. These main lines are to be found, much to our own astonishment, in the framework of the classic distinction between antiquity (to which we can join the high Middle Ages), the classical Middle Ages, and modern times.

I

ANTIQUITY AND THE HIGH MIDDLE AGES

In the primitive Church there was a function of a doctor, *didaskalos*, probably analogous to that exercised by rabbis in the synagogues of the Hellenic world (cf. 1 Cor. 12:28; Rom. 12:7; Eph. 4:11; Acts 13:1),[1] but such activity had to be more like our catechesis than theological speculation. It is not certain that the schools that flourished in the second and third centuries are a continuation of them.[2] These schools, which were opened on the initiative of the masters without direction by the pastoral authorities,[3] were at first simply centers to illustrate the faith. There arose among them however a kind of speculation which attracted control by the community and its pastors. Origen, who continues the Alexandrian line of didascales, places bishops in command of their activities.[4]

In the second half of the second century there was a certain tension between the speculation of the doctors and the apostolic testimony linked to the succession of ordained ministers; this testimony had as its objective "teaching in conformity with piety" (1 Tim. 6:3; Tit. 1:1), *hypotyposis* (1 Tim. 1:16) or the systèma (Irenaeus), that is to say, the type or schema of interpretation of God's plan of salvation. As early as the time of Ignatius and Polycarp, but even in the time of the apostles, there were interpretations that the faithful resented as perversions. That is how orthodoxy became established: by exclusion and rejection of what did not agree with their understanding of the faith.[5] "True gnosis," says St. Irenaeus, "is the teaching of the apostles and the plan (systèma) the Church has had from the beginning in accordance with the dimensions of the universe, and its identification with the body of Christ, which consists in the chain of succession by which bishops have traditionally founded the Church in each place."[6]

The succession of bishops or presbyters (for Clement of Alexandria, masters) is the guarantee of faithful transmission (cf. 2 Tim. 2:2). We know that St. Irenaeus formulated the doctrine of apostolic succession of ministers as the form and guarantee of the authenticity of tradition, against gnosticism.[7]

Also at this period what characteristizes the bishop is the *cathedra*, the chair. This is certified in the *Pastor,* around 150, and in the fragment of Muratori, around 200 (lines 75-76): "Hermas conscripsit sedente cathedra urbis Romae ecclesiae Pio episcopo fratre eius."[8] The *cathedra* is the episcopal function, its continuity, succession, *doctrina.*[9] We can speak in a special way of the *cathedra Petri,* for Peter is the first to confess Christ and on his confession Christ builds his Church. And he is still in Rome in his representatives (*vicarii*) or successors.[10] *Cathedra* is the equivalent of what we call "magisterium." The apostolic succession of ministers involves an authority, which is conditional on faithful transmission of the trust. As J. Ratzinger has written, "Succession is the form (Gestalt) of tradition; tradition is the content (Gehalt) of succession."[11] In this sense, it is tradition taken as transmitted truth which is genuine authority; the magisterium is considered not as a juridical authority possessing as such a power to compel, but as a function through which the Church receives the faith inherited from the apostles. This results from several considerations: (a) The "rule of faith" or of truth is not a formal principle of authority, but *what* the Church believes, having received it from the apostles and preserved it thanks to the succession of presbyters.[12] As B. Häggelund says, *regula fidei* is not a rule for faith (objective genitive) but is the rule which is faith (subjective genitive).[13] (b) There is debate on the meaning of "charisma veritatis certum" in Irenaeus. [14] D. van den Eynde and H. von Campenhausen understand by it the spiritual gift of truth, in the objective sense of the word. But other interpretations are perhaps correct.[15] (c) When St. Athanasius speaks of the Council of Nicaea, he does not base his argument on intrinsic authority, but on the fact that Nicaea expressed the faith received from the apostles and the Fathers.[16]

Let us here cite some relevant texts:

> The Fathers, in matters of faith, never said: Thus it has been decreed, but: This is what the Catholic Church believes; and they confessed what they believed directly, so as to show unmistakably that their thought was not new, but apostolic.[17]

> We have a more than sufficient guarantee of the truth of our teaching tradition, that is, the truth that has come down to us from the apostles, in succession, like an inheritance.[18]

> If someone does not confess in the right way and in truth, following the holy Fathers, everything received by tradition and preached in the holy, catholic and apostolic Church of God . . . let him be condemned.[19]

The action of the magister consists in preaching, teaching, and comparing the more elaborate interpretations which come to light through the faith of the Church. This happens in treatises: St. Gregory of Nyssa and St. Basil wrote a *Contra Eunomium,* St. Jerome a *Contra Iovinianum*, St. Augustine a *Contra Faustum* and a *Contra Iulianum,* and so forth. It is eventually brought to a conclusion in a council: ecumenical councils, all held in the East, Roman councils, national councils in Visigothic Spain, provincial councils in the ˙West, like those of Orange in 529, Quierzy in 853, and Valence in 855. Nonetheless Roman bishops intervened by expositions of Trinitarian and Christological doctrines (Dionysius in 262, Damascus, Leo, Hormisdas, Agathonus) and they required people to write to them (Julius I, 341: DSch 132). Their vocabulary to establish a proper magisterium is "auctoritas" (Zosimus, 418; Simplicius, 476: DSch 221, 343), "iudicium" (Boniface I: DSch 232, 235).

If there was harsh opposition by pastors and councils to erroneous speculation by doctors, even if the Fathers did not stop denouncing "philosophy" as the inspiration of heresies,[20] there was no statutory separation or opposition *a priori* between pastors and doctors. St. Augustine (*Epist.* 149, 11: PL 33, 635) and St. Jerome (PL 26, 510) identify pastors and doctors in Ephesians 4:11: "Non enim ait: alios autem pastores et alios magistros, ut qui pastor esse debeat et magister" (For he does not say: some as pastors, others as masters, so that he who is a pastor ought also to be a master. This derives first from the fact that the two categories practice a similar theology, dominated by commentary on the Scriptures and reference to the collective sense of revelation and administration. It derives next from the fact that at the very least from the fourth century onward, theologians are most often bishops and important bishops are theologians. Thus theology cooperates in the effort for dogmatic clarification; the complex history of Christological debates before Chalcedon shows this. Non-pastors, such as Tertullian, cooperated in this with Theodore of Mopsuestia and the Cappadocians. Since authority rests on truth and tradition, a non-bishop is listened to: Athanasius participates at Nicaea as a simple deacon, St. Augustine asserts his right to invoke Jerome against Pelagius, Vincent of Lérins calls "patres" non-bishops.[21]

II
THE MIDDLE AGES

From the point of view which interests us, two traits seem dominant: (1) We limit our attention to the Latin West, from now on not interacting with the East. (2) A decisive event is the development of schools, and hence of Scholasticism: Tours, Le Bec, Laon, Abelard, later on the universities, the *studia* of religious orders.

Scholasticism is the passage "from symbol to dialectic," analyzed by de Lubac.[22] It is the development of analytical *doctrina,* questioning, seeking the *rationes*, bringing to bear genuinely philosophical resources, not only in reasoning but in content and thought.

Thus we are led to reformulate a distinction already known between doctrinal-scholarly teaching and pastoral teaching. Innocent III, writing to Archbishop Peter of Compostella on a Christological question, declares: "Haec ergo tibi scholastico more respondemus. Sed si oportet nos more apostolico respondere, simplicius quidem sed cautius respondemus" (Therefore we will reply to you on these matters in Scholastic fashion. But if it is necessary for us to answer in apostolic fashion, we will certainly answer more simply but more cautiously.)[23] Thomas Aquinas distinguishes the "magisterium cathedrae pastoralis" or "pontificalis" (magisterium of the pastoral or pontifical chair) from the "magisterium cathedrae magistralis" (magisterium of a master's chair).[24] The former is power par excellence, the latter is personal competence recognized publicly. The magisterium of a theologian can in fact be recognized and be a public office in the Church, but its substance comes from his scholarly competence. The pastoral magisterium is linked to the public office of *praelatio,* that is, superiority or authority, to which belongs jurisdiction.[25]

Let us sum up here in a few words what the preceding article establishes clearly. The word "magisterium" did not then signify what we call "the magisterium." In the Fathers, in the Middle Ages and up until the 1820's and 1830's, *magisterium* means simply the situation, the function or the activity of someone who is in the position of a *magister*, that is, of authority in a particular area. In antiquity there was a "magister equitum" (master of the horsemen) and a "magister militum" (commander of troops). The activity could be that of teaching. In this case, *magisterium* shared materially in the modern sense of "magisterium," but before the nineteenth century it never meant precisely what we call *"the* magisterium."

Preaching was a public act of teaching the Gospel which belonged primarily and principally to bishops (who were designated as "ordo praedicatorum," "ordo doctorum" — order of preachers, order of doctors) [26] and then generally *ex officio* to those who had a *cura animarum* (cure of souls). This public act supposed a *missio* (authorization) received either immediately with the *cura animarum,* or "mediante auctoritate praelatorum qui gerunt vicem Dei" (by the authority of bishops who act in place of God). [27] A fierce criticism was formulated against sects, Waldensian or otherwise, who preached without authorization. [28]

Yet we must date from the thirteenth century, with a prehistory in the twelfth, the beginning of what we can call the magisterium of Doctors in the Church. In addition to their function of scholarly teaching, Doctors and universities acquired a position and a role of authority to make decisions or to call for submission. The *studium* is a third authority beside the *sacerdotium* (priesthood) and the *regnum* (kingship). [29] The Popes themselves rely on the universities to publish collections of decretals (for example, Gregory IX in 1234) or councils (those of Lyon I and II, in 1245 and 1274, and of Vienna, under John XXII). There is more than one way of influencing opinion by this means. Faculties judge doctrinal theses. Gerson affirmed the right of doctors to "scholastice determinare ea quae sunt fidei" (to decide scholastically those things which pertain to the faith) before the "praelati Ecclesiae" (bishops of the Church). This role of Doctors will reach its apogee, a peak sufficiently unhealthy, at the Council of Basle: at the thirty-fourth session, on June 25, 1439, there were three hundred Doctors as against thirteen priests and seven bishops! It explains the importance Luther attached to his title (his function and authority) as a Doctor. [30] A theologian as balanced as Godefroid of Fontaines (died 1306) maintained the right of masters not to comply with an episcopal decision [31] and to "determine" things in the Pope's jurisdiction because "ea quae condita sunt a Papa possunt esse dubia" (those things which have been established by the Pope may be doubtful). [32]

E. Delaruelle suggests that the autonomy and the role assumed by speculation or theological *doctrina* led to the institution of an office of surveillance and repression, the Inquisition.[33] But the Inquisition functioned first against heresy and especially heresy among the people. For surveillance and repression of scholarly errors, Popes proceeded rather by prompt inquiry and councils and then by commissions. See the cases of Beranger, Abelard, Gilbert of la Porrée and even Peter Lombard and Joachim of Flores (councils), then the eternal Gospel, Seculars against Mendicants, Olivi, Eckhart, Ockham, Nicolas of Autrecourt (papal commissions and censure of "propositions"); next papal censure of Wycliffe's theses and the intervention again of a council (Constance). Under the threat of possible censures, theologians who thought they might be suspected extricated themselves by saying they would submit their writings to the judgment of the Roman Church (thus Joachim of Flore, Guillaume of Saint-Amour, Olivi, Ockham, Marsiglio, Peter Auriol, Durand of Saint-Pourçain), or by protesting that they had simply offered propositions, not asserted them (Taddeo of Parma, Nicolas of Lyre, John XXII): this acquitted them of "persistence" and so of heresy. In the case of Luther, there was condemnation of the theses by universities (Louvain, Paris), then preparation of a papal document (bull *Exsurge Domine,* 15.6.1520), by university documents (Cologne, Louvain) and by theologians (Eck, Cajetan). The result was, as H. Jedin notes, that theses which were strictly *theological,* scholarly positions were condemned in the name of the Catholic faith (thus theses 5 and 37) and that *Christian* elements in Luther were neither recognized nor accepted.[34]

In reality, Popes had been introducing theology in their pastoral teaching for more than three centuries. From Alexander III onward, almost all popes are canon lawyers, "masters." The universities provided numerous bishops, which, in itself, was good. The result was the entry into dogma of concepts, or at least of theological terms: *transsubstantiatio,* "anima forma corporis" (soul as the form of the body), decretal of 1439 "pro Armenis," largely recopied from *De articulis fidei et Ecclesiae sacramentis* (On the articles of faith and the sacraments of the Church) by St. Thomas. This will hold true into our own time. The encyclicals of Leo XIII and Pius XII are theology. They are not purely an expression of apostolic witness according to the needs of the time, but a *doctrina* of "cathedra magistralis" assuming the principles of natural law, human wisdom, and classical theology.

Throughout the Middle Ages, papal authority grew not only in fact but in its theoretical expression—unfortunately, in a very imperfect knowledge of history. This produced at the same time a development of ideas which concerns the theory of what we call the papal magisterium. Let us emphasize the four following points: (a) A broad sense of "heresy" understood, since the Gregorian reform, as any idea or attitude "qui Romanae Ecclesiae non concordat" (which does not agree with the Roman Church).[35] (b) Repeated affirmation that the Roman Church has never erred in faith. But this falls a long way short of the idea that "Roman Church" is defined by or interchangeable with "sedes Romana" (Roman throne), or with "Papa" (the Pope). (c) Progressive insistence on the aspect of *judgment* putting an end to debate, which takes primacy compared with a function of preaching and witness. People will speak of "auctoritas declarandi dubia (auctoritate)" (authority to declare what is of dubious authority) (Hervé Nédellec, died 1323), "potestas definitiva ad declarandas veritates fidei" (definitive power to declare the truths of the faith) (Bañez, died 1604). Completing the papal victory over the conciliar tide, Cajetan established a clear distinction between personal faith, which the theologian puts forward, and the authority which alone can pass judgment, which Cajetan finds is that of the Pope.[36] (d) The *False Decretals* did not create the claim for the Pope to approve, or even to authorize and convoke councils, but they gave a decided support to this claim.[37] But if the Pope convoked, presided over and confirmed councils, it was ultimately by his authority that, conciliarly or directly, judgments were reached which decided controverted points of dogma; it was for him to "finaliter determinare ea quae sunt fidei" (decide finally those things which are part of the faith) and to "novum symbolum edere" (declare a new article of faith).[38]We are on the road which leads to the dogma of 1870. The text of John Olivi undoubtedly had historically the role B. Tierney attributes to it, but it is, with those of Guy Terré (before 1328) and of Hermann of Schildesche, testimony to the progress of the idea of an infallibility in the doctrinal pronouncements of the Pope, who personifies the impossibility of a mistake by the Church.[39]

III
Modern Times

The Council of Trent achieved a happy collaboration between theologians and Fathers. First, theologians were admitted to congregations partly composed of bishops; then congregations of lesser theologians were established, that is to say, not conciliar Fathers, ahead of legates and prelates. The opinion of theologians was considered; then the Fathers drafted a decree and, before publishing it, submitted the text to the theologians. Then, the theologians were allowed to speak in assemblies, which brought the difficulty of limiting their interventions.[40] Among the bishops, several were good theologians. All in all, after a period of resistance by the Fathers, the interventions and importance of theologians have been growing.

With the reactions against the Protestants, the Council of Trent, the Society of Jesus, and then the necessity of meeting the challenges from rationalism and popular and social movements, the four centuries preceding Vatican II developed under the aegis of the affirmation of this authority just as much in its form of "magisterium." Let us note, a little schematically, seven points.

1. Faculties of theology remain active until the French Revolution. They continue to condemn theses (Alcala and Salamanca on the subject of Baius, Louvain and Paris against overtolerant morality), but sometimes they intervene in Rome: Louvain about Baius, 1567; on permissiveness, 1677; with the bishop of Ghent on attritionism, 1682ff. Whether invited or not, Rome intervenes in a number of theological questions by censuring propositions: Pius V against Baius, 1567 (DSch 1901ff.), Innocent X against Jansenism, 1633 (2001ff.), against permissiveness, 1665-1666 and 1679 (2021ff., 2101ff.); Rome against Molinos and quietism, 1687 and 1698 (2201ff., 2351), Alexander VIII against Jansenism, 1690 (2291ff.), Clement XI against Quesnel, 1713 (101 propositions: 2400ff.) and finally the rather bland condemnation of the theses of the Jansenist synod of Pistoia. Theology is watched, at least when it bears with consequences for the behavior of clerks and the faithful. But since the days of Paul IV and Pius IV (1564), the Index of prohibited books exists. The papacy disposes of an organism to repress errors.

The situation will change as a result of the suppression of most faculties of theology by the French Revolution and Napoleon — all those in France, thirteen of eighteen in Germany. A restoration of faculties will take place in the nineteenth century, at Rome first (Roman College, 1824) and in large part under the authority of the papacy and from Rome. The problem of the independence of the "cathedrae magistrales" will not arise again as in the past.

2. The discussions stirred up by Jansenism brought about the emergence of a new category, that of "dogmatic facts." Moreover, in the context of the progress of the idea of the infallibility of the papal magisterium, the distinction between the infallibility of the body of the faithful and that of the Pope and pastors is made more precise. This culminated in the distinction between *Ecclesia docens* (the teaching Church) and *Ecclesia credens* or *discens* (the believing or learning Church) (in the middle of the eighteenth century), a distinction which was to become common in the nineteenth, including in catechisms and into our own time, often in debatable formulations such as active and passive infallibility. These are categories and a vocabulary to reconsider.

3. We have sketched out elsewhere the changes in ideas by which, in modern times, we have replaced consideration of the principle or the *quod* by that of the teaching or defining authority, that is, the *quo*. This has been expressed in the categories, valid in themselves, of "living magisterium" and of "active tradition" as distinct from "passive tradition," or again by *regula proxima* as distinct from *regula remota*.[41] Thus there was a tendency to give "magisterium" an autonomous and absolute value, whereas soundness consists in not separating the form of the apostolic ministry from the content of tradition (cf. *supra*, n. 11). What Luther wrote to Prierias does all the same deserve attention: "I do not know what you mean by calling the Roman Church the rule of faith, I have always believed that faith was the rule of the Roman Church and of all Churches" (WA 1, 662). Let us note that many official texts state that the magisterium only guards, proposes and ultimately interprets what is objectively given.[42] Nevertheless, the meaning we have just given was indeed that of a whole train of thought which it is proper to criticize. Of the two classic activities of the magisterium, preserving and defining, the second has been

privileged. It seemed under Pius XII that the objective of theology was to prepare "definitions" and that the purpose of the magisterium was to define. At that time it was forgotten that the essential and first function is *to bear witness to what has been received*. Definition should be handled cautiously, occurring only when required by necessity in order to protect the truth of apostolic witness under threat.[43]

4. The word "magisterium" appeared in its modern sense, *"the* magisterium." Our historical and semantic essay expounds and illustrates that. The distinction between ordinary magisterium and extraordinary magisterium is classical. Vatican I introduced the category of "ordinary and universal magisterium" (DSch 3011) already used by Pius IX to indicate the magisterium of the scattered college of bishops.

5. Vatican I defined, certainly not, as is said popularly, the infallibility of the Pope, but that of his teaching when, acting in his capacity as pastor and teacher of all Christians, he commits his supreme authority in the universal Church on a question of faith or morals.[44] Vatican I distinguished two powers: order and jurisdiction. It made infallibility an attribute of primacy (DSch 3065). "Deducimus ex primatu supremam potestatem docendi tamquam speciem a suo genere" (We deduce from the primacy the supreme power of teaching as a species from its genus), said Gasser on July 11, 1870 (Mansi 52, 1221 A). This approach, as Pottmeyer has shown, is part of the stream of ideas expressed with as much brilliance as sophistry by J. de Maistre, de Bonald, and the first Lamennais, ideas whose roots plunge into the *modern* concept of sovereignty (Bodin, Hobbes). Vatican I took place in a general context of restoration, of opposition to movements of liberation, of affirmation to the highest degree of authority.[45] Such sociohistorical conditioning, such unilateralism, call for us to consider Vatican I again, both positively and critically, with good historical studies, even with the questions asked by H. Küng or after him. It will be particularly necessary to define theologically the status of "magisterium" or what M. J. Scheeben called "Lehrapostolat" (the teaching apostolate) and to distinguish it from the *genus* "primatus jurisdictionis" (primacy of jurisdiction). On the other hand the Council speaks (DSch 3072 and 3074) of "summum

pastorale officium" (the highest pastoral office), which is more satisfactory.

6. Vatican I made no precise statement concerning the "ordinary magisterium" of the bishop of Rome.[46] *In point of fact,* as the "ordinary magisterium" of Popes has been exercised by excellent Pontiffs in an incredible flow of encyclicals, speeches, and various interjections, this magisterium has assumed preponderant importance and, in the light of an intense "devotion to the Pope,"[47] has been almost assimilated, in current opinion, to the prerogatives of the extraordinary magisterium. Besides, Pius XII, who carried it to its furthest point, expressed in the encyclical *Humani Generis* (August 12, 1950) his position on two points of great importance: (1) The ordinary magisterium of the Pope requires total obedience: "He who listens to you listens to me." When the Pope has expressed his *sententia* on a point previously controversial, "quaestionem liberae inter theologos disceptationis iam haberi non posse" (there can no longer be any question of free discussion between theologians) (DSch 3884-3885). (2) The (or a) role of theologians is to justify the declarations of the magisterium: "eorum est indicare qua ratione ea quae a vivo magisterio docentur, in Sacris Litteris et in divina 'traditione' sive explicite, sive implicite inveniantur" (their task is to indicate for what reason those things which are taught by the living magisterium are found in Holy Scripture and divine "tradition," whether explicitly or implicitly) (DSch 3886). This was already to be found in Pius IX, in the letter *Gravissimas inter* of December 11, 1862 against Frohschammer (ASS 8 [1874] 429). Pius XII saw the theologian teaching only by delegation from the "magisterium" and doing so strictly in his service and under his control.[48] Is this consonant with what nineteen centuries of the Church's life tell us about the function of "didascale" or doctor? No, not exactly.

These positions were all the more serious in that, in their encyclicals (the series begins with *Mirari Vos* of Gregory XVI, 1832), modern Popes have done *theology*—and a determined theology, which the Roman schools practiced, their personnel being recruited and supervised according to a very definite line. It is not very easy to define the significance of encyclicals in theological terms. On the one hand there are many kinds; on the other they do not fit the classical frameworks of treatises of theological criteriology. Sometimes they simply express a common conviction that has already been reached; at other times they formulate a doctrine that has not yet been accepted. They are intended to be the means, for the Pope, of realizing unity among bishops and, through them, of the body of the faithful around them.[49] There are several books and articles on the value of encyclicals.[50] The present article does not have to deal with this issue in itself.

Yet it is necessary, from the historical point of view, to add that if there has been an unfitting inflation of encyclicals' authority, there is now a relativization and criticism of them. People have practically applied to them what Vatican I had said on extraordinary papal magisterium.[51] Today in contrast we find refusal to accept, at least partially, such documents as *Humanae Vitae*. It is true that we can invoke texts of classical theologians on the right not to assent to a non-infallible teaching.[52]

7. Vatican II has renewed in sufficiently striking fashion collaboration between theologians and conciliar Fathers. "You are the teaching Church, but we are the informing Church." The bishops have become aware of the importance of theologians.[53]

The Council itself insists on the necessity of a very frank openness to the questions and resources of our world, and on the vitality and freedom of theological work.[54] Concerning the magisterium, the Council re-established the traditional relationship of subordination of pastoral authority to the given or to the object, in short the primacy of *quod* over *quo*: either by affirming that the magisterium is linked to the Word of God and his serivce (*Lumen Gentium*, n. 25; *Dei Verbum*, n. 10), or by not taking up (*Dei Verbum*, n 25) the affirmation that the preparatory schema of 1962 had borrowed from *Humani Generis* the idea that the magisterium is "proxima veritatis norma" (the proximate norm of truth). This restoration of *quod* in its traditional sovereignty has allowed recognition of a "hierarchia veritatum" (hierarchy of truths) (*Unitatis Redintegratio*, n. 11).

Paul VI often spoke of the relations between the magisterium and theologians. At first he spoke along the same lines as Pius XII,[55] still denying all private judgment and insisting on obedient and docile dependence toward the magisterium. Paul VI on several occasions was severe about certain theological researches.[56] In his speech to the International Congress on the theology of Vatican II,[57] he dealt expressly with the relations of theologians and the magisterium. He regarded theology as a function *of the Church*, taking place in the morphology and physiology of the Church. It mediates in a way between the magisterium and the faithful or the world of men: on the one hand, discerning faith as it is lived by the Christian community, its problems and the resources culture offers, in order to answer men's questions in the light of revelation and tradition, and thus to help the magisterium to fulfill its task more amply; on the other hand, to transmit and explain, by elaborating and justifying it in scholarly fashion, the teaching of the magisterium. For these two mediations there must be an active theology, carried on in a religious climate, fraternally trusting and communicating.

But the period since the Council has been marked by argument, the breaking up of what had represented Catholic unity up to and including Pius XII. With new means of information, men are shaping their ideas by a host of means other than official teaching. This seems insufficient faced with what the critical sciences, philosophy and the social sciences produce as problems and bring as data. The general democratic climate is changing the meaning of authority, which is perceived less as the right to determine the thought and life of subordinates. Former beliefs and practices are no longer effective by virtue of their own weight; people want to do and say other things than they have been taught. People appreciate nevertheless the endeavors of authority and the texts of the magisterium in the light of disciplines such as the sociology of knowledge of K. Mannheim, and notice that affirmation by itself of the magisterium such as it has been practiced is subject to ideological criticism.[58] We cannot not take into account the critical historical study of the magisterium in modern times. Its pretentions seem excessive and unreal. For one thing, the current crisis is to be explained as a reaction against them. Today, theologians are going beyond the ecclesiastical work-category formulated for them by Pius XII and Paul VI; they are living according to a common standard of scholarly research. Obviously it is no longer enough to explain decisions already reached ("Denzinger-theology"); it is a matter of rejoining men in their critical questions with reference to revelation in Jesus Christ. In these conditions the work of theologians is still tied to faith as transmitted and defined, but it cannot be a simple commentary on pontifical teachings. The period since the Council has seen several declarations of the freedom of theological work. Consult also the criticism of that made by *Concilium* in December 1968 by G. Chantraine.[59] Neither these declarations nor his criticism can resolve the real questions facing us today.

If we may conclude an historical article with a theological perspective, we will say: the relationship between scholars and the magisterium calls for reconsideration. This supposes that we will first define the status of the "magisterium" in the Church, and that it will not be isolated from the living reality of the Church. It will be necessary to recognize the fundamental character of the charisma and service of theologians, the necessary specificity of their work within the faith of the Church, to define the conditions for a healthy exercise of their service: an awareness of responsibility, of communion with the concrete life of the faithful, the doxological context and celebration of mysteries, a mutual criticism actively performed. We cannot define the dependent condition of theologians only with reference to the "magisterium," even while this retains its truth. In this area as in that of obedience we must not think of the issue just in two terms: authority and theologians. We must think in three terms: above, the truth, the transmitted apostolic faith, confessed, preached and celebrated. Beneath this, at its service, the "magisterium" of the apostolic ministry, and the work or the teaching of theologians, as well as the faith of the faithful. It is a differentiated service, articulated organically, like all the life of the Church.

Notes

1. P. V. Dias, *Vielfalt der Kirche in der Vielfalt der Jünger, Zeugen und Diener* (Freiburg, 1968), pp. 262ff.
2. Cf. K. H. Rengstorf, in Kittel, *ThWNT*, II, p. 162 on Alexandria.
3. D. van den Eynde, *op. cit., infra*, n. 7, pp. 59ff.
4. *Ibid.*, p. 233.
5. This is what is true in the thesis of W. Bauer, *Rechtgläubigkeit und Ketzerei im ältesten Christentum* (Tübingen, 1934).

6. *A.H.* IV, 33, 8; PG 7, 1077; Harvey 2, 262.

7. D. van den Eynde, *Les normes de l'enseignement chrétien dans la littérature patristique des trois premiers siècles* (Gambloux-Paris, 1933), pp. 57-67; J. Beumer, "Heilige Schrift und kirchliche Lehrautorität," in *Scholastik* 25 (1950), pp. 40-72; A. Ehrhardt, *The Apostolic Succession in the First Two Centuries of the Church* (London, 1953), pp. 107-131.

8. Cf. E. Stommel, "Die bischöfliche Kathedra im christlichen Altertum," in *Münch. Theol. Zeitschr.* 3 (1952), pp. 17-32.

9. "Cathedram pro doctrina posuit," Augustine, *Sermo Guelferb.* 32, 10, ed. Morin, p. 572.

10. M. Maccarone, "'Cathedra Petri' und die Entwicklung der Idee des päpstlichen Primats vom 2, bis 4. Jahrhundert," in *Saeculum 13 (1962), pp.* 278-292.

11. "Primat, Episkopat und Successio apostolica," in J. Ratzinger, K. Rahner, *Episkopat und Primat* (Freiburg, 1961), p. 49.

12. See texts and references in my *La Tradition et les traditions. I. Essai historique* (Paris, 1968), pp. 44ff. and notes, p. 97.

13. B. Häggelund, "Die Bedeutung der 'regula fidei' als Grundlage theologischer Aussagen," in *Studia theologica* 12 (1958), pp. 1-44. See also H. de Lubac, commentary on *Dei Verbum* in *La Révélation divine* (Paris, 1968), I, pp. 63-66 and 88.

14. *A.H.* IV, 25, 2: PG 7, 1053; Harvey, 2, 236.

15. References in our *L'Eglise une, sainte, catholique et apostolique* in *Mysterium salutis* (Paris, 1970), p. 210, n. 73.

16. Cf. J. Sieben, "Zur Entwicklung der Konzilsidee. I. Werden und Eigenart der Konzilsidee des Athanasius von Alexandrien," in *Theol. u. Phil.* 45 (1970), pp. 353-389.

17. St. Athanasius, *De synodis*, 5; PG 26, 688.

18. St. Gregory of Nyssa, *Contra Eunomium*, c. 4; PG 45, 653.

19. Lateran Council under Martin I, in 649, can. 17; DSch 517.

20. References in my *La foi et la théologie* (Paris, 1962), p. 215, n. 2.

21. *Common.*, c. 29-31: PL 50, 675-683.

22. *Corpus mysticum*, Paris, 1944.

23. *Decr.*1a compil., tit. 1 (PL 216, 1178). Compare, in another context, distinctly antidialectical, Anastasius the Sinaite, around 700: "Sancta Ecclesia, fugiens aristotelicas et graecancias vaniloquentias, evangelice et apostolice . . . tractat" (Holy Church, fleeing Aristotelian and Greek grandiloquence, deals evangelically and apostolically) (*Hodegos* c. 9: PG 89, 147 Latin, 148 Greek).

24. *Contra Impugn.* c. 2 et *Quodl. III*, 9, ad 3.

25. Cf. Thomas, *IV Sent.* d. 19 q. 2 a. 2 q^a, 2 ad 4.

26. Cf. P. Mandonnet, R. Ladner, in *Saint Dominique. L'idée, l'homme et l'œuvre* (Paris, 1938). Vol. II, pp. 50-68.

27. Thomas, *In Rom.* c. 10, lect. 2; and cf. *In 1 Cor.* c. 12, lect. 2; *IV Sent.* d. 19 q. 2 a. 2 q^a 2 ad 4; *Quodl.* XII 27. J. Leclercq, "Le Magistère du prédicateur au XIIIe siècle," in *ADLMA* 15 (1946), pp. 120, 131-132, 134ff.

28. Cf. Lateran IV, c. 3: DSch 809.

29. Cf. E. Gilson, "Humanisme médiéval et Renaissance," in *Les et les Lettres* (Paris, 1952), pp. 171-196; H. Grundmann, "Sacerdotium, Regnum, Studium. Zur Wertung der Wissenschaft im XIII. Jahrhundert," in *Archiv f. Kulturgesch* 34 (1951-52), pp. 5-21; A. G. Jongkens, "'Translatio Studii': les avatars d'un thème médiéval," in *Miscellanea Mediaev. in hon. J. F. Niermeyer* (Groningen, 1967), pp. 41-52; G. Le Bras, "Paris, seconde capitale de la Chrétienté," in *Rev. Hist. Eglise de France* 37 (1951), pp. 5-17.

30. Cf. our *Vraie et fausse réforme dans l'Eglise* (Paris, 1969), pp. 455-459, 461-463; *L'Eglise de S. Augustin à l'époque moderne* (Paris, 1970), pp. 241-244.

31. *Quodl. VII*, 18.

32. *Quodl. III,* 10, ed. De Wulf and Pulzer, 1904, p. 218.

33. E. Delaruelle, in *Hist. du Catholicisme en France I* (Paris, 1957), p. 335.

34. H. Jedin, "Theologie und Lehramt" (lecture given on August 31, 1972 at the archiepiscopal academy of Bensberg; I do not know if this text has been printed in a journal).

35. Gregory VII, *Reg. VII,* 24, ed. Casper, p. 504; compare *Dictatus Papae XXVI.*

36. *De comparatione auctoritatis Papae et Concilii* in 1511, c. IX n. 135 in Pollet's edition.

37. Cf. Y. Congar, *L'ecclésiologie du haut moyen âge* (Paris, 1968), pp. 229ff., 212-214, and also our article cited in the following note: p. 90, n. 22.

38. St. Thomas, *II^a-II^ae* q. 1 a. 10. Y. Congar, "St. Thomas Aquinas and the Infallibility of the Papal Magisterium," in *The Thomist* 38 (1974), pp. 81-105.

39. Cf. our *L'Eglise de S. Augustin à l'époque moderne*, pp. 244-248.

40. Cf. H. Lennerz, "De congregationibus theologorum in Concilio Tridentino," in *Gregorianum* 26 (1945), pp. 7-21; H. Jedin, in the article cited above, stresses the freedom that bishops exercising their responsibility kept.

41. See *La Tradition et les traditions. I. Essai historique* (Paris, 1960), pp. 233-242, 253-257; compare W. Kasper, *Die Lehre von der Tradition in der römischen Schule* (Freiburg, 1962), p. 44, and H. Kümmering, "Es ist Sache der Kirche iudicare de vero sensu et interpretatione Scripturarum sanctarum," in *Theol. Quartalschr.* 148 (1968), pp. 282-296, which shows the change in meaning of this maxim between Trent and Vatican I.

42. Cf. *La Tradition . . . ,* pp. 257ff.

43. Tradition states that "definitio" is to be handled cautiously, occurring only when compelled by the necessity of excluding an error; cf. A. Liégé, article "Dogme" in *Catholicisme* III, 956-957; our *La Foi et la Théologie* (Paris, 1962), p. 48.

44. Dogmatic Constitution *Pastor Aeternus,* c. 4: DSch 3074.

45. Cf. our study "L'ecclésiologie de la Révolution française au concile du Vatican sous le signe de l'affirmation de l'autorité," *L'Ecclésiologie au XIXᵉ siècle* (Paris, 1961), pp. 77-114.

46. M. Caudron, "Magistère ordinaire et infaillibilité d'après la constitution Dei Filius," in *Ephem. Theol. Lovan.* 36 (1960), pp. 393-431.

47. Remarkable documentation on this subject is found in R. Zinnhobler, "Pius IX in der katholischen Literatur seiner Zeit. Ein Baustein zur Geschichte des Triumphalismus," in *Konzil und Papst. Historische Beiträge zur Frage der höchsten Gewalt in der Kirche* (Munich-Paderborn, 1975), pp. 387-432.

48. Cf. M. Seckler, "Die Theologie als kirchliche Wissenschaft nach Pius XII und Paul VI," in *Theol. Quartalschr.* 149 (1969), pp. 209-234.

49. P. Nau, *Une source doctrinale: les Encycliques. Essai sur l'autorité de leur enseignement* (Paris, 1952).

50. See especially F. M. Gallati, *Wenn die Päpste sprechen* (Freiburg, 1960); A. Pfeiffer, *Die Enzykliken und ihr formaler Wert für die dogmatische Methode. Ein Beitrag zur theologischen Erkenntnislehre* (Fribourg, 1968), which, on a broad base (233 encyclicals, up to only 1962!), deals with our current problem.

51. Thus, for example, A. Vacant, *Le magistère ordinaire de l'Eglise et ses organes* (Paris, 1899), pp. 97-116; less massively, J. Salaverri, *Sacrae Theologiae Summa I,* n. 647-648; J. Fenton, "Humani Generis and the Holy Father's Ordinary Magisterium," in *The American Ecclesiastical Revue* 124 (1951), pp. 33-62.

52. H. J. McSorley in *Bijdragen* 30 (1969), pp. 3-8, has collected a variety of texts of modern theologians, from 1877 to 1966; he also cites those of Vatican II on the freedom of research in areas where theologians are competent.

53. R. Caporale, *Les hommes du Concile* (Paris, 1965), pp. 111ff.

54. Pastoral Constitution *Gaudium et Spes,* nn. 44 and 62; Declaration *Gravissimum Educationis,* nn. 10 and 11.

55. Cf. quoted article by M. Seckler, pp. 222ff., 227ff.

56. Cf. opening speech at the Synod (September 29, 1967); message to German Catholics (September 8, 1968), etc.

57. October 1, 1966: AAS 58 (1966) 892-894.

58. Cf. for example P. Thibaut, *Savoir et Pouvoir. Philosophie thomiste et politique cléricale au XIXᵉ siècle* (Quebec, 1972), and our review, *Rev. Sc. ph. th.* 59 (1975), pp. 164-166; P. Hégy, *L'autorité dans le catholicisme contemporain. Du Syllabus a Vatican II* (Paris, 1975). Review: *Rev. Sc. ph. th.* 59 (1975), pp. 486-488.

59. *Vraie et fausse liberté du théologien. Un essai.* (Paris-Bruges, 1969).

The State of Moral Theology: A Critical Appraisal

Thomas Dubay, S.M.

It is well known in the circles of professional education that educators are too specialized and too close to their work to assess in broad vision the overall thrust and direction in which they are going. And so it is customary that college boards of directors be made up of businessmen and housewives, lawyers and dentists, as well as of academics of one type or another.

Few theologians would now contest the proposition that modern theology must be interdisciplinary. Bernard Lonergan's *Method in Theology* presents an impressive account of why this is so. There is no need to repeat the point here. I wish in this article to suggest some reasons why we may not evaluate the general thrust and trends in moral theology from the vantage point of moral theology alone. Charles E. Curran has written an assessment of the current condition of moral theology that strikes this observer much as would an evaluation of education offered by an educator.[1] His article expresses an enlightened awareness of details, but it is less successful in assessing overall import. While he describes the trees well, he says less about the forest.

I
RESUME OF THE ASSESSMENT

Curran describes what he envisages as the present self-identity of the discipline we call moral theology. He believes that this discipline has changed enormously, even drastically, in the last decade (p. 446), and to show the present state of the field he writes under three headings: natural law, authoritarianism, theological presuppositions. He thinks that the present plurality of theories and methodologies in Catholic ethics will expand and become even more manifold in the future (pp. 450, 466). One can welcome his admonition that as we disagree with elements in our past we must also adopt a critical stance in the light of a current pluralism in approaches and thus not succumb to the danger of forgetting the complexity of moral reality (pp. 451-52). Curran finds the papal concept of natural law defective (pp. 447-48), and he notes the considerable number of theologians who now often reject magisterial teaching:

> Catholic theologians frequently deny the existing teaching of the hierarchical magisterium on such issues as contraception, sterilization, artifical insemination, masturbation, and the generic gravity of sexual sins. Newer approaches have been taken to the question of homosexuality. Some Catholic theologians have argued against the moral norm condemning all sexual relationships outside marriage. . . . Another absolute norm in Catholic moral teaching that has been questioned is the prohibition of euthanasia in all cases. . . . A plurality of opinions also exists in other questions where previously there was *the* Catholic opinion. Contemporary theologians are calling for a rethinking of the absolute prohibition against divorce. . . . In questions of social and political morality there is also a divergence of opinions among Catholic theologians (pp. 456-457).

Curran rightly notes, therefore, that the rejection of papal teaching on contraception is no isolated event. What was formerly considered to be an exception has today become routine and normal.

This, of course, suggests the problem of the Catholic teaching on the obligation to respond to non-infallible authentic teaching of the magisterium with an inner religious assent. Curran considers that the American bishops' discussion of this matter is presented in "a confused and inaccurate manner" (p. 459). He says little about the main theological point of an obligation to give this inner assent to authentic teaching and much about the comparatively incidental point of a right to dissent from it. He believes apparently that the formerly granted right to dissent in isolated cases should be extended so that it becomes a principle of usual theological activity:

> Even when the hierarchical magisterium has spoken on a particular issue, there can still be a pluralism of Catholic thinking on this issue. Thus, from the viewpoint of a proper understanding of the moral teaching office of the hierarchical magisterium, it will be impossible to speak about *the* Roman Catholic position on a particular moral issue as if there could not be any other possible position (p. 460).

The past exception becomes the future norm. No one, it would seem, can any longer articulate in moral matters the mind of the Catholic Church. If I understand rightly, this is no insignificant conclusion.

Because the differences in the theological presuppositions of Protestant and Catholic ethics are much less today, "there really are no outstanding pertinent theological differences between some Protestant and some Catholic ethicians" (p. 461).

Before I proceed to an assessment of Curran's evaluation, I make a few less central observations. One may regret the caricature involved in speaking of "some who reject any change in the methodology or the practical conclusions of the manuals of moral theology" (p. 447). If there are some who reject "any change," I do not know of them. To name Kippley as one of these is, in my opinion, unjust. I can only wonder if Curran has read all of Kippley's careful work. One can also regret the use of the weighted word "authoritarianism" to describe a position Curran does not share. We may wonder, too, how one could write of pluralism in moral theology and not discuss at length the statement of the International Theological Commission of October 1972. This statement, "The Unity of Faith and Theological Pluralism," has a section, numbers 13 through 15, which deals expressly with pluralism in moral theology. It would have been helpful, too, if Curran had discussed the thinking expressed in a number of recent studies on pluralism in theology.[2] Reporting on them (if they were available at the time of his writing) would have added no little balance to his account.

II
PLURALISM IN MORAL THEOLOGY

For the most part I have no problem with Curran's factual description of the pluralism situation. My difficulties arise chiefly with his interpretation of the facts. I shall discuss these difficulties under five headings: (1) lack of distinctions; (2) New Testament on pluralism and unity; (3) unconvincing rationale for undifferentiated pluralism; (4) the magisterium's position; (5) healthy and unhealthy pluralism.

Lack of Distinctions

That there has always been a pluralism in the moral theology practiced in the Catholic Church is clear. But the pluralism of the schools is just as clearly not the pluralism of which Curran writes. He includes the former but goes considerably beyond it. This requires, therefore, that we identify the levels of unity-diversity that may be operative in our problem. Delhaye, for example, distinguishes four levels of thematic or lived morality: fundamental orientation, particular personal laws, social and political concerns, individual judgments of prudence. He notes that the exigencies of unity and diversity are evidently not the same on the several levels, and he feels that one of the causes of our moral disarray is that many Christians do not make these distinctions in the levels of their moral commitment.[3] Curran unfortunately does not make these needed distinctions in his evaluation.

Another distinction appears to me fundamental to our problem, namely, that between what we may call complementary pluralism and contradictory pluralism. The first is enriching, the second is destructive. The second suggests that someone is out of touch with reality. To affirm and deny at the same time and in the same sense that a road leads to San Francisco suggests that one party is in for bad news. A complementary pluralism regarding our picture of God can only enrich our understanding, whereas a contradictory pluralism means that one of the parties is partially out of touch with the real God. If two ethicians affirm and deny in the same sense, it is not a happy situation for one of them.

One may possibly respond at this point that there are few, if any, contradictory positions among ethicists. Since every set of circumstances is unique, they are not really at odds with one another. This I strongly doubt. But even if one grants the allegation, the response suffers from all the weaknesses that have recently been uncovered in situation ethics. Furthermore, if Curran is not speaking of contradictory pluralism, he is not saying anything new or significant. We may presume, therefore, that he is speaking of contradictory positions.

Jorge Medina Estevez, dean of the faculty of theology of Santiago, Chile, and member of the International Theological Commission, points out a further distinction: between pluralism and plurality. These terms are often taken as equivalent, but there is a difference at least in some languages. Pluralism suggests the character of principle, namely, that diversities are legitimate, whereas plurality mainly reflects the factual situation. The question of legitimacy, he remarks, refers to both meanings.[4]

My final distinction refers to the pluralism found in the local churches throughout the world. In its proposition 9, the International Theological Commission noted that the local churches contribute an enriching diversity to the universal Church. When it retains its communion with the universal Church of the past and the present, the local congregation helps to lead the human race in all its diversities toward the unity God wishes for his people.

New Testament on Pluralism and Unity

The presence of complementary diversity in Gospel theologies is so well known that we need not dwell on it. What is not so well known or spoken about is the astonishing (and, to our ears, shocking) insistence on unity of mind and practice. Because this is not the place for a thorough study, I shall merely summarize this thought and then add a few words from recent Scripture commentators. Moral theology needs this input from biblical studies.

St. Paul sees the community as coming to a maturity in Christ precisely because it achieves a unity in faith and in knowledge (Eph. 4:11-13). For the apostle, factions in the Church are a sure proof that some are not being led by the Spirit, for disagreements arise from self-indulgence (Gal. 5:19-21). Paul knows that the Corinthians are immature because they are divided; their divisions spring from their worldliness, from their being men of the "flesh" (1 Cor. 3:1-3). When the community has the Holy Spirit, it has harmony and peace (Gal. 5:22). Paul insists that the factioned Corinthian church put aside its divisions and be united again in its "belief and practice" (1 Cor. 1:10). The Greek for this verse is strong: Paul demands a "perfect agreement" even in mind. In a solemn plea he asks here for an extraordinary (to our modern mind) unity, a perfect agreement in belief and practice. The apostle's "all say the same thing" is not, of course, a mere external harmony. Richard Kugelman remarks that "this common Greek expression does not refer to agreement in words only, but means 'to be in perfect agreement.' . . . Christians must be united in their thinking (*nous*) and in the goal and direction (*gnome*) of their lives."[5]

Paul pleads in another letter with no little emotion that the Philippians "be united in your convictions and united in your love, with a common purpose and a common mind" (Phil. 2:2). Jesus had already implicitly prayed for this kind of oneness when he asked the Father that his disciples would have a unity so remarkable that it would be explicable only by a divine intervention: "May they be so *completely* one that the world will realize that it was you who sent me" (Jn. 17:23).[6] Not by the widest stretch of imagination could we call that ecclesial community "completely one" if in it some members are at odds habitually and in important moral and disciplinary matters with those whose duty it is to articulate the faith and morals for and to the community. A pluralism in moral theology that fails to reckon with this New Treatment insistence is failing to reckon with its sources.

John L. McKenzie is probably correct in observing that the disunity in the Corinthian church against which Paul wrote so vigorously was likely enough not deep by our standards, that is, no more than we now consider normal. The difference, notes McKenzie, is between Paul and us.[7] What we consider normal, a contradictory pluralism regarding important issues, Paul would not tolerate. Like Jesus, he wanted us to be completely one—at least in important matters. Max Zerwick is of the same mind as McKenzie.

He finds in Paul a consuming concern about unity, a concern that is "beyond all else." Zerwick does not see in the apostle's insistence on oneness any special reason to suppose particular dangers to unity in the eastern regions. No, it is just Paul's great sensitivity to the need for perfect oneness in the new creation, and "it therefore forces its way to the front. It is all the more important, therefore," says Zerwick, "that we should yield to this insistence of the apostle, and make his interest our own."[8] I regret not finding in Curran's evaluation an indication of this Pauline concern in the important areas of moral theology. Lionel Swain goes so far as to say that "the essence of the Christian's vocation described in Ephesians 1:3-3:21 is unity: unity among men (cf. 2:13-17) established by union with the Father, through Christ in the Spirit (2:18)."[9] It seems to me that the trinitarian-ecclesial unity may serve as an example of where moral theology should learn from doctrinal theology. Christian ethics is not the same as secular ethics. McKenzie adds that the concept of unity entertained in the early *ekklesia* did not favor divisive influences. While Paul admits that they are inevitable, "he does not praise them (1 Cor. 11:19), and they are mentioned together with dissension and envy in a list of the most serious vices (Gal. 5:20). They are called destructive parties or divisions (2 Pet. 2:1)."[10] All this sounds very different indeed from an undifferentiated commendation of pluralism in important matters of ethical theory and practice.[11]

An adequate evaluation of pluralism in moral theology would, therefore, consider this New Testament heritage. An insistence on oneness of mind and practice would seem to pose no little problem to a concept of diversity that eliminates a shared vision regarding doctrine and practice.

Unconvincing Rationale for Undifferentiated Pluralism

Curran is too competent a thinker to argue for a wide pluralism in moral theology simply on the basis of its popularity. He does seem to be somewhat impressed by factual plurality, but he does not in his article offer this as the main reason. Rather:

The basic reason for such a pluralism is the complexity of moral issues and the need for relational and empirical considerations, which involve many aspects and afford the possibility of arriving at different ethical judgments. In the past, when forbidden actions were described solely in terms of the physical structure of the act, it was possible to speak about certain actions which were always and everywhere wrong. A relational understanding or morality of an empirical calculus cannot admit such absoluteness. In the midst of all the circumstances which must be considered in complex questions, one must admit a possible diversity of concrete, ethical judgments (pp. 460-61).

I find this reasoning unpersuasive. Though he does not make any distinctions (such as I think are needed), Curran seems to envision or at least include contradictory pluralism about basic matters or norms. If he means only complementary pluralism, he is not saying anything we have not known for centuries. Catholic theologians have for centuries taught that circumstances change many moral judgments, and that those circumstances included relational and empirical considerations (e.g., manner of dress at home, on the beach, or in center city). If, consequently, he is thinking of contradictory pluralism, what I have already said at some length is applicable here.

But his rationale is unconvincing for other reasons also. First, it makes practical pastoral guidance next to impossible. Whether in the confessional or in the pulpit, a priest could hardly give clear moral guidance, because in principle a contradictory answer is always possible. Stanley Hauerwas is correct in speaking of "the disastrously vague character of the new moral theology." [12] To see that this is not an unkind characterization, one need only ask typical young people about the morality involved in areas Curran discusses. Many of them will decide issues according to "how one feels about" the matter. There is something wrong in a theory that does not work in practice.

Second, on the premise of contradictory pluralism together with a denial of moral absolutes, a secure knowledge of the moral implications of many acts becomes impossible. Who could possibly weigh the "relational and empirical considerations" involving "many aspects" of a given situation? Who would care to do it if he could, since this complexity affords "the possibility of arriving at different ethical judgments"? The matter becomes ludicrous when one transfers it from the library study to the rush of daily life.

Third, one cannot be prophetic with this stance. We Catholics have been accused of humanism, and not without reason. If there were no absolutes other than love in Gospel morality, how could one proclaim the holy will of God as an Amos or an Isaiah or a Jeremiah proclaimed? A proclamation that begins "In my opinion" is hardly going to be prophetic.

Further, although it is not so intended, a contradictory pluralism issues practically in people concluding that almost anything is permissible, given the right circumstances. If there is no teaching authority that may not be contradicted, people will commonly consider their case either to be supported by somebody or to be the exception. If abortion were permitted in one percent of hard cases, large numbers would consider their case to be that hard one. One need not even say "would consider"—current history makes it obvious that they do so consider.

Lastly, who would care to listen to a Church in which contradictory pluralism flourishes in important matters? A hierarchy that may in principle and therefore as a matter of course be contradicted in its official teaching is a pitiable hierarchy. Its position is so weak, diluted, and ineffectual that few will take it seriously. That this is a clean break with Catholic tradition is hardly obscure.

Magisterium on Unity and Diversity in Moral Matters

We may be brief here, for the reader knows that Curran's view of pluralism is not shared by the magisterium. This needs no demonstration. A statement recently issued by the papal Secretariat of State may, however, serve as an illustration. Speaking of the 1974 World Population Year and the teaching of *Humanae Vitae*, it asserted that "those who deal with such subjects without heeding the authentic, established teaching cannot claim to represent Catholic viewpoints." [13]

Curran himself expresses awareness that his view of pluralism is not shared by the magisterium. He writes: "Recently an American bishop has recognized the fact of this growing pluralism, although his reaction to the fact is *much different* from the general approving tone of this paper" (p. 457; italics added). And further on he explains how thoroughgoing the differences are:

> The problem seems more acute on the level of the life of the Church, especially in terms of a recognition of the present self-understanding of moral theology by the hierarchical magisterium. If the assessment of contemporary moral theology elaborated in this article is accurate, then there must be important repercussions and changes in the life of the Roman Catholic Church. The differences between theologians and the hierarchical magisterium on the condemnation of artificial contraception in *Humanae Vitae* does not represent merely one isolated and unfortunate event; it points to the understanding of moral theology developed in these pages (p. 466).

Here Curran is quite correct. And this is another reason why I am maintaining that moral theology must be criticized by biblical studies and doctrinal theology. Curran is raising issues deeper than ethics. In this issue of theologians versus magisterium the above citation makes it clear (and I wish this to be gently said and understood) who is to learn from whom, that is, who are expected to change their position.

Criteria of Healthy Pluralism

For all these reasons it would seem that we ought not to speak about theological pluralism unless we have made some distinctions and unless we have integrated a careful use of the term into our concept of the Church itself. We may at this point suggest some criteria by which we may judge in given areas of scholarly inquiry what is a healthy as distinguished from an unhealthy pluralism. I may begin by briefly reporting several norms offered by the International

Theological Commission in its study of pluralism in theology. From their overall discussion I find four statements that may serve as criteria. The first two here mentioned are concerned with theology as a whole, the last two with moral theology as such.[14]

1. The Church is the subject in whom the unity of New Testament theologies is had as well as of the dogmas presented through the centuries (6).

2. The criterion which distinguishes true from false pluralism is the faith of the Church expressed in its normative pronouncements. The fundamental criterion is Sacred Scripture in relation to the confession of the believing and praying Church (7).

3. The unity of Christian morality is founded on constant principles contained in Scripture, explained by tradition, presented in each age by the magisterium (14). Regarding this criterion Delhaye remarkes: "Il était donc indiqué de rechercher dans l'Ecriture et la Tradition relayées par le Magistère les normes essentielles de la praxis chrétienne qui, comme nous l'avons dit plus haut, assurent à la fois l'unité de la morale et le cadre d'un pluralisme sain."[15]

4. This unity does not prevent a diversity of vocations and personal preferences in living the mystery of Christ. There is also within this unity a possibility in the temporal realm of a diversity in analyses and options among Christians (15).[16]

To these criteria I may add several others. Although there is some overlapping between the Commission's propositions and what I shall say, the criteria of the former, correct as they are, do not exhaust what needs to be said.

5. A contradictory pluralism tends to destroy ecclesial unity, since unity is just another aspect of reality, and between contradictory positions there is no middle ground—one of them is out of touch with the real. The deeper the contradictions, the weaker the unity. Hence, if pluralism means not only a rare questioning of non-infallible authoritative teaching but also the permissibility of routine dissent, it is difficult to see where one could speak of anything more than an occasional pragmatic unity in ethical matters. Even more, if the pluralism means that private theologians may entertain a concept of ecclesial unity at odds with that of the official teaching office, that unity is still more deeply damaged.

6. Numbers do not make a position. The dissent of a given

number of theologians and/or laity cannot automatically be assumed to be a basis for reassessing moral teaching. As I shall note later, in the history of divine revelation the prophets were constantly inveighing against the immoral positions of large numbers of the chosen people. One gets the impression that they were a minority condemning the majority. Richard McCormick is correct in noting that even a "massive dissent" from the magisterium's teaching is not necessarily a work of the Holy Spirit. He does ask that such a dissent be taken seriously, be tested, and be examined in a new communal reflection.[17] One should further ask that the dissenters take seriously the obligation so often mentioned in the wisdom literature and assumed in Paul that we welcome correction and be ready to learn from the official teachers in the Church.

7. A healthy unity-in-diversity (that takes both elements seriously, not just the latter) leaves the *ekklesia* strong in its mission to the world. A debilitating fragmentation cannot be of the Spirit. To see this we may look at the worth of contradictory pluralism from another point of view, namely, from that of a secular outsider. How would he view an institution in which no one can speak for the group in basic, fundamental matters? Would he consider it a weakness or a strength that a strong condemnation issuing from leadership had little impact on membership? We may imagine with a recent observer that the Pope issued some vigorous statement on doctrine:

> A promising test of the likely effect would be to survey the members of various departments in a Catholic university or college, not directly under the control of Rome or of a bishop, on their expected reaction to a strong condemnation of certain doctrines advanced in the theology department. Neither the theologians nor their Catholic colleagues are apt, as a group, to be jarred by the condemnation unless this latter could lead indirectly to attacks on academic freedom or job security.[18]

Some may feel that this is a healthy situation. I think our secular outsider (who, we may note, cares nothing about the doctrines involved) would find the situation pitiful. At the very least he would consider the Church weak, as having nothing to say to the world. I think he would be close to the truth. After all, who would pay much attention to statements from France or Russia if no one could speak for those nations? Who pays any attention to any group that cannot speak out authoritatively and with one voice in important matters (Rom. 15:6)? A contradictory pluralism in ethics is a weakness when limited, a disaster when widespread.

Though it is surely far from the intentions of ethicians, the weakness of the discipline and its practical ineffectiveness is such that a recent European periodical with over 700,000 readers has seriously engaged in a study entitled "Do We Still Have a Moral Theology Today?"[19] Paul Toinet wryly observes that if the Catholic Church had ever renounced its right and duty to pronounce on truth and falsity of previous theological debates, there would exist today no debate on pluralism. Any notion of imperative Catholic truth would have long ago disappeared from the earth.[20]

8. Healthy pluralism, whether complementary or contradictory, is characterized by non-evasive encounter. Each side learns from the other, addresses its attention to the other's noteworthy affirmations and criticisms, does not evade embarrassing points brought against it. Some of our current debates pass muster here and some do not. The former do not need illustration, the latter do. James Hitchcock has written with devastating detail of the aberrations of the religious left during the last few years, and yet no one to my knowledge has seriously contested most of what he has said. John Kippley in 1970 wrote a strong theological support of Catholic teaching on contraception, a book that merited the following comment:

> I hope the book will sell and be widely read, for Kippley does not present a simple apologetic for authoritative Catholic teaching. Rather, his book shows that he has read widely on both sides of the question, that he has given much thought to both sides, and that hard planning has gone into the exposition of his thought. . . . The book is recommended.[21]

We are still awaiting an adequate reply. In the years intervening we find many theologians and non-theologians repeating that Pope Paul was wrong in *Humanae Vitae*, but I have found no one dealing with what Kippley has said. Possibly answers have been given, but I have not come across them. Several years later Kippley reminds us again (as he had done in his book) that the majority position of the papal birth control commission "was so untenable that it has never been adopted in serious theology by the dissenters, who have admitted that their position is only as good as their reasons."[22] The evasion of what Kippley is saying is hardly a sign of a healthy pluralism. Raymond Brown accurately put his finger on two of the chief dangers confronting renewal efforts in the Church when in his now well-known address before the National Catholic Educational Association he observed that "the real danger is from those ultra-liberals who scorn serious theology and from those ultra-conservatives who see in every investigation a threat to faith."[23] Curran does not scorn serious theology; nonetheless one would have expected a discussion of pluralism in moral theology to wrestle with some of these criteria. This seems especially true when the opinions of the private theologian run counter to the teachings of the magisterium and even, it seems to me, to the criteria of the International Theological Commission.

9. We may complete our criteria with an interesting one mentioned by Toinet. A "dissolving pluralism," he notes, will either fail to perceive or will evade crucial issues that touch at the very heart of the Catholic enterprise. "Une théorie pluraliste dissolvante aura pour caractéristique de ne pas percevoir ou d'éluder certaines questions cruciales touchant les exigences internes d'une pensée théologique d'essence catholique."[24] I find this quite true of Curran's discussion.

III
IS MORAL THEOLOGY PROPHETIC?

My purpose in this essay is not to take up individual issues in Christian ethics (except by way of illustration) but to back away and look at the forest instead of concentrating on the trees. I am examining main thrusts, one of which is the pluralism question. I turn at this point to still another long-range matter. Since biblical prophecy is concerned especially with proclaiming the holy will of the

Lord, and since moral theology is concerned with ascertaining this holy will in all the intricacies of modern life, we may expect that the one will exhibit certain similarities to the other—though there are obviously some differences too. These latter are so clear that we need not dwell on them.

We may say that for God's people a prophet was a charismatic man called and sent by the Lord to proclaim his will. This concept seems broad enough to cover prophets of both Testaments.[25] Scripture scholars seem of one mind as to what characterized the genuine prophet of the Lord. I discuss these traits here because it seems to me that since we all say that prophecy is important in the contemporary Church, we would expect those who deal with the knowledge of right and wrong to be prophetic in their teaching if not in the exact manner of its proclamation.

1. *The prophet is a man sent, a man commissioned to proclaim the Lord's holy will.* Joachim Jeremias notes that for the synagogue the possession of the holy spirit of God was *the* mark of prophecy. "To possess the spirit of God was to be a prophet. In fact, Jesus repeatedly made an explicit claim that he himself *possessed the spirit.*"[26] John L. McKenzie points out that the true prophet has an immediate experience of God, and that the false prophet, sincere though he may be, is false because he lacks this awareness. He therefore "lacks the prophetic insight into the moral will of Yahweh and the reality of sin, [and so] the false prophet sees no evil where it is. . . . "[27] Beauchamp offers a brief definition of the false prophets: "those who speak in their own name (Jer. 14:14f.; 23:16), without having been sent (Jer. 27:15), following their own inspirations (Ez. 13:3), are false prophets."[28] Being sent is in the new dispensation as well a necessary requirement for being authorized to proclaim the message. As the Father has sent the Son, so the Son sends those who are to declare him to the whole world.[29] A Catholic theologian is always sent, if not juridically through diocesan faculties (a lay theologian), at least through being in communion with the bishop and through the bishop with the Holy See. Insofar as theologians are at odds with the sending magisterium, they are not sent. They lack the first note of a prophet among God's people. If a private person feels he has a direct commission from the Holy Spirit to admonish an officer about disciplinary matters, even

then he will be humble and willing to be corrected himself (1 Jn. 4:1-6).

2. *The prophet does not conform his message to popular morality or to what men will accept.* This must be the case, since God's thoughts are not men's thoughts, and his ways are above ours as the heavens are above the earth.[30] The full Gospel has never been popular, and even though we are happily living in the midst of a biblical renewal, the picture has not substantially changed. Guy Couturier, commenting on Jeremiah 23:9-40, notes that among the scriptural signs of the false prophets is that their moral conduct is lacking and their message flatters the popular passions.[31] James puts it starkly: anyone who makes the world his friend is making God his enemy.[32]

It is perhaps significant that not a few of the current divergences from the magisterium in moral theology tend to make the Gospel teaching easier to take. I do not doubt that this is due to a well-intentioned effort to present a picture of the Gospel acceptable to modern men and women. But what seems not sufficiently realized is that this aim is exactly what the prophets did not try to do. For St. Paul, seeking the approval of men is a sign of failing to serve Christ. Speaking in vigorous language of those who were introducing a new version of the good news into the community, Paul pronounces an anathema on them. Then he asks: "So now, whom am I trying to please—man or God? Would you say it is men's approval I am looking for? If I still wanted that, I should not be what I am—a servant of Christ."[33] It is difficult to locate in the prophetic tradition theologians who seem to begin with "what modern men will accept" and then delve into the tradition to find rare statements among the older theologians and thus build them into principles that run counter to the great thrust of those same older theologians. It is still more difficult to consider prophetic this kind of procedure when in the search for more permissive ways one chooses to set aside clear magisterial statements regarding the same matter. The disciple has become the teacher.

Tailoring ethics to the expectations of majorities is a desalting of the salt. It has no basis in Scripture. A moral theology that moves smoothly with popular wisdom, with what men and women want to hear, is unpersuasive, unimpressive, dull. It has the marks of compromise all over it. While he may not be uncritical, the true prophet is independent, unapologetic, fearless. He will contradict and run counter to the stream because he loves truth and is driven to proclaim the holy will of the Lord. A recent reviewer of Paul Minear's *Commands of Christ* has observed:

> In my darker moments at any rate, it seems to me that, whatever its advancing technical merit, New Testament scholarship since Strauss has functioned in the main to deflect the crippling objections which the biblical text would otherwise pose to post-Enlightenment and contemporary redefinitions of Christianity. Nevertheless, there regularly appear works that travel in the opposite direction—independent, out-of-season, unapologetically calculated to give the Bible back its cutting edge. The modest but substantial book here under review belongs to that class. Consider the title: not the "principles" nor "ethics" nor even the "challenge," but the "commands of Christ." The book's very project, then, crosses the grain of our culture, exposing and contradicting it and us. Moreover, the commands in question are specific, concrete, and clear.[34]

This I find refreshing. It is prophetic. There is something unreal about conformism. The prophet of the Lord is never a slave to popularity or style.

What I am saying has not gone unnoticed in the literature. Speaking of the tendency we have to confuse ethics and apologetics, Stanley Hauerwas notes the temptation we have to baptize the secular in the name of relevance and that for the glory of God:

> The new morality is a response to the feeling that the Church has misled the world by its stubborn defense of a system of unintelligible symbols and of values eroded beyond recognition. It is naturally assumed that the way to expurge our guilt in this respect is by fondly embracing "modern man's self-understanding." . . . What we have here is not apologetics, but capitulation. As such, it betrays not only the task of Christian ethics, but also the "modern" man it wishes to address. For such a man exists only in rhetoric.[35]

This reminds me of Tom F. Driver's comment on Andrew Greeley's *Sexual Intimacy*; parts of it are based, he thinks, "on an erroneous theological assumption—namely, that the God we have known all along as Yahweh is the same who presides over the modern sexual revolution. It sounds to me like the old game of baptizing everything in sight."[36]

3. *The prophet is rejected by the majority.* Though this trait is so well known in biblical circles that I hesitate to write of it here, yet we find in theological circles the curious assumption (it is never proved) that Christian ethics should be acceptable to the majority. Just as curiously, it is further assumed that if the majority do as a matter of fact reject Gospel morality, the fault could not be with the majority's morals—it must be the fault of our previous understanding of the Gospel. By any revealed standard, this is odd. Scripture does not tire of telling us over and over that the Gospel will be rejected by most people. The crowd hounded and ridiculed and abused Jeremiah because he proclaimed the will of the Lord.[37] Jesus recalled that his ancestors routinely murdered the prophets, and he warned that his own representatives would be rejected by many and even be persecuted.[38] He said that few walk the hard road and find the narrow gate that leads to life.[39] The author of 2 Timothy makes it clear that those who are faithful to Christ are certainly (not probably) going to be persecuted.[40] Paul says the same thing to the Thessalonians: he warned them that they should expect persecution.[41] Commenting on Hosea 9:7, Denis McCarthy remarks that in rejecting the whole line of the prophets, Israel was showing "the natural, hostile response of the guilty to the reprover."[42] Bruce Vawter writes that "the vicars of Bray, too, have reacted in their perennially predictable way, obediently furnishing texts as required to bless whatever deeds their masters care to have clothed with respectability."[43]

A genuine ethics worthy of the Gospel must be ready to contradict what the majority wishes. As Hauerwas rightly notes, "we cannot start with the question of what modern man will accept as true. . . . An apologetic that is not first based on truth is but propaganda."[44] Though the moral theologian rightly tries to present the word in attractive terms and in new thought patterns, he must be prepared to see that men and women no longer walk with the Lord because "this word is intolerable; who can hear it?"[45] Not only is Gospel doctrine difficult; so is practice. But they alone lead to life.[46]

4. *The prophet proclaims absolute precepts.* There are so many absolutely worded precepts in both Testaments that I shall not mention one. I am aware, of course, that some ethicians who deny absolutes other than love consider their positions compatible with biblical morality. Others disagree. I merely add that the attempt to explain away some of the absolute precepts in Scripture strikes me as unreal, as doing exegesis with a pre-conceived thesis that forces meaning into texts.

The need for a greater immersion into Scripture on the part of moral theology may be illustrated by Bright's perceptive study of the apodictic prohibition in the Old Testament.[47] He deals in no little detail with the two main ways Hebrew expressed a prohibition: *'al* with the jussive and *lō'* with the imperfect. It is generally agreed that the *lō'* prohibitive has a far stronger force than the *'al* prohibitive. Careful study of biblical linguistic usages suggests, as one would expect, a wide range of intent all the way from the weak to the strong: wish, request, plea, earnest entreaty, exhortation, solemn admonition, stern warning, flat order, apodictic prohibition. Among his conclusions Bright notes:

> The legal prohibitive and the wisdom admonition move in different worlds and have different concerns. The one lays down the normative policy to which members of the community must at all times conform; the other urges youth to wise and right living and warns of the consequences of folly. The one carries with it the sternest of sanctions, supported by the righteous will of Yahweh himself; in the other, where motivation is supplied or implied, it is generally prudential.[48]

In my opinion, it would be helpful if those who accept a divine revelation would deal with this sort of biblical distinction in their efforts to develop a religiously orientated ethics. And it seems indispensable that they would explore thoroughly what Scripture has to say about the motivational aspects of divine law. Bright adds:

Nowhere is the difference between apodictic prohibition and wisdom admonition more clearly evident than in the motivation attached to each. Here we move in two different worlds. In the bare apodictic sentence no motivation is given: you simply will not do it; it is so ordered! Where motivation is supplied in an apodictic context, it is all but invariably because Yahweh had forbidden it and requires its punishment. In the wisdom admonition a motive clause is frequently added. Though this may occasionally be warning that Yahweh will take action in the event of transgression, in the overwhelming majority of cases the motivation is purely prudential.[49]

The significance of these distinctions for the consequentialism discussion is hardly arcane. The prudential admonition cites consequences, the apodictic command need not and does not. In revealed morality "the apodictic prohibition is a binding command of absolute validity; it needs no motive save that its giver has given it and demands that it be obeyed."[50] Scripture takes absolute moral norms for granted. And it also takes for granted that the individual person must accept moral direction from those who have the authority to give it. Philbin is surely right when he observes that "there is no support in the Scriptures or in Church tradition for the view that all questions of conduct, as opposed to those of belief, are to be decided by personal assessment of each case. The indications are all in the other direction."[51]

5. *The prophet is faithful to his tradition.* We may take it as widely known, as Vawter points out, that "both in the Old Testament and in the New Testament it is recognized that prophecy in order to be true must be consistent with known revelation."[52] Weber notes that the biblical prophets were so dependent on those who had gone before them that their works were filled with references and allusions to the earlier prophets. These "men of tradition," he adds, "were not essentially innovators; they called men *back* to the authentic faith."[53] We may not conclude that authentic, prophetic persons today must only call men back to the past, but we may conclude that they must be faithful to their past. The pastoral epistles repeatedly insist on clinging to the tradition and adhering to what has been taught. Luke makes a point that the

early faithful did cling to the teaching of the apostles, and Paul calls the Galatians foolish because they did not adhere to the teaching they had heard.[54] There is no doubt that a binding teaching authority is already operative in the apostolic *ekklesia*.

If our use of the term *sensus fidelium* is in accord with scriptural thinking, we may raise the question as to who the faithful are. Richard McCormick refers to the *sensus fidelium* as a source of religious truth, but he does not mention who the faithful are. Though I am confident that he does have in mind a clear concept, yet I would like to see moral theologians discuss the question as such. I would presume that both theology and common sense would reply that "the faithful" are precisely that, namely, faithful. They are, it seems to me, those who accept the whole Gospel, who are willing to carry the cross every day, who lead a serious prayer life, who accept the teaching magisterium commissioned by Christ. We could hardly call faithful those who reject knowingly anything Jesus has taught or established.

6. *The true prophet proclaims authentic teaching.* In our age of great emphasis on subjectivity we assume that a true position manifests itself through our own personal insight into and our experience of it. While biblical men did not deny the value of subjectivity, they demanded objective evidence, and especially a faithfulness to what they knew Yahweh had already revealed of his holy will. Hence the genuine prophet is known by this trait also: he proclaims truth. Deuteronomy 13:1-6 is a classical locus for this criterion: the false prophet is known to be such, even if he works a sign or wonder, in that he declares a false doctrine. McCarthy comments on this passage: "Deuteronomy attempts to establish a more universal, even theoretical norm by which a prophet might be judged: the self-proclaimed prophet whose words led the people astray from strict Yahwism must be false."[55] Commenting on the same passage, Beauchamp is of like mind: "Even in the Old Testament, did not the Deuteronomist see in the doctrine preached by the prophets the authentic sign of their mission (Dt. 13:2-6)? Thus it remains today."[56] Beauchamp's last sentence is pregnant with significance.

This criterion continues on into the New Testament. The Johannine letters emphasize the point that there are false prophets in the world of the latter part of the first century, and doctrine is an effective way to distinguish the true from the false. We find a little treatise on the subject in 1 John 4:1-6, and it occurs again in 2 John 8-9. On this last verse Vawter remarks that "'progress' was probably one of the slogans of the false teachers, implying the superiority of their doctrine. On the contrary, fellowship with God (see 1 Jn. 2:23) is only to be achieved by adhering to the true doctrine of Christ and his Church."[57] Commenting on 2 Peter 2:1, Stoger offers some hard words that theologians need to ponder in prayer: "The teaching spread by false prophets leads to divisions within the Church; it destroys the unity of the Church. . . . He who tampers with the teaching of Christ condemns himself; his deed is his condemnation."[58] Discussing the "sound teaching" idea found often in the pastoral letters, Dibelius and Conzelmann remark that 1 Timothy 1:10f. "provides the concrete criterion: the Gospel which is a firm part of the Church's teaching tradition."[59] Citations like this abound in current biblical scholarship.[60] I have cited some of them here to indicate that my critique of Curran's article is not based on mere personal opinion. Any theory of pluralism in theology that neglects an honest confrontation with this and other prophetic traits in Scripture cannot be considered adequate. Moral theology needs a critique from outside itself.

If one is looking for an example of one who exemplifies the biblical traits of a prophet in his person, surely the best known is Pope Paul VI. Like all biblical prophets, he has a commission from the Lord to teach and he is faithful to his religious tradition. Like them, he proclaims the holy will of God whether people find it to their liking or not. Like them, he is widely rejected because he openly speaks against the immorality of our day—in the sexual area as well as in any other. Like them, he does not dilute either doctrine or moral teaching.

SOME UNANSWERED QUESTIONS

We may now turn to several questions that moral theologians should explore and answer. Mere assertions such as "modern men think that" or "there are many ethicists who" are a new authoritarianism. We are asked to accept premises without proof. I should like to suggest some assumptions and premises that need to be tested and justified, together with a few questions that beg for answers.

1. *Is habitual and frequent dissent from authentic, non-infallible teaching in the Church biblically or theologically justified?*

In his assessment of current Catholic ethics, Curran makes it clear that dissent is not now what it occasionally was in the past, a rare phenomenon considered permissible only within narrow limits and confined to the pages of scholarly publications. He seems to be trying to establish that there is now in principle a right to dissent (and so to teach publicly) frequently and as a matter of normal procedure. Is there such a right?

I find neither in Scripture nor in the magisterium any basis for this practice. On the contrary, we read so frequently that I shall not cite texts both in Paul's major letters and in the pastorals an adamant insistence that the faithful accept and cling to what they are taught by those who articulate the faith to the community. The same is true in magisterial teaching. It is academically unacceptable that an exception be blown up into a rule.

2. *Does not a "right" to frequent dissent and public teaching of it postulate two magisteria in the Church?*

There are a number of reasons why the response to this question must be affirmative. One is the practical and indisputable fact that many Catholic priests and religious and laity do accept the teaching of dissenting theologians as against that of the Pope and bishops. Even if one attempts no theoretical justification, the fact is plain to see.

Then there is the current custom among some theologians of considering episcopal and papal statements as merely opinionative when they are intended to be much more. These statements are discussed alongside those of private theologians, and no special import is granted to them. Curran's article may serve as an example.[61] He expresses little concern that his view of pluralism is not that of the bishops.[62]

The same affirmative answer follows if one holds that contradictory pluralism is desirable. I may illustrate the point that we really and for all practical purposes have two magisteria operating in the Church with the example of the contraception controversy. It is now widely admitted that the majority opinion in the papal birth control commission was based on weak reasons. Even if one counters with the remark that the reasoning of our best dissenters is now based on other considerations, it still remains that the vast majority of married (or single) persons who follow their advice are doing so with an act of faith. One can confidently say that not one percent of our married laity have read and understood for themselves what Fuchs, Schüller, Knauer, McCormick, Janssens, and Chirico have written about the matter. If they make the judgment that contraceptives are permissible in some circumstances, they can be doing this only on the basis of their own private insight or on a human faith in the theologians who teach this or in the priests who filter the latter's teaching to them. The large majority of Catholic people entertain their position on contraception through an act of faith either in the magisterium or in dissenting theologians and priests. But this is practically to have two magisteria — even when the latter declare that they have no intention of substituting for the official teaching authority. We should notice how this principle is now operating not in one confined area of dispute but quite generally: Sunday worship, nature and practice of religious life, premarital sexual relations, sterilization, and others.

Fourth, this affirmative response may be suggested by Curran's interesting and repeated references to the "hierarchical magisterium," a characterization that seems to imply there is some other magisterium in the Church. As a matter of fact, he even refers to "the so-called authentic or authoritative, non-infallible hierarchical magisterium."[63] I do not wish to push this too far. If he does not mean to suggest that there is a second magisterium in the Catholic Church, it would be well to use other terminology. If, on the other hand, he does wish so to imply, I would like it clearly said and then established in a competent theological manner. In any event, his position on pluralism does postulate two magisteria in practice.

One need hardly demonstrate that the theory or practice of two magisteria runs flatly counter to the teaching of the one magisterium we do know. I may cite one recent example. Speaking to the

General Superior of the Sulpicians, Pope Paul VI mentions only one teaching authority to which other teachers must conform: "Thus two things must be done by teachers in the seminary: maintain fidelity toward revealed truth, of which the authentic interpretation is in the hands of the teaching authority of the Church, and keep one's mind open to the problems which are being discussed in this world in continual change." [64]

3. *Is a "Catholic's position" necessarily a Catholic position?*

When one puts the question as plainly as I have it here, the answer is obviously negative. But this is not a useless question. We find it widely assumed that because individual Catholics hold a particular view, theirs is a Catholic view. This is to use the word "Catholic" analogously, if not equivocally. To suppose an affirmative answer to this question, as Curran does, once again implies two or more magisteria in the Church.

4. *Is a contradictory moral pluralism a weak effort to make a virtue of necessity?*

I think it is. We find in the literature of religious pluralism the common argument "is to ought." We have pluralism; therefore it is good. In a recent analysis of decadent societies, an historian has written:

> Decadence is dissipation in the literal sense, in which the center disintegrates and the parts fly off in all directions. "Pluralism" is welcomed as a positive good, because it is imposed as an historical necessity. Societies which are young, vigorous, purposeful, and possessed of a great dream are rarely pluralistic. . . . The loss of the vital center, while it can hardly go unnoticed, is nonetheless little discussed and, since the recognition is so traumatic, is by tacit consent ignored as much as possible. [65]

5. *Is an ethics without absolutes anything more than a homiletics?*

We have seen from Bright's study that Scripture has a prominent place for the apodictic prohibition that binds always and everywhere. This is one reason among many why the Bible is a perennial best seller: it says something. It seems to me that the alternative to an ethics with some apodictic teaching is an ethics of exhortation. To say invariably to common people "There may be an exception to this norm" or "Some theologians say yes and some say no to your question" is perhaps to comfort them, but it cannot be called a prophetic, challenging stance. When an ethics knows only a contradictory pluralism and/or a whole series of "maybes," it ceases to be interesting. It becomes quite unlike biblical morality, which in the wisdom literature is detailed in saying what courses of action are good and what are bad. It becomes quite unlike St. Paul, who terms extramarital relations fornication or adultery and does not suggest that tender love changes the situation. Hauerwas is correct in referring to the "disastrously vague character of the new moral theology." [66]

6. *What does moral theology say of the "new creation"?*

It seems to me that much of contemporary pluralism in moral theology pays too little attention to the close intertwining of Gospel morality with Gospel faith. When Paul speaks of us as new creatures, he is not merely referring to an invisible grace transformation but also to a mode of living unknown to the pagan. When he wants us to put off the old man and to die with Christ, he is referring to ethical action and not simply to a doctrinal/sacramental reality. Christian morality is a revolution, not merely a restatement of non-Christian ethics. In my judgment, one can say that Gospel morality is not unique only if, on the one hand, he divorces it from doctrinal theology, or, on the other, he looks on it as minimalistic. If one does not think that ascetisicm, contemplation, passive purifications, and discernment of the Spirit are part and parcel of Christian morality, he may indeed think that it is substantially the same as a secular ethics. If does think that the content of the teaching of a St. John of the Cross is an essential part of practical Christian living, he could hardly avoid viewing Gospel morality as far advanced beyond the content of secular ethics.

7. *What is the place of the cross and self-denial in Christian morality?*

One finds in the literature supporting premarital sexual relations, contraception, and abortion little or nothing about common Gospel themes: carrying the cross *every day* (Lk. 9:23), the seed dying in the ground as a condition of its fruitfulness (Jn. 12:24), renouncing all things to be a disciple (Lk. 14:33), chastising our bodies lest we become castaways (1 Cor. 9:24-27), following the hard road and entering the narrow gate (Mt. 7:13-14), crucifying ourselves with Christ (Rom. 6:5-6), giving up our old selves and our illusory desires (Eph. 4:22), and a host of other texts. One could hardly argue that these ideas are not to be operative in practical everyday life. Yet they rarely appear in discussions of moral problems. A selective use of Scripture is always suspect. Pope Paul has spoken of this problem: "We are also confronted with the growing tendency to prune away from the Christian life everything that requires effort or causes inconvenience. It rejects as vain and futile the practice of Christian asceticism and the contemplation of the things of God."[67]

8. *May moral theology neglect contemplation?*

Almost never do we read in contemporary Christian moralists how their discipline relates to the contemplation themes of the great mystics. Rarely is ethics discussed in reference to prayerful communion with God, an idea prominent in Paul and the greatest theologians of our twenty-century theological tradition. Ethicians are not sufficiently aware of how this-worldly their ethics appears or how impersonal their discussions seem when they make no reference to the "one thing," gazing on the beauty of the Lord (Ps. 27:4; Lk. 10:38-42). The prophets proclaimed the holy will of Yahweh for what it was, the holy will of Yahweh. What men did or did not do bore directly on their personal relations with the Lord God. We have now instead in moral theology an artifical divorce between interpersonal relations with God and the everyday business of life, between adoration and activity. It is remarkable how few are the points of contact with our extremely rich prayer-action heritage of Origen, Gregory of Nyssa, Augustine, Basil, Gregory the Great, Bonaventure, Thomas, Suso, Tauler, John of the Cross, and Teresa of Avila.

Almost all of current ethics is ethics of action, of means. It has little to say about the end, the purpose. The situation is not unlike taking a trip from New York to San Francisco, all the while talking about maps and tires and water and gasoline but never about the loved ones to be seen in San Francisco. There is something deeply wrong with a morality so truncated.

It is not enough to respond to my objection by saying that spiritual theology deals with prayer. It does. But if one accepts the conciliar teaching that in the Church "action is directed and subordinated to contemplation,"[68] it is difficult to grasp how he could fail to fault a moral system that rarely looks to the end of the whole operation. Once again we see how very different Gospel morality ought to be from a secular ethics. And it is not likely that a contradictory pluralism will further a more prayerful community life.

V

CONCLUSION

We may take it as obvious that there are many fine developments in the moral theology of the last decade, and the biblical renewal is not the least of them. So also do we welcome the far more friendly and cooperative work done by secular, Protestant, and Catholic ethicians. But it is difficult to appreciate Curran's judgment that "the present state of moral theology as described here is in keeping with the best of the Roman Catholic theological tradition" (p. 467). I refer to the questions I have just asked, but especially to Curran's judgment on pluralism. A neutral outside observer would consider that an organization that cannot speak with one voice on important matters is weak at best, chaotic at worst. I think he would tend to accept the judgment of Hauerwas that "this new emphasis [in ethics] that acceptance of the other is good in itself entails a parallel conception of God. God is viewed as the great understander, the paradigm liberal, who perceives all and is committed to nothing."[69] If Curran were correct, our observer would probably wonder with the publication we have cited "Y a-t-il encore une morale?"

The vast preponderance of Catholic tradition has held that theologians must, as a normal rule, learn from papal teaching, accept and defend it. To reject this and then appeal to an exceptional case in that tradition as "the best" is neither impressive argumentation nor model use of the sources. The level of pluralism found in this tradition (schools and opinions) was surely not on the level envisioned by Curran. Thomas Aquinas, whom Curran often cites in selected areas, would have repudiated a great deal of current pluralism in moral theology. Whatever else we may say, we can hardly avoid saying that the acceptance of a contradictory pluralism is a break with the Catholic tradition. Nor can I reconcile it with the position of the International Theological Commission.

Finally, one can hardly consider a moral theology which neglects crucial and primary Gospel themes as completely "in keeping with the best" in our tradition. This is settling for far too little. I submit we should be as critical of our own age and methods as we are of our forebears'.

Notes

1. Charles E. Curran, "Moral Theology: The Present State of the Discipline," *Theological Studies* 34 (1973), pp. 446-67.

2. Among the more recent studies dealing with pluralism in moral theology we may include Paul Toinet, "Implications philosophiques de la question du pluralisme," *Esprit et vie* 83 (1973), pp. 177-81; Eugene Hillman, C.S.Sp., "Pluriformity in Ethics: A Modern Missionary Problem," *Irish Theological Quarterly*, 1973, pp. 264-75; Luigi Lombardi, "A proposito di fede e pluralismo teologico: Saggio di neo-teologia controversista," *Palestra del clero*, 1973, pp. 1022-38; Ph. Delhaye, "Unité et diversité en morale," *Esprit et vie* 83 (1973), pp. 321-28, 337-42; "Pluralism, Polarization and Communication in the Church," *Pro mundi vita*, no. 45, pp. 1-39. Delhaye adds two other references: S. Olejnik, "Pluralizm teologicny a jednosc chrzescijanskiej moralnosci," with a French résumé, "Le pluralisme théologique et l'unité de la morale chrétienne," *Collectanea theologica*, 1972, pp. 19-37; D. Capone, "Nota sul pluralismo in morale," in *Studia moralia* of the Alphonsiana.

3. Delhaye, "Unité et diversité en morale," p. 322.

4. Jorge Medina Estevez, "Brève introduction aux 'Propositions' de la Commission théologique," *Esprit et vie* 83 (1973), p. 373.

5. Richard Kugelman, C.P., in *Jerome Biblical Commentary* (Englewood Cliffs, N.J., 1968) 51:15.

5. Richard Kugelman, C.P., in *Jerome Biblical Commentary* (Englewood Cliffs, N.J., 1968) 51:15.

6. For some reflections on and examples of shared vision together with complementary diversity in New Testament thought, see Raymond Brown, "The Unity and Diversity in New Testament Ecclesiology," *New Testament Essays* (Milwaukee, 1965), chap. 3.

7. John L. McKenzie, in the preface to Eugene Walter, *The First Epistle to the Corinthians* (New York, 1971), p. 6.

8. Max Zerwick, *The Epistle to the Ephesians* (New York, 1969), p. 99.

9. Lionel Swain, in *New Catholic Commentary on Holy Scripture*, ed. Reginald C. Fuller, Leonard Johnston, and Conleth Kearns (London, 1969), p. 1188.

10. John L. McKenzie, *Dictionary of the Bible* (Milwaukee, 1965), p. 353.

11. For other statements of the same kind, see Franz Mussner, *The Epistle to the Colossians* (New York, 1971), p. 130, and Otto Knoch, *The Epistle of St. James* (New York, 1969), pp. 203-04.

12. Stanley Hauerwas, "Correctives for the New Morality," *Theology Digest*, 1973, p. 228.

13. Reported in the Chicago *New World*, Feb. 1, 1974, p. 1. Paul Toinet, writing of the magisterium's right to judge "compatibilities and incompatibilities," is of the same mind: "C'est bien pourquoi il apparaît inconcevable que la Magistère renonce aujourd'hui à exercer son jugement doctrinal sur les formes de théologie qui réclameraient, au nom du pluralisme, d'avoir en elle droit de cité" (*art. cit.*, p. 179).

14. The propositions of the Commission are reported in *Esprit et vie* 83 (1973), pp. 371-72.

15. Delhaye, *art. cit.*, p. 339.

16. In his commentary on this proposition, Medina Estevez, a member of the Commission, notes that the characteristic sphere of moral pluralism is that of temporal activities (*art. cit.*, p. 375). Karl Rahner has also pointed out that neither the Gospel nor the Church presents a blueprint for the temporal order.

17. Richard McCormick, S.J., "State of the Question," *America*, Oct. 20, 1973, p. 290.

18. Michael J. Kerlin, "A New Modernist Crisis? Hardly," *America*, Oct. 6, 1973, p. 242.

19. Cf. Delhaye, *art. cit.*, p. 321. He adds in a footnote: "un résumé de l'enquête et des réflexions sur celle-ci ont été récemment publiés en un dossier: *Y a-t-il encore une morale?* par A. Chottin et R. Masson, Paris, Le Centurion, 1972."

20. Toinet, *art. cit.*, p. 180.

21. Robert H. Dailey, *Theological Studies* 32 (1971), pp. 343-44.

22. John Kippley, "State of the Question," *America*, Oct. 20, 1973, p. 288.

23. *National Catholic Reporter*, May 11, 1973, p. 10.

24. Toinet, *art. cit.*, p. 181.

25. See M. Eugene Boring, "How May We Identify Oracles of Christian Prophets in the Synoptic Tradition? Mark 3:28-29 as a Test Case," *Journal of Biblical Literature*, 1972, p. 502.

26. Joachim Jeremias, *New Testament Theology* (New York, 1971) p. 78.

27. McKenzie, *Dictionary of the Bible* p. 697. Commenting on Hosea 4:6, D. Ryan makes much the same point in *New Catholic Commentary*, p. 681.

28. Paul Beauchamp, *Dictionary of Biblical Theology* (New York, 1967), p. 415.

29. Jn. 20:21; Mk. 16:15; Mt. 28:18-20; Rom. 10:14-15. Alois Stoger, *The Second Epistle of Peter* (New York, 1969), p. 158, notes the deviousness of false prophets and their abusive accounts of moral freedom and power of the spirit. He is commenting on 2 Peter 2:2-3.

30. Is. 55:8-9.

31. Guy Couturier, C.S.C., in *Jerome Biblical Commentary* 19:71.

32. Jas. 4:4. See also 1 Jn. 2:15-17. For a somewhat extended discussion of the New Testament meaning of "world," see Rudolf Schnackenburg, *Christian Existence in the New Testament* (Notre Dame, 1968), pp. 190-228.

33. Gal. 1:9-10.

34. Ben F. Meyer, in *Catholic Biblical Quarterly*, July 1973, p. 400.

35. Hauerwas, *art. cit.*, p. 229.

36. Tom F. Driver, book review, *America*, Dec. 8, 1973, p. 448. For more biblical commentary on this issue, see, regarding Micah 3:5-8, D. Ryan, in *New Catholic Commentary*, p. 709, and, regarding Jeremiah 23:17, Beauchamp, *Dictionary of Biblical Theology*, p. 416.

37. Jer. 20:7-8; see also 6:10 and 23:28-29. The NAB footnote on this last reference is interesting.

38. Mt. 23:29-32; 10:17-25.

39. Mt. 7:13-14.

40. 2 Tim. 3:12.

41. 1 Th. 3:3-4.

42. Denis J. McCarthy, S.J., in *Jerome Biblical Commentary* 15:25.

43. Bruce Vawter, C.M., *The Conscience of Israel* (New York, 1961), pp. 147-48. Alois Stoger, *The Gospel According to St. Luke 2*, p. 153, recalls how the young Church clashed with the worldwide Roman Empire and thus impressed the historian Tacitus so that he could say that the Christians incurred "the hatred of the human race." Even in its youth the Gospel was not popular. See also Couturier, in *Jerome Biblical Commentary* 19:61; Stoger, *op. cit.* 1, p. 116; W. J. Harrington, O.P., in *New Catholic Commentary*, p. 1004; Wilhelm Thusing, *The Three Epistles of St. John* (New York, 1971) p. 65; Beauchamp, *op. cit.*, p. 415. We find this same human trait likewise in the civil sphere: the thoroughly honest man will make enemies. A young federal prosecutor, George Beall, known to be unafraid of going after the mighty, remarked upon accepting his post as United States Attorney: "If I leave this office without enemies, I will not have done the job properly" (reported in *U.S. News and World Report*, Oct. 1, 1973, p. 21).

44. Hauerwas, *art. cit.*, p. 230.

45. Jn. 6:60.

46. Jn. 6:67-69.

47. John Bright, "The Apodictic Prohibition: Some Observations," *Journal of Biblical Literature*, June 1973, pp. 185-204.

48. *Ibid.*, p. 200.

49. *Ibid.*, p. 201.

50. *Ibid.*

51. William J. Philbin, "The Way of Faith," in Paul Surlis, ed., *Faith: Its Nature and Meaning* (Dublin, 1972), p. 160.

52. Vawter, in *Jerome Biblical Commentary* 62:22.

53. Paul J. Weber, S. J., "Of Prophets Now and Then," *Review for Religious* 31 (1972), p. 982.

54. Acts 2:42; Gal. 1:6-9; 3:1-5.

55. D. J. McCarthy, "Prophetism (in the Bible)," *New Catholic Encyclopedia* 11 (1967), p. 871.

56. *Op. Cit.*, p. 419.

57. Vawter, in *Jerome Biblical Commentary* 62:32.

58. Stoger, *The Second Epistle of Peter*, pp. 156-57.

59. Martin Dibelius and Hans Conzelmann, *The Pastoral Epistles* (4th ed.; Philadelphia, 1972), p. 25.

60. I may offer several examples: Joseph A. Fitzmyer, S.J., regarding Gal. 1:6, in *Jerome Biblical Commentary* 49:11; Joseph A. Grassi, regarding Col. 2:8, *ibid.* 55:23; Bruce Vawter, regarding 1 Jn. 2:24-25, *ibid.* 62:17; W. J. Dalton, regarding Jude 3-4, in *New Catholic Commentary*, p. 1264; Franz Mussner, regarding Col. 2:8, in *The Epistle to the Colossians,* p. 134; John L. McKenzie, "Teach, Teaching," and "Truth," *Dictionary of the Bible*, pp. 871 and 902; Lucien Cerfaux, *The Spiritual Journey of St. Paul* (New York, 1968), pp. 213-16.

61. See, e.g., pp. 466-67.

62. Pp. 456, 457, 458, 460.

63. P. 457.

64. This document, issued July 6, 1973, is published in *Review for Religious*, November 1973, pp. 1230-33.

65. James Hitchcock, "The Problem of Decadence in Catholicism," *Critic*, Sept.-Oct. 1973, p. 16.

66. Hauerwas, *art. cit.*, p. 228.

67. Pope Paul VI, Aug. 6, 1964; included among the documents presented by Joseph F. Gallen, S.J., *Review for Religious*, November 1973, p. 1278.

68. *Constitution on the Sacred Liturgy*, n. 2.

69. Hauerwas, *art. cit.*, p. 231.

Pluralism in Catholic Moral Theology

Charles E. Curran

In a recent assessment of contemporary Catholic moral theology I pointed out that pluralism now characterizes Catholic moral teaching both in methodologies employed and in the solutions to particular moral questions involving such issues as medical ethics, abortion, conflict situations which had previously been solved in terms of the principle of double effect, and some questions of sexuality and divorce. Pluralism on these specific moral questions was justified from the viewpoints of ecclesiology and of moral methodology.[1]

In reacting to this assessment Thomas Dubay has acknowledged the accuracy of the description of pluralism on specific moral questions in the writings of Roman Catholic theologians, but he disagrees with the evaluation given to this fact.[2] Dubay closes his article with several unanswered questions that moral theologians should explore (pp. 501-506). In the interest of pursuing the present discussion and hopefully of clarifying some of the reasons proposed, I will respond to the more important questions he raised.

I
THE FIRST QUESTION

Dubay proposes his first question: "Is habitual and frequent dissent from authentic, non-infallible teaching in the Church

364

biblically or theologically justified?" (p. 501). Dissent in the past was a rare phenomenon considered permissible only within narrow limits and confined to the pages of scholarly publications. It is academically unacceptable that an exception should now be blown up into a rule (pp. 501-502).

Yes, the possibility of frequent dissent from existing teachings of the authentic, hierarchical magisterium on specific moral matters is theologically justified today. Dubay and all Catholic theologians admit in theory the possibility of dissent from such authentic, non-infallible teaching of the hierarchical magisterium. The disagreement centers on whether or not such dissent can be frequent.

What is the ultimate theological reason for the possibility of dissent — be it rare or frequent? In my judgment the ultimate reason is epistemological. On specific moral questions one cannot have a certitude which excludes the possibility of error. Such an epistemological approach distinguishes the degree of certitude which can be had depending on the degree of generality of specificity with which one is dealing. As one goes from the general to the more specific, the possibility of a certitude which excludes error is less. One can be quite certain, for example, that murder is always wrong, but the problem is to determine in practice what is murder.

One can assert with great certitude that a Christian should be a loving, self-sacrificing person of hope and a sign of the fruits of the Spirit to the world, but one cannot know with great certitude how to solve conflict situations involving human lives. Roman Catholic theology in the past has solved the question of conflict situations which might involve killing or abortion on the basis of the understanding of the principle of double effect. Such a solution rests on a philosophical understanding of human actions in which the meaning of direct effect is defined in terms of the physical structure of the act itself. Such a solution is based on one philosophical understanding of the human act, but many people, including Roman Catholic theologians today, point out the inadequacy of that particular philosophical understanding as a solution to conflict situations.[3]

Catholic teaching should, in season and out of season, with great certitude, proclaim that the Christian must respect life. One, however, cannot have such certitude in determining precisely when death occurs. Catholic moral theology has been willing to recognize the difficulties in determining precisely when death does occur.[4] In a somewhat similar way it seems that one cannot have absolute certitude about when human life begins. The solution to the question of abortion ultimately rests on determining the beginning of human life. The judgment about the beginning of human life cannot claim to be so certain that it excludes the possibility of error.[5] One cannot exclude from the Church of Jesus Christ a person who holds that the test for the existence of individual human life is the same at the beginning of life as at the end of life—that is, the presence of brain waves. Even though I personally would not hold such an opinion, I cannot exclude anyone who does from the Church of Jesus Christ.

Why is the possibility of such dissent now recognized to be much more frequent than in the past? There are three factors contributing to this changed understanding. First, the emphasis on historical consciousness in moral theology has affected theological methodology and the understanding of certitude in the area of theological ethics. A more historically conscious methodology, as illustrated in the *Pastoral Constitution on the Church in the Modern World* which begins its consideration of substantive questions by discerning the signs of the times, employs a more inductive methodology. The old methodology in Catholic moral theology tended to be more deductive so that the conclusion that one reached was just as certain as the premises from which one started, provided the logic was correct. A historically conscious methodology gives greater appreciation to the reality of continuing historical change and the need to begin, not with an abstract, universal, essentialist statement, but rather with the concrete, historical realities with which we live. Such a changing methodology with its emphasis on a more inductive approach will never be able to achieve the type of certitude which a more deductive methodology claimed to achieve.[6]

Second, contemporary moral theology recognizes the impossibility of an absolute identification between the physical aspect of the act and the moral description of the act. In fairness it should be pointed out that for the most part Catholic moral theology has avoided the problem of identifying the physical structure of the act with the moral aspect. Thus, for example, our theology never claimed that all killing is wrong but only that all murder is wrong. One can have great certitude in claiming that all murder is wrong, but there might be more difficulty in determining in particular cases whether a specific act is murder or not.

In a similar way Catholic moral theology taught that lying is always wrong, but in the last few decades many theologians do not define a lie as the lack of correspondence between what I say and what is in my mind. The malice of lying consists in the violation of my neighbor's right to truth. Not every falsehood (defined in a somewhat physical way as the correspondence between what is uttered and what is in my mind) is a lie (defined in a moral sense).[7] However, the physical is a very important aspect of the human or the moral, and at times the moral is the same as the physical. In this world, my humanity cannot be separated from my physical, corporeal existence. There is a definite danger in some contemporary ethical discussions of not giving enough importance to the physical aspect, but one cannot merely assert that the physical is always the same as the moral.

In my judgment the areas of questioning today in Catholic moral theology are especially those areas in which the human moral act has been identified with the physical structure of the act itself. The areas under discussion today can generally be reduced to five—medical ethics, the solution of conflict situations which traditionally were solved by the application of the principle of double effect, abortion, sexuality, and divorce. There is not an opportunity here to develop fully an approach to these different questions, but rather the aim of this particular section is merely to seek intelligibility. Why is there questioning today about these particular issues?

Why is it that it will be very difficult to achieve on these questions the certitude which we thought we had in the past? The answer is that in all of these questions one cannot automatically make the identification of the human moral act with the physical structure of the act itself. In medical ethics involving questions such as contraception and sterilization, the older Catholic approach defines the morally wrong act in terms of its physical structure. The principle of the double effect understands the direct effect as the *finis operis* of the external act itself. In the question of sexuality, some ask why the physical act of sexual intercourse alone is permitted only between husband and wife even though many other acts such as revealing most intimate secrets can be done with one who is not a spouse? Some people today argue that human life does not begin at conception because according to them the human is more than just the biological, the physical and the genetic. I do not agree with all these new approaches. At times the human act is the same as the physical structure of the act, but such an identity cannot be accepted with a certitude that excludes the possibility of error.

Here, again, there are a number of different epistemological approaches being taken by contemporary moral theologians on the basis of which they deny the position that the moral aspect is always identifiable with the physical aspect of the act itself. Moral theologians such as Milhaven, McCormick, and Schüller have insisted on the need to judge the morality of actions in terms of the consequences and seek justification for good acts in terms of proportionate reasons.[8] A more relational or phenomenological approach judges the morality of actions not in terms of the physical structure of the act but rather in terms of the manifold relationships with God, neighbor, the world, and self.[9] Other Catholic theologians such as Capone, Fuchs, Janssens and Knauer agree in distinguishing between moral evil and ontic evil although they might not all employ the same terminology. Such authors often appeal to the Thomistic distinction between the interior act and the exterior act. The decisive factor in determining the moral act is the internal act, especially the intention, and not just the external act itself.[10]

All of these approaches to the evaluation of the moral act differ from the approach of the past which often spoke of intrinsically evil actions in terms of the physical structure of the act itself. These contemporary approaches differ among themselves, but they agree in proposing an evaluation of the human moral act which includes so many other considerations that one cannot identify the human moral act and the physical structure of the act with such certitude that the possibility of error is excluded.

In a sense the debate about contraception in the Roman Catholic Church in the 1960's necessarily involved more than just the question of contraception. Some "conservative" Catholics, perhaps in an exaggerated way, pointed out that a change in the teaching on contraception would involve a change in other teachings of the Catholic Church. In one sense they were correct. The methodological approach employed in justifying the condemnation of artificial contraception was the same general approach used to justify some other Catholic teachings. Logically, the call for a change in the teaching on contraception will also have reverberations in other matters where the same methodological difficulties occur. Even if one does not advocate different conclusions on the specific questions mentioned above, at least the newer methodological approaches realize that one's conclusions on these questions cannot have the same type of certitude as that proposed in the older methodology.

Third, contemporary Catholic theology acknowledges the overly authoritarian understanding of the Church which prevailed in the Catholic ethos until the last few decades. This authoritarian overemphasis also had its ramifications in the area of moral theology. Free theological discussion on many questions, such as the possibility of parvity of matter in sexual sins or the solution of conflict situations in the question of abortion, was not allowed. In an earlier article I tried to show at great length how an overemphasis on an authoritarian imposition of moral methodology and of solutions to particular moral problems arose and intensified from the time of the nineteenth century. Decisions of the Holy Office were sufficient to prevent any discussion of the particular questions mentioned above and other questions such as direct sterilization. Since older Catholic teachings on specific moral questions were often based on a monolithic methodology which is no longer accepted and were imposed in an extrinsic and authoritarian way, one must now expect that there will be greater disagreement with such teachings.

II
The Second Question

The second question proposed by Dubay is: "Does not a 'right' to frequent dissent and public teaching of it postulate two magisteria in the Church?" (p. 502). Dubay correctly notes my intentional references to the "hierarchical magisterium" and concludes that my position does postulate two magisteria in practice.

Again one must recall that Dubay acknowledges the possibility of dissent from authentic, authoritative, non-infallible Church teaching. Anyone who admits such a possibility must deal with the same question. In theory one can at times go against the hierarchical magisterium and thus appeal to other criteria or sources of teaching. The question thus stands not only for one who would admit more frequent dissent but for anyone who in conformity with the Roman Catholic self-understanding admits the possibility of dissent from authentic, non-infallible Church teaching.

The key to the solution of such a question again involves a consideration of the reasons justifying the possibility of dissent. The theological reason for dissent rests on the epistemological recognition that on specific moral questions one cannot have that degree of certitude which excludes the possibility of error. The ultimate ecclesiological reason justifying dissent is that the hierarchical magisterium is not the only way in which the Church teaches and learns. A loyal Roman Catholic must acknowledge the hierarchical teaching office and the special assistance given by the Holy Spirit to such an office. However, since the hierarchical teaching office is not the only way in which the Church teaches and learns, the loyal Catholic can, and at times should, test this teaching in the light of a broader perspective.

The teachings of the Second Vatican Council show that the hierarchical magisterium is not the only way in which the Church teaches and learns. The *Declaration on Religious Freedom* begins by recognizing in the conscience of contemporary human beings the demand for a responsible freedom with regard to free exercise of religion in society. "This Vatican Synod takes careful note of these desires in the minds of men. It proposes to declare them to be greatly in accord with truth and justice" (n. 1). In the light of this assertion, one can ask when the teaching on religious liberty became true. The moment a document was signed in Rome? No, the teaching had to be true before that time. The hierarchical magisterium changed because it learned from the experience of people of good will.

Many of the documents of the Second Vatican Council insist

on the importance of dialogue, not only with other Christians, but with non-believers, professionals, scientists, and others. Dialogue implies that one can and does learn from others. History illustrates the truth of the assertion, for the Roman Catholic Church has been taught by others, even non-believers. One should not wonder at this because a basic Catholic premise in moral theology is that our moral teaching is often based on our humanity and human reason which we share with all persons.

The *Constitution on the Church* proclaims that the holy people of God shares in the prophetic office of Christ (n. 12). Theology has traditionally spoken about the threefold office of Jesus as priest, prophet, and king. Through baptism the individual Christian shares in these threefold functions of Jesus. The liturgical movement found a deep theological basis in the fact that through baptism all Christians share in the priestly office of Jesus. The existence of the priesthood of all believers does not deny the need for a special hierarchical priesthood, but the complete priestly ministry in the Church cannot be identified solely with the hierarchical office of priesthood. So too, the fact that all Christians share in the prophetic teaching office of Jesus does not take away from the need for a hierarchical teaching office, but such a hierarchical teaching office cannot be identified with the totality of the teaching office and function in the Church.

The ultimate theological reason why all Christians share in the teaching function of Jesus comes from the fact that the primary teacher in the Church is the Holy Spirit, but the Spirit dwells in the hearts of all the baptized and in some way in all persons of good will. The possibility of dissent from authoritative, authentic, non-infallible Church teaching rests on the theological reality that all the baptized share in the gift of the Spirit, and the hierarchical, non-infallible teaching office in the Church has never claimed to have a total monopoly on the Spirit.

The *Constitution on the Church* acknowledges that all people in the Church are given different gifts (n. 12). We are reminded of St. Paul's recognition of the different charisms and gifts which are given in the Church—some are called as apostles, prophets, teachers, workers of miracles, healers, helpers, administrators, speakers in various kinds of tongues (1 Cor. 12:27ff). The role of the prophet exists in the Church and is not always identified with the hierarchical teaching function. The prophets both in the past and in the present have continually taught the whole Church. There arises the difficult question of the discernment of the Spirit and the discernment of the true prophet. But at least one has to admit that the acceptance of the authoritative, non-infallible teaching of the hierarchical magisterium cannot always be an ultimate test of the true prophet, although the prophet, like all others, must give due weight to this consideration.

The ecclesiology proposed in the Second Vatican Council clearly indicates that the hierarchical teaching office is not the only way in which the Church teaches and learns. This is the theological foundation for the teaching also accepted in the *Constitution on the Church* that dissent from authoritative, authentic, non-infallible Church teaching is a possibility for the Roman Catholic. The frequency of such dissent will depend on the other factors mentioned in response to the first question. In this connection, Dubay also raises the question of public dissent but elsewhere at great length I have justified public dissent in the Church.[11]

III
THE THIRD QUESTION

Dubay proposes a third question: "Is a contradictory moral pluralism a weak effort to make a virtue of necessity?" (p. 503). Earlier, Dubay has recognized the need to distinguish between complementary pluralism which is a healthy part of the life of the Church and contradictory pluralism which destroys the unity of the Church. Such a contradictory pluralism also diminishes the support of a secular observer who will not pay attention to a group who cannot speak out authoritatively and with one voice on important matters (pp. 91-92).

As an introductory note, it is important to point out that here and in other matters Dubay's differences are not only with my interpretation but with the approaches taken by many well-recognized Roman Catholic moral theologians writing today. Dubay expressly admits, "For the most part, I have no problem with Curran's factual description of the pluralism situation" (p. 484). My explanation of this situation attempts to give meaning and intelligibility to the fact of pluralism which we both admit. Dubay does not want to admit the legitimacy of such contradictory pluralism which he recognized does exist in the writings of many Roman Catholic moral theologians today.

The consequences of Dubay's position are staggering—the many Catholic moral theologians today who are questioning various teachings of the Church and proposing alternate solutions are not truly within the pale of true Catholicity. In the light of such an interpretation, the Roman Catholic Church would be in the awkward position of acknowledging that probably the majority of Roman Catholic moral theologians who actually contribute to theological journals are not truly Catholic. But his question still remains—am I and many others merely making a virtue out of necessity?

While recognizing the rightful need and place for complementary pluralism, Dubay denies the possibility of contradictory pluralism on important moral questions. I contend that the Roman Catholic Church has now and always has had a contradictory pluralism even on important moral issues. The Catholic Church has been catholic enough to embrace both a William Buckley and a Dorothy Day, or in a wider context a Generalissimo Franco and President Julius Nyerere. There are Catholics who are for capital punishment and Catholics who are against it. The majority of Roman Catholics (rightly, in my judgment) were against the open shop, but some Catholics approved it. There are Roman Catholics who were in favor of the American involvement in Vietnam and Roman Catholics who were opposed to it. Some Roman Catholics are pacifists; others accept various forms of a just war theory. Some Catholics favor busing as a means of overcoming racial imbalance in schools; others are opposed. Some Catholics believe that smoking is morally wrong because it is harmful to health, while other Catholics are willing to justify cigarette smoking.

There can be no doubt that a contradictory pluralism already does exist within the Roman Catholic Church on important moral matters. Many of the issues mentioned above pertain to the area of social ethics, but they constitute very important issues facing

Catholics and the total society. It is strange that so often one tends to think of moral theology only in terms of personal morality and forgets the very important aspect of social morality. However, some of the examples above belong to the realm of personal morality, so it is not sufficient to say that contradictory pluralism can exist on the level of social morality but not in the sphere of personal morality.

The reason explaining the possibility of such pluralism in both cases is the same — the epistemological reason because of which on specific moral questions it is impossible to have the type of certitude that excludes all possibility of error. The unity of the Church has co-existed in the past and even now in the present with contradictory pluralism on very important moral issues. All references to the need for unity in the Church as proposed in Scripture and mentioned by Dubay must take account of this fact — contradictory pluralism on important moral questions does not destroy the basic unity of the Church.

How can one attempt a more positive explanation and reconciliation of the unity of the Church and the possibility of pluralism on specific questions? A good starting point for such an explanation would be the well-accepted axiom — *in necessariis, unitas; in dubiis, libertas; in omnibus, caritas.* There can and should be unity in terms of the general values, goals, attitudes, and dispositions that the Gospel and human experience call for. Here attention centers on such things as the Beatitudes of Matthew, the fruits of the Spirit proposed by Paul, or those basic Christian attitudes such as care, love, hope, forgiveness and compassion which should characterize the life of the Christian. However, as one descends to specifics and to more particular acts, then it is impossible to have the type of certitude that exists on the level of greater generality. the question of unity and pluralism finds its solution in terms of the epistemological question. Unity is present at the level of greater generality, but as one descends to particulars the possibility of pluralism arises because in the midst of such complexity one cannot exclude the possibility of error.

Once one recognizes that even contradictory pluralism has existed in the Roman Catholic Church in the past on important moral matters, both social and personal, it is now helpful to try to indicate the scope of the new areas in which pluralism is emerging. A survey of the literature seems to limit these questions to the following areas — medical ethics, direct and indirect voluntary as a solution to conflict situations, sexuality, abortion, and divorce. These questions cover only a comparatively small part of the Christian life and should not be identified in any way with the totality of the Christian life or with the totality of the concerns of Christian ethics.

Too often in the past few years moral theology has so riveted attention on the situation ethics debate that occasionally moral theologians have forgotten the many other aspects of Christian ethics such as attitudes, virtues, goals, dispositions, and values in the Christian life which can never be simplistically reduced to the one question of whether or not there is a norm. Likewise, as Dubay also points out, there are many more important topics and concerns in the Christian life such as the paschal mystery, the imitation of Jesus, and the Christian's call to perfection.

Although the questions mentioned above in which there is now a growing pluralism are comparatively few and not the most important considerations involved in moral theology, nevertheless, they do have some importance. Why is pluralism now beginning to arise in these questions? Once again the answer to this question attempts to give some intelligibility to the fact which has been observed and to understand better some of the reasons justifying such pluralism. In my judgment there is a common denominator which is present in all these questions, although it limps somewhat in the question of divorce, which in some ways is a different type of question. In all these other questions there has been an identification of the moral or human aspect with the physical structure of the act itself. As mentioned earlier, I do not deny that at times, but not always, the moral act is the same as the physical structure of the act. When one does conclude that the moral or the human is identical with the physical, such an identification cannot be made with the same type of certitude that an older methodology claimed. It is precisely the possible questioning of this fact of identification which is the reason for the contradictory pluralism that is now existing on all these questions.

It is also interesting to note that in these limited questions, again excluding the question of divorce, the appeal in Roman

Catholic theology has always been based on the natural law. In other words, the Roman Catholic Church has traditionally claimed that it is human reason by which one is able to arrive at these particular truths and conclusions. No great appeal has been made to Scripture or revelation in determining these questions. It should only be natural then that changing understandings of humanity and changing perceptions of human reason might also have important effects in these areas. Again I want to underline that my own approach to such problems cannot be fully developed in the short space available here. Sometimes the human is identified with the physical, but even when such identification is made I cannot do it with the degree of certitude which excludes the possibility of error. Likewise, the hierarchical Church can and should teach on these issues. Roman Catholics must attach special importance to such teaching, but dissent cannot be excluded.

In conclusion, there has been a contradictory pluralism on many important specific moral questions within Roman Catholicism. There is a tendency today to extend this pluralism to a comparatively few other areas where it did not exist before, but the same epistemological reason justifies the pluralism in these new areas just as it did in the more numerous areas where pluralism has existed in the past.

IV
A Fourth Consideration

There are several other questions raised by Dubay, but I believe I have answered the most significant questions and at the same time responded to other comments he raised on the whole question of pluralism. There remains to be considered a comparatively large section of his article which begins with the heading—"Is Moral Theology Prophetic?" (pp. 493-500). This question has great importance and deserves attention, although Dubay himself develops this section not in terms of moral theology, but in terms of the moral theologian. Nonetheless, one should first say a few words about moral theology.

Dubay asks what the moral theologian says of the new creation and what is the place of the cross and self-denial in Christian morality. He goes on to point out that in the literature supporting premarital sexual relations, contraception, and abortion, little or nothing appears about common Gospel themes such as carrying the cross every day or renouncing all things to be a disciple or chastising our bodies lest we become castaways (pp. 504-505).

In response to this it should be noted that even in the teachings of the manuals of moral theology on the same questions there are no similar quotations or references. As already pointed out, these moral teachings were based primarily on human reason, and the older manuals of moral theology refer to the Scriptures in a very occasional and peripheral way.

One cannot deny the importance of these aspects mentioned by Dubay and the fact that they must be always integrated into a full development of moral theology. Moral theology as the systematic reflection upon the Christian life must always insist on the basic call to perfection and to the following of Christ. Christians are called to be perfect even as the heavenly Father is perfect. Catholic moral theology in the last few decades has overcome the former separation between moral and spiritual theology so that one can no longer talk about two classes of citizens in the kingdom of God. However, in the light of the fact that the fullness of the eschaton is not yet here, the Christian will never fully live up to the complete Gospel teaching. We are often made aware that in the times in between the two comings of Jesus we experience ourselves as being *simul justus et peccator.* The radical ethical teaching of Jesus challenges us with the Gospel call to perfection, reminds us of our own continued need for the mercy and forgiveness of God, and calls us to change of heart and conversion. A true moral theology can never neglect or omit these most significant considerations.

The paschal mystery calls for the Christian, who is united in baptism with the risen Lord, to live the Christian life by dying to self and rising in the newness of life. The Christian knows that in union with Jesus suffering and tragedy will always be a part of the Christian life. The paschal mystery remains our hope because in Jesus the Father has changed death into life, and we as Christians are called to share in the promise of that same risen life. However, one must be extremely careful in applying the very important but broad theme of the paschal mystery to particular moral questions.

In response to Dubay's contention that mention of the cross does not appear in literature on these questions, I might refer to an article I wrote over ten years ago in which I first urged a change in the Catholic teaching on contraception. The article began by saying that my previous arguments in favor of the official teaching of the Church developed along the lines of the controlling influence of love with regard to sexuality. Sacrificing love and self-control will always form part of human existence. True Christian asceticism does not constrain the individual; rather it enables the Christian to participate ever more in the freedom of the children of God which only the life-giving Spirit can produce. Like Christ, we die to self and rise in the newness of life. But then my consideration went on to indicate that such an argument was more of a defense of an already accepted position rather than an argument for the truth of that position. The reasoning assumes the official teaching of the Church and then tries to explain it within the whole context of the paschal mystery. But then, as now, theologians cannot merely assume the truth of the official teaching of the Church.[12]

The above paragraph illustrates that very often the paschal mystery or the cross has been used in a pastoral way to help the Christian find some meaning in the midst of a moral crisis or of suffering. In fact, reference to the cross or suffering in the Christian life is often in terms of such a pastoral approach. The Christian has no obligation to look for suffering or even to avoid the possible means of overcoming suffering. For example, in the case of a person who is sick, one immediately recommends that such a person try to be cured. However, if the best of medical knowledge testifies that the disease is incurable and that the individual person will suffer and die, then one understands this in the light of the cross and of the paschal mystery. The paschal mystery also has direct moral implications, but great prudence is required in applying it. Catholic moral theology in its history has tried to avoid the extremes of laxism and rigorism. A moral theologian cannot forget the new life in Jesus or the paschal mystery, but particular moral questions must be considered in the light of the total Christian perspective. For example, if one wanted to solve every ethical problem by appealing to the biblical text of the need to deny oneself, then there would be no room for legitimate self-love or pleasure which Roman Catholic theology has always upheld. One thus must be very careful in the way in which such texts and the ideas behind them are applied in moral theology.

Also, from the strictly moral perspective, the paschal mystery itself does not always call for self-renunciation and self-denial. The paschal mystery involves us in the dying and the rising of Jesus. We as Christians do not yet participate in the fullness of the resurrection, but, nonetheless, through baptism we already have the first fruits of the resurrection. Roman Catholic moral theology, to its great credit, has never seen the paschal mystery as indicating an incompatibility between Gospel values and human values. Catholic moral theology with its acceptance of the natural law and the goodness of man has seen that the values of the "supernatural order" do not deny or contradict the values of the "natural order" but rather build on them and thus surpass them. The cross does not stand as a denial and refutation of all that is truly human. In my judgment, the relationship should be seen in terms of the transforming of the human in the light of the paschal mystery itself.

In conclusion, any Catholic moral theology must give due place and importance to the new life which we share in Jesus. This constitutes the fundamental attitude, disposition and value in the Christian life. On specific moral questions such as cigarette smoking or the drinking of alcohol, one really cannot always appeal directly to the cross and paschal mystery alone to find a solution to such a question. Often on particular questions, once one realizes the difficulty and suffering involved, then the Christian seeks to understand it in view of the paschal mystery itself. The paschal mystery does have a meaning and intelligibility from the strictly moral viewpoint, but even here the cross of Jesus in the Catholic tradition does not always stand in contradiction to human values so that one cannot always interpret the meaning of the cross in moral theology in such a way.

Dubay in this section of his article concentrates his attention on the Catholic theologian and tries to see if the Catholic moral theologian fulfills the six traits of the prophet which he describes. I can agree with some of the six characteristics provided they are properly interpreted. The second characteristic maintains that "the prophet does not conform his message to popular morality or to what men will accept" (p. 495). No one should affirm that a majority belief in a particular teaching makes it correct.

However, an ethics which in the past has claimed that most of its teaching is based on human reason which is common to all human beings and an official teaching which has lately been addressed to all men of good will must recognize that at times one can and should learn from the experience of others. Likewise, the recognition that the Spirit dwells in the hearts of all men of good will also gives an important theological significance to the experience of people, although this can never be the absolute or ultimate determining factor any more than can the non-infallible teaching of the hierarchical magisterium. The fact that a majority of practicing Catholics in France do not accept the teaching of the Church on divorce does not make their opinion correct, but a theologian must consider this datum as well as other important aspects, especially the hierarchical teaching, in arriving at his conclusions.

Other criteria of the true prophet proposed by Dubay have some truth for the moral theologian but they cannot be accepted absolutely. The third criterion is that "the prophet is rejected by the majority" (p. 497). Often the prophet is rejected, but not always. Think of the universal acclaim given to Pope John XXIII on the occasion of his encyclical *Pacem in Terris*. At times, though, the prophet should speak out against the sinful conduct of the majority such as the consumerism so present in our society. The fourth criterion is that the prophet proclaims absolute precepts (p. 498). Dubay ends his whole section on the prophet by remarking that Pope Paul VI best exemplifies the biblical traits of a prophet in his person (p. 501). However, take the example of the very moving speech of Pope Paul VI to the United Nations in which he uttered those very memorable words: "War—never again." Was this an absolute precept? Did the Pope require all nations of the world immediately to put down all their arms and destroy them? No, the prophetic utterance in this case was a moving prayer and not an absolute precept.

The other three criteria proposed by Dubay—"(1) The prophet is a man sent, a man commissioned to proclaim the Lord's holy will" (p. 494); "(5) The prophet is faithful to his tradition" (499); "(6) The true prophet proclaims authentic teaching" (500)—can all be accepted by me but not with the interpretation given them by Dubay. What is the criterion of this being sent, of being faithful to the tradition and of proclaiming authentic teaching? Dubay explicitly and implicitly makes agreement with all the teaching of the hierarchical magisterium, including the authoritative, non-infallible, hierarchical teaching, the criterion in all these cases. "Insofar as theologians are at odds with the magisterium they are not sent. They lack the first note of a prophet among God's people" (p. 495). The faithful are "those who accept the whole Gospel, who are willing to carry the cross every day, who lead a serious prayer life, who accept the teaching magisterium commissioned by Christ" (p. 500). Finally, Dubay cites scriptural warnings about false prophets and concludes that any theory of pluralism which neglects an honest confrontation with these texts cannot be considered adequate (pp. 500-501).

In all these cases, Dubay thus presupposes that true authentic teaching is identified with the teaching of the hierarchical magisterium even when it is a question of authoritative, non-infallible teaching. Catholic theology and the hierarchical teaching office do not make such claims today. As I have pointed out in my earlier article, the Fathers of Vatican II purposely rejected the simple application of the biblical phrase, "He who hears you hears me," to the authoritative, non-infallible, hierarchical teaching function. Dubay's argument is vitiated because he is presupposing what he wants to prove—that the proclamation of a teaching by the authentic, non-infallible teaching office is an absolute guarantee that such a teaching is truly the will of God.

One could make a very strong case on the basis of the prophetic function of the theologian for the fact that at times the theologian will have to stand up and disagree with authentic, non-infallible teaching. There can be no doubt that at times in the Old Testament the prophets did speak against what was proposed by the duly constituted religious authorities. The *Constitution on the Church* explicitly recognizes the existence of the prophetic office in the Church as separate from the hierarchical teaching office, thus indicating the existence of a possible friction between the prophet and the hierarchical teaching office. In the light of the whole understanding of the response due to authentic, non-infallible Church teaching one cannot deny that at times the theologian as prophet must speak in a way contrary to that proposed by the teaching office. The theologian should never do this lightly but must try to discern what God is truly asking of us. The rules for the discernment of spirits and the recognition of true prophets from false are very important, but their very complexity is such that they can never be reduced to the one criterion of the ordinary, non-infallible hierarchical magisterium, as important a criterion as this is.

One must consider the prophetic aspect not only of moral theology itself and of the moral theologian but also the prophetic role of the hierarchical teaching office in the Church. Granted that the prophetic function and the hierarchical teaching function are not identical, nonetheless there should be a prophetic aspect, along with other aspects, to the hierarchical magisterium.

In the past few years it is precisely this prophetic element in the hierarchical teaching function which has been lacking in the opinion of many. The American bishops have often been criticized for speaking publicly and often on such questions as abortion but keeping silent on many other questions facing our society. Today it seems that the American bishops are beginning to speak up more on other issues (e.g., going on record against capital punishment at their November 1974 meeting in Washington), but for a long time the American bishops were silent on the issue of the Vietnam War which was probably the most significant moral issue that arose in the United States in the decade of the 1960's.

Why such silence on so important a moral question? In fairness, I believe there is a very plausible explanation. Although the American bishops frequently and loudly spoke on the question of abortion, they were for a long time silent on the war in Southeast Asia. On questions such as abortion the bishops were convinced that Church teaching was certain, so they had a duty to speak out and inform their people what is the certain teaching of the Church in this matter. In other areas where they realized that such certitude cannot be obtained, they tended not to speak out. They did not want to place any unnecessary burdens on the Catholic people, and, therefore, where a freedom of opinion exists, they felt it better not to speak.

In a true sense the need for absolute certitude has become an albatross around the neck of the teaching office of the hierarchical magisterium. If one waits for such certitude before speaking in to-day's fast-changing world, one can be certain of only one thing—by the time an utterance is made, it will be irrelevant. The problem will long since have gone by and no longer be a pressing, urgent contemporary problem. The prophetic voice addressing the complexities of modern existence must be willing to accept the risk of being wrong but still speak out in the light of the best possible understanding of the Gospel, of human experience, and of the concrete facts of the situation. Again, it is the epistemological reason which will prevent the possibility of certitude in these cases, but still some type of direction and guidance on some important issues should be given by the hierarchical teaching office in the Church. Such teaching should stress the general Christian attitudes, goals and ideals and then descend into the particularities with the recognition that specific proposals cannot claim to be absolutely certain.

In an earlier period it seems that the American bishops did exercise a more prophetic role in questions of social justice. The administrative committee of the National Catholic War Council in 1919 issued a call for a reconstruction of the American social order which was called "The Bishops' Program of Social Reconstruction: A General Review of the Problems and Survey of Remedies." Aaron A. Abell, one of the foremost historians of the Catholic social movement in the United States, mentions that some charged that this document was socialistic and revolutionary, even Marxist, rather than Christian in its approaches.[13] In 1940 the administrative board of the American bishops issued a statement entitled "The Church and the Social Order" which called for far-reaching reforms in the American economic system.[14]

In a sense these were not official statements of the whole American hierarchy exercising its teaching office, but they were truly prophetic utterances. There is a continued need today for official statements by the bishops as hierarchical Church teachers on important issues of our day, but such teachings will be possible only if the hierarchical teaching office recognizes that its teaching might be wrong; but with the best insights of the Gospel, human experience, and the assistance of the Holy Spirit it should nevertheless speak out on some of the important moral issues facing society and the world. Note that the bishops cannot and should not speak out on every issue, but they should strive to discern the most important moral issues and must always acquire a competent knowledge before speaking out.

In conclusion, the prophetic is an important aspect of moral theology, of the role of the moral theologian, and of the role of the hierarchical magisterium. But a proper understanding of the prophetic aspect coincides with the accepted Catholic teaching that at times and for sufficient reasons dissent from authoritative, authentic, non-infallible Church teaching is permitted. The prophetic aspect of the theologian's role at times might require the theologian to dissent from such teaching. The prophetic aspect of the hierarchical teaching office will be better accomplished if one acknowledges that such a teaching on specific questions cannot achieve the degree of certitude which excludes the possibility of error.

V
CONCLUSIONS

Two final points deserve brief mention. Some would argue that only the theologian is competent to dissent or disagree with the authentic, non-infallible teaching of the hierarchical magisterium. Such a proposition harbors a poor understanding of the function of the moral theologian. The moral theologian studies Christian decision-making in a thematic, reflexive and systematic way. Every single Christian is called upon to make moral decisions and try to follow the Gospel call in a non-thematic, non-reflexive and non-systematic way (these are non-pejorative terms).

Perhaps a comparison might be helpful. The psychiatrist is the person who professionally studies in a thematic, reflexive and systematic way the questions of human maturity and emotional balance. One can ask the question: Are psychiatrists the most emotionally mature and balanced human persons in the world? Without any degrading of a profession as such, I think most people would conclude that psychiatrists are not necessarily the most mature and balanced persons. There are many people who have never heard of Freud who are much more emotionally mature and balanced than those who have read his complete works. This is not to belittle psychiatric knowledge, but it is to show the difference between the more reflexive role of the theorist and the practical day-to-day life situation. There are many Christian people who have never read Thomas Aquinas who are "better Christians" than many theologians. All Christians are called to follow out the Gospel and respond to it with conscientious decisions. One does not need the type of thematic, reflexive and systematic theological knowledge in order to make such decisions, but a prudent person would give some consideration to this particular source of knowledge.

The second point concerns the teaching function of the Church and the conscience of the individual Roman Catholic. There are many different ways in which the Church can and should exercise its teaching function. The liturgy remains a very important teaching instrument of the Church, although not the only one. The Church also teaches by the witness of its individual members and the corporate witness of the institution. The Church in so many different ways, in season and out of season, should exercise its teaching function. Likewise, the hierarchical teaching office has many different ways of exercising its teaching function in addition to those mentioned above. Sometimes it might raise a challenging question or point to the danger of motivation which is not truly Christian. At other times it might speak out on specific matters with the limitations we have already discussed.

In traditional Roman Catholic moral theology the ultimate moral decision rests with the properly formed conscience of the individual. Every individual must acknowledge the twofold limitations of finitude and of sinfulness which affect all human beings. The individual person is limited and thus can never see the total picture but only a part of it. Likewise, sin affects all of us and impairs the possibility of complete objectivity. In making ethical decisions the individual thus seeks help from other sources. The community of the Church strives to overcome the twofold limitations of finitude and sinfulness which can affect the individual conscience. The believing Catholic recognizes the God-given role of the hierarchical magisterium but also realizes that the teaching on specific moral questions cannot absolutely exclude the possibility of error. The prudent person will pay significant attention to this teaching and only act against such teaching after a careful and prayerful investigation.

The hierarchical teaching office must also recognize its God-given function as well as its limitations. The authentic or authoritative teaching of the hierarchical magisterium on specific moral questions receives the assistance of the Holy Spirit. In the future the hierarchical magisterium must operate more in accord with the newer theological methodologies and with the ecclesial self-understanding as proposed in the Second Vatican Council.

However, even recognizing newer theological methodologies and following an ecclesiological search for moral truth as described in the documents of the Second Vatican Council, the authoritative, non-infallible, hierarchical teaching on specific issues can never claim to exclude the possibility of error. The Catholic can never hope to have that type of certitude because of the complexities involved in specific moral questions but must be content with the moral certitude and risk becoming involved in such specific decisions. The Catholic should gratefully receive the teaching of the hierarchical magisterium and only for serious reasons and after commensurate reflection make a conscience decision in opposition to it.

Notes

1. Charles E. Curran, "Moral Theology: The Present State of the Discipline," *Theological Studies,* XXXIV (1973), pp. 446-467. A slightly expanded version of this article may be found in my *New Perspectives in Moral Theology* (Notre Dame, Indiana: Fides Publishers, 1974), pp. 1-46.

2. Thomas Dubay, "The State of Moral Theology: A Critical Appraisal," *Theological Studies,* XXXV (1974), pp. 482-506.

3. Cornelius J. van der Poel, "The Principle of Double Effect," in *Absolutes in Moral Theology?* ed. C. E. Curran (Washington: Corpus Books, 1968), pp. 186-210; Leandro Rossi, "Diretto e indiretto in teologia morale," *Rivista di Teologia Morale,* III (1971), pp. 37-65.

4. Edwin F. Healy, S.J., *Medical Ethics* (Chicago: Loyola University Press, 1956), pp. 380-383.

5. For indications of some diversity already existing among contemporary Roman Catholic authors on the question of the beginning of human life, see *Abtreibung—Pro und Contra,* ed. J. Gründel (Würzburg: Echter, 1971); *Avortement et respect de la vie humaine,* Colloque du Centre Catholique des Médecins Français (Paris: Editions du Seuil, 1972); D. Mongillo, F. D'Agostine, F. Compagnoni, "L'Aborto," *Rivista di Teologia Morale,* IV (1972), pp. 355-392; Richard A. McCormick, S.J., "Notes on Moral Theology: The Abortion Dossier," *Theological Studies,* XXXV (1974), pp. 312-359.

6. Bernard J. F. Lonergan, *Method in Theology* (New York: Herder and Herder, 1972), pp. 153-234.

7. J. A. Dorszynski, *Catholic Teaching about the Morality of Falsehood* (Washington: Catholic University of America Press, 1949).

8. Richard A. McCormick, S.J., *Ambiguity in Moral Choice,* The 1973 Père Marquette Theology Lecture (Milwaukee: Marquette University, 1973); John Giles Milhaven, "Objective Moral Evaluation of Consequences," *Theological Studies* XXXII (1971), pp. 407-430; Bruno Schüller, S.J., "Zur Problematik allgemein verbindlicher ethischer Grundsätze," *Theologie und Philosophie,* XLV (1970), pp. 1-23; Schüller, "Typen ethischer Argumentation in der katholischen Moral Theologie," *Theologie und Philosophie,* XLV (1970), pp. 526-550.

9. William H. Van der Marck, *Toward a Christian Ethic* (Westminster, Md.: Newman Press, 1967), pp. 41-79.

10. Domenico Capone, "Il pluralismo in teologia morale," *Rivista di Teologia Morale,* VI (1974), pp. 289-302; Joseph Fuchs, "The Absoluteness of Moral Terms," *Gregorianum,* LII (1971, pp. 415-458; Louis Janssens, "Ontic Evil and Moral Evil," *Louvain Studies,* IV (1972), pp. 115-156; Peter Knauer, S.J., "La détermination du bien et du mal moral par le principe du double effet," *Nouvelle Revue Théologique,* LXXXVII (1965), pp. 356-376; Knauer, "The Hermeneutic Function of the Principle of the Double Effect," *Natural Law Forum* XII (1967), pp. 132-162.

11. Charles E. Curran, Robert E. Hunt, et al., *Dissent In and For the Church: Theologians and Humanae Vitae* (New York: Sheed and Ward, 1969), pp. 133-153.

12. "Personal Reflections on Birth Control," *The Current,* V (1965), pp. 5-12. This was later reprinted in a number of places including my book *Christian Morality Today* (Notre Dame, Indiana: Fides Publishers, 1966), pp. 66-76. For a more extended treatment of the paschal mystery in Christian life, see my *Crisis in Priestly Ministry* (Notre Dame, Indiana: Fides Publishers, 1972), pp. 51-102.

13. *American Catholic Thought on Social Questions,* ed. Aaron I. Abell (Indianapolis: Bobbs-Merrill Company, 1968), pp. 325-348.

14. Francis L. Broderick, *Right Reverend New Dealer John A. Ryan* (New York: Macmillan, 1963), pp. 256-257.

Academic Freedom:
The Catholic University
and Catholic Theology

Charles E. Curran

Freedom has been a perennial topic of discussion in Catholic thought. Ever fearful of individualistic license and of the dangers of denying an objective morality based on the law of God, Roman Catholic theology in the nineteenth century opposed the modern freedoms — freedom of worship, freedom of speech, of teaching, of the press, and of conscience. However, in the last few decades the Roman Catholic Church has become a staunch defender of human dignity and of human freedom. In the light of this changing emphasis on freedom, the Second Vatican Council accepted religious liberty for all peoples. Discussions about academic freedom took place in the context of this developing attitude toward freedom in general and toward the concrete manifestations of freedom.

The purpose of this study is to examine the relationship of academic freedom to the Catholic university and to Roman Catholic theology. The topic seems quite limited, but actually there are many significant questions connected with it which can only be presented in a summary fashion. This study will consist of four parts: (I) the meaning of academic freedom; (II) the relationship of the Catholic university to academic freedom; (III) Roman Catholic theology and academic freedom; (IV) academic freedom as related to *Sapientia Christiana*, the recent apostolic constitution on norms for ecclesiastical universities and faculties, and also to the proposed new code of canon law.

I
MEANING OF ACADEMIC FREEDOM

Academic freedom is related to all other aspects of freedom, but what specifies academic freedom is its relationship to the university. The university in this context is generally understood to include all institutions of higher learning such as undergraduate colleges and universities. A university exists to preserve, impart, and discover truth. To achieve its purpose, the university as a community of scholars needs a proper academic environment. Academic freedom is essential for the very existence of a university and is what distinguishes a university from a propaganda institution or a center of indoctrination. The university as such must be a free and autonomous center of study with no external constraints limiting either its autonomy or its freedom. An often-cited definition of academic freedom is the following:

> Academic freedom is the freedom of the teacher or research worker in higher institutions of learning to investigate and discuss the problems of his science and to express his conclusions, whether through publication or in the instruction of students, without interference from political or ecclesiastical authority, or the administrative officials of the institution in which he is employed, unless his methods are found by qualified bodies of his own profession to be clearly incompetent or contrary to professional ethics [1]

Academic freedom is based not on the personal privilege of academics but on the common good of society. Society is best served by institutions of higher learning in which there is a free search for truth and free expression. The only limit is the truth itself and nothing else. Academic freedom applies to the teaching, research and extramural utterances of the professor. The teacher is to be guided only by truth and its understanding. The integrity of the faculty member and the rights of the students are violated if the teacher is not allowed to express his own ideas and hypotheses based on scientific knowledge and investigation. Freedom in research is fundamental to the advancement of all knowledge. Nor can a faculty member's freedom be summarily taken away because of controversial extramural utterances which might upset some of the different publics served by the university. However the right of academic freedom carries with it corresponding duties. In general, the right to freedom involves the duty to use that freedom responsibly. More specifically in terms of academic freedom, the individual professor's responsibility is spelled out in terms of competency as a teacher and researcher.

The concept of academic freedom briefly described here has been developed in the United States in the light of historical circumstances and of the growth of higher education. One of the functions of a university is to be critical, but in the process influential and powerful people might be upset by such criticism or new hypotheses. Problems have arisen in many different subject areas including religion, science, history, politics, economics, sexual ethics, business, race questions, and various types of radicalism in different areas.[2]

In the United States the work of developing and spelling out the procedures and institutions needed to protect the autonomy of the university and academic freedom has been done especially by the American Assocaition of University Professors (AAUP). It should be pointed out that structures and procedures are the minimal safeguards needed to protect academic freedom. A vigorous intellectual community with highly competent and dedicated scholars cannot be brought about through legal procedures alone. At the time of the founding of the AAUP in 1915, a committee on academic freedom and tenure formulated "A Declaration of Principles" which set forth the concerns of the Association for academic freedom, tenure, proper procedures, and professional responsibilities. From a meeting called by the American Council on Education in 1925, there emerged the "Conference Statement on Academic Freedom and Tenure," which because of its endorsement by the Association of American Colleges and by the AAUP was quite generally supported within American higher education. This somewhat unwieldy statement of rules and regulations designed to be incorporated by institutions of higher learning was replaced in 1940 by a set of principles approved by both associations and known as the 1940 *Statement of Principles on Academic Freedom and Tenure.* This statement, which has been endorsed by the most significant academic associations, is generally accepted as governing higher education in the United States. The AAUP has also issued further statements and proposed regulations based on the 1940 *Statement, especially the 1958 Statement on Procedural Standards in Faculty Dismissal Proceedings* and the *1976 Recommended Institutional Regulations on Academic Freedom and Tenure.* In addition to its work of proposing principles and regulations, the AAUP also investigates alleged violations of academic freedom, trying to work out amicable solutions in accord with its principles, but at times having to take the more drastic action of censuring institutions which violate the principles of academic freedom.[3]

The two instrumentalities designed to protect academic freedom are tenure and academic due process. After a probationary period, the professor is entitled to a permanent or tenured appointment if the institution decides to keep such a professor. A tenured professor can be dismissed only for adequate cause. Adequate cause is not precisely defined but certainly includes the notion of competency and the fitness to teach and do research. Although one of the purposes of tenure is to safeguard the academic freedom of the professor, full academic freedom is also demanded for faculty on probationary appointments.

Academic due process, as explained in the 1958 AAUP *Statement* and elsewhere, spells out the procedure to be employed in attempting to dismiss a professor for adequate cause. Academic due process calls for a judgment by academic peers together with all the other legal safeguards and procedures connected with due process. It is normally expected that the governing board of the institution will accept the decision of the faculty committee. In recognizing incompetency and unfitness as grounds for dismissal, this procedure legally enshrines the fundamental responsibility which it is the duty of all faculty members to exercise. To dismiss a professor after incompetency has been demonstrated and accepted by a committee of peers in accord with academic due process in no way constitutes a violation of academic freedom.[4] The principles and procedures briefly described here are generally accepted by all in dealing with the meaning and actual protection of academic freedom in American higher education. Today there are some who want to modify or even abolish the tenure system, but they still insist on safeguarding academic freedom.

II
CATHOLIC HIGHER EDUCATION AND ACADEMIC FREEDOM

From the beginning, defenders of academic freedom have been very wary of denominational institutions of higher learning. The 1915 "Declaration of Principles" firmly stated the principle that if a church establishes a college with the express understanding that the college will be used as an instrument of propaganda and indoctrination in the interests of the religious faith, such an institution does not allow academic freedom and is not truly a university. However, the Declaration goes on to note that such institutions are rare and are becoming more rare. The 1940 *Statement* recognized a problem and attempted to solve it by a general statement that "limitations of academic freedom because of religious or other aims of the institution should be clearly stated in writing at the time of the appointment."[5]

Before the 1960's there was a widespread feeling among college and university educators in general and among Catholic leaders in these fields that the Catholic institution of higher education was incompatible with the full or absolute academic freedom existing in American institutions of higher education. Some non-Catholic educators accepted the Shavian dictum that a Catholic university is a contradiction in terms. Sidney Hook affirmed that academic freedom does not exist in Catholic institutions.[6] Robert M. MacIver, director of the American Academic Freedom Project housed at Columbia University in the early 1950's, in his influential volume *Academic Freedom in Our Time* includes statements by Catholics to illustrate the religious line of attack on academic freedom.[7]

From the Catholic side before 1960 there was also general agreement that full academic freedom could not exist in Catholic institutions. The president of Georgetown University in 1950 referred to the sacred fetish of academic freedom and called for sensible limitations to preserve the future of the nation from fatal consequences.[8] The immediate context of his remarks was the controversy about communists and academic freedom, which was quite widespread during those years. The incompatibility between Catholic colleges and full academic freedom was accepted as a matter of course. There were very few studies of academic freedom and Catholic higher education until the 1950's. Before 1960, only one Catholic institution was censured by the AAUP for violating academic freedom, and there were no *ad hoc* committee reports about possible violations which did not result in censure. The two most in-depth studies of academic freedom from the Catholic perspective in the 1950's proposed an understanding of academic freedom which is opposed to and destructive of the accepted understanding in American academe. According to these studies, academic freedom is limited not only by the competency and responsibility of the individual scholar but also by a specific doctrinal test of a religious nature. Ecclesiastical authority, from which there is no appeal, can be invoked to settle controverted cases in academe. One of the pedagogical functions of the teacher is to solidify and deepen the faith of the student. Loss of faith by students reflects unfavorably on a Catholic college teacher.[9]

In the 1960's great changes occurred. Catholic scholarly organizations began to endorse the 1940 *Statement*. Faculties at Catholic institutions frequently called in the AAUP to vindicate their rights and their academic freedom. In 1965 Gerald F. Kreyche published a paper in the *National Catholic Education Association Bulletin* that called for Catholic institutions to accept the concept of full academic freedom. More favorable articles together with some dissent followed.[10] A symposium at the University of Notre Dame in 1966 heard from many speakers who saw the need for Catholic institutions of higher learning to incorporate the principles of complete academic freedom." A thesis accepted at The Catholic Univeristy of America in 1969 made the case for full academic freedom even for Roman Catholic theology, a position which had been rejected in 1958 dissertation.[12]

Perhaps the strongest indication of the extent of the changes is found in what is called the Land O'Lakes Statement, "The Nature of the Contemporary Catholic University," which was signed in 1967 by twenty-six leaders in Catholic higher education in the United States and Canada, including the presidents and representatives of the major institutions. The very first paragraph states the position on academic freedom bluntly and clearly:

> The Catholic university today must be a university in the full modern sense of the word, with a strong commitment to and concern for academic excellence. To perform its teaching and research functions effectively, the Catholic university must have a true autonomy and academic freedom in the face of authority of whatever kind, lay or clerical, external to the academic community itself. To say this is simply to assert that institutional autonomy and academic freedom are essential conditions of life and growth and indeed of survival for Catholic universities as for all universities.[13]

A 1971 report of the North American Region of the International Federation of Catholic Universities (IFCU) emphasizes the need for the autonomy of the university as such. "The Catholic university is not simply a pastoral arm of the Church. It is an independent organization serving Christian purposes but not subject to ecclesiastical-juridical control, censorship or supervision." In a university without statutory relationships to Rome, the hierarchical magisterium might in an extreme case issue a public warning about the theologizing activity of a particular theologian, but there can be "no question of juridical intervention in the institutional affairs of the university itself."[14]

Although there continued to exist occasional dissenting voices, the mainstream of American Catholics involved in higher education accepted the imperative for the Catholic institution to be autonomous and affirmed for themselves the same academic freedom as existed in other universities. What explains such a sudden and massive change on the part of Catholic educators? Three generic types of reasons—cultural changes, changes in Catholic higher education, and philosophical and theological changes—appear to have contributed to this abrupt change.

Cultural changes include especially the general attitude of Catholics to American institutions and culture. After the Second World War, the American Catholic population was being assimilated into the mainstream of American life. The Church of the immigrants was moving out of the ghetto. On the one hand, the fears of some Catholics about incompatibility between Catholicism and the American ethos were greatly dissipated. On the other hand, Americans as a whole no longer looked on Catholics primarily with suspicion and mistrust. The election of a Catholic as president of the United States in 1960 symbolically indicated there was no incompatibility between Catholicism and the American ethos with its emphasis on political freedoms and human rights and its important institutions such as universities. Many Catholics matriculated at these non-Catholic institutions and did not find the environment inimical to their faith.

Since the 1950's, John Tracy Ellis, Walter Ong, and Thomas O'Dea had pointed out the failure of Catholics to contribute to American intellectual life.[15] This criticism was a sign of a growing maturity which enabled Catholics to be self-critical, and at the same time it encouraged Catholic institutions of higher education to take a critical look at themselves.

Significant developments were occurring in Catholic higher education itself. The number of Catholic institutions and the number of students in such colleges increased dramatically after the Second World War. At the same time, Catholic institutions became more interested in graduate education with its emphasis on research, investigation, and discovery. In the light of the increasing number and size of Catholic institutions, religious and clerical teachers and even administrators were supplemented by an ever-growing number of lay people, many of whom had been trained at prestigious non-Catholic schools with their strong traditions of autonomy and freedom. The same time period saw the breakdown in the old curriculum in Catholic colleges which attempted to hand down the classical wisdom to the new generation. Changes in governance not only included a greater role for laity in the faculty and administration, but also the ownership and incorporation of number and size of Catholic institutions, religious and clerical community or group to boards of trustees which often even had a majority of lay members. Catholic institutions in the 1960's experienced the same problems and questions that were present on all campuses. Even in Catholic colleges, for example, greater freedom and responsibility were given to students not only in curriculum but also in terms of their lifestyles on campus, for many rejected the understanding of the college as existing *in loco parentis*.

Above all, in the 1960's, Catholic higher educators recognized that the primary purpose of their institutions was intellectual and that they should not be seen as juridically serving under and subordinate to the pastoral mission of the Church. They could best serve the Church by being good institutions of higher learning and holding on to their autonomy as such. Many factors contributed to this new understanding and focus: in competition with other colleges and universities, Catholic institutions accepted the goal of striving for academic excellence; accrediting agencies emphasized such intellectual goals and purposes; federal and state monies were available to institutions of higher learning which did not exist primarily to carry on indoctrination; the cultural and other changes in Catholic higher education also pointed toward the primary academic and intellectual purposes of Catholic institutions.

Changing theological factors, especially as illustrated in the Second Vatican Council, also influenced the acceptance of full academic freedom as an essential aspect of Catholic colleges and universities. The *Pastoral Constitution on the Church in the Modern World* (nn. 36, 59) affirms the legitimate autonomy of earthly affairs, created things, culture, and the sciences. All things are endowed with their own stability, truth, goodness, proper laws, and order. Catholics should not divert these realities from their own natural purposes and functions. In this perspective one can argue that the Church should accept the university as it is with its own nature and purposes. The Catholic university should not change the nature of a university and thereby violate the autonomy of the natural or created order.

Roman Catholic theology traditionally has maintained that faith and reason cannot contradict one another. According to both the *Pastoral Constitution on the Church in the Modern World* (n.59) and the *Declaration on Christian Education* (n.10) the human sciences in using their own proper principles and method can never be in contradiction with the faith.

Roman Catholic theology, which in the nineteenth century had opposed modern liberties, by the time of the Second Vatican Council had become a staunch defender of human freedom and dignity. This emphasis appears in all the conciliar documents but especially in the *Pastoral Constitution on the Church in the Modern World* and in the *Declaration on Religious Freedom*, which begins by recognizing the demand for freedom in human society regarding chiefly the quest for the values proper to the human spirit (n. 1). The emphasis on freedom and dignity in general, together with the responsibility and role of the laity in the Church, stimulated the need to protect the rights of all in the Church. As a result, due process was often called for in settling disputes within the Church. Without spelling out its meaning, the *Pastoral Constitution on the Church in the Modern World* (n. 62) maintained that all the faithful, whether clerical or lay, possess a lawful freedom of inquiry, freedom of thought and of expressing their mind with humility and fortitude in those matters on which they enjoy competence.

In retrospect, there is an intriguing analogy between the acceptance of religious liberty in the Roman Catholic Church and the acceptance of academic freedom by the mainstream of Catholic educators in the United States. Proponents of religious liberty in the nineteenth century often based their position on a theory that there was no place for faith, religion, or the Church in society. Finally, in the middle of the twentieth century, a different rationale was proposed for religious liberty based on the dignity of the human person and on the presupposition of a limited constitutional state which is not competent in matters of religion, but which allows freedom for religion to flourish in society.

There can be no doubt that some of the proponents of academic freedom in the beginning were opposed to faith and dogma of any kind. At the very least, it was often asserted that true knowledge could come only from the scientific method and not from faith. Faith was an unjustified intrusion on scientific inquiry with its heavy empirical orientation. Robert MacIver in his often-cited book stoutly argues against a positivistic notion of science, but on the other·hand betrays the one-sidedness of his approach when he asserts that what the scholar investigates is not values but evidences.[16] Also American Catholics were aware that academic freedom and the autonomy of institutions of higher learning had gone hand in hand with the fact that many colleges and universities which were originally started by Protestant denominations were no longer, or only nominally, related to the Church. In addition, Catholics feared the secularism they saw in non-Catholic higher education.

By the late 1960's, many Catholics recognized that the acceptance of academic freedom did not necessarily involve these other unfortunate consequences which in many ways were unacceptable to Catholics. First, faith and academic freedom were not necessarily opposed. The limitations of the scientific method and the value-free approach of much of earlier American higher education were coming under increasing criticism. The search for values, meaning, and the human is a most important academic function. Scientists themselves began to acknowledge that even the empirical sciences have their own presuppositions. Theology with its presupposition of faith is not the only academic discipline that functions on presuppositions that cannot be proved by the scientific method. Second, in Catholic circles discussions about academic freedom occurred in a context within which educators were discussing the Catholic identity of their institutions. The majority of Catholic educators were convinced that a Catholic identity can remain and be efficacious in a free and autonomous institution of higher learning. Academic freedom was championed without having to endorse some of the negative aspects often associated with it in the past.

III

ACADEMIC FREEDOM AND ROMAN CATHOLIC THEOLOGY

Statements by Catholic educators affirmed the need and the place for full academic freedom in Catholic colleges and universities, but such statements did not develop a theological rationale for the most difficult aspect of the question—the academic freedom of Roman Catholic theology in the university setting. Not only Roman Catholic thinkers but most secular academics were convinced that Roman Catholic theology on the campus could not enjoy a complete academic freedom. This section will argue that the academic freedom of the Catholic theologian in the university is not only legitimate but in the long run is most beneficial for the Catholic institution, for theology, and for the Church.

The defense of the academic freedom of the Catholic theologian was worked out amid a number of practical controversies at Catholic colleges and universities in the United States in the 1960's, especially at The Catholic University of America and at the University of Dayton.[17] The problem can be succinctly stated. Roman Catholic faith gives a God-given role to the hierarchical magisterium of Pope and bishops as the official and at times even infallible teachers on questions of faith and morals. The Roman Catholic theologian precisely as such must recognize the role of the hierarchical magisterium and therefore is not and cannot be free to come to a conclusion in opposition to Catholic faith or to the divinely constituted hierarchical teaching office in the Church.

Some attempts that were made to justify the academic freedom of the Roman Catholic theologian seem to me to be inadequate. According to John E. Walsh, the Catholic university should not be seen as an instrument of the Church's teaching mission. Such an approach rightly tries to distinguish and separate the roles of academic theology and of the hierarchical teaching Church, but Walsh solves the problem by seeing the university as the Church learning in distinction from the hierarchical magisterium as the Church teaching.[18] The teaching function of the Church cannot be reduced only to the teaching function of the hierarchical magisterium. In one sense all the baptized also share in the teaching function of Jesus.

A second inadequate justification overemphasizes the secularization of the university so that the theology taught in a Catholic university is not merely Roman Catholic theology. In my judgment, such an approach goes too far and destroys not only the academic discipline of Roman Catholic theology but also any real notion of a Catholic university. My justification rests on contemporary but quite widely accepted notions of the science of theology and of the relationship between the hierarchical magisterium and the role of theology. Both of these are disputed questions, but the position outlined below is in conformity with a very sizable part of contemporary Roman Catholic theologizing.[19]

Theology is a scientific discipline, a human activity which presupposes faith. Faith itself is not primarily the revelation of propositions or even of truths. Faith is primarily the saving encounter with the living God. But there is a truth dimension to faith. The object of faith is the totally other mystery of God, so that our knowledge of God will never be perfect in this world. In addition to the lack of completion in our knowledge and concepts of God and faith, there is also the imperfection of the language and symbols used to express this faith. The acceptance of hermeneutics reminds us of the historically and culturally conditioned nature of our knowledge and of our verbal and symbolic expression of this knowledge. Theology has the never-ending task of trying to interpret better and understand more adequately the mystery of faith in the light of contemporary realities. No longer is theology understood in the light of a science seeking certitude based on a deductive methodology. Interpretation of the sources of revelation and of the teaching of the hierarchical magisterium in the light of the signs of the times is theology's function.

All must admit the God-given role of the hierarchical magisterium, but its relationship with the role of the theologians has been proposed in a different way by many contemporary theologians. To this day, many bishops and Roman authorities follow an approach proposed by the theologians of the Roman school in the nineteenth century, according to which the role of theology is seen in terms of complete subordination to the hierarchical magisterium. Theology sets forth and defends the teaching of the hierarchical magisterium.

Many contemporary theologians see a more complex relationship. Theology itself also has a pastoral dimension and is not merely a scientific discipline. The hierarchical magisterium has the function of teacher in faith and morals, but that teaching cannot avoid theology. History reminds us that the hierarchical Church has been dependent upon theology for its own formulations. The interpretative function of theology must deal with and give correct weight to the teachings of the hierarchical magisterium so that through theological speculation our understanding may grow and deepen. Part of the theological function of interpretation of the hierarchical teaching involves the possibility of dissent from authoritative, non-infallible Church teaching.[20] Theology must be free to exercise this interpretative function responsibly.

This understanding of the relationship of theology to the hierarchical magisterium acknowledges important aspects of subordination but also includes an interpretative function which should deepen and increase our understanding, but which might possibly involve dissent from authoritative teaching. Here is the ultimate reason for the need of responsible freedom for Catholic theologians. Many proponents of this approach point out that historically there were mistakes and errors in some aspects of authoritative teachings which were corrected, thanks at least partly to the work of theologians — e.g., the cases of Popes Liberium, Vigilius, Honorius, Alexander III, and thirteenth-century condemnations of Aristotle. Official Church teaching has changed on a number of issues, at least partly with the assistance of theology — war and peace in the early Church; reasons justifying sexual relations between spouses; interest taking; the right of the accused to keep silent; religious liberty. In the context of the Second Vatican Council it was easy to see the detrimental effects on the life of the Church caused by the silencing and condemnation of many theologians not only during the anti-Modernist period but until the Council itself. In the United States, John Tracy Ellis has chronicled the most significant cases in which the autonomy of the academic enterprise of Roman Catholic theology has not been respected by the hierarchical authorities in the Church.[21]

The procedure and institutions connected with academic freedom in American academe seem very apt for safeguarding the legitimate freedom of Roman Catholic theology and at the same time for recognizing the God-given teaching function of the hierarchical magisterium in faith and morals. How should this work in practice? The Roman Catholic theologian who enjoys academic freedom in the college or university has the correlative duties of responsibility and competency. Competency requires that one be true to the presuppositions, sources, and methods of the discipline. Specifically, the theologian should distinguish between the data of revelation and theories or hypotheses that have been proposed. The official teaching of the Church should be carefully spelled out and interpreted in accord with accepted hermeneutic principles. Personal hypotheses and opinions should be labeled as such. The personal responsibility of the competent theologian forms the best safeguard for protecting the rights of all concerned.

If the Roman Catholic theologian is not competent, then the professor can be dismissed for cause just as an incompetent physicist or anthropologist can be dismissed for cause in accord with the principles of academic due process. However, the judgment about incompetency must be made by academic peers. In the case of the theologian, the peers must give due weight to all official Church teaching in arriving at their judgment. Church authority as such has no direct power to intervene juridically in academe, for then the autonomy of academe is violated. Church teaching authority can point out for the good of the Church that the theory of a particular theologian is erroneous, but the judgment about dismissal must be made by academic peers giving due weight to official Church teaching. Such procedures, although not perfect, safeguard both the God-given hierarchical teaching function and the role of theology.

In practice many have accepted the procedure protecting the academic freedom of the Roman Catholic theologian in academe as explained above. In this light there is no need to require any limitation on the academic freedom of the Roman Catholic theologian. "The Catholic University in the Modern World," a statement issued by the Second International Congress of Delegates of Catholic Universities, outlines such a process for institutions not juridically erected by Rome.[22] The Faculty Inquiry Board at The Catholic University of America proposed such an approach in its decision about the theologians who dissented from aspects of the papal teaching in *Humanae Vitae* condemning artificial contraception.[23] This section has attempted to establish the need of academic freedom for the Roman Catholic theologian in academe not merely on pragmatic grounds but on a theological consideration of the role of theology and its relation to the hierarchical magisterium. Such academic freedom should exist not only for the good of the Catholic university but also for the good of theology and of the whole Church.

IV

NEW CHURCH REGULATIONS, THEOLOGY, AND ACADEMIC FREEDOM

On April 15, 1979, Pope John Paul II issued *Sapientia Christiana*, an apostolic constitution containing the new law and regulations for ecclesiastical universities which are canonically erected and approved.[24] On the basis of these regulations, universities and faculties are to submit their statutes to the Sacred Congregation for Education for approval. All those who teach disciplines concerning faith or morals must receive a canonical mission from the chancellor of the university, "for they do not teach on their own authority but by virtue of the mission they have received from the Church" (art. 27). To acquire a tenured position or the highest faculty rank, the candidate needs a declaration of *nihil obstat* from the Holy See (art. 27). Also the document stresses that teachers are to carry on their work in full communion with the authentic magisterium of the Church (arts. 26, 70).

If interpreted literally and without any accommodation to local academic conditions, the constitution stands in opposition to the understanding proposed in this paper. According to the most obvious interpretation of the new apostolic constitution, the Catholic college and university is not autonomous but is a continuation of the teaching function of the hierarchical magisterium. Such a relationship explains why teachers need the *nihil obstat* from Rome and teachers in disciplines concerning faith and morals also need a canonical mission. In such a situation, there is no academic freedom because judgments about competency are not made by peers, and promotion and tenure depend on judgments made by Church authority as such.

In the light of this new document, one can point out clear differences emerging between the constitution and many Catholic educators. In the 1960's, the International Federation of Catholic Universities (IFCU) began considering the question of the nature and structure of a Catholic university. The Land O'Lakes statement quoted above was prepared by the North American region of the Federation in preparation for the meeting at Kinshasa in 1968, but that meeting did not accept the notion of autonomy and academic freedom proposed in the North American document. At the First International Congress of Delegates of Catholic Universities held in Rome in 1969 the positions proposed in the Land O'Lakes statement were generally acknowledged, but the Congregation for Education did not accept this document. Finally, the Second Congress issued its statement, "The Catholic University in the Modern

World," which accepted the basic wording of the Land O'Lakes statement calling for true autonomy and academic freedom in the Catholic university (n. 20). For institutions which are not canonically erected by Rome, the Congress document calls for procedures similar to those developed in the previous section of this article (n. 59). The Congregation had some misgivings about these aspects of the document, but allowed the document to be circulated as the work of the Congress.[25]

If the apostolic constitution is literally applied, it will mean that such canonically erected Catholic institutions cannot be true universities in the accepted sense of the term in the United States. Likewise, the theology done in such institutions will not have the necessary academic freedom to perform its function properly. As a result, canonically erected universities, Roman Catholic theology, and the good of the whole Church will suffer.

The apostolic constitution *Sapientia Christiana* applies only to pontifical universities and faculties, and hence would not affect most Catholic institutions of higher learning in the United States. However, the proposed new code of canon law, which will probably go into effect in the near future, in Canon 64 of Book III states that all who teach theology or disciplines related to theology in any Catholic institution of higher learning need a canonical mission. Again, if applied literally and without any accommodation to American academic principles, this legislation threatens the autonomy of all Catholic colleges and universities.

Notes

1. Arthur O. Lovejoy, "Academic Freedom," *Encyclopedia of the Social Sciences*, ed. by Edwin R. A. Seligman and Alvin Johnson (New York: Macmillan Co., 1930), p. 384.

2. Richard Hofstadter and Walter P. Metzger, *Academic Freedom in the United States* (New York: Columbia University Press, 1955).

3. For the significant documents, statements and actions of the AAUP together with important essays on academic freedom, see *Academic Freedom and Tenure: A Handbook of the American Association of University Professors*, ed. by Louis Joughin (Madison, Wisconsin: University of Wisconsin Press, 1969). Subsequent statements and actions of the AAUP are found in the *AAUP Bulletin*, which since 1979 is called *Academe: Bulletin of the AAUP*.

4. Louis Joughin, "Academic Due Process," in *Academic Freedom and Tenure*, pp. 264-305.

5. *Academic Freedom and Tenure*, p. 36.

6. Sidney Hook, *Heresy, Yes—Conspiracy, No* (New York: John Day Co., 1953), p. 220.

7. Robert M. McIver, *Academic Freedom in Our Time* (New York: Columbia University Press, 1955), pp. 134-146.

8. Cited by MacIver, p. 135.

9. Charles Donahue, "Freedom and Education: The Pluralist Background," *Thought*, 27 (1952-1953), pp. 542-560; "Freedom and Education: The Sacral Problem," *Thought*, 28 (1953-1954), pp. 209-233; "Freedom and Education, III: Catholicism and Academic Freedom," *Thought*, 29 (1954-1955), pp. 555-573; also, "Heresy and Conspiracy," *Thought*, 28 (1953-1954), pp. 528-546; Aldo J. Toss, "A Critical Study of American Views on Academic Freedom" (Ph.D. dissertation, The Catholic University of America, 1958).

10. Gerard F. Kreyche, "American Catholic Higher Learning and Academic Freedom," *National Catholic Education Association Bulletin*, 62 (August 1965), pp. 211-222. For historical information on academic freedom and Catholic institutions in the United States, see various writings of Philip Gleason including "Academic Freedom and the Crisis in Catholic Universities" in *Academic Freedom and the Catholic University*, ed. by Edward Manier and John W. Houck, (Notre Dame, Ind.: Fides Publishers, 1967), pp. 33-56. "Academic Freedom Survey, Retrospect and Prospects," *National Catholic Education Association Bulletin*, 64 (August 1967), pp. 67-74; "Freedom and the Catholic University," *National Catholic Education Association Bulletin*, 65 (November 1968), pp. 21-29.

11. For a book of significant articles based on that symposium and for a summary of the discussions that occurred, see *Academic Freedom and the Catholic University*, ed. by Edward Manier and John W. Houck.

12. Frederick Walter Gunti, "Academic Freedom as an Operative Principle for the Catholic Theologian" (S.T.D. dissertation, The Catholic University of America, 1969). For the 1958 dissertation, see Toss in note 9.

13. This document has been reprinted in many places. For the text of this and other documents on Catholic universities, together with significant essays on various aspects of academic freedom and the Catholic university in the contemporary world, see *The Catholic University: A Modern Appraisal*, ed. by Neil G. McCluskey (Notre Dame, Ind.: University of Notre Dame Press, 1970), p. 336.

14. "Freedom, Autonomy and the University," *IDOC International: North American edition*, 39 (January 15, 1972), pp. 86, 83.

15. John Tracy Ellis sparked the debate with his provocative article, "American Catholics and the Intellectual Life," *Thought*, 30 (1955), pp. 351-388. See also Walter J. Ong, *Frontiers in American Catholicism* (New York: Macmillan Co., 1957); Thomas F. O'Dea, *American Catholic Dilem-*

ma: An Inquiry into the Intellectual Life (New York: Sheed and Ward, 1958).

16. MacIver, Academic Freedom in Our Time, p. 141.

17. For an overview of these and other problems, see John Kelley, "Academic Freedom and the Catholic College Theologian" in Theology in Revolution, ed. by George Devine (Staten Island, New York: Alba House, 1970); pp. 169-183; John Tracy Ellis, "A tradition of Autonomy?" in The Catholic University: A Modern Appraisal, especially pp. 252-270. In 1967, the trustees of Catholic University did not renew the contract of a professor who had been unanimously approved by all the academic committees of the university for promotion. After a faculty and student strike lasting almost a week, the professor was given his contract and promotion. In 1968, twenty Catholic University professors signed a public statement of dissent from the specific teaching of Humanae Vitae condemning artificial contraception. Despite some significant abuses in procedures, the Catholic University trustees followed academic due process and ordered a hearing by a faculty board of inquiry which vindicated the statement and actions of the professors. See Charles E. Curran, Robert E. Hun, et al., Dissent In and For The Church: Theologians and "Humanae Vitae" (New York: Sheed and Ward, 1969), and John F. Hunt and Terence R. Connelly, The Reponsibility of Dissent: The Church and Academic Freedom (New York: Sheed and Ward, 1969). At Dayton one of the lay instructors charged several of his colleagues with heresy.

18. John E. Walsh, "The University and the Church" in Academic Freedom and the Catholic University, pp. 103-118.

19. My position here summarizes what has been developed at much greater length in the volumes mentioned in note 17. For similar approaches, see Gunti and Robert E. Hunt, "Academic Freedom and the Theologian," Proceedings of the Catholic Theological Society of America, 23 (1968), pp. 261-267.

20. For a recent summary of present-day discussions on the nature of hierarchical magisterium, see Chicago Studies, 17 (Summer 1978). This special issue is entitled "The Magisterium, the Theologian, and the Educator."

21. John Tracy Ellis, "A Tradition of Autonomy?" in The Catholic University: A Modern Appraisal, pp. 206-270.

22. This statement is published in a number of places including Catholic Mind, 71 (May 1973), pp. 25-44. This particular point is made at n. 59, pp. 42-43.

23. "Report of Catholic University Board of Inquiry Regarding Expressions of Theological Dissent by Faculty Members on Encyclical Humanae Vitae," AAUP Bulletin, 55 (June 1969), pp. 264-266. Interpretative comments by relevant committees on the 1940 Statement of AAUP show that most Church-related institutions no longer need or desire the departure from the principle of academic freedom implied in the 1940 Statement and the AAUP does not endorse such a departing. AAUP Bulletin, 56 (1970), pp. 166-167.

24. For an English translation, see *Origins: N.C. Documentary Service* 9, n. 3 (June 7, 1979), pp. 34-45.

25. For the history of these developments within regional and international groups of Catholic educators, see Neil G. McCluskey, "Introduction: This Is How It Happened," in *The Catholic University: A Modern Appraisal,* pp. 1-28, and Robert J. Henle, "Catholic Universities and the Vatican," *America,* 136 (April 9, 1977), pp. 315-322. It should be reported that a December 1976 meeting in Rome attended only by delegates of canonically erected universities and faculties (almost all American Catholic colleges and universities are not canonically erected except for some faculties at The Catholic University of America) voted in favor of a *nihil obstat* for tenured professors and for professors in the highest rank. See "Delegates Approve Vatican Consent for Professors," *Our Sunday Visitor,* 65 (December 19, 1976), p. 1.

The Collaboration of the Hierarchy and All Christians in Formulating Moral Norms

Philippe Delhaye

One of the current and truly relevant issues of our day has to do with the respective impact of the hierarchy, priests, and the faithful on the formulation and authority of moral and juridical norms. I should like to consider several aspects of the issue here.

There is a great temptation to view the problem under consideration in terms of a certain dualism. There on one side we have the hierarchy formulating laws and precepts and giving orders. Here on the other side we have those who are not part of the teaching Church: priests and lay people have no active role to play; they must rest content with a purely passive role. Within a sociological perspective which places almost exclusive stress on authority and its rights, priests and lay people have only one possibility open to them: they must obey and execute. Humorists, of course, observe that "all the force of superiors is tempered by the ill will of inferiors," and there is a tendency to stay within that basic outlook. I don't think we get away from it when we try to institutionalize that resistance with the theory of *receptio*. The French *parlements* did that with the disciplinary decrees of Trent (with the exception of *Tametsi*); later on, Gallicanism and Febronianism combined to extend it far beyond the purely disciplinary domain. There was talk about the necessity of the doctrinal teachings of Popes and councils being accepted. Quite recently some theologians arrogated to themselves the right of *receptio* or *non-receptio*. They claimed that a fair number of episcopal letters expressed prudent regrets about *Humanae Vitae*,[1] and they themselves went so far as to set themselves up as judges of the magisterium, as *magistri magisterii*.

It is not just that I find it difficult to reconcile such a claim with the teachings of conciliar and papal tradition.[2] I also find two major flaws which vitiate this effort at its very core. First of all, this claim for the necessity of acceptance (*receptio*) adopts the standpoint and outlook of a false dualism. Of course there is a duality between the hierarchy and the other members of the Church. However, the Church is one, first and foremost, and it carries out its praxis and its work of formulation in an ongoing process of exchange and collaboration.[3] More serious still is the fact that the theory of absolute obedience and the theory of *receptio* totally ignore concrete facts. Take the conciliar and post-conciliar experience of collaboration, the work of committees created by episcopal conferences. For people who have had these experiences the distinction urged in the above view becomes increasingly blurred in the concrete, however much it may retain its value in principle. Consider how many conciliar and episcopal texts have been drawn up by *periti*, inspired by pastoral teams, and endorsed by Church authorities with little or no modification. And this phenomenon is not a new one, though there may be a little more publicity about it all today. Just recently we saw the publication of the rough drafts of certain interventions by Pius XII. His statements were particularly clear-cut, yet they were wholly drawn up by a Jesuit professor at the Gregorian.[4]

What I want to do, then, is explore a different tack: not the approach of dualism and opposition but rather the approach of collaboration. I mean authentic, energetic collaboration, which nevertheless respects the specific nature of the roles involved. I can only hope to hit the high points here, of course. So I will consider the following aspects of collaboration: (1) Christ, the hierarchy, and the faithful in their threefold dimension as prophets, priests, and kings; (2) the "sociology" or concrete aspects of hierarchical teaching; (3) the magisterium and dialogue.

I

CHRIST, THE HIERARCHY, AND THE FAITHFUL
IN THEIR THREEFOLD DIMENSION
AS PROPHETS, PRIESTS, AND KINGS

If we are attentive to the aspect of *koinonia* in the Christian moral effort, then we have every reason to show how the Church is a milieu of divine-moral life in accordance with Christ's threefold dimension as prophet, priest, and king. It is true, of course, that these prerogatives and responsibilities are found in the Church, in continuity with Christ, on different grounds and terms (*Lumen Gentium*, Chapters 3 and 4). But the fact remains that this classic division offers us a clearer picture of the different facets of the transformation wrought in human praxis by the Lord Jesus, the Revealer and Redeemer.

Some have feared that the influence of Calvin might be at work here.[5] They forget that back in the fourteenth century the *Roman Catechism* developed this theme at length.[6] Moreover, the formula itself is used by Thomas Aquinas[7] to point up the perfection of Christ's work vis-à-vis the divine envoys who preceded him: "Quantum ad alios pertinet, alius est legislator, et alius sacerdos, et alius rex, sed haec omnia in Christo tanquam in fonte omnium gratiarum." Christ is simultaneously the successor and the surpasser of Moses, Aaron, and David. Eusebius of Caesarea[8] is credited with being the first to explicitly propose this tripartite systematization, but he merely codified what Christian art and thought had been expressing for a long time. Christ is presented as the prophet, the *didaskalos*, the teacher. Holding a volume in his hand, he is surrounded by the apostles, his historical witnesses, and by the faithful, his witnesses in the world. The shepherd and king is both the one who finds the lost sheep and the chief who rules the flock. The crucified Christ is the priest who may be surrounded by Mary, the holy women, and John or who may be surrounded by the faithful in the Sacrifice of the Mass. It is because of its theocentric character and its summons to collaboration on the part of the faithful that the theme of Christ as priest, king, and revealer took on such importance in Catholic Action during the pontificates of Pius XI and Pius XII. The work of Catholic Action clearly had an impact on the redaction of *Lumen Gentium*, and of Chapter 4 in particular.

Thus let us consider briefly how the faithful, priests, bishops, and the Pope may collaborate—in differing but real ways—in the sanctifying work of Christ under the three headings of teaching, ministerial or common priesthood, and "kingship."

Christ's *opus propheticum* is carried out in a primordial way by the apostles and their successors: "Euntes ergo docete omnes gentes, baptizantes eos . . . docentes eos servare omnia quaecumque mandavi vobis" (Mt. 28:18). One need only read Paul's letters to see that the apostle to the pagans is aware that he is exercising a real kind of authority in this domain (see 1 Thes. 1:5; 1 Cor. 2:1-4; Rom. 1:16; also see 1 Thes. 2:2, 7, 11-13; 4:11). The apostle speaks in the name of the Lord and teaches commandments. But we must also note another point of view. The Holy Spirit teaches morality in the hearts of the faithful (1 Thes. 3:3; 4:9, 11). The word of God is at work in Christians (1 Thes. 2:13). The latter engage in witness and rivalry vis-à-vis those without and those within (1 Thes. 1:3, 7-9; 3:6-7; 4:12). The faithful offer each other mutual comfort through the faith they believe and practice (1 Thes. 4:18), and they display courage (1 Thes. 5:8). Imitation goes on between them (1 Thes. 1:6; 2:14). We note here a more clear-cut collaboration than that of which we were speaking above. But this collaboration is not just horizontal, as some put it today; it is also vertical.

This verticalness surfaces even more clearly in the Letter to the Galatians. The apostle is in conflict with this particular community. He recalls his authority, which is not attached to his person but to the Lord's revelation, to the demands of faith, and to the action of the divine *pneuma* (Gal. 1:1, 8-9, 11-12; 2:8-9; 4:14; 5:6). Within the confines of this divine action there is still room for an area of possible confrontation between Paul and the other apostles, between Paul and Peter himself (Gal. 1:13–2:14), and among the faithful (Gal. 6:1-6).

The ecclesial aspect of the Christian moral life shows up also in the *opus sacaerdotale*. One merit of the liturgical movement has been its stress on the link between the sacramental life and the moral life (Heb. 7:12). Once upon a time people only talked about the link between the two insofar as it derived from the virtue of religion; here religion, as was the case with Cicero, was viewed merely as a duty of justice. The Christian moral life is the existential and logical result of the divinization of the human being by the Spirit: "Caritas diffusa est in cordibus nostris per Spiritum Sanctum qui datus est nobis" (Rom. 5:5). Now this divine life, which is to be translated into a moral life, is given to us essentially through the sacraments: baptism, the Eucharist, confirmation, penance, etc. To the sacrament of the sacrifice of the Eucharist, liturgical gatherings add sacramentals and the word of God. The Emmaus meal is indeed the sign of this action through the explication of the word and the breaking of bread. To this action, which exists principally in the pastors and ministers of the New Testament, is added the collaboration of the faithful through the exercise of their common priesthood (*Lumen Gentium*, nn. 11, 33-34). It is not certain that the post-conciliar period has always understood this doctrine correctly. Some may well have fallen back into Lutheran excesses. But the active link between the sacramental and moral life avoids this danger. It even has the advantage of forewarning Christians against any secularization of morality.

Sacerdotium regale (royal priesthood): the term is true of Christ and the hierarchy even before being applicable to all the faithful. Christ is to realize his primacy through his Church (Col. 1:18). Once upon a time people may well have made the mistake of applying the juridical concepts of political states to the Church without sufficient analogy. Today, however, the danger is that people will make the opposite mistake, that they will deny any institutional, juridical structure to the Church. But even a community of faith and charity cannot live without laws and norms. St. Paul gives precepts. Under the leadership of the apostles, the first Christian communities immediately formulated laws: e.g., on the preconditions for entering ministries, on the weekly celebration of the resurrection on Sunday rather than Saturday, and on the concrete conditions of marriages. But we can also learn some lessons from other viewpoints to be found in the communities headed by the apostles and the *viri apostolici*. The aim of those laws and the precepts is not domination but charity: "Finis praecepti caritas" (1 Tim. 1:5). The aim is to promote the kingdom of charity and grace, the kingdom of justice, love, and peace, as *Lumen Gentium* reminds us (n. 36, echoing the Preface for the Feast of Christ the King) in discussing the *opus regale* specifically. In this connection we should perhaps encourage fresh, more energetic reflection on the function of laws. Their aim is to point up the practical and communitarian consequences of certain fundamental requirements (e.g., the prayer specified by the Sunday law, the breviary). Their aim is also to establish a minimum below which one cannot go, and to make people aware of the sin committed (1 Tim. 1:8-11).

A second lesson from the apostolic era is undoubtedly that of collaboration between the faithful and their pastors. Without doubt it is the latter who have the right and the duty to pass judgment in the first instance; however, merely on the level of pastoral care and effectiveness, they do well to take into account the *praxis fidelium*, their customs.

As numerous canonists have shown, this is how a good portion of ecclesiastical legislation has taken shape, grounded on the base and nurtured with the critical judgment of the hierarchy.

II
The "Sociology" or Concrete Aspects of Hierarchical Teaching

One of the most striking features of our time is the tendency to look at problems in their concrete reality and to attribute less importance to legal aspects.

One reason for this is that people have abandoned an essentialist, deductive type of philosophy for an existential, inductive one. This may be done unconsciously, but it is a worldwide trend. Another reason is the indiscretion of the media of social communication, which have broadcast the underside of things. When a papal document appears, people are more readily inclined to ask who the author of the text is than to consider what teaching the Pope wants to present. It is very significant that Hans Küng's attacks on the infallibility of the Pope take as their starting point a document that is not infallible but that Catholic opinion readily treats as infallible.

Here, then, I would like to consider the concrete conditions in which Catholic opinion experienced the publication of papal and episcopal documents over the past twenty years or so. Three periods should be distinguished, in my opinion: the period which runs from Pius IX to Pius XII, the period of conciliar "reorientation," and, finally, a period of post-conciliar suspicion.

From Pius XI to Pius XII

Insofar as documents of the last century are concerned, we can see this official pattern unfolding almost universally. First a group of Christians poses some question to the Pope (and to the Pope alone). He then gives a response. This response is commented on by bishops and theologians. Let us look at this pattern in greater detail.

First of all a question is raised, often because of new circumstances. In the nineteenth century the condition of workers was deteriorating. Marxism presented its solution: class struggle. Closer to today, contraception spread and people sought "Catholic" solutions in the Ogino or Chanson method. Doctors perfected techniques of painless childbirth, but Catholics were worried about them: "In pain you shall bring forth children" (Gen. 3:16). Sometimes circumstances forced a question into the open; sometimes opinion was the motivating factor. During the pontificate of Pius XII, we not infrequently saw conventions in Rome publicly or privately posing questions to the Pope. He alluded to this in his discourses.

At the second stage, Roman authority intervened. Leo XIII published the encyclical *Rerum Novarum*. It was taken over with adaptations in *Quadragesimo Anno* (Pius XI) and *Pacem in Terris* (John XXIII). Contraception was condemned by Pius XI on December 31, 1929, in *Casti Connubii*, in a polemical tone directed against Lambeth. But Pius XII allowed for the regulation of births and justified the Ogino method, still suspect to some, in his discourse to Italian midwives, who had presented their case of conscience to him (1951). The therapeutic use of the anovulant pill was permitted in 1958, but recourse to it as a means of birth control was condemned in a discourse to physicians who had raised the problem. The troubles surrounding decolonization raised the problem of the raping of nuns in tragic terms. The Holy Office did not intervene directly, but three theologians belonging to that tribunal offered a positive response in a concerted way and with a noticeably authoritative tone. By contrast the Chanson method was declared suspect by the Holy Office in an official decree.

This second stage, clearly enough, was typically Roman. It involved interventions of varying degrees. To stay with the examples cited above, there were the encyclicals of Leo XIII, Pius XI, and John XXIII. There were discourses by Pius XII, who liked this type of teaching and who excelled at it. There were decrees of Roman Congregations, such as those of the Holy Office. The latter has gained a monopoly over this type of intervention, which it still shared with the Sacred Penitentiary in the nineteenth century. And there were interventions by authorized theologians.

In the mind of a theologian who studies the *loci theologici* or who ponders the methodology of his discipline, there are real differences among these four types of expression by the magisterium. But we must admit the fact that all these documents were put on almost exactly the same footing by the vast majority of Catholics. A French journalist, Ageorge, used to write a "Paris Bulletin" for *La Libre Belgique*, a conservative Catholic journal in Brussels. Shortly before the 1940 war he stated: "Some would like to make a distinction between acts of the magisterium in which the Pope is infallible and those in which he is not. This idea won't stand up. If the Pope is infallible then, to me he is infallible always."

At most some people might have dared to question the religious authority of papal theologians and to judge their remarks on the basis of their arguments. But they were reminded that theologians possessed authority provided that the Pope recognized them as such and did not censure them. The *Institutiones morales* of Fr. Genicot and Fr. Salsmans used the same idea to advocate probabilism: this "moral system" had been taught since the seventeenth century at the Roman College, which later became the Gregorian University. The Popes would never have permitted so close to home the teaching of a false doctrine that would be broadcast throughout the world with the prestige of Rome behind it. Hence that system is correct.

Now, in the third stage, this curial teaching was to move on to the "peripheral" Church. Professors of theology and Scholastic philosophy, in particular, were asked to provide commentaries on the papal documents and to defend them against objections. Intellectual obedience applied not only to the theses but also to methods and arguments. The angry attack of Rev. Huerth against Jacques Leclercq, who wanted to give value to the evangelical argument and inject social dimensions in a "privative" moraltiy, was total and decisive. The work on the *Teaching of Christian Morality* had to be withdrawn from circulation.

The argument from authority (*ex magisterio*, often linked up with the argument *ex patribus*) of dogmatic theologians did not occupy a place between Scripture and natural law. It was everything. Furthermore, it was this argument that transformed natural law into a doctrine of the Church. No critical reflection was allowed. Indeed professors of theology were so conditioned by their training that they did not dream of indulging in personal reflection.

Through current controversies we get a better picture of certain aspects that once were taken for granted. Under Pius XII the real theologians were the curialists, and they alone. Concretely that meant certain professors in the Roman universities and Congregations, particularly those who were consultors of the Holy Office. They would have been astonished to see bishops giving preference to experts or *periti* chosen by the bishops themselves during Vatican II, or in the theological commissions of the post-conciliar period. They would never have granted that some professor should be recognized as a theologian on the sole basis of his scholarly competence.

Moreover, at that point in time the work of the theologian was viewed primarily under the heading of teaching as determined by the theologian's *missio canonica*. Little thought was given to the aspects of research or contact with modern culture, which would require greater liberty and personal responsibility.

The Period of the Council

Here we must first note a calling into question (not always explicit but real enough) of the conditions surrounding the exercise of the magisterium in Pius XII's manner.

For example, insofar as the first stage is concerned, people noted that the role of lay people, priests, peripheral theologians, and bishops for that matter did not consist solely in posing questions to Rome (or denouncing people who disagreed with them to Rome). They also had to think and live as lucid Christians, to accept their responsibilities, and to search for solutions. Of course authority had the right to have the last word, but that did not mean it always or even frequently had the first word. Consider *Rerum Novarum*, for example. From the study of the archives we know today that this encyclical was prepared in direct conjunction with bishops and social groups of Catholics. Their involvement was evident on the two planes of thought and action (Bishop Ketteler, the Fribourg Union).

At the second stage, people now relativized the *motu proprio* character of papal acts. Very few thought that the Pope was the "prisoner of the Curia," though some claimed it was so. Only as a joke did people recount the harsh remark of Luc Verus in 1932: "Holy Father, have you read your encyclicals?" They knew that Pius XII and Paul VI realized very well what they had in mind when they prepared their documents. But they also were aware of the importance of the preliminary work done under Pius XII by the group of Jesuit priests under the direction of Father Leiber. When one wanted to know the exact meaning of an ambiguous phrase in John XXIII's *Pacem in Terris* concerning religious liberty, one now found it natural to ask Msgr. Pavan, the chief drafter of the encyclical. And one was hardly astonished when he replied that an ambiguous phrasing was finally chosen so as not to arouse the annoyance of the Holy Office. Every French newspaper presented *Populorum Progressio* as the work of the late Father Lebret. The "Roman" theologians—or the "Curia" theologians to be more exact, since the two groups are not identical—vaunted their supremacy by presenting their prefabricated schemas to the bishops arriving for Vatican II. And when the wind turned against them, it was with some chagrin and pain that the participants observed the tortuous maneuvers of some of those Curia theologians to win alterations in already approved texts by non-conciliar means. All that certainly has "relativized" the interventions of Church authority. But the principles remain and they can be safeguarded while still integrating them into a new analysis.

It must be pointed out clearly that Vatican II in no way called into question the hierarchical character of the Church and the essential, decisive role of the magisterium. Chapter 3 (n. 25) of *Lumen Gentium* provides a terse teaching on this matter. More than any other Council it insists upon the duty of the faithful to give religious assent of intellect and will to the non-infallible teachings of the Pope, ecumenical councils, and the universal ordinary magisterium of the episcopal body gathered around Peter's successor. This has particular importance in the area of morals, where infallible decisions are rare.

But while the responsibilities of the magisterium were reaffirmed in the most solemn manner, the conditions for exercising this responsibility were modified. Alongside documents from the Pope and the Roman Congregations we now have the teaching of episcopal conferences. The scope and authority of the latter are far greater than that of "pastoral letters" in an earlier day. The case is blatantly obvious with regard to problems of marriage and sexuality. The expositions are more positive, biblical, and pastoral. They relate to questions from the faithful now, rather than to questions asked by priests. In drawing up these texts bishops often give theologians a degree of responsibility akin to that of people who are consultors. The synods are places where reflection and research go on in a new style, and lay people have been invited to express themselves in a dialogue that is authentic even if a bit asymmetric (*Lumen Gentium*, n. 37).

So whence comes the general impression that Vatican II and the hierarchical Church have become totally lax, abdicating their authority in favor of permissiveness? The answer is undoubtedly complicated and cannot be fully given here.

1. It can hardly be denied that there is a crisis of authority in this area. One day Cardinal Daniélou said to me: "I pointed out certain specific errors to three top people. They replied: 'Mistakes have been made so often in condemning theologians that it is much better not to do that any more.'" Others will point to pressures from the media of social communications, which force a hands-off

policy with regard to the very things taught that snub the faith of the Church.

2. Alongside this crisis there is the fact that the conciliar Church, as some imagine it, wanted to experiment with a style of doctrinal and moral teaching akin to that exercised in Protestant denominations. Instead of condemning the errors of the time, said John XXIII at the opening of Vatican II, let us teach the truth in a positive way. Linking up with the ancient tradition, Vatican II did not pronounce anathemas. Above all, I think, we must note the Council's new way of expressing itself. The Council did not teach in its own name, make affirmations in the name of its own authority, or offer arguments of its own stamp. Its teaching was presented essentially as a relaying of God's word, of which the bishops wanted to be witnesses and servants. To some who were used to the older way the difference was great because at first it seemed as if they were listening to a pious exhortation. Time for reflection was needed for them to realize that the authority invoked was still there, not so much on the level of the bishops as pastors but on the more remote level of the Gospel message, of which the bishops are the interpreters.

3. Finally, and this must be said, the novelty of the method was particularly apparent in the area of morals. The Council did not enact precise laws. Following the evangelical approach, it placed the main stress on the basic framework behind the laws, on the chief motivations, principles and intentions. On that basis it summoned each person to assume his responsibilities. Canon law did not lose its utility or necessity, of course, but it was to be re-examined in a new perspective, and the colonialism it had exercised over morality was to be ended.

After Ten Years of Concrete Experience

Now we see signs of startled alarm. People are beginning to realize that the experiment with permissiveness needs to be criticized. After ten years of a new style in the exercise of doctrinal, moral, and pastoral authority, very different tendencies are manifesting themselves. These, too, deserve mention here.

As we celebrate the tenth anniversary of the closing of Vatican II, some prelates, theologians, and lay people have taken stock and expressed reservations about what has been going on. It is not a matter of wiping away Vatican II but rather of making a distinction between it and a post-conciliar thrust that has given it a meaning quite different from that intended by the Council Fathers. Moreover, some feel that the lessons learned from experience are inescapable: i.e., that we must add shadings to the measures of liberalization. History has always known such swings of the pendulum.

In some countries a crisis of authority is observed. Bishops and the Pope are suspect from the very outset. They take a back seat to the media of social communication (which often are in the hands of leftists or former seminarians with complexes). Certain pastors, therefore, are afraid to intervene or they believe that it is useless. Their warning call, however, would tell many distressed priests and lay people where the faith of the Church lies and what morality they should follow. It should be made with all fairness and prudence, of course. If certain Christians have doubts about the divinity of Jesus or the apostolicity of ministers, they invoke the authority of a Schillebeeckx or a Hans Küng; the latter would not be permitted to teach if they were in error, say these Christians. This points up the necessity of finding effective ways to issue admonitions while still respecting persons and freedom of research.

Many theologians, priests, and lay people feel an unhealthy need to release their pent-up problems and to provoke authority. "Nothing has ever been gained," they say, "except by disobedience." All people and things Christian are suspect to them in their identity crisis; on the other hand all other people and things seem to be right every time, whether they be protesters, advocates of secularization, or Marxists. It reminds one very much of the symptoms evident at the time of the French Revoltuion in 1789. Many priests and lay people had already joined the *philosophes* in spirit before ten years of collective madness broke upon all of Europe.

To combat this trend of thought and emotion, a twofold course of action is clearly needed: one on the level of thought, the other on the level of affectivity. We must stress the purity, the authenticity of the faith and explore it more deeply in the light of the magisterium. The latter must teach tirelessly, as Paul VI did on behalf of Christian morality. Many episcopates did likewise.

An effort at clarification and putting things in their proper place is necessary. Theologians must be reminded that their scholarly competence and their academic freedom, properly recognized, remain subject to the magisterium. Priestly and pastoral councils as well as pressure groups must remember that they are valuable organs of dialogue and information but that they do not constitute a parliament.

We need not believe that every wave of opinion is necessarily a sign of the times or a message from God. Christ spoke against the prevailing current and refused to say what the Jews were expecting from the Messiah. Nor need we believe that the human being is naturally good (as did Jean Jacques Rousseau), or that everything is already in human beings before the activity of the Church and Christ. *Veritas et gratia per Jesum Christum factae sunt* (Jn. 1:17). Revelation and grace come through the Church even though the Spirit prepares human beings within.

Authority should not end up as the spirit of domination; its spirit is that of the Gospel message itself. By the same token, however, an authority that lacks force and evinces self-doubt does not fulfill its mission. Christ speaks in the Father's name, the apostles in Christ's name and the Pope and the bishops in the name of Christ and the apostles.

Without being pessimistic, one finds it difficult to avoid the conclusion that we are far from riding the crest of the wave. But we must be clear-eyed. We must never cease to believe in the Spirit's work of assisting the Church or in Christ's privileged presence in our midst through the ministry of his Vicar and other representatives. It is very likely that historians with the eyes of faith will one day be able to detect the finger of God in all the data mentioned above. Then they will be able to sort matters out. They will be able to point out the essentials pertaining to Christ as revealer, Savior, and pastor, who is always present in his Church through the various hierarchical ministries and the fervor of all. And they will be able to distinguish those essentials from the transient historical and cultural aspects of his presence which must be revitalized and revivified in new forms.

III
THE MAGISTERIUM AND DIALOGUE

Here we might be tempted to mark a transition by saying something like this: Having talked about theologians and *periti*, let us now consider the place of lay people. The point would be well taken insofar as lay people do enjoy a certain preeminence, but we would be falsifying the problem nevertheless because we would be falling back into the dualism we wished to avoid. For dialogue does not just bring lay people on the one hand into contact with the Pope and the bishops on the other. It is also a reality among priests, who stand at the junction between two "orders." It takes place between lay people themselves, just as it takes place between bishops themselves (e.g., in the Synod of Bishops or in episcopal conferences). To go even further, we can say that it allows those who intend to remain outside the visible Church to express themselves and have some impact on the life of Christians. Here, too, the vital and necessary viewpoint based on ecclesial institutions must be complemented by perspectives of a more psychological nature.

I certainly have no illusions about the ambiguity of the term "dialogue" and the consequences resulting from the distortions to which it has been subjected over the past fifteen years. But this is not the first time in the history of ideas that years were needed to refine a theme and spell it out correctly. What should be pointed out here, briefly at least, is the fact that praxis has its contribution to make to the enunciation of principles and laws. It tells us the impact of a common mentality that we will call the voice or signs of the time, and even of a certain manifestation of that mentality in surveys and inquiries. To repeat, here lay people occupy a choice place, but it is not theirs exclusively. Rather than going back over this point, I would merely remind you what *Lumen Gentium* had to say on the matter. It clearly indicated that the term "people of God" is not to be equated completely with the laity. Bishops, too, have a moral experience of the utmost value, and it cannot help but guide them in issuing their directives. Moreover, in surveys and inquiries those outside the visible Church can suggest questions and pose challenges to the magisterium, priests, and the faithful. Thus it is on several levels and in several directions that this inquiry, or projected inquiry at least, is pursued.

Fides Moribus Applicanda

More than one text of Vatican II shows us that the people of God are not ones who merely carry out the directives given by the hierarchy. To this exterior action of structures corresponds the interior action of the divine *pneuma*. Since the law has been interiorized, it is normal that it be assumed, understood, mulled over, and judged. When St. John addresses his directives and his counsels to the readers of his First Epistle, he indicates that he is counting on the assistance of this inner teacher: "But the anointing which you received from him abides in you, and you have no need that anyone should teach you; as his anointing teaches you about everything, and is true, and is no lie, just as it has taught you, abide in him" (1 Jn. 2:27). The Johannine context makes clear that faith entails truths not only to be believed but also lived.

Lumen Gentium underlined this point somewhat insistently. Just consider the phrase *fidem credendam et moribus applicandam* (n. 25). The *sensus fidei* has a moral aspect as well: "The holy people of God shares also in Christ's prophetic office. It spreads abroad a living witness to him, especially by means of *a life of faith and charity*. . . . The body of the faithful as a whole, anointed as they are by the Holy One (cf. Jn. 2:20, 27), cannot err in matters of belief. Thanks to a supernatural sense of the faith, which characterizes the people as a whole, it manifests this unerring quality when, 'from the bishops down to the last member of the laity,' it shows universal agreement in matters of *faith and morals*. For, by this sense of faith . . . God's people . . . clings without fail to the faith once delivered to the saints, penetrates it more deeply by accurate insights, and *applies it more thoroughly to life*. And this it does under the lead of a sacred teaching authority to which it loyally defers" (*Lumen Gentium*, n. 12).

Under these conditions obedience in no way rules out exchanges of views, shouldering of responsibilities, and appeals to experience. We read that a bit further on in the same document: "By reason of their knowledge, their competence, and their worthy position, lay people are permitted and sometimes even obliged to state their opinion on those matters which concern the welfare of the Church. . . . In the spirit of Christian obedience the laity, as all the faithful, should promptly accept the things which their bishops decide as teachers and rulers in the Church. . . . A great many benefits are to be expected from this familiar exchange between lay people and their bishops. It will strengthen the laity's *sense of personal responsibility*, stimulate enthusiasm, and make it easier to link up their abilities with the work of their bishops. The latter, aided by the *laity's experience*, can make clearer and better judgments on both spiritual and temporal matters . . . " (*Lumen Gentium*, n. 37; my italics).

The Signs of the Times

Another aspect of the dialogue mentality shows up in what has come to be called the "signs of the times" since John XXIII used the term. It is an effort in the "discernment of spirits," to use the sixteenth-century term, or, more profoundly, of *dokimazein* in Paul's sense.[10] This effort takes place on different levels. It may be the whole structured people of God—the Pope, bishops, priests, and faithful—confronting the ensemble of human beings (the "world of today," as *Gaudium et Spes* put it). It may be the pastors of the Church meeting the laity. Or it may be lay people dealing with each other. The distinctions are all the more inept insofar as a bishop is also one of Christ's faithful, in the sense used by St. Augustine and noted earlier (see note 3) as well as a person living in a certain age and culture.

In any case it seems we must distinguish two main stages in talking about the signs of the times. The first stage is primarily sociological, the second primarily theological.

First of all, one must take cognizance of facts and events and try to grasp their import. On July 14, 1789, a crowd of Parisians took over the Bastille, the royal fortress and state prison which symbolized autocratic power. King Louis XVI kept a personal diary in which he recorded events and his own reactions to them. That day he wrote in his diary: "Nothing." Some people certainly saw the event as far more significant, as signaling the start of a more thoroughgoing revolution than the labors of the Estates-General might suggest. Nevertheless it is doubtful that many people of the day attributed to the event the profound sense that the Third Republic did later when that date was established as the great national holiday of the French nation.

Who of us is capable of saying what import should be given to the cultural revolution at the Sorbonne in May 1968? Some see it as little more than a "highway accident"; some see it as the initial outbreak of a new world; others view it as a menace that must be combated. What we are dealing with here is an instance for the "discernment of spirits" which spirituality has tended to apply to the level of the individual alone. Where is the grace of God manifesting its power? Toward what is God guiding human beings? John XXIII seems at times to have had recourse to the criterion of how generalized a datum was. Human beings as a whole, amid their most varied circumstances, are particularly sensitive today to the whole issue of personal dignity. To some extent women everywhere are protesting against the inferior situation foisted upon them. Efforts on behalf of the rights of the human person, and of women in particular, would thus be "signs of the time."

A second stage (and criterion) would be theological. The ensemble of human beings forces Christian reflection to ponder a particular fact or event in the light of the Gospel message. Cardijn sees in the suffering of laborers the inescapable need for social reform. Helder Camara probes the scandal of non-development in a "charismatic" manner. The task of grasping the meaning of human history in order to perceive there the import of salvation history is a task incumbent on all Christians. It calls for lofty spiritual appreciation, but also for ongoing contact with phenomena. In that sense it is indeed the business of all Christians who want to know what God expects of them. This aspect must be increasingly stressed in the face of certain post-conciliar abuses. In the light of the abuses, this second stage becomes increasingly important and necessary. John XXIII took it for normal and natural because the controlling influence of the faith was quite strong in the context where he was speaking. Within a system of authority he inserted recourse to lived experience and public opinion. Not long afterward, however, Paul VI saw a need to lay stress on this second stage of hierarachical control. Indeed he began to do so even before Vatican II was over.

How much more necessary that is today! For the problem is not simply that of the exercise of authority; it has to do with essential Christian themes that are being jeopardized.

For example, some implicitly or explicitly assert that Christian revelation did not close with the age of Christ, the apostles, and the *viri apostolici*. They say that it continues in history today. In the evolution of outlooks and events God allegedly enables us to perceive what he expects of us in the future.[11]

More generally, we hear people claiming that every idea, even a "revealed" one, reflects a certain culture. If that culture changes or disappears, then the religious or moral idea is changed by that very fact. May I spell out my own thinking here by citing an example which I myself was confronted with quite recently? A Catholic man, noted for his fervor and enlightened outlook, told me that the discovery of the birth-control pill had changed sexual morality. In his eyes it had broken the divinely willed link between conjugal intimacy and procreation. Hence premarital relations could be permitted. There was no danger of an unexpected birth.

One possible doctrinal backdrop for the theory of the signs of the time might be mentioned: i.e., the Hegelian idea that there is no objective truth but rather an equivalence of contraries through evolution. Every idea goes through three stages: thesis, antithesis, synthesis. All are equally worthwhile on the plane of praxis, which is the criterion of Christianity. Orthopraxis takes priority over orthodoxy.

Finally, we see here a rebirth of sociologism. The old theory of Auguste Comte has come back to life. What everyone thinks is true and objective is so; what everyone does is moral.

Sociological Surveys

Some people readily move from "signs of the time" to sociological surveys. Recently one professor told me how shocked and annoyed he was to find some of his priest students identifying the two in such naive fashion. Paul VI spoke about sociological surveys on several occasions, most notably in his Apostolic Exhortation of December 8, 1970. He pointed up their usefulness for becoming acquainted with people's opinions, but he also denied their validity as a norm.

Experience increasingly proves that this type of investigation can be very dangerous. To begin with, there is the problem of the selection and competence of the people surveyed. When *Humanae Vitae* was issued, a peripheral radio station quickly organized a survey among merchants of a particular neighborhood and passengers on a bus.

Moreover, when it is not a question of morality, we constantly find people indulging in the sophistry of moving from fact to norm: "That is done; therefore it is permissible to do it." Since that is the way people live today, one can live that way. It is today's way of inverting the old idea of emulating one's betters: *Quod isti, cur non ego?*

A recent publication offered several criteria and counsels with regard to this whole subject:[12]

• A distinction must be made between what is sociologically normal (indicated by averages) and what is morally normal.

• Any reading of averages must be complemented by an examination of distribution figures. Alongside a broad average group of lukewarm people we find minorities composed of great sinners and great saints.

• Behavior patterns must be distinguished from opinions. A division into two or three relatively equal groups may simply indicate a confused or baffled opinion.

• Different interpretations must be compared.

• Turn the questions back on the questioners.

• Exercise normal judgment in examining why and in what way we are interested in this particular question; figure out the moral values at issue; explore where the tendencies presented as models lead.

• Apply the rules for the discernment of spirits. They can be found in many places: e.g., the discussion of charisms in 1 and 2 Corinthians, modern spiritual writers and, of course, Ignatius of Loyola.

Notes

1. Very much is made of a statement by Newman about the rights of conscience vis-à-vis the authority of the Pope (Letter to the Duke of Norfolk, Longman's edition, 1891, II, p. 285), which was cited by the bishops of the United States and by Bishop Heusclein (*Pour relire Humanae Vitae*, nn. 3-5). However, it seems that there are substantial differences between conscientious doubt and *receptio*. (a) The theory of *receptio* turns the opinion of the faithful into a criterion superior to that of the hierarchy. (b) *Receptio* confuses truth and value considered in themselves with the way in which human beings gain access to them. Today we again find a tendency to deny an objective truth in the name of the rights of the subject. (c) Conscientious doubt, be it doctrinal or practical, is an individual matter. One changes its entire meaning and goes beyond its limits when one turns it into a "collective conscience" setting itself up as an anti-authority.

2. Both at Vatican I (DS 3074) and at Vatican II the necessity of any *receptio* by the Church was ruled out in the case of infallible definitions. Remember what *Lumen Gentium* (n. 25) said: "This is the infallibility which is enjoyed by the Roman Pontiff, the head of the episcopal college in virtue of his office when, as the supreme pastor and teacher of all Christ's faithful who confirms his brethren in the faith (cf. Lk. 22:32), he makes a definitive pronouncement on a doctrine of faith and morals. Thus his definitions, of themselves and not from the Church's consent, are rightly called unalterable — for they are propounded with the assistance of the Holy Spirit promised to him in the person of St. Peter, and hence they do not need any approval from others; nor do they allow for recourse to another judgment. In these instances the Roman Pontiff is not pronouncing judgment as a private person; rather, as the supreme teacher of the universal Church in whom the Church's charism of infallibility resides in a singular way, he is propounding or preserving the teaching of the Catholic faith." The Pope's non-infallible teaching is discussed just prior to the above remarks in the same section of *Lumen Gentium*. Such teaching is to be given "religious assent of intellect and will" (n. 25).

3. This is brought out nicely in another section where *Lumen Gentium* is speaking of the laity (n. 32): "By God's good pleasure, then, the laity have Christ for their brother. He, though he is the Lord of all, came not to be served but to serve (cf. Mt. 20:28). The laity also have for their brothers those in the sacred ministry who, by teaching, sanctifying and ruling with Christ's authority, nourish God's family so that the new commandment of charity may be fulfilled by all. St. Augustine puts it very beautifully: "My relationship to you frightens me, my association with you consoles me. For I am linked to you as your bishop, associated with you as a Christian. The former represents a duty, the latter a grace. The former is a source of danger, the latter a source of salvation."

4. See J. Schwarte, *Gustav Gundlach, S.J.: Massgeblicher Repräsentant der Katholischen Soziallehre während der Pontificate Pius XI*

und Pius XII (Coll. *Abhandlungen zur Sozialethik*, 9) (Munich, 1975). See the comments by E. Elders in the *Revue de théologie de Louvain-la-Neuve, 1977*, pp. 240-41. We all know of the important role played during the reign of Pius XII by the private secretariat composed of about twenty Jesuits under the direction of Father Leiber, who had once been the secretary of the former nuncio in Munich. Father Huërth provided documentation and orientation for many texts regarding morals.

5. In his *Institutions Chrétiennes* (II, 15, 1), Calvin does in fact attribute major importance to Christ's and the Church's functions as priest, prophet, and king. He also reproaches papists for not taking account of those functions.

6. *Catechismus Romanus*. In the Italian edition of 1946, see pp. 57-59.

7. Thomas Aquinas, *Summa theologiae*, III, 22, 1, ad 30.

8. Eusebius of Caesarea, *Demonstratio evangelica*, IV, 15f.

9. The whole notion of dialogue, as old as the life of thought itself (see the dialogues of Plato and the Synoptics), was brought back to prominence in this century by personalism (that of Mounier, for example). It was presented as an effort to foster communication between persons, to get people to listen to each other, and to counteract the tendency of most individuals to close in upon themselves and assume that they know everything about everything. At that point in time it tolerated asymmetry, such as that of the doctor-patient relationship. It also called for a well-grounded personal conviction which was capable of offering reasons for its position. Very soon, however, the dynamics of our own era sought to suppress all differences between the partners in dialogue. Criticism was leveled against the alleged "one who knows" and the father or parent role. Under the pretext of a common search, people saw personal conviction as a refusal to engage in dialogue and sought to impose an attitude of universal doubt.

10. See, for example, Rom. 12:1-2.

11. Here we link up with another aspect of the present cultural revolution: i.e., the attempt to cut human beings off from their roots completely. This effort would deny history altogether even though history explains many things.

12. *Cahiers de l'Actualité Religieuse et Sociale*, August 15, 1976.

The Natural Law
and the Magisterium

John Boyle

The June 1978 issue of *Theological Studies* contained two articles[1] which reflected on theological issues raised by the encyclical *Humanae Vitae* and its teaching on contraception. Because the modern teaching of the Roman magisterium and its explanation and defense by Catholic theologians have cited the natural law as the source of the teaching on contraception,[2] the controversy over the status of that teaching is also a controversy about the relationship of the magisterium and the natural law.

But contraception and related questions of sexual ethics are by no means the only moral questions on which the Roman magisterium has based its teaching on the natural law. The corpus of Catholic social teaching elaborated by the Popes since Leo XIII and by the Second Vatican Council has also been presented as natural law doctrine.

Such teaching by the magisterium, with its attendant claims to the assent of the faithful, raises important epistemological questions. Since the magisterium in modern Catholic theology has been understood as a function of the Pope and the bishops,[3] do they know about the natural law in a way not open to other members of the Church, or, for that matter, to men and women generally? How can a *natural* law be taught with special authority by religious leaders? And since many of the social ethical questions to which modern Catholic magisterial teaching has offered answers drawn from the natural law are peculiar to our own historical period, how do authoritative religious teachers find solutions to concrete historical problems from the general principles of a natural law?

This study will approach these questions in four steps. In the first the teaching of the modern magisterium and Catholic theologians about the authority and competence of the magisterium will be reviewed. In the second the study will locate this teaching in its broader historical and theological context. The third step will summarize various elements of a doctrine about the magisterium, and the fourth step will be to offer some critical and constructive reflections on the epistemological questions relating to the magisterium and the natural law.

I

The brief statement at the beginning of *Humanae Vitae* asserting the competence of the magisterium to interpret the natural law, and citing for support a series of papal documents from Pius IX to John XXIII, is typical of such statements in documents of the ordinary papal magisterium in the nineteenth and twentieth centuries.

In the earlier study I have traced the first use in a papal document of the term "ordinary magisterium" and I have argued that the term and its meaning can be traced to the work of the German Jesuit Scholastic theologian Joseph Kleutgen.[4]

For Kleutgen, the teaching authority of the Church in matters of natural law was not problematic at all. The Church is the authoritative teacher and guardian of revelation, and the natural law is revealed. Kleutgen further argues that the ordinary teaching authority of the Pope and bishops in natural law matters could also be established from the holiness of the Church, which is an essential mark and therefore requires that the Church not declare something to be a virtue or a vice when it is not.[5]

Kleutgen's view that the natural law is revealed was shared by other theologians whose views were influential under Pius IX, Leo XIII, and Pius X, when the theology of the magisterium that dominated Catholic theology in the first half of this century developed. Their notions of biblical inspiration,[6] revelation,[7] and tradition[8] cohere with their view of the magisterium.[9] To cite only one, John Baptist Franzelin, S.J. states clearly that the natural law is contained in the deposit of faith.[10]

Franzelin also devotes some pages to an explanation of why the natural law must be revealed.[11] The first reason is that the truths of natural religion, which includes natural morality and hence the natural law, must be known even if human beings had no supernatural end. Therefore, just as the natural end of human beings has been elevated by God to a supernatural end and natural religion is contained at least implicitly in the revelation of supernatural religion, so natural morality must also be included in that revelation at least implicitly. Second, the supernatural end of human beings demands that knowledge of that end be the knowledge of faith, i.e., supernatural knowledge. Likewise, the way in which morality is known must be similarly proportionate to that supernatural end. Therefore the truths of natural religion and morality must be revealed and held by faith. Third, even though human beings have the physical capacity to know the truths of natural religion and morality, they are morally impotent to do so. Therefore, in order that these truths be known by everyone in a timely way, fully, with adequate clarity and full certitude and without admixture of error, their revelation is necessary. There is an allusion to but no citation of Romans 1 in support of this last argument, since Paul there affirms the possibility of knowing God but simultaneously affirms that human beings through their own fault have not known or served him.

In Franzelin's view, Christ's revelation was given to the apostles and to their successors the bishops. It is through the authoritative teaching of the body of bishops that revelation is known to the rest of the Church.[12]

Kleutgen makes another observation about the teaching authority of the Church that should be noted here. He writes that revelation must not only be accepted with pious faith but must also order our acts and works. But this demands the concrete application of revelation to life. The Church, declares Kleutgen, is structured in virtue of its pastoral office (*Hirtamt*) to do this. Similarly, the Church has the power to prohibit not only those errors which directly clash with revelation, but also those which can be recognized as pernicious in the light of revelation.[13] There can be little doubt in the context of Kleutgen's repeated insistence on the infallibility and indefectibility of the Church that such actions will be without error, but it is significant that Kleutgen describes the application to the concrete as an exercise of the pastoral office (*Hirtamt*) and not the teaching office (*Lehramt*).

II

The dependence of the nineteenth-century Roman Jesuit theologians on the work of the baroque Scholastics, in particular, Francesco Suarez, S.J. and Juan de Lugo, S.J., is well known and can be quickly verified from the numerous references to them in writers such as Kleutgen and Franzelin. In this section the study will locate the views of Kleutgen and Franzelin on the magisterium and natural law in the broader context of the more developed theology of the human person and grace found in the earlier writers, especially Suarez.

For our purpose, it will be useful to locate what Suarez teaches about the natural law in the larger context of his theology of grace—as he does himself in discussing the promulgation of the natural law.[14] Much of Suarez's theology of the human person is to be found in the treatise on grace.

The treatise on grace recalls Catholic teaching on the fallen state of the human race and the impact of that fall on the ability of human beings to know and to carry out the precepts of the natural law. It recalls also that the destiny of human beings is not merely a natural one but a supernatural destiny available by God's gracious design. Grace is required as the result of sin and of this supernatural destiny if human beings are to obey even the natural law.[15]

As a result of the fallen state of the human race, grace is needed to know all practical moral truths and to make moral judgments without error. Indeed, such is the imperfect nature of human beings that God's grace would be needed even in a hypothetical state of pure nature in order to know the whole range of moral principles. In the state of "integral nature" in which Adam and Eve were in fact created, a state graced in various ways and thus superior to "pure nature," humans could know and obey the natural law, but since the fall they cannot.

Thus, even apart from the supernatural destiny of humans, there is both a defect of the practical intellect and an impotence of the will which makes it impossible for human beings afflicted with original sin to know and observe the natural law.

But God's grace has not been wanting. One form of grace is revelation.[16] In fact in his treatise on law[17] Suarez declares that Christ has revealed the whole of the moral law, and then he immediately adds that in the law of grace no positive moral precept has been added by Christ to the natural moral law.[18] But that law, in principle still accessible to the natural light of reason, when revealed can be accepted by faith.[19]

Matters which are revealed must be proposed for acceptance in faith by the Church's infallible teaching authority, which is the living oracle of revealed truth for believers.[20] Suarez is, of course, only repeating what had become a common theme in Catholic controversial writing, especially during and after the Protestant Reformation. Against the Protestant principle of *sola Scriptura* and private interpretation, Catholic controversialists insisted on the mediation of revelation through the Church. The Church, of course, meant Pope and bishops.[21]

III

If Kleutgen and Franzelin played major roles in the development of a theology of the Church's teaching authority, they were not alone. We turn now to other elements of this theology which pertain to the epistemological questions we raised at the beginning. Clearly, for the nineteenth-century theologians the authority of the Pope and bishops to teach about matters of moral practice which included the natural law was not in doubt. The theological explanation of that fact included several elements, which can be summarized as follows: (1) the natural law has been revealed; (2) revelation has been given by Christ to the Pope and bishops as successors of the apostles; (3) therefore the Pope and bishops teach about moral questions relating to the natural law with special authority; (4) the Pope and bishops teach with an authority rooted in their episcopal ordination and jurisdiction and with the help of special teaching insights given with the grace of holy orders.

We turn now briefly to each of these points:

1. That the natural law is revealed was commonly held by Catholic theologians including Suarez, Kleutgen and Franzelin. In support of this view the theologians cited scriptural passages, including the decalogue, the Sermon on the Mount and the parenetic passages of St. Paul. These impose moral commands or prohibitions such as those against murder, adultery or theft which were held by Catholic theologians to pertain to the natural law. The whole of the Bible was regarded, of course, as revealed.

Suarez's view that Christ has revealed the whole of the moral law should be understood in the context of his view that natural law includes precepts at various levels of generality, not only the primary precept that good is to be done and evil avoided, but secondary and even tertiary precepts of the natural law.[22] Suarez notes that some conclusions from the natural law are known to everyone, but that some others, for example that fornication is an intrinsic evil, are arrived at only by the wiser and more experienced. Suarez does not imply that every specific precept or prohibition of the moral law as it applies to particular moral problems is somehow revealed. There is nothing in his citations of Scripture and nothing in his view of the natural law which would demand that conclusion. However, his argument does seem to imply that all the principles needed to guide moral decisions are revealed. Given the two-source theory of revelation commonly held by theologians of the post-Reformation period and by the Roman school in the nineteenth century, both Scripture and tradition would be sources of revealed moral doctrine.[23]

2. Franzelin's influential work *De sacra traditione et scriptura*, published in 1870, asserts that the revelation contained in tradition and Scripture has been given by Christ to his apostles and by them to their successors, the Pope and bishops. Revelation has not been given to the whole Church but to the body of bishops, who together with the Pope as chief bishop constitute the authoritative teachers in the Church, the *Ecclesia docens*, which proposes the divine revelation for belief by the rest of the Church, the *Ecclesia discens*.[24]

Nonetheless, it seems clear enough from what Franzelin writes that the Pope and bishops are bearers of revelation in a rather juridical sense. The Pope and episcopal college receive the revelation in receiving Scripture and tradition from an earlier generation. Franzelin gives special prominence to tradition as this process of handing down from generation to generation the revelation of Christ. Even the Pope and bishops are first of all learners, i.e., they do not receive revelation directly from Christ in each generation but rather they hand on what has been handed down to them by a succession of authorized teachers in the Church.[25]

The assistance of the Holy Spirit insures the integrity of this transmission as well as the infallibility of the proclamation and defense of revelation by the Pope and the college of bishops. But this charism of the Spirit is to be distinguished from both revelation and inspiration.[26]

It follows from the revelation of the natural law that it is included in the deposit of faith thus handed on by the Pope and the college of bishops.

3. From the role of the Pope and bishops as authentic or authoritative teachers of God's revelation it follows that their teaching role vis-à-vis the natural law invests their pronouncements with special authority. The assent of faith is owed to the teaching of divine revelation by the authoritative teachers of the Church. It is less clear what qualification ought to be given to teaching derived from the natural law which is not presented as revealed. The usual term is "religious assent," which needs further explanation.[27]

The Pope and bishops are not only teachers in the Church but also pastors. They are therefore not only authoritative teachers of divine revelation but also authoritative guides in the Christian life for the faithful. In the field of moral decision there is a close and not always very clear relationship between the *potestas docendi* of the bishops as teachers and the *potestas regiminis* or *pastoralis* of the same bishops as pastors. In a passage cited above Kleutgen appealed to the pastoral office (*Hirtamt*) of the Pope and bishops for their authority in applying revelation to everyday life. Franzelin discusses at length the relationship between these two powers as subdivisions of the more general power of jurisdiction. For both Kleutgen and Franzelin the indefectibility and infallibility of the Church protect both the teaching and pastoral roles of the Pope and bishops from error, at least in those cases in which a definitive judgment or discipline is in question, since the genuineness of the Christian life and doctrine is at stake.[28]

4. Although not all writers on the subject of the magisterium give the same prominence to the question of the sources of magisterial authority, a number of them root that authority in the episcopal ordination of the Pope and bishops. Kleutgen and Franzelin, whose view of the Church is highly juridical, move rather directly from the magisterial or pastoral offices of the Church to the assurance of its infallibility in exercising those offices in virtue of the promises of Christ to be with the Church and to send the Holy Spirit upon it.[29] While this argument for the "Catholic principle" of mediation by the Church which is assured by the Holy Spirit is very much in the line of post-Reformation Catholic thought, the mode in which it takes place is not given much elaboration by these authors, though Franzelin does relate the various *potestates* of those in orders as bishops to the character of the sacrament of orders.[30] Still, he is not willing to make the reception of orders even a prerequisite for full jurisdiction in the Church, since under the canon law in force until quite recently, even a layman elected Pope was said to receive the fullness of the papal jurisdiction upon his acceptance of election, not from his episcopal ordination.[31]

For a fuller exploration one must look elsewhere, and so we turn to the study of the relationship between the teaching authority and holy orders by Joseph Fuchs, S.J.[32]

Fuchs outlines the special relationship of the sacrament of orders to the teaching authority of bishops. It is through ordination that the bishop becomes a sharer in the continuing offices of Christ as priest, teacher and pastor. The powers he receives over the eucharistic body of Christ are the ground of his related authority over the mystical body of Christ, whose unity the Eucharist both symbolizes and brings about. The bishop acts *in persona Christi* especially in celebrating the Sacrifice of the Mass. It is his priestly role of leadership in the Church community that gives rise to the power of jurisdiction.

Although the sacrament of orders does not confer jurisdiction, it does create a positive disposition in the ordained for the active power of jurisdiction. This positive disposition arises from the character given by the sacrament of orders.

For our present purposes, however, it is Fuchs' discussion of the relation of orders to the teaching authority of the ordained that is of greatest interest. In the words of Matthias Scheeben, the question is: Does the sacrament of orders itself mediate a specific power of witnessing which fits the ordained for an authentic mediation of doctrine?

Fuchs responds with an analysis of the effects of orders, with special reference to the relationship of these effects to the teaching authority.

It is common doctrine that the sacraments produce an increase in sanctifying grace, including the infused virtues and the gifts of the Holy Spirit. These are significant for the role of teaching:

> On the other hand one cannot lose sight of the fact that a minister of Christ and of the Church is called by orders to the highest and the holiest; the grace is given him to be able to respond to his high calling with personal worthiness. Is there not in the very increase of the virtues and gifts a greater warrant for the authority of the doctrine which the ordained presents? The power of faith is always increased by the sacraments; love grows, which stimulates him to deeper knowledge, to truthfulness and fidelity; and there grows ease in penetrating revealed truths, in a supernatural evaluation of natural and supernatural realities, in the courage and zeal to proclaim them, in the readiness to risk everything in searching out and proclaiming them.[33]

In addition to the increase of sanctifying grace and the virtues, there is the special sacramental grace of orders. Here, as in his discussion of sanctifying grace and the virtues, Fuchs takes guidance from a dictum of St. Thomas: To whomever a power is divinely given, there are also given those things by which the exercise of that power can be suitably done.[34] Thus the special sacramental grace means an increase in precisely those graces and gifts which are most needed for the worthy exercise of the office of teacher in the Church. The virtues of faith and love, of prudence and the gift of fear of the Lord come to mind.

All contribute to forming a teacher of truth, who, deeply rooted in faith, draws from that faith, lives out of faith and love, and is thus an instrument of God conjoined to God.[35]

Again these gifts and graces become a powerful warrant for the genuineness of the doctrine taught by the ordained.

There is a further question whether, in addition to the increase of sanctifying grace and the virtues and gifts of the Holy Spirit, there are also *gratiae gratis datae*, genuinely charismatic gifts of the Spirit, which arise from holy orders and relate to the teaching office of the ordained. After offering several examples of theologians from the nineteenth century (including Scheeben) to the thirteenth who appear to have held the view that such graces do arise from the sacrament of orders, Fuchs judges it "not improbable" that such charismatic graces underlie a power of witnessing which is based on orders.

This sketch of a theology of orders and its relationship to teaching authority is important for our interests. It provides another ingredient for a coherent reply to the epistemological questions we raised at the beginning drawn from theologians who flourished from the period of the restoration of Scholasticism in the nineteenth century to the Second Vatican Council. At many points they in turn drew upon a theological tradition dating back to the post-Reformation period and before.

In summary of this traditional position, the following points seem to be widely accepted:

1. Members of the hierarchy (Pope and bishops) who exercise the teaching authority of the Church know with certitude of the natural law, at least in its fundamental principles, because the natural law is revealed.

2. The Pope and bishops know of revelation not by some special inspiration or new revelatory experience but as members of the community of believers in which the apostolic tradition is transmitted by authorized teachers and preachers and those delegated by them. Before being called to office as bishop or Pope a person is first a learner within a community of believers. There is a succession of authorized teachers.

3. The natural law, or at least its basic principles, does not

acquire new material content when taught by the authoritative teachers of the Church. Rather these fundamental principles are known by all easily and accurately with the help of the Church. In addition, since the response to the teaching authority is one grounded in faith (and setting aside here the question of the usefulness of the notion of a *fides ecclesiastica*), assent to the teaching of the Church adds to purely natural knowledge the formality of supernatural faith, thus elevating it to the supernatural destiny of human beings.

4. The authorized teachers of the Church do possess, in virtue of their ordination to office, special insight into those matters on which they must teach. Some theologians who take an especially juridical view of the Church argue directly from the indefectibility and infallibility of the Church to an infallibility in teaching by the Pope and bishops and explain it only in general terms as the work of Christ and the Holy Spirit. The classic *assistentia Spiritus per se negativa* appears rather external but prevents the teaching of erroneous doctrine.

But other theologians relate the teaching authority to a *potestas docendi* given in holy orders and rooted in the *character indelibilis* of orders, especially the episcopacy. In this view the sacramental grace of orders includes special and charismatic helps of the Spirit for those who teach with authority in the Church, a real modification of the knowing subject.

It should be noted that such theological views would appear applicable to the pastoral office of the Pope and bishops as well as to their teaching office, even if there is no direct claim to infallibility in pastoral decisions. There does seem to be a claim that in making pastoral decisions binding on the whole Church the authoritative pastors will be prevented from leading the Church astray from the authentic Christian life.

5. The tradition has not been consistent in attributing specific moral applications of the natural law to the teaching authority or to the pastoral authority of the bishops and the Pope.[36]

Taken together, these elements offer a coherent and comprehensive account of the authoritative actions of the Pope and bishops as teachers of the natural law. They explain the knowledge of the natural law peculiar to authoritative teachers through revelation and offer an account of the special insights into the faith and its application to particular moral questions that could respond to epistemological problems about the teaching of the magisterium on particular moral questions that is said to be derived from the moral law.

IV

We turn now to some critical and constructive reflections on the epistemological questions related to Church teaching authority and the natural law. The issues, however, cannot be separated from basic questions in theological anthropology, ecclesiology and ethics. We will take up each of these and then return to a summary of the epistemological questions which are our basic concern.

Theological Anthropology

Reflecting on the Scriptures, Catholic theology has described the indwelling Holy Spirit as "uncreated grace." Karl Rahner has written of the indwelling Spirit as a quasi-formal cause and the primary meaning of grace in human beings and their world to which God has determined to communicate himself.[37]

We noted above that the decrees of the First Vatican Council held that natural law was accessible to reason without the aid of grace and faith—at least in principle.

However, much contemporary Catholic theology agrees with Rahner's criticism of the traditional conception of the relation of nature and grace. In Rahner's view there is in fact no nature apart from grace. God's decision to communicate himself to human beings constitutes a "supernatural existential," i.e., a component of concrete human existence prior to any human action. Therefore the only world, the only human nature there is, is graced. Suarez's "pure nature" is only an abstraction, a "remainder concept" arrived at by peeling away the effects of grace by careful theological analysis. Whatever may be the possibilities of human nature in principle, the fact is that we have no experience of nature apart from grace.[38]

It is the work of the Holy Spirit that produces the effects of grace ("created grace") in those who have accepted the offer of God's self-communication. The question we must address now is whether this grace affects a person's ability to know, and in particular one's ability to know what is morally right and wrong.

In an earlier study[39] we reviewed the work of Rahner and Bernard Lonergan and concluded that in their view Christian faith does indeed affect the believer's moral perception, judgment and action. When Rahner speaks of faith and Lonergan of conversion, both are talking about a transformation of subjectivity by grace which produces an opening out of the subject's world of meaning and the transvaluation of his or her values. Such is the transformation worked by faith that the believer and the unbeliever perceive the world, meanings and values differently. Even if their words are the same at times, their meanings are different nonetheless, since they are defined by different horizons of meaning.

This work of transformation is, of course, most conspicuous in those whose faith is explicit and who have associated themselves with the community of believers. But it should be noted here that both Rahner and Lonergan insist that God's grace is offered to every human being and that some accept that offer of grace, if only implicitly, as they follow their consciences enlightened by God's grace. Whether or not the term "anonymous Christian" is apt, the point to be made here is that the sort of transformed subject described here can surely be found outside the institution of the Church.

Ecclesiology

The action of the Holy Spirit sent by the Father and the Son is fundamental for an understanding of the role of the Church vis-à-vis the natural law. We turn now to the work of the Spirit in the community of believers.[40]

It is the Church community which is the body of Christ animated by the Spirit of Christ. The Church is, in Rahner's phrase, the sacrament of the eschatologically victorious grace of God in Jesus Christ.[41] Therefore the Church, not just those who are bishops, is the indefectible bearer of the revelation of God in Christ. This is the teaching of the Second Vatican Council, which thus corrected the teaching of Franzelin and of *Humani Generis*.[42]

In this community of faith animated by the Spirit there exists a "collective consciousness" of God's revelation of himself in Jesus Christ.[43] In its article on tradition,[44] Vatican II points out that tradition develops in the Church, in part through a growth in understanding of the realities and of the words which have been handed down. The apostolic tradition, however, includes whatever contributes not only to Christian faith but also to Christian life. It follows that there is growth in the understanding of the Christian life too. The discernment of moral norms consonant with the Christian *kerygma* is a collective process.

Moral discernment, like other kinds of human knowing, can usefully be thought of in Bernard Lonergan's terms as a self-correcting process of learning.[45] Such a view seems especially appropriate in the theological context which considers the activity of the Spirit by grace in both the individual and the community but which also considers the realities of human finitude, history and sin.

The limits of the work of the Spirit must also be acknowledged, for in coming among us the Spirit takes on certain human limitations.[46] As humanity and divinity in Jesus are, in the words of the Council of Chalcedon, unconfused and undivided,[47] so by analogy is the Spirit unconfused with, yet undivided from, the limitations of the persons in whom he dwells. Mühlen writes of a *kenosis* of the Spirit among us analogous to the *kenosis* of the Logos in becoming man.

Moreover, the Spirit in coming upon Jesus in his anointing has entered into time and therefore into history.[48] Yet he remains unconfused with history, even if inseparable from it. Therefore the Church cannot dispose of or manipulate the Spirit. The Church is not the "continuation of the incarnation" as J. A. Möhler held—with the perilous suggestions of a kind of "communication of idioms" that the phrase suggests. Rather the Church shares in the anointing of the Spirit that first came upon Jesus.

There remains therefore an inevitable eschatological expectation in the Church. For it, the perfection of the gifts of the Spirit is "not yet." But the work of the Spirit goes on in the Church in the word, in Church office and in the sacraments.[49]

For our question of the relationship of the Church and its teaching office to the natural law, these are important assertions. They emphasize the unfinished state of the work of the Spirit in the Church and in the world. They emphasize that we cannot forget that the Church remains a community of sinners, that with the nature of the Church there is always the shadow of what Hans Küng has called its "unnature"[50] of human sinfulness and imperfection. The believer and the community of believers can and does suffer from what Lonergan has termed a scotosis of the intellect and an impotence of the will.[51] To say that is not to deny the traditional doctrines of the indefectibility and infallibility of the Church; it is only to point out that these doctrines stand in tension with others which assert that the eschaton is not yet. The Church's perception and thematization of moral values is therefore in need of correction and reformulation, especially at the level of specific moral directives, as we shall see. Given the multiplicity of the gifts of the Spirit in the Church, the community must be one of ongoing moral discernment as it seeks the implications of its Christian commitment for its life.

It is entirely consonant with this view of the Church as a community of moral discernment with its multiple gifts of the Spirit that some in the Church should be called to various offices, including the teaching office, to which gifts of the Spirit are given through the reception of the sacrament of orders. The same transformation of subjectivity which is brought about by the gift of grace and faith can be carried further by the work of the Spirit in this sacrament. Indeed Vatican II emphasized the fundamental role of the sacrament of orders in its discussion of hierarchical office.[52] There is nothing incongruous in the claim that the college of bishops with the Pope at its head possesses in virtue of the sacrament of orders and the charismatic gifts of the Spirit appropriate to their role in the Church special insight into the moral demands and implications of the Christian life. Such insights can complement or at times correct those of the community. Indeed the explication of the implications of the *kerygma* in a continuing *didache* has been a feature of life in the Church from the beginning.[53] The view of orders and the effect of the work of the Spirit in the ordained suggested by Scheeben seems sound.

If that is true, it suggests a view of the Church as a community of moral discernment in which a dialogue exists between the authoritative proposition and explication of the Christian faith and its implications by authoritative teachers and the reception of that teaching by the Church community—which also possesses the gifts of the Spirit. It is the experience and reflection of the community in turn which produces further insights and discernment by the community, which stimulates on the part of the authoritative teachers their own discernment and a new, perhaps modified proposition of the Christian faith and its implications.[54] Indeed the limits of the community of discernment cannot be too narrowly drawn, since grace and the gifts of the Spirit are not confined to the institutional limits of the Church. And it is an obvious fact of Church life in the twentieth century that the Church learns from the culture in which it lives.[55]

There is also a role for the theologian in this community of moral discernment. Scholars bring that variety of competencies to their work that Bernard Lonergan has described as "functional specialties," together with their "scholarly differentiation of consciousness." Both the community as a whole and the authoritative teachers look to scholars to insure not only adequacy to the Christian tradition, but also the scientific and philosophical adequacy to the Church's work of moral discernment.[56]

The relationship of the community of faith and the authoritative teachers has often been conceived in too narrowly juridical terms. The college of bishops was thought of in post-Reformation apologetcs in ways that separated it from the community of the faithful—an excess that the Second Vatican Council has corrected with its teaching in *Lumen Gentium* about the people of God and the role of hierarchical office. Officeholders are first of all believers, who have themselves learned the Christian faith from the community. They do not receive it by special inspiration or some new revelation.

The result is a far more dialogic model of the relationship between officeholders and the community which does not at all exclude the possibility of authoritative teaching so fully assisted by the Spirit as to be infallible and thus demanding of the assent of faith. The Council has pointed out that this protection of the Spirit extends also into the community, which is infallible in believing, so that its assent to infallible teaching will never be lacking.[57]

Here we can note that if the Church is a community of moral discernment in which there is an ongoing, self-correcting process of moral learning under the influence of the Spirit and under the conditions and limitations discussed above, then it is no simple matter to develop purely formal criteria for infallible moral teaching, as Grisez and Ford have attempted to do.

Ethics

Our discussion thus far has centered on the knowing subject, the community of moral discernment, and the action of the Holy Spirit upon them in their moral perceptions and judgments. Now we must touch on several ethical issues pertinent to our question.

We turn first to the natural law. We have reviewed elsewhere a range of views among contemporary Catholic theologians about the natural law and the appropriate method to be followed in knowing it.[58] It is neither possible nor necessary to adjudicate here disputes between those who argue for a transcendental method in defining human nature and those who follow the more traditional view that human beings can know the good to which human nature inclines and by reflecting on those inclinations can come to know moral obligation based on the dictates of reason.

Other contemporary Catholic thinkers ground moral obligation on human relationships or on objective values, especially the value of the person. The influence of Max Scheler and Dietrich von Hildebrand on these latter writers is often explicit.[59]

Any of these approaches seems consonant with the definition of Vatican I that *in principle* the natural law is accessible to human reason without the aid of grace or faith. The Council's definition was aimed at traditionalism; it did not address itself to the question of fact.

Contemporary theology is marked by a consciousness that nature is not simply a "given" which has come just as it now is from the hand of the Creator. The historicity of the world and everything in it, human beings included, is more apparent to us than to generations past. This explains in part why the contemporary discussion of natural law has taken a transcendental turn. It seeks to locate a constant or at least a reference point in the flux of history.[60]

In any event, many contemporary theologians insist that the natural law and the law of Christ ought not to be envisioned as two juxtaposed fields, but as two points of a continuum on which faith is the ultimate and all-encompassing degree.[61] Other theologians see the relationship as one of sublation, with nature being taken up into the order of grace as a condition is taken up by the conditioned.[62]

As a logical construct a "natural law" is still a possibility, but in the real order there is no "natural" morality; there is only an order of grace in which the law of Christ is the law — at least for believers.

Contemporary theologians in large part agree with Suarez and the older tradition that the "law of Christ" adds no new material norms to the natural law. What is specific to Christian ethics must therefore lie at another level.[63]

Two points can be made at once. The first is that it is a mistake to conceive of the natural law as something which the Church knows by reason alone. "Natural law" is the product of extended theological reflection. The second is that the authority of those who hold the teaching office must admit of degrees, ranging from those utterances for which infallibility might be claimed, with its attendant obligation to the assent of faith, to those dealing with the natural law which can claim only a lesser certitude and therefore a lesser assent.[64]

Both of these points cohere with a view of the Church as a community of moral discernment and with the view of the work of the Holy Spirit in the Church which transforms the knowing subject, and with the eschatological "not yet" outlined above. They cohere too with the role we have suggested for authorized teachers in the Church in dialogue with the community of faith. Their authority is grounded in the Spirit's work: jurisdiction flows from ordination; it is not the result of mere organizational arrangements.

There is one further point. Moral decisions must be made about specific concrete matters. In making such decisions a moral agent must consider all the relevant factors, including conflicting values and principles. For a member of the Church community, the moral insights and convictions of that community, its view of the world, of human beings and their relationship with God, will be important factors. Yet it is essential to the notion of moral agency that the agent ultimately assume the burden and responsibility of moral decision.

If that is true, it suggests a limit to the knowledge of the Church and its authorized teachers in the field of morals, for whatever the competence of the Church with respect to the natural law, the nature of moral decision would seem to exclude a notion of official teaching which can claim authority to descend to such particulars as to effectively substitute itself for the moral agency of the believer.[65]

There are other limits. Karl Rahner has written of an existential ethic, of moral commands given by God to the individual person precisely as such. Such commands are not in conflict with general moral principles, but neither are they derivable from them. Existential ethical obligations have a personal and individual character which puts them outside the limits of Church authority without putting them in conflict with general moral law. Each person's conscience has the function of discerning these personal moral obligations. For our purposes the point is that there exists a field of moral obligation in harmony with general moral principles but not derived directly from them and which cannot be discerned, much less imposed, by Church authority.

An ethics which looks to an adequate anthropology must also take note of what Rahner, Lonergan and others have said about the horizon of our knowledge which is transformed by grace and about the relationship between our global unthematic knowledge of moral values and the rational arguments we offer in defense of our moral choices. Rahner has explicated this latter aspect of our moral knowledge in his writings on moral instinct and its implications for a method of moral argument.

Rahner is interested not only in his contention that moral argument often seems to assume what it is attempting to prove, but also in the fact that moral arguments so often seem unpersuasive. These issues are akin to those treated by Bernard Lonergan in his chapter on "dialectic" in *Method in Theology*, in which he offers an account of similar problems and proposes to deal with them in terms of differing horizons grounded in the presence or absence of his multiple conversions and also in terms of what Lonergan calls "differentiations of consciousness." [66]

We cannot pursue these matters here. We draw attention to them only to indicate the multiplicity of factors which affect the ability of the knowing moral agent to perceive moral values and make judgments and decisions about them. Since believers and officeholders in the Church are such agents, these facets of moral knowledge affect them too.

Summary: Epistemological Issues

We began by asking epistemological questions raised by the teaching of the hierarchical magisterium based on the natural law. *Humanae Vitae* is the most discussed example, but the corpus of modern Catholic social teaching would serve as well. We conclude by addressing a series of epistemological issues.

1. What is it that authoritative teachers know when they know the "natural law"?

Bruno Schüller[67] has suggested that "natural law" be understood as the whole of those moral norms which human beings can know in a way at least logically independent of divine revelation. Moreover, the Catholic tradition asserts that moral obligation for human beings is grounded in human existence, although that is not essential to Schüller's definition of natural law.

We have pointed out that Catholic theologians today understand the natural law and roots of moral obligation in a variety of ways. For our present interests, it is enough to hold that authoritative teachers in the Church can know the moral obligations of the Christian life which are not derivable, certainly not directly, from divine revelation.

We can point to the corpus of Catholic social teaching in the nineteenth and twentieth centuries as an example, together with much Catholic sexual ethical teaching. For the most part the warrant for this teaching is explicitly the natural law, not revelation as transmitted by Scripture or tradition.

It is not necessary to hold exclusively to one of several possible theories of the origin and nature of natural law obligations, the ontological status of moral values and the like, to hold at least this much. What is basic is the objective, given character of moral value.

We would hold further that this knowledge includes insight into the implications of the Christian life as this is defined by the Christian proclamation (*kerygma*). Whether or not such insights are logically independent of revelation is a question not germane to our present interest, and we do not pursue it here.

2. Who can know about the natural law?

First, it is basic to the Catholic position on the natural law that it is accessible, at least in its general principles, to every human person. We have suggested above the problem of accounting for the influence of grace in the lives of those who are not explicitly Christians, but it is enough to define our problem by noting that even unbelievers can and do know of the natural law.[68]

Second, every believer who has received the gift of grace and faith and therefore has experienced the horizon shift effected by faith as discussed above also can know the natural law—but within a quite different horizon of meanings and values. The moral perceptions of the believing Christian are informed moreover by his faith in Jesus Christ and acceptance of his commandments, by his experience of the demands of the kingdom of God announced by Jesus, and by the presence and power of the Holy Spirit.[69]

These are the believers whose global perception of moral values may or may not be in harmony with their enunciation of reasons for their moral judgments, as Rahner has pointed out. It is the community of these believers, with their experience of the Christian life and its demands in a changing world, which provides one side of the dialogue with Church officeholders.

Third, it seems possible to speak of a kind of "collective consciousness," a sedimentation of moral experience within the community of belief which is something larger than the experience of numerous individuals.[70] This collective or corporate consciousness extends, we would argue, not only to matters of belief and matters of practice clearly related to belief, but also to moral knowledge which is logically independent of revelation but often presupposed by it.

Rahner has pointed to the role of theologians in criticizing the adequacy of the thematizations of this collective moral consciousness both by believers generally and also by the Church's authoritative teachers. Theologians bring their various scholarly competencies to this critical task.

Fourth, the natural law is known by those who are authoritative teachers in the Church. We pointed out above that these officeholders are first of all believers and members of the Church community. Their knowledge is not therefore the result of personal revelation, and it is distinguished from the inspiration of the writers of Scripture. Like other believers, officeholders have experienced the transformation of consciousness we have described for all believers.

But, in addition, the officeholders who are bishops have experienced the further action of the Spirit rooted in holy orders which further transforms their consciousness. In virtue of this action of the Spirit, and in dialogue with the community of believers they serve, officeholders do have insight into the moral demands of the Christian life correlative to the historical situation of the world in which the community finds itself.[71]

These insights are related to their office of apostolic preaching (*kerygma*) but extend, as the example of the New Testament itself shows, to a continuation of the apostolic instruction (*didache*) as well. There is an element of mystagogy in this instruction which clearly relates to the priestly office of bishops as stewards and celebrants of the Christian mysteries. We observe, however, that a purely kerygmatic notion of the authoritative teaching office of bishops does not seem adequate either to a notion of the teaching office (as distinct from a preaching office) precisely as authoritative, nor to the practice of the Church, which certainly has not limited the authoritative teaching of bishops to the apostolic kerygma.[72]

Two observations are in order. One is that the traditional distinction of the three offices of the Church, the prophetic, priestly and pastoral, cannot be pressed; clearly the roles of preaching/teaching, liturgical and other priestly acting, and pastoral direction are closely linked.[73] The second is that both the sources and the authority of the practical pastoral directives of teachers and pastors in the Church have not been adequately clarified. Karl Rahner has suggested in his essays on the Pastoral Constitution of Vatican II that such directives are a kind of existential ethic for the Church community, recognized as representing the binding will of God by the charismatic action of the Spirit in the Church. Especially those directives in the fields of politics, economics and the like, in which the Church possesses no special competence, are the Church's response to the binding will of God in a particular time and place but are not conclusions drawn from general principles. Because they are God's will and are known as such, they are indeed obligatory, yet they are known only through the charismatic action of the Spirit—and therefore are not general principles binding on everyone. Thus they do not meet the definition of "natural law" despite the fact that such modern Church social teaching has offered the natural as its warrant.[74]

The role of authoritative teachers in this process of formulating pastoral directives is clearly one of discernment and articulation, a function fully in harmony with the gifts of the Spirit given to bishops by their ordination.

We cannot pursue this matter further. It suffices to illustrate the complexity of the epistemological questions which arise in an examination of the role of the Church's authoritative teachers in the teaching of the natural law.

Conclusion

The very complexity of the issues of theological anthropology, ecclesiology and ethics which arise in a study of epistemological problems assures us that no simple solution to these problems is available.

Nonetheless it does seem to us that the inadequacy of a purely juridical approach to the magisterium and its exercise in the area of the natural law is apparent. The multiple actions and gifts of the Spirit in the Church (and outside it) suggest rather that a dialogic model of magisterium is needed. In such a model the bishops' proposition of Christian belief and practice guided and protected by the Spirit is received by a community which has also received the gifts of the Spirit. It is scarcely an accident that Vatican II could teach with such confidence that, because of the work of the Holy Spirit, the consent of the Church will never be lacking to infallible teaching.

But the function of the community is not purely receptive. The community is the bearer of revelation and it is through the experience of the community that the implications of this revelation develop in the Church. Therefore the moral experience of the community is of profound religious significance, precisely because it is the experience of a community gifted by the Spirit.

This experience includes that of the natural law, however it may be precisely defined, at least as the presupposition of grace. Since this knowledge is available to the community of believers, and indeed to human beings generally, it is impossible to claim for the Church community or for its authoritative teachers exclusive knowledge of natural law.

But because its knowledge is not exclusive, the Church can and must appeal to the moral perceptions both of its own community and of humanity generally. What our study suggests is not exclusive knowledge, but gifts of the Spirit that can enable believing individuals, the community of belief and its authoritative teachers to have an insight into the demands of the moral life at a given time and place that may be absent in the larger community. Thus the role of the Church will often be a prophetic one, calling attention to dimensions of the moral life that are neglected. Since the notion of a natural law affirms a commonality of moral experience and moral judgment among human beings, that prophetic role of the Church can hope to elicit a response in the larger human community.

Karl Rahner has written of the "liberating modesty" of an attitude of the Church to the world which respects its legitimate autonomy.[75] It is our judgment that a teaching authority which recognizes both its own function and limits in the field of natural law morality will find itself both liberated from pretensions to omniscience false to the historical experience of the Church and at the same time freed for a perhaps more modest but indispensable prophetic role in modern society.

Notes

1. J. A. Komonchak, *"Humanae Vitae* and Its Reception: Ecclesiological Reflections," pp. 221-57, and J. C. Ford, S.J., and G. Grisez, "Contraception and the Infallibility of the Ordinary Magisterium," pp. 258-312.

2. See *Casti Connubii,* nn. 54, 56; *Humanae Vitae,* nn. 4, 11; J. C. Ford, S.J. and G. Kelly, S.J., *Contemporary Moral Theology,* Vol. 2 (Westminister: Newman, 1963), pp. 276-78; and G. Grisez, *Contraception and the Natural Law* (Milwaukee: Bruce, 1964). Ford and Grisez, "Contraception and Infallibility," introduce some qualifications in their discussion at pp. 285, 290-91.

3. See Y. Congar, O. P., "Pour une historie sémantique du terme 'Magisterium,' " *RSPT,* 60 (1976), pp. 85-98.

4. J. P. Boyle, "The Ordinary Magisterium: Toward a History of the Concept," *Hey J,* Fall 1979 and Winter 1979.

5. J. Kleutgen, S.J., *Die Theologie der Vorzeit verteidigt,* Vol. I (2nd ed., Innsbruck, 1878), p. 146. The argument strongly resembles that made by Bellarmine, "Controversiarum de Summo Pontifice," lib. 4 cap. V, "de decretis morum." Bellamine's proposition is: "The Soverign Pontiff cannot err not only in his decrees in matters of faith, but also in moral precepts (*praecepta morum*) which are prescribed for the whole Church and which deal with matters necessary for salvation or with those which are good or evil per se." Bellamine's arguments are drawn from the divine promises to the Church and from the holiness which is a mark of the Church in the creeds.

Bellarmine's examples are these: "It cannot be that the Pontiff would err by commanding some vice like usury or forbidding a virtue like restitution, because these things are good or evil per se. Nor can it be that he would err by commanding something contrary to salvation like circumcision or the Sabbath (observance), or by forbidding something necessary to salvation like baptism or the Eucharist. But that he might command something which is not good or evil ex se, nor contrary to salvation, but which is nonetheless useless, or that he might command it under a penalty which is too severe: it is not absurd to say that that could happen, although it is not for subjects to judge in this matter but simply to obey" (in J. Favre, ed., *Bellarmini Opera,* Vol. 2 [1870; reprint ed., Frankfurt: Minerva, 1965], pp. 87-88).

6. See J. T. Burchaell, *Catholic Theories of Biblical Inspiration Since 1810* (Cambridge: Cambridge University Press, 1969).

7. See R. Latourelle, S.J., *Theology of Revelation* (New York: Alba House, 1966).

8. See W. Kasper, *Die Lehre von der Tradition in der Römische Schule* (Freiburg: Herder, 1962).

9. See T. H. Sanks, *Authority in the Church: A Study in Changing Paradigms,* American Academy of Religion Dissertation Series, 2 (Missoula: Scholars Press, 1974).

10. J. B. Franzelin, S.J., *De Divina Traditione et Scriptura* (Rome: Propaganda Fide Press, 1870), p. 110.

11. *Ibid.,* pp. 547-51. This same line of reasoning also underlies the teaching of the First Vatican Council's constitution *Dei Filius,* of which Franzelin was a major author. His contributions have been conveniently collected by H. J. Pottmeyer. *Der Glaube vor dem Anspruch der Wissenschaft* (Freiburg: Herder, 1968), who includes in an appendix the *votum* prepared by Franzelin for the preparatory commission of the Council as well as his first schema of the constitution on the Catholic faith.

During the discussion of Chapter 2, paragraphs 1 and 2, of the constitution, the Deputation for the Faith rejected efforts to insert explicit reference to the natural law into the chapter which defined the power of human reason to know of God's existence from the things which he has made. The *Relator* for the Deputation, Bishop Vincent Gasser, explained that the amendments were superfluous, since a knowledge of God, "the beginning and end of all things," included knowledge of at least one's principal moral duties toward God, and the phrase *ea quae in rebus divinis humanae rationi per se impervia non sunt* in paragraph 2 was broader than and thus included the natural law. See *Sacrorum conciliorum nova et amplissima collectio,* ed. by J. Mansi et al. Vol. 53 (1923-27; reprint ed., Graz: Akademische Druck, 1961), cols. 276D, 279C, and *DS* 3004, 3005.

Pottmeyer also indicates the important contributions of Kleutgen to the development of the constitution, pp. 171-89.

12. *De Divine Traditione,* p. 28.

13. *Die Theologie der Vorzeit,* Vol. 1, pp. 62-63.

14. *Tractatus de legibus,* lib. 1, cap. IX, n. 4 in *Opera Omnia,* Vol. 5 (Paris: Vives, 1856), p. 51.

15. *Tractatus de gratia,* lib. 1, "De necessitate gratiae ad perficienda opera moraliter bona ordinis naturalis, et ad contraria peccata vitanda," *Opera Omnia,* Vol. 7, pp. 355-583.

16. *Tractatus de gratia,* lib. 2, "De necessitate gratiae ad actus divini ordinis eliciendos, servanda supernaturalia praecepta, et peccata contraria vitanda," *Opera Omnia,* Vol. 7, pp. 585-718, esp. cap. I, n. 10, p. 588.

17. Lib. 10, cap. II, n. 3, *Opera Omnia,* Vol. 6, p. 554.

18. Lib. 10, cap. I, n. 5, *Opera Omnia,* Vol. 6, p. 555.

19. *Tractatus de fide,* disp. II, sec. 2, n. 7, *Opera Omnia,* Vol. 12, p. 20.

20. *Tractatus de fide,* disp. V, sec. 5, *Opera Omnia,* Vol. 12, pp. 152-54.

21. Tracing this development would take us beyond the scope of this study. See Y. Congar, O.P., *Tradition and Traditions* (New York: Macmillan, 1967), esp. pp. 86-176; P. de Vooght, O.S.B., *Les Sources de la doctrine chrétienne d'après les théologiens du XIVᵉ siècle et du début du XVᵉ avec le texte intégral des XII premières questions de la summa inédite de Gérard de Bologne* (Paris: Desclée de Brower, 1954); J. Murphy, *The Notion of Tradition in John Driedo* (Milwaukee: 1959); and H. Schützeichel,

Wesen und Gegenstand der kirchlichen Lehrautorität nach Thomas Stapleton: Ein Beitrag zur Geschichte der Kontroverstheologie im 16. Jahrhundert, Trierer Theologische Studien, 20 (Trier: Paulinus Verlag, 1966), esp. the useful short history, pp. 8-28.

22. *Tractatus de legibus,* lib. 2. cap. VII, n. 5, *Opera Omnia,* Vol. 5, p. 113.

23. See F. Suarez, *Tractatus de fide,* disp. V, sects. 3 and 4, *Opera Omnia,* Vol. 12, pp. 142-52; J. de Lugo, *Tractatus de virtute fidei divinae,* disp. III, sect. 5, *Disputationes Scholasticae et Morales,* Vol. 1 (Paris: Vives, 1891), p. 258.

24. *De sacra traditione,* thesis V, p. 28. This doctrine passed into the official teaching of the papal magisterium in Pius XII's encyclical *Humani Generis* in 1950. See Max Seckler, "Die Theologie als kirchliche Wissenschaft nach Pius XII und Paul VI," in *TQ* 149 (1969), 212-214.

25. *De sacra traditione,* p. 31.

26. *Ibid.,* pp. 33-37. The distinction of the charism of infallibility from revelation or inspiration was noted in the discussions of the First Vatican Council on papal infallibility. Bishop Gasser mentions the distinction in his presentation of chapter 4 of *Pastor Aeternus* and proposed amendments. See Mansi, 52, col. 1213D. That the assistance of the Spirit is therefore *per se negativa* is asserted by many Catholic theologians. See H. Dieckmann, S.J., *De Ecclesia, II: De Ecclesiae Magisterio* (Freiburg: Herder, 1925), pp. 36-37; I. Salaverri, S.J., *De Ecclesia Christi,* in Patres S.J. Facultatum Theologicarum in Hispania Professores, eds., *Sacrae Theologiae Summae,* Vol. 1 (Madrid: BAC, 1952), p. 563; T. Zapelena, S.J., *De Ecclesia Christi,* Pars Altera Apologetico-Dogmatica (Rome: Gregorian University Press, 1954), pp. 133-34. Zapelena notes on p. 134 that while no positive divine influence on the authoritative teachers is required, neither is it excluded.

That point is made more emphatically by Charles Journet, who distinguishes three degrees of divine assistance: an "absolute" assistance which protects the proposition of divine revelation by the Church, a "prudential assistance" which protects the multitude of pastoral decisions taken by the authority of the Church from error in matters essential to the holiness of the Church and protects such decisions as a whole from error—at least collectively and in the majority of cases, and finally a "biological assistance" which protects the Church authorities in making decisions essential to its survival—a field which embraces quite practical political decisions. Journet concludes that the notion of "divine assistance" is extrinsic, analogous and positive—taking a great variety of forms that cannot be satisfactorily enumerated. "It would be a mistake to think that the divine assistance can consist only of a negative help. The better theologians affirm on the contrary that Divine Providence sustains God's Church more by positive graces of light and of power than by negative interventions that would be limited to checking dangerous measures and reducing their authors to impotence" (*L'Eglise du Verbe Incarné,* Vol. 1

[Paris: Desclée de Brouwer, 1962-69], pp. 426-35, citation at pp. 433-34; see also Vol. 2, pp. 634-43).

Clearly this more expansive notion of the divine assistance to the teaching of the Church has important implications for this study.

Nevertheless it seems agreed by Catholic theologians that, whatever the assistance of the Holy Spirit to the Church, it is not of such a kind as to produce new revelations to supplement, much less to correct, the apostolic deposit of faith which is transmitted in the Church.

27. An explicit demand for internal, assent to papal doctrinal definitions has its origins in the Jansenist controversies and in the bull *Vineam Domini Sabaoth* pubished by Clement XI in 1705, cited in *DS* at n. 2390. The discussion of the assent due to authentic but not infallible propositions of the magisterium is often located in a thesis dealing with the authority of the Roman congregations. See J. Salaverri, thesis 15, pp. 696-705: H. Dieckmann, assertion 29, pp. 112-27; J. B. Franzelin, *De divina traditione*, pp. 117-18. Franzelin argues directly from the papal letter *Tuas Libenter*.

28. J. B. Franzelin, *De Ecclesia Christi*, thesis 5, pp. 43-64; for Kleutgen, see n. 12.

29. See also the *relatio* of Bishop Gasser in Mansi, 52, col. 1213B.

30. J. B. Franzelin, *Tractatus de sacramentis in genere* (Rome: Propaganda Fide Press, 1878), pp. 170-73; see also W. Van Roo, S.J., *De sacramentis in genere* (Rome: Gregorian University Press, 1957) scholion A: "Ordo, Jurisdictio, Character, Gratia," pp. 260-62.

31. *De Ecclesia*, p. 51.

32. "Weihesakramentale Grundlegung kirchlicher Rechtsgewalt," *Scholastik* 16 (1941) 496-520. What follows is derived from the article.

33. *Ibid.*, p. 515.

34. *Summa theologica,* Supplement, q. 35, art. 1 in corp.

35. "Weihesakramentale Grundlegung," p. 516.

36. The allocution of Pius XII, "Magnificate Dominum mecum," of November 2, 1954 (*The Pope Speaks* 1 [1954] 375-85) locates the power of the Church to proclaim the natural law in its pastoral authority; the encyclical *Humanae Vitae*, of July 25, 1968, n. 4, puts the natural law under the *teaching* authority.

The pastoral office is emphasized by Jacob David, S.J., *Loi naturelle et autorité de l'église* (Paris: Cerf, 1968) [*Das Naturrecht in Krise und Läuterung* (Cologne: Bachem, 1967)]. On David, see J. P. Boyle, *The Sterilization Controversy* (New York: Paulist Press, 1977), pp. 62-64. David holds that only the general principles of the natural law are revealed and pertain to the teaching authority. Other problems of the natural law pertain to the pastoral authority and thus bind only as disciplinary matters do.

37. K. Rahner, "Some Implications of the Scholastic Doctrine of Uncreated Grace," *Theological Investigations*, Vol. 1 (New York: Seabury, 1961-79), pp. 319-46.

38. See K. Rahner, "Concerning the Relationship between Nature and Grace," in *Theological Investigations* I, pp. 297-317; and "Nature and

Grace," in D. Wharton, trans., *Nature and Grace: Dilemmas in the Modern Church* (New York: Sheed & Ward, 1964), pp. 114-49.

39. J. P. Boyle, "Faith and Christian Ethics in Rahner and Lonergan," *Thought* 50 (1975), 247-65.

40. For what follows on the work of the Spirit I am indebted to H. Mühlen, *Una Persona Mystica: Eine Person in vielen Personen* (3rd ed., Munich: Schönigh, 1968).

41. K. Rahner, *The Church and the Sacraments,* Quaestiones Disputatae, 9, trans. W. J. O'Hara (New York: Herder & Herder, 1963), p. 18.

42. See *Dei Verbum,* no. 10. See the texts together with their *relationes* in *Acta Synodalia Sacrosancti Concilii Oecumenici Vaticani Secundi,* 3/3 (Vatican Press, 1970-78), 80-81, 87; 4/1; 350-51, 354; and M. Löhrer, "Träger der Vermittlung," in J. Feiner and M. Löhler, eds., *Mysterium Salutis* (Einsiedeln: Benziger, 1965-76), Vol. 1, pp. 545-87.

43. The notion of a *sensus fidei* or collective consciousness was exploited by J. A. Möhler, *Einheit in der Kirche,* ed. by J. R. Geiselman (Darmstadt: Wissenschaftliche Buchgesellschaft, 1957) and after him by Karl Rahner, especially in his treatment of "faith-instinct." See J. P. Boyle, "Faith and Christian Ethics," pp. 252-54. See also *Lumen Gentium,* n. 12.

44. *Dei Verbum,* n. 8.

45. See *Insight* (3rd ed., New York: Philosophical Library, 1970), p. 286.

46. See H. Mühlen, *Una Persona Mystica,* pp. 255-56.

47. *DS* 302.

48. H. Mühlen, *Una Persona Mystica,* p. 272.

49. *Ibid.,* p. 278.

50. H. Küng, *The Church,* trans. by Ray and Rosaleen Ockenden (London: Burns & Oates, 1967), p. 28.

51. *Insight,* pp. 191, 627-30.

52. *Lumen Gentium,* chapter 3. See B. Dupuy, "Theologie der kirchlichen Ämter," in *Mysterium Salutis,* 4:2, pp. 488-523, esp. p. 517. Dupuy's discussion of the sacramental character is very brief and is undeveloped with respect to the teaching role of the bishop. The view presented here of the relationship of the community to its authoritative teachers resembles the view of the Church found in the Agreed Statement by the Anglican-Roman Catholic International Commission dated January 17, 1977 and published in *Worship* 51 (1977), pp. 90-102. See esp. Part II which describes the relationship of *episcope* and *koinonia.*

53. See D. M. Stanley, S.J., "*Didache* as a Constitutive Element of the Gospel-Form," *CBQ* 17 (1955), pp. 336-438.

54. The reality of historical development even in the field of defined dogma has been explicitly acknowledged in the "Declaration in Defense of the Catholic Doctrine on the Church Against Certain Errors of the Present Day (*Mysterium Ecclesiae*)" issued by the Congregation for the Doctrine of the Faith, June 24, 1973, n. 5. Such a view of the Church community ac-

cords with Vatican II's teaching on the development of doctrine in *Dei Verbum*, n. 8.

55. This is acknowledged by Vatican II, *Gaudium et Spes,* n. 44.

56. See B. Lonergan, *Method in Theology* (London: Darton, Longman and Todd, 1972) and J. Gustafson, *Protestant and Roman Catholic Ethics* (Chicago: University of Chicago Press, 1978).

57. *Lumen Gentium,* n. 25. The same point is made in chapter 2 on the transmission of revelation in *Dei Verbum.*

58. See J. P. Boyle, *The Sterilization Controversy,* pp. 30-50. See also B. Schüller, "La théologie morale peut-elle se passer du droit naturel?" *NRT* 88 (1966), pp. 449-75, and "Zur theologischen Diskussion über die lex naturalis," *TP* 41 (1966), pp. 481-503.

59. On human relationships see H. Rotter, "Zum Erkenntnisproblem in der Moraltheologie," in J. Lotz, ed., *Neue Erkenntnisprobleme in Philosophie und Theologie* (Freiburg: Herder, 1968), pp. 226-47. Value theory appears in both Rahner and Lonergan; see J. P. Boyle, "Faith and Christian Ethics." On Lonergan see also F. E. Crowe, "An Exploration of Lonergan's New Notion of Value," *ScEs* 29 (1977), pp. 123-43, and W. E. Conn, "Bernard Lonergan on Value," *The Thomist* 40 (1976), pp. 243-57.

60. See A. Auer, "Die Erfahrung der Geschichtlichkeit und die Krise der Moral," *TQ* 149 (1969), pp. 4-22.

61. See K. Demmer, "Kirchliches Lehramt und Naturrecht," *TGl* 59 (1969), pp. 191-213.

62. See the articles by Bruno Schüller cited in n. 58 above. We cannot pursue here the critique of Schüller by Demmer.

63. See, for example, J. Fuchs, S.J., "Gibt es eine spezifische christliche Moral?" *SZ* 185 (1970), pp. 99-112.

64. This view of the teaching authority is in contrast to an older one which drew a very hard distinction between infallible teaching and that which is only authentic. See J. Beumer, S.J., "Das authentische Lehramt der Kirche," *TGl* 38 (1948), pp. 273-89. Demmer argues strongly for a distinction of degree and not of kind. See n. 60.

65. See E. Anscombe, "Authority in Morals," in J. M. Todd, ed., *Problems of Authority* (Baltimore: Helicon, 1962), pp. 179-88.

66. See J. P. Boyle, "Faith and Christian Ethics." See also K. Rahner, "Über die schlechte Argumentation in der Moraltheologie," *Schriften zur Theologie,* Vol. 13 (Einsiedeln: Benziger, 1954-78), pp. 93-107. In this recent article Rahner has further explored the role of unthematized, global moral knowledge in making moral arguments convincing or not. He again points out that the Church may know moral right and wrong better than it can formulate arguments for its point of view, but he now argues that the reverse can also be true: the Church may be offering arguments convincing only to those whose pre-thematic knowledge disposes them to accept the arguments. If that knowledge is incomplete, the arguments may in fact be bad ones. Rahner concludes to a critical—and thankless—role for moral theology vis-à-vis the moral pronouncements of the magisterium.

67. See n. 57 above.

68. *Ibid.*

69. See R. Collins, "Scriptures and the Christian Ethic," *CTSA Proceedings* 29 (1974), pp. 215-41.

70. H. Mühlen, *Una Persona Mystica*, pp. 74-88, discusses the problems of the notion of "collective personality." Mühlen prefers his own *Gross-Ich* to H. Wheeler Robinson's "corporate personality." Notions of the Church as the body of Christ and the people of God suggest that some such notion is widely accepted in Catholic theology.

71. *Ibid.*, pp. 342-58; on sacramental character, *Dei Verbum,* chapter 2, and *Lumen Gentium,* esp. chapters 1, 2, and 3.

72. See Cardinal William W. Baum. "Magisterium and Life of Faith," *Origins* 8 (1979), 76-80. The address was given to the Fellowship of Christian Scholars, April 28, 1978.

73. See M. Löhrer, *Mysterium Salutis,* Vol. 1, pp. 555-57.

74. We have dealt with this theology of pastoral directives in *Faith and Community in the Ethical Theory of Karl Rahner and Bernard Lonergan* (Ann Arbor: University Microfilms, 1972), pp. 97-103.

75. K. Rahner. "Church and World," *Sacramentum Mundi,* Vol. 1, pp. 346-57.

Reflections on the Literature

Richard A. McCormick, S.J.

1
Thomas Dubay and the State of Moral Theology

Dubay's major concerns, I think it fair to say, are the following: a contradictory and destructive pluralism inconsistent with the magisterium's notion of pluralism; the disappearance of the prophetic element in moral theology for an unevangelical ethics of accommodation to the expectations of the majority; the inadmissible appearance of two magisteria in the Church (theologians, hierarchy); the failure of moral theology to include in its concerns the ascetic and spiritual dimensions of Christian living. In the course of developing these objections against Curran—and to some extent against a large segment of the community of moral theologians —Dubay touches on a whole series of delicate and difficult theological themes: dissent in the Church, the existence of moral absolutes, the formation of conscience, etc.

I am glad Dubay composed his thoughtful critique. Moral theology does need criticism from outside its own ranks. Furthermore, and more importantly, Dubay has formulated his objections in a way that represents the attitudes and theological presuppositions of very many concerned and intelligent thinkers, Catholic and non-Catholic. Therefore the attempt to bring these issues into sharper focus at some length may throw light on matters that are a cause of concern and even division in the contemporary Church. Dubay has raised some very good questions. For instance, his insistence that the notion of *sensus fidelium* be made more precise is altogether salutary. However, I have very serious reservations about several of the substantial points in his study. The following remarks may be organized under three titles: pluralism, theologians vs. the magisterium, and prophecy.

Pluralism

Dubay has some important things to say here. One certainly is the distinction between complementary and contradictory pluralism. The latter, which he attributes to Curran, he regards as inconsistent with scriptural insistence on unity, destructive of practical pastoral guidance, and deadening to the Church's commission to speak out authoritatively on important moral matters.

For instance, where unity is concerned Dubay writes: "Not by the widest stretch of imagination could we call that ecclesial community 'completely one' (Jn.17:23) if in it some members are at odds habitually and in important moral and disciplinary matters with those whose duty it is to articulate the faith and morals for and to the community. A pluralism in moral theology that fails to reckon with this New Testament insistence is failing to reckon with its sources." [1] Or, again, with a contradictory pluralism "a secure knowledge of the moral implications of many acts becomes impossible."

Dubay is looking for unity in "important moral and disciplinary matters," a unity based on a "a secure knowledge of the moral implications of many acts. . . ." Here I believe we must ask: What are these "important moral and disciplinary matters"? What are these "basic matters or norms" confused by a contradictory pluralism? Are they rather detailed and concrete conclusions representing the application of moral general norms? Or are they the more general norms themselves? His terminology ("basic matters or norms") suggests the latter, but I suspect he really is looking for unity and security at the level of application, for he speaks of "a secure knowledge of the moral implications *of many acts*. . . ." So, how basic is basic?

Here I make three points. First, a past tradition easily led us to believe that "basic" had to do with matters such as self-stimulation for sperm-testing, removal of ectopic fetuses, actions that are *per se graviter excitantes*, cooperation in contraception, punitive sterilization, and a host of very concrete applications. We felt that we ought to possess and did possess a kind of certainty and subsequent security in these matters, and that our certainty was founded on the natural law. These, I submit, are not "basic matters or norms," if by this term is meant material on which we must agree if our Christian unity is to remain integral. There is plenty of room for doubt and hesitation and change, even contradictory pluralism, at this level of moral discourse. And yet, because the magisterium did get involved in such detailed practical applications in the past (e.g., the moral allocutions of Pius XII, responses of the Holy Office), and in a way that was authoritative, it gave credence to the notion that our moral unity is or ought to be located at this level, and that disagreement or pluralism at this level is a threat to unity. It is unclear to me whether Dubay is insisting on unity at this level. But there are certainly many who are so insisting and who will use Dubay and the biblical texts he cites to support the necessity of such unity. If it is unity at this level that Dubay has in mind as necessary when he says " 'In my opinion' is hardly going to be prophetic," it must be urged that the best way to eviscerate true prophecy is to attempt to be prohetic in areas where true prophecy cannot be objectively founded and persuasively argued.

Second, in the contemporary world we are faced with a great number of truly new moral problems. The scope and many-sidedness of these problems means that we must struggle our way through to new insights and a new vocabulary capable of conceptualizing new data within the value perceptions and commitments of the Christian tradition. To approach this task with an overriding concern for unity and a corresponding intolerance of pluralism is in some sense to suppose that we already have the answers. In other words, in many areas of contemporary moral concern unity is not a present possession but a difficult, often elusive, perhaps impossible goal.

Third, Vatican II reinserted the Church into the world, into history, and into Christendom. This insertion calls necessarily for a rethinking of certain moral formulations and pastoral practices. A process of rethinking, because it is in human hands, is precisely a process—often halting, painful, imperfect. It requires a tolerance for the tentative and ambiguous. Many persons in the Church experience this as "confusion" because there has been very little in our past ways of doing things that educates to this tolerance.

Theologians vs. the Magisterium

This theme runs throughout Dubay's study. Only a few of the more important items can be raised here. First, he criticizes Curran for supporting a right to frequent and habitual dissent from authentic, non-infallible teaching. Dubay argues that this equivalently establishes two magisteria in the Church. I agree with this, but much more needs to be said. I have always been uncomfortable with the term "right to dissent." We are concerned, as believers, with the behavioral implications of our being-in-Christ, with moral truth. The magisterium is a vehicle for this purpose and therefore subordinated to it. To isolate this vehicle from other sources of reflection and knowledge in the Church is to forget this purpose, to subordinate the vehicle to superior-subject relationships, and thus to juridicize the search for truth. To speak of a "right to dissent" tends to accept this juridical narrowing by establishing rights against the teacher or his authoritative teaching. Therefore it would be much better, I believe, to speak of a duty and right to exercise a truly personal reflection within the teaching-learning process of the Church, a duty and right that belong to all who possess proportionate competence. Bishops, as well as theologians, are not exempt from this arduous task. To reduce this duty to "supporting Rome," "being loyal to the Holy Father," is both to misconceive loyalty and to undermine the magisterium.

This personal reflection can end in inability to assent to the formulations of the magisterium, as any number of episcopal conferences have pointed out. How frequent and habitual this might be depends on several factors. First, if the magisterium is functioning in a healthy manner, such dissent ought to be relatively rare, a point made convincingly by Schüller.[2] Otherwise it would cease to be authoritative in any theologically acceptable sense of the word. Second, the notions of "difference" and "dissent" demand a distinction, clearly made by Pope John XXIII and Vatican II, between the substance of a teaching and its formulation. Dissent with regard to substance will be a rare phenomenon, though it might occur with regard to formulation somewhat more frequently. For instance, the substance of the Church's teaching on abortion is one thing; its formulation by Pius XI and Pius XII or even the Sacred Congregation for the Doctrine of the Faith is not necessarily identical with that substance (e.g., where the life of the mother is at stake). Finally, how much qualification and dissent is present will likely depend on how detailed the documents of the magisterium become. There has been a real difference here in recent pontificates. Pius XII, in his many allocutions and discourses, went into some very detailed applications of medical ethics; this has not been the style of Pope John XXIII or Pope Paul VI. Indeed there are many theologians who believe that the detailed application of perennially valid moral principles should generally not be the concern of the magisterium, or that if the magisterium chooses to undertake this, it must do so with a tentativeness proportionate to the contingency of the material.

But Dubay's concern with the existence of two magisteria needs yet further comment. Speaking of the prophet as one who is sent, Dubay notes that a Catholic theologian is always sent, if not by diocesan faculties, then "at least through being in communion with the bishop and through the bishop with the Holy See." He then adds that "insofar as theologians are at odds with the sending magisterium, they are not sent." Being at odds with the magisterium, they constitute a second magisterium, a notion Dubay rejects.

I do too, but I believe he has not explored the possibility of a third alternative. If the magisterium can *per accidens* err in its authentic, non-infallible teaching (and it can), and if such error is detectable by someone other than the magisterium (and it could be), then it is clear that others in the Church do participate in the teaching-learning process of the Church without thereby becoming a second, competitive magisterium. By framing the matter as he has (either the hierarchical magisterium or the magisterium of dissenting theologians), Dubay has fragmented the teaching-learning process in the Church into camps of competitive interests and prerogatives. That is improper. We all have a part to play in a healthily functioning magisterium, and to view that part—even and especially when it takes the form of dissent—as a second and competitive magisterium is to fail to see the teaching-learning function of the Church in appropriately processive and cooperative terms. It is to see one group in the Church in prior and independent possession of the truth. One need not hold that notion to treasure and support a genuinely authoritative teaching office in the Church and to locate that office in the person of the Pope and the bishops in communion with the Pope. For this reason I think it is simply false to say that theologians who disagree with the magisterium on a particular point "are not sent." They are honestly, even if very noninfallibly, making their contribution to the teaching-learning process of the Church. And that is their proper task, that for which they "are sent." In this sense there are indeed two magisteria in the Church, but two that have different if not unrelated functions. When these two functions are confused and identified and the magisterium seen in either-or terms (either bishops or theologians), the response should not be denial of one magisterium, but a clarification of both.

Prophecy

My most serious reservations on Dubay's study are in this area. First, in discussing theologians who have found themselves in a position of dissent, Dubay uses phrases such as "tailoring ethics to the expectations of majorities," "theologians who seem to begin with 'what modern man will accept,'" "the curious assumption . . . that Christian ethics would be acceptable to the majority." This Dubay sees as unworthy of the true prophet.

Since the theologian is human, there is always the danger that such tailoring will occur. But that being admitted, one could wish that such phrases with their motivational overtones would disappear from serious theological discourse. This or that theologian may be wrong—and the better the theologian he is, the more ready he is to admit this. But it is precisely rightness or wrongness that is his concern and should be the issue, not attitudes of accommodation and compromise alleged to be his point of departure by those who disagree with him.

Second, Dubay contrasts "prophetic" with "conformism." "The prophet of the Lord is never a slave to popularity or style." True enough. But there is a hidden and, I believe, false argument buried in such statements. It is this: all that is difficult is right; all that is not is conformism.

Third — and very similar to the above — Dubay, in speaking of moral prophecy, makes it appear that the more alone, isolated, and rejected a position, the more prophetic and true it is. Here great caution is required. Prophetic statements and actions, it is true, are often lonely ones. But the fact that prophetic statements are countercultural does not guarantee that every countercultural statement is truly prophetic.

Fourth, Dubay repeatedly warns that the prophet (i.e., prophetic theologian) is faithful to the Gospel. "The full Gospel has never been popular." He cites Stöger: "He who tampers with the teaching of Christ condemns himself." In the context of the discussion, one must wonder what Dubay has in mind. Disagreements on things like contraception, masturbation, direct-indirect killing, artificial insemination, sterilization, and pastoral policies for homosexual problems are the areas of liveliest disagreement cited by Dubay. But if the Gospel dictates one particular answer to these problems, I am not familiar with such an answer. Thus to face these problems with appeals to the uncompromising and prophetic demands of the Gospel is either to suggest that the Gospel answers these questions or is overkill. In these areas the Gospel informs reasoning processes; it does not replace them. Therefore in all of the above points Dubay seems guilty of *ignorantia elenchi*; he misses the point.

Fifth, Dubay insists that the prophet (and the prophetic theologian) proclaims absolute precepts. Hence theologians who question these absolutes are departing from the Gospel and abandoning their own prophetic responsibility. In developing this, he states that "Scripture takes absolute moral norms for granted" and that "there are so many absolutely worded precepts in both Testaments that I shall not mention one." He cites and supports Bright's study on apodictic prohibitions that bind always and everywhere. His conclusion: "It seems to me that the alternative to an ethics with some apodictic teaching is an ethics of exhortation."[3]

It would have been well if Dubay had become specific here, for the term "absolute" is treacherous when applied to biblical or any morality.[4] For instance, when speaking of "absolute moral norms," does one mean formal (e.g., never act unjustly) or material norms (e.g., never tell a falsehood)? Put somewhat differently, in discussing norms we must be careful to distinguish between parenetic discourse and explanatory discourse or moral reasoning.[5] Explanatory discourse deals with the pros and cons of a position, with argumentation, with the normative validity of a precept. Parenetic discourse is not concerned with the normative validity of a moral command. Such validity is taken for granted and then the precept is used to pass judgment on a person's behavior. A good instance is the Johannine pericope on the woman taken in adultery. The question is not whether adultery is right or wrong; all the participants agree that it is wrong. The validity of the command is acknowledged. The only question is whether the woman has committed the act and what should be done.

Thus parenetic discourse makes use of rules to accuse, convict, condemn, and urge repentance. Positively, rules are used to praise, advise, implore, encourage, and strengthen. Such discourse can succeed only if genuine agreement exists on what is right or wrong.

Because parenesis supposes agreement on what is morally obligatory and what is not, its language can be very concise and clipped. For instance, in the commands "You shall not kill. Neither shall you commit adultery. Neither shall you steal" (Dt. 5:17-19), the words "kill," "adultery," and "steal" contain compressed and complicated value judgments. "Killing" (or, better, "murder") must be defined in terms of what killing was regarded as morally licit by Israel. Similarly, "adultery" is understood only if one first understands the institution of marriage that prevailed in Israel. For example, a husband having intercourse with an unmarried woman was not considered an adulterer.[6]

Now the decalogue presumes that all these matters are settled and contents itself with uttering the words "kill," "adultery," "steal," etc. Thus the emphasis falls on the "You shall not," an emphasis highlighting the absolute, unconditional character of the precept. But this absoluteness is that of parenetic discourse. It does not convey information about the specific content of various moral demands. That it takes for granted.

The upshot of these remarks is that Dubay's opposition between absolutes (apodictic teaching) and exhortation is a false opposition, for the precepts of biblical morality are themselves heavily parenetic — hortatory to what is presumed to be known and agreed on. One can hardly use their absolute and unconditional character to discredit the contemporary discussion of absolute moral norms, for this discussion is concerned precisely about what ought to count as "murder," "theft," "unchastity," etc., about what is the content of parenetic discourse. It is a discussion within the area of *moral reasoning.* So when Dubay says "When an ethics knows only a contradictory pluralism and/or a whole series of 'maybes,' it ceases to be interesting. It becomes quite unlike biblical morality . . . " [7] he is identifying and therefore confusing in the term "ethics" two forms of discourse: parenesis and moral reasoning.

Notes

1. Thomas Dubay, S.M., "The State of Moral Theology," *Theological Studies* 35 (1974), pp. 482-506.
2. Bruno Schüller, "Bemerkungen zur authentischen Verkündigung des kirchlichen Lehramtes," *Theologie und Philosophie* 42 (1967), (pp. 534-51. Cf. Also *Theology Digest* 16 (1968) pp. 328-32.
3. *Art. cit.,* p. 504.
4. There is a sense, for instance, in which every moral norm is "absolute." That is, it is absolute because it imposes a categorical imperative in contrast to a mere prudential suggestion.
5. I owe these remarks to Bruno Schüller's lectures at the Gregorian University in 1973. For some helpful remarks on parenesis cf. Norman Perrin, *The New Testament — An Introduction* (New York: Harcourt Brace Jovanovich, 1974), pp. 20-21.
6. Dubay's rather sweeping statement about extramarital sex is, I believe, in error. He writes: "It [an ethics without absolutes] becomes quite unlike St. Paul, who terms extramarital relations fornication or adultery . . . ." (p. 504). Cf. Bruce Malina, "Does *Porneia* Mean Fornication?" *Novum Testamentum* 14 (1972), pp. 10-17.
7. *Art. cit.,* p. 504.

2
Theologians and the Magisterium

The Church is and ought to be a teacher of Christian morality; no one doubts this. But what is a matter of continuing adaptation and perennial dispute is how this is to be done most effectively. This "how" touches closely and sensitively on the very notion of magisterium, especially as the notion relates to several components in the Church, most particularly theologians. Thus the relationship of theologians and bishops will have a good deal to say about how Christian morality is conceived, implemented, and received in the Church.

This relationship has always been somewhat tense. Robert B. Eno, S.S., in a useful historical study of the early Church, passes in review some of the conflicts of the time.[1] It was in the third century that the Church saw the rise of what Eno calls "conscious theologizing." The rise of theological reflection as another form of expertise or authority was almost bound to lead to tension with established authority, and that tension has been with us ever since. Eno has no pat answers to the problem except to hold up the patristic ideal stamping the consciousness of both theologian and bishop. The theologian is above all a churchman; the bishop is one who is above all concerned with *prodesse*, not *praeesse* (care for others, not precedence over them).

The magisterium, the Church's teaching function, will reflect the situation of the world in which it lives. How one analyzes this situation differs markedly, apparently with the preoccupations of the analyzer. Francis X. Murphy, C.SS.R., reviews this situation, with its tensions and inconsistencies, through the attitudes and actions of Pope Paul VI, which he paints as full of tensions and inconsistencies.[2] George Kelly blames it all on dissenting theologians.[3] In the face of such differences, I recommend an essay by Bishop B. C. Butler.[4] It takes the form of a letter to a convert distressed by changes in the Church. He points out, with historical precedents and great compassion, how the shift to a more historical understanding requires patience. It is a cultural, not a faith, crisis. Incidentally, it is refreshing to see an intensely loyal Catholic bishop write that "it is possible to have grave reservations about particular papal decisions and policies" at the very time he is insisting on the indispensability of papal authority.

Paul VI has repeatedly addressed himself to this subject. For instance, in his general audience of August 4, 1976, he reasserted the hierarchical structure of the Church as deriving from Christ.[5] He expressed his grave concern for those who deny "the existence within the Church of legitimate, or rather obligatory, authoritative functions," and in some of the strongest language he has ever used castigated those who sit in judgment on this hierarchical function. It is hard to believe that he did not have Archbishop Lefebvre in mind.

Before turning to the longer, more systematic studies, I note several interesting entries. Cardinal François Marty (Paris) argues that the dialogue between theologians and bishops must be "institutionalized."[6] Jerome Theisen, O.S.B. proposes the notion of "reliability" as best describing the Catholic attitude toward the ministry of the Holy Father.[7] In a study remarkably different in tone, Dario Composta (Pontificia Università Salesiana) insists, against what he takes to be the position of Franz Böckle, that the magisterium does not "merely inform" but teaches.[8]

The following literature touching the relation of theology and the magisterium falls into two divisions: groups (International Theological Commission, Sacred Congregation for Catholic Education) and individuals (Coffy, Whealon, Palazzini, Congar, Dulles, Lanne).

During October 1975, the International Theological Commission met in Rome. The subject of its deliberations: the relationship between the magisterium and theologians. The Commission drafted twelve theses in an attempt to state this relationship.[9] In its introductory statement it noted that this relationship has shown considerable variations through history. In the patristic age, for example, Popes and many bishops were often the great theologians. At other times a greater separation of functions could be noted, research into matters of faith pertaining to the function of specialists. Faculties of theology were at times in conflict with Popes—e.g., with John XXII on eschatology. This separation of expertise probably peaked in the Councils of Constance and Basle.

At the thirty-fourth session of Basle (June 25, 1439) there were three hundred doctors of theology, thirteen priests, and seven bishops.

The International Commission treats three points: (1) elements common to theology and the magisterium; (2) differences between theology and the magisterium; (3) principles of a trusting collaboration between the two. Under the second heading, the Commission points out that the magisterium "draws its authority from sacramental ordination." Theologians, on the other hand, owe their "specifically theological authority to their scientific qualification." The Commission admits that tensions can arise between theologians and the magisterium but sees this realistically as a vital creative force in the Church. It concludes by urging more efficacious dialogue and lists some threats to such dialogue.

Maurizio Flick, S.J. has provided a thoughtful commentary on this document.[10] He concentrates on the relationship between the magisterium and theologians. There are two functions the theologian performs in the Church: (1) he mediates between Pope-and-bishops and the people; (2) he contributes to the magisterium's formation of opinion. What I find refreshing about Flick's presentation is his ability to spell out these functions in a realistic, satisfying way.

As for the first function, he notes two objections against this notion of theology. First, it "reduces" the theologian to a vulgarizer of magisterial opinion. Flick responds convincingly in several ways, especially by showing the absolute necessity of an "ascending communication" (*divulgazione ascendente*), the need to relate basic ecclesial judgments to the community of the well-informed. The second objection sees this theological function as a kind of ideology — an approach which forms its positions to support the interests of an institution or movement. Not so, he says, because the theologian exercises his interpretative function in a *critical* way. Here Flick is especially good. This function requires that the theologian show not only the authority behind the teaching but also its incomplete and to-be-completed aspects. Indeed, where dogma is not involved, "the theologian can and ought (in particular circumstances) to manifest his own dissent."[11]

The second task of the theologian, to precede and prepare the opinions of the magisterium, derives from the fact that revelation "is not to be considered as a static deposit . . . but is always confronted with new questions which demand that it be continually developed." In this development, the actions, opinions, and inclinations of the people of God have a special place, but not without discernment. In this discernment both the magisterium and theology have a true *authority*.

Flick next notes that the two functions of theologians (mediation and preparation) "are not separate," i.e., normally theological research reflects and supports both functions. Thus, in dealing with the crisis of the sacrament of penance, the theologian interprets the past teaching of the Church, but in doing so also suggests to the magisterium the proper way to explain reconciliation with the Church.

In trying to relate this double function of the theologian to the magisterium, Flick cites the interesting condemnation of George Hermes (*DB* 2738-40). Some of Hermes' disciples, so goes the anecdote, came to Rome to determine why he was condemned. A Roman official asked whether "they had come to the Holy See to instruct the Holy See or be instructed by it." Flick sees this as a false statement of the question, since it presupposes that the truth is in the prior possession of one of the conversationalists. After insisting on the need for dialogue, Flick shows that classical ecclesiology had the tendency to describe the relations of magisterium and theologians in juridical terms: "the duty and therefore the right of the magisterium to direct the entire theological project." The Commission has qualified this, and this switch in the methodological aspect of the question "constitutes the principal novelty of the document."

On February 22, 1976, the Sacred Congregation for Catholic Education issued a fifty-page document, "The Theological Formation of Future Priests."[12] Within it the relationship of the magisterium and theologians is explicitly treated. Several statements are made about theology and its relation to the magisterium. First, the Church has the "right and duty to demand of theologians a loyalty to the magisterium," which has the function of guaranteeing that research will promote the authentic building up of the body of Christ. Second, the *munus docendi* belongs to "the bishops united in collegiality with the Supreme Pontiff." This episcopal magisterium cannot be replaced by individual thought. The latter has the "limited function only of investigating, illustrating, and developing objective data which come from God." Third, theologians have the task of research and critical reflection. But "they can receive from the magisterium a share in its *munus docendi (missio canonica docendi)*." However, the magisterium must maintain its "authority to judge the relation of theological speculation to the word of God."

If I interpret this document correctly, its view of the relationship between theology and the magisterium seems to be that theology is at the service of the magisterium. This is a view explicitly rejected by Archbishop Coffy (see below) and the episcopal discussions that followed his study. As will be clear, Coffy sees the relationship as one of complementarity. Whatever the term used, the substantial idea is that both the magisterium and theology are at the service of the revealed word of God; they have the same tasks (*custos* and *promotor*) but from different levels, with different tools, and sometimes with different conversation partners.

The Congregation's perspective is one of subordination, wherein the official magisterium grants a share in its charge to theologians. Thus, the Congregation says that "the episcopal magisterium cannot be replaced by individual thought." True, and every theologian knows it and ought to admit it. But "replaced by" seems a defensive and uneasy way of framing the matter. One wonders why it was not immediately added that the magisterium cannot fulfill its function without theological thought.

Another problem sharpens the issue. The document states that the magisterium has the power to judge the conformity of the results of research, etc., with revelation. Few would deny this, but the problem is more complex. If, as nearly everyone concedes, it is impossible to conceive and speak of revelation without a theology (i.e., the very statement of revelation, *Glaubenssprache*, implies *a* theology, as is clear from the Gospels themselves), then clearly those who judge the conformity of theological research and reflection with revelation are doing so *with a theology*. That there are problems here is obvious. For instance, what is the theology of the Congregation for the Doctrine of the Faith when it issues a decree on human sexuality, or apostolic succession, etc.? Is it self-validating as a theology because it is official? I do not raise this question out of any desire to undermine the function of the magisterium. I raise it only to sharpen the issue and thus to strengthen the function of the magisterium in the Church. The question raised suggests that the real issue is not captured with words like "replaced by individual thought," etc. This is a juridical vocabulary that ends up pitting theologians competitively against bishops. The real issue is what form their indispensable cooperation ought to take if the word of God and its implications in our time are to be preached (*promotor*) and protected (*custos*).

In the spring of 1975, the third Symposium of European Bishops met outside of Rome to discuss the relationship of bishops and theologians. Archbishop Robert Coffy (Albi) delivered a very interesting paper, which first appeared in the *Bulletin du secrétariat de la Conférence épiscopale française* but is now available in *Orientierung*.

Coffy proceeds in two steps: the problem, then suggestions toward a solution. Some of the causes of the problem are: the changing cultural climate, which demands a new faith-language (*Glaubenssprache*); theological pluralism involving different language, different philosophical assumptions, different use of empirical sciences; the demand by theologians that "the ecclesial office be executed in a new way" more in keeping with our time. Furthermore, the very understanding of the faith is involved.

> Every understanding of the faith necessarily implies a theology. There are no sharp lines of demarcation between the faith and the theological understanding of the faith. This clarifies the reaction of theologians to certain interventions of the magisterium. Theologians have the impression that the magisterium imposes its own theology. Therefore they demand that the magisterium admit its theological preferences and then grant that it is not the only way to express the faith.[14]

The most profound cause of the magisterium's problems Coffy sees in the very notion of revealed truth. In the recent past, perhaps under certain Platonic influences, revelation was conceived in a way that allowed it to be encapsulated in objective formulated truths. Thus by the very statement of the question the magisterium was positioned to distinguish clearly between the true and the false. It conceived its task as comparing certain formulations with eternal truths thus conceived (*ewige Wahrheiten*). Our time, however, is much more sensitive to the historical character of truth—which means that magisterial interventions can no longer be beyond discussion, as they were thought to be in the past.

Against this background Coffy sees the relationship of theology to the magisterium as one of complementarity. Both the magisterium and theologians are involved as guardians (*custos*) and promoters (*promotor*) of the faith, not as rivals but in different ways. Coffy rejects the idea that theologians are in the service of the magisterium; both theologians and the magisterium are in service of the word of God. After insisting on respectful cooperation, he suggests that fewer magisterial interventions might be in order. In our time "must we not allow for a long-enduring, indispensable maturing process for many questions?" Clearly Coffy thinks so.

Coffy's presentation was followed by individual discussion groups drawn up along common-language lines. This is reported by Ludwig Kaufman.[15] For instance, the bishops noted that pluralism existed not only among theologians but also among bishops. The suggestion was also made that episcopal conferences need theological commissions chosen by theological societies and faculties. Furthermore, there was broad agreement with Coffy that magisterial interventions ought to be reduced if the magisterium is not to undermine its own authority.

Archbishop John F. Whealon (Hartford) presents an interesting study of the magisterium, not the extraordinary magisterium, but the year-to-year reformable teaching of the Pope, the college of bishops, and the local diocesan bishop in union with Rome.[16] After stating that relations between bishops and theologians ought to be better, Whealon makes several points. First, the priest (and bishop and deacon) are expected to "teach and preach as the Church's doctrine only that which the magisterium has presented as the Church's doctrine . . . not our own ideas or speculations, or the ideas and speculations of theologians." Second, where do we find this teaching? "A rule of thumb for the Catholic laity is to accept the teaching of a deacon or priest if he is in agreement with the local bishop, and to accept the teaching of the local bishop if he is in agreement with Rome." [17] Third, Whealon sees the source of confusion in the contemporary Church as located in those priests who do "not reflect or express the official teaching in [their] public and private utterances." Finally, he adds a few after-thoughts on the magisterium. Statements of national episcopal conferences do not have juridical authority of themselves. They have "magisterial import only if accepted by the local bishop and taught by him to the local church. A statement from another episcopal conference has no direct relevance for bishops, priests, and laity of another nation—and in every instance enjoys validity only if it is in harmony with Peter." [18]

Archbishop Whealon then mentions the imprimatur. The guarantee that the faith is being safeguarded "is the *imprimatur*—a review of the manuscript by a *censor deputatus* who notifies the bishop that this manuscript holds nothing contrary to Catholic teaching." For this reason he faults the recently published *An American Catholic Catechism*. "It demonstrates sadly the lack of external discipline through an *imprimatur* granted after needed revisions were made." His judgment of the book is extremely severe, especially in its "cavalier attitude toward the magisterium." [19] In summary, then, Archbishop Whealon concludes, contrary to Archbishop Coffy and others, that "theologians are at the service of the magisterium."

I have cited this interesting study at some length because I believe it represents the approach of very many non-theologians and at least some bishops. It is in rather sharp contrast to the approach taken by Archbishop Coffy, Bishop Descamps, Congar, and Dulles (see below), as are the remarks of Cardinal Pietro Palazzini on the subject. [20]

Specifically, what I miss in Whealon's reflections is a sense of magisterium rooted in the history of teaching in the Church such as one notes in Congar, Dulles, Coffy, and others. The sense of the term "magisterium" as defined by a single, recent, historically conditioned theological current and formulated only by recent Popes is accepted as normative, as God's will for things. In other words, it seems to me that Archbishop Whealon has accepted a *theology* of the magisterium without attending to the possibility that there have been and still can be other such theologies. And the theology he adopts is precisely the theology identified by Congar, Dulles, and others as one which has a history dating to only the nineteenth century. I respect this view and its proponent; indeed, with many others, I have been brought up with it and still "think it," I am sure, in many ways without adverting to it.

The overall approach, however, is heavily juridical, and this appears in Archbishop Whealon's presentation of it. Item: the emphasis on the imprimatur. This too easily overlooks the fact that a *censor deputatus* will make his assessments within the confines of his own theology. Item: the attitude toward statements of national episcopal conferences. While they may have no juridical status, it seems clear that they are used by many episcopates as genuine teaching devices.[21] Furthermore, I know of no theologian who would accept Whealon's assertion that "a statement from another episcopal conference has no direct relevance for bishops, priests and laity of another nation." It has a great deal to say about the status of a particular conviction or formulation of conviction *in the Church as a whole.*

Finally, a one-sidedly juridical approach to the teaching office of the Church, while it has elements of truth, hides more problems than it solves. Item: it opposes the doctrine of the Church and the opinions of theologians. I believe all would admit that no theologian can speak for the Church, but that is not really the issue. The issue is the truth or, in the context of doctrine, the completeness or even accuracy of a particular officially-proposed teaching. If what is officially proposed is true up to the point where it is officially changed, then "officialness" has assumed a primacy in our thought patterns that distorts the teaching function of the Church and eventually the truth.

Concretely, was the teaching of *Mirari Vos* and that of the Syllabus of Errors on religious liberty right until they were corrected by *Dignitatis Humanae?* Or is it not that we came to see through experience and theological reflection what is right and then it could be authenticated by the magisterium? Even more concretely, what was John Courtney Murray to say when he was convinced of the truth of the doctrine eventually enshrined in *Dignitatis Humanae?* Should he have said that it is not the doctrine of the Church but it is right — or it is not the doctrine of the Church and *therefore not right?* Surely not this latter. But unilateral emphasis on past formulated doctrine too easily leads to this cul-de-sac.[22]

The more important point in all of this is that our problems in relating the magisterium to theology depend on our ability to see the recent shape of the magisterium as but a single, culturally conditioned way of viewing the magisterium, and hence, too, its relationships to other segments of the people of God. If we fail here, we are victimized by ecclesiastical ideology, i.e., the use of time-conditioned formulations to support present practices and concepts in a way that sacralizes the *status quo* and thereby makes it difficult, if not impossible, to speak meaningfully of a *living* teaching office in the Church.

These brief footnotes on Archbishop Whealon's reflections are less a critique of the theology of these notions than an occasion for a respectful invitation to all of us (bishops, theologians, lay people) to be more open, not to lock ourselves into a single, historically-conditioned understanding of magisterium. In openness we may be able to discover understandings that are better calculated to serve the word of God in our time. And that is what this discussion is all about.

Yves Congar submitted a paper (really two papers) to the International Theological Commission, and his colleagues rightly urged him to publish it.[23] What distinguishes the study is the profound historical learning out of which it originates. It is both detailed and ranging, and in both aspects richly documented. There is no way that the study can be adequately digested; it can only be translated. All I can do here is indicate *some* points of interest and emphasis.

Let us start at the end of Congar's paper. He concludes his historical study as follows:

> The relationship between theologians (*docteurs*) and the magisterium calls for a reconsideration. This supposes first that the status of the "magisterium" in the Church is made more precise, that it is not isolated in the living reality of the Church. . . . One cannot define the dependent condition of theologians solely with reference to the "magisterium," even though there is a truth here. In this domain, as in that of obedience, one ought not frame the question in two terms only:

authority, obedience. It is necessary to think in three terms: above, the truth, the apostolic faith passed on, confessed, preached, celebrated; beneath it, at its service, the "magisterium" of the apostolic ministry and the work or teaching of theologians, as well as the faith of believers.[24]

How did Congar arrive at this conclusion? Historically. He first studies the use of the word "magisterium." Until the nineteenth century, the word signified the activity of one in authority in a specific area (*magister equitum, magister militum*). "Never before the nineteenth century did the word signify what we call '*the* magisterium,' even though the reality existed."

Congar next approaches the forms which teaching in the Church assumed at various times. In the early Church there were *didáskaloi,* whose activity was more catechetic then speculative. In the second and third centuries the schools began to appear and with them a certain element of theological speculation. But from the same period "that which characterized the bishop is the *cathedra,* the chair." This was the guarantor of the transmission of the apostolic message. But, Congar argues, this was not conceived primarily as juridical authority "possessing a power to obligate, but as a function by which the Church receives the faith inherited from the apostles." The tradition, in the sense of transmitted truth, was the true authority. There was no statutory separation or opposition between pastors and doctoṛs. Thus, Athanasius participated at Nicaea as a simple deacon.

The Middle Ages witnessed the full development of the schools and the birth of Scholasticism—a form of doctrine analytic and questioning. Thus there was formulated the distinction between teaching that is scientific in character and that which is pastoral. Thus, too, Thomas' distinction between *magisterium cathedrae pastoralis* and *magisterium cathedrae magistralis.* This latter was a true public office in the Church, but one based on scientific competence, whereas the "pastoral magisterium is tied to the public office of *praelatio,* i.e., of superiority or authority." Thus it is from this time that we can date a "magisterium of theologians in the Church." Theological faculties judged doctrinal theses. Gerson affirmed the right of theologians "scholastice determinare ea quae sunt fidei." This development, Congar notes, took one-sidedly unhealthy turns (e.g., Council of Basle, 1439).

In the course of time, properly theological theses, the positions of theological schools, had a place in condemnations issued in the name of the faith itself (e. g. Luther). This development continued into recent times, so that Congar notes: "The encyclicals of Leo XIII and Pius XII are theological. They are not purely the expression of apostolic witness according to the needs of the time, but a *doctrine* of the 'cathedrae magistralis' incorporating data from natural law, human wisdom, and classical theology." [25]

Congar traces the historical currents from Trent to our time, currents that led to Vatican I and subsequently to *Humani Generis,* with the growing unilateralism represented in these developments. *Humani Generis* brought these developments to a high point in two ways: (1) "The ordinary magisterium of the Pope demands a total obedience: 'He who hears you hears me.' " (2) "The (or one) role of theologians is to justify the pronouncements of the magisterium." Pius XII did not view the theologian as teacher, Congar notes, "except by delegation of the 'magisterium' and purely, narrowly at its service and under its control. Is this in conformity with that which nineteen centuries of Church life tell us about the function of the 'didaskalos' or doctor?" Congar's answer: "No, not exactly."

Congar sees in these developments a gradual supremacy of the *quo* (formal pastoral authority) over the *quod* (the word of God).[26] This was all the more threatening, he believes, because since 1832 the modern Popes have done theology—and a theology identified with that of the Roman schools, "whose personnel was recruited and watched according to a well-defined line." Vatican II, however, has restored the supremacy of the *quod* over the *quo,* and with it raised afresh the question of the true magisterium of theologians.

This article is indispensable and will, I hope, eventually be made available in English.

Many of the same themes are taken up by Bishop A. L. Descamps in a very long study.[27] He describes what he calls the classical view of the relationship between theologians and magisterium. The task of the hierarchy is to preserve and define the essentials of revelation (the *minimum minimorum*), and its habitual mode of expression is preaching. Thus in the Middle Ages the episcopate was called the *ordo praedicatorum*. According to classical views, "the theologian—nearly always a priest— drew his authority from his share in the sacred power of the bishop, which could concretize itself in a more explicit delegation (*missio canonica*)." Both this *missio* and his own competence were subordinate to the magisterium.

These and other emphases, he states, have changed in our time. The response to authoritative pronouncements is much less obediential. Instead of the classical *missio canonica* (a product of mixing the episcopal teaching and jurisdictional functions), Descamps states that "in a sense every theologian—even the lay person —providing that that person works within the faith and in the communion of the Church, can be said to be called by God, by revelation, by the Church, even by the hierarchy." [28] Thus, without becoming an elite or challenging the principle of doctrinal authority, the theologian no longer views himself as "sent by the hierachy" but as the "word-bearer of the people of God."

Avery Dulles, S.J., begins his forthright but courteous study of the magisterium and theologians by noting that the relationship is still fraught with tension, misunderstanding, distrust, and occasional bitterness. [29] Dulles notes two symptoms of this malaise. First, "certain official statements seem to evade in a calculated way the findings of modern scholarship. They are drawn up without broad consultation with the theological community. Instead, a few carefully selected theologians are asked to defend a pre-established position. . . . " Second, many Catholics have lost all interest in official ecclesiastical statements and do not expect any light from the magisterium on their real problems. Dulles sees this situation as alarming, and so do I.

Many factors and causes are at work here. Dulles highlights one: the notion of tradition and the magisterium being followed by the Pope and many bishops. It is a neo-Scholastic theory which was "devised by the theologians of the Roman school in the second half of the nineteenth century," as Congar also notes. According to this theory, the Pope and bishops have the "charism of truth." Theologians are subordinate and instrumental, their chief function being to "set forth and defend the teaching of the papal and episcopal magisterium." They are not teachers in the Church or part of the magisterium.

While Vatican II did not directly (in *Lumen Gentium,* n. 25) undermine this theory, Dulles believes that it did so in practice, modifying or reversing previously-taught views and rehabilitating the very theologians who made this possible.[30] Thus, the Council "implicitly taught the legitimacy and even the value of dissent. In effect," he continues, "the Council said that the ordinary magisterium of the Roman Pontiff had fallen into error and had unjustly harmed the careers of loyal and able theologians." Contemporary theological developments have revealed the weaknesses of this neo-Scholastic theory, especially as making insufficient allowance for error in the ordinary teaching of Popes and bishops.

Dulles' second step is to recover from history some elements that may aid in the construction of the post-juridical magisterium. He notes that Thomas used the term *magisterium* primarily for those who are licensed to teach theology in the schools. Thus Thomas distinguishes *officium praelationis,* possessed by the bishop, and the *officium magisterii,,* which belongs to the professional theologian. Thus, too, the distinction already noted between *magisterium cathedrae pastoralis* and *magisterium cathedrae magistralis.* The former has juridical authority behind it but is concerned with preaching and public order. The latter is concerned with teaching by argument and knowledge rather than official status. Thus Thomas would not say that prelates alone possess the charism of truth. Theologians have their own sphere of competence. "Within this sphere the theologian is a genuine teacher, not a mouthpiece or apologist for higher officers." Dulles finds this more in conformity with the great Catholic tradition and biblical evidence than the neo-Scholastic theory.

On the basis of the existence of many charisms in the Church, Dulles admits that bishops have a "legitimate doctrinal concern," but they are not the dominant voices on all doctrinal questions. Rather, "the *magistri,* teachers by training and by profession, have a scientific magisterium but they are subject to the pastors in what pertains to the good order of the Church as a community of faith and witness."[31] These two magisteria are complementary and mutually corrective.

Dulles' third step consists in a variety of reflections and suggestions on the magisterium in the post-juridical world. For instance, the theological community itself should have a greater voice in who is to represent it. Similarly, in certain areas where the preaching of the faith and technical theology are inseparably interwined and a pronouncement is called for, it "could most suitably be drawn up by a cooperation between representatives of the pastoral and of the theological magisterium." In brief, Dulles is very close to the historical perspectives of Congar. Congar is more historically detailed, Dulles more constructive in that he draws from history to create the outlines of a model of the future magisterium.

Archbishop Joseph Bernardin, in a symposium at Notre Dame University (January 1976), granted that we have much to learn about the way that others besides Pope and bishops fit into the "magisterial function in the Church." But he denied that this meant "multiple magisteria." Not only does this cause confusion; "it undermines valid complementarity—between the respective roles of the magisterium and the scholarly community—and at its worst could actually lead to painful and broadly destructive competition at the expense of the entire Church."[32]

Dom Emmanuel Lanne points up certain recent changes in emphasis in the notion of magisterium (e.g., collegiality, theology of the local Church).[33] Recent challenges to magisterial documents (*Humanae Vitae*, 1968; *Mysterium Ecclesiae*, 1973; *Persona Humana*, 1976) do not represent a questioning of the privileged role of the magisterium, but "disappointment at the result of the exercise of the teaching authority." In the course of his essay Lanne discusses the function of theologians in the magisterium. That function is "not that of 'doctor' (teacher) in the full sense of the term. The bishops alone are the 'doctors' of the faith." But then Lanne raises precisely the questions to which such assertions lead, e.g., is it possible to dissociate the content of faith, taught by the magisterium, from its theological presentation? Furthermore, what does the Church mean in declaring St. Teresa of Avila a Doctor of the Church?

Thus far the literature; here a final comment or two. First, all the literature would agree that there is a "magisterial function" (Bernardin's phrase) in the Church. Similarly, all would agree that the Pope and the bishops have a special place within this function, though the "magisterial function" is not simply identifiable with hierarchical status. That is, the function necessarily includes more than Pope and bishops; specifically, it must also include theologians. It is the *manner* of that inclusion that is most interesting. Some, adhering to a neo-Scholastic or classical view, describe the inclusion in terms of "subordination" and often in a highly juridical way. Others speak of pertinence of theologians to the "magisterial function" as one of complementarity, of convergence, or even of another distinct (scientific) magisterium. What these latter phrases—shared by bishops (e.g., Coffy, Descamps) and theologians (e.g., Congar, Dulles)—have in common is fear that the term "*the* magisterium," because of its relatively recent history, too easily identifies the teaching function of the Church with, and limits it to, a single group in the Church, and by implication excludes or seriously underestimates the indispensable place of theology and the theologian, to the ultimate detriment of the "magisterial function" of the Church.

There is probably a variety of ways of formulating the relationship between bishops and theologians. But recent literature agrees on two points: the relationship reached an enviable and ideal peak in Vatican II, and it has worsened since and needs improvement. For that improvement to occur, I believe, with Coffy and others, that "a new status is necessary for theology" in our time. That probably means also a new (different from the neo-Scholastic) status for the hierarchy. What these statuses ought to be will probably have to be discovered *in the process of cooperation*. As Archbishop Basil Hume of London put it, "The Church is so riddled with tensions and problems at the moment that any man who says he can give final answers to these problems is deluding himself. I really hope to be able to call on the best minds to guide me in forming attitudes and statements that I should be expected to make. I don't see myself as a great person. I see myself far more as a member of a team."[34]

"Members of a team" may be an identifiably American, but not altogether bad, way of formulating the matter: members with different but converging functions. If it is not the best formulation, it is a good way to begin a cooperative relationship that might eventually yield a more adequate theological formulation. Whatever the case, several things can be done to move toward a more harmonious cooperation. First, there should be broad dissemination of the studies of Congar, Dulles, and Descamps. These essays reveal the historically conditioned and very late character of the neo-Scholastic understanding of magisterium. Second, we theologians need to be more critical of one another—in a courteous and disciplined way, of course—so that the hierarchy does not bear the whole responsibility of correcting one-sidedness or irresponsibility, and therefore get forced into a dominantly negative role. Third, it is important that our best theologians devote themselves to stating more clearly papal and episcopal prerogatives and duties within the "magisterial function" of the Church. In rejecting the heavily juridical notion of these prerogatives, we must not reject their substance. Appeal is made repeatedly to n. 25 of *Lumen Gentium*, but it is widely, even if quietly, admitted in the theological community that this paragraph represents a dated and very discussable notion of the Church's teaching office.

Finally—and this is delicate—something must be done to liberate Roman congregations from a single theological language and perspective. The International Theological Commission was conceived in part to perform this service; yet there is little evidence that this has worked.[35] More radically, one can wonder whether congregations as such should be involved in doing theology. The temptation is almost irresistible for such groups to support the theological views of the officeholders whom they serve, as Dulles observes. Concretely, there is danger of a rather narrow notion of orthodoxy, one which compares present vocabulary with past vocabulary, thus unduly narrowing revelation to "statements" and disallowing an active, historical notion of the revelation event—"acculturation of faith," as Coffy words it.

To some this continuing theological concern with magisterium may seem otiose, a sterile postponement of the real problems of the world. I am convinced that this is terribly short-sighted. More than ever, we need a *strong* "magisterial function" in the Church, but it remains an unfinished task to determine what "strong" means in our time.

Notes

1. Robert B. Eno, S.S., "Authority and Conflict in the Early Church," *Eglise et théologie* 7 (1976), pp. 41-60.

2. Francis X. Murphy, C.SS.R., "The Pope and Our Common Future," *Catholic Mind* 74, no. 1300 (Feb. 1976), pp. 29-38.

3. George A. Kelly, "An Uncertain Church: The New Catholic Problem," *Critic* 35, no. 1 (Fall 1976), pp. 14-26. One commentator (Andrew Greeley) referred to this article as "demented drivel." To this Kelly responded that "the article is serious." One hates to be confronted with such desperate alternatives; but if pressed, I would have to say the article is not "serious," and represents the collapse of theological courtesy.

4. B. C. Butler, "Letter to a Distressed Catholic," *Tablet* 230 (1976), pp. 735-36, 757-58.

5. Cf. *L'Osservatore Romano*, Aug. 12, 1976, p. 8 (English edition).

6. Cardinal François Marty, "La Charge particulière du théologien dans l'église," *Documentation catholique* 73 (1976), pp. 572-75.

7. Jerome Theisen, O.S.B., "Models of Papal Ministry and Reliability," *American Benedictine Review* 27 (1976), pp. 270-84.

8. Dario Composta, "Il magistero ecclesiastico informa o insegna la morale?" *Divinitas* 20 (1976), pp. 199-203.

9. "Theses de magisterii ecclesiastici et theologiae ad invicem relatione," *Gregorianum* 57 (1976), pp. 549-63; also *Documentation catholique* 73 (1976), pp. 658-65.

10. Maurizio Flick, S.J., "Due funzioni della theologia secondo il recente documento della Commissione Theologica Internationale," *Civiltà cattolica* (1976), pp. 472-83.

11. *Ibid.*, p. 476.

12. *Origins* 6 (1976), pp. 173-80, 181-90.

13. Robert Coffy, "Lehramt und Theologie—die Situation heute," *Orientierung* 40 (1976), pp. 63-66, 80-83.

14. *Ibid.*, p. 65.

15. *Ibid.*, pp. 83-84.

16. John F. Whealon, "Magisterium," *Homiletic and Pastoral Review* 76, no. 10 (July 1976), pp. 10-19.

17. *Ibid.*, p. 15.

18. *Ibid.*, p. 16.

19. He states: "The special problem in this book is its occasional attempt to set up 'reputable theologians' as a second teaching authority in the Church, and its occasional presentation of the hierarachical magisterium as that which a Catholic should *in conscience be schooled not to obey rather than to obey* (pp. 181-187)" (emphasis added). A curious reader who consulted the pages referred to would discover that they were written by the author of these reflections. I shall leave it to the reader to determine whether the italicized words bear any relationship to the content of those pages. But one thing needs saying: the material presented there on the magisterium and

theologians represents by far the dominant theological position in the Church today.

20. Pietro Palazzini, "Rome e l'insostituibile magistero universale del Papa," *Divinitas* 20 (1976), pp. 5-8.

21. Cf. my "Abortion Dossier," *Theological Studies* 35 (1974), pp. 312-59, where the point is made by many episcopates.

22. Something similar could be said about Archbishop Whealon's criterion ("accept the teaching of the local bishop if he is in agreement with Rome"). The question immediately suggests itself: Rome at what time—under Pius XII perhaps? I mean to suggest, of course, that there are some formulations of the Popes that are commonly qualified or rejected by nearly all theologians. And if that is the case, *when* was such qualification or rejection appropriate? Was it not when the matter became reasonably clear? But that is not simply convertible with "agreement with Rome."

23. Y. Congar, "Pour une histoire sémantique du terme 'magisterium,'" *Revue des sciences philosophiques et théologiques* 60 (1976) pp. 85-98, and "Bref historique des formes du 'magistère' et de ses relations avec les docteurs," *ibid.*, pp. 99-112.

24. *Ibid.*, p. 112.

25. *Ibid.*, p. 105.

26. Cf. also Robert B. Eno, S.S., "Ecclesia docens: Structures of Doctrinal Authority in Tertullian and Vincent," *Thomist* 40 (1976), pp. 96-115; John F. Quinn, "St. Bonaventure and the Magisterium of the Church," *Miscellanea Francescana* 75 (1975), pp. 597-610.

27. A. L. Descamps, "Théologie et magistère," *Ephemerides theologicae Lovanienses* 52 (1976), pp. 82-133.

28. *Ibid.*, p. 109.

29. Avery Dulles, S.J., "What Is Magisterium?" *Origins* 6 (1976), pp. 81-87.

30. Cf. Cl. Dagens, "Le ministère théologique et l'expérience spirituelle des chrétiens," *Nouvelle revue théologique* 98 (1976), pp. 530-43. This article studies the work of Congar and M. Chenu.

31. *Art. cit.,* p. 86.

32. Cf. *Origins* 6 (1976), p. 87.

33. Dom Emmanuel Lanne, "Evolution of the Magisterium in the Roman Catholic Church," *One in Christ* 12 (1976), pp. 249-58.

34. Cited in Descamps (n. 27 above) p. 103.

35. E.g., it may be questioned whether the inclusion of *missio canonica* in the theses of the International Theological Commission (n. 67 above) is due to the full Commission.

3
The Ordinary Magisterium
in History

Nearly everyone who comments on the tenth anniversary of *Humanae Vitae* calls attention to the fact that the past ten years have led to a reconsideration of authority in the Church, and particularly the nature of the magisterium. This traces, of course, to the fact that there was so much dissent associated with *Humanae Vitae*. A few entries here will have to suffice.

Richard M. Gula, S.S. reviews the teaching of the manualists on dissent.[1] They do not see dissent as undermining the teaching of the ordinary magisterium, and at least one (Lercher) recognizes that suspending assent may be one way of protecting the Church from error.[2] Furthermore, Gula correctly notes that the responses to the *modi* on *Lumen Gentium* (n. 25) state the very same thing. The charismatic structure of the Church further supports this notion. Gula argues that we must develop an approach to public dissent that is more realistic and adequate to our time.

One of the more interesting statements on the meaning of dissent from authentic teaching of the magisterium was made by Bishop Juan Arzube at the Catholic Press Association Convention Mass.[3] He notes that, in contrast to infallible teaching, ordinary teaching has sometimes to "undergo correction and change." As an example Arzube offers *Dignitatis Humanae* and the teaching of previous Popes on religious liberty. Such development could not have occurred "unless theologians and bishops had been free to be critical of papal teaching, to express views at variance with it. . . . " Our faculty of judgment cannot give assent to a proposition that it judges to be inaccurate or untrue. After detailing the conditions for legitimate dissent (competence, sincere effort to assent, convincing contrary reasons), Arzube argues that dissent must be viewed "as something positive and constructive" in the life of the Church.

Arzube's statement strikes this reviewer as being realistic, calm, and theologically correct. It is particularly encouraging because it comes from a bishop. Theologians also received very warmly the remarks of Archbishop John Roach at the opening of the Catholic Theological Society of America meeting. Roach touched enlighteningly on the public he felt obliged as bishop to listen to carefully, even if at times critically.[4]

An entire issue of *Chicago Studies* is devoted to the theme "The Magisterium, the Theologian and the Educator."[5] It is one of the finest issues of that seventeen-year-old journal that we have had. Here only a few highlights can be reported.

After Archbishop Joseph Bernardin's introductory essay, there follow useful "setting the stage" articles by Carl Peter and John F. Meyers. Eugene A. LaVerdière, S.S.S. has a fine treatment of teaching authority in the New Testament period. This is followed by John Lynch's detailed study of the magisterium and theologians from the Apostolic Fathers to the Gregorian Reform. During this period it was the councils that promulgated creeds and dogmatic definitions, but "it was the theological teachers who carried on the vital interpretative task." Indeed, with the exception of Tertullian, Origen, and Jerome, one cannot speak of a differentiation of the magisterial and theological functions. That came with the rise of the universities.

Yves Congar covers the following period up to Trent. It was in this period that a new form of teaching developed, "the 'magisterium' of the theologians, the schools and the universities." This reflects what Congar calls "two different modes of teaching." Thus, the University of Paris considered itself and was generally thought of as exercising an authentic theological authority in Christianity. As a result, properly theological terms were employed by the councils to express the data of the faith (*transsubstantiatio, anima forma corporis*). Trent achieved a balance between *inquisitio* and *auctoritas*, but a balance conditioned by four centuries of Scholastic theology. The result: "The teaching of the magisterium has been woven with 'theology' which has gone far beyond the pure witness of the word of God and apostolic tradition." Congar concludes that the distinction of charisms must be preserved but within a necessary and felicitous collaboration.

Michael Place traces developments in the relationship between scholars and what he calls "the authoritative hierarchical solicitude" (for the faith) from Trent to Vatican I. The upshot of these developments was a growing isolation of the papal and episcopal competency from the rest of the Church. Place outlines the political and theological threads that led to an increasingly powerful papacy. For instance, in the late eighteenth century the key category by which papal action in matters of faith was understood was that of jurisdiction—the concern of one who was not first a teacher but was to provide for unity. As Place puts it: "The theologian is the teacher. The papacy is the ruler that provides for the right ordering necessary to preserve ecclesial unity." However, early in the nineteenth century, categories from Germany (teach, rule, sanctify) were introduced rather than the powers of orders and jurisdiction. With this came also the usage "magisterium" around 1830, and it was "situated in the cultural milieu where the papacy is understood as having absolute spiritual sovereignty. . . . " In this new context the function of a theologian is differently understood. He is now related not to the "governor of ecclesial unity" but to a supreme teacher. In such a context his role changes. It is Place's thesis that the relationship of magisterium to theologians is determined by the manner in which the Church perceives itself at a given time in history.

T. Howland Sanks, S.J. treats the relationship of theologians and the magisterium from Vatican I to 1978. He argues, rightly I think, that the conflicts that existed, and still exist, are between various forms of theology, various theological paradigms, not precisely or first of all between theologians and the magisterium. During this period (up to Vatican II) the a-historical, neo-Scholastic theology of the Roman school achieved an ascendency. It got enshrined in official statements. It is present in Vatican I (*Dei Filius, Pastor Aeternus*) and continued to be the official theology used by the magisterium in its dealings with the historically conscious leanings of Loisy, Tyrrell, and Pierre Rousselot. Furthermore, it was responsible for the suppression of Teilhard and John Courtney Murray (as well as de Lubac, Bouillard, and their colleagues at Fourvière). In *Humani Generis* (August 12, 1950) this a-historical approach peaked. Vatican II constituted a definitive break with such an approach, but Sanks believes that the problem is far from gone, because this theology has "formed the thinking and attitudes of many of the hierarchy."

Avery Dulles provides a theological reflection on the magisterium in history. His overall conclusion is that "the structures commonly regarded as Catholic today are relatively new and thus do not reflect God's unalterable design for his Church." Dulles passes in review the salient features of the models of the Church in various periods and uses these features to raise questions for our time. In the patristic period, for example, what Dulles calls a "representational model" prevailed. The Catholic faith is identified with the unanimous belief of all the churches—and the bishops were the responsible heads of such local churches. The bishops were seen as teaching with full authority when they gather in councils representing the churches of the entire Christian world. On the basis of this model (not without imperfections) Dulles asks: Can we reactivate the idea of a unity achieved "from below" through consensus? Furthermore, instead of thinking of the bishop as the representative of the Holy See, should we not see him more as the local community's representative? Or, again, Dulles wonders whether we can credibly view the bishop as the "chief teacher" in our time. This notion fits more easily the fourth and fifth centuries, when prominent theologians were bishops.

When he discusses the medieval model characterized by the rise of the universities, Dulles asks: "Could theologians, individually or at least corporately, be acknowledged as possessing true doctrinal or magisterial authority?" The notion, he insists, is well founded in tradition. He criticizes the excessive privatizing of theology as if theologians "indulge in nothing other than airy speculations." He suggests that statements could occasionally be issued jointly by bishops and non-bishops, by the Pope with the International Theological Commission. This would reduce the cleavage between the pastoral magisterium and theology.

The neo-Scholastic period (nineteenth and twentieth centuries) saw the magisterium as a power distinct from orders and government. Thus it regarded the hierarchy not simply as judges but as true teachers, whereas in the eighteenth century teaching was viewed as a command or along more disciplinary lines. Under this neo-Scholastic model the Holy See exercised a vigorous doctrinal leadership. But because papal teaching was drawn up by theologians of the Roman school, they "gave official status to their own opinions." Vatican II changed many of the perspectives associated with the neo-Scholastic approach, especially the identification between magisterium and jurisdiction. It neither affirmed nor denied a complementary magisterium of theologians. However, it is clear that Dulles (along with Congar) believes such a notion is valid. "The concept of a distinct magisterium of theologians, as we have seen, is not simply a medieval theory; it is accepted in neo-Scholastic manuals of the twentieth century."

These papers were discussed at a seminar of the Catholic Theological Society of America (June 1978) in Milwaukee. Timothy O'Connell reports the results of those discussions in the same issue of *Chicago Studies*. The key issue in relating theology to the magisterium was seen to be doctrinal development. Specifically, the seminarists asked: How do we account for the various changes in teaching that have occurred in the past? Can we develop a theology of Church teaching which accommodates without embarrassment the twin phenomena of divided opinion and ignorance?

The issue concludes with the address of Raymond Brown, S.S. to the National Catholic Education Association (March 29, 1978).[6] The prestigious exegete argues that the dispute among theologians and bishops has been "greatly exaggerated." He identifies four fictions that surround the dispute: belief that the main opponents in matters of doctrine are the magisterium and theologians, that their prevailing relationship is one of disagreement, that theologians and magisterium can be spoken of as if they were monolithic groups, and that they conflict because even centrist Catholic theologians deny many matters of Church doctrine. Brown argues — persuasively, in my judgment — that third parties such as the secular media and the ultraconservative Catholic press are more damaging than any polarization of bishops and theologians. Furthermore, though there has been dissent (especially in matters of sexual morality), Brown asserts that this has been seriously exaggerated. With regard to centrist theologians denying many matters of Church doctrine, Brown insists that we must not inflate (as many do) what constitutes Catholic doctrine and that we must realize that doctrines change. In his words, "seeking a new formulation to meet a new problem" is hardly a denial of a teaching.

Though his paper was delivered to religious educators, both theologians and bishops could read it with profit. Brown approaches delicate problems with a combination of precision, wisdom, and pastoral sensitivity that is admirable. Those on the extreme right or left will not be happy with his reflections. But that reflects more on the geography of their position than on the accuracy of Brown's analysis. One point might deserve more emphasis than Brown's irenic analysis suggests: the differences on a single issue such as *Humanae Vitae* have enormous implications with regard to moral theological method, notions of pluralism and authority, notions of the Church. Increasingly it is these issues that come to the fore in moral discussions and that perhaps account for the impression of polarization between some bishops and some theologians.

In another symposium (held in Philadelphia, January 6-8, 1978) William May discusses the moral magisterium.[7] He insists, quite rightly, that the Church expects that the faithful "will, in faith, make their own through acts of faithful understanding" the teachings of the Church. However, dissent remains possible. But this does not mean that there is a "double truth." He takes issue with Congar, Dulles, and this compositor, who "speak of two magisteria within the Church." The unity of the Church demands one magisterium, and the scholar must be willing to allow his or her positions to be judged by this one magisterium.

Any differences between May and myself on this subject appear to be non-substantial and a matter of emphasis. However, two comments might be in place. First, while May admits the possibility of dissent, he does not carry this far enough. That is, he does not relate it to the development of doctrine. It remains privatized. Concretely, if dissent on a particular point is widespread, does this not suggest to us that perhaps the official formulation is in need of improvement? To say otherwise is to say that scholarly (and other) reflection has no relation to the Church's ongoing search for truth and application of its message. As Bishop Arzube notes, we would never have gotten to *Dignitatis Humanae* if the reflections of John Courtney Murray had been merely tolerated and not taken as a new source of evidence.

This leads to the second point: May's rejection of two magisteria in the Church. It is easy to understand how this can be a confusing verbal vehicle, and I, for one, am not wedded to it. Raymond Brown notes: "Magisterium is a fighting word. I think the attempt to reclaim it for theologians will not succeed; and I personally do not think the battle worth fighting so long as, under any other name, the legitimate role of theologians in shaping the teaching of the Church is respected."[8] I agree with that statement of things and with Brown's subsequent addition: "All that I want is that scholarly evidence be taken into account in the formulation and reformulation of Catholic doctrine."

What is important, then, is not the word; it is the idea beneath it. That is, the Church in its teaching makes use of (and probably must) theologies and philosophical concepts, as Congar repeatedly reminds us. In moral theology, an example would be *direct* killing, *direct* sterilization. These formulations are only more or less adequate and may even be wrong at times. It is one of theology's (and philosophy's) tasks to make that determination, not precisely the magisterium's.

Here an example is in place. Masturbation for infertility testing has been condemned officially (the Holy Office, Pius XII). Yet, very few theologians of my acquaintance see this procedure as having the malice of masturbation. When theologians say this, they are stating (at least they think they are) a truth, and in this sense they are teaching. Or must one wait until something is officially modified to recognize that it is true or false? Personally, I would have no hesitation in saying to an individual that that condemnation is obsolete, even if it has not been modified by the Church's more official teaching organs.

What theologians (and other scholars) have been searching for is a formula which would incorporate two things: (1) the practical admission of an independent competence for theology and other disciplines; (2) the admission of the indispensability of this competence for the formation, defense, and critique of magisterial statements. They are not interested in arrogating the kerygmatic function of the Holy Father and the bishops.[9] By "independent" I do not mean "in isolation from" the body of believers or the hierarchy. Theologians are first and foremost believers, members of the faithful. By "independent" competence is meant one with its own proper purpose, tools, and training. The word "practical" is used because most people would admit this in theory.

In practice, however, this is not always the case. This practical problem can manifest itself in three ways. First, theologians are selected according to a pre-determined position to be proposed, what Sanks calls "cooptation." Second, moral positions are formulated against a significant theological opinion or consensus in the Church. Such opinion should lead us to conclude that the matter has not matured sufficiently to be stated by the authentic magisterium. Third, when theologians sometimes critique official formulations, that is viewed as out of order, arrogating the teaching role of the hierarchy, disloyalty, etc. Actually, it is performing one of theology's tasks. All three of these manifestations are practical denials of the independent competence of theology.

As for the third manifestation mentioned above, it ought to be said that when a particular critique becomes one shared by many competent and demonstrably loyal scholars, it is part of the public opinion in the Church, a source of new knowledge and reflection. Surely this source of new knowledge and reflection cannot be excluded from those sources we draw upon to enlighten and form our consciences, for conscience is formed *within the Church*.[10]

An unsolicited suggestion might not be irrelevant here. Bishops should be conservative, in the best sense of that word. They should not endorse every fad, or even every theological theory. They should "conserve," but to do so in a way that fosters faith, they must be vulnerably open and deeply involved in a process of creative and critical absorption. In some, perhaps increasingly many, instances, they must take risks, the risks of being tentative or even quite uncertain, and, above all, reliant on others in a complex world. Such a process of clarification and settling takes time, patience, and courage. Its greatest enemy is ideology, the comfort of being clear, and, above all, the posture of pure defense of received formulations.

In all fairness, at this point something should be added about theologians. Amid the variation of their modest function in the Church, they must never lose the courage to be led. "Courage" seems appropriate, because being led in our times means sharing the burdens of the leader—and that can be passingly painful. They should speak their mind knowing that there are other and certainly more significant minds. In other words, they must not lose the nerve to make and admit an honest mistake. They should trust their intuitions and their hearts, but always within a sharp remembrance that the announcement of the faith and its implications in our times must come from the melding of many hearts and minds. The Church needs a thinking arm, so to speak; but that arm is dead if it is detached.

Notes

1. Richard M. Gula, S.S,, "The Right to Private and Public Dissent from Specific Pronouncements of the Ordinary Magisterium," *Eglise et théologie* 9 (1978), pp. 319-43.

2. "It is not absolutely out of the question that error might be excluded by the Holy Spirit in this way, namely, by the subjects of the decree detecting its error and ceasing to give it their internal assent" (L. Lercher, *Institutiones theologiae dogmaticae* 1 [4th ed.; Barcelona: Herder, 1945], p. 297).

3. Juan Arzube, "When Is Dissent Legitimate?" *Catholic Journalist* (June 1978), p. 5.

4. John Roach, "On Hearing the Voices That Echo God," *Origins 8* (1978), pp. 81-86.

5. *Chicago Studies* 17 (1978), pp. 149-307. The issue includes articles by Joseph L. Bernardin, Carl J. Peter, John F. Meyers, Eugene LaVerdière, S.S.S., John E. Lynch, C.S.P., Yves Congar, O.P., Michael D. Place, T. Howland Sanks, S.J., Avery Dulles, S.J., Timothy O'Connell, and Raymond E. Brown, S.S.

6. Cf. also *Origins* 7 (1978), pp. 673-82.

7. William E. May, "The Magisterium and Moral Theology," in *Symposium on the Magisterium: A Positive Statement*, ed. John J. O'Rourke and Thomas Greenburg (Boston: Daughters of St. Paul, 1978), pp. 71-94.

8. Brown, as in *Origins* 7 (n. 6 above), p. 675.

9. William Cardinal Baum has a thoughtful paper on the episcopal magisterium. He suggests that the theology of this magisterium must be based on the evangelical notion of the proclamation of the kerygma and on the sacramental nature of the episcopal order. "The episcopal magisterium is thus not above, below, or alongside the role of theologians and others. It is a reality of a different order. It pertains to the sacramental transmission of the divine realities. . . . " Cf. "Magisterium and the Life of Faith," *Origins* 8 (1978), pp. 76-80. A similar analysis was made by the then Archbishop Karol Wojtyla. He emphasizes the magisterium of bishops as proclamation, leading people to Christ. Bishops are first of all *fidei*

praecones and only secondly *doctores.* The faithful defense of the *depositum* and its proclamation "entails its growing understanding, in tune with the demands of every age and responding to them according to the progress of theology and human science." He argues that the magisterium "as systematic and doctrinal teaching should be put at the service of the announcement of the Gospel." Cf. "Bishops as Servants of the Faith," *Irish Theological Quarterly* 43 (1976), pp. 260-73.

10. In "The 'New Morality' vs. Objective Morality," *Homiletic and Pastoral Review* 79 (1978) pp. 27-31, Joseph Farraher, S.J. states: "Most present-day liberals in both dogmatic and moral theology . . . treat his [the Pope's] statement with no more acceptance than they would the statements of any individual theologian who disagrees with them." That statement is, I believe, simply false.

4
Theologians and Academic Freedom

John Paul II addressed himself to the relation of theologians to the teaching office of the Church in his address to Catholic educators at Catholic University, October 7, 1979.[1] Joseph Fitzmyer, S.J., the distinguished exegete, offers a commentary on that address.[2] The Holy Father stated his gratitude for theological work ("We all need your work, your dedication, and the fruits of your reflection"). He also insisted on high standards and freedom of investigation. Finally, John Paul II referred to theological "theories and hypotheses" and to "the right of the faithful not to be troubled" by them.

Fitzmyer points to a real problem in the papal address. "How can he insist on the 'eminent role of the university' and its 'undiminished dedication to intellectual honesty and academic excellence' and still caution the theological faculty of a Catholic university about theories and hypotheses? They are, after all, the stuff of 'scientific research' and 'freedom of investigation' . . . We can only wish that he had addressed himself more explicitly to this tension that is reflected in his address."[3]

Fitzmyer's own approach to this tension is to put both magisterium and theologians in a position of reciprocal need and mutual stimulation. Theologians need the magisterium to keep them dedicated to honesty and responsible scholarship. The magisterium and the faithful need theologians to make them reflect on their need for constant updating. The real enemy of this harmonious symbiosis is, according to Fitzmyer, "the right-wing mass that would vie for authority in catechetics and teaching with both bishops and theologians."

Pope John Paul II returned to this subject in his address to the International Theological Commission.[4] He referred to the work of theologians as participating "to a certain extent" in the magisterium. But he then added: "We say 'to a certain extent' because, as our predecessor Paul VI wisely said, the authentic magisterium, whose origin is divine, 'is endowed with a certain charism of truth that cannot be communicated to others and for which none other can substitute.'" The Holy Father praised a "healthy pluralism" in theology and repeated what he had stated in *Sapientia Christiana*: that theologians in institutions of higher education (*in altiorum studiorum sedibus*) "do not teach on their own authority but by virtue of a mission received from the Church."

Charles Curran examines the relationship between academic freedom, the Catholic university, and Catholic theology.[5] After accepting the standard definition of such freedom, he notes that the two instrumentalities designed to protect it are tenure and academic due process. Before the 1960's it was widely accepted that full academic freedom could not exist in Catholic institutions of higher learning. This began to change in the 1960's and culminated with the signing, by twenty-six leaders in Catholic education, of the Land O'Lakes statement, "The Nature of the Contemporary Catholic University." In this statement full academic freedom is endorsed, "in the face of authority of whatever kind, lay or clerical, external to the academic community itself."

Curran's next move is to apply this to theology in the Catholic university, an area where it would seem most difficult to justify full freedom. He justifies full academic freedom by appeal to a contemporary understanding of theology (interpretation of the sources of revelation in light of the signs of the times vs. a deductive method highlighting clear and certain propositions) and of the magisterium (where the interpretative function of theology in relating to the magisterium involves the possibility of dissent).

Curran's final reflection is on *Sapientia Christiana*.[6] The document requires that those who teach disciplines concerning faith or morals receive a canonical mission,[7] "for they do not teach on their own authority but by virtue of the mission they have received from the Church" (n. 27). Furthermore, to acquire a tenured position or the highest faculty rank, the candidate needs a *nihil obstat* from the Holy See (n. 27). Curran sees in these stipulations a view of the university as "a continuation of the teaching function of the hierarchical magisterium." He concludes: "In such a situation, there is no academic freedom because judgments about competence are not made by peers, and promotion and tenure depend on judgments made by Church authority as such." He argues that canonically erected universities, Catholic theology, and the good of the whole Church will suffer as a result of the literal application of this apostolic constitution.

Joseph Farraher, S.J. takes a point of view poles apart from that of Curran.[8] A questioner had asked why bishops allow their own Catholic universities and some seminaries to retain teachers who contradict their teaching. Farraher replies that removal should not be the first step. First there should be a fraternal warning "that professors at Catholic universities and seminaries . . . are considered and are representatives of the Church and as such should not promote opinions contrary to the teaching of the magisterium." Farraher is clearly opposed to *promoting* one's ideas "while acting in a situation where he represents the Church." If dissenters feel that they must propose a contradictory opinion, they should resign their position "where they are considered a representative of the Church." If they persist, Farraher argues, "all efforts" should be used to remove them.

The key phrase in Farraher's analysis is "professors at Catholic universities and seminaries . . . *are considered and are representatives of the Church.*" The phrase is extremely general and loose. If it means that a Catholic theologian ought to take his or her tradition seriously, be aware of, respect, and study official Catholic documents, and be sensitive to the pastoral implications and repercussions of his or her work, then no one can question the phrase. If, however, "representatives of the Church" is taken to mean official spokespersons of the Church within the university community—and this is the implication of Farraher's conclusion—I believe it is simply erroneous to say that this is the proper description of the theologian's function.

Furthermore, the word "promote" is loaded. It suggests a political contest with the magisterium as the opposing candidate. Does one who states his or her own opinion honestly and presents the reasons for it as persuasively as possible "promote" it? Behind my problems with Farraher's analysis there are undoubtedly deeper disagreements about the notion of Church, of magisterium, and of teaching in general.

Kenneth Baker goes even further. He reviews the contemporary theological scene and sees it as one of "open defiance now being shown by supposedly 'Catholic' theologians. . . . "[9] "Rebellion by theologians against the supreme magisterium" is the rule, not the exception. His examples: Hans Küng, Charles Curran, Avery Dulles, Stephen Kelleher, Anthony Kosnik. Later the list is expanded to include Andrew Greeley, John Milhaven, John Dedek, and the author of these reflections. And this list "is just to scratch the surface." In this Baker is correct. A deeper scratch would expand the list with names such as B. Häring, Joseph Fuchs, B. Schüller, Karl Rahner, J.-M. Aubert, Louis Janssens, D. Maguire, Walter Burghardt, David Tracy, Franz Schölz, Franz Böckle, A. Auer, and on and on.

After explaining the nature and function of the magisterium, Baker considers the role of the theologian. Theologians attracted an exaggerated respect during Vatican II, one that intimidated the bishops. The result: bishops have largely abandoned their teaching function to theological experts. Baker relies on the paper of the International Theological Commission in attempting to elaborate the role of theologians. But, unfortunately, he feels that the rules governing the theologian's role are being violated "with impunity from coast to coast, in almost every diocese. . . . " Baker concludes that theologians and intellectuals who "refuse to submit to the magisterium of the Church" should, after adequate dialogue, be excommunicated.

"Remove," "excommunicate"—these are strong words aimed indiscriminately at all kinds of targets. One would think that there is a slight difference in questioning the divinity of Christ and questioning, e.g., the teaching of Pius XII on artificial insemination by the husband. This latter has been done, and done carefully, by theologians of demonstrated competence and loyalty. The Farraher-Baker perspective would reverse the procedure and judge competence and loyalty by failure to question. This makes official formulation the judge of truth, rather than truth the judge of authentic formulation.[10]

At this point a very traditional and, in my judgment, still to be revered theology would have spoken of something like probabilism. The abiding and liberating value of such a concept is that it is issue-oriented, not primarily authority-oriented, even though its advocates had great respect for authority. They simply viewed it as the job of theologians to say what they honestly thought. And if enough people of genuine theological authority said the same thing, it was a presumptive sign that there was something to it. Perhaps those days are gone. Perhaps issues will be discussed with the stereotypic slogans loyal-disloyal and orthodox-deviant, but I hope not. For if that is the case, theology will have been transformed into institutional rhetoric, and truth will have become subordinate to the instruments of its search. That sort of thing is much more at home in a society that makes no pretenses about its objectivity and freedom.

In the matter of dismissal-excommunication, therefore, I am sure that theologians would prefer to follow the counsels of John Paul II. In urging Catholics to reconcile their internal theological differences, the Holy Father stated in Chicago, as noted above, that "no one in the ecclesiastical community should ever feel alienated or unloved, even when tensions arise in the course of common efforts to bring the fruits of the Gospel to society around us."

This attitude of John Paul II should not come as a surprise. In his book *The Acting Person*,[11] the then Cardinal Wojtyla discusses authentic community. There are three characteristics that distinguish authentic community: solidarity, opposition, dialogue. Solidarity "is the attitude of a community, in which the common good properly conditions and initiates participation." It refers to a readiness "to accept and realize one's share in the community."

Opposition Wojtyla sees as "essentially an attitude of solidarity." It is the attitude of those who, because they are deeply devoted to the common good, disagree with official ideas and policies. Of such opposition the cardinal of Krakow makes several statements: "The one who voices his opposition to the general or particular rules or regulations of the community does not thereby reject his membership."[12] Indeed, such opposition is vital to the community's growth and well-being. It is "essentially constructive." He continues:

> In order for opposition to be constructive, the structure, and beyond it the system of communities of a given society, must be such as to allow opposition that emerges from the soil of solidarity not only to *express* itself within the framework of the given community but also to *operate* for its benefit. The structure of a human community is correct only if it admits not just the presence of a justified opposition but also that practical effectiveness of opposition required by the common good and the right of participation.[13]

Then there is dialogue. Dialogue allows us to "select and bring to light what in controversial situations is right and true." Wojtyla admits that dialogue involves strains and difficulties and is sometimes messy. But a "constructive communal life" cannot exist without it. Opposed to solidarity and opposition are "unauthentic" attitudes of "servile conformism" and "non-involvement." For example, "conformism brings uniformity rather than unity."

Cardinal Wojtyla did not apply this analysis to the ecclesial community. "But," as Gregory Baum notes, "the characteristics of authenticity defined for a true community, any true community, secular or religious, ought to apply *a fortiori* to the Church, which is the divine revelation of the model of community in the world."[14] Baum's point was also made tellingly by both Ronald Modras and Edward Cuddy.[15] For instance, Modras, adverting to *The Acting Person*, correctly asserts that "loyal opposition can serve the well-being of a church as well as of a state." But the situation in Poland did not allow Cardinal Wojtyla to highlight the critical function of theology. The militant hostility of a Marxist regime required a united resistance.

Baum's reflection is supported by John Howard Yoder in a

different context.[16] In discussing a Christian approach to social ethics, he suggests that a powerful beginning to the problems of the wider social order has been made when Christians have seen their believing community as a paradigm and pilot processing plant for the models of culture and service which later could be commended to a wider society. As he noted:

> Freedom of speech must first of all be realized in the puritan assembly before we can explain how it would be a good way to run a civil democracy. Care for the hungry must first develop as a commitment of the body of believers before it will occur to anyone to propose moving toward a welfare state. Christians must first be ready to forgive those who have trespassed against them for the sake of the forgiveness of Christ before there is any hope for a new effort to reform the treatment of offenders.[17]

Similarly, Gerard O'Connell states that the Church's proclamation of rights should first be verified in the Church itself.[18] He specifically refers this to, among other things, dissenting opinions.

Just so. If creative and courteous exchange and opposition is the ordinary way of progress in human knowledge and growth in any society, as the then Cardinal Wojtyla insisted, should it not first find its most splendid exemplar in the Church? I believe so.

One of the standard responses to this direction of thought is that the people have a "right not to be confused" ("troubled" is the word used by the Holy Father). The implication frequently made is that theologians should cease expressing their views publicly if those views deviate at all from official formulations. That is, I think, unrealistic and intolerable.[19] As for the "confusion" of the people, several things need to be said. First, reality is sometimes confusing and it takes time and groping before a truly satisfactory Christian and Catholic response can be formulated. Second, rather than silence free thought and speech in the Church, people must be educated to the idea that differing times do suggest differing perspectives and analyses, especially where very detailed moral norms are concerned, and that what seems a closed question very often is not.[20] Third, they must be educated to the idea that our unity as a community does not ride or fall with absolute uniformity on the application of moral norms to very detailed questions (e.g., *in vitro* fertilization with embryo transfer). Otherwise the Holy Father's notion of opposition would be only destructive.[21] Finally, they must be educated to take theologians seriously, but not all that seriously. If theologians are mistakenly thought to be the ultimate teachers in the Church, they risk losing, besides their freedom to probe and question, their humility.[22]

One final word about the notion of *missio canonica*. This term needs a great deal of careful questioning. It is a very general phrase capable of remarkably loose and eventually abusive understanding and use. As it is used in *Sapientia Christiana*, it refers to "a canonical mission from the chancellor or his delegate" (n. 27). While the terms "chancellor" and "delegate" are somewhat obscure, at least in some instances they would apply to the local ordinary or religious superior (e.g., Catholic University of America). Of this *missio* it is said that they "must receive" it. Presumably that means that professors may not teach without it.

If all this means is that the *formal* appointment comes from the chancellor, who must be guided by the judgment of the professor's academic peers, then there is no problem. If, however, the chancellor may grant or deny this *missio* on his own, then the notion of academic freedom disappears as we know it in this country, for the chancellor could grant or deny the *missio* on warrants unacceptable to sound theology.[23]

For instance, does the *missio canonica* exclude the possibility of responsible dissent? There are those who argue this way[24] and undoubtedly some chancellors would act this way.[25] But that would be unacceptable to all theologians of my acquaintance, and at variance with traditional manualist theology, as well as with the principles stated by Pope John Paul II in *The Acting Person*.

Or, again, does this *missio* mean that in their scholarly tasks theologians are an extension of the magisterium into the academic world? Few would accept this self-description, although there are signs that some chancellors or potential chancellors might. Does the term suggest that theology's main task is to mediate the teachings of the magisterium? This was clearly the view of Pius XII in *Humani Generis*, but it has been repeatedly criticized by theologians as a one-sided view.[26] Yet it is not rash to think that some chancellors might share Pius XII's theology. Finally, does it mean that only a theologian acceptable to the local bishop gets this *missio*? It should not mean this, or any of the above things, if academic freedom in any meaningful sense is to be preserved.

These are some of the possible senses of the term *missio canonica* and they are cumulatively the reasons why theologians legitimately fear the notion.

There is, on the other hand, a quite acceptable notion of *missio ab Ecclesia*. At one point in his discussion of the common responsibilities of theologians and the magisterium, the Pope asserted:

> In their service to the truth, theologians and the magisterium are constrained by common bonds: the word of God; the "sense of faith" that flourished in the Church of the past and still flourishes now; the documents of tradition in which the common faith of the people was proposed; and, finally, pastoral and missionary care, which both [theologians and magisterium] must attend to.[27]

I would think that those theologians whose work takes account of these bonds (*vinculis*) are, in the most profound sense of the term, "sent." Few theologians would have any difficulty with such "bonds." Indeed, they simply outline theological responsibility. But what many would object to is the extension of such constraints into a *missio* given by a per se non-academic person, and into a *nihil obstat* from the Holy See.

Here it must be remembered that *Sapientia Christiana* is dealing with pontifical faculties (and these are faculties involved with the training of future priests). Such faculties relate somewhat differently to episcopal authority than does the Catholic university in general. In other words, the bishop does indeed have responsibilities with regard to orthodoxy in such faculties. But it can still be doubted whether *missio canonica* is the appropriate way to implement such responsibilities. Concretely, it is an extremely dangerous weapon, especially in light of the sanctions some ultra-right groups are calling for and pressuring the bishops to use. University structures are designed to protect the faculty against precisely this type of thing.

One point is to be noted. Both *Sapientia Christiana* and John Paul II regard theology in Catholic institutions of higher learning as a kind of continuation of the mission of the magisterium. *Sapientia* restricts this to canonically erected faculties. The Holy Father more generally speaks of institutions of higher learning (*in altiorum studiorum sedibus*). This is not the self-understanding of the Catholic university in the United States. In a 1971 report of the North American Region of the International Federation of Catholic Universities (IFCU), stress is put on the need for university autonomy. "The Catholic university is not simply a pastoral arm of the Church. It is an independent organization serving Christian purposes but not subject to ecclesiastical-juridical control, censorship or supervision."[28]

Therefore I agree with Curran that certain understandings of *missio canonica* and the requirement of a *nihil obstat* from the Holy See for tenure on pontifical faculties are incompatible with academic freedom as this is commonly understood in university circles in the United States.[29] Clearly, theologians must be responsible in the exercise of their freedom. But to threaten such freedom and thereby the causes for which it exists — among them, the vitality and integrity of theology — strikes this reviewer as killing the patient to cure the disease. With concerns such as this in mind, the Catholic Theological Society of America, at its 1979 convention in Atlanta, passed a resolution on academic freedom that included two principles:

1. No theologian should be censured or deprived of that liberty acknowledged to be necessary for theological inquiry without due process which respects fundamental fairness and equity.
2. No theologian holding an academic appointment should be censured or otherwise deprived of any right except as a result of due process which is in accordance with publicly stated standards and is consonant with generally accepted academic practice in the United States and Canada.[30]

These views represent a sampling of theological perspectives from many points of view. It is probably safe to say that they also represent a division in the Catholic, and even larger, public. What might be said at this point? Much depends on one's ecclesiological presuppositions. But one thing is clear. The use of stereotypic language has no place in serious theological discussions. When those with whom one disagrees are summarily classified as "dissenters" or "deviants," we see an instance of such language and the collapse of theological courtesy. One is tempted to respond by dubbing other discussants as "conformers." That is a kind of game. The regrettable aspect of such semantics is, as I noted, that the issue gets lost. When that happens, nobody wins, and something seriously detrimental to the Church prevails.

Notes

1. *Origins* 9 (1979), pp. 306-08.
2. Joseph A. Fitzmyer, S.J., "John Paul II, Academic Freedom and the Magisterium," *America* 141 (1979), pp. 247-49.
3. *Ibid.*, p. 249.
4. *L'Osservatore Romano*, Oct. 27, 1979.
5. Curran's study is to appear in the *Furrow;* I cite from the unpublished manuscript which he kindly forwarded to me.
6. *Origins* 9 (1979), pp. 33-45.
7. For a discussion of *missio canonica* in various contexts, cf. Francisco Javier Urrutia, S.J., "De magisterio ecclesiastico: Observationes quaedam ad propositam reformationem partis IV, libri III, CIC," *Periodica* 68 (1979), pp. 327-67.
8. Joseph Farraher, S.J., "Why Don't Bishops Take Action against Dissenters?" *Homiletic and Pastoral Review* 79, No. 7 (April 1979), pp. 64-66.
9. Kenneth Baker, S.J., "Magisterium and Theologians," *ibid.*, pp. 14-23.
10. Norbert Rigali has, I believe, a much more realistic and balanced view of dissent in the Church. He points out that the theologian's role is that of explorer and discoverer, "of seeking for ways to advance the understanding or intellectual life of the Church, of proposing new theories." He refers to "better or fuller ways of understanding the meaning of faith in relation to an ever-changing world." Such work "must involve at times the proposing of theories that conflict with current official (non-infallible) teachings of

the Church." Clearly these probes must be weighed against a background of experience and reflection much broader than that of any individual theologian; but to do so, these proposals must "get into the open." Rigali rightly notes that a theologian can act irresponsibly. He concludes: "However, it also would be irresponsible, and indeed cruel, to regard a theologian as irresponsible or disloyal to the Church simply because there is being proposed an opinion that conflicts with official theological teaching in the Church." I think Rigali has it exactly right. Cf. "Faith and the Theologian," *Priest* 34, No. 4 (April 1978), pp. 10-14.

11. Karol Wojtyla, *The Acting Person* (Boston: D. Reidel, 1979).

12. *Ibid.*, p. 286.

13. *Ibid.*, pp. 286-87.

14. Gregory Baum, "Le pape et la dissidence," *Relations* 39 (1979), pp. 250-51.

15. Ronald Modras, "Solidarity and Opposition in a Pluralistic Church," *Commonweal* 106 (1979), pp. 493-95; Edward Cuddy, "The Rebel Function in the Church," *ibid.*, pp. 495-97.

16. This was a response to Scott Paradise in *Anglican Theological Review* 61 (1979), pp. 118-26.

17. Yoder, *ibid.*, p. 125.

18. Gerard O'Connell, "The Church and Human Rights," *Way* 17 (1979), pp. 273-82.

19. In an editorial in the *St. Louis Review*, Msgr. Joseph W. Baker writes: "Dissenting opinions are not to become a matter of public scandal, but are to be presented to appropriate ecclesiastical authorities, avoiding troubling the consciences of other members of the Church." In Baker's perspectives public dissent is equivalent to public scandal; for he contrasts as the only alternatives "presenting to appropriate ecclesiastical authorities" and "public scandal." And this is said to accord with the norms for licit dissent. If taken seriously, Baker's norms would utterly destroy public discussion in the Church and with it the very possibility of doctrinal development. Cf. *St. Louis Review*, Oct. 19, 1979.

20. Karl Rahner, "Open Questions in Dogma Considered by the Institutional Church as Definitively Answered," *Catholic Mind* 77, No. 1331 (March 1979), pp. 8-26. Rahner has some illuminating things to say about the rules to be followed in arriving at formulations in moral and dogmatic questions.

21. In an inventive editorial, *America* puts in the mouth of John Paul II the following lines in an imagined speech in the U.S.: "But I would urge you, above all, not to let those differences that divide you distract you from the central faith in the Gospel of Jesus Christ that unites you" (*America* 141 [1979], p. 145).

22. Cf. Richard A. McCormick, S.J., "Moral Theology since Vatican II: Clarity or Chaos?" *Cross Currents* 29 (1979), pp. 15-27.

23. Cf. *National Catholic Reporter*, Nov. 23, 1979, for Karl Rahner's accusations (of injustice) against Cardinal Joseph Ratzinger; also Manuel

Alcalá, "La tensión teologíamagisterio en la vida y obre de Karl Rahner," *Estudios eclesiásticos* 54 (1979), pp. 3-17.

24. Thomas Dubay, S.M., "The State of Moral Theology," *TS* 35 (1974), pp. 482-506.

25. It must be remembered that there are still bishops in this country who exclude theologians from their dioceses because of dissent on this or that point.

26. *TS* 38 (1977), pp. 85ff.

27. Cf. n. 4 above.

28. "Freedom, Autonomy and the University," *IDOC International*, North American edition, 39 (Jan. 15, 1972), p. 83.

29. Cf. Josef Georg Ziegler, "'Rolle' oder 'Sendung' des Moraltheologen: Versuch einer Selbstreflexion," *Theologie und Glaube* 69 (1979), pp. 272-88.

30. Cf. *Bulletin of the Council on the Study of Religion* 10 (1979), p. 114.

Biographical Notes

John C. Ford, S.J. and the late Gerald Kelly, S.J. were for many years professors of moral theology at Weston College and St. Mary's College respectively.

Bruno Schüller, S.J. is professor of moral theology at the University of Münster, West Germany.

Daniel C. Maguire is professor of Christian ethics at Marquette University.

Joseph A. Komonchak is associate professor in the Department of Religion and Religious Education at The Catholic University of America.

Antonio di Marino, S.J. is professor of moral theology in the Pontifical Theological Faculty of St. Louis at Posillipo.

Karl Rahner, formerly of the University of Munich, is the author of *Theological Investigations* and *Foundations of Christian Faith.*

Karl Lehmann is professor of systematic theology at Freiburg.

Otto Semmelroth, S.J. is professor of systematic theology at St. Georgen, Frankfurt.

Christopher Butler, O.S.B. is the former abbot of Downside and auxiliary bishop of Westminster.

John Francis Whealon is the archbishop of Hartford.

Juan Arzube is auxiliary bishop of Los Angeles.

Robert Coffy is the archbishop of Albi.

Giovanni B. Guzzetti is professor of moral theology at the Interregional Theological Faculty of Milan.

Avery Dulles, S.J. is professor of systematic theology at The Catholic University of America.

John R. Quinn is archbishop of San Francisco.

Raymond Brown, S.S. is Auburn Professor of Biblical Studies at Union Theological Seminary.

Yves Congar, O.P. is the author of many books, including most recently a three-volume work on the Holy Spirit.

Thomas Dubay, S.M., with a Ph.D. from Catholic University, writes frequently on the spiritual life.

Charles E. Curran is professor of moral theology at Catholic University of America.

Philippe Delhaye is professor of moral theology at the University of Louvain.

John Boyle is professor of Christian ethics and chairman of the Department of Religion at the University of Iowa.

Richard A. McCormick, S.J. is Rose F. Kennedy Professor of Christian Ethics, Kennedy Institute of Ethics, Georgetown University.